Rainer Bendel, Norbert Spannenberger (Hg.)

Kirchen als Integrationsfaktor für die Migranten im Südosten der Habsburgermonarchie im 18. Jahrhundert

Kirche und Gesellschaft im Karpaten-Donauraum

herausgegeben von

PD Dr. Rainer Bendel (Tübingen),
Dr. Jaroslav Šebek (Praha)
und
Dr. Norbert Spannenberger (Leipzig)

Band 1

LIT

Rainer Bendel, Norbert Spannenberger (Hg.)

Kirchen als Integrationsfaktor für die Migranten im Südosten der Habsburgermonarchie im 18. Jahrhundert

LIT

Gedruckt mit Förderung durch den Beauftragten der Bundesregierung für Kultur und Medien

Bibliografische Information der Deutschen Nationalbibliothek
Die Deutsche Nationalbibliothek verzeichnet diese Publikation in der Deutschen Nationalbibliografie; detaillierte bibliografische Daten sind im Internet über http://dnb.d-nb.de abrufbar.

ISBN 978-3-643-10045-0

Verlagskontakt:
Fresnostr. 2 D-48159 Münster
Tel. +49 (0) 2 51-620 320 Fax +49 (0) 2 51-922 60 99
e-Mail: lit@lit-verlag.de http://www.lit-verlag.de

Auslieferung:
Deutschland: LIT Verlag Fresnostr. 2, D-48159 Münster
Tel. +49 (0) 2 51-620 32 22, Fax +49 (0) 2 51-922 60 99, e-Mail: vertrieb@lit-verlag.de
Österreich: Medienlogistik Pichler-ÖBZ, e-Mail: mlo@medien-logistik.at
Schweiz: B + M Buch- und Medienvertrieb, e-Mail: order@buch-medien.ch

Inhalt

Auf dem Weg in die europäische Integration erinnert sich Europa der Pluriformität der verbindenden geistigen, kulturellen und religiösen Werte, um Antworten auf die Anforderungen der Zukunft finden zu können. Die EU-Osterweiterung, der Beitritt zahlreicher ostmittel – und südosteuropäischer Staaten zur Europäischen Union, ist für zehn Staaten vollzogen, weitere stehen in absehbarer Zeit bevor. Alle Beitrittsländer bringen ihre jeweils eigene Kultur, Geschichte und Mentalität, spezifische historische Erfahrungen und Identitäten ihrer Gesellschaften ein.
Parallel zu dieser integrativen Entwicklung ist die Angst vor der Sogwirkung eines gigantischen Zentralstaates wahrzunehmen; eine Antwort mag die Betonung des Europa der Regionen sein. Regionalbewußtsein und Regionalgeschichte kommen verstärkt in den öffentlichen Diskurs. Dabei ist auf dem Hintergrund der Nationalgeschichten des 20. Jahrhunderts die Chance zu sehen, dass Regionalgeschichten von ihrem Zugriff her erst einmal anational sind.
Die Entwicklungen innerhalb der Historiographie in den vergangenen Jahrzehnten zeigen das gewachsene Bewußtsein für die Realitäten schaffende Kraft geistiger Prozesse, die Prozesse der Sinn- und Bedeutungskonstituierung. Fragestellungen und methodisches Instrumentar suchen gegen eine klare Scheidung verschiedener Wirklichkeitsdimensionen gerade ihrer inneren Verflochtenheit in der Dynamik von Kräftefeldern, Mechanismen, frei gesetzten oder zufälligen Impulsen ansichtig zu werden. Religiöse Lebensformen und -vollzüge werden in ihrer Verflechtung mit Politik, Wirtschaft und Kultur untersucht. Von der historischen Anthropologie und kulturwissenschaftlichen Ansätzen in der Historiographie wird die Bedeutung der Theologie unterstrichen, um das jeweilige Selbst- und Weltverständnis des Menschen zu erkennen.
Beschäftigung mit Religion, mit Kirchen und Konfessionen erscheint gerade jüngeren Fachvertretern wieder als lohnend. Ihnen soll hier ein Publikationsforum geboten werden.
Gegenüber partikularisierenden, aus- und abgrenzenden Geschichtsbildern muß der ostmitteleuropäische Raum als Begegnungs- und Brückenraum verschiedener Völker, Sprachen, Kulturen, Religionen und Bekenntnisse betont, die Themen Religion und Kultur in ihren integrativen Leistungen und teils auch Versagen untersucht werden. In Vergleichen von west- und ostmittel- und südosteuropäischen Modellen gesellschaftlicher und staatlicher Entwicklung können aufschlußreiche Erkenntnisse für integrierende und desintegrierende Faktoren und Prozesse in multiethnischen, -religiösen und –kulturellen Ländern und Regionen erwartet werden.

Rainer Bendel und Norbert Spannenberger

Einführung

„Alle und jede, was Standts, Nation und Religion, inn- oder außer Landts die seynd" wurden nach dem *Kaiserlichen Impopulationspatent* von 1689 eingeladen, sich in den sog. *Neoaquistica*, also von den Osmanen zurückeroberten Gebieten des Königreiches Ungarn niederzulassen.[1] Dieses Patent, ein Werk des Kardinal Leopold Kollonich, stützte sich inhaltlich auf das *Einrichtungswerk des Königreichs Hungarn* mit 500 Seiten. In fünf Kapiteln gegliedert – Justiz, Kirche, Politik, Militär und Wirtschaft – wurden die wichtigsten Bereiche problematisiert, wie diese „Vormauer der Christenheit" nach der Osmanenherrschaft und den Befreiungskriegen aufgebaut werden sollte.[2] Tatsächlich wurde im Kapitel *Politicum* festgehalten, dass „am Beispiel der Römer" keine „einzige Nation diskriminiert" und auch alle Konfessionen unter den Katholiken auf dem Lande, nicht aber in den Städten toleriert werden sollte.[3] Der sog. Rákóczi-Aufstand 1703-1711 machte den ersten, zaghaften Erfolgen dieses Vorhabens ein blutiges Ende, so dass unmittelbar nach der Niederwerfung dieser „Rebellion" nunmehr Vertreter des ungarischen Adels zu diesen Ansätzen zurückgriffen und auf dem Reichstag von Pressburg 1722/23 erneut das Thema Immigration als dringende Aufgabe artikulierten.[4]

Die von diesen politischen Prozessen vorgegebenen Rahmenbedingungen vermochten stimulierend zu wirken, gingen aber stets von einem Idealzustand aus, den es aber auf der Mikroebene nie gegeben hat. Denn die praktische Umsetzung war ein komplexer Prozess von Re- und Neuorganisation. Vordergründig ging es um eine „Reorganisation", argumentativ konnte nämlich damit die Legitimation untermauert und somit eine Kontinuität suggeriert werden.[5] Hierbei spielten die Kirchen, allem voran die römisch-katholische Kirche eine Schlüsselrolle. Vordergründig ging es um eine Reorganisation der Zustände aus der Vorosmanenzeit in der Politik und in der Verwaltung. Die Kircheninstitution hatte lebhaftes Interesse daran, sich als Akteur

[1] Abgedruckt bei TAFFERNER, Anton: Quellenbuch zur donauschwäbischen Geschichte. Bd. I. München 1974, 53-55.

[2] MAYER, Theodor: Verwaltungsreform in Ungarn nach der Türkenzeit. Sigmaringen 1980, 98. – Zum zeitgenössischen Diskurs der Einrichtungsalternativen siehe pars pro toto BAHLCKE, Joachim: Hungaria eliberata? Zum Zusammenstoß von altständischer Libertät und monarchischer Autorität in Ungarn an der Wende vom 17. zum 18. Jahrhundert. In: Die Habsburgermonarchie 1620 bis 1740. Leistungen und Grenzen des Absolutismusparadigmas. Hg. v. Petr MAT`A und Thomas WINKELBAUER. Stuttgart 2006, 301-317.

[3] Vgl. MAYER: Verwaltungsreform, 113-114.

[4] Das Gesetz *De impopulatione regni 103 ex 1723* siehe bei TAFFERNER: Quellenbuch Bd. I., 95.

[5] Dazu gehören etwa die Wiederherstellung der Diözesangrenzen, die Klärung der Jurisdiktionskompetenz in der Pastoration zwischen konkurrierenden Einrichtungen oder die sozio-politische Selbstdefinition des Klerus. Indem die alten Sitten und Traditionen der Bevölkerung auf der Lokalebene fortgesetzt wurden, wurde diese suggerierte Kontinuität von ihr als solche erlebt und durchaus mitgetragen.

an dieser Aufbauarbeit zu profilieren, wobei dies ohne staatliche Hilfe nicht möglich gewesen wäre. Umgekehrt war auch der Staat bei der Herrschaftserrichtung auf diese angewiesen.[6] Die Kirche wirkte dabei nicht allein im spirituellen, sondern auch im politischen, verwaltungstechnischen und ökonomischen Bereich mit. Auch wenn ideell eine „Reorganisation" stattfand war allen Beteiligten bewusst, dass es sich letztlich oft um einen Neuanfang handelte, was nicht zuletzt die zahlreichen Schwierigkeiten in der Praxis belegten. Seit dem *Tridentinum* galt für die Geistlichkeit das Residenzprinzip, also die Residenzpflicht, die in den ohnehin schwierigen Transformationsprozessen eine besondere Herausforderung darstellte.[7] Dazu gesellten sich Multikonfessionalität und Multiethnizität als weitere besondere Herausforderungen, die bewältigt werden mussten.

Genau deshalb war es aber allen staatlichen Instanzen wie Herrschaftseinrichtungen die schnelle Einbindung der Geistlichen als Ordnungsfaktor von oberster Priorität. Sie wirkten intermediär zwischen Herrschaft, staatlicher Autorität und Untertanen, in den Pfarreien übten sie eine wichtige Funktion für die Verwaltungsprozesse aus und insbesondere in der langen Phase der Konsolidierung waren sie nicht selten Kreditgeber für die bäuerlichen Untertanen. Das z.B. ursprünglich kirchenrechtlich relevante Prinzip des „constanter residet" des Pfarrers erhielt somit eine soziopolitische Dimension, denn dafür trat auch der jeweilige Grundherr – natürlich aus anderen Gründen wie der Bischof – ein. Indem der Priester seine integrative Rolle ausübte, konnte die Konsolidierung der Gemeinde beschleunigt und deren ökonomische Belastbarkeit auf sichere Grundlagen gestellt werden. Somit wurde den Geistlichen auf der Mikroebene eine indirekte Rolle der Sozialdisziplinierung zugewiesen, der sie in der Regel auch nachkamen.

Dieses Wechselspiel der Makro- und Mikroebene bildeten die Rahmenbedingungen (nicht nur) für die deutschen Immigranten ab 1690. „Damit also dieses neuungarische Volk [sic!] seiner christlichen Pflicht entsprechend Gott gebe, was Gott gebührt, und dieses Prädium nicht auch eine Einöde bleibe, wie es früher für Tiere war, hat sich der Graf um einen Priester umgesehen" brachte es in seiner zeitgenössischen Chronik Pfarrer Wilhelm Winkler auf den Punkt.[8] Für einen gelungenen Integrationsprozess waren besonders die Gegebenheiten auf der Mezzo- (Komitate und Herrschaften) und der Mikroebene (Gemeinden) maßgeblich. Der Dialog wie die Kooperation zwischen dem „doctus et pius" Priester und seiner Gemeinde galt als Ideal. Migration impliziert Ankommen in einem Ort, in einem Territorium, einem Raum, der geographisch, politisch, religiös, in der Mentalität der Bewohner differiert vom Herkunftsort. An diesem Ort müssen sich die Emigranten eine neue Existenz aufbauen, müssen sich also mit dieser Differenz zurecht finden, sie zu überwinden suchen; hier werden Lebenswelten weiter gepflegt, modifiziert, geraten in

---

[6] Diese komplementäre Entwicklung siehe bei BAHLCKE, Joachim: Ungarischer Episkopat und österreichische Monarchie. Von einer Partnerschaft zur Konfrontation (1686-1790). Stuttgart 2005.

[7] Pars pro toto siehe dazu ausführlich GÁRDONYI, Máté: A papi élet reformja a Trienti Zsinat korában. [Reform des priesterlichen Lebens zur Zeit des Konzils von Trient]. Budapest 2001.

[8] Glaube und Kirche in der Schwäbischen Türkei des 18. Jahrhunderts. Aufzeichnungen von Michael Winkler in den Pfarrchroniken von Szakadát, Bonyhád und Gödre. Hg. v. Franz GALAMBOS. München 1987, 25.

Konflikt. Migranten müssen sich einfügen oder sie werden verändern oder sie werden verändert. Religion, Glaubenshaltung, religiöse Praxis, Frömmigkeitsformen spielten eine wichtige Rolle im Leben derer, die migrierten. Sie konnten also ihre Glaubenshaltung, ihre religiöse Praxis auch an dem Ort, an dem sie ankommen, nicht einfach und rasch ablegen. Wie gestaltet sich in dieser Begegnung die Aufnahme? Wurden die Migranten mit ihrer religiösen Praxis ernst genommen? Konnten die Migranten ihre Eigenart bewahren und mit einbringen oder mussten sie sich einfügen und unterwerfen?

Die Erforschung der Rolle der Kirchen für die Migrationsprozesse im Königreich Ungarn im 18. Jahrhundert bildete bisher keinen Gegenstand wissenschaftlicher Fragestellung. Selbst Grundlageforschungen für die Kirchengeschichte des 18. Jahrhunderts auf der Mikroebene sind äußerst rar.[9] So wagt dieser Sammelband insgesamt Neuland zu betreten. Konzeption und Durchführung dieses Vorhabens war stark determiniert von den Forschungsschwerpunkten der Referenten, die jedoch dem Vorschlag gerne nachkamen, im Sinne der vorgegebenen Fragestellung ihre eigene bisherige Arbeit zu hinterfragen.

Die komplementären Prozesse der Herrschaftseinrichtungen, demographischer Entwicklungen, Zerstörung der Kulturlandschaften und Migrationen beleuchtet *Szabolcs Varga* am Beispiel zweier besonders in Mitleidenschaft gezogenen Regionen, nämlich Süd-Transdanubiens und Slawoniens im 16. und 17. Jahrhundert. Unterschiedliche Entwicklungslinien begünstigten in diesen Regionen auch die Reorganisation der Kirchenstrukturen, die die Weichen für das 18. Jahrhundert gestellt hatten. Im Kontext staatlicher Ansiedlungspolitik thematisiert *Norbert Spannenberger* das interkonfessionelle Zusammenleben deutscher Einwanderer im 18. Jahrhundert in Süd-Transdanubien. Hierbei spielten nicht nur bereits vorhandene protestantische, meist kalvinistische Siedlungen eine wichtige Rolle, sondern auch die Bereitschaft säkularer Grundherrschaften, durchaus Protestanten bei sich aufzunehmen. Die Rahmenbedingungen für diese Prozesse bildete das Programm der Rekatholisierung, die natürlich an Dynamik und Tempo je nach Region unterschiedlich zur Geltung kam. *Zoltán Gőzsy* untersucht am Beispiel der Diözesen Veszprém und Fünfkirchen (ung. Pécs) die Möglichkeiten dieses Prozesses in einem multiethnischen Umfeld bis Ende des 18. Jahrhunderts. Dabei kommt er zum Ergebnis, dass Konflikte diverser Provenienz natürlich stattfanden, doch diese nicht den Alltag bestimmten und keineswegs vorprogrammiert waren. Die Einwanderung der Serben Ende des 17. Jahrhunderts ins Königreich Ungarn ist ein bis heute weitgehend unerforschtes Gebiet. *Branko Bešlin* stellt in seinem Beitrag Wandel und Wirkung der „süßen Orthodoxie" als geistige Komponente serbischer Immigranten nach der sog. „Großen Wanderung" im Spiegel des aktuellen Forschungsstandes dar.

[9] Eine erfreuliche Ausnahme bildet A pécsi egyházmegye a 17-18. században [Die Diözese Fünfkirchen im 17.-18. Jahrhundert]. Hg. v. Tamás FEDELES und Szabolcs VARGA. Pécs 2005. – Auch die Grundlagenforschung steckt noch in den Kinderschuhen. Eine Ausnahme bildet die jüngere Quellenedition Visitatio canonica Dioecesis Quinqueecclesiensis 1738-1742. Hg. v. Zoltán GŐZSY und Szabolcs VARGA. Pécs 2009.

Von ganz wenigen Ausnahmen abgesehen handelten kirchliche Grundherrschaften nach anderem Muster als die privaten: Bei ihnen war nämlich die konfessionelle Zugehörigkeit der Immigranten von besonderer Relevanz, wie das *András Forgó* in seinem Beitrag am Beispiel der Zisterzienserabtei Zirc nördlich vom Plattensee und der Pauliner im Gebirge Pilis zeigt. Während in Süd-Transdanubien infolge der Einwanderungspolitik der privaten Herrschaften die Anzahl der evangelisch-lutherischen Bevölkerung quantitativ deutlich zunahm, führten die interkonfessionellen Konflikte in der Herrschaft Zirc zum Terrainverlust der Kalvinisten. Doch ausschließlich eine bipolare Konfliktkonstellation zwischen Katholiken auf der einen und Protestanten auf der anderen Seite zu suggerieren wäre verfehlt, wie dies *Zoltán Csepregi* in seiner Arbeit belegt und charakterisiert die beiden protestantischen Konfessionen im süd-transdanubischen Komitat „brüderlich verfeindet". Damit korrigiert er nicht nur die etablierte Auffassung evangelischer Geschichtsschreibung, sondern zeigt der Forschung andere Wege, die sich aus der Auswertung der Korrespondenz pietistischer Geistlicher ergeben können.

Ethnische und konfessionelle Ausdifferenzierungen hatten zur Folge die großen Wanderungswellen im Nordosten des Königreiches Ungarn. Obwohl diese Region von der Osmanenherrschaft nicht betroffen gewesen war, erfolgten nach 1690 auch hier Migrationsvorgänge, die nach wenigen Jahrzehnten zu gravierenden Veränderungen in der Bevölkerungszusammensetzung führten. *Peter Šoltes* geht in seinem Beitrag der Frage nach, was die Gründe für die erfolgreiche Selbstbehauptung griechisch-katholischer Ruthenen in dieser Region waren. Lebenswelten und Konfessionen konfrontierten sich selbst wenn es keine ethnischen Unterschiede gab. *Sándor Őze* stellt die wenig bekannte Migration von Süd-Transdanubien Richtung Osten, wo auf der ungarischen Großen Tiefebene konfessionelle Merkmale als Alteritätskomponenten ihre Langzeitwirkung zeigten.

Unter Migrationen des 18. Jahrhunderts versteht man in erster Linie freiwillige, spontane und/oder geplante Bewegungen. *Mathias Beers* Beitrag ist selbst in diesem Sammelband eine Ausnahme, da er die Geschichte der „Transmigranten" und deren „rechtlich abgesicherte Kriminalisierungsmaßnahmen" thematisiert. Er kommt zum Ergebnis, dass eben diese der Grund dafür waren, dass trotz gemeinsamer ethnischer und konfessioneller Zugehörigkeit eine vollständige Integration nicht zu erfolgen vermochte. „Die gleiche Stammes- und Glaubenszugehörigkeit führte zugespitzt formuliert nicht zur Erleichterung und Beschleunigung der Integration, sondern eher zu ihrer Verzögerung und der Herausbildung einer eigenen kulturellen Identität der Transmigranten." Bei der Rekonstruktion der Institution Kirche spielte die Kompetenz des Ehegerichts für die Mikroebene eine Schlüsselrolle. *Karl-Peter Krauss* untersucht am Beispiel von ehemals Kameralgemeinden in der Batschka welche Rolle Ehegerichtsbarkeit für Konsolidierung und Disziplinierung hatte. Ihre Funktionstüchtigkeit setzte einen von der Bevölkerung verinnerlichten religiösen und sozialen Wertekanon voraus. *György Kurucz* wertet einen einzigartigen Quellenbestand aus dem Budapester *Evangelischen Landesarchiv* aus und stellt eine Deskription des Evangelischen Seniorats im Banat aus dem Jahr 1836 vor. Er resümiert, dass diese

canonica visitatio eine stabile Kirchenstruktur mit gefestigten multiethnischen Gemeinden widerspiegelt.
Kreuzwege und Kalvarienberge bilden feste Bestandteile katholischer Frömmigkeitspraxis. *Klaus Loderer* konstatiert in seinem Beitrag eine starke Kontinuität der Kalvarienberge in den ungarndeutschen Gemeinden bis ins 20. Jahrhundert und stellt die Frage, ob solche nicht von deutschen Migrantenpriestern nach Ungarn gebracht worden war? *Swantje Volkmann* wendet sich der „Peripherie der Habsburgermonarchie" zu und untersucht das Banat im Spiegel barocker Kirchenbauten. Als Ergebnis stellt sie die Schaffung einer „einzigartigen Kulturlandschaft" bis Ende des 18. Jahrhunderts fest. *Tiborc Fazekas* thematisiert die Rolle der Einwanderungen in die Kameralgebiete Batschka und Banat in der schöngeistigen Literatur als „Reflexion über die Reflexionen". Er geht dabei der Frage nach, warum diese Autoren bzw. Werke keinen „festen Bestandteil der nationalen oder weltliterarischen Kanones" werden konnten und vor allem von ihrem „jeweiligen politischen oder gesellschaftlichen Umfeld" rezipiert wurden, also im Milieu ähnlicher Erfahrungen blieben.
Krista Zachs Abhandlung über konfessionelle Raumkonfigurationen im südöstlichen Europa konstatiert den Abschluss der Quellenausgaben aber noch fehlende Auswertungen in der Forschung und plädiert für internationale Kooperation. *Tamás Tóth* präsentiert die Forschungsergebnisse über die Aufbauarbeit der Erzbischöfe Gabriel und Adam Patachich von Kalocsa-Batsch zwischen Donau und Theiß. Dank zielstrebiger Reformarbeiten galt die mehrsprachige und multikonfessionelle Erzdiözese 1784 als konsolidiert und blühend. Auch *Tamás Véghseő* zeigt die Ergebnisse seiner Dissertation und zeichnet die wichtigsten Maßnahmen des Bischofs von Wardein, Augustin Benkovich, in den letzten Dezennien des 17. Jahrhunderts nach, die die Union mit den Rumänen – trotz störender Zwischenfälle wie dem Rákóczi-Aufstand (1703-1711) – ermöglichen sollten.
Die Frage nach dem Gebrauch von Orts- und Personennamen stellt sich hinsichtlich des multiethnischen und -konfessionellen Donauraumes stets neu. Bei den Ortsnamen wurden – soweit welche existieren – die historischen deutschen Namen verwendet. Bei der Erstnennung wurden sie allerdings in Klammern auch in den jeweiligen Landessprachen hinzugefügt. Bei historischen Namen blieb dem einzelnen Autor überlassen, welche Form er verwenden wollte.
Bei der redaktionellen Arbeit leisteten den Herausgebern Martin Wambsganß (Tübingen) sowie Robert Pech und Marcus Fischer (Leipzig) eine große Hilfe, wofür ihnen ausdrücklich gedankt werden soll. Ebenso danken möchten die Herausgeber dem Beauftragten der Bundesregierung für Kultur und Medien für die finanzielle Förderung dieses Sammelbandes. Für vielseitige Hilfe danken wir Herrn Klaus Loderer und dem Ungarndeutschen Sozial- und Kulturwerk (USK), Backnang-München.

Leipzig und Tübingen
Rainer Bendel, Norbert Spannenberger

Osmanenzeit, Herrschaftswechsel und interkonfessionelle Konflikte

Szabolcs Varga

Ethnic Groups, Denominations and Migration in South Transdanubia and Slavonia in the 16th-17th Centuries

This study identifies the causes of the formation of various denominations in South Transdanubia and Slavonia in the early modern age.[1] It is, to a great extent, based on the latest results of research focusing on the dynamics of the emergence of these denominations[2] and thus, fundamentally changing the picture gained from positivist historical works often written for self-justification.[3]

The starting point for this study is the late medieval religious and ethnic division of the territory. At the beginning of the 16th century, South Transdanubia, which consisted of the counties of Tolna and Baranya, was primarily inhabited by Catholic Hungarians. Neither the inchoate Serbian migration, nor the German population of Pécs, considered as the centre of the region, influenced strongly this ethnic picture. However, Slavonia was in a different state of affairs.[4] It was predominantly populated by people speaking various South Slav dialects.[5] Their number was further increased by the Croatian migration brought about by the Ottoman advance

[1] Mainly historians dealing with military and church history have noticed the similarities between the two regions. PÁLFFY, Géza: Egy szlavóniai köznemesi família két ország szolgálatában: A budróci Budor család a XV-XVIII. században [A Slavonian Noble Family in Service of Two Countries: The Budors from Budróc in the 15th-18th Centuries.]. In: Hadtörténeti Közlemények 115/4 (2002), 923-1007. – MOLNÁR, Antal: Katolikus misszók a hódolt Magyarországon I. (1572-1647) [Catholic Missions in the Part of Hungary under Ottoman Rule vol. I (1572-1647). Budapest 2002 (Humanizmus és reformáció 26). – An abridged edition is French is also available MOLNÁR, Antal: Le Saint-Siège, Raguse et les missions catholiques de la Hongrie Ottomane 1572–1647. Roma – Budapest 2007 (Bibliotheca Academiae Hungariae Roma, Studia 1).

[2] MOLNÁR, Antal: Mezőváros és katolicizmus. Katolikus egyház az egri püspökség hódoltsági területein a 17. században [Market Town and Catholicism. The Catholic Church in Part of the Diocese of Eger under Ottoman Rule in the 17th Century. Budapest 2005 (METEM Könyvek 49.), 9-15. – BALÁZS, Mihály: Felekezetiség és fikció [Denominations and Fiction]. Budapest 2006 (Régi Magyar Könyvtár Tanulmányok 8).

[3] PAYR, Sándor: A dunántúli református egyházkerület története I. [The History of the Transdanubian Reformed District vol. I]. Sopron 1924. – KATHONA, Géza: Fejezetek a török hódoltsági reformáció történetéből [Chapters from the History of the Reformation under the Ottoman Rule]. Budapest 1974 (Humanizmus és reformáció 4). – THURY, Etele: A Dunántúli Református Egyházkerület története I-II. [The History of the Transdanubian Reformed District vol. I-II]. Pozsony 1998. – KANYARÓ, Ferencz: Unitáriusok Magyarországon tekintettel az unitarizmus általános történetére [Unitarians in Hungary Considering the General History of Unitarianism]. Kolozsvár 1891.

[4] Medieval Slavonia did not include the county of Požega. Nevertheless, this study discusses this territory as part of Slavonia to make possible a more complex understanding of the issue at hand.

[5] ŠTEFANEC, Nataša: Demographic Changes on the Habsburg-Ottoman Border in Slavonia (c. 1570-1640). In: Das Osmanische Reich und die Habsburgermonarchie. Akten des internationalen Kongresses zum 150-jährigen Bestehen des Instituts für Österreichische Geschichtsforschung Wien, 22-25. September 2004. Ed. by Marlene KURZ et alii. Wien-München 2005 (Mitteilungen des Instituts für Österreichische Geschichtsforschung Ergänzungsband 48), 550-578.

as early as the 15th century, and by the Bosnian refugees after 1528. Moreover, the Serbs also started to flow into the region at that time, though the majority of them settled in Sriem or on the estates of the Serbian despot before 1541.[6] The Slavonian landed nobility was ethnically mixed, but as a result of the nationalism of the Hungarian political estates, they were all members of the „*natio Hungarica*". They mastered both the Croatian and Hungarian languages, and due to the universality of Latin culture and literacy, ethnicity did not play a part in the formation their identity at that time.[7]

Although the late medieval South Transdanubian and Slavonian societies were ethnically divided, they mainly followed the Latin rite as the subjects of the Kingdom of Hungary. This uniform religious picture became shattered during the Ottoman rule, and the most coloured ethnic and religious patterns in Europe developed in the region by the 18th century.[8]

The fact that many members of the first great generation of the Reformation in the conquered part of Hungary came from the counties of Tolna and Baranya, and several famous preachers working in the region beyond the River Tisza had the same origin, is well known. It is also evident that the change of religion took place rather quickly in South Transdanubia. Historians explain its reasons in several different ways.[9] However, they have seldom examined the Reformation from the recipients' point of view; thus, it is worth looking at the local inhabitants, as well.

South Transdanubia was one of the richest territories of the Kingdom of Hungary at the end of the Midle Ages, in great part due to its location and its hospitable climate. Thanks to the features of the terrain, Baranya and Tolna were famous for their vineyards, and the population could eke out a good living from viticulture, which provided the basis for the development of market towns in the region, and had a

---

[6] The fact that the nobles of Baranya expelled the Serbs they considered unreliable in 1529, also played a part in this. It is not clear whether it was the order of Szapolyai or a private action. IVIĆ, Aleksa: Spomenici (...) Novi Sad 1910, 23-25. 17 July 1529. Lak. Pál Bakics to King Ferdinánd. – About Serbian immigration see Ferenc SZAKÁLY: Szerb bevándorlás a török kori Magyarországra. In: Szomszédaink között Kelet-Európában. Emlékkönyv Niederhauser Emil 70. születésnapjára. [Serbian Immigration into Hungary under the Ottoman Rule In: Among Our Neighbours in Eastern Europe. Studies for the 70th Birthday of Emil Niederhauser]. Ed. by Ferenc GLATZ. Budapest 1993, 75-78. – This study does not deal with the Uskok-Vlach population settled in Žumberak (Sichelburg) because at that time this area was in Austrian hands. For the best summary of the issue, see KASER, Karl: Freier Bauer und Soldat. Die Militarisierung der agrarischen Gesellschaft an der kroatisch-slawonischen Militärgrenze (1535-1881). Wien-Köln-Weimar 1997 (Zur Kunde Südosteuropas Band II/22).

[7] KLANICZAY, Tibor: Irodalom és nemzetiség. [Literature and Ethnicity]. In: IDEM.: Stílus, nemzet és civilizáció. Budapest 2001 (Régi Magyar Könyvtár, Tanulmányok 4), 14-17.

[8] For the state of affairs at the beginning of the 18th century, see: Magyar Kódex III. Szultán és császár birodalmában. Magyarország művelődéstörténete 1526-1790 [Hungarian Codex vol. III. In the Empires of the Sultan and the Emperor. The Cultural History of Hungary 1526-1790]. Ed. By József SZENTPÉTERY. Budapest 2000, 315-330.

[9] The majority of Protestant church historians think that the fervour of the preachers was the cause of the successful conversion. „E vidék reformálását mégis a Sztárai Mihály lankadást és félelmet nem ismerő buzgalma hajtotta végre...". ZOVÁNYI, Jenő: A reformáczió Magyarországon 1565-ig [The Reformation in Hungary up to 1565]. Budapest é.n., 218.

great influence on the culture of the middle classes.[10] The church also assisted this process of development as several monastic orders preferred to settle in South Transdanubia, and they established an elaborate system of institutions in the area. The religious institutions operated a well-functioning school-network, the centre of which was the chapter school in Pécs. The quality of local education is well-proved by the fact that many students from the diocese of Pécs continued their studies at foreign universities. Thus, a rich middle class, which encouraged its members to gain foreign experience, existed in the market towns of South Transdanubia. This shows a strong need for culture, and at the same time it denies the premise that the population was ignorant in the century of the Reformation.[11] Therefore, the question is the following: why only the Protestant ministers could cover this need? Historical research offers several explanations for this, and it is worth considering them one by one.

The prevailing view is that believers became disappointed with the Catholic Church. However, many historians have already denied this 19th-century opinion,[12] and now there is only one point to highlight. At the end of the Middle Ages, the majority of the people from the Kingdom of Hungary visiting the Papal Court to get absolution came from the dioceses of Zagreb and Pécs. The archives of the Office of the *Sacra Poenitentiaria Apostolica* preserve 652 petitions from the diocese of Zagreb and 377 requests from the episcopacy of Pécs, which, considering all the petitions from the Kingdom of Hungary, is 22 per cent and 13 per cent respectively,.[13] It was not secular law that made people set out on this journey, which means that they were willing to make financial sacrifices in exchange for the mediation of the Church. Nonetheless, interestingly enough, the Reformation quickly gained ground in a region maintaining such an intense relationship with Rome. It was not turning away from religion, but rather the opposite: the heightened spiritual expectation that might have provided a favourable background to the Reformation.

Another often-mentioned argument concerning the success of the Reformation is the landlords' change of religion. However, recent research has revealed that the principle *cuius regio eius religio* did not apply to Hungary, and the change of religion was a private decision. Irrespective of denomination, landlords were the patrons of the churches on their estates.[14] Moreover, Hungarian serfs had a greater freedom than their western European contemporaries because they were tied to the landlords only through their lands but not their persons. Thus, landlords could not interfere in their choice of religion, and the Ottomans did not limit this right in the

---

[10] SZAKÁLY, Ferenc: Mezőváros és reformáció [Market Towns and the Reformation]. Budapest 1995 (Humanizmus és reformáció 23), 13-92.

[11] PÉTER, Katalin: kényszer vagy választás [The Reformation: Coercion Or Choice]. Budapest 2004.

[12] PÁSZTOR, Lajos: A magyarság vallásos élete a Jagellók korában [Hungarian Religious Life in the Jagiellonian Period]. Budapest 2000.

[13] ERDÉLYI, Gabriella: A „Sacra Poenitentiaria Apostolica" hivatala és magyar kérvényei a 15-16. században II [The Office of the „Sacra Poenitentiaria Apostolica" and Its Hungarian Requests in the 15th-16th Centuries vol. II.] In: Levéltári Közlemények 76/1 (2005), 82.

[14] PÉTER: A reformáció, 32.

16th century, either.[15] Hence the question remains: why was it not the Catholic priest that the congregation chose?

The Catholic loss of space in the conquered area, which was the result of the Ottoman devastation, is the most frequent answer for this question. Tax records also support this premise: they suggest that nearly 70 per cent of the Catholic institutions perished in the 16th century, and thus, Protestant preachers could easily convert the inhabitants of the region.[16]

Beside the devastation, another argument suggests the invaders' friendly attitude towards the Protestants.[17] However, Antal Molnár has in many cases proved the lack of a uniform Ottoman religious policy, and has shown that their decisions were based on pragmatism.[18] The conquerors' aim was to pacify the region, and as a result, they attempted to avoid conflicts with local people. Therefore, they supported the new denominations in the Protestant areas, whereas in Jászberény, Gyöngyös and Szeged, where Catholics formed the majority, they backed these congregations. The Ottomans' only concern was to have a maximum of two denominations within one community, possibly a stronger and a weaker one,[19] so that both would seek the support of the Ottomans.[20]

Hence, apart from the damage suffered by the Catholic infrastructure, the most important reason for the quick success of the Reformation lay in the fact that Protestants got ahead of their rivals in the cultural contest of the denominations. Protestant preachers were much more prepared than Catholics, their argumentation techniques were more sophisticated, and they could rely early on printing.[21] As a result of the change of religion, the new ministers were charged with the supervision of parochial schools, and they were entrusted with the local children's education, which might also have influenced the inhabitants' decision. The generation grown up in these schools already called for Hungarian literature, the birth of which had

[15] PÉTER: A reformáció, 99.

[16] SZAKÁLY, Ferenc: Török uralom és reformáció Magyarországon a 16. század közepe táján [Ottoman Rule and Reformation in Hungary around the Middle of the 16th Century]. In: Világosság 25 (1984), 52-54. – The state of affairs was similar in Somogy where half of the recorded 58 parishes were empty as early as 1546. SOLYMOSI, László: A hódoltság néhány somogyi település történetében [Ottoman Rule in the History of Some Villages in Somogy.]. In: Somogy Megye Múltjából 8 (1977), 51.

[17] SZAKÁLY: Török uralom, 51-59.

[18] MOLNÁR: Katolikus missziók, 108. – MOLNÁR: Le Saint-Siège, 95. It offers further studies to read.

[19] For this reason, they did not let the Calvinists to practise their religion freely. MOLNÁR, Antal: Jezsuiták a hódolt Pécsett. [Jesuits in Pécs under the Ottoman Rule.]. In: IDEM: A katolikus egyház a hódolt Dunántúlon. Budapest 2003 (METEM Könyvek 44), 21.

[20] This mainly had financial reasons: the Ottomans expected further income from these congregations this way. MOLNÁR: Katolikus missziók, 110-114. – MOLNÁR: Le Saint-Siège, 97–100.

[21] There were thirty printing-houses in the territory of the Kingdom of Hungary in the 16th century, only one of which was Catholic, in Nagyszombat. PÉTER, Katalin: A reformáció Magyarországon [The Reformation in Hungary]. In: Papok és nemesek. Magyar művelődéstörténeti tanulmányok a reformációval kezdődő másfél évszázadból]. Budapest 1995, 26. – Also in German PÉTER, Katalin: Die Reformation in Ungarn. In: Études Historiques Hongroises 1990 publiées à l'occasion du XVIIe Congrés International des Sciences Historiques par le Comité National des Historiens Hongrois. IV. European Intellectual Trends and Hungary. Ed. by Ferenc GLATZ. Budapest 1990, 47.

also been the result of the Protestant ministers' operation.[22] Although this question still requires further research, cultural issues also contributed to the success of the Reformation.

On the whole, there was a rich middle class interested in religious matters in 16th-century South Transdanubia who could decide freely about the denominations they wanted to join. The Protestants could meet their cultural demands and that is why they became the members of the Calvinist or the Unitarian denominations. Unitarianism won through in the region, and Pécs became the home of the Unitarian bishop, which indicated the level of literacy of the people in Baranya, because only the highly educated population could understand the complex argumentation of Unitarianism.[23] The intellectual dominance of Pécs made the county of Baranya become fundamentally Unitarian by the end of the 16th century, whereas the county of Tolna and the Hungarian population along the Danube mainly joined Calvinist congregations. Only two large blocks of Hungarian Catholics survived the ordeals of the century.[24]

The Reformation, however, was not so successful south to the Drava[25] despite the fact that in the first decades it seemed that the new doctrines would easily gain ground in this region, too.[26] When examining the reasons why, it is worth looking separately at the conquered territories and the areas retained by the Christians.

---

[22] Protestant teachers translated the works of Homer and Plutarch into Hungarian. They were also the ones who wrote about Ban Bánk, Miklós Toldi and King Matthias, although the Catholics could also have done it. Gáspár Heltai translated Antonio Bonfini into Hungarian, while his Catholic contemporary, Miklós Oláh wrote only in Latin. The peak of the publication of such books was the last 30 years of the 16th century, when eigthty per cent of the Hungarian society belonged to some Protestant denomination. Thus, Protestantism went hand in hand with arousing the interest in culture. For a detailed analysis of the question, see: MAGYARORSZÁG TÖRTÉNETE III/1. 1526-1686 [The History of Hungary vol. III/1. 1526-1686]. Ed. by Zsigmond Pál PACH. Budapest 1986, 583-593.

[23] Recent research has shown that the nonadorantist wing of Unitarianism spread in Transdanubia as early as the 1570s. This group denied the divinity of Jesus Christ and strove for syncretism with the Jewish and Muslim religions. BALÁZS, Mihály: Teológia és irodalom. Az Erdélyen kívüli antitrinitarizmus kezdetei [Theology and Literature. The Beginnings of Antitrinitarianism Outside Transylvania]. Budapest 1998 (Humanizmus és Reformáció 25), 98-102. – For the Unitarian congregation in Pécs see VÁLASZÚTI, György: Pécsi Disputa [The Dispute of Pécs]. Ed. by Katalin NÉMETH S. Budapest 1981 (Régi magyar prózai emlékek 5), 12-26. – BALÁZS, Mihály: A szekér és az ökör. Adalék a baranyai antitrinitarizmus történetéhez [The Cart and the Ox. Additional Data for the History of Antitrinitarianism in Baranya]. In: Pécs a törökkorban. Ed. by Szakály Ferenc. Pécs 1999 (Tanulmányok Pécs történetéből 7), 265-266. – For the Unitarians in Baranya see BENDA, Kálmán: Unitáriusok a hódoltság-kori Dél-Baranyában [Unitarians in South Baranya under the Ottoman Rule]. Baranya IV/1-2 (1991), 87-97.

[24] The first group of the Catholic congregations lay east of Pécs, to the Danube. Hosszúhetény, Bogád, Kozár (today: Egyházaskozár) and the other Kozár (Nagykozár) formed its western border, while Szebény, Somberek and Szekcső lay in the eastern part. The other block lay west and north-west of Pécs in a semicircle. Its most southern point was Bicsérd, and the northernmost villages were Vásárosdombó and Alsómocsolád. MOLNÁR: Jezsuiták, 33.

[25] For a summary see TARCZAY, Erzsébet: A reformáció Horvát-Szlavonországban [The Reformation in Croatia and Slavonia]. In: Theológiai Szemle 5/3 (1929), 195-287.

[26] On 25 April 1533, the Palatine and the Supreme Comes of Virovitica, János Bánffy wrote to Clement VII that heresy had already appeared in Slavonia as well. BUNYITAY, Vince – RAPAICS, Rajmund – KARÁCSONYI, János – KOLLÁNYI, Ferenc – LUKCSICS, József: Egyháztörténelmi emlékek a magyarországi hitújítás korából II. (1530-1534.) [Church Historical Memories from the Age of the Reformation in Hungary. Vol. II. (1530-1534.)]. Budapest 1904, 244-245.

In the territory retained by the Habsburgs, the causes of the failure are extremely complex. First, the Catholic hierarchy did not collapse in the region at the time of the Ottoman conquests, and the Episcopal centre, Zagreb, remained in Christian hands. While in 16th-century Hungary the Catholic clergy became impoverished, , the bishop of Zagreb was one of the wealthiest landed proprietors due to the special Slavonian land structure.

The early beginning of the Catholic revival also relates to this question. György Draskovich, Bishop of Zagreb,[27] issued the decrees of the Council of Trent in his diocese[28] as early as 1574, and he made some crucial steps to reform the life of the clergy. The early starting date of the Catholic revival stopped reaping the fruits of the activities of Hans Ungnad von Sonneck, a patron of the arts, and the translator Primus Truber.[29] Draskovich's position was further strengthened when he was appointed as Ban in 1567, and as a consequence, he held both the secular and the religious power over the region. It was Draskovich who suggested the codification of Act 300 of 1576, which forbade Protestants from obtaining estates or holding any offices in the territory under his authority.

The close cultural links with Rome, the centre of the Catholic Church, also promoted Catholic reform. Croatian students kept studying at Italian universities, while only few of them attended Protestant schools in the German territories. The University of Vienna, favoured by the Croats, became a stronghold of Catholic theology in 1552, when the Jesuit College opened there. Moreover, Croatian priests were still educated in Italy, especially after 1553, when Paulus Zondinus established the Collegium Hungaricum et Illiricum in Bologna.[30] This institution had a key role in 17th-century Catholic revival.

Another difference between Slavonia and South Transdanubia lay in the fact that in the former, the centres of the Franciscan order were left more intact after the Ottoman conquest,[31] and the Jesuits also appeared in the region rather early. The first Jesuit college opened in Zagreb in 1606, to be followed by several others. The well-trained monks established schools where they could teach a newer generation of missionaries. However, there were no Protestant schools in Slavonia, and as a result, Protestants could not spread their religious tenets so effectively. In the towns along the border, Koprivnica and Jastrebarsk, Franciscan monasteries operated all

[27] BATELJA, Juraj et alii: Zagrebački biskupi i nadbiskupi. Zagreb 1995.

[28] He was the first one to do this in the Kingdom of Hungary, but Hungarian surveys of church history usually do not mention this deed. Instead, they generally regard the announcement in the diocese of Győr in 1579 as the first of this kind. However, it is also connected to Draskovich. KOLTAI, András: A győri egyházmegye 1579. évi szombathelyi zsinata [The Synod of the Diocese of Győr in Szombathely in 1579.]. In: Magyar egyháztörténeti vázlatok 7/3-4 (1995), 41-60.

[29] For the latest study on his life see BAHLCKE, Joachim: Aussenpolitik, Konfession und Kollektive Identitätsbildung: Kroatien und Innerösterreich im historischen Vergleich. In: Konfessionalisierung in Ostmitteleuropa. Wirkungen des religiösen Wandels im 16. und 17. Jahrhundert in Staat, Gesellschaft und Kultur. Ed. by Joachim BAHLCKE and Arno STROHMAYER. Stuttgart 1999, 193-211.

[30] VERESS, Endre: Olasz egyetemi városok magyar vonatkozásai [Hungarian Connections of Some Italian University Towns]. Pécs 1941, LXXI.

[31] HOŠKO, Franjo Emanuel: Franjevci u kontinentalnoj Hrvatskoj kroz stoljeća [Franciscans in kontinental Croatia trough the centuries]. Zagreb 2000, 24-29.

the while and they could meet local people's spiritual demands. Only foreign soldiers serving in the border fortresses were Protestants, but their abuses did not, in any case, make the new religion attractive. The strength of the Catholic hierarchy, the proximity to Italy, and the custody of schools all suggest that Protestantism suffered a similar defeat in the cultural field to Catholicism north of the Drava.

Some linguistic factors were also responsible for the failure of the Reformation. Preaching in the Old Slav language was a peculiarity of Croatian Catholicism, thus, the Protestant program of giving sermons in the national language did not offer any novelties. In addition, Protestantism could not stimulate the birth of the national literature either, as Croats spoke three different regional dialects and there were no possible ways of their unification. Moreover, the Bishop of Zagreb proclaimed in 1570 that priests had to celebrate the mass in Croatian, „*croatica lingua missa decantabitur*".[32] There was an interesting addition to the language problems: the Croatian Ban Péter Erdődy, who had his sympathies with the Reformation, received a Protestant Bible but could not read it since it was printed in Cyrillic letters.[33]

In spite of the multitude of languages, there is still a national aspect of Slavonian Catholicism, and the migration of the Croatian nobility into Slavonia played an important role in it. As a result of this migration, the administrative systems and the ideologies of the two regions, which had previously differed greatly, merged.[34] By the beginning of the 17th century, in opposition to the Protestant Hungarian political estates, Catholicism became one of the cornerstones of the identity of the Croatian-Slavonian nobility, and they used it to develop their own self-consciousness within the Kingdom of Hungary. Thus, Catholicism, one of the bases of the modern Croatian national identity, did not principally take shape against Serbian orthodoxy, but rather against the Protestant Hungarian estates. Although the Croatian struggle against the Ottomans also had some role in this development, it mainly appeared in literature and in some works written with the aim of propaganda.[35] Unlike the act passed in 1604 by the Diet of Pozsony that guaranteed religious freedom for Protestants, the Croatian Sabor declared that Croats would not re-employ the dismissed Protestant ministers, and it renewed the act which had been passed in 1567. This decision was greatly influenced by the fact that the Croatian estates could only rely on the assistance of the Austrian provinces in the struggle against the Ottomans, and the Counter-Reformation of the latter territories intensified the Slavonian development.[36] In 1625, Protestants were also expelled from Međimurska, which had been the South Slav citadel of Protestant culture, and by then, only the

[32] TKALČIĆ, Ivan Krst: Prilog za povjest zagrebačkih sinoda u XV. i XVI. vieku. In: Starine XVI (1884), 117-129.

[33] TARCZAY: A reformáció, 216.

[34] PÁLFFY, Géza: Hrvatska i Slavonija u sklopu Ugarske Kraljevine u 16.-17. stoljeću [Croatia and Slavonia in the structure of the Hungarian Kingdom in the 16.-17. centuries]. In: Hrvatsko-mađarski odnosi 1102-1918. Zbornik radova. Ed. by Milan KRUHEK. Zagreb 2004, 113-123.

[35] Evidence for the latter is that the Protestant Hungarian political estates used the same anti-Ottoman terminology as the Catholic Croatian nobility.

[36] For the relationship between Croatian foreign policy and the formation of the denominations see: BAHLCKE: Aussenpolitik, passim.

German soldiers stationed in the border castles practised the Lutheran faith in the region whose centres were Karlovac and Žumberak.[37]

A completely different development took place in the conquered parts of Slavonia,[38] where the influences of both neighbouring regions were felt. Parallel to the events of South Transdanubia, Protestant ministers soon appeared in the area after the collapse of the Catholic infrastructure. As in Baranya and Tolna, Mihály Sztáray managed to convert local people. The first generation of the missionaries, Mihály Sztáray, Imre Szigeti and Illés Szerémi, could also master the South Slav language and due to this bilingualism, they were effective in the South Slav territories as well, which helped the early success of the Protestant denominations.[39] In 1550, Sztáray held a local synod in Vaskaszentmárton and then another one in 1551 in Torjanci (between Vuka and Vukovar), where he enlisted a lot of congregations thanks to his argumentation skills. He proudly wrote in 1551, „*centum viginti ecclesias aedificavi*". Following the Catholic pattern, he organised his own religious district in 1554, which included the counties of Požega and Vuka.[40] However, Protestantism lost much of its impetus after his death, and the number of the Reformed South Slav communities declined gradually. The fact that the second generation of the Reformers could no longer address and integrate all the inhabitants of Slavonia under Ottoman control was the reason of their failure. This had both linguistic and pastoral causes. By the end of the 16th century, Calvinism dominated the Protestant denominations, and it mainly met the demands of the Hungarian-speaking population. The spread of Unitarianism, which was considered as a fairly extreme religion by the majority of Christians, also deterred South Slavs. Interestingly enough, no Unitarian works written in Croatian were published, which showed that Unitarians made no attempts to convert South Slavs.

These events projected the change of religion of the Slavonian South Slavs, and it was further strengthened by the existence of a strong Catholic infrastructure beyond the border, for its influence was felt in the conquered territories, too. The migration of the Balkan Catholics into Slavonia, as revealed by the Ottoman tax records, was an even more important factor, because the Bosnian Franciscans, who provided their pastoral care, also arrived in the territory. Apart from taking over the vacant parishes, these monks revived the network of monasteries with Velika and Našice as centres. This movement enabled Catholicism to survive in the region, and also largely contributed to the formation of the current denominational and ethnic borders. As a result, Protestant communities that had flourished in the 16th century vanished during the next hundred years. Tax collectors found Protestants only in

[37] It is important to mention that the miners around Samobor (Sichelburg) and Gvozdánszkó (Gvozdansko) were also mainly German Lutherans in the 17th century still. TARCZAY: A reformáció, 240-241.

[38] This term includes the counties of Virovitica and Požega, the major part of Križevci and the conquered part of the county of Zagreb.

[39] KISS Z., Géza: Történeti vázlat egy ormánsági filia (Kemse) mindennapjaihoz (1550-1914) [A Historical Outline of the Everyday Life of a Filia (Kemse) in the Ormánság (1550-1914)]. In: A Ráday Gyűjtemény Évkönyve 8 (1997), 32.

[40] BOTTA, István: Sztáray Mihály baranyai püspöksége [Mihály Sztáray's Episcopacy in Baranya]. In: Theológiai Szemle 32 (1989), 150-154.

Vaskaszentmárton in the floodplain of the Drava and in eighteen villages along the Karasica around Valpovo.[41]

The South Slav migration is strongly related to wartime destructions. The 16th-century Ottoman advance caused less devastation north of the Drava (except for the military route along the Danube and the area of inner Somogy) than between the Drava and the Sava.[42] The Ottoman campaigns induced a larger scale population movement between the two rivers because of geographical and political reasons. As early as the 1530s, tens of thousands of people had fled from Slavonia to safer areas because the territories controlled by Ferdinand were regularly ravaged.[43] Meanwhile, South Transdanubia, ruled by János Szapolyai at that time, was mainly spared.[44] The invading armies could make their way only with difficulties in Slavonia, which was defended by a dense network of castles and was watered by several rivers. Thus, the front could only advance slowly and it caused enormous damage to local people. Permanent warfare made Požega and the occupied areas of the county of Križevci almost completely deserted in 1541, and Catholic Bosnians and Orthodox Serbs fleeing from the South could settle down freely in the region.[45] The register of the Ottoman defters suggests that the population in this territory completely changed by the end of the 16th century,[46] and the new inhabitants were followed by the appearance of the Balkan church infrastructure. The Bosnian Franciscans provided pastoral care for the Catholics, while the Orthodox Church, controlled by the patriarch of Ipek from 1557 on, dealt with the Orthodox people. In the meantime, even the memories of the medieval parishes faded several times.[47]

With the migration of the southern groups, new divisions were created within local society. These were not caused by conflicts between the denominations but rather by the rivalries between the Catholic infrastructures. The local inhabitants with their different origins, identities and cultures lived together mostly in peace, and a special syncretism appeared in their set of religious beliefs. However, there were permanent clashes between the institutions dealing with their pastoral care, namely, the Bosnian

---

[41] The latter might have been the largest South Slav Calvinist community which survived in the region until the end of the Ottoman rule. BUTURAC, Josip: Katolička Crkva u Slavoniji za turskoga vladanja [The Catholic Church in Slavonia during the Ottoman Rule]. Zagreb 1970, 204-205.

[42] DÁVID, Zoltán: Adatok a török háborúk pusztításának értékeléséhez [Data for the Assessment of the Devastations of the Ottoman Wars]. In: Keletkutatás (1993), 56-68.

[43] MAŽURAN, Ive: Turska osvajanja u Slavoniji (1526-1552) [Turkish Rule in Slavonia (1526-1552)]. In: Osječki Zbornik VI (1958), 93-135.

[44] It is typical that while Suleyman the Great forbade his army to plunder Transdanubia, the retreating troops caused great damage in Slavonia.

[45] MOAČANIN, Nenad: Požega i požeština u sklopu osmanlijskoga Carstva (1537-1691) [Posegha in the structure of the Ottoman Empire]. Jastrebarsko 1997.

[46] In the Sancak of Požega, the proportion of Hungarians was only eight per cent in 1579, although they lived in bigger villages. Thus, one can conclude that the population of larger towns had better chances to survive the military campaigns. DÁVID, Géza: Magyarország népessége a 16-17. században [The Population of Hungary in the 16th-17th Centuries]. In: IDEM.: Pasák és bégek uralma alatt. Demográfiai és közigazgatás-történeti tanulmányok. Budapest 2005, 48.

[47] HADROVICS, László: Magyar és déli szláv szellemi kapcsolatok [Hungarian and South Slav Intellectual Connections]. Budapest 1944.

Franciscan province[48] and the missionary diocese of Smederevo whose seat was in Belgrade and which was directed by Rome. This struggle had both ethnic and economic causes: Raguzan merchants, enjoying special privileges in the Ottoman Empire, supported the activities of Rome, whereas the Bosnian Catholic tradespeople, who had become a relevant factor by the 17th century, backed the Franciscans.[49] The conflict ended in 1647. Although the Raguzan merchants achieved a certain amount of success, Rome entrusted the Franciscans with the pastoral care of the conquered areas. Typically, the competent authority, the bishop of Pécs, was not asked about the control of these areas which had had formerly belonged to him. The migration following the Ottoman devastation wiped out the memory of the medieval church infrastructure from the historic awareness, and this memory was substituted with Balkan elements.

On the other hand, the change of population was not so dramatic in South Transdanubia. Peace prevailed in the counties of Baranya and Tolna until 1541, and due to the characteristics of the terrain, the front could easily make its way in the region.[50] People could survive the first and bloodiest period of the conquest more easily. Although Balkan groups started to migrate also into this region in the years of consolidation, their proportion did not increase to 25 per cent by the end of the 16th century.[51] Contrary to the general view, the Hungarian network of villages could recover from wartime shock rather quickly and reorganisation started as early as the end of the century.[52] The reality was a bit less grim behind the startling numbers of the tax records. The disappearance of small villages (Hung. *pusztásodás*) had already started in the 15th century, and this process continued in the next century, irrespective of the fights.[53] The population of these small villages chose to move to the nearby bigger communities, and only 25 per cent of them moved to further than twenty kilometres.[54] Thus, these people did not leave the occupied areas en masse, and the 16th century, being such a bitter period in Slavonia, did not make the

---

[48] The most relevant work for the Bosnian Franciscans' role in parts of Hungary under Ottoman rule is MOLNÁR: Katolikus misszók, 142-144 and 224-426. – MOLNÁR: Le Saint-Siège, 124–126 and 198–328.

[49] MOLNÁR, Antal: A Katolikus Egyház intézményrendszere a hódolt Magyarországon [The Institutions of the Catholic Church in the Parts of Hungary under Ottoman Rule]. In: A pécsi egyházmegye a 17-18. században. Ed. by Tamás FEDELES – Szabolcs VARGA. Pécs 2005 (Seria Historiae Diocesis Quinqueecclesiensis 1), 7-18.

[50] SZAKÁLY, Ferenc: Pécs török uralom alá kerülésének történetéhez. [On the History of Pécs Passing under Turkish Rule]. In: In Memoriam Barta Gábor. Tanulmányok Barta Gábor emlékére. Ed. by István LENGVÁRI. Pécs 1996, 158.

[51] DÁVID: Magyarország népessége, 47.

[52] According to the records, the devastation affected twenty per cent of the villages in the Sancak of Simontornya. DÁVID: Magyarország népessége, 39.

[53] Within the modern borders of Nagybajom (in Somogy), six villages had been deserted as early as the Middle Ages. This tendency also continued in the 16th century and their inhabitants generally chose Nagybajom as their new home. SOLYMOSI: A hódoltság, 37-38.

[54] DÁVID, Géza: A népesség vándormozgalma a Budai szandzsákban, 1546-1559 [Population Migration in the Sancak of Buda]. In: IDEM: Pasák és bégek uralma alatt. Demográfiai és közigazgatás-történeti tanulmányok. Budapest 2005, 66-67. See also an English version of this study: Géza DÁVID: Data on the Continuity and Migration of the Population in 16th Century Ottoman Hungary. In: Acta Orientalia Hungarica 45 (1991), 219–252.

population decrease in South Transdanubia; rather, their number stagnated in the era. However, this statement can be further refined in light of the fact that there were certain areas in inner Somogy and in the county of Tolna that became deserted due to the warfare and the disappearance of small villages. A South Slav group of people called the Vlachs settled in these areas in the 1580s.[55] Nonetheless, their appearance did not mean a change of structures for several reasons. First, the vlachs did not outnumber the local inhabitants in the examined period because they settled only in deserted areas and did not form a coherent ethnic block. Second, the former inhabitants who had moved to the nearby villages often came back to cultivate the deserted lands and thus the sense of community preserved the memory of the church administration of these areas. The third factor is closely related to the second one. Unlike the conquered parts of Slavonia, Hungarian nobles did not completely leave their South Transdanubian landed properties during the Ottoman rule, and they could vindicate their rights as landlords all along. Therefore, they could many times force the newly settled Balkan people, who had so far been privileged, to pay taxes. As a result, the idea of settlement in these areas was not very attractive to them. Due to the efficiency of the taxation by the landlords, South Slav migration stopped, and by the beginning of the 17th century, several groups moved back to south of the Drava.[56] Only those Serbs remained in Transdanubia who had settled in deserted villages and accepted to pay rent to the landlord. Hungarian nobles clearly differentiated this group from the so-called „unyielded Serbs", and they offered them legal defence similar to their Hungarian serfs. However, Hungarian landlords acted harshly against the Serbs who insisted on their privileges and served in the Ottoman army: they were handled the same way as the Ottoman soldiers.[57] Obviously, this group tied their existence to the Ottoman conquest, and at the end of the Ottoman rule they disappeared, too.

Beside its demographic and economic significance, the South Slav migration to Baranya and Tolna was also very important for the Catholic survival, as, in contrast to previous assumptions, the majority of this population was Catholic and not Orthodox. The Catholic migration promoted the survival of the Catholic Church in South Transdanubia, and a new Catholic block developed along the River Drava by the 17th century.[58]

The presence of this block made the denominational map of South Transdanubia complete. Beside native Hungarians, Catholic South Slavs, Orthodox Serbs and – only in the towns – perfunctorily Islamised Muslims lived in the region during the Ottoman rule. The population numbers can only be estimated. In 1591, 20,000

---

[55] DÁVID, Géza: A simontornyai szandzsák a 16. században [The Sancak of Simontornya in the 16th Century]. Budapest 1982, 67.

[56] SZAKÁLY, Ferenc: Magyar adóztatás a török hódoltságban [Hungarian Taxation in the Parts of Hungary under Ottoman Rule]. Budapest 1981, 183.

[57] IBID., 182.

[58] BOROS GYEVI, László: A pécsi egyházmegye horvátjai a XVII. század végéig [Croats in the Diocese of Pécs up to the End of the 17th Century]. In: A pécsi egyházmegye schematizmusa 1981. Pécs 1981, 128-151.

taxable men were listed in the tax record of the Sancak of Mohács.[59] On the basis of the method applied by Géza Dávid, 43 per cent has to be added to it to get the number of families.[60] Then, this sum has to be multiplied by five to get the number of the population. According to this method, in this period, 143,000 people lived in the Sancak of Mohács, which included the counties of Baranya and Tolna. 25 per cent of them were of South Slav origin, i.e. about 38,000 people, and only half of this group was Orthodox. They lived in hamlets and dealt with animal husbandry.[61] The number of the Muslims is estimated to be 50,000[62] in the part of Hungary under Ottoman rule, ie. in 120,000 km^2. When one wants to get the number of the Muslims in Baranya and Tolna whose size was about 9,000 km^2, one has to divide the total number of Muslims by 120,000/9,000, ie. by 13. Although this method is extremely hypothetical, one gets an approximate number of 4250. It means that about 100,000 Hungarians lived in this region at the end of the 16th century, and the majority of them were Protestants. Therefore, the appearance of 20,000 Catholics was very significant, and while it generated new impulses, it also led to new conflicts in the area.

The effect of the Catholic South Slavs' migration is best illustrated with the example of Pécs. The Catholic Church was present all along the 16th century in this town which had been conquered by the Ottomans in 1543. However, the number of Catholics gradually declined and they even lost their suburban church by the turn of the century. The South Slav immigration and the appearance of the Raguzan merchants, however, ensured the survival of the denomination. Beside Tolna, Požega and Beograd, the Raguzan tradesmen also established a colony in Pécs. It was due to them that Stjepan Radobilja, a Catholic priest, worked in the town between 1609 and 1612. Using the church together with the Unitarians, he provided the South Slav inhabitants with spiritual service.

The Jesuit settlement in town in 1612 further strengthened Catholic positions. As a result of their modern pastoration and valuable work, they managed to achieve considerable success not only in Pécs but also in the nearby villages.[63] The Jesuits started to reorganise the Hungarian Catholic infrastructure in this diocese, but their activity provoked fierce debates about authority among the members of the Balkan Catholic infrastructure, who had arrived in the region with the South Slav immigrants.

This conflict had both economic and jurisdictional causes, similarly to the clash between the Bosnian Franciscan and the missionaries directed by the Holy See in Slavonia. In South Transdanubia, the debate took part between the Jesuit monks who accepted the Hungarian Catholic hierarchy and acted as vicars of the bishop of Pécs, and the South Slavs who supported the authority of the bishop of Smederevo. There

[59] VASS, Előd: A szekcsői-mohácsi szandzsák 1591. évi adóösszeírása [The Tax Record of the Sancak of Szekcső-Mohács from 1591]. In: Baranyai Helytörténetírás (1977), 25-26.
[60] DÁVID: Magyarország népessége, 48.
[61] VASS: A szekcsői-mohácsi, 26.
[62] DÁVID: Magyarország népessége, 22.
[63] For the history of the Jesuits in Pécs see: MOLNÁR: A katolikus egyház.

were only a few Bosnian Franciscans in this area, since they did not deal with the pastoral care of Hungarians, and much fewer South Slav refugees moved to South Transdanubian villages than to Slavonia. Nevertheless, the relationship of the Jesuits and the Franciscans was not undisturbed in the region. This conflict, in addition to the language differences and different cultural traditions, caused conflicts between the South Slavs and the Catholic Hungarians. Thus, the Jesuits' attempt to attract the former group was in vain, in spite of some of the missionaries' bilingualism. The debate between the different church authorities well indicates that the memory of the medieval church infrastructure survived in South Transdanubia, and the continuity of the population enabled the bishop of Pécs to revive his claims in the 17th century. The fact that the Jesuit monks had conflicts not only with the members of the Balkan church infrastructure or the Protestant denominations, but even with their own followers, further refines the picture of Transdanubian Catholicism under the Ottoman rule. The Hungarian Catholics refused to introduce the new calendar reformed by Gregory XIII because in the Protestant economic space the market-days had been adjusted to the old calendar. This change could have meant economic failure for them. Only the Raguzan merchants supported the Jesuits in this question, and in the end, the monks had to give up their plans because of the Hungarian Catholics' resistance.

Paradoxically, the Jesuit missionaries of Pécs were mostly supported by the Ottoman authorities in the hostile milieu. The main reason for this is that the Ottoman soldiers in the conquered part of Hungary were actually recruited from the perfunctorily Islamised Balkan Orthodox population, and they were not satisfied with Muslim religious infrastructure.[64] Their system of beliefs was rooted in traditional popular religiosity based on miracles and healing. Thus, the Jesuit monks using these kinds of abilities in their pastoral care enjoyed huge popularity. The majority of the soldiers serving in the border castles in South Transdanubia came from Bosnia,[65] and brought the cult of the Holy Virgin with them.[66] Another reason why the Muslims backed the Jesuits was that the Orthodox church infrastructure was incomplete in the region, and the monks of the monastery of Grábóc, which was built in 1587, could not fulfil the tasks falling on them.[67] Although considerable Orthodox population had filtered into Transdanubia, their settlement was not

---

[64] HEGYI, Klára: Etnikum, vallás, iszlamizáció. (A budai vilájet várkatonaságának eredete és utánpótlása) [Ethnicity, Religion, Islamisation. (The Origin and Supply of the Soldiers Serving in the Castles of the Vilayet of Buda]. In: Történelmi Szemle 40/3-4 (1998), 229-256.

[65] VARGA, Szabolcs: Popular Religiosity and Religious Syncretism in South Transdanubia and in the Southern Part of the Kingdom of Hungary in the 16th-17th Centuries. (under publication)

[66] For the 17th-century significance of the shrine to the Holy Virgin in Olovo see TÓTH, István György: Athanasio Georgiceo álruhás császári megbízott útleírása a magyarországi török hódoltságról, 1626-ból [Athanasio Georgiceo, Disguised Imperial Commissioner's Travelogue about the Part of Hungary under Ottoman Rule in 1626]. In: Századok 132/2 (1998), 837-859.

[67] The monastery was established by monks coming from Dalmatia in 1587. DUJMOV, Milán: A szerb ortodox egyház helyzete Baranyában az 1690-es években [The Position of the Serbian Orthodox Church in Baranya in the 1690s]. In: A pécsi egyházmegye a 17-18 században. Ed. by Tamás FEDELES and Szabolcs VARGA. Pécs 2005 (Seria Historiae Diocesis Quinqueecclesiensis 1), 117-134.

followed by the establishment of the Orthodox church infrastructure,[68] which resulted in their disappearance from the region almost by the end of the Ottoman rule. They survived only in some particularly important villages along the Danube. Later, these Orthodox people did not have to flee far from the attacks of the Catholic and Kuruc troops, for by the end of the 17th century, a well-functioning network of monasteries had been set up in Sriem and in Slavonia (with its centre in Orahovica).[69] These monks successfully dealt with the pastoral care of Orthodox people[70] and made the region inviting for the migrating Serbs. However, their activity also prepared the ground for the bloody ethnic and denominational conflicts of the 20th century.

The last part of this study investigates the the similarities and differences between the social and church history of South Transdanubia and Slavonia under the Ottoman domination. As previously shown, the medieval denominational picture was shattered in both regions. Nevertheless, the population north of the Drava welcomed the immigrants who were willing to accept the local value system, but during the war of liberation they rejected those who were incapable of living together. The continuity of the majority of the population enabled the religious and secular reorganisation of South Transdanubia after the expulsion of the Turks because it preserved the sense of belonging to the Kingdom of Hungary, and this became more important than any denominational identity. A solid church infrastructure whose task would have been to deal with the settled Muslim and Orthodox population was not formed in the region – thus, these people remained outsiders all along.

In Slavonia, the almost complete change of population brought about fundamental transformations. During the Ottoman rule, the original inhabitants of the region were almost completely perished, and the newly arrived population brought different values and a new culture. Therefore, the memories of the medieval systems could not survive. It is not by chance that there are only little data concerning the Islamisation of village people north of the Drava, whereas in the last decades of the Ottoman rule, half of the Slavonian population and that of Sriem were Muslims, only a third of them belonged to the Catholic Church, fourteen per cent were Orthodox, and the proportion of the Protestants living next to Valpovo decreased to five per cent. Although Slavonian society was more homogenous from the aspects of ethnicity and denomination, reorganisation was more difficult in this region than north of the Drava. The borders of the medieval church and secular administrative units had disappeared, and the borders of the new dioceses and the counties became established as late as the middle of the 18th century in the Catholic areas. A military

---

[68] In the sources found up to now there have been no signs of any Orthodox churches built in villages inhabited by Serbs under the Ottoman conquest.

[69] MILEUSNIĆ, Slobodan: Manastir Orahovica kao duhovno i kulturno središte Srba u Slavoniji u vriejeme turske vladavine [The monastery Orahovica as a spiritual and cultural center of the Serbs at the times of the ottoman rule]. In: Peti znanstveni sabor Slavonije i Baranje. Zbornik radova. Osijek 1991.

[70] ZIROJEVIĆ, Olga: Crkve i manastiri na pòdručju pečke patrijaršije do 1683 [Churches and monasteries in the area of the Patriarchat of Pec until 1683]. Beograd, no date of publication.

frontier was formed from the areas where the Orthodox frontiersmen had lived, and therefore, the formerly uniform region became divided on denominational basis.

In summary, the continuity of the population was more significant than the denominational division in early modern South Transdanubia. The parallel church infrastructures strengthened one another, and as a result, dynamised their followers and compelled them to preserve their identities under the Ottoman rule. The discontinuity of the population in the reconquered Slavonian area hindered reorganisation, and the Bosnian Franciscan infrastructure was not adequate to develop and preserve any ideologies. Only the Orthodox Church could achieve this in the 18th century, and thus formed the basis of the religious and ethnic conflicts the influence of which is still at work today.

Norbert Spannenberger

Immigrationspolitik und interkonfessionelles Zusammenleben im 18. Jahrhundert in Süd-Transdanubien

Nach einer Anekdote aus Kölesd, im Komitat Tolna, fragte der Grundherr, Graf Claudius Florimund Mercy, einige Jahre nach der Besiedlung des Ortes einen alten Ungarn aus dem benachbarten Nagydorog, wie man ein Dorf am schnellsten zur Blüte bringt. Der alte Ungar erwiderte, in einer Gemeinde dürften nur Angehörige der gleichen Konfession zusammenleben. Mercy soll diesen Rat beherzigt und die Siedlungen seiner Grundherrschaft tatsächlich nach konfessionellen Kriterien angeordnet haben.[1] Diese Anekdote suggeriert ein von vornherein gegebenes Konfliktpotential unter den Konfessionen. Dies jedoch widerspiegelt keineswegs die tatsächlichen Zustände in Transdanubien in der ersten Hälfte des 18. Jahrhunderts, sondern die imaginären Bilder der in der Nationalromantik beheimateten ungarischen Historiographie des 19. Jahrhunderts, die ihre Aufgabe mitunter darin sah, Komponenten für eine verklärte Erinnerungskultur zu kreieren.
Zugleich verrät aber diese Anekdote – ungewollt – einen zu weiteren Überlegungen anregenden Aspekt: Wenn der Grundherr, hier Graf Mercy, Anlass zu einer Trennung der Konfessionen hatte, so müssen die Neusiedler konfessionell doch bis zu einem gewissen Grade heterogen gewesen sein. Im Gegensatz zum *ceterum censeo* der ungarischen Historiographie kamen nicht ausschließlich katholische deutsche Siedler, um die einheimischen ungarischen Protestanten zu marginalisieren, sondern ein „Fleckerlteppich" von Konfessionen erwartete die ohnehin schon konfessionell heterogenen Gruppen der Neusiedler.[2] Die mit der Vertreibung der Osmanen eingeleitete intensive Immigrationspolitik des ungarischen Adels und des Wiener Hofes führte zur quantitativen Zunahme verschiedener Konfessionen, womit die ohnehin vorhandene konfessionelle Vielfalt nur weiter vertieft wurde. Doch nicht diese Quantifizierung, sondern die aus dem Anspruch der *Herrschaftsintensivierung* abgeleitete *Konfessionalisierung* war der Grund dafür, dass die Form des interkonfessionellen Zusammenlebens neu geregelt werden musste, und zwar von oben nach unten, d.h. auf der Makroebene seitens des Staates und auf der Mikroebene seitens der Herrschaft.
Die unter Kaiser Ferdinand II. ab 1619 auf das ganze Habsburgerreich ausgedehnte Politik des konfessionellen Absolutismus setzte sich mit der Schlacht auf dem Wei-

[1] WEIDLEIN, Johann: Die Schwäbische Türkei. Bd. I. Beiträge zu ihrer Geschichte und Siedlungsgeographie. München 1967, 60f. – Zu den Mercys in Ungarn siehe: SEEWANN, Gerhard: Zur Familiengeschichte der Grafen Mercy und Mercy-Argentau. In: Südostdeutsches Archiv XIX/XX (1976/1977), 53-70.
[2] Zu den Rahmenbedingungen siehe pars pro toto WELLMANN, Imre: Merkantilistische Vorstellungen im 17. Jahrhundert und Ungarn. In: Nouvelles Études Historiques Hongroises 1 (1965), 315-354.

ßen Berg 1620 gegenüber den protestantischen böhmischen Ständen als das neue politische System durch. In der Folge wurden alle politischen Schlüsselpositionen mit der im Geiste des tridentinischen Katholizismus erzogenen Elite des Hofadels besetzt. Zusehens wurde dem Prinzip der religiösen Einheit der Vorrang gegenüber dem Prinzip der politischen Einheit eingeräumt.[3] Doch ausgerechnet in Ungarn gelang dies der kaiserlichen Regierung am wenigsten. In der Verteidigung ihrer Privilegien, allem voran der Steuerfreiheit, widersetzten sich die Stände für lange Zeit den als Absolutismus und Despotismus verteufelten Modernisierungsbemühungen des Wiener Hofes. Aus diesem Grunde scheute man sich auch nicht, ein Bündnis mit den Osmanen einzugehen und in diversen Aufständen gegen Wien ins Feld zu ziehen. Wenn auch diese sog. Kuruzzenaufstände scheiterten, verhinderten sie dennoch die Integration Ungarns in einen habsburgischen Einheitsstaat.[4]
Die nach der Vertreibung der Osmanen in Ungarn einsetzende, frühmoderne Staatsbildung war nicht frei von jenen soziokulturellen Gegebenheiten, die gesamteuropäische Züge aufwiesen. Daher ist die von Wolfgang Reinhard und Heinz Schilling in den 1970er und 1980er Jahren herausgearbeitete Theorie der *Konfessionalisierung* durchaus – wenn auch mit regionaltypischen Differenzierungen – anwendbar. Die „kausale Verknüpfung zwischen dem Streben nach konfessioneller Vereinheitlichung der frühneuzeitlichen Gesellschaft einerseits und weiteren sozialen, politischen und kulturellen Integrationsprozessen andererseits“[5] war nicht nur seitens des Wiener Hofes, sondern auch in der katholischen ungarischen Elite vorhanden. Als Hinweis möge hier nur das im Jahre 1688 erschienene *Einrichtungswerk* des Kardinal Kollonich erwähnt werden, was János J. Varga, László Benczédi und János Kalmár in etlichen Publikationen herausgearbeitet haben.[6] Wenn eine konfessionelle Homogenisierung selbst für Kollonich als unmöglich erschien – was aus dem *Einrichtungswerk* deutlich hervorgeht, in der ungarischen Historiographie jedoch bis vor kurzem mit bemerkenswerter Hartnäckigkeit negiert wurde und sich in der Erinnerungskultur noch immer behauptet – bleibt doch für das 18. Jahrhundert in Ungarn gültig, dass die „tiefgreifende politisch-soziale Auseinandersetzung“ oft in „konfes-

---

[3] SEEWANN, Gerhard: Habsburgermonarchie. In: Lexikon zur Geschichte Südosteuropas. Hg. v. Edgar HÖSCH, Karl NEHRING und Holm SUNDHAUSSEN. Wien-Köln-Weimar 2004, 264-269, hier 265.

[4] Wie polarisierend bis Ende des 17. Jahrhunderts die Konfession wirkte, belegte auch der ungarische Historiker Ignácz Acsády, der darauf hinwies, dass die Ungarn unter sich mit Schimpfwörtern begegneten: Die Katholiken nannten die Protestantischen als „Türken“, diese wiederum die Katholiken als „Deutsche“. Vgl. ACSÁDY, Ignácz: Magyarország belállapota 1680 [Die inneren Zustände Ungarns 1680]. In: Századok 19 (1885), 549-562 und 631-654, hier 641.

[5] BAHLCKE, Joachim/STROHMEYER, Arno: Zur Einführung. In: Konfessionalisierung in Ostmitteleuropa. Wirkungen des religiösen Wandels im 16. und 17. Jahrhundert in Staat, Gesellschaft und Kultur. Hg. v. Dens. Stuttgart 1999, 7-10, hier 7.

[6] VARGA J., János: Államhatalmi és rendi kísérletek a közigazgatás és az igazságszolgáltatás reformjára a török kiűzésének időszakában (1688-1723) [Staatliche und ständische Reformversuche in der Verwaltung und der Justiz in der Zeit der Vertreibung der Osmanen (1688-1723)]. In: A magyar államiság első ezer éve. Hg. v. Márta FONT und István KAJTÁR. Pécs 2000, 147-159. – BENCZÉDI, László: Kollonich Lipót és az „Einrichtungswerk“ [Leopold Kollonich und das „Einrichtungswerk“]. In: Gazdaság és mentalitás Magyarországon a török kiűzésének idején [Wirtschaft und Mentalität in Ungarn zur Zeit der Vertreibung der Osmanen]. Hg. v. Mihály PRAZNOVSZKY und Istvánné BAGYINSZKY. Salgótarján 1987 (Diskussiones Neogradienses 4), 153-158.

sionelle Frontenbildungen mündete", so dass das Konfessionelle in der Gesellschaft sehr wohl „konfliktleitend" fungierte.[7] Im Vergleich zu Mitteleuropa handelte es sich um eine retardierte Entwicklung, deren Erforschung bisher erst in Ansätzen erfolgt ist.

Wo die Grenzen dieses Ansatzes waren, zeigte auch die fehlgeschlagene „Bekehrung" der griechisch-orthodoxen Serben, die sich als erste große Migrantengruppe während und nach der Vertreibung der Osmanen in Ungarn niederließen. Während der Osmanenzeit sowie der Wende vom 17. zum 18. Jahrhundert machten die Raitzen in den südtransdanubischen Komitaten Tolna und Baranya einen beträchtlichen Anteil der Bevölkerung aus. Ein weiterer Aufschwung erfolgte im Zuge der *velika seoba*, der „Großen Wanderung" unter dem Patriarchen Arsenije III. Čarnojević nach 1690.[8] Die meisten von ihnen ließen sich zwar in Szentendre und Pest nieder, doch die Donau entlang waren sie von Norden bis nach Süden ebenfalls aufzufinden.[9] Nach einer Konskription der Hofkammer von 1695 lebten in den 22 Gemeinden der Baranya 139 serbische Familien, wobei die Städte nicht berücksichtigt wurden. 1696 zählte man im Komitat Tolna insgesamt 459 raitzische Familien.[10] Die eigentliche Anzahl dürfte aber deutlich höher gelegen haben, da lediglich die Steuerzahlenden, und auch diese nicht genau, berücksichtigt wurden. Das ethnische Bild Süd-Transdanubiens veränderte sich zugunsten der Raitzen. Nach Seewanns Schätzung machte die raitzische Bevölkerung um 1700 etwa eine halbe Million Menschen aus, was mehr als die Hälfte in den von den Osmanen zurückeroberten Gebieten bedeutete.[11]

---

[7] BAHLCKE/STROHMEYER: Zur Einführung, 7. – Der ungarische Historiker Kálmán Benda sieht diese Fragestellung insgesamt wenig erforscht und fokussiert den Einfluss des Kalvinismus auf den Adel. Vgl. BENDA, Kálmán: A nemzeti hivatástudat nyomában [Auf der Spur des Bewusstseins der nationalen Berufung]. Hg. v. János LUKÁTS. Budapest 2004, 52-54.

[8] Zur *velika seoba* siehe pars pro toto VESELINOVIĆ, Rajko L.: Срби у великом рату 1683-1699 [Die Serben im großen Krieg 1683-1699]. In: Историја српског народа [Geschichte des serbischen Volkes]. Bd. III/1. Београд 1993, 530-552. – MARIJAN, Vlado St.: Србска историйска читанка 2 [Serbisches historisches Lesebuch]. Београд 2001, 276-287. – Eine kritische Auseinandersetzung mit dieser in der serbischen Erinnerungskultur stark mythologisierten Wanderung aus dem Kosovo siehe MALCOLM, Noel: Kosovo. A Short History. New York 1998, 160-163. Demnach begaben sich 30.000-40.000 Menschen ins Königreich Ungarn, während eine serbische Klosterchronik von 37.000 Familien sprach, was auch Eingang in die Erinnerungskultur fand.

[9] Kollonich schrieb in seinem Brief an Papst Clemens XI. über den „Patriarchen der Raitzen, welcher mit mehr als 60.000 Köpfen unter den Schutz des Kaisers aus der türkischen Knechtschaft sich geflüchtet hat". Zitiert nach MAURER, Joseph: Cardinal Leopold Kollonitsch, Primas von Ungarn. Sein Leben und sein Wirken. Innsbruck 1887, 370.

[10] SZILÁGYI, Mihály: Az újratelepülő Tolna megye 1710-1720 [Das wiederbesiedelte Komitat Tolna]. In: Tanulmányok Tolna megye történetéből (1983), 33-168, hier 50. – DUJMOV, Milán: A szerb ortodox egyház helyzete Baranyában az 1690-es években [Die Lage der serbisch.orthodoxen Kirche in der Baranya in den 1690er Jahre]. In: A pécsi egyházmegye a 17-18. században. Hg. v. Tamás FEDELES und Szabolcs VARGA. Pécs 2005, 117-134, hier 129.

[11] SEEWANN, Gerhard: Serbische Nord-Süd-Migration in Südosteuropa als Voraussetzung für die deutsche Ansiedlung im 18. Jahrhundert. In: DERS.: Ungarndeutsche und Ethnopolitik. Ausgewählte Aufsätze. Budapest 2000, 237-256, hier 244. – Seewann betont zugleich, gestützt auf Ferenc Szakály und Klára Hegyi, die Unzuverlässigkeit der Aussagekraft damaliger Konskriptionen und will diese Zahlen als „Orientierungsgröße" verstehen.

Die Situation der Raitzen war jedoch ambivalent, rechnete sie doch der Wiener Hof, genauer der Hofkriegsrat, nach deren Ansiedlung in Ungarn als Militärpotential und Reserve für die geplanten Türkenkriege. Schon im August 1690 sicherte Kaiser Leopold den Serben diverse Privilegien zu, die eine religiös-kulturelle Autonomie beinhalteten: So hatten sie das Recht auf eine freie Wahl des Patriarchen und auf eine freie Kalenderbenutzung. Der Patriarch erhielt die Befugnis, Priester zu weihen, die Gläubigen befreite man vom Zehent, allen Steuern und der Einquartierung von Soldaten. Am 4. März 1695 wurde im Leopoldinischen Diplom sogar eine eigenständige Kircheninstitution nördlich der Donau-Drau-Linie mit sieben Diözesen festgelegt. 1696 ernannte man Jefrem Janković zum *rascianorum Quinque Ecclesiarum Graeci Ritus Episcopus.*[12] Bis 1700 wurde also die orthodoxe Kircheninstitution aufgebaut, die während des Rákóczi-Aufstandes großteils wieder vernichtet werden sollte. Mit Hilfe der Jesuiten zwang Bischof Radanay von Fünfkirchen am 18. Januar 1690 „den Griechen" eine „Kirchenunion" auf, die aber bis auf einen Streit innerhalb der serbisch-orthodoxen Kirche keine praktischen Folgen hatte. Als Patriarch Arsenije sich diesem Druck zur Wehr setzte, nannte ihn Kardinal Leopold Kollonich *exkommunikatus et solius Diaboli filius.*[13] Wenn auch Teilerfolge dieser Katholisierung zu verzeichnen waren, insgesamt blieb der Ansatz erfolglos.

Wie sehr eine alles Andere in den Hintergrund verdrängende Konfliktkonstellation der großen Migrationen der Nachosmanenzeit die Historiographie heute noch beherrscht, bezeugt die Gratwanderung zwischen Konfessionellem und Nationalem: Seit dem späten 19. Jahrhundert bzw. frühem 20. Jahrhundert trat – nicht zuletzt im Zusammenhang mit dem *Einrichtungswerk* und geltend für die Migrationen insgesamt – der konfessionelle Aspekt in den Hintergrund und der imaginäre Konflikt wurde „ethnisiert": Demnach ging es seitens des Wiener Hofes nicht vornehmlich um die „Zurückdrängung" des Protestantismus mit der Hilfe katholischer Siedler, sondern um die „Germanisierung" des „Magyarentums", dessen williges Werkzeug die deutschen Einwanderer gewesen sein sollen.[14] Diese Interpretation fügte sich nahtlos in das seit 1848/49 vorherrschende antihabsburgische Geschichtsbild, konnte aber erst nach 1867 im Zuge der Schaffung eines ungarischen Nationalstaates und der damit einhergehenden Aufwertung einer umfassenden und vom Staat inszenierten und gesteuerten Assimilationspolitik an Popularität gewinnen.[15]

---

[12] Vgl. DUJMOV: A szerb, 127.
[13] EBD., 125.
[14] Diesen Standpunkt vertrat auch Benda noch 1981. BENDA: A nemzeti hivatástudat, 25. – Damit stützte er sich auf eine Interpretation, die auf Mihály Horváth zurückging, der in den 1860er Jahren – verbittert von der Niederschlagung des ungarischen Aufstandes von 1848/49 – zum ersten Mal die Herrschaftserrichtung der Habsburger an der Wende vom 17. zum 18. Jahrhundert mit überwiegend negativen Konnotationen versehen hatte. Hier zitiert nach HORVÁTH, Mihály: Magyarország történelme [Geschichte Ungarns]. Bd. 6. Pest 1872, 253 und 255. – Die Interpretation der „Instrumentalisierung der Kolonisten durch den Wiener Hof zwecks „Germanisierung" der Einheimischen, in diesem Fall südslawischen Bevölkerung übernahm auch die jugoslawische Geschichtsschreibung. Vgl. JANJETOVIC, Zoran: Between Hitler and Tito. The disappearance of the Vojvodina Germans. Belgrade 2000, 21f.
[15] Zur Verteufelung von Kollonich siehe u. a. MIHÁLYI, Ernő: Koldusországgá akarta-e tenni Kolonics Magyarországot? [Wollte Kollonich aus Ungarn ein Betteland machen?]. Pannonhalma 1927. – Zur Biographie des Kardinals MAURER, Joseph: Cardinal Leopold Graf Kollonitsch, Primas von Ungarn. Sein Leben

Staatliche Richtlinien der Ansiedlungspolitik

In den seltensten Fällen wird in den Meistererzählungen allerdings darauf hingewiesen, dass – abgesehen von den Kameralgebieten – nicht der Wiener Hof, sondern der ungarische Adel Initiator und Akteur der nachosmanischen Immigrationspolitik war. Die Rolle des Adels wird in der Historiographie wegen der absoluten Dominanz des *Einrichtungswerkes* ignoriert. Dies ist aus zwei Gründen anfechtbar: Erstens wurde das umstrittene *Einrichtungswerk* vom Kaiserhaus selbst zu Fall gebracht und somit gar nicht in die Praxis umgesetzt. Zweitens übte ausgerechnet dieses Opus auf die Kommissionen des Reichstages von Pressburg (1722/23) eine wegweisende und nachhaltige Wirkung aus. Für die Immigrationspolitik Ungarns stellte der Reichstag eine entscheidende Rolle dar, waren doch die Mitglieder der Kommissionen Angehörige des Adels, meist des Hochadels.[16]

Nach dem Intermezzo des Rákóczi-Aufstandes (1703-1711), der nicht nur den Abbruch der bisherigen Ansiedlungen zu Ende gebracht sondern auch die ersten Erfolge fast spurlos ausgerottet hatte, begann ein zweiter, systematischer Anlauf auf Initiative des ungarischen Adels. Dabei spielte der ehemalige „Kuruzzengeneral" und reichste Magnat in Ostungarn, Graf Alexander Károlyi, eine führende Rolle.[17] Der ungarische Großgrundbesitz brauchte mehr denn je Arbeitskräfte für den Wiederaufbau. Schon auf dem Reichstag 1712 bis 1715 wurden deshalb Subkommissionen aufgestellt, die auch ältere Arbeiten wie etwa das *Einrichtungswerk* berücksichtigten. Doch die eigentliche Arbeit konnte erst nach diesem Reichstag beginnen. Die fachliche Hintergrundarbeit versahen sogenannte „systematische Kommissionen", denen jeweils einzelne Fachgebiete zugewiesen wurden. Das von dieser Kommission ausgearbeitete Entwurf zeugt von profunden volkswirtschaftlichen Kenntnissen der Autoren, die sich an den Lehren des Merkantilismus orientiert hatten.[18] Nach

und sein Wirken. Innsbruck 1887. – Zur passenden Historiographie des Dualismus siehe pars pro toto GRÜNWALD, Béla: A régi Magyarország 1711-1825 [Das alte Ungarn 1711-1825]. Hg. v. János POÓR. Reprint Budapest 2001. – MARCZALI, Henrik: Magyarország története a Szatmári békétől a Bécsi Congresszusig 1711-1815 [Geschichte Ungarns vom Frieden von Sathmar bis zum Wiener Kongreß]. In: A magyar nemzet története. Hg. v. Sándor SZILÁGYI. Bd. V. [Budapest 1895.] Reprint Budapest 2000.

[16] Dieser Reichstag wird in der Regel in der Historiographie aus dem Blickwinkel der Migrationen unterschätzt, da im Mittelpunkt die Auseinandersetzungen um die *Pragmatica sanctio* sowie um diverse Adelsprivilegien standen. Dabei setzte sich schon der Reichstag von 1711 zum Ziel, die Besteuerung neu zu regeln, was die „Peuplierung" wieder interessant machte. Da die Konskription von 1715 sehr fragwürdige Ergebnisse aufwies, wurde sie 1720 wiederholt. Dies bildete die Grundlage für den Reichstag von 1722/23. Vgl. ausführlich BÉRENGER, Jean / KECSKEMÉTI, Károly: Országgyűlés és parlamenti élet Magyraországon 1608-1918 [Reichstag und Parlamentsleben in Ungarn 1608-1918]. Budapest 2008, 154-159.

[17] Károlyi arbeitete in der Landeskommission praktisch ganz allein die Vorschläge aus: „[...] ich arbeite wie zurzeit von Franz [II. Rákóczi], kaum habe ich Zeit zum Speisen. Wenn Gott nur meine Arbeit segnen würde, meine Bemühungen zum Wohle der armen Untertanen und des ganzen Landes", schrieb er an seine Gattin. ÉBLE, Gábor: Károlyi Ferencz gróf és kora 1705-1758 [Graf Franz Károlyi und seine Zeit 1705-1758]. Band I. Budapest 1893, 137-138.

[18] Vgl. SCHÜNEMANN, Konrad: Die Einstellung der theresianischen Impopulation (1770/71). In: A bécsi gr. Klebelsberg Kuno Magyar Történetkutató Intézet évkönyve (1931), 167-213, hier 211. – Károlyi analysierte die Probleme nach Ursache und Wirkung, berücksichtigte dabei auch die Erkenntnisse des *Einrichtungswerk*es von Kollonich, und schlug die Ansiedlung von 100.000 Kolonisten in ganz Ungarn vor, nämlich 36.400 Personen in Städten und Burgen, und 63.600 auf dem Lande. Vgl. TAKÁTS, Sándor: A dohány elter-

diesen Vorarbeiten wurden auf dem Landtag in Pressburg 1722/23 die grundlegenden Gesetzesartikel zwecks Vermehrung der Bevölkerung des Ungarischen Königreiches verabschiedet.

Die Gesetzesbeschlüsse des Reichstages hinsichtlich der Einwanderungspolitik bildeten eine zwar nie betonte, aber unverkennbare Kontinuität zu den Maßnahmen des Wiener Hofes nach der Vertreibung der Osmanen. In dem am 11. August 1689 herausgegebenen, übrigens von Kollonich verfassten sog. *Ersten Kaiserlichen Impopulationspatent* wurde ausdrücklich hervorgehoben, dass das „so großer sowohl feindlicher, als eigener Armaden und Hilfs- Völcker, fast gänzlich zu Grund gerichteten und abgeödten Erb-Königreichs Hungarn" schleunigst mit Siedlern „popularisiert" werden soll, wobei „alle und jede, was Stands, Nation, und Religion, inn- oder außer Landts die seind" willkommen seien.[19] Eine aktive Bevölkerungspolitik befürwortete Artikel 103 *De impopulatione regni*. Im Gesetzentwurf hieß es noch ausführlich: „Weil dieses Königreich mit dem, was landtagsmäßig seiner Heiligen Krone unterworfen ist, in seiner weiten Ausdehnung des genügenden Volkes entbehrt, das in seinem Raume Aufnahme finden könnte und zu seiner Bebauung notwendig wäre und weil wegen dieses Menschenmangels nur lauter weit ausgedehnte Wüsten zu sehen sind, die durch eine anzuordnende Wiederbevölkerung sowohl dem Königreich wie Eurer Hoch Geheiligten Majestät bedeutenden Nutzen bringen könnten", sollten explizit freie Personen eingeladen werden und diese sechs Jahre Befreiung von allen öffentlichen Abgaben genießen. In den Erbländern sollte der Kaiser für die Bekanntmachung der neuen Einwanderungspolitik Sorge tragen.

In der Gesetzgebung des Reichstages blieb die Auffassung von Kollonich verbindlich, wonach die 1681 auf dem Ödenburger Reichstag beschlossenen Religionsgesetze dahingehend zu interpretieren seien, dass protestantische Pfarrer lediglich an den vorher bestimmten sog. „Artikularorten" (an je 2 Orten eines Komitates) ihren Gottesdienst abhalten durften, wobei die Stolgebühren weiterhin den katholischen Priestern zu entrichten waren.[20] In den übrigen Gemeinden durfte zwar der Grundherr ein Oratorium oder Bethaus für die protestantischen Untertanen erbauen, aber keinen Prediger anstellen. 1701 bestätigte Kaiser Leopold I. in seiner *Explanatio*, dass in den *Neoacquistici*, also in den von den Türken neu erworbenen Gebieten, keine freie Religionsausübung gestattet sei, sondern die 1681 angenommenen Richtlinien gelten. Die Fundamente für die im konfessionellen „Europa typischen Zusammenarbeit von Staat und Kirche"[21] waren damit auch in der ungarischen Immigrationspolitik gelegt. Die Doppelzüngigkeit in der Siedlungspolitik bestand eben darin, dass – wie es auch aus dem *Einrichtungswerk* hervorgeht – sehr wohl mit pro-

---

jedése s az első dohány-monopólium hazánkban [Die Verbreitung des Tabaks und das erste Tabakmonopol in unserem Land]. Teil 2. In: Magyar Mezőgazdasági Szemle V/2 (1898), 121-145, hier 124.

[19] TAFFERNER, Anton: Quellenbuch zur donauschwäbischen Geschichte. Bd. I. München 1974, 112.

[20] Ausführlich siehe BARTA, János ifj.: A tizennyolcadik század története [Geschichte des 18. Jahrhunderts]. Budapest 2000, 27 und 32.

[21] SCHILLING, Heinz: Das konfessionelle Europa. Die Konfessionalisierung der europäischen Länder seit Mitte des 16. Jahrhunderts und ihre Folgen für Kirche, Staat, Gesellschaft und Kultur. In: BAHLCKE/STROHMEYER: Konfessionalisierung, 13-63, hier 18.

testantischen Siedlern gerechnet wurde, doch in der Anwerbung sämtliche Hinweise auf derlei Beschränkungen in der Religionsausübung fehlten. Somit war der praktischen Umsetzung der gültigen Gesetze seitens der Grundherren doch ein gewisser Spielraum gelassen, woraus diese durchaus Gebrauch zu machen wussten.

Immigrationspolitik der Grundherren

Angesichts der quantitativ bescheidenen Untersuchungen ist es noch verfrüht, generelle Aussagen über die Zusammenhänge der Immigrationspolitik der privaten Herrschaften und der Komponenten der Konfessionen zu machen. Viel mehr können lediglich hypothetische Überlegungen anhand von Einzelfällen oder wenigen Einzelstudien angestellt werden. Man kann aber grob festhalten, dass der katholische Klerus und religiös-eifrige Grundherren explizit und ausschließlich katholische Siedler bevorzugten, während eher ökonomisch dominierte Grundherren – sehr wohl auch katholischer Konfession – durchaus auch Protestanten aufnahmen.
Zu den frühen Ansiedlungen gehörte die Herrschaft Petschwar (ung. Pécsvárad) im Komitat Baranya. Der Abt der Benediktinerabtei, Francesco Giani oder in der ungarischen Form Ferenc Jány, wurde am 11. Oktober 1688 in seinen Besitz eingeführt. Schon am 26. Januar 1689 berichtete ihm sein Agent, Dionysius von Rehlingen aus Augsburg über die Fortschritte in der Anwerbung von Kolonisten. „Hochwürdiger Fürstlicher Gnädigster Fürst und Herr. Weilen ich kain andtwort von Ihro Hochfürstlichen gnaden auf mein gethanes schreiben erhalten, als hab ich nochmahlen gehorsamb berichten wollen, daß ich nuhr af 30 oder 40 familien habe, so sich auf dero habenden grundt und boden in Vngaren wirdtlich ansetzen, und gethrewe onderthanen abgeben wollen.“ Natürlich war das nur ein Teilerfolg, da der Agent davon ausging, dass er noch mehr als 100 Familien anwerben könne, damit „eine ganze herrschaft in kuzer Zeit mit lauter redlichen, arbeitsamben katholischen hochdaischen zue besetzen“ sei. Letztlich blieb der Agent erfolgreich, die Abtei Petschwar wie übrigens auch die benachbarten Ländereien des Bischofs und des Domkapitels von Fünfkirchen wurden mit katholischen Deutschen besiedelt.[22]
Keinerlei konfessionelle Beschränkung gab es in den „frühen“ Ansiedlungsverträgen von Budakeszi (1701) oder Grossturwall (ung. Törökbálint 1701), die vor dem Rákóczi-Aufstand ausgestellt wurden. Bei der Neubesiedlung der Gemeinde Harta im Komitat Pest vom 9. Juni 1724, also dreizehn Jahre nach dem Rákóczi-Aufstand, wurde sogar als erster Punkt das Privileg der protestantischen Kolonisten wie folgt verankert: „Wird denenselben erlaubt, ein Bethauß aufzubauen und nach ihrer Religion Prediger zu berufen und anzunehmen“.[23] Der hiesige Grundherr, Graf Pál Ráday, setzte in seiner Anwerbung bewusst auf evangelisch-lutherische und kalvinistisch-reformierte Kolonisten aus der Pfalz, aus Württemberg und Speyer. In der

[22] HERRMANN, Ägid: Erste Spuren der Kolonisation in Pécsvárad. In: Deutsch-Ungarische Heimatsblätter 1/1 (1929), 48-52.
[23] Hier zitiert nach BRANDTER, Paul: Buch der deutschen Forschungen in Ungarn. Budapest 1940, 272.

Forschung intensiver behandelt wurde die Kolonisationspolitik des Grafen Mercy, der im Komitat Tolna protestantische Siedler bevorzugte und damit überhaupt die Gründung eines evangelischen Seniorats in Süd-Transdanubien ermöglichte.[24] Er hatte im Komitat Tolna etwa 25 Dörfer gekauft und war damit zu einem der mächtigsten Grundherren aufgestiegen. 1722 bestimmte er sein Gut Högyész, auch Mercystetten genannt, zum Zentrum, wozu die Orte Pálfa, Schar- St. Lorenz (ung. Sárszentlörinc), Rácegres, Kleintormasch (ung. Kistormás), Teile von Köleschd (ung. Kölesd), Warschad (ung. Varsád), Gallas (ung. Kalaznó), Obernana (ung. Felsönána), Mucsi, Isming (ung. Izmény), Mutschwang (ung. Mucsfa) und Kleinmangarth (ung. Kismányok) gehörten.

Diese Strategie des katholischen Mercy war allerdings keineswegs eine singuläre Erscheinung: Im öffentlichen Bewusstsein galt der protestantische Fleiß, der Hang zur Ordnung, Disziplin und Mäßigkeit als Schlüssel der unbestreitbaren ökonomischen Erfolge zeitgenössischer protestantischer Länder. So schrieb der evangelische Pfarrer aus dem hohenlohischen Kupferzell, Johann Friedrich Mayer: „Der catholische Ackermann vermisset also den Gewinn aus 60 Tagen, den der protestantische machet, und da der catholische an den Feyertagen von 60 Tägen in den Wirtshäusern schmauset, oder festlicher zu Hause isset, trinkt, und sich kleidet, Besuche annimmt oder gibt und dergleichen, so ist unterdessen der Protestante mit seinem Alltagsbrod zu frieden und arbeitet sich weniger schadhaft in seinem alltäglichen Kittel.“[25] Evangelisch-lutherische, vornehmlich pietistische Pfarrer verstanden es durchaus, Frömmigkeit mit dem zeitgenössischen Ideal der *industria* zu verbinden und auf diesem Fundament einen Wertekatalog zu kreieren, der zur Steigerung von religiöser Besinnung, Fleiß, Effizienz, kollektiver Solidarität etc. anspornte.[26]

Dennoch bleibt die Frage, ob man tatsächlich vor Ort darauf geachtet hat, möglichst homogene Siedlungen in konfessioneller oder ethnischer Hinsicht zu schaffen. Die Relevanz dieser Frage lässt sich auch daran ermessen, dass in der Propaganda der Kolonistenagenten die konfessionelle und manchmal auch die ethnische Homogenität in den Siedlungsgebieten durchaus als ein attraktives Angebot und eine bewusste Strategie der Grundherren erschienen. So hieß es etwa 1718 auf einem Werbezettel im schwäbischen Biberach: „An diesem Orth (nämlich auf den Gütern des Döry im Komitat Tolna) ist auch bereits ein Teutscher Catholischer Geistlicher und 29 Schwäbische Ehen, und braucht man noch daselbst biß 2000 Ehen, darunter von allerhand Handtirungen könne gerechnet werden; welche Herrschaft zumahl von einem Schwäbischen Ambtmann wird verwaltet und gar keine Ungar, auch lauter Catholische Leute angenommen werden.“[27] Die Anekdote von Kölesd hat also inso-

[24] Zur Aktivität der Mercys beim Aufbau einer katholischen Infrastruktur ihrer Untertanen siehe: LANTOSNÉ IMRE, Mária: Két világi kegyúr a hitélet megújításáért [Zwei weltliche Patronatsherren für die Erneuerung des religiösen Lebens]. In: A pécsi egyházmegye a 17-18. században. Hg. v. Tamás FEDELES und Szabolcs VARGA. Pécs 2005, 185-204.

[25] MÜNCH, Paul: Lebensformen in der frühen Neuzeit. Berlin 1998, 366.

[26] Siehe dazu ausführlich GŐZSY, Zoltán/ SPANNENBERGER, Norbert: „Discipulus Teschedikianus huc pro experientia mitti deberet“. Das Prinzip der *ordo* in den Entwürfen deutscher und ungarischer Aufklärer. In: Ungarn-Jahrbuch 29 (2008), 59-72.

[27] TAFFERNER: Quellenbuch, Bd. I., 68.

fern einen Wahrheitsgehalt, als vor allem konfessionell einheitliche Dorfgemeinschaften – und zwar sowohl von den Grundherren als auch für die Siedler selbst – bevorzugt wurden.

Eine weitere Frage betrifft die Möglichkeit seitens der Herrschaft, eine konfessionell (wie auch ethnisch) homogene Siedlung zu schaffen. Allzu oft war das nämlich einfach nicht umsetzbar. Wenn auch die Methode, ein Dorf umzusiedeln, um den neuen Kolonisten Platz zu schaffen, nicht unbekannt war, trachtete man dennoch vor allem nach der „Auffüllung" der vorhandenen, meist dünn besiedelten Gemeinden.[28] Das ist die Erklärung dafür, warum 1720 im gesamten Komitat Gran (ung. Esztergom) in insgesamt neun Siedlungen Deutsche lebten, dabei aber allein in Dorog eine ethnisch homogene Gemeinschaft bildeten. Sonst lebten sie mit Ungarn zusammen.[29]

Es scheint erst in der zweiten Hälfte des 18. Jahrhunderts, als genügend Bauern zur Verfügung standen, die Regel geworden zu sein, dass der Grundherr bereits in der Anwerbung nur Katholiken (oder nur Protestanten) ansiedeln ließ, so beispielsweise in Szulok im Komitat Somogy.[30] Anders gesagt: In der Notsituation wurde seitens der Herrschaft eine restriktive Auslegung der konfessionellen Freiheit beliebig bzw. „flexibel" angewandt. Doch sobald die Lücken gefüllt waren und die Lage sich stabilisiert hatte, wurde auch dieser Aspekt strenger genommen. Spätestens ab diesem Zeitpunkt waren die protestantischen *Neoadveniae* auf den Schutz ihrer Grundherren angewiesen. Diese Funktion eines Schirmherrn der Protestanten erfüllten allerdings nicht nur protestantische sondern auch katholische Grundherren. Graf Mercy nahm dabei bewusst heftige Konflikte mit dem Bischof von Fünfkirchen in Kauf, der nicht nur als geistlicher Oberhirte, sondern auch als Obergespan des Komitates Tolna fungierte. Nachdem sein Sohn, Graf Claudius Florimund Mercy II., 1773 die Güter des Komitats verkauft hatte, begann unter den Apponyis teilweise ein Exodus der Lutheraner. Nicht zuletzt profitierten die Esterházys davon, wie das bereits davor der Fall war. So wurde schon die Gründung des Dorfes Mekényes wie folgt interpretiert: „[...] dieses neue Mekényes hat seinen Anfang genommen Anno Christi 1735 durch die deutschen evangelischen Emigranten aus Gyönk. Ursach ihrer daherigen Emigration war die Bedrückung von der Grundherrschaft, der hiesigen Niederlassung aber die Erlaubniss des Fürsten Esterházy de Galánta".[31] In diesem Fall demonstrierte der reformierte Grundherr Péter Magyary-Kossa sein Unverständnis gegenüber dem Wunsch der Evangelischen, ein Bethaus zu errichten. Der religiösen Toleranz

---

[28] So verfuhren etwa die Károlyis im Sathmar oder die Hofkammer in der Batschka. In Batschsentiwa z.B. wurden 1755 die insgesamt 22 serbisch-orthodoxen Familien auf die Puszta Gyurity umgesiedelt. MAHR, Jakob: Kleine Chronik unserer Heimatgemeinde. In: Heimatbuch Batschsentiwan. Geschichte einer donauschwäbischen Großgemeinde in der Batschka zwischen Donau und Theiß. Hg. v. Anton TAFFERNER. Heidelberg 1980, 9-22, hier 10.

[29] Diese Orte waren Csolnok, Dorog, Dömös, Esztergom-Víziváros, Magyarszőgyén, Nyergesújfalu, Süttő, Szentgyörgymező und Szenttamáshegy. Esztergom vármegye [Das Komitat Gran]. Hg. v. Samu BOROVSZKY. (Budapest 1908). Reprint Budapest 1989 (Magyarország vármegyéi és városai. Magyarország monográfiája. A Magyar Korona országai történetének, földrajzi, képzőművészeti, néprajzi, hadügyi és természeti viszonyainak, közművelődési és közgazdasági állapotának encziklopédiája), 386.

[30] HUBER, Anton: Der Ansiedlungsvertrag der Gemeinde Szulok. In: Unser Hauskalender 56 (2004), 50.

[31] Gedenkblatt auf das Jubiläumsjahr der evang. Gemeinde Mekenyes. Mekényes 1935, 3.

des katholischen Grundherrn, Johann Nepomuk Hunyady, verdankte auch die evangelische Gemeinde Döröcske ihre Existenz im Komitat Somogy.
Insgesamt kann man also keineswegs von einer bipolaren Konfliktkonstellation zwischen Katholiken und Protestanten sprechen, sondern vielmehr von einer multipolaren, wobei jede einzelne Konfession unter den konkreten Umständen als Konkurrenz aber auch als Partner einer anderen fungieren konnte. Auf keinen Fall lässt sich eine „Einheitsfront" der beiden protestantischen Konfessionen konstatieren.[32] Zwei konkrete Beispiele mögen die Tragweite von lokalen Konflikten unter Protestanten, hier im Komitat Somogy, veranschaulichen: 1772 wandte sich György Markos an das Consilium des Komitates mit der Beschwerde, dass der katholische Priester die Haiducken des Grundherren auf ihn gehetzt habe. „Mein Vater wurde als Kind während seiner Dienstzeit in Kroatien als kranker Mensch mit Gewalt zum römisch-katholischen Glauben gezwungen, auch ich wurde mit Anwendung von Hunger und Durst dazu gezwungen. Doch ich habe noch vier Söhne, die ich in der Helvetischen Konfession erzog, in der auch ich wie auch meine alte Familie gelebt hatte und gestorben war. Doch sowohl die Herrschaft als auch Pfarrer Baboltsai bedrohen sie ständig mit Verfolgung und Gefängnis Tag und Nacht. Sie sind aber eher bereit zu fliehen als die bereits angeeignete Wahrheit zu verleugnen."[33] Schon ein Jahr später wandte sich die Gattin von József Blaskovics an das Komitat, weil der lutherische Grundherr János Börsönyi sie wegen ihrer katholischen Religion schwer misshandelt hatte. „Der Herr Börsönyi will nach freier lutherischer Manier [...] das Fest kündigen. [...] Er [der Grundherr] verprügelte mich mit einer Eisenstange und Holzstange, die selbst für ein Rindvieh ausgereicht hätte und nicht einem Frauenzimmer, wie mir [...] er brach mir die Knochen, so dass ich seither nicht mehr arbeiten kann."[34] Interkonfessionelles als Konfliktpotential war also nicht ethnisch definiert, die hier zitierten Beispiele spiegeln Fälle aus ungarischen Gemeinden wider.

[32] Siehe den Beitrag von Zoltán Csepregi in diesem Band.

[33] „Atyám gyermekségében Horváth orszàgban szolgálván az Romai Catholica hitre betegségében eröszakosan reá hajtották, engemet is éhséggel, szomjusággal arra kénszeritettek. Már ezek meg estek, de még vannak négy fiaim, kiket az Helvétiai Confessióban neveltem, melyben mint magam éltem, mint régi Fámiliám abban éltek, s – abban haltak meg. Már mostan mind az Uraság, mind Baboltsai Plbanos Ur nem szünnek meg fiaimat, üldözéssel fenyegetni, fogsággal, tömlöczözéssel, ejjel nappal reájok jár, már csak nem földön futok, pedig készszebbek el bujdosni, hogy sem az egyszer meg ismért igazságot vissza tagadni". Hier zitiert nach SZILI, Ferenc: Somogy megye „láthatalan" történelme a 18-19. században. In: Népek együttélése Dél-Pannóniában. Tanulmányok Szita László 70. születésnapjára. Pécs 2003, 435-453, hier 450.

[34] „Börsönyi Ur pediglen Szabad Lutheri modon akarja pápista cselédjével az ünnepet föll bontatni, még azt modja, sem pap sem barát eö neki nem parancsol, mi pedig Catholikusok a` mi modunk szerént Istennek szolgálunk, és Luther szolgállyon ugy a`mint Luthernek szokott szolgálni az eö modja [...] irtoztató vasnyárs és fa bottal valo veréssét melly both elégh lett volna marhának, nem egy hozzám hasonlo nyomorult Aszszon álathoz [...] mellyel öszve vert, és kereszt csontomat el törvén az utátul fogvást semmit sem dolgozhatom". EBD., 451.

Interkonfessionelles Zusammenleben als Konfliktpotential

Frühneuzeitliches Leben spielte sich – im Gegensatz zu heute – in Gruppen und Verbänden, also kollektiv ab, weil eine ausschließlich auf sich gestellte Existenz praktisch nicht realisierbar war. Kirchlich-religiöse Gemeinschaften boten den geeigneten Rahmen für das Gruppenerlebnis, sie wirkten also nicht nur bei den Kolonisten integrativ. Fast alle Vorstellungen, Hoffnungen und Träume, die sich im 18. Jahrhundert mit dem Ablauf des menschlichen Lebens verbanden, waren religiös fundiert. Der Bedarf an religiösen Einrichtungen unter den Neusiedlern war folglich ausgeprägt: Religion gehörte zum Alltag, sie war identitätsstiftend und -pflegend. Deshalb gehörte zur Konsolidierung der Ansiedlung die Installierung eines religiösen Netzwerkes, oder wie Pfarrer Michael Winkler über die deutsche Gemeinde in Sagethal (ung. Szakadát) im Komitat Tolna schrieb: „Damit also dieses neuungarische Volk [sic!] seiner christlichen Pflicht entsprechend Gott gebe, was Gott gebührt, und dieses Prädium nicht auch eine Einöde bleibe, wie es früher für Tiere war, hat sich der Graf um einen Priester umgesehen."[35] Diese Gemeinde selbst war zwar schon 1723 neu gegründet worden, erhielt jedoch erst vier Jahre später einen eigenen Seelsorger. Dieser musste die Heilige Messe in der alten Kirchenruine oder in einem Privathaus lesen. In Berin (ung. Diósberény) hielt die einheimische Bevölkerung Gebetsandachten mit Ansprachen oder Lesungen aus einem Predigtbuch in einem Privathaus ab. Die feierlichen Prozessionen wurden um die Ruine der verwahrlosten raitzischen Kirche veranstaltet.[36] Man baute andernorts – wenn es nicht anders ging – Kirchen aus Holz als Notlösung für eine „Übergangszeit". Der spätere Bau von Kirchen aus Stein und Ziegeln war auch ein äußeres Zeichen der vollendeten Integration. In Sagethal konnte im Juli 1765 und damit erst Jahrzehnte nach ihrer Besiedlung eine solche Kirche geweiht werden.

Dass im Konfliktfall die ethnische Komponente gegenüber dem Konfessionellen in den Hintergrund trat, zeigt eine äußerst wertvolle Quelle, nämlich die zeitgenössische Pfarrchronik des römisch-katholischen Priesters Michael Winkler. Winkler selbst war ein glühender Gegenreformator und seine zwei Pfarrgemeinden, Szárazd und Udvari, bekamen diese Sinnung auch zu spüren. Die Gemeinde Száraszd im Komitat Tolna war konfessionell gemischt. Die 1735 gegründete Tochtersiedlung von Kéty bewohnten laut Konskription zunächst nur Katholiken. Bald siedelten sich jedoch auch Protestanten an, die zwar für die Kosten einer gemeinsamen Glocke aufkamen, die Oberhoheit des katholischen Priesters aber laut dessen Aussage nicht akzeptieren wollten. Dieser wirkte auch nicht integrativ, denn er war „auch bemüht zu verhindern, dass sie [die Protestanten] einen eigenen Gottesdienstraum bekamen".[37] Udvari wiederum war eine Filiale von Sagethal. Zu den einheimischen katholischen Ungarn kamen deutsche Lutheraner hinzu. Der deutsche Winkler be-

---

[35] GALAMBOS, Franz: Glaube und Kirche in der Schwäbischen Türkei des 18. Jahrhunderts. Aufzeichnungen von Michael Winkler in den Pfarrchroniken von Szakadát, Bonyhád und Gödre. München 1987, 25.
[36] EBD., 29.
[37] EBD., 30.

kämpfte mit allen Mitteln die deutschen Lutheraner und förderte demonstrativ die katholischen Ungarn. Natürlich bezog sich das nicht allein auf kultische Handlungen, sondern auf alle Lebensbereiche. Als die Lutheraner einen eigenen Schulmeister wünschten – der einheimische war des Deutschen nicht mächtig – konnten sie trotz des Widerstandes seitens des Priesters erreichen, dass aus der Gemeinde ein Schulmeister, der „einzig und allein lesen und schreiben lerne und nichts weiteres informiere", erwählt werden durfte. Wenn man auch diese Konstellation nicht verabsolutieren darf, so spielte doch die Religion im Zweifelsfalle eine relevantere Rolle als eine etwaige ethnische Zugehörigkeit.
Der Alltag im Ungarn des 18. Jahrhunderts zeigte, dass Regelungen und Vorschriften „von oben" unwirksam waren, wenn die Verwaltungsbeamten oder die Obrigkeit nicht deren Überwachung gewährleisteten. So wurde zwar festgelegt, dass in Mischehen die Kinder katholisch zu erziehen seien, doch wenn der Vizegespan nicht auf die Einhaltung dieser Bestimmung bestand, war der katholische Geistliche machtlos. Zumindest klagte darüber Winkler, der auch anhand anderer Beispiele belegt, dass ohne die tatkräftige Mitwirkung der Behörden die restriktiven gesetzlichen Vorschriften in der Praxis unwirksam waren. Im protestantischen Jink (ung. Gyönk) im Komitat Tolna z.B. konvertierte ein gewisser Stephan S. zum Katholischen. Er wurde daraufhin von den Dorfbewohnern in Ketten gelegt und im Haus der Grundherrin, der kalvinistischen Witwe des Péter Magyary-Kossa, eingesperrt und danach von der Bevölkerung verprügelt. Zudem wurde er gezwungen, sein Haus innerhalb von 15 Tagen zu verkaufen und aus der Gemeinde wegzuziehen. Umsonst wandte er sich an den Vizegespan, der zwar Hilfe versprach, praktisch aber nichts erreichen konnte. Schließlich wurde ihm nach zwei Wochen eine Pauschalsumme für sein Haus von der Gemeinde überreicht, sein Hab und Gut auf ein Pferdegespann geladen und an der Dorfgrenze abgeladen. Weder die Ermahnungen des Bischofs von Fünfkirchen an den Vizegespan noch die Interventionen bei der Statthalterei bewirkten eine Veränderung – der Mann blieb ein Ausgestoßener, seine Vertreibung war irreversibel.[38]

Interkonfessionelle Begegnungen auf interethnischer Ebene

Es wäre aber verfehlt, interkonfessionelle Koexistenz ausschließlich als Konfliktpotential zu sehen. Haus oder Familie, also die Mikroebene der Sozialgefüge, waren für sich nicht lebensfähig zu jener Zeit. Sie musste durch weitere Formen der Sozialität, durch ein Netz außerhäuslicher Kontakte ergänzt werden. Solche waren die enge und aktive Pflege von Nachbarschaft, Verwandtschaft oder sämtliche Verbandsformen innerhalb der Gemeinde. Die Verwandtschaften ersetzten die Familie, wenn deren Mitglieder Schutz, Unterhalt oder Fortkommen bedurften. Die fast ebenso wichtige Nachbarschaft konnte durchaus auch religiöse Differenzen überbrücken. Die simpelsten Situationen boten dabei die Möglichkeit zur Annäherung, so wurde etwa seitens der Geistlichkeit darüber geklagt, dass Katholiken mit Andersgläubigen

[38] Ebd., 44f.

im Wirtshaus, einem Kulminationspunkt gesellschaftlichen Umgangs, in Kontakt kamen. „Geselligkeit“ und „Gesellschaft“ waren die Zauberworte des 18. Jahrhunderts, die längerfristig auf die Herausbildung von gut funktionierenden Dorfgemeinschaften hinwirkten und konfessionelle Schranken aufzuheben wussten.
Die Nachbarschaft beruhte auf Gegenseitigkeit und verlangte daher auch Respekt vor dem Anderen. Sie waren in der Zeit des „Ökonomie des Überlebens“ (Michael Stürmer), also in der frühen Ansiedlungszeit, als es um die nackte Existenzsicherung ging, unumgänglich.[39] Als Beleg soll hier das Matrikelbuch der Gemeinde Kozár in der Baranya, eines Dorfes der Esterházys, dienen. In der Zeit von 1751 bis 1756 gab es sieben Sterbefälle, von 1735 bis 1755 22 Taufen und von 1737 bis 1746 drei Eheschließungen. Von diesen drei war nur eine einzige konfessionell „homogen“, d.h. sowohl das Ehepaar als auch die Zeugen gehörten der gleichen – hier der katholischen – Religion an. In den anderen Fällen waren ein Lutheraner und ein Katholik Trauzeuge bei einem evangelischen Brautpaar und zwei Orthodoxe, also Serben, Trauzeugen bei einem katholischen Brautpaar. Von den 22 Taufen waren in 18 Fällen die Religion der Getauften wie der Taufpaten die gleiche, doch insbesondere in der „Frühphase“, nämlich 1735 und 1739 waren jeweils evangelische Taufpaten zu katholischen Familien eingeladen. In weiteren zwei Fällen (1749 und 1752) standen orthodoxe Taufpaten katholischen Eltern zur Seite.[40] Ebenso befürwortete der orthodoxe, also serbische Gemeindevorstand die Errichtung von evangelischen Kirchen für die deutschen Mitbewohner.[41]
Diese Fakten zeugen nicht nur von einem friedlichen Nebeneinander, sondern von einem aktiven Miteinander der Konfessionen und der Ethnien. Konflikte waren zwar häufig, aber nicht zwingend vorhanden.[42] Auch der wirtschaftliche Zwang brachte die Menschen zueinander, denn konfessionell einheitliche Höfe verloren durch die Einstellung konfessionell unterschiedlicher Knechte oder Mägde ihren konfessionell trennenden Charakter. Religiöse Schranken innerhalb einer Gemeinde aufrechtzuerhalten war schon deshalb unmöglich geworden, weil die demographischen Verhältnisse ebenso einer Änderung unterworfen waren. „Die Nichtkatholiken haben sich auf erstaunliche Weise vermehrt. Sie scheinen sich im Stillen vorgenommen zu haben, die Katholiken zu verdrängen“, beklagte sich Pfarrer Winkler über die Verhält-

---

[39] Hier zitiert nach MÜNCH: Lebensformen, 270.
[40] Matrikelbücher der Pfarrei Bikal: Copulationes et Baptisati.; Auch in der zweiten Hälfte kamen solche interethnische Berührungspunkte vor, wenn sich auch die Genese bzw. die Indikatoren nicht mehr eruieren lassen. Am 24. April 1769 wurde der Sohn Markus des kroatischen Ehepaares Nikolaus und Anna Polyak getauft, als Taufpaten standen ihnen die Deutschen Mathias und Helena Pranger zur Seite. Oder am 29. Mai d. J. wurde der Sohn Johannes des ungarischen Ehepaares Johannes und Marianna Szekeres im raitzisch-ungarischen Dorf Hajmás getauft, und als Taufpaten fungierten Stipan und Katharina Stravunacz. Matrikelbuch der Pfarrei Bikal. Bapt. II. 1751-1772.
[41] Solche interkonfessionellen Berührungen waren den serbischen Orthodoxie nicht fremd und sie verdankte dieser Tatsache einen quantitativen Zuwachs unter der Osmanenherrschaft, indem sich Katholiken den Orthodoxen angeschlossen hatten. Vgl. HADROVICS, László: Vallás, egyház, nemzettudat. A szerb egyház nemzeti szerepe a török uralom alatt [Religion, Kirche, Nationalbewusstsein. Die nationale Rolle der serbischen Kirche während der Osmanenherrschaft]. Budapest 1991, 21-22.
[42] Formen solcher Kooperation siehe auch im Beitrag von Peter Šoltes in diesem Band.

nisse in Száraszd.[43] 1735 wurden hier anlässlich der Visitation 89 Katholiken gezählt und Protestanten gar nicht erwähnt. Im zweiten Drittel des 18. Jahrhunderts gab es 16 katholische und 72 protestantische Paare, 1783 insgesamt 71 Katholiken und 380 Protestanten. Eine starke Expansion der Evangelischen ähnlichen Ausmaßes war auch in den Herrschaften der Esterházys zu beobachten.[44]
Mit der sozialen und wirtschaftlichen Konsolidierung gegen Ende des 18. Jahrhunderts war noch ein weiterer Prozess verbunden: Die interkonfessionellen Streitigkeiten wurden ganz deutlich reduziert, denn die interkulturellen Spielregeln machten diese nicht mehr notwendig. Anders gesagt: Die Bevölkerung war nicht mehr in einem solchen Maße aufeinander angewiesen. Im Matrikelbuch von Bikal z.B. waren zwischen 1756 und 1761 nur noch in zwei Fällen die Taufpaten anderer Konfession als die Eltern. Dasselbe gilt auch für Trauzeugen bei Eheschließungen. Zugleich förderten demographische und ökonomische Entwicklungen eine größere Mobilität innerhalb einer Region. Diese Binnenwanderung führte gezwungenermaßen zur Entstehung multikonfessioneller Siedlungen. Soziale Stabilisierung, Aufklärung und ökonomischer Aufschwung nahmen dem konfessionellen Konflikt aber die Spitze, er barg somit nicht mehr automatisch Konfliktpotential. Damit schließt sich der Kreis: Was um die Wende des 17. zum 18. Jahrhundert noch als modern galt, nämlich ethnisch und konfessionell homogene Siedlungen, war im darauf folgenden Jahrhundert schon ein überholtes Modell. Das aus unterschiedlichen Gründen erzwungene Zusammenleben verlangte nach Formen des modus vivendi. Um die Koexistenz nicht zu gefährden, aber die eigene Konfession dennoch zu bewahren akzeptiert man in den gemischten Siedlungen die Aufrechterhaltung trennender Komponenten als Maßstab soziokultureller Barrieren.[45] So verlief der Alltag der Bevölkerung jenseits solcher Differenzen nach festen Formen: Man heiratete ausschließlich untereinander und das soziale Netzwerk wurde in der eigenen konfessionellen Gruppe ausgebaut bzw. weitergeführt. Die konfessionelle Schranke blieb also weiterhin intakt, löste jedoch kaum mehr offene Konflikte aus.

[43] GALAMBOS: Glaube, 30.
[44] Siehe dazu ausführlich SPANNENBERGER, Norbert: Zur Siedlungspolitik der Fürstenfamilie Esterházy im 18. Jahrhundert. In: Specimina nova dissertationum ex instituto historico Universitatis Quinqueecclesiensis 2005, 121-142.
[45] Zu diesem Ergebnis kommt auch eine Studie über die Ansiedlung der Deutschen in der Region nördlich vom Plattensee. PÉTERDI, Ottó: A Balaton-Felvidék német falvai. (Dűlőnévkutatási tanulmány) [Die deutschen Dörfer des Balaton-Oberlandes. (Eine Flurnamenstudie)]. In: Századok 69 (1935), 693-714.

Zoltán Gőzsy

Grenzen und Wirkungsradius der Rekatholisierung in Südtransdanubien nach der Osmanenzeit

In der vorliegenden Studie geht es um die integrative Tätigkeit der katholischen Pfarrämter und der einzelnen Pfarrer bzw. um die Möglichkeiten und Rahmenbedingungen der Katholisierung bzw. Rekatholisierung in Südtransdanubien in der ersten Hälfte des 18. Jahrhunderts. Es werden auch die Ursachen jenes Phänomens untersucht, infolge dessen in der zweiten Hälfte des 18. Jahrhunderts in der südtransdanubischen Region sowohl die Anzahl der Pfarrämter, als auch der Anteil der Katholiken bedeutend angewachsen ist. Meinen Untersuchungen liegen in erster Linie die Protokolle der Visitationen (*Canonicae Visitationes*),[1] und die Kirchenuntersuchungen der Komitate, bzw. der Diözesen (*Inquisitiones Ecclesiastici*) zugrunde.[2]
Die meisten Pfarrämter im Komitat Schomodei (ung. Somogy) gehörten zur Diözese Wesprim (ung. Veszprém) und die in den Komitaten Tolnau (ung. Tolna) und Branau (ung. Baranya) zur Diözese Fünfkirchen (ung. Pécs). Der Verfall und die Auflösung der Institutionen der katholischen Kirche begann bereits vor der osmanischen Eroberung.[3] Dieser Prozess erreichte unter der türkischen Besatzung seinen Höhepunkt. Die Ära der osmanischen Okkupation verursachte in den Einrichtungen der katholischen Kirche Südtransdanubiens enorme Schäden. In den zum Oberdekanat Schomodei gehörenden 10 Dekanatsbezirken waren 188 bzw. 189 Pfarrämter, von denen kein einziges die Zeit der Eroberung überstand.[4] Die Klöster, die im religiösen Leben des Komitats eine immense Rolle spielten, sind auch untergegangen.[5]
Die katholische Konfession verschwand jedoch nicht gänzlich aus dem Komitat; mehrere Dörfer blieben im 16. und 17. Jahrhundert dem Katholizismus treu und die

[1] Bezüglich der Diözese Fünfkirchen siehe: GŐZSY, Zoltán/VARGA, Szabolcs: 1738-42 között készült egyházlátogatási jegyzőkönyv [Protokolle der Visitation 1738-1742.] (in Vorbereitung). – Bezüglich der Diözese Wesprim siehe PFEIFFER, János: A Veszprémi egyházmegye legrégibb egyházlátogatásai (1554-1760). [Die ältesten Visitationen der Diözese Wesprim (1554-1760)]. Veszprém 1947 (A Veszprémi egyházmegye múltjából 10).
[2] Baranya Megyei Levéltár [Archiv des Komitates Baranya]. (fortan: BML). IV. 1. f. 3. Akten der Adelsversammlung des Komitats Branau und deren Subkommission; Gerichtliche Untersuchungen (Inquisitiones) – Somogy Megyei Levéltár [Archiv des Komitates Somogy]. (fortan: SML) IV. 10. bb. Akten des Gerichtsstuhls (Sedria) des Komitates 1488-1848 (1855); Inquisitionales 1654-1848. 60. Bündel. 1715-1784. ohne Signatur. – Veszprém Érseki Levéltár [Erzbischöfliches Archiv Wesprim]. (fortan VÉL). Miscellanea 14. a. Inquisitio Comitatus Simighiensis intuitu Acatholicorum 1721.
[3] MOLNÁR, Antal: A katolikus egyház a hódolt Dunántúlon. [Die katholische Kirche im osmanischen Transdanubien]. Budapest 2003 (METEM könyvek 44), 141.
[4] Das Pfarramtregister der Diözese Wesprim aus dem Jahre 1550 berichtet über die 188 einstigen Pfarrämter des Oberdekanats Schomodei bereits in Vergangenheitsform. EBD., 141.
[5] A veszprémi püspökség papjainak névjegyzéke [Namensregister der Pfarrer der Diözese Wesprim]. Veszprém 1975, 16. (fortan: VESZPRÉMI).

Quellen berichten auch über bedeutendere katholische Siedlungsgebiete. Problematisch war allerdings, dass sie über keinen Pfarrer verfügten.[6] Seit den 1620er Jahren sind Angaben vorhanden, die bestätigen, dass das religiöse Leben der Schomodei und der Branau durch Missionen der Franziskanerpriester bzw. der Jesuiten gefördert wurde. Die Bistümer Wesprim und Fünfkirchen gewährten den Katholiken der Region zu jener Zeit weder materielle noch religiöse Unterstützung. Bis zu den Rückeroberungskriegen waren es lediglich die Jesuiten, die ihnen Pastoraldienst leisteten.[7]

Die Reorganisierung der kirchlichen Institutionen nach der Zeit der osmanischen Eroberung erfolgte am Ende des 17. bzw. in den ersten Jahrzehnten des 18. Jahrhunderts. Pál Széchényi gab sein Amt als Bischof von Fünfkirchen auf und war ab dem 26. April 1687 als Bischof von Wesprim tätig.[8] Bis zu seinem Tode im Jahre 1710 legte er großen Wert auf die Neuorganisierung der Pfarrämter in der Schomodei.[9] Sein Nachfolger Otto Volkra wurde am 28. Mai 1710 von Joseph I. ernannt.[10] Der neue Bischof engagierte sich sehr für die Rückgewinnung der verlorenen Pfarrämter, für die Wiederbelebung der inaktiven Pfarreien sowie für den Schutz der Güter der Diözese.[11] Bezeichnend für den Eifer des Bischofs ist, dass er in seiner zehnjährigen Amtszeit alleine in der Schomodei 18 Pfarrämter einrichten und 11 Kirchen erbauen ließ.[12] Der Bischof ließ sich bereits von Anfang des Jahrhunderts an durch seinen Gutsverwalter (*Episcopi bonorum provisor*) auf den Komitatsversammlungen vertreten.[13]
Ähnliche Tendenzen kann man auch am Ende des 17. Jahrhunderts nach den Rückeroberungskriegen sowie nach dem Rákóczi-Aufstand in der Diözese Fünfkirchen feststellen. Bischof Radanay wandte sich sehr intensiv der Bekehrung der Nichtkatholiken zu. Im letzten Jahrzehnt des 17. Jahrhunderts spielten bei der Katholisierung die Jesuiten eine wichtige Rolle, wobei sie in erster Linie aus den unitarischen

---

[6] MOLNÁR: A katolikus egyház, 141-142.
[7] EBD., 147.
[8] Am 24. November 1687 erhielt er auch die päpstliche Bestätigung. PFEIFFER, János: A veszprémi egyházmegye történeti névtára (1630-1950) püspökei, kanonokjai, papjai. [Historisches Namensregister der Diözese Wesprim (1630-1950) ihre Bischöfe, Kanoniker, Pfarrer.] München 1987 (Dissertationes Hungaricae ex historia Ecclesiae VIII), 59.
[9] Er ließ mehr als 10 Pfarrämter reorganisieren. VESZPRÉMI, 35.
[10] PFEIFFER: A veszprémi, 62. – Über Volkra KÖRMENDY, József: Gr. Volkra Ottó Ker. János veszprémi püspök élete és munkássága 1665-1720 [Leben und Wirken des Wesprimer Bischofs Graf Otto Volkra 1665-1720]. Veszprém 1995.
[11] 1718 protestierten die Dörfer Kötcse und Patca bei der Komitatsversammlung Schomodei gegen die Enteignung der bischöflichen Güter. PFEIFFER: A veszprémi, 63-64. – SML, Komitatsprotokolle. 1658-1728. 577-581 und 865-869.
[12] PFEIFFER: A veszprémi, 63. – VESZPRÉMI, 36-40. – Die wachsende Bevölkerung in den Gemeinden der zurückeroberten Gebiete errichtete einfache Holzkirchen zwecks Abhaltung der heiligen Messen bzw. Gottesdienste. Vgl. GÁRDONYI, Máté: A katolikus egyház a XVIII. században. [Die katholische Kirche im 18. Jahrhundert]. In: Nagyatád monográfiája I. Hg v. Sándor BŐSZE. Nagyatád 2001, 172. – KÖRMENDY, József: Fa- és sövénytemplomok a Veszprémi Egyházmegye területén a XVIII. században. [Holz- und Buschkirchen auf dem Gebiet der Diözese Wesprim im 18. Jahrhundert]. In: Veszprém Megyei Múzeumok Közleményei 10, 53-78.
[13] SML, Komitatsprotokolle. 1658-1728. 868-869.

(in den Quellen: arianisch) Gemeinden des Komitats Branau neue Gläubigen in größerer Zahl warben. Währenddessen war die Reorganisierung des katholischen Institutionennetzwerks auf dem Gebiet des Bistums weniger erfolgreich; nach dem Tode von Radanay betrug die Zahl der Pfarrämter – die Stadt Fünfkirchen nicht einberechnet – kaum mehr als zehn.[14] Unter diesen Umständen erschien der Rundbrief des neuen Bischofs Vilmos Nesselrode, in dem er die Geistlichen des Bistums zur Diözcsansynodc einlud.[15] Bei der Renovierung der zerstörten Kirchen, in der Administration der Pfarrämter, in der Seelsorge kamen so viele Probleme zum Vorschein, dass der Klerus diese unter Leitung des Bischofs im Rahmen einer solchen Diözesansynode klären musste.[16] Die im Jahre 1714 abgehaltene Synode war im Leben der Diözese auch in jener Hinsicht wichtig, dass die Pfarrämter, die Pfarrer und sowohl die intakten als auch die zerstörten Kirchen aufgelistet und ermessen wurden. Laut Inventur gab es damals im Bistum 23 Pfarrämter, 144 Filialkirchen, 28 weltliche Pfarrer, Mönche, sowie 7 Lizentiaten. Aufgrund dieser Bestandsaufnahme erarbeitete man den Plan der Diözese, in dem festgelegt wurde, welche Pfarrämter renoviert bzw. wo neue aufgestellt werden müssten.

Damit die ungarischen Diözesen wieder tatsächlich funktionieren konnten, musste man sie neu organisieren.[17] In der Konsolidierung der katholischen Kirche spielten die Beschlüsse des Tridentinums eine wichtige Rolle und bildeten deren Fundament.[18] Zum einen musste das „Residentia-Prinzip" (Residenzprinzip) zur Geltung kommen, was im Falle des hohen Klerus – im Sinne der ursprünglichen Bedeutung des Wortes – die Rückkehr in den alten Bischofssitz, von seiten der niederen Geistlichkeit die Inbesitznahme der Pfarrämter bedeutete. Andererseits musste man auch Priesterseminare einrichten, denn zur Behebung des Priestermangels waren im Bistum qualifizierte Pfarrer notwendig. Das „Visitatio-Prinzip" (Visitationsprinzip) musste auch zur Geltung gebracht werden. Die Leiter der Diözese mussten in erster Linie die Konsolidierung des kirchlichen Lebens bzw. den Wirkungsradius der Katholisierung kontrollieren.

---

[14] Grundlegende Fachliteratur über Radanay vgl. BABICS, András: Radanay Mátyás pécsi püspök kinevezése [Die Ernennung von Mátyás Radanay zum Bischof von Fünfkirchen]. In: Regnum 2 (1937), 187-205. – FRICSY, Ádám: A török utáni első pécsi püspök, Radanay Mátyás Ignác. [Mátyás Ignác Radanay, erster Bischof von Fünfkirchen nach den Türken]. In: Tanulmányok a pécsi egyházmegye történetéből I. Hg. v. Ádám FRICSY. Pécs 1983, 115-130.

[15] MERÉNYI, Ferenc: Domsics Mátyás egyházlátogatása (Canonica Visitatio) Baranyában 1729-ben [Der Kirchenbesuch (canonica visitatio) von Mátyás Domsics in der Branau 1729]. Pécs 1939, 10-11.

[16] „(...) Ecclesiarum passim dirutarum reparatione, verum etiam multoque magis in debita Parochiarum administratione cura animarum, ac Parochorum necessaria provisione adeo disturbata ac confusa esse videatur". Pécsi Püspöki Levéltár [Bischöfliches Archiv Fünfkirchen]. (fortan: PPL). Archiv des Domkapitels. Fasc. CLIV:15. – Der lateinische Text zitiert nach Josephus Koller: Historia Episcopatus Quinqueecclesiensis. VII. 220.

[17] Zur Neuorganisierung der katholischen Kirche siehe kürzlich BAHLCKE, Joachim: Ungarischer Episkopat und österreichische Monarchie. Von einer Partnerschaft zur Konfrontation (1686-1790). Stuttgart 2005, 44-64.

[18] Grundlegendes Werk zum Konzil von Trient JEDIN, Hubert: Geschichte des Konzils von Trient. I-IV. Freiburg 1949-1974. – In ungarischer Sprache GÁRDONYI, Máté: A papi élet reformja a Trienti Zsinat korában [Reform des priesterlichen Lebens zur Zeit des Konzils von Trient]. Budapest 2001.

Die Neuorganisierung der Bistümer begann selbstverständlich mit der Grenzziehung und der Klärung der Frage der Rechtshoheit; diese zogen jedoch zahlreiche Kontroversen und Konflikte nach sich. In den Neoacquistica-Gebieten riefen die Visitationen Rechts- und Zuständigkeitskonflikte hervor. Das war darauf zurückzuführen, dass während der Osmanenherrschaft die Grenzen der Diözesen verschwanden beziehungsweise einzelne Bistümer ihr Gebiet auf Kosten der anderen erweiterten. Die Bischöfe von Zagreb/Agram führten im 17. Jahrhundert im Süden der südtransdanubischen Komitate Visitationen durch. Nach 1686 betrieben neben den kroatischen *Franziskanern* auch Diözesanpriester aus Zagreb/Agram Seelsorge und wegen des einst zur Diözese Fünfkirchen gehörenden Komitats Pozsega stritten die Missionsbistümer Zagreb/Agram und Belgrad. Nach den Rückeroberungskriegen mussten also die genauen Grenzen festgelegt werden, um zu klären, auf welche Pfarrämter sich die Kompetenz des Wesprimer bzw. des Fünfkirchener Bischofs erstreckte. Denn dies war bei Weitem nicht eindeutig.[19] Der Bischof von Zagreb erhob lange Zeit Anspruch darauf, Visitationen in den südlichen Gebieten der Komitate Schomodei und Zala durchzuführen. Ab den 1730er Jahren ergaben sich dadurch immer mehr Konflikte zwischen dem Bischof von Zagreb beziehungsweise den Bischöfen von Wesprim und Fünfkirchen. Am Ende der 1720er Jahre festigten sich die Besitzverhältnisse im Drau-Gebiet und man begann auch dort mit dem Ausbau der kirchlichen Infrastruktur.

Die Bischöfe von Wesprim und Fünfkirchen legten vor allem deshalb großen Wert auf die Neuorganisierung, Gründung und Förderung der südtransdanubischen Pfarrämter, besonders im Drau-Gebiet, weil sie dadurch gleichzeitig an zwei Fronten Siege verbuchen konnten. Einerseits gelang es ihnen, den katholischen Glauben in einer größtenteils von Protestanten bewohnten Region zu festigen, andererseits konnte der Bischof von Wesprim seinen Rechtsanspruch und seinen Machtstatus gegenüber der Diözese von Zagreb demonstrieren. Im ersten Viertel des 18. Jahrhunderts wurden die katholischen Pfarrämter in den größeren und daher strategisch wichtigen protestantischen Siedlungen an der Drau, wie in Csurgó, Berzence, Babócsa, Lakócsa, Nagybajom beziehungsweise in Szigetvár organisiert.[20]

Beide Bischöfe erhoben Anspruch auf Visitationen in Südtransdanubien. Der Bischof von Wesprim berief sich dabei auf die bei der mittelalterlichen Gründung festgelegten Grenzen der Diözese, der Bischof von Zagreb auf die herausgebildete Praxis (usus) sowie auf die in diesem Gebiet in großer Anzahl lebende kroatische Bevölkerung. Solange die Bischöfe das Schicksal der Pfarrämter an der Drau mit großer Aufmerksamkeit verfolgten, war hier die Fluktuation der Pfarrer viel größer. Das Moorgebiet, die zerstreut liegenden Gemeinden waren den Priestern recht unbehaglich, vor allem denen, die etwas andere Umstände gewohnt waren. Nicht von ungefähr bat der aus Dalmatien stammende und für die Gemeinde Lakócsa zuständige

[19] Volkra reichte 1717 ein Memorandum bezüglich der Grenzen der Diözese Wesprim beim Kaiser ein. PFEIFFER: A veszprémi, 63.

[20] Csököly (reorganisiert 1718), Babócsa (gegründet 1723), Nagyatád (gegründet 1720), Berzence (reorganisiert 1708), Csurgó (gegründet 1722), sowie das zum Bistum Fünfkirchen gehörende Lakócsa (gegründet 1717).

Mazurani, ihn ins Bistum Syrmien zu versetzen, weil er dort mit einem etwas bequemeren Amt rechnete.[21] Wegen der geringen Anzahl der Pfarrämter gab es viele zugehörige Filialkirchen, deren pastorale Versorgung eine große Belastung für die Priester war. Darunter litt des Öfteren die Qualität ihrer Arbeit.

Der Amtsnachfolger des Bischofs von Wesprim Otto Volkra, Ádám Acsády, führte 1734 in Kanizsa eine Visitation durch, genauso wie der Bischof von Zagreb. Die Gemeinde Nagyatád in der Schomodei zeigt exemplarisch die Tendenzen, sowie die Ursachen der Konflikte. Der Grundherr, Ignác Ferenc Czindery (zugleich der Vizegespan des Komitats Varasd) organisierte 1722 in der von Kroaten und Ungarn bewohnten Gemeinde das Pfarramt. Als Schirmherr beauftragte er die kroatischen Priester der Diözese Zagreb mit dem Pfarrdienst. Später aber wollte er, anstelle der lediglich das Kroatische beherrschenden weltlichen Priester, sowohl kroatisch- als auch ungarischsprechende, im Kreise der Gläubigen mehr akzeptierte Mönche mit der Leitung des Pfarramtes beauftragen.[22] 1731 bat er im Einvernehmen mit dem Wesprimer Bischof das Kanizsaer Zentrum der slawonischen Ordensprovinz der Franziskaner, die nach dem Heiligen Ladislaus benannt war, Mönche nach Nagyatád zu schicken. Seine Entscheidung war von rationalem, besitzpolitischem Prinzip geleitet; in der allmählich ungarisch werdenden Gemeinde wollte er der ganzen Bevölkerung das entsprechende religiöse Leben sichern.
Die aus Kanizsa, dem ungarischen Zentrum der slawonischen Franziskaner-Ordensprovinz, kommenden Franziskaner, die ihr eigentliches Zentrum in Agram hatten, wollten weitere Visitationen aus Kroatien verhindern. Die weltlichen Priester aus der Diözese Zagreb beklagten sich jedoch des Öfteren darüber, dass die ungarischen Mönche weder bei der Rekatholisierung noch bei der Gestaltung der entsprechenden Kirchenordnung effektiv genug seien. Der Konflikt erreichte 1745 seinen Höhepunkt, als Adam Patachich, der Kanoniker von Zagreb, die Kirche von Nagyatád nicht betreten durfte. Patachich ließ daraufhin das Schloss und den Tabernakel aufbrechen, welchen er auch mitnehmen wollte. Die Mönche verhinderten dieses und jagten die Delegation aus Zagreb fort. Das Problem wurde vom Bischof von Wesprim, Márton Padányi Bíró – der eine sehr entschlossene Kirchenpolitik betrieb – gelöst, der die südtransdanubischen Ambitionen des Zagreber Bischofs dadurch kompensierte, dass er Rechtsanspruch auf das zum Bistum von Zagreb gehörende Mur-Gebiet erhob. Der Streit wurde 1754 durch einen Kompromiss beigelegt; jeder blieb hinter den mittelalterlichen Diözesangrenzen und Márton Padányi Bíró stattete dem Pfarramt einen demonstrativen Kirchenbesuch ab.

---

[21] Die 30 Sept. 1751 exponit officio vicariali se parochiam Lakocsensem propter difficilem administrationem in dissitis filialibus per loca paludinosa amplius tenere haud posse. BRÜSZTLE, Joseph: Recensio universi cleri Dioecesis Quinque-Ecclesiensis [...]. Bd. II. Pécs 1874-1880, 500.

[22] Varii idiomatis populo ut illyrico videlicet et ungarico. P. TAKÁCS, J. Ince O.F.M./PFEIFFER, János: Szent Ferenc fiai a veszprémi egyházmegyében a 17-18. században. Pápa-Zalaegerszeg 2001, 3. – GÁRDONYI: A katolikus egyház, 173.

In der Diözese Fünfkirchen verordnete der Bischof Nesselrode 1720 eine Visitation, die im folgenden Jahr vom Domkanoniker Imre Bohuss durchgeführt wurde. Acht Jahre später setzte der Bischof eine erneute Visitation an, um über das sich entwikkelnde, aber nach wie vor mit zahlreichen Problemen kämpfende Bistum ein genaueres Bild zu bekommen. Diese wurde vom Kanoniker Mátyás Domsics durchgeführt.[23] In der ersten Hälfte des 18. Jahrhunderts erfolgte noch ein Kirchenbesuch zwischen 1738 und 1742.[24]

Das Residenzprinzip, das auf dem Konzil von Trident verkündet wurde, bedeutete auf der unteren Ebene die Organisierung von Pfarrämtern und die Anstellung von Priestern. In der zweiten Hälfte des 17. Jahrhunderts und am Anfang des 18. Jahrhunderts war die Anzahl der besetzten Pfarrämter in Südtransdanubien jedoch außerordentlich niedrig. Geeignete Pfarrer in den Gemeinden, die ihre priesterlichen Aufgaben pflichtbewusst versahen, standen sowohl im Interesse des Staates als auch der Kirche, des Grundherrn und der Gläubigen. Das Ziel des Staates, der Kirche und im Allgemeinen auch das des Grundherrn war ferner, dass der Priester die ethnisch und konfessionell heterogene Bevölkerung homogenisierte und integrierte. Gerade aus diesen Gründen spielten in dieser Region bei der Auswahl eines Pfarrers mehrere Aspekte eine Rolle. Am Anfang des Jahrhunderts wurden infolge des Priestermangels von Grundherren, die das religiöse Leben für wichtig hielten, Lizentiaten angestellt, die mit der Leitung der Gemeinde beauftragt wurden.
Der Grundherr erwartete vom Priester, dass er mit dem Ausbau der entsprechenden Infrastruktur, mit fleißiger Arbeit zum friedlichen Leben der Gemeinde, zum Prosperieren und zur Entwicklung beitrug. Die Vorsteher der Diözese forderten von ihm die Vertiefung des religiösen Lebens, die Verbreitung des katholischen Glaubens sowie die Bekehrung der Andersgläubigen zum Katholizismus.
Es wurde zum Ziel gesetzt, dass die Pfarrer sich möglichst lange an einem Ort aufhalten sollten, wodurch man die Fluktuation – je nach Möglichkeit – reduzieren wollte. In der ersten Hälfte des 18. Jahrhunderts gab es bereits Priester mit langen Amtszeiten. Bei solchen Fällen betonen die Quellen stets die Geeignetheit und die positiven Eigenschaften des Pfarrers.[25]
Die Ortsgebundenheit der Pfarrer wurde auch in der Hinsicht betont, dass sie sich möglichst regelmäßig und intensiv an ihren Dienstorten aufhalten sollten. Laut

---

[23] Die erste Visitation führte der Domkanoniker Imre Bohuss 1721 durch, die Protokolle sind jedoch nicht mehr vorhanden. Diese Daten verwendeten Mihály Haas, Josephus Koller und Josephus Brüsztle. HAAS, Mihály: Baranya földirati, statisticai és történeti tekintetben. [Die Branau hinsichtlich ihrer Geographie, Statistik und Geschichte.] Pécs 1845. – Die erste vollständige Visitation stammt aus dem Jahr 1729, deren sich auf die Branau beziehende Teile von Ferenc Merényi frei übersetzt und veröffentlicht wurden. MERÉNYI: Domsics.

[24] Protokoll der Visitation 1738-42 der Diözese Fünfkirchen. Visitatio Parochorum diocesis Quinque Ecclesiensis in inclyto Comitatu Baranyiensi 1738 Deo auspice inchoata. Die Veröffentlichung der Visitation 1738-1742 ist in Vorbereitung im Institut für Kirchengeschichte Pécs/Fünfkirchen von Zoltán GŐZSY und Szabolcs VARGA (fortan: Can. Vis. 1738-1742).

[25] József Gergely Fekete etwa, der länger als 30 Jahre in Várpalota als „plebanus fidelissimus" tätig war. PFEIFFER: A veszprémi, 402.

Standpunkt der Bischöfe benötigten die Gläubigen die tägliche Präsenz ihrer Priester. Márton Padányi Bíró genehmigte dem Pfarrer Franz Littenberger zum Beispiel nicht die geplante Heimreise nach Deutschland, um zu vermeiden, dass seine Gläubigen für die anstehende Fastenzeit ohne Seelsorge blieben.[26]
Gleichzeitig kam es auch vor, dass geeignete Pfarrer in solche Gemeinden oder Regionen versetzt wurden, wo die bisherige Tätigkeit der Kirche weniger erfolgreich war. Diese Priester bewegten sich nicht nur innerhalb einer Diözese. Sowohl der Grundherr als auch der Bischof konnte diese Geistlichen versetzen. Ein Grund für die Mobilität zwischen den Bistümern konnte jedoch die Untauglichkeit sein. Pfarrer wurden im ersten Viertel des Jahrhunderts wegen Mangelhaftigkeiten, negativer Meinungsäußerungen aus ihren Ämtern bzw. von ihren Dienstorten entlassen, dieselben wurden aber in andere Diözesen aufgenommen, teils aus großem Priestermangel, teils aus nicht eindeutig geklärtem Entlassungsgrund.
Der 1689 in Fünfkirchen geborene János Keresztes studierte in Nagyszombat und Raab (ung. Győr). Er diente an mehreren Pfarrämtern der Diözese Wesprim, und hatte diese sehr häufig gewechselt. In Gölle, in der Schomodei wurde er seiner Kommende beraubt und aus der Diözese entlassen.[27] Danach kam er ins Bistum Fünfkirchen, wo er in Sumony und Mindszent tätig war, aber in den Gemeinden war man mit ihm auch unzufrieden. Wegen diverser Probleme hat man ihn auf Pilgerfahrt auf den Jakobsweg geschickt und aus der Diözese Fünfkirchen entlassen. Nach der Wallfahrt kam er ins Bistum Wesprim zurück, wo er wiederum an mehreren Orten als Pfarrer diente, bis er 1747 selber um seine Entlassung bat.[28]
Die Versetzungsabsichten der Bischöfe verliefen jedoch nicht immer im vollen Einvernehmen. Es gab Fälle, in denen eine Gemeinde die Versetzung des gewohnten und akzeptierten Pfarrers nicht guthieß, bzw. der Pfarrer seinen designierten Dienstort nicht annahm. Gegen den Südtiroler Wilhelm Federspiel, der in Werischwar (ung. Pilisvörösvár), Großnaarad (ung. Nagynyárád) und in Hedjeß (ung. Hőgyész) Pfarrer war, wurde vom Fünfkirchner Bischof deshalb ein Untersuchungsverfahren eingeleitet, weil er seine Versetzung nach Marok (ung. Márok) nicht zu akzeptieren bereit war. Schließlich verließ Federspiel die Diözese und ging ins Bistum Raab bzw. Csanád.[29]
Beim Wechsel der Pfarrämter und der Diözese spielten aber auch andere Gründe und Gesichtspunkte eine Rolle. Igal in der Schomodei wurde wegen der konfessionellen Konflikte während des Rákóczi-Aufstandes am Anfang des 18. Jahrhunderts sogar von zwei Pfarrern verlassen.[30] András Kazó war zwischen 1701 und 1706

[26] PFEIFFER: A veszprémi, 679.
[27] Brüsztle benutzt den Terminus „Vertreibung" (eliminavit). BRÜSZTLE: Recensio II, 710.
[28] PFEIFFER: A veszprémi, 586.
[29] BRÜSZTLE: Recensio II, 963. – PFEIFFER: A veszprémi, 399.
[30] Vgl. GŐZSY, Zoltán: A Rákóczi-szabadságharc eseményei Somogyban [Die Ereignisse des Rákócsi-Freiheitskampfes im Komitat Schomodei.] In: A Rákóczi-szabadságharc a numizmatika tükrében 1703-2003. Hg. v. Ernő SZABÓ. Kaposvár 2003. – GŐZSY, Zoltán: A pécsi egyházmegye nyugati határainak problémái a 18. század elején [Die Problematik der Westgrenzen der Diözese Fünfkirchen am Anfang des 18. Jahrhunderts]. In: A pécsi egyházmegye a 17-18. században. Hg. v. Tamás FEDELES und Szabolcs VARGA. Pécs 2005 (Series Historia Dioecesis Quinqueecclesiensis I).

Pfarrer in Igal; er beanstandete, dass weder die Gläubigen, noch der Grundherr bereit waren, einen Beitrag zum Aufbau des Pfarrhauses zu leisten. Deshalb verlegte er seinen Sitz nach Szentkirály, das sich im Bistum Fünfkirchen befindet und in der Nähe der Komitatsstadt liegt; er wurde zum ersten Priester der Gemeinde nach der Befreiung.[31] Interessanterweise verließ der Amtsvorgänger von Kazó, Benedek Tokay, auch die Pfarrei von Igal. Tokay flüchtete vor den Unruhen des Rákóczi-Aufstandes und suchte Zuflucht in der Diözese Fünfkirchen, wo er sich lange Zeit am Pfarramt von Hosszúhetény aufhielt.[32] Auf Vorschlag von Kazó übernahm er nach dessen Abdankung die Leitung der Pfarrei Szentkirály.[33] Diese Beispiele machen deutlich, dass zu Beginn des 18. Jahrhunderts in manchen Fällen wegen Priestermangels und ungeordneter Verhältnisse in der kirchlichen Infrastruktur die Pfarrer über größeren Freiraum verfügten. Der aus Dalmatien stammende Anton Gesich ging aus Angst vor Banditen vom Pfarramt Beremend in seine Heimat zurück.[34]
Unmittelbar vor dem bzw. während des Rákóczi-Aufstandes kam es öfters vor, dass katholische Pfarrer insultiert wurden. In erster Linie sind uns die Beschwerden der Priester am Plattensee-Ufer überliefert, dessen Gebiet vom Kriegsgeschehen ohnehin stark betroffen war.[35] Die mehrheitlich protestantischen Kuruzzen strömten am Südostufer des Plattensees in die Schomodei, genau dort, wo die katholische Bevölkerung auch unter der osmanischen Eroberung intakt erhalten blieb und wo sogar noch Pfarrämter tätig waren.[36] Die Soldaten waren – wie es die Quellen bezeugen – den katholischen Pfarrern gegenüber sehr feindlich gesinnt. Szaniszló János Podszklanszky, der Priester von Kiliti, wurde von den Kuruzzen bzw. den jungen Protestanten der Ortschaft gezwungen, die Soldaten auf allen vieren kriechend auf seinem Rücken zu tragen.[37] Die örtlichen Katholiken konnten ihn nur äußerst mühsam in Sicherheit bringen.[38] Er wurde aus dem Dorf gebracht und von einem Gläubigen nach Wesprim gefahren, wohin man nicht nur ihn sondern genauso „*die zur Messe notwendigen Gegenstände und noch sonstige ähnliche Sachen der Kirche*" transportierte. In Wesprim stellte sich heraus, dass die Kuruzzen in der Plattensee-Region andere Pfarrer in ähnlicher Weise belästigten.[39] Die Vertreibung des katholischen Priesters aus Kiliti zog ernsthafte Konsequenzen nach sich; das Pfarramt wur-

---

[31] BRÜSZTLE:_Recensio IV, 621. – PFEIFFER: A veszprémi, 580.
[32] Anno 1704. exortis disturbiis Rakoczyanis ex parochia illa profligatus ad oras dioecesis Quinqueeccles. appulit, in parochia Hosszu-Hetény diutius delitescens. BRÜSZTLE:_Recensio I, 622.
[33] EBD.
[34] MERÉNYI: Domsics, 81.
[35] Über die Konflikte siehe ausführlich GŐZSY: A pécsi egyházmegye.
[36] Über die Lage der Katholiken im Balaton-Gebiet in der Osmanenzeit MOLNÁR: A katolikus egyház, 139-162.
[37] SML, IV. 1. x. Miscellanea. Fasz. 130. – VÉL. Acta Parochialia. Ab initiio archivi ad usque 1770. – PFEIFFER: A veszprémi, 847.
[38] Ein interessanter Beitrag aus dem Untersuchungsprotokoll: solange die männlichen Zeugen behaupten, dass der Pfarrer von den Würdenträgern der Gemeinde gerettet wurde, beteuert im Gegensatz dazu die Zeugin Sára Rozs, dass der Geistliche seine Rettung der Intervention der Frauen verdanke, die ihn auf abenteuerliche Weise, unter Anwendung von List, davontrugen (man steckte ihn unter eine Mulde – eine flache Holzwanne – und schob ihn durch das Fenster). SML IV. 1. x. Miscellanea. 130. Fasz.
[39] SML IV. 1. x. Miscellanea. 130. Fasz. – András Ignác Nagy, der Pfarrer von Fokszabadi (1701-1703), wurde von den Kuruzzen ebenfalls vertrieben. PFEIFFER: A veszprémi, 750.

de danach nämlich nicht mehr besetzt und mit der Zeit nahmen die Kalvinisten die katholische Kirche in Besitz. Podszklanszkys Schicksal wurde von den geschilderten Geschehnissen auch negativ beeinflusst. Laut Quellen verstarb er an seinem nächsten Dienstort (in Szigliget oder in Káptalanszabadi) anderthalb Jahre nach seiner Demütigung.[40]

Bei der Belästigung der Pfarrer durch die Bevölkerung spielten noch andere Gründe mit. János Mihalik, der Seelsorger von Balatonfőkajár, wurde 1702 von den Protestanten der Gemeinde angegriffen, nachdem im Jahre 1700 die Jesuiten (als Grundherren) ihnen die Kirche weg- bzw. zurücknahmen.[41]

Der Staat signalisierte unter anderem mit der Regelung der Dotierung der Priester, dass er die Konsolidierung der Pfarrämter für wichtig hielt. Karl III. verordnete, dass das Jahreseinkommen eines Dorfpfarrers mindestens 150 Forint betragen solle und weil das Gehalt der meisten Priester nicht einmal diese Summe erreichte, wurde 1733 die „Kasse der Pfarrer" (*Cassa parochorum*) erneut ins Leben gerufen, aus der das Einkommen der Dorfpfarrer ergänzt wurde. Die Bischöfe mussten einen Teil ihres Einkommens in diese Kasse einzahlen.[42]

Der Ausbau eines Netzes von Pfarrämtern war nicht nur für den Staat und die Kirche von großer Wichtigkeit, es lag ebenso im Interesse der Grundherren. Sie waren sich nämlich der Tatsache bewusst, dass die Sicherung der Religionsausübung zur Integration und Konsolidierung der angesiedelten Bevölkerung sowie zur erfolgreichen Koexistenz der Gemeinden beitrug. Genau deshalb waren sie es bzw. die Gutsverwalter, die in den von den Diözesanzentren entfernteren Dörfern die Pfarrer auswählten, empfahlen und diese sogar einsetzten. Im ersten Drittel des Jahrhunderts legte die Diözese Agram größeren Wert auf die Einsetzung der Priester. Die Vertreter des Dekanbezirks Kamarcs bekräftigten die Einsetzung der Pfarrer der Diözese Agram auch durch ihre persönliche Präsenz. Parallel zur Zurückdrängung Agrams durch die Bistümer Fünfkirchen und Wesprim waren diese transdanubischen Diözesen bei den Einsetzungen immer intensiver anwesend.

Durch die Kongruenz grundherrlicher und kirchlicher Interessen bei der Auswahl der Priester wurde immer wichtiger, dass die in Frage kommende Person die gegenseitige Akzeptanz fand. Im Visitationsprotokoll von Michael Modrussan, dem Pfarrer von Babócsa, der aus Karlovac stammte, können wir lesen, dass er nach seiner Vorstellung und Einsetzung (*praesentatio et installatio*) durch den Hauptdekan von Kamarcsa auch vom Grundherrn akzeptiert wurde (*post tamen per dominium acceptatus*).[43] Das bedeutete noch nicht, dass der durch Konsens erwählte Pfarrer fähig war, sein Amt zu versehen. Modrussan erwies sich zum Beispiel als völlig unfähig.

---

[40] VÉL. Acta parochialia. Fasz. V.; „(...) wegen der vielen Quälerei lebte er nur anderthalb Jahr, und dort starb er". Zitiert nach PFEIFFER: A veszprémi, 847.

[41] Mihalik wurde später 27 Jahre lang, zwischen 1714 und 1741, der Pfarrer von Tapolca. EBD., 718.

[42] Siehe dazu den Briefwechsel von Karl III. und Imre Esterházy zu diesem Thema bei HODINKA, Antal: Történelmi Tár (1879), 4-6.

[43] PFEIFFER, János: A veszprémi egyházmegye legrégibb egyházlátogatásai (1554-1760) [Die ältesten Visitationen der Diözese Wesprim (1554-1760)]. Veszprém 1947 (A Veszprémi egyházmegye múltjából 10), 54.

Die 1728 durchgeführte Visitation warf ihm Trunksucht, Jähzorn und Diebstahl vor (*Homo est vino deditus, qui saepius ingurgiatus, insanit et furit*). Er verwickelte sich in skandalöse Angelegenheiten, die sowohl die Beurteilung der Kirche als auch die seiner eigenen Person negativ beeinflusste (*scandalaque publica et percussiones committit, cum magna indecentia status ecclesiastici et turpidine propriae personae*).[44] Nicht von ungefähr schlug der Visitator vor, ihn von seinem Dienstort zu entfernen (*si populus hic in fide catholica novellus conservari debet, amoveri oportebit*).[45]

Die entsprechenden Sprachkompetenzen waren von besonderer Wichtigkeit, da ein Pfarrer fähig sein musste, nicht nur Predigten in der Kirche abzuhalten, sondern auch auf die Probleme der Bevölkerung einzugehen. In den südlichen Gebieten der Komitate Zala, Schomodei und Branau, in den überwiegend von Kroaten bewohnten Gemeinden waren bis zur Mitte des 18. Jahrhunderts kroatische und in Agram ausgebildete Seelsorger in Überzahl. Es handelte sich um Priester, die sehr eng an die katholischen Institutionen Kroatiens gebunden waren, in Zagreb ausgebildet und von den Bischöfen von Zengg, Agram oder Syrmien zum Priester geweiht wurden.
Ihre Präsenz im ungarischen Raum hatte mehrere Ursachen. Zum einen war dieser zu jener Zeit bereits ein traditionelles Wirkungsgebiet für Pfarrer aus dem katholischen Kroatien, zum anderen gab es in der Region außer der 1606 gegründeten Theologischen Akademie in Zagreb keine andere Möglichkeit, einen kirchlichen Abschluss zu erlangen, denn in Wesprim und in Fünfkirchen nahmen die Priesterseminare ihre Tätigkeit erst ab den 1740er Jahren auf. Nachdem aber die ersten Jahrgänge ihre Studien absolviert hatten, änderte sich die Tendenz und die südtransdanubischen Bistümer konnten selber für ihren Priesternachwuchs sorgen. Der Fall von Gábor Bedekovics steht beispielhaft dafür. Bedekovics war in Fünfkirchen geboren, sein Vater war der Oberrichter der Stadt. Er besuchte die Mittelschule in Fünfkirchen, studierte Philosophie in Zagreb, danach war er Student der Theologischen Fakultät der Universität Nagyszombat. Zuerst diente er als Administrator in Katoll (ung. Kátoly) östlich von Fünfkirchen, dann war er 1722 am neu errichteten (*neo-erecta*) Pfarramt von Babarcszőlős tätig.[46] Babarcszőlős war durch seine Nähe zur Drau für das Bistum strategisch wichtig, gleichzeitig aber aus besitzpolitischen Gründen auch für die katholische Familie Pálffy bedeutend. Deshalb ernannte man einen gebildeten, verlässlichen, kroatisch sprechenden Pfarrer. Da die kirchliche Struktur noch nicht herausgebildet war, wurde der Geistliche in sein Amt vom ebenfalls zuständigen, die Verhältnisse vor Ort besser kennenden Gutsverwalter der Grundherrschaft eingesetzt (*investituram habet nullam pro Parochia ista nec est Installatus per Personam Ecclesiasticam, verum per officialem Dominӱ propositus*

[44] Arhiv Zagrebačke Nadbiskupije [Erzbischöfliches Archiv Zagreb]. (fortan: AZN). Archidiaconatus Camarcensis, anno 1716-1731 et Vaska 1731-1733. – PFEIFFER: A veszprémi, 54. Zu Weihnachten 1727 benahm er sich im betrunkenen Zustand absolut skandalös, er machte die Nachtandacht zunichte.
[45] EBD.
[46] BRÜSZTLE: Recensio II, 78.

est).[47] Bedekovics wurde den Erwartungen in allerlei Hinsicht gerecht, von seiner Ausbildung bis zur Sprachkompetenz (*Gnarus lingvarum Hungaricae, Croaticae, et Slavonicae*), und war dort 23 Jahre lang der Pfarrer der Gemeinde.[48] Man muss aber hinzufügen, dass die Bevölkerung mit seiner Tätigkeit nicht ganz zufrieden war (*non tamen optimum sparsit odorem*).[49]

Die kroatischen Seelsorger der kroatischen Siedlungen waren in mehreren Bistümer aktiv. Der aus Dalmatien stammende Stefan Brozovics war zum Beispiel ab 1721 der Pfarrer in Felsőszentmárton in der Branau. 1725 verlegte er seinen Sitz in die ebenfalls kroatische Gemeinde Buzsák, die sich allerdings schon in der Schomodei befindet und zur Diözese Wesprim gehörte.[50] Die Bischöfe von Wesprim bemühten sich in der Regel, aus Kroatien stammende oder Kroatisch sprechende Priester nach Buzsák zu ernennen. Jakob Kozarics, in Zagreb ausgebildet, wurde von Márton Padányi Bíró in die Diözese aufgenommen und versah seine priesterlichen Aufgaben unter anderem in Lengyeltóti ud Karád.[51] Paul Lepi (Liepi), der in Raguza geboren war und in Wien studierte, war ab 1712 Pfarrer in Lúcs, Komitat Branau. Hier war er auch für die Gemeinden Beremend und Kásád zuständig. Ab 1726 war er bereits auf dem Gebiet der Diözese Wesprim, im Dorf Lengyeltóti, und ab 1734 in Tótszentpál, in einer Siedlung mit ebenfalls kroatischer Bevölkerung.[52]

Das Schicksal der Geistlichen kroatischer Abstammung stellt exemplarisch die kroatische Familie Hrnchevich (Hernecsevics) dar, aus der sich mehrere Mitglieder für eine kirchliche Laufbahn entschieden. Matthias Hrnchevich studierte in Graz und wurde zum Pfarrer von Karlovica (Diözese Agram). Auf Empfehlung des aus Raguza stammenden Nikolaus Gigovics, Weihbischof von Syrmien und Großpropst von Fünfkirchen, wurde er in die Diözese Wesprim aufgenommen.[53] Hrnchevich war zwischen 1751 und 1759 am Pfarramt von Tótszentpál. Von hier aus ging er in die Diözese Fünfkirchen und war bis 1768 in Bikal tätig, wo er jedoch vom Bischof entlassen wurde.[54] Danach ging er in die Diözese Wesprim zurück und wurde mit bischöflicher Genehmigung – da seine Arbeit hier gefragt war, gemeinsam mit dem Pfarrer von Tapsony – der Seelsorger der teils kroatischen Gemeinde Gadány im Komitat Schomodei.[55] Sein Bruder Michael war auch als Priester in der Diözese Zagreb tätig (Orahovica, Komitat Verőce), wurde ab 1724 Pfarrer in der kroatischen

[47] Can. Vis. 1738-1742, 202.
[48] Can. Vis. 1738-1742, 202-203.
[49] BRÜSZTLE: Recensio II, 78.
[50] BRÜSZTLE: Recensio II, 445. – PFEIFFER: A veszprémi, 316.
[51] EBD., 636-637.
[52] BRÜSZTLE: Recensio III, 597-598. – PFEIFFER: A veszprémi, 673-674. In Lengyeltóti ließ er die Pfarrei auf eigene Kosten aufbauen.
[53] Gigovics war ab 1753 Bischof von Syrmien. Vgl. BRÜSZTLE: Recensio I, 581. – FEDELES, Tamás: Die Kanoniker Domherren des Domkapitels zu Pécs in der ersten Hälfte des 18. Jahrhunderts. In: A pécsi egyházmegye a 17-18. században. Hg. v. Tamás FEDELES und Szabolcs VARGA. Pécs 2005 (Series Historia Dioecesis Quinqueecclesiensis I), 228-229.
[54] Anno 1767. die 5. Septembr. rursus in facie consistorii constitutus, tandem in sessione die 7. Januar 1768. pronunciatur finalis sententia, qua Herncsevics parochia privatus e diocesi hac dimittititur. BRÜSZTLE: Recensio II, 239.
[55] PFEIFFER: A veszprémi, 533-534. – BRÜSZTLE: Recensio II, 239.

Gemeinde Öreglak, dann im Dorf Somogyvár, beide im Komitat Schomodei im Bistum Wesprim. Zu seiner Amtszeit in Somogyvár versah er die Seelsorge zahlreicher kroatischer Filialkirchen der Schomodei, unter anderem der (später selbstständige Pfarreien habenden) Gemeinden Buzsák, Lengyeltóti, Mernye, Osztopán, Tótszentpál. 1744 verließ er Somogyvár und wurde zum Hauskaplan in Bonyhád/Bonhard, bei József Perczel, Vizegespan des Komitats Tolnau.[56]
Ab Mitte der 1720er Jahre, als die Zahl der Ungarn anstieg und die Kroaten sich teilweise assimilierten, gewann die Frage der ungarischen Sprachkompetenz der Priester an Aktualität. Deren Mangel verursachte nämlich Probleme. Die Quellen zeugen davon, dass die Kroatisch sprechenden Priester keinen Anschluss an die ungarische Bevölkerung ihres Pfarramtes fanden bzw. nur bescheidene Ergebnisse bei der Bekehrung der Protestanten erzielen konnten. In einer Visitation aus dem Jahre 1728 in Berzence, Komitat Schomodei, können wir über die Rekatholisierung Folgendes lesen: „*Das Ergebnis wäre besser, wenn der Pfarrer der ungarischen Sprache mächtig wäre.*"[57] In Kanizsa zum Beispiel war der Priester damals kroatischsprachig, seine Gläubigen aber Ungarn. Deshalb zelebrierte er die Messe, die Predigt aber hielt ein Jesuit aus der Burg in ungarischer Sprache. In Szilvás, im Komitat Branau konnte ein Pfarrer gerade wegen der sprachlichen Barrieren nicht predigen.[58] Für die Gläubigen war es auch wichtig, dass der Pfarrer ihre Beichten auf Ungarisch anhörte.[59] Eben deshalb wurde es im 18. Jahrhundert gang und gäbe, dass die Priester in drei, vier, ja sogar in fünf Sprachen predigten und all dieser mächtig waren, angepasst an den jeweiligen ethnischen Charakter eines Dorfes.[60] Sie sprachen vor allem Latein, Ungarisch, Deutsch sowie Serbisch und Kroatisch, eventuell Italienisch, Spanisch. Es kam auch vor, dass einige Pfarrer sowohl des Kroatischen als auch des Slawonischen mächtig waren, das heißt, sie sprachen den Kajkaw- sowie den Stokaw-Dialekt. Der Priester von Szigetvár, der fünf Sprachen beherrschte, gab in der Mitte des Jahrhunderts auch ehrlich zu, dass er ohne diese Fähigkeit seine Pflichten nicht erfolgreich versehen könnte.[61] Josephus Antonius Mazorani, Pfarrer in Lakócsa, konnte ebenfalls fünf Sprachen sprechen. Der aus Dalmatien stammende Geistliche studierte in Fünfkirchen und unter anderem wegen seiner Sprachkompe-

---

[56] PFEIFFER: A veszprémi, 534.

[57] et fieret fructus uberior, si linguae etiam hungaricae gnarus haberi posset administrator. EBD., 15.

[58] In eo tamen conqueritur populus pure Ungaricus, quod Parochus idiomatae illorum nunquam concionetur. Can. Vis. 1738-1742, 3.

[59] Bezüglich des Priesters von Lakócsa, Josephus Mazoranyi, z.B. Gnarus linguarum Latinae, Italicae Illyricae, et Germanicae in tantum ut confessiones Fidelium excipere possit. Can. Vis. 1738-1742, 143. Über János Keresztes in Sumony: in casu necessitatis fidelium confessiones excipere possit. EBD., 166.

[60] In den ausschließlich von einer Ethnie – Ungarn, Deutschen oder Südslawen – bewohnten Ortschaften findet man auch zweisprachige Priester, wie z.B. im Fall von Görcsöny, den Pfarrer Mathias Tariany. Gnarus Linquarum Latinae, Hungariae. Can. Vis. 1738-1742, 30.

[61] Vgl. GŐZSY, Zoltán: Szigetvár története 1715-1825 között. [Die Geschichte von Szigetvár zwischen 1715 und 1825.] In: Szigetvár története. Tanulmányok a város múltjából. Hg. v. Sándor BŐSZE, László RAVAZDI und László SZITA. Szigetvár 2006, 170-172. – Can. Vis. 1738-1742, 128.

tenzen wurde er 1738 in die Gemeinde an der Drau versetzt.[62] Zusammenfassend können wir feststellen, dass bei den Pfarrern weniger die Herkunft und Nationalität, sondern viel mehr die damit selbstverständlich zusammenhängenden Sprachkenntnisse sowie ihre Befähigung die ausschlaggebenden Faktoren für ihren Erfolg waren. Der aus der Diözese Zagreb stammende, in Zagreb ausgebildete Pál Bíró kam zum Beispiel 1742 nach Csurgó, wo er 1778 als Pfarrer diente.[63] Der Dalmatier Johannes Bobus studierte in Agram und Ofen (ung. Buda) und war Priester im ungarisch-kroatischen Lengyeltóti, dann in Felsősegesd.[64] Der gebürtige Agramer Pál Jurash diente vor allem in südslawischen Ortschaften und das sogar in drei Diözesen, in der von Fünfkirchen, Wesprim und Csanád.[65]

Die entsprechende Befähigung der einzelnen Pfarrer stand sogar über den kirchenpolitischen Interessen. Die bewährten Geistlichen versuchte man unbedingt in der Diözese zu halten. Parallel zur Aufstellung und Konsolidierung der Priesterseminare in Wesprim und Fünfkirchen und zur Zunahme der Zahl der dortigen Absolventen änderte sich die Situation. Die Bischöfe konnten von nun an aus den Kandidaten eine Auswahl treffen. Die Möglichkeiten der Entlassenen, Abgesetzten oder der aus anderen Diözesen Zurückehrenden wurden beschränkt, die Bischöfe bevorzugten die Absolventen der eigenen Seminare. Der 1705 in Ofen geborene Georg Latinicsich war zuerst in Mohatsch (ung. Mohács), dann in Katoll Pfarrer. Danach war er in Syrmien aufzufinden; er war am zur Diözese Diakovar gehörenden Pfarramt Karlovica tätig, wartete dann in Pétervárad vergebens auf ein kirchliches Amt. Schließlich verlegte er 1744 seinen Sitz in die Schomodei, nach Legyeltóti. Zuvor aber, im Jahre 1743 schrieb er einen Brief ans Bistum Fünfkirchen, in dem er um seine Wiederaufnahme in die Diözese ersuchte, was jedoch vom Vikar mit der Begründung abgelehnt wurde, dass momentan eher die Entsendung von Seminaristen als die Zurücknahme der Davongegangenen bevorzugtwerde.[66] Nachdem die Priesterseminare ihre Tätigkeit aufgenommen hatten, finden wir des Öfteren Fälle, in denen Priester entlassen wurden bzw. die Dotation ihnen weggenommen wurde.
Die aus kroatischen Bistümern kommenden Pfarrer mussten nach dem Amtsantritt des Bischofs Márton Padányi Bíró eine Synodenprüfung ablegen und durften erst nach dieser den Kirchendienstaufnehmen. Die Prüfung musste vor den sog. Synodenprüfern absolviert werden. Padányi schrieb diese offensichtlich deshalb vor, um seine eigene Rechtshoheit dem Bischof von Zagreb gegenüber zu demonstrieren. Die Prüfung hatte aber auch eine andere, spezifische Bedeutung: Der Bischof genehmigte die Tätigkeit nur jener Pfarrer, die nicht „vagus" waren, d.h. die der

[62] BRÜSZTLE: RECENSIO II, 500. Der Pfarrer der Hauptdiözese Gran/Esztergom, Márton Rostás, wurde 1731 gerade wegen seiner mangelnden Kompetenzen in der deutschen und den illyrischen Sprachen entlassen. Danach ging er ins Bistum Wesprim. PFEIFFER: A veszprémi, 881-882.
[63] EBD., 291.
[64] EBD., 294.
[65] BRÜSZTLE: RECENSIO III, 665-666. – PFEIFFER: A veszprémi, 559.
[66] „Nunc esse potius cogitandum de Alumnis ad curam mittendis et dislocandis, quam de dimissis ad dioecesim recipiendis" BRÜSZTLE: RECENSIO II, 251-252.

Rechtshoheit eines Bischofs unterstanden. Jeder einzelne Priester musste einer Diözese angehören (incardinatio); so waren seine hierarchischen Verhältnisse klar bzw. auch, wer sich um die Versorgung des Geistlichen kümmern musste. (Letzteres bezog sich nur auf die, die auf den Titel der Diözese geweiht wurden nicht für Inhaber von Benefizien oder die für die Mission bestimmt waren.)
Die „excardinatio“, d.h. die Entlassung aus der Diözese erfolgte durch ein amtliches Schreiben und war nur mit dem Aufnahmeschreiben eines anderen Bischofs gültig; also rein theoretisch durften die Pfarrer eine Pfarrei nicht willkürlich verlassen. Der aus der Diözese Zagreb stammende Péter Fehér musste z.B. diese Prüfung ablegen, bevor er in Csurgó Kaplan wurde, dann im kroatisch-ungarischen Miháld in der Schomodei die Leitung des Pfarramtes übernahm.[67]

In den von Deutschen bewohnten Siedlungen galt der deutschsprachige Pfarrer deutscher Herkunft als Selbstverständlichkeit. Die deutschen Seelsorger trugen zur Konsolidierung der deutschen Ansiedlung in großem Maße bei. Die ersten Priester kamen zum Teil mit den Einwanderern, zum Teil zogen sie aus den bereits integrierten deutschen Gemeinden an ihre Dienststellen. Der erste Pfarrer der Gemeinde Tevel im Komitat Tolnau kam zusammen mit den deutschen Kolonisten.[68] Der erste Pfarrer der Gemeinde Großnaarad im Komitat Branau war in Fulda geboren und kam mit den Siedlern nach Ungarn. Solange das Priesterseminar im Bistum Fünfkirchen seine Tätigkeit noch nicht aufgenommen hatte, kamen oft Seelsorger aus den deutschen Gemeinden in der Umgebung von Pest, vor allem aus Solymár, Pilisborosjenő und Zsámbék. Der aus Bayern stammende Christophorus Puck kam aus dem zur Diözese Wesprim gehörenden Zsámbék ins Bistum Fünfkirchen. 1732 war er in Apar, im darauffolgenden Jahr bereits in Hímesháza tätig.[69] Deutsche Geistliche kamen auch aus anderen Gebieten in die Branau, zum Beispiel über Nordungarn aus Mähren und Schlesien. Der 1702 in Schlesien geborene Joannes Venkler/Vinkler kam an Ostern 1738 nach Dárda, von wo er später nach Hímesházára ging.[70] Er predigte auf Deutsch, aber im Notfall war er in der Lage, sich sowohl auf Ungarisch als auch in einer südslawischen Sprache zu äußern.[71] In solchen Gemeinden aber, wo neben den Deutschen auch Gläubige anderer Nationalität lebten, bedeuteten die mangelnden Fremdsprachenkenntnisse ein ernsthaftes Problem. Karl Kiener bat selber um seine Entlassung aus der Marktgemeinde Tolna, da er kein Ungarisch sprechen konnte (*ob*

---

[67] Nach Mihald kam er auf Empfehlung des Grundbesitzers Károly Inkey. PFEIFFER: A veszprémi, 401.
[68] Joannes Henricus Mack anno 1713 cum neocolonia ex Svevia ad Tevel veniens curam animarum ibidem inchoavit. Hujus sacerdotis mentionem facit synodus anni 1714. his verbis: „Admodum Reverendus D. Neo-Parochus in Possessione Tevel, in comitatu Tolnensi, absque ecclesia. BRÜSZTLE: RECENSIO I, 696.
[69] EBD. II, 30 und III, 62. – PFEIFFER: A veszprémi, 859.
[70] Joannes Vinkler. Geboren 1702 in Schlesien. Ostern 1738 kam er nach Dárda, von dort ging er später nach Hímesháza.
[71] Dedit operam studÿs Philosophicis Vratislaviae Theologiae speculativae pro ut etiam Morali Viennae gnarus lingvarum Latinae, Germanicae aliquid etiam Hungaricae ut confessiones audire possit et Illiricae ut in casu necessitatis. Can. Vis. 1738-1742, 274.

defectum linguae hungaricae a petito suo dimoveretur). Aus dem Grund versetzte man ihn lieber ins deutsche Dorf Nadasch (ung. Mecseknádasd).[72]

Eine interessante Tendenz_der Zeit, in der häufig Priester aus der Umgebung von Ofen und Pest in die deutschen Gemeinden der Branau und nach Tolnau kamen,[73] ist es, dass dies in der umgekehrten Richtung nicht mehr funktionierte.[74] Dieselbe ist auch bei den kroatischen Pfarrern festzustellen. Wenn ein im Komitat Branau oder Schomodei tätiger Priester aus irgendeinem Grund nach Slawonien oder Kroatien versetzt wurde, kam er sehr selten nach Ungarn zurück.[75]

Seit der Mitte des 18. Jahrhunderts war unter den deutschen Pfarrern eine Art Fluktuation festzustellen. Die Grundherren deutscher Gemeinden oder die Gemeinden selber riefen oft geeignete und bewährte Priester zu sich. Der in Wien geborene Henricus Muth kam zum Beispiel auf Wunsch des Florimundus Mercy 1740 nach Hőgyész, wo das Pfarramt gerade unbesetzt war (*per comitem Claudium Florimundum Mercy pro Hőgyész destinatus et praesentatus*). Die Amtsträger der Grundherrschaften legten einen großen Wert auf die Anstellung eines geeigneten Pfarrers, wenn die Interessen der Grundherrschaften eines bedurften.[76] Gleichzeitig entfernten sie die von ihnen wenig akzeptierten Geistlichen. In Lakócsa zum Beispiel geriet der Pfarrer Jakob Spanics in einen Dauerkonflikt mit dem Gutsverwalter, weshalb er sein Amt aufgeben und Monate lang in Fünfkirchen weilen musste, bis er endlich nach Egerág versetzt wurde.[77] Der sehr erfolgreich katholisierende, agile János Kereszturi erweckte die Aufmerksamkeit des Wesprimer Bischofs, Ádám Acsády, der

[72] BRÜSZTLE: Recensio II, 116-117.

[73] Es kamen vor allem aus Solymár, Pilisvörösvár, Pilisborosjenő Priester hierher.

[74] Johannes Bayermann kam nach seinen Diensten in Solymár, Városlőd, und Perjámos (Komitat Csanád) nach Naarad/Nyárád, dann nach Mucsi, von wo er 1750 nach zur Diözese Wesprim gehörendem Pesthidegkút ging, um dort als Pfarrer zu dienen. PFEIFFER: A veszprémi, 271.
Anton Gabrieli (geb. 1693 in Sachsenfeld) leitete zwischen 1716 und 1725 das Pfarramt von Solymár. Danach kam er ins Bistum Fünfkirchen, zuerst nach Tevel, dann nach Hímesháza, wo er zwischen 1729 und 1733 tätig war. Von dort ging er zurück in die Diözese Wesprim. Ab 1781 war er der Hauptdekan von Buda. PFEIFFER: A veszprémi, 425. – BRÜSZTLE: Recensio I, 699. – Karl Kiener wurde 1678 in Wien geboren, war Pfarrer in Pilisborosjenő; von hier kam er ins Bistum Fünfkirchen. Er war Priester in Hőgyész, dann in Mecseknádasd. Er verstarb in Fünfkirchen 1748. BRÜSZTLE: Recensio II, 116-117; PFEIFFER: A veszprémi, 594. – Der Benediktiner aus Bayern, Benedikt Strelle, kam aus Deutschland nach Ungarn, wurde Pfarrer im zum Bistum Waitzen/Vác gehörenden Dunaharaszti; von hier kam er nach Adony, in die Wesprimer Diözese, schließlich ins Bistum Fünfkirchen nach Tevel. – Es gab auch deutsche Geistliche, die – laut Quellen – verschollen sind. Johann Rascher kam 1735 nach Kakasd, Komitat Tolnau, nachdem er in Piliscsaba und in Budajenő als Pfarrer tätig war; nach 1738 sind über ihn allerdings keine Angaben mehr in den ungarischen kirchlichen Quellen zu finden (isthinc disparet, quin sciatur, quo devenerit). BRÜSZTLE: Recensio II, 198. – PFEIFFER: A veszprémi, 870-871.

[75] Es kam vor, dass ungeeignete, bzw. ihren Dienstort verlassende kroatische Pfarrer nach Slawonien geschickt wurden. Stefan (Stephanus) Pauletics, der Pfarrer von Lúcs, wurde zum Beispiel, nachdem er das dortige Pfarramt verließ, nach Kukoljevci beordert („curam animarum penitus negligens, variis impicitus processibus, ante annum 1738. hunc locum deserere, coactus ad Kukojevci in Slavonia ut administrator dirigitur.) BRÜSZTLE: Recensio II, 599.

[76] Joannes Manhalt ex parochia Bikal huc venit. Eodem tempore J.M. ad occupandam parochiam Egerágh invitatur … ad Joannem Drakovics provisorem dominalem in Bólly dimitteret litteras. EBD. II, 561-562.

[77] Cum hic loci continuas cum officialibus dominalibus altercationes, instituta 28. Mart. 1754. ex parte ordinariatus inquisitione, administrator mense Junio e.a. isthinc discedere jussus, pluribusque mensibus Quinque-Ecclesiis commorari coactus, tandem mense Aprili 1755 in Egeragh iterum ut administrator accomodatur. EBD. II, 501.

ihn in seine Diözese aufnahm, in der er ab 1740 das Pfarramt von Attala leitete. Wahrscheinlich fiel er hier dem Provisor der Esterházy-Herrschaft, Gábor Gyulai Gaál, auf, der ihn nach der Familie Esterházy gehörendem Keszi, Komitat Tolnau, mitnahm. Dagegen legte der Bischof von Fünfkirchen Protest ein. Kereszturi blieb schließlich nicht in Keszi, sondern wurde ab 1742 der Priester von Szentbalázs in der Schomodei, wo er eine enorm wichtige Tätigkeit ausübte: Er pastorierte beinahe die gesamte Zselic-Region, indem er sie von Dorf zu Dorf bereiste, auch in den Wintermonaten (*19 pagis laboriose inservit ferme per totum Zselicz, saepe quidem cum manifesto vitae periculo*). Nicht von ungefähr wurde bezüglich seiner Person gesagt: „*Der zweite Radonay ist auferstanden*!"[78] Ein letztes Beispiel ist Tamás Pápai, der 45 Jahre Priester in Bagod, Komitat Wesprim, war. Der lange Zeit aktive Pfarrer diente auf Wunsch der Familie Zichy auch in Nagyvázsony noch einige Jahre.[79]

Die Priester der deutschen Gemeinden des Bistums Fünfkirchen sind in der zweiten Hälfte des 18. Jahrhunderts im Allgemeinen bereits auf dem Gebiet ihrer Diözese geboren und absolvierten ihre Schulen in Fünfkirchen. Davon zeugen die Pfarrer der Gemeinde Závod: Matthias Spreng war 1758 in Hőgyész geboren, besuchte das Priesterseminar in Fünfkirchen und wurde zum Pfarrer in Závod. Der ihm folgende Georgius Klie war in Bozsok geboren, machte seinen Abschluss in Fünfkirchen, war ab 1799 Pfarrer in Závod, starb 1810 in Fünfkirchen.

Ab den 30er Jahren des 18. Jahrhunderts war festzustellen, dass nicht ausschließlich in Agram ausgebildete, kroatische Pfarrer in die Pfarrämter der Branau und der Schomodei kamen, sondern auch solche, die nach einem Zagreber Grundstudium an ungarischen Hochschuleinrichtungen weitergebildet wurden. Ab der Mitte des Jahrhunderts nahm die Anzahl der aus Kroatien kommenden und in Zagreb ausgebildeten Pfarrer eindeutig ab. Das hatte mehrere Gründe: Erstens nahmen die Priesterseminare in Fünfkirchen, in Wesprim bzw. an anderen Bischofssitzen ihre Tätigkeit auf,[80]

Zweitens hatten die dortigen Bischöfe positive Erwartungen gegenüber der ungarischen Priesterausbildung, drittens verfolgten die Grundherren Integrationsabsichten bezüglich der konfessionellen und ethnischen Zusammensetzung der Bevölkerung. Hinzu kam noch, dass die Bischöfe Márton Padányi Bíró und György Klimó solche agile, zielbewusste und starke Kirchenpolitik betreibende Persönlichkeiten waren, die den Einfluss des Bistums Zagreb auch durch die entsprechende Auswahl der Priester minimieren wollten. Gleichzeitig aber legten die Bischöfe von Fünfkirchen

---

[78] PFEIFFER: A veszprémi, 587.

[79] EBD., 815.

[80] In Fünfkirchen begann 1736 der Lehrbetrieb an der Fakultät für Theologie. In Wesprim richtete 1711 Bischof Volkra das Seminar ein, das allerdings 1722 geschlossen wurde. Márton Padányi Bíró richtete 1745 mit Hilfe der Sankt-Anna-Stiftung von Volkra das Seminar erneut ein und beauftragte mit seiner Führung die Piaristen. Vgl. A veszprémi papnevelő intézet emlékkönyve Magyarország fennálásának ezredéves ünnepére [Festschrift des Priesterseminars zu Wesprim zur Feier des Ungarischen Milleniums.]. Veszprém 1907, 17-18. – KÖRMENDY, József: Gr. Volkra Ottó Ker. János veszprémi püspök élete és munkássága 1665-1720 [Das Leben und Wirken des Wesprimer Bischofs Graf Otto Volkra 1665-1720.]. Veszprém 1995, 23-24.

Wert darauf, dass in die kroatischen Gemeinden kroatischsprachige Absolventen des Fünfkirchner Priesterseminars entsendet wurden.[81]
In den Pfarrämtern nahe dem bischöflichen Zentrum dienten Priester, die in Nagyszombat studierten und dort gute Ergebnisse erzielten. Sie versahen auch Kanoniker-Aufgaben am Bischofssitz. Bei diesen Pfarrämtern kam die Personalpolitik eines Bischofs oder einer anderen leitenden kirchlichen Persönlichkeit besser zur Geltung. Ein gutes Beispiel für die Patronage begabter Nachwuchspfarrer bietet der Fall des Joannes Visa de Mátha. Er entstammte einer adeligen Familie aus Gyöngyös, Komitat Heves, studierte in Wien im Pázmáneum. Der Bischof von Fünfkirchen, Pál Széchényi, nahm ihn zu sich (*in clientalem acceptum*) und versetzte ihn als Pfarrer nach Kővágószőlős, nahe Fünfkirchen. Später wurde er Lektor des Fünfkirchner Domkapitels.[82]
Im Falle der niederen Geistlichkeit bedeutete das Residenz-Prinzip die Besetzung eines Pfarramtes und beinhaltete auch jene Erwartung, nach der sich ein ernannter Pfarrer tatsächlich an seinem Dienstort aufhalten sollte und diesen nur in begründeten Fällen auf längere Zeit verlassen durfte.[83] Bezüglich des Schlesiers Josephus Brozsek, der der Einladung des Bischofs von Csanád, Miklós Stanislavich, folgend nach Ungarn, später in die Diözese Fünfkirchen kam, können wir in einem Vikar-Brief die Bemerkung lesen, dass er zu viel unterwegs sei und selten Sakramente spende (*multum peregrinatur, raro sanctificatur*).[84]
Wie lange ein Pfarrer an einem Ort blieb, war von der Einstellung und vom Verhalten der Gläubigen sehr beeinflusst. Die psychisch labilen, den Dienstort nicht zu akzeptieren bereiten Geistlichen taten sich oft schwer. Diese Seelsorger wechselten oft ihre Pfarrämter und waren meistens auch von der Gemeinde wenig akzeptiert.[85] In der ersten Hälfte des Jahrhunderts kamen jedoch auch solche Konflikte vor, die weit über einen simplen religiösen Widerstand hinausgingen.[86]

Hinsichtlich der Rechtshoheit und der Pastoration ist die Präsenz der verschiedenen Ordensprovinzen des Franziskanerordens in der Region interessant und belehrend.[87] Manche ungarische Grundherren riefen in der ersten Hälfte des Jahrhunderts logi-

---

[81] Der Pfarrer von Lúcs, Martinus Turkovics, war in Zagreb geboren, studierte auch dort, dann kam er ins Bistum Fünfkirchen, wo er in ein kroatisches Dorf der Branau entsendet wurde. Das gleiche galt für Stefan (Stephanus) Pauletics, der Turkovics in seinem Amt folgte. BRÜSZTLE: Recensio II, 598-599.
[82] EBD. III, 410-411. – FEDELES: Die Kanoniker, 239.
[83] In den Visitationen kommen Bemerkungen häufig vor, wie z.B. Parochus in Parochia constanter residet. Can. Vis. 1738-1742, 22 und 33.
[84] BRÜSZTLE: Recensio II, 445.
[85] Der in Fünfkirchen geborene, „oft an etwas kränkelnde und schwächelnde" Jakob Issl wurde sogar aus dem Seminar von Kalocsa entlassen, weil er unter seinen Kommilitonen Entsetzen auslöste. Danach wechselte er oft seinen Dienstort, Márok verließ er wegen unbequemer Zustände (discessit ob inamoenitates in Márok perpessas). BRÜSZTLE: Recensio, II, 688 und III, 687-688. – PFEIFFER: A veszprémi, 545.
[86] Der zwischen 1735 und 1750 in Gölle dienende György Fejérváry wurde wahnsinnig und starb wenig später. 1740 plünderten Unbekannte das Pfarramt und setzten es in Brand (die ab 1710 geführten Matrikelbücher gingen in den Flammen auf), 1750 wurde die Pfarrei in der Abwesenheit des Geistlichen erneut geplündert. PFEIFFER: A veszprémi, 401.
[87] Vö. BONITIUS, (Ivan) Rupčič: Entstehung der Franziskanerpfarreien in Bosnien und der Herzegowina und ihre Entwicklung bis zum Jahre 1878. Breslau 1937.

scherweise die nach dem Heiligen Ladislaus benannte slawonische Ordensprovinz (*Patrum Franciscanum provinciae Slavonicae*) ins Land. In Kanizsa, Szigetvár und Nagyatád war die Präsenz der über Pastorations-Erfahrungen verfügenden, wegen ihrer Sprachkenntnisse im Kreise der kroatischen und ungarischen Bevölkerung akzeptierten Franziskanermönche dringend benötigt. In Szigetvár zum Beispiel hielten sie die Reden in kroatischer Sprache (*Alius autem Populus Croaticus Praedicationi Verbi Divini apud Patres Franciscanos interesset*).[88] Bis zur Mitte des Jahrhunderts unterstützten jedoch die ungarischen Bischöfe die nach der Heiligen Maria benannte Ordensprovinz, also die Marianer, im Gegensatz zur kroatisch-slawonischen Provinz jenseits der Drau, benannt nach dem Heiligen Ladislaus.

Man muss die Franziskaner in Szigetvár gesondert erwähnen, die in der ersten Hälfte des 18. Jahrhunderts im religiösen Leben der Schomodei eine besondere Rolle spielten. Diese bestand darin, dass sie die katholische Diaspora in der Umgebung von Szigetvár, in einer vorwiegend kalvinistischen Region, förderten und somit die Gläubigen für die katholische Kirche gewannen, indem sie das religiöse Leben gerade dort unterstützten, wo es noch keine Pfarrämter gab und die Seelsorge noch nicht herausgebildet war.[89] Sie übten in mehr als neun Dörfern der Diözese Wesprim ihre Tätigkeit aus, in der ersten Hälfte des 18. Jahrhunderts waren sie für die Administration der Pfarrämter in Kadarkút, in Németlad, in Németújfalu, in Somogyhárságy und in Szulok zuständig. Aus den im Archiv des Ordenshauses aufbewahrten Matrikelbüchern geht klar hervor, dass die Franziskaner in einer großen Zahl von Dörfern, von Nemeske und Kacsóta in der Branau bis Kőröshegy in der Nordschomodei, tauften. Nachdem die Bischöfe von Wesprim die Tätigkeit der Franziskaner von Szigetvár ermessen und ausgewertet hatten, gaben sie ihnen noch mehr Privilegien: Sie durften als Beichtväter fungieren, die Aufgaben von Dorfpriestern versehen und weitere Sakramente spenden.[90]

Die Bischöfe legten großen Wert auf die Bekehrung der Nichtkatholiken. Aus diesem Grund wurden in den protestantischen Gebieten Pfarrämter in größerer Anzahl gegründet bzw. den Protestanten wurden ihre Kirchen weggenommen. Daraus resultierten viele Konflikte. Ein weiteres Problem bestand in der Uneindeutigkeit der Gesetze zum Kirchennutzungsrecht der Protestanten. 1681 regelte Leopold I. lediglich in den unter Habsburg-Hoheit stehenden ungarischen Gebieten die Frage der Religionsausübung. Laut Gesetz durften die Protestanten nur an je zwei Orten pro Komitat Gottesdienste abhalten; damit wurde der sogenannte „Artikularis-Ort" zum Rechtsbegriff. Das betraf damals freilich nicht das Territorium, welches noch unter osmanischer Herrschaft stand.

---

[88] Can. Vis. 1738-1742, 128.

[89] P. TAKÁCS-PFEIFFER: Szent Ferenc fiai, 208 und 343. – Die Oberhäupter des Ordens sind uns aus den Quellen des Diözesenarchivs Wesprim bekannt: 1754 Antal P. Antony, 1770; Adorján P. Szigetvári, 1778; Antal P. Fabsits, 1779; Lajos P. Schwartz.

[90] EBD., 345-348. – GŐZSY: Szigetvár.

Die Konsolidierung der Kirchenverwaltung in Südtransdanubien bedeutete eine besonders große Aufgabe sowohl für den Herrscher als auch für die Kirchenelite. Leopold I. unterstützte im Dienste der konfessionellen Homogenisierung die Katholische Kirche. Die vom Kaiser Leopold und Kardinal Kollonich angekündigte und forcierte Rekatholisierung vertiefte jedoch die Grabenkämpfe zwischen den Konfessionen. Kardinal Kollonich zum Beispiel wies zwischen 1700 und 1702 die Komitate in Transdanubien an, die Protestanten zu vertreiben. Man kam natürlich dieser Aufforderung nicht nach, doch die Richtlinien dieser Religionspolitik trugen dazu bei, dass der Komitatsadel Rákóczis Kuruzzen unterstützte.
Genau deshalb kamen konfessionelle Gegensätze während des Rákóczi-Aufstandes oft an die Oberfläche. In mehreren transdanubischen Gemeinden vertrieben die protestantischen Kuruzzen die katholischen Priester und nahmen Kirchen zurück bzw. besetzten sie. Nicht umsonst trat auf königlichen Befehl Anfang der 1720er Jahre in Pest eine Kommission zusammen, die sich mit Religionsfragen befasste (Pester Kommission). Auf Anweisung dieser Kommission hatte jedes Komitat zu überprüfen, mit welchem Recht Protestanten Kirchen oder Bethäuser benutzten. Diese Untersuchungen dauerten bis in die 1760er Jahre, zogen aber keine ernsthaften Konsequenzen nach sich. In Südtransdanubien wurden diese Untersuchungen gerade im 18. Jahrhundert immer häufiger, als die Bischöfe ihre Macht immer weiter stärkten.[91]

Der Ausbau der Pfarrämter, die Ernennung der entsprechenden Pfarrer war – wie Obiges klar zeigt – für die Katholisierung von hoher Bedeutung. Es gab unter den weltlichen wie unter den kirchlichen Grundherren solche, die darauf großen Wert legten. Die Gemeinde Gölle in der Schomodei war zum Beispiel Eigentum des Custodiat von Stuhlweißenburg (ung. Székesfehérvár). Tamás Nádasdy, Bischof von Csanád und Kanoniker von Stuhlweißenburg, überwachte persönlich die Bekehrung der reformierten Bevölkerung der Gemeinde und beauftragte den Lizentiaten Miklós Jókai mit der Konsolidierung der erreichten Ergebnisse. Jókai ging seinen Aufgaben gewissenhaft nach; er taufte, traute, beerdigte, den Neubekehrten las er den Katechismus von András Illés und die Sammlung der Predigten des Péter Pázmány vor. Kurz danach, 1718, wurde schon das Pfarramt in Gölle gegründet.[92]
Die Frage der Kirchennutzung sorgte in der ersten Hälfte des Jahrhunderts für heftige Debatten. Es kam vor, dass der Grundherr die protestantische Religionsausübung nicht zuließ und die auf seinem Grundbesitz befindliche Kirche dem katholischen Pfarrer übergab. Zsigmond Széchényi verbannte beispielsweise den kalvinistischen Priester von seinem Grundbesitz in Látrány in der Schomodei; der Bischof begründete daraufhin das dortige Pfarramt und ernannte Imre Gomba zum Pfarrer, der sehr eifrig an der Bekehrung der Protestanten arbeitete und der in dieser Aufgabe eine

[91] Über die Untersuchungen in der Schomodei siehe LADÁNYI, Sándor: 1721. évi vallásügyi vizsgálat Somogy vármegyében [Die konfessionelle Untersuchung in der Schomodei im Jahre 1721.]. Somogy megye múltjából 3 (1972), 91-118.
[92] PFEIFFER: A veszprémi, 556.

große Herausforderung sah. Er nahm also seine Versetzung vom bereits katholisierten Gölle nach Látrány sehr gerne an. Gomba machte aus dem hölzernen Gebetshaus der Protestanten eine katholische Kirche und besetzte gleichzeitig die Wohnung des Praedikators.[93]

Neben den Bischöfen waren auch die Priester sehr darauf bedacht, die Nichtkatholiken zu bekehren. Sie machten das sehr fleißig und eifrig, infolge dessen viele Familienoberhäupter rekatholisiert wurden. Es kam aber gleichzeitig auch vor, dass Säuglinge *„offen und heimtückisch"* getauft wurden (*praetextatus baptismus*). Dabei spielten die katholischen Hebammen (*obstetrices*) eine bedeutende Rolle, die unter fiktiven oder realen Umständen beim Baden den Säugling tauften. Sie beriefen sich in allen Fällen darauf, dass die Neugeborenen nicht gesund gewesen seien (*„ihre Farbe wurde blau und schwarz"*) und wegen ihrer eigenen Seeligkeit bzw. ihres eigenen Gewissens mussten sie dringend getauft werden (*„Oh, wenn ich bloß eine Möglichkeit fände, dieses unschuldige Kind ins Himmelreich zu schicken..."*).[94] Die Hebammen erzählten mit großem Stolz und großer religiöser Überzeugung über ihre solchen Taten.

Solange die Rekatholisierung der Protestanten bereits ab dem Ende des 17. Jahrhunderts im Komitat Schomodei sehr intensiv erfolgte,[95] wurde die Bekehrung der Juden zum katholischen Christentum erst ab den 1740er Jahren gang und gäbe. Erstens, weil sie in dieser Zeit in immer größerer Anzahl in den südtransdanubischen Komitaten erschienen, zweitens betonte der Bischof von Wesprim, Márton Padányi Bíró, die Wichtigkeit der Konversion der *„Ungläubigen"*.[96] Maria Theresia verbot jedoch 1762 durch Verordnung die gewaltsame Bekehrung der jüdischen Kinder und 1763 ordnete sie dem katholischen Klerus an, von Andersgläubigen kein Stollengeld mehr zu fordern.[97] Da die königliche Verordnung lediglich die gewaltsame und willkürliche (*„violens"*) Taufe nicht erlaubte, setzte die katholische Priesterschaft ihre Missionstätigkeit mit großem Eifer fort.[98]

Am Ende des 18. Jahrhunderts wuchs die Anzahl der Pfarrämter im südtransdanubischen Raum erheblich, die Infrastruktur der katholischen Kirche wurde besser. Im Kreise der Bevölkerung erhöhte sich der Anteil der Katholiken zwar, jedoch blieben die Gemeinden, die am Anfang des Jahrhunderts protestantisch waren, nach wie vor protestantisch geprägt. Für die Konversionen spielten die barocke Religiosität, die Prozessionen, die Kirchweihfeste eine wichtige Rolle. Bei den Priestern ist

---

[93] PFEIFFER: A veszprémi, 445-446.

[94] SML Komitatsprotokolle. 36. 1776. I. 783 p.

[95] Siehe die Visitation der Pfarrämter an der Drau. AZN. Archidiaconatus Camarcensis 1716-1731. – PFEIFFER: A veszprémi, 41-121.

[96] Über die Konversion der Juden im Bistum Wesprim in der Zeit von PADÁNYI BÍRÓ, Márton: De numero Judaeorum Weszprimii in Cathedrali Ecclesia per memet baptizatorum. 286-288 und 319-320.

[97] GATES-COON, Rebecca: The Landed Estates of the Esterházy Princes. Hungary during the reforms of Maria Theresia and Joseph II. Baltimore-London 1994, 115-133 und 126-127.

[98] GŐZSY, Zoltán: A zsidóság Somogy megyei megtelepedésétől 1815-ig [Das Judentum von seiner Ansiedlung in der Schomodei bis 1815]. In: Újrakezdések. Zsidósors Somogy megyében a XVIII. századtól napjainkig. Hg. v. Sándor Bősze. Kaposvár 2005, 9-38.

das Bild der ethnischen und sprachlichen Kompetenzen eher differenzierter, sie spielen aber nach wie vor eine wichtige Rolle.

Branko Bešlin

The baroque Form of „sweet Orthodoxy". The Church and the transformation of serbian society after the Great Migration of 1690

I shall begin my study with a scene from the novel «Migrations» by Miloš Crnjanski, because it is indicative of the subject of my paper, and also because, as a rule, literary works have a stronger influence on the formation of historical consciousness among the popular masses than historical writings.[1] The majority of educated Serbs know well what Crnjanski wrote about their compatriots in the Habsburg Monarchy in the 18th century. He is one of the greatest Serbian writers and the work I am referring to is one of the best in Serbian Literature, and has been mandatory reading in schools for decades. The main hero is Vuk Isakovič, an Austrian officer, commander of a regiment of Serbian frontier militia who start a campaign against the French in 1744. In Pécs, he and his officers are invited by the local bishop and the uncouth veteran soldiers from the borders of the Christian world attend the mass. They are enchanted by the sound of the organ, the appearance of the church, and the brilliance of the Catholic service. They remember their «strange, wooden churches, in which the crowd sang, spat loudly, and their unruly, uncontrollable priests». After the mass, they are enthusiastic and sad at the same time. At supper at the bishop's, Vuk Isakovič is additionaly embarrassed by the setting and his conversation with the dignified, learned bishop, who invites him to become a Catholic. The «ferocious borderer» begins to sweat and drink excessively («If they convert him by force, at least they won't get him sober, he thought»). Finally, under the influence of drink, he begins to speak, disconnectedly and awkwardly but resolutely, about «sweet Orthodoxy». The phrase emphasizes the peculiar beauty of the tradition of the Eastern Church and people's devotion to it. The complete spiritual life of the Serbian people, from its first appearance on the historical scene of Europe until the 18th century, had been based on the Byzantine cultural sphere. The centre of Serbian religious, cultural and political life in the 18th century was in the Habsurg Monarchy, because during the great Migration of 1690, church dignitaries and many prominent personalities left the Ottoman Empire together with the people. The Serbs found themselves in a completely different legal, social and cultural state than the one in which they had been living earlier, and they began to adapt to it gradually. A national elite was created, consisiting of church dignitaries, frontier officers and affluent citizens. The Orthodox Church was also the leading spiritual and political force among the Serbs north of the Sava and

[1] CRNJANSKI, Miloš: Seobe [Migrations]. Beograd 1978, 40-47.

the Danube, and it would join the reforming trends in the Habsburg Monarchy which would transform the whole Serbian society. It did not do this willingly – high church dignitaries had been very traditional in the Ottoman Empire. The church accepted the reforms and energetically carried them out from sheer necessity. In order to withstand Catholic proselytism which it feared most, and to represent the Serbian people successfully in the Monarchy, the church had to work hard on its internal organization, discipline and education of its clergy and the people. «In that maelstrom of different events, the process of the adaptation of the Serbs to Western European culture in the Danubian region was accomplished. [...] The Danube and its region were of paramount importance for the formation of modern Serbian culture. Broadly speaking, in this region, in recent Serbian history, our exclusively Byzantine mediaeval spiritual orientation vanished for ever [...] Briefly, modern Serbian culture was born along the Danubian roads ».[2]

I used the word «Baroque» in the title. The term might create confusion, the more so because many different opinions by historians of art and culture have been voiced about it, and the debate is far from finished. The question threatens to become even more complex if «Baroque» is discussed in regional or national contexts. I am not talking now about Baroque as a stylistic, but a historical category: as a comprehensive cultural model of an epoch demonstrated not only in art but in all aspects of life – religious, political and social.[3] The term «Baroque» was first used by prominent Serbian historians of the history of art, literature and culture – Dejan Medaković, Dinko Davidov, Miroslav Timotijević, and Milorad Pavić – to denote a whole epoch in the history of the Serbs in the Habsburg Monarchy. However, the term became fully legitimate in historiography. Most scholars, first of all those dealing with political history, continue to use simple chronological and topographical definitions. Methodologically, they are justified – this periodization cannot be applied to the whole of the Serbian nation. In the 18th century, Serbs developed in different cultural and historical circumstances. Among the Serbs in the Ottoman Empire, only a feeble influence of the Baroque can be traced, originating indirectly from the Greco-Levant regions. The influence of the Baroque is more pronounced in the art of the Serbs living under Venetian rule. However, «only the Serbs in the Habsburg Monarchy adopted Baroque as a comprehensive historical-cultural model...»[4] Therefore, some authors (D. Medaković, M. Timotijević) speak of the «Baroquization» of Serbian culture and society. As for chronology, the epoch of the Baroque in Serbian cultural history begins with the Migration of 1690 and ends with the convocation of the Assembly of Temesvar in 1790. Western influences were not immediately accepted directly from the cultural centres of the Habsburg Monarchy. In the beginning, especially in sacral painting and literature, Baroque, in an already «transformed» form, arrived from Russia and Ukraine. On the basis of this, the

[2] МЕДАКОВИЋ, Дејан: Дунавски путеви српске културе XVIII века [Danubian Roads of Serbian Culture in 18th Century] in: Путеви српског барока [Roads of Serbian Baroque]. Београд 1971, 46.
[3] ТИМОТИЈЕВИЋ, Мирослав: Српско барокно сликарство [Serbian Baroque Painting]. Нови Сад 1996, 12-13.
[4] IBID., 22.

internal periodization of the Baroque epoch among the Serbs consists of two periods. During the first, until 1769, Russian cultural influences had still been dominant. In the second, the Austrian influence prevailed.[5]

*****

The settlement of the Serbs and the strengthening and organization of the Orthodox Church in the regions north of the Sava and the Danube did not begin during the Great Migration, but towards the end of the 14th century, when the Turks began to destroy the medieval state of Serbia. The migrations of the Serbs to Hungary were both spontaneous and organized. The Serbian ruler, Despot Stefan Lazarević, took advantage of the great defeat of the Turks by the Mongols at Angora (1402) and the struggles among the sultan's successors, and turned to Hungary. He accepted (1404) its suzerainty and was given Belgrade and Mačva in return. He and his successor Djuradj Branković were also given numerous estates in Hungary. Many Serbs came to Hungary fleeing the Turks, but the despot had some of them settled on their estates. Djuradj Branković also granted his compatriots high places in spite of the opposition on the part of the Hungarian nobility. After the final fall of the Serbian medieval state in 1459, the number of Serbs in southern Hungary increased and was rising steadily during the following 100 years, parallel to the Turkish conquest. During the 15th and 16th centuries, Serbs played an important role in the defence of the Hungarian frontiers. However, a great number of them was in Turkish service, in the advancing Turkish army. After the conquest, new waves of immigrants arrived from the South. The Hungarian population was very sparse; they either perished or fled before the Turks. In the second half of the 15th and the beginning of the 16th century, the Serbian despots from the House of Branković, together with masses of peasants, also left Serbia and retained that title in Hungary. Together with other prominent families, they would become part of the new feudal system, which contributed to the strengthening of the Serbian Orthodox Church in southern Hungary. At the end of the 15th and the beginning of the 16th century, a number of new monasteries were built. The Metropolitanate of Karlovci-Belgrade was founded in the beginning of the 16th century, with the Sirmian monastery of Krušedol as its seat. Its head was Maksim Branković, who renounced his title of despot. «The Branković family from Sirmium», in their lifetime and later as well, played an important part in the political and spiritual life of the Serbs in Hungary. Within the church and among the population, a cult developed, which would last until the present.

The Turkish conquest brought about an increase in the number of Orthodox Christians and the strengthening of Orthodoxy, but it did not strengthen the Serbian Church itself, which was passing through one of the most difficult periods of its history at the time. During the Turkish conquest, numerous churches and monasteries were partially or completely destroyed, and many priests and believers perished.

[5] IBID., 434.

This was followed a period of adaptation to the norms of the Turkish Empire, that is, to the status of a religion and subjects of a lower order. Parallel to this, there was a process of islamization within the population. Besides, between 1459 and 1557, after the fall of the Serbian medieval state, the Serbian Church lost its autocephalous status. The autocephalous Serbian Church had been established in 1219 by St. Sava, and from 1346, it was elevated to the rank of patriarchate.[6] After Serbia had obtained church independence, a specific branch of Orthodox spirituality and culture was developed – «Svetosavlje». The first Serbian archbishop, St. Sava, the son of the Serbian ruler, had the official authority to initiate the Christian renaissance in Serbia, stabilize Church organization and discipline, eradicate heresy and the forms of primitive Christian living, and suppress the encroachment of the western church. Based on Byzantine culture, – with more or less marked characteristics – legislature, literature, architecture and painting developed. It led to the formation of the idea of the Serbian state, which implied insistence on the unity of dynasty, church, and the people. The church sanctified the Nemanjić dynasty, and the people embraced that idea even during the centuries when the Serbian state did not exist. The questions of how the Serbian Orthodox Church lost it autocephalous character, or how the Patriarchate of Peć was abolished have not been solved completely. The Patriarchate had been gradually weakening, and due to Turkish conquests, it lost teritories under its jurisdiction. Some of these territories were under the jurisdiction of the Archbishopric of Okhrid, and others were under the jurisdiction of the Patriarchate of Constantinople, which was already under Turkish rule. Soon after the final collapse of the Serbian state, the last Patriarch of Peć died. The disorganized Serbian Church came under the jurisdiction of the Archbishopric of Okhrid, and indirectly under the Patriarchate of Constantinople. The universal Patriarchate of Constantinople had since Byzantine times enjoyed the prestige of being the leader of the Orthodox churches. Its dominant position was recognized by Mehmed II after the fall of Constantinople. Its efforts to impose its administrative dominance over all Orthodox churches were only partially successful; nevertheless, its spiritual leadership was mostly undisputed. The loss of independence did not mean the complete disappearance of the peculiarities of the Serbian Church. The Greek high clergy was adamant concerning their jurisdiction and fiscal rights, but they showed understanding for the spiritual needs of Slav Christians – they were allowed to conduct services and educate not only in Greek. Besides, although not as old or powerful as the Greek Church, the Serbian Church had its own fairly strong tradition which could not be obliterated. Finally, the Porte had the final say about everything, and its decisions depended on the interests of the Empire or powerful court cliques.

The most important factor in the reinstatement of the Patriarchate of Peć was the fact that in that period the Grand Vizier was Mehmed-Pasha Sokolović, of Serbian origin. He achieved his military successes in Hungary, notably in the conquest of the Banat in 1552, mostly with the help of his compatriots. There was a great number of

[6] САМАРЏИЋ, Радован: Српска православна црква у XVI и XVII веку [Serbian Ortodox Church in 16th and 17th Century]. In: Историја српског народа. III/2. Beograd 1993, 11.

Serbs in the Turkish army, and also in the garrisons defending the towns, so he had no difficulty in establishing contacts with them. This shows that the Serbs had a great military and economic importance in the establishment of Turkish rule on the periphery of the Empire. As Greek influence with the Porte had already been weakened, the powerful Grand Vizier had no problems in effecting the re-establishment of the autocephalous Patriarchate of Peć in 1557. For the Turks, this meant a more efficient way of using the Serbs for the interests of the Empire. The Patriarchate of Peć was a legitimate institution, included in the state system, and its heads were obliged to cooperate with and be resposible to the Porte. The patriarchs had a similar status to the one enjoyed by Genadious Scholaris, the first Patriarch of Constantinople after the fall of the Byzantine capital in 1453. The Serbian Church continued to recognize the supremacy of the Patriarchate of Constantinople in the Orthodox world, but became completely independent in the regions of its jurisdiction and its obligations towards the Sultan. It had clearly defined territory on which it exercised its jurisdiction, its internal organization, its right to independent political and, to a great extent, canonical decisions.[7] The first patriarch was Makarije Sokolović, a relative of the Grand Vizier. Apart from Makarije, patriarchs were elected at assemblies attended by the clergy and prominent laymen, which gave additional strength to the political legitimacy and influence of the Patriarchate among the Serbs. This was followed by a cultural renaissance: churches and monasteries were restored, sacral architecture and painting reached a higher level, liturgical and legal writings multiplied. The newly created lay élite of patriarchal leaders and prosperous merchants accepted the traditional role of sponsorship formerly practiced by the nobility, which, in the meantime, had disappeared from the historical scene. However, this did not mean the acceptance of new cultural models, but rather the restoration of the old ones, established in the time of the Nemanjić rulers. The cult of this dynasty, but also that of later rulers, the Lazarević and Branković, was systematically promoted in literature and sacral painting. Therefore, the restoration of the Patriarchate is considered as one of the most crucial events in Serbian national history. Around the middle of the 15th century, the Serbs lost their state. The re-establishment of the Patriarchate of Peć did not mean the restoration of Serbian statehood, but it did restore, at least partially, political subjectivity and created an impression that it was a mark of continuity from the medieval state. In any case, the idea of statehood, based on the unity of the Church, dynasty and people, received its final form during these times. The Serbian clergy gave the Church a more pronounced national character, whereas the population often equalizied Orthodoxy with ethnic origin, which had far reaching consequences. Naturally, since the disappearance of the state, many things had changed. After 150 years of mass migrations, the Serbs found themselves in distant northern and western regions; thus, the territories under the jurisdiction of the Patriarchate of Peć greatly exceeded the frontiers of the Serbian medieval state. Due to our lack of documents, it is difficult to precisely reconstruct its organizational structure, which

[7] IBID., 53.

changed during the following century. Generally, it had eight metropolitanates and 32 bishoprics in the 17th century. Some were far in the north (at Buda, Siget (heute ung. Szigetvár), Fünfkirchen (ung. Pécs), Szeged, Arad, Temeswar, Lipova, Gyula). The political and spiritual influence of the Patriarchate of Peć spread beyond the Ottoman Empire – due to migration. Great numbers of Serbs settled in the territories of the neighbouring countries, the Habsburg Monarchy and Venice. Vast territories of Central Europe, where western church and culture were present for centuries, were also under the jurisdiction of the Patriarchate. This one had direct contacts with the territories on the borders of the Ottoman Empire. It did not affect either the Church or the other classes of Serbian society too much. The achievements of western culture were mostly destroyed by Turkish conquest. The seat of the patriarch, which means of political and social life, remained far south, in Peć and on the territory of the Serbian medieval state.
The period of good relations between the Patriarchate of Peć and the Porte did not last long. The Ottoman Empire passed its zenith in the last third of the 16th century. The first patriarch to seek support from the West was Jovan Kantul (1592-1614). He had strong contacts with the Habsburgs, Venice, Spain, and Russia. During the war between Austria and Turkey (1593-1606), the Serbs in the Banat, loyal to the Turks until then, rose in arms. The insurgents – which is indicative – carried flags with the picture of St. Sava on them.[8] The policy of reliance on the West was continued by successive Patriarchs more or less intensely. It is typical for the representatives of the Patriarchate of Peć that they sought political support and abstained from discussing religious questions in their talks with the Papal Curia. On the other hand, the Curia insisted on the union which enjoyed the support of some bishops and popular leaders. In their talks, the patriarchs demonstrated much tact, but rejected the union resolutely. Catholic propaganda was active in two regions. One was Dalmatia, Montenegro, and Northern Albania. In the second, the Military Frontier in Croatia, the Vretanian (Marča, Uskok) Orthodox bishopric was founded. Its bishops had long avoided to accept the union, although they recognized the Pope together with the Patriarch of Peć. This transitional period lasted until 1671, when the Marčan bishop finally accepted the union with Rome. Seeking ways to continue the struggle against the Turks and to avoid the pressure of the Catholic church, the Patriarchs of Peć had intensive relations with Russia, where priests often travelled, on diplomatic missions and for material support.
The next decisive moment was the great war between Austria and Turkey (1683-1699). As the Austrian army triumphantly advanced towards the Southeast, great numbers of Serbs joined it. Patriarch Arsenije III Čarnojević was indecisive and cautious during the first years of the war. He feared Turkish retaliations, which had already begun – and he himself was persecuted. He was also worried by the news from the bishoprics liberated from the Turks, which came immediately under the pressure of Catholic propaganda. When the Austrian army invaded Serbia and

[8] Слијепчевић, Ђоко: Историја Српске православне цркве [History of the Serbian Ortodox Church] I. Беорад 1991, 320-327.

reached Kosovo, the Patriarch entered into talks on the insistence of the Austrian military authorities, and decided to support Austria. In 1690, the Turks started a counter-offensive, and great masses of population left Serbia to settle in the Pannonian Basin. This exodus, known as the Great Migration, is not so important because of the number of people who migrated, although Serbia suffered a demographic catastrophy; migrations to the North had been very intense in the previous 200 years, too. Throughout the 18th century, the Serbs of Bosnia, Croatia, and Montenegro also migrated in different directions. However, almost the whole élite left Serbia in 1690: the high clergy and most of the ordinary priests, heads of patriarchal communities, and rich merchants. This meant that the centre of Serbian spiritual and political life was transferred from the South, where it had been established for centuries, to the North – from Serbia to the Habsburg Monarchy. Formally, even after the Great Migration, the seat of the church was at Peć. The Ottoman authorities appointed a new patriarch already in 1691, instead of Arsenije, who had fled. On the other hand, the Serbian Orthodox Church in the Habsburg Monarchy was organized through the Metropolitanate of Karlovci. The Viennese Court insisted on its complete separation from the Patriarchate in Peć, which was on Ottoman territory, but the clergy resisted this quite resolutely. Finally, a compromise was found: the Metropolitanate of Karlovci did not became autocephalous, only an autonomous institution within the Patriarchate of Peć, which means that administrative unity was abolished, but spiritual unity with the Patriarchate of Peć was preserved.[9] However, the Patriarchate of Peć was not a strong spiritual and political centre any more. First, the Serbian people were not united in the Ottoman Empire but were separated by state frontiers instead. Secondly, Serbia was devastated by wars and migrations. Greek high clergy was increasingly present in the place of the exiled Serbian, and the Patriarchate of Peć was gradually losing its national character. Finally, in 1766, it was abolished and its territory was placed under the jurisdiction of the Patriarchate of Constantinople. Therefore, the Metropolitanate of Karlovci was the spiritual, political, and cultural centre of Serbs for more than a century. The political centre of the Serbian people would return to the South, to Serbia, after the national revolution of 1804, but the Serbs from the Habsburg Monarchy would dominate Serbian cultural life until the 1860s.

While Serbs were not among the most numerous ethnic groups in the Monarchy, they were nonetheless already politically organized and supplied considerable military contingents. As previously in the Ottoman Empire, members of the high clergy were accepted in the Habsburg Monarchy as legitimate representatives of the Serbian people. The legal basis for this were a number of normative acts issued since 1690 by the Habsburg rulers, known under the name «Privileges». Serbs were allowed to remain Orthodox and were exempt from paying the tithe to the Catholic Church; they were also given the right to elect their metropolitan and bishops, and to have their own civic authorities and education. These privileges were eventually reduced, but they provided the basis for the preservation and practice of their

[9] IBID., 370.

religion and nationality. Their wish for territorial autonomy was not realized. The representative body through which the religious and educational autonomy was realized was the Church and the Popular Assembly.[10] Its legal authority was not precisely defined, and neither was the number of representatives or the way of their election. The ruler allowed the convocation of the Assembly in person, through his rescript, which usually determined the agenda, time and place of the session. The imperial commissioner controlled whether it worked in accordance with the approved agenda (it was rarely a representative of the Hungarian Court Office). Essentially, the views of the Assembly, depending on the circumstances, had some political importance, but it was not legally binding for anybody. The most important and the only right of the Assemby, legally based on the «Privileges», was the right to elect the Serbian Metropolitan. Formally, as it was customary in the Monarchy, there were three candidates. One usually enjoyed the patronage of the Court, and most frequently it was this person who would be elected. As for the members of the Assembly, it consisted of the representatives of the high clergy at first. On the initiative of the Court, the Assembly assumed the characteristics of an assembly of estates by virtue of its members and ceremonial. The distribution of representatives was done in accordance with the social circumstances among the Serbs in Hungary – 25 hierarchs, 25 members of the Military Frontier, and 25 representatives of the «provincials».[11] The Frontier was represented by officers. From the Provincials came citizens and noblemen, the former group being far more numerous in Serbian society and thus in the Assembly, too. The way the representatives from the provincials in the Assembly were elected is little known. The first two estates were conservative and consistently supported the absolutism of the Court. The Metropolitan of Karlovci and the bishops thought that the «Privileges» gave them the right to regulate the lives of their fold and thus behaved as «princes of the Church». The third estate, especially the middle class, grew rich, made considerable progress, and became educated; they accepted the ideas of enlightenment and liberal tendencies relatively quickly. Already about the middle of the 18th century, the middle class tried to challenge the absolute supremacy of the clergy in making decisions –without any success. At the Assembly of Temeswar in 1790, this division of the conservative-clerical and liberal wings was evident. The clergy defended their role as the traditional defenders of Serbian nationality and in this they enjoyed the backing of the Court, so that the «third estate» would always be outvoted in the Assembly until the 1860s.

The functioning of the Metropolitanate of Karlovci had faced two major problems from the beginning: first, taking sides in the conflict between the Viennese Court

[10] In the 18th century, there were 19 altogether, and in the 19th, until 1861, two, in 1837 and 1842. Поповић, Душан: Срби у Војводини [Serbs in Vojvodina]. II. Нови Сад 1990, 372-380. – Форишковић, Александар: Политички, правни и друштвени односи код Срба у Хабзбуршкој монархији [Political, Legal and Social Relationns of the Serbs in the Habsburg Monarchy]. In: Историја српског народа. IV/1. Београд 1994, 269-280.

[11] This became practise in 1708, on the basis of instructions the commissioners received from the Court. This form of the Assembly received legal form by the Edict of 1779.

and the Hungarians, and second, resisting Catholic proselytism. The regions where the Serbs had settled belonged to Hungary with regard to state and law. The Habsburgs wanted to rule absolutely; on the other hand, Hungarian nobility vehemently resisted absolutism and defended Hungarian statehood. From the very beginning, the leaders of the Church supported the Court as the guarantor of the Privileges, and they followed this policy until the Compromise of 1867. The price was high, though. Soon after the Migration, the Serbs participated in the suppression of Rákoczi's rebellion (1703-1711) and were almost eradicated in some parts of Hungary as a consequence. However, this decreased the pressure by the Catholic Church to which they had been subjected in the previous decade. The recatholization of the Monarchy – directed at first towards Hungarian Calvinists, then towards Orthodox believers, was considered by the ruling circles the crucial factor of the cohesion of the state. The process was carried out consistently – not always with the same intensity and means, of course. In this, the Metropolitanate demonstrated great dogmatic tenacity and at the same time great adaptability with regard to western traditions. «Adaptation to the political and church model of the Habsburg Monarchy was one of the key conditions for the survival of the Orthodox Church and its believers [...] The idea behind all church reforms was to change the Orthodox Church thoroughly and to identify it with the ideal of *ecclesia militans*.»[12] As I have already mentioned, this departure from tradition was not motivated by a desire for change. The Orthodox Church wanted to resist Catholic proselytism but at the same time had to accept reforms in the spirit of the enlightened absolutism pursued energetically by the state. The transformation of Serbian society was not only the result of the reforms. The population accepted many customs and ways of the new surroundings.

During the first decades after the Migration of 1690, Patriarch Arsenije III Čarnojević and his successorrs still conducted religious and political activities in accordance with the traditions of the Eastern Church, which they had partially and spontaneously adapted to the new state, its laws and culture. The Orthodox Church began radical and sytematic internal reforms in the early 1720s, but their efforts met with success only around the middle of the century. The basic idea of the reform was to strengthen the spiritual and political authority of the religious leader as the legitimate leader of the nation. Subordination and discipline within the church became stronger, and the clergy were better educated and enjoyed greater prestige. The method of working with the believers was strictly prescribed and controlled; the believers were systematically instructed in the spirit of institutionalized piety. «It was a mechanism already well established in the Jesuit pedagogy of the Catholic religious revival».[13] The first Regulations for the clergy were published already in 1724, and they were based on the Spiritual Regulations issued in Russia in the time of Peter the Great. The revised Regulations were published in 1733, and then also

---

[12] ТИМОТИЈЕВИЋ, М: У Хабсбуршкој монархији од барока до просветитељства [In the Habsburg Monarchy from the Baroque to the Enlightenment]. In: Приватни живот у српским земљама у освит модерног доба. Ed. By А. ФОТИЋ. Београд 2005, 659.

[13] IBID., 625.

the Regulations for sextons and the Regulations for tutors in towns appeared. A series of measures were taken – including fines and physical punishment – in order to force the believers to attend Sunday service regularly.[14] Special attention was paid to the eradication of the remnants of paganism which were deeply rooted and widely practised among the people: for instance, the exhumation of the dead who were considered to be vampires, hunts for witches and ghouls. The church also began to fight negative practices in public morality – violations of canon law (partnership relations autside of marriage, bigamy, blasphemy) and bad customs (extravagant waste of money on weddings, feasts for soul, patron saints' days, or immoderate drinking). The change is evident in the names given to children – instead of Serbian popular names, biblical names prevail during the 18th century. Some reforms were not initiated by the Church, but by the state authorities. According to the Regulations of 1777, Serbs were not allowed to carry the dead in open coffins as previously. The Church protested, and there were open riots of the believers in some places.[15] The number of feast days was reduced in accordance with the principles of enlightened absolutism. The authorities imposed the Regulations on all churches, including the official one: the Roman Catholic church. After the Migration, the Serbs had had as many as 164 feast days every year. Due to great resistance of the clergy and the believers, the Synod gradually and unwillingly decreased their number (in 1769, 1774, and 1786), so that the number of feast days was finally reduced to 27 (not including Sundays).[16]

The development of the educational system was particularly important. Many priests were barely literate, and there was a great number of illiterate priests – there were even some who did not know the basic principles of religion. The Church was not the only part of society in the need for education. The middle class also supported the opening of schools since they successfuly participated in economic competition of the new state.[17] The first elementary schools were opened spontaneously soon after the Great Migration, towards the end of the 17th and the beginning of the 18th century, and they functioned in a disorganized way. The Serbian Church had neither the qualified staff nor the necessary textbooks to organize systematic education, because besides elementary education, secondary schools were also necessary to educate teachers and priests. Therefore, the metropolitans asked for help from the coreligionst Russia. The first teachers arrived in 1726 from Russia and opened a secondary school at Karlovci. They were poorly paid and had no understanding of the social surroundings. Part of the Serbian clergy maintained that their teaching, which included Latin, was unnecessary. The majority of pupils shared this view, and many left the school before finishing it in order to become priests. The school at Karlovci gradually weakened and was ultimately closed in 1731. A new secondary

[14] Скерлић, Јован: Српска књижевност у XVIII веку [Serbian Literature in the 18th Century]. Београд 1966, 61-64.

[15] Ibid., 63.

[16] Ibid., 61.

[17] The Serbs from Buda sent an address to the Church-Popular Assembly in 1744, in which they sharply criticized the high clergy for their authoritarian methods and abuses and requested the opening of schools.

school, also with Russian faculty, lasted only a few years as well, from 1733 to 1737. Progress was only made when a permanent fund was established for the maintenance of schools – it was created from voluntary contributions and the progressive taxation of the clergy and believers. While elementary schools, although not organized systematically, worked, secondary schools were all shortlived.[18] From 1721 to 1762, 28 Serbs attended the Theology Seminary in Kijev. Changes were introduced in 1774 in accordance with the educational reforms of Maria Theresia. Education was in the hands of the Orthodox Church, but the curriculum was reformed in accordance with the ambition of the state that its subjects accept some social and political norms. The first Serbian secondary school was founded in 1791 at Sremski Karlovci, the seat of the Metropolitanate, and the second in Novi Sad in 1810. The Theoological Seminary was founded in 1794, and the teachers' college 1778. There were about 200 schools in parishes towards the end of the century.[19]

Although the educational system was finally completed due to these reforms, the Metropolitanate of Karlovci faced a new problem. According to the Education Act of 1776, foreigners could not be employed as teachers, and only textbooks approved by the censor could be used. This meant the suppresion of Russian influence, as most qualified teachers, textbooks and other literature were from Russia. The Serbian Orthodox Church thus turned to the Protestants, whose higher education system was well developed, and established contacts with the pietists at Halle as early as in the first half of the 18th century. That was the *Kollegium Orientale*, where Old Slavonic and living Slav languages were taught. The first four headmasters of the secondary school at Karlovci were Protestants, as well as a considerable number of teachers in both Serbian secondary schools. Most Serbian students continued their education in Protestant high schools, mostly in Northern Hungary (Slovakia today). It is estimated that between 2.000 and 2.500 Serbs were educated there from 1735 to 1914.

Until the 1770s, Russo-Ukrainian literary influences were very strong. They spread through textbooks and other literature. As there were cases of Catholic propaganda through church books printed in Serbian, in Cyrillic, the Serbian metroplitans permitted only the use of books published in Russia authorized by their church authorities. A considerable number of books arrived from Ukraine, where Catholic propaganda had been active, so their Orthodox theological and polemical literature was very developed. After the Theresian reforms and the ban on the import of Russian books, new textbooks – by Serbian authors, or translated from German – were published,. A lasting consequence of Russian influence was a change in literary language. The old Serbo-Slavonic language was forced out of the Curch and literacy by Russian-Slavonic. The idea that the Russian-Slavonic was the true Serbian language and that the popular language was only its corrupted form – a

[18] A secondary school existed in Novi Sad in 1732, in 1732 and 1749-1768 at Karlovci. A theological seminary was founded for the diocese of Bačka in Novi Sad in 1765, which was soon closed. There was a secondary school at Ruma in 1770, a teachers' college ws founded in Sombor in 1776 but was closed a few months later.

[19] СКЕРЛИЋ: Српска, 92.

vulgar «Hungaro-Turco-German-Serbian» -- became more and more accepted. Via the Church, Russian-Slavonic was introduced in literature. The educated circles modified it and its middle class variety known as «Slaveno-Serbian». Thus, class distinctions which had been increasingly evident after the migration to the new territories manifested themselves in language, which had three variants: church, middle-class, and popular. The resistance of the Church and a part the of middle class elite to the reform of language and orthography was mostly interpreted as a departure from tradition and Russia, introducing Catholicism in a roundabout way. In any case, Serbian writers in the second half of the 18th century did not follow Russian, but rather Western European models – mostly German, then French, and to a minor degree, English. Thus, the spirit of enlightenment and rationalism prevailed in Serbian literature.

The high clergy, as well as the Serbian economic and military elite, were very anxious to demonstrate their status by their appearance and way of life – according to the cultural models of their new surroundings. «Baroque culture was accepted already in the first years after the Migration. Baroque was first noticeable in politics, in the behaviour of popular leaders and church dignitaries, and soon after in other areas of spiritual, cultural, and artistic life.»[20] Having arrived from the depths of the Balkans, many of them began to trace their origin to medieval Serbian ruling and aristocratic families, and mystified history by providing forged documents to prove their claims. They behaved pompously in order to emphasize their position. Thus, when he arrived in Vienna soon after the Migration, Arsenije III Čarnojević ordered his official portrait, in which he is shown with all the insignia of an Orthodox patriarch.[21] He and the members of his family maintained that they descended from the Crnojević dynasty, which ruled in Montenegro towards the end of the Middle Ages, which was probably true. Later metropolitans imitated in their dress and way of life the dignitaries of the Catholic Church. In an official portrait painted around 1731, Vikentije Jovanović Vidak is shown in purple-black robe with a red tiara (similar to that of a cardinal), which only a decade earlier would have been impossible as part of the official robe of a Metropolitan of Karlovci. Round his neck, he wears a richly decorated cross and his hand lies on a big crown, a symbol of his spiritual and worldly power. Similar portraits of some other church dignitaries – such as those of Metropolitan Mojsije Petrović (around 1726) and Patriarch Arsenije Jovanović Šakabenta (1746-48) – have been preserved. The residences of bishops in the exterior and interior, as well as in the ceremonial, resemble the palaces of European aristocracy. Metropolitan Vikentije Jovanović issued a detailed instruction entitled *Duties and Rights of Courtiers and Court Servants* in 1741, which describes in detail daily duties, way of behaviour and wages. Of course, rude Serbian peasants and frontier soldiers were not well qualified enough to be courtiers. Already during the 1720s, all court servants of the Metropolitan Mojsije Petrović were Austrian.

[20] ТИМОТИЈЕВИЋ: Српско барокно сликарство, 27. – Самарџић, Радован: Барок и Срби [Baroque an the Serbs]. In: Западноевропски барок и византијски свет. Београд 1991, 13-17.
[21] ТИМОТИЈЕВИЋ: У Хабсбуршкој монархији, 660.

That was also the case with Vikentije Jovanović, who had a personal valet, a personal physician, and even three cooks. One of them, who was Viennnese, had a salary of 180 forints. The Serbian cook had a salary of 42 forints, and the headmaster of the Latin school earned 250 forints. Expensive furniture, dinner services and coaches were ordered from the West for the residences of the metroplitan's and bishop's residences. Feasts at the Metropolitan's residence were also organized in imitation of those of European aristocracy. Gargantuan quantities of venison and wine from the monasteries were ordered for sumptuous banquets and balls. The Patriarch Arsenije IV organized balls not only for foreigners, but also for his birthday – although birtrhdays were unusual in the Serbian tradition up to the 20th century. The appearance and way of life of the lower clergy also changed. In the years after the Migration, Serbian priests looked fairly strange to foreigners. «Many had hair reaching their waist, and when they spread it, they could use it as a cover», and some could not be distinguished from laymen in their manner of clothing. The Synod of Belgrade decreed in 1730 that priests had to wear priests' robes in public places, clip their beards, carry a comb, and behave in accordance to what their position requires. Of course, the results were not immediately visible – Jovan Jovanović, the Bishop of Karlovci, issued an epistle in 1784 in which he prescribed precisely what a priest's robe should look like in terms of the cassock, shirt, footwear, and toilet articles.[22] An indication of the role of the Church in the Habsburg Monarchy in the 18th century is the great number of priests – one to 150 families. They were not only relatively, more numerous than towards the end of the 19th and the beginning of the 20th century.[23]

Baroque influences are very visible in the sacral architecture of the period. Soon after the Migration, churches were built by foreign builders in the Austrian Baroque style. Baroque adaptations were carried out on the oldest churches built in the 16th and 17th centuries in various variants of the late Serbian-Byzantine style (mostly Moravian) – belfries were built, windows were opened, decorations were added. Yet, occasionally traditionalistic ideas were dominant, so up to the middle of the 18th century, architectural elements of the Morava school are discernible on many churches built in the period.[24] The development of Serbian painting, especially sacral, does not coincide with the time of the formation and duration of Baroque culture. The influence of the Baroque is first seen in portraits ordered by noblemen, rich citizens, and church dignitaries from foreign artists. However, when religious painting is concerned, the high clergy were much more conservarive – iconographic representations were closely connected to dogma and tradition, that is, with the very

[22] Скерлић: Српска, 73-74.

[23] Екмечић, Милорад: Стварање Југославије 1790-1918 [Creating of Yugoslavia 1790-1918]. Београд 1989, 36. – In the Eparchy of Srem in 1732- 1733 there were 138 villages, 111 churches, 7.785 houses and 179 priests– in the same eparchy in 1900 there were 187 villages, 171 churches, 29.289 houses, and 139 priests. In the Eparchy of Bačka, in 1785 there were 83.316 Serbs and 169 priests, while in 1892 there were 130.383 Serbs and 92 priests. Скерлић: Српска, 78.

[24] Медаковић, Дејан: Путеви српског барока [Roads of the Serbian Baroque]. Београд 1971, 179-199.

essence of religious identity.[25] In the beginning, the Church rejected Central European, Catholic models in painting, which means that they only accepted moderate changes to the late Byzantine heritage of painting done in the style of Baroque traditions.[26] Changes set in in the 1740s, when there was an increase in Russian cultural influence. The Metropolitanate engaged artists from Ukraine, where Baroque influences had already been accepted and adapted to the needs of the Orthodox Church. These models were accepted by a generation of Serbian painters who were active until the 1790s. A second generation of painters educated in the Viennese Academy of Painting appeared in the 1770s (when Russian cultural influences began to give way to Western influences), and they continued to be active in the beginning of the 19th century. Church painting also serves a political programme in its insistence on the continuity of the Metropolitanate of Karlovci with the Patriarchate of Peć and the Serbian medieval state. More than before, portraits of Serbian rulers and saints, from the Nemanjić and Branković dynasties, were painted on prominent places – in the very iconostasis.[27]

Liturgical brilliance was evident in church chanting, to which metropolitans paid great attention. The best singers among the monks and pupils of the Theological Seminary were gathered and educated. Novelties were introduced in the Serbo-Byzantine chanting under the influence of West European musical tradition. As in the case of church painting, here, too, western influence entered directly and indirectly – from Russia and Ukraine. «The developed melodic ornamentation so characterisatic of the Baroque reached its heights in the form called 'the great chant of Karlovci'.»[28]

---

[25] ТИМОТИЈЕВИЋ: Српско барокно сликарство, 27.
[26] IBID., 435.
[27] МЕДАКОВИЋ: Путеви српског барока, 71-83.
[28] PETROVIĆ, Danica: Baroque and Serbian Chant in the 17th and 18th Centuries. In: Западноевропски барок и византијски свет [West-European Baroque and the Byzantine World], 93-102.

Migrationen und Integrationsprozesse

András Forgó

Ansiedlungspolitik und konfessionelle Konflikte auf den Landgütern der geistlichen Orden in Ungarn (am Beispiel der Tätigkeit der Zisterzienser und der Pauliner)

Ein besonderes Kapitel in der Geschichte der Wiederbesiedlung des Karpatenbeckens und der Rekatholisierung der Bevölkerung bildet die Tätigkeit der geistlichen Orden im 18. Jahrhundert. Die mit königlicher und kirchlicher Unterstützung wirkenden Ordensgemeinschaften trugen erheblich dazu bei, dass das in Folge der osmanischen Eroberung und der Befreiungskriege verödete Land mit einheimischen und ausländischen Kolonisten wieder bevölkert wurde und die Katholische Kirche ihre nach der Verbreitung der Reformation verlorene führende Stellung wiedergewann.

Der Schwerpunkt bei der folgenden Untersuchung wird in erster Linie auf die Zisterzienserabtei Zirc gelegt, wo in der zweiten Hälfte des 18. Jahrhunderts die organisierte Migration zu konfessionellen Konflikten führte und diese Konflikte in die Zurückdrängung des Protestantismus mündeten. Als Gegenbeispiel steht im zweiten Teil dieser Analyse ein Einblick in die Ansiedlungspolitik der Pauliner im Gebirge Pilis, die wegen der verschiedenen Gegebenheiten vor Ort keine konfessionellen Auseinandersetzungen verursachte. Schließlich wird die Tätigkeit der Pauliner in Pápa kurz behandelt, um zu zeigen, welche Methoden die geistlichen Orden für die Rekatholisierung anwenden konnten, wenn sie wegen der fremden Herrschaftszugehörigkeit des betroffenen Gebietes kein Mittel für die Veränderung der Bevölkerungszusammensetzung einsetzen konnten.

Ansiedlungspolitik der Zisterzienser von Zirc

Die Zisterzienser in der Herrschaft Zirc

Die ausländischen Weltlichen und Geistlichen, die bei den osmanischen Befreiungskriegen für den Wiener Hof Waffenhilfe geleistet hatten, wurden in den wiedereroberten Territorien mit erheblichen Landgütern entschädigt. Außerdem forderte Wien seine Untertanen auf, sich in Ungarn an der Arbeit des Wiederaufbaus zu beteiligen. Der Ankauf öder ungarischer Gebiete bot den Landbesitzern langfristig eine lukrative Investition; so fand die Aufforderung des Kaisers bei vielen ein offenes Ohr. Auch die österreichischen, mährischen und schlesischen Zisterzienserabteien zeigten ein wachsendes Interesse, ehemalige Zisterziensergüter in Ungarn wiederzufinden und die Tradition des Ordens im Land wieder ins Leben zu rufen.[1]

Seit dem 12. Jahrhundert ist im Karpatenbecken die Anwesenheit von Zisterziensermönchen nachzuweisen, in der Blütezeit existierten über zwanzig Zisterzienserabteien im Königreich Ungarn.[2] Der Niedergang begann bereits im Spätmittelalter und wurde durch die osmanische Eroberung beschleunigt. Bis zur Mitte des 16. Jahrhunderts verschwanden die Zisterzienser aus Ungarn. Die Abteien bzw. die Ländereien der einzelnen Konvente wurden durch die Herrscher an geistliche und weltliche Kommendatare (Verwalter) verschenkt und viele Landgüter wurden von den Nachbarbesitzern widerrechtlich übernommen. Auch die Güter der Zisterzienserabtei Zirc, die spätestens zur Zeit der Eroberung Ofens (1541) von den Zisterziensern verlassen wurden, gerieten während des Zeitalters der Osmanenherrschaft in die Hände mehrerer weltlicher Familien.[3]

Die ausländischen Zisterzienserabteien informierten sich bereits in den 60er Jahren des 17. Jahrhunderts über den Zustand der ehemaligen Ländereien in Ungarn; so begann zunächst die niederösterreichische Abtei Lilienfeld damit, die ehemaligen Landgüter von Zirc ausfindig zu machen und anzukaufen. Der Bevollmächtigte des Abtes kaufte auch ein Haus in Pápa, das bis zum Wiederaufbau des Klosters in Zirc (1726) als Quartier der Zisterzienser diente.[4] Aber die Kriegswirren und die fehlenden materiellen Quellen zwangen den Abt, die betreffenden Ländereien weiterzuverkaufen. So erhielt die Abtei Heinrichau in Schlesien gegen Zahlung von über 30.000 Gulden die Güter von Zirc.[5]

Zwischen 1700 und 1814 war also die ungarische Abtei Zirc ein Tochterkloster der schlesischen Abtei Heinrichau. Der Abtstitel beider Institutionen wurde vom Abt in Heinrichau getragen, das Kloster Zirc wurde durch einen Administrator, seit 1750, als die Anzahl der in Zirc tätigen Mönche die zwölf erreichte und ein Konvent errichtet werden konnte, durch einen Prior geleitet.[6]

Die Mutterabtei Heinrichau befand sich um die Wende des 18. Jahrhunderts in einer sehr günstigen finanziellen Lage. Der Abt Viktor Kahlert bewies sich als erfolgreicher Geschäftsmann: Während seiner Amtszeit erfolgten in Schlesien und in Ungarn viele Investitionen, die die Blüte der Doppelabtei für eine lange Zeit sicherten. Auch die Personenzahl im Heinrichauer Konvent stieg in dieser Zeit: Während 1682 27

[1] HERVAY, Ferenc Levente: A ciszterci rend története Magyarországon [Geschichte des Zisterzienserordens in Ungarn]. In: LÉKAI, Lajos: A ciszterciek. Eszmény és valóság. Budapest 1991, 470-492, hier 481-482.
[2] Vgl. HERVAY, Ferenc Levente: Repertorium historicum ordinis cisterciensis in Hungaria. Roma 1984 (Bibliotheca Cisterciensis 7).
[3] HORVÁTH, Konstantin: Zirc története [Geschichte von Zirc]. Veszprém 1930 (Zirci könyvek 1), 69-110.
[4] GRÜGER, Heinrich: Heinrichau. Geschichte eines schlesischen Zisterzienserklosters 1227-1977. Köln, Wien 1978 (Forschungen und Quellen zur Kirchen- und Kulturgeschichte Ostdeutschlands 16), 66.
[5] MUSSBACHER, Norbert: Die Bemühungen Lilienfelds um die Wiedererrichtung der Abtei Zirc 1659-1814. In: Analecta Cisterciensia 38 (1982), 22-42.
[6] ALPÁR, Lucián: A zirci apátság függetlenítésének kérdése [Die Frage der Unabhängigkeit der Abtei Zirc]. Budapest 1942, 25.

Professen in der Abtei lebten, zählte der Konvent 1749 bereits 55 Mitglieder.[7] Dies ermöglichte auch die Übernahme der Aufgaben in der ungarischen Tochterabtei. Aber Heinrichau war nicht die einzige ausländische Zisterzienserabtei, die durch den Ankauf ehemaliger Ordensbesitzungen in Ungarn in Erscheinung trat. Lilienfeld erhielt das Kloster Marienberg (ung. Borsmonostor), das unter dem Patronat der Herzöge Esterházy stand,[8] die mährische Abtei Velehrad kaufte die Landgüter der Abteien Pásztó und Pilis[9] und die niederösterreichische Zisterzienserabtei Heiligenkreuz erhielt 1734 die Klosterherrschaft Sankt Gotthard (ung. Szentgotthárd).[10] Die erste Aufgabe in Ungarn war für Heinrichau das Zurückgewinnen der ehemaligen Landgüter der Abtei Zirc. Wie behandelt, resultierte aus den Wirren der Osmanenkriege, später des Rákóczi-Aufstandes (1703 – 1711) eine sehr ungünstige Situation für die rechtmäßigen Grundbesitzer. Zum Glück für Heinrichau hatten die Äbte von Lilienfeld in den vorausgegangenen Jahrzehnten, während ihrer Zeit der Herrschaft über Zirc, hervorragende Arbeit geleistet und die ehemaligen Güter dieser Abtei größtenteils zurückgewinnen können. Die Kämpfe um einige Dörfer wurden aber auch in der ersten Hälfte des 18. Jahrhunderts fortgesetzt. Einer der heftigsten Gegner in diesem Kampf war die in der Nachbarschaft liegende Benediktinerabtei Bakonybél, dessen Abt sogar auf mehreren Landtagen gegen die Zircer (Wieder-) Inbesitznahme von Dörfern seiner Abtei protestierte.[11] Dank der geschickten Politik und der groß angelegten Investitionen konnten aber die Rechte der Abtei Zirc im Laufe des Jahrhunderts gesichert werden. So bewirtschafteten die Zisterzienser von Zirc in zwei Herrschaften – Herrschaft Wesprim (ung. Veszprém) im Komitat Wesprim und Herrschaft Előszállás im Komitat Fejér – rund 50.000 Hektar.[12] Wir beschäftigen uns im Folgenden mit der Herrschaft Wesprim, die aus neun Gutshöfen (Zirc, Akli, Eplény, Polány, Berénd, (Bakony)Koppány, Borsod, Sóly, (Nagy)Tevel) bestand.[13] Im Mittelpunkt steht das Dorf Polány, an dessen Beispiel die Ansiedlungs- und Konfessionspolitik der Abtei dargestellt werden soll.

[7] GRÜGER: Heinrichau, 63-65.
[8] Siehe dazu KOVÁCS, Ignác: A borsmonostori apátság története [Geschichte der Abtei Marienberg]. Sopron 1910.
[9] BÉKEFI, Remig: A pilisi apátság története 1541-1814. [Geschichte der Abtei Pilis] Budapest 1892. – DERS.: A pásztói apátság története 1702-1814 [Geschichte der Abtei Pásztó]. Budapest 1902.
[10] ZLINSZKYNÉ STERNEGG, Mária: A szentgotthárdi ciszterci apátság története és művészetének emlékei (1183-1878) [Geschichte der Zisterzienserabtei Sankt Gotthard und der Denkmäler ihrer Kunst]. In: Szentgotthárd. Helytörténeti, művelődéstörténeti, helyismereti tanulmányok. Hg. v. Lajos KUNTÁR und László SZABÓ. Szombathely 1981, 365-540.
[11] Magyar Országos Levéltár, Budapest [Ungarisches Landesarchiv]. (fortan: MOL). Mikrofilmsammlung 32872/4. Abtei Zirc. Historia domus, 14 und 17.
[12] DÓKA Klára: Egyházi birtokok Magyarországon a 18-19. században [Kirchliche Landgüter in Ungarn im 18.-19. Jh.]. Budapest 1997 (METEM Könyvek 19), 96.
[13] GRÜGER: Heinrichau, 120.

Das Dorf Polány im Besitz der Zisterzienser

Das Dorf Polány stand seit dem 12. Jahrhundert unter der Herrschaft der Benediktinerabtei Bakonybél. Die Existenz seiner Kirche, St. Johannes, ist seit der Mitte des 13. Jahrhunderts belegt.[14] Nachdem die Abtei von den Mönchen verlassen worden war, geriet auch Polány unter weltliche Herrschaft. Mit Tevel wurden bereits 1563 die Güter von Zirc an den Hauptmann von Palota verschenkt.[15] Die Bewohner des Dorfes blieben lange Zeit von den Verwüstungen des Türkenkrieges überwiegend verschont. Der Verwalterabt von Martinsberg erwähnt Polány noch 1575 als einen bewohnten Ort;[16] während des langen Türkenkrieges (1593 – 1606) musste aber das Dorf große Verluste erleiden: 1603 wurden in Polány bloß fünf, 1609 nur noch vier Steuerpforten konskribiert.[17] Zu dieser Zeit geriet Wesprim wieder unter osmanische Herrschaft,[18] was auch die Zugehörigkeit der nebenan liegenden Dörfer beeinflusste. Der nächste Schlag für die Bewohner des Gebietes kam mit den Befreiungskriegen. Die Einquartierung des kaiserlichen Heeres bedeutete für die Dörfer eine ähnliche Verwüstung wie die Streifzüge der osmanischen Truppen. So berichtete Bernard Keczer, der erste Novize des durch Lilienfeld ernannten Abtes von Zirc, Martin Újfalussy, dass die im Zusammenhang mit der Rücknahme von Stuhlweißenburg erfolgte Einquartierung das Dorf Sóly vollkommen verwüstet habe, die Einwohner von Polány ihren Heimatort verlassen mussten und seitdem im Wald in Hütten lebten.[19]

Die erste Visitation von Polány ist aus dem Jahr 1698 bekannt. Das Dorf hatte bis 1777 eine komplizierte Stellung in der Verwaltung: Es lag auf dem Gebiet des Komitats Wesprim, wo der sog. Ewige Obergespan[20] der jeweilige Bischof von Wesprim war; das Erzdekanat Pápa, in dem auch das Dorf Polány lag, gehörte aber zur Diözese Raab, bis Maria Theresia das Erzdekanat 1777 im Rahmen ihrer Diözesanreform mit 14 Pfarreien der Diözese Wesprim anschloss.[21]

Nachdem die Türkenkriege in Westungarn abgeschlossen waren, befahl König Leopold I. die Visitation der Diözese Raab, die nach der Anweisung des Bischofs Christian August von Sachsen zwischen 1696 und 1698 durchgeführt wurde. Die Beauftragten suchten außer dem Erzdekanat Komorn das ganze Bistum auf und lieferten

---

[14] RAINER, Pál: Magyarpolány község története [Geschichte der Gemeinde Ungarisch-Polány]. Veszprém 1990, 6-7.

[15] SÖRÖS, Pongrác: A bakonybéli apátság története II. A Pannonhalmától való függés kora 1548-tól napjainkig [Geschichte der Abtei Bakonybél. Das Zeitalter der Abhängigkeit von Martinsberg von 1548 bis heute]. Budapest 1904 (A Panonhalmi Szent-Benedek-Rend története 9), 10.

[16] EBD., 12.

[17] RAINER: Magyarpolány, 19.

[18] HUNGLER, József: A török kori Veszprém [Wesprim in der Türkenzeit]. Veszprém 1986 (A Veszprém Megyei Levéltár Kiadványai 4).

[19] HORVÁTH: Zirc, 121.

[20] Die Würde eines ewigen Obergespans (*supremus et perpetuus comes*) hatten vom hohen Klerus die zwei Erzbischöfe und mehrere Bischöfe inne, die in dem Komitat (ständischer Verwaltungsbezirk), wo ihre Bischofssitze lagen, das Amt des Obergespans erfüllten, waren also die Vertreter des Königs und die ersten Würdenträger im Komitat.

[21] DÓKA, Klára: A Győri Egyházmegye területi változásai [Die territorialen Änderungen der Diözese Raab]. In: A Győri Egyházmegye ezer éve. Hg. v. Tamás KISS. Győr 2000, 9-22, hier 13.

zahlreiche wertvolle Informationen über den Zustand des Gebietes. Demnach war fast die ganze Diözese protestantisch, überwiegend evangelisch.[22] Das Erzdekanat Pápa wurde 1698 visitiert. Am 7. Juni kam der Visitator in Polány an, fand hier zwölf bewohnte Häuser und einen lutherischen Prediger Namens Georg Némety (Nimety). Die Bewohner, die laut der Visitation alle „akatholisch" waren, hatten eine Kirche – die schon erwähnte, aus dem Mittelalter stammende Johanneskirche – die in dieser Zeit mit Stroh bedeckt war. Das Dorf stand bereits unter der Herrschaft der „Zisterzienser des Komitats Wesprim", also der Abtei Zirc, noch bis 1699 zu Lilienfeld gehörig und mit dem Sitz in Pápa.[23]

Während der Lilienfelder Herrschaft konnte keine große Änderung in Bezug auf die Bewohnerzahl und die konfessionelle Zugehörigkeit erfolgt sein. Der aus Lilienfeld geschickte Abt Újfalussy wirkte seit den 60er Jahren in Ungarn und kaufte im Mai 1666 das Haus in Pápa, auf dem Herrschaftsgebiet der Familie Esterházy. Die ersten Professen legten 1672 und 1673 das Gelübde ab. Nach dem Tod des Abtes während eines Osmanenstreifzugs ernannte der Abt von Lilienfeld einen Administrator in Pápa, der aber bereits 1681 wegen des Thököly-Aufstandes das Land verlassen musste. Nach 1685 konnte sein Nachfolger nach Pápa zurückkehren und begann die Residenz in Zirc neu zu bauen, konnte aber trotz der finanziellen Unterstützung von Lilienfeld keine genügende Anzahl von Arbeitern finden. 1697 begannen bereits die Verhandlungen mit Heinrichau betreffs der Übergabe der Herrschaft.[24]

Konkrete Schritte der Ansiedlungspolitik

Die Administratoren versuchten zwar 1687 und 1696 Bauern um Zirc, in Berénd, Olaszfalu und Sóly anzusiedeln,[25] die riesige Arbeit des Wiederaufbaus und der Besiedlung der Dörfer musste aber die Abtei Heinrichau übernehmen. Das Gebiet, das damals außer dem Grundstück und Haus in Pápa und den Weinbergen in Badacsony noch aus zehn weiteren Dörfern bestand, war zwar größer als das Stiftsland in Heinrichau, allerdings lebten in den bewohnten Ortschaften, in Berénd, Olaszfalu, Polány und Sóly um die Jahrhundertwende bloß etwa 30 untertänige Besitzer, von denen viele noch über das Privileg der sog. Freijahre verfügten, also keinerlei Abgaben lieferten. Die jährliche Zehnt- und Zinseinnahme der für über 30.000 Gulden erkauften

[22] EBD., 11.

[23] Visitatio ecclesiarum et parochiarum in archidiaconatu Papensi, in comitatu Wesprimiensi existentium, in anno Dominicae Incarnationis 1698. a die 3. Junii usque ad diem 12. eiusdem... In: A Veszprémi Egyházmegye legrégibb egyházlátogatásai (1554-1760) [Die ältesten Visitationen der Diözese Wesprim]. Hg. v. János PFEIFFER. Veszprém 1947 (A Veszprémi Egyházmegye múltjából 10), 121-144, hier 136. – Das Protokoll, das insgesamt 22 Pfarreien und 17 Filialen erwähnt, wurde vom Erzdekan Franz Mikos aufgenommen. EBD. 121.

[24] MUSSBACHER: Bemühungen, 25-31.

[25] GRÜGER, Heinrich: Der Beginn der Union von Heinrichau und Zirc. In: Analecta Cisterciensia 38 (1982), 43-75, hier 45-46.

Herrschaften betrug 206 Gulden, dazu kamen die Erträge der Weinberge von etwa 270 Gulden und eine Verpachtung in Előszállás brachte 250 Gulden jährlich.[26]
Der erste schlesische Administrator, Abraham Wabrzig übernahm 1701 mit seinem Mitbruder Wilhelm Sebastian das Haus in Pápa, begann mit dem Aufbau der Dörfer und siedelte schlesische Kolonisten an. Die beiden mußten eigentlich alles, inklusive Teller und Kleidungsstücke aus Heinrichau zuschicken lassen, da es in der neuen Heimat an allem fehlte. Sie erhielten auch in den folgenden Jahren materielle Unterstützung für den persönlichen Unterhalt und den Ankauf von Vieh für die Kolonisten. Die ersten Bemühungen wurden aber durch den Rákóczi-Aufstand zunichte gemacht. Der Administrator musste nach Schlesien flüchten und der Konfrater wurde von den Kuruzzen gefangen genommen.[27] Als der neue Administrator Heinrich Schneider 1711 nach Ungarn kam, fand er in Polány elf Familien, in Berénd nur fünf. Unter ihm und vor allem seinem Nachfolger Gregor Regnard, der mit 37 Jahren die Administration übernahm und auch die ungarische Sprache erlernte, blühte aber die Herrschaft auf. Im Jahr 1723 berichtete P. Regnard seinem Abt über die neu besiedelten Dörfer in der Herrschaft Wesprim: Laut dem lebten in Zirc bereits 31 Familien, in Polány 48, in Berénd 41, in Sóly 47 und in Olaszfalu 23. Die Kolonisten waren Katholiken aus Schlesien und Krain.[28]
Die Zisterzienser übernahmen auch die Seelsorge in den Dörfern der Herrschaft von Zirc. In mehreren Ortschaften errichteten sie neue Gotteshäuser.[29] Die Mehrheit der Zisterzienserdörfer lag auf dem Gebiet der Diözese Wesprim. Bis zu den 80er Jahren sind bis auf eine Ausnahme[30] keine Auseinandersetzungen zwischen der Abtei und dem Bistum bekannt, die wegen der Exemtion der Zisterzienser in anderen Gebieten festzustellen sind; nachdem aber das Ordenszentrum Cîteaux aufgelöst wurde, versuchten die Bischöfe Josef Bajzáth, dann David Zsolnay die Abtei Zirc der Diözesanverwaltung zu unterstellen.[31] Dies stimmte mit dem Versuch der ungarischen Stände überein, die auch die anderen Abteien der Benediktiner, Zisterzienser und Prämonstratenser von den ausländischen Mutterklöstern abtrennen wollten. Besonders nach dem Frieden von Aachen, seit dem das schlesische Heinrichau zum feindlichen Preußen gehörte, wurde die Abtei Zirc den Ständen ein Dorn im Auge. Wie auch in anderen Diözesen, brach der Konflikt um die Bestellung der Pfarrer aus, und bis zur Auflösung der Union mit Heinrichau waren die Beziehungen zwischen Abtei und Bistum angespannt.[32]

---

[26] GRÜGER: Heinrichau, 202.
[27] EBD. 205-207.
[28] GRÜGER: Beginn, 62.
[29] Emlékkönyv, melyet Magyarország ezeréves fennállásának ünnepén közrebocsát a hazai czisztercz rend [Festschrift, die aus Anlass der Feierlichkeiten des Millenniums Ungarns durch den einheimischen Zisterzienserorden veröffentlicht wurde]. Hg. v. Remig BÉKEFI. Budapest 1896, 28.
[30] Siehe Anm. 45.
[31] GRÜGER: Heinrichau, 69.
[32] HORVÁTH: Zirc, 155.

Die juristischen Grundlagen der Rekatholisierung

Bevor wir uns mit den konfessionellen Konflikten in der Herrschaft der Abtei Zirc beschäftigen, müssen wir auf die Religionspolitik in Ungarn im zu behandelnden Zeitalter einen Blick werfen.

Bekanntlich änderte sich die konfessionelle Situation im Karpatenbecken in den ersten Jahrzehnten des 16. Jahrhunderts rasch: Während vor der Verbreitung des Protestantismus etwa 80 Prozent der Gesamtbevölkerung des Königreichs zur katholischen Konfession gehörte, wurde das Land im Laufe des Jahrhunderts weitgehend protestantisch: ungefähr 70-80 Prozent. Die harten Beschlüsse des ungarischen Landtags, die den Anhängern der lutherischen Lehren den Scheiterhaufen angedroht hatten, wurden abgesehen von Einzelfällen nicht vollstreckt; so konnte der Protestantismus parallel mit dem Niedergang des in Folge der osmanischen Eroberung zerfallenden katholischen Kirchenwesens[33] im Land endgültig Fuß fassen und seine Institutionen errichten. Interessant ist der Ablauf der Verbreitung der protestantischen Glaubensrichtungen in Ungarn: Obwohl das Reformationsrecht den Grundbesitzern im Gegensatz zu den Landesfürsten im Heiligen Römischen Reich gesetzlich nicht zugesichert wurde, verursachte der Übertritt des Landesherren in Folge des auch in Ungarn üblichen Patronatsrechtes den Konfessionswechsel des ganzen Herrschaftsgebiets.[34] Daneben finden wir aber auch die bewusste Entscheidung der Bevölkerung für die Reformation, wie es die Bestellung der Pfarreien in den königlichen Freistädten und teilweise in den Marktflecken beweist.[35]

Weil die Mehrheit der ungarischen Stände des Jahrhunderts protestantisch wurde, konnten die Habsburger auf dem ungarischen Landtag keine Beschlüsse gegen die Verbreitung der nichtkatholischen Konfessionen verabschieden lassen.[36] Der nach dem Aufstand des siebenbürgischen Fürsten Bocskai geschlossene Wiener Friede (1606) sicherte außerdem den Magnaten, den Adeligen, den Städten, den Dörfern und den Soldaten die freie Religionsausübung und den Erhalt der kirchlichen Institutionen zu. Diese Zugeständnisse, weswegen dem Wiener Hof vom Heiligen Stuhl

---

[33] Siehe ADRIÁNYI, Gabriel: Zu den Auswirkungen der osmanischen Expansion. In: Ungarn Jahrbuch 23 (1997), 361-374.

[34] Zur Funktion des Patronatsrechtes im Konfessionswechsel: FAZEKAS, István: Dorfgemeinde und Glaubenswechsel in Ungarn im späten 16. und 17. Jahrhundert. In: Konfessionalisierung in Ostmitteleuropa. Wirkungen des religiösen Wandels im 16. und 17. Jahrhundert in Staat, Gesellschaft und Kultur. Hg. v. Joachim BAHLCKE und Arno STROHMEYER. Stuttgart 1999 (Forschungen zur Geschichte und Kultur des östlichen Mitteleuropa 7), 339-351.

[35] Siehe SZAKÁLY, Ferenc: Mezőváros és reformáció. Tanulmányok a korai magyar polgárosodás kérdéséhez [Marktflecken und Reformation. Studien zur Frage der frühen ungarischen Verbürgerlichung]. Budapest 1995 (Humanizmus és reformáció 23), 10-13. – Zu Präzisierung dieser These MOLNÁR, Antal: Mezőváros és katolicizmus. Katolikus egyház az egri püspökség hódoltsági területein a 17. században [Marktflecken und Katholizismus. Die katholische Kirche auf den osmanischen Gebieten der Diözese Erlau im 17. Jahrhundert]. Budapest 2005 (METEM Könyvek 49), 9-21. – Ferner KOWALSKÁ, Eva: Die ungarischen Städte und das Problem der Konfessionalisierung aus kulturpolitischer Sicht. In: BAHLCKE/STROHMEYER: Konfessionalisierung, 351-367.

[36] Vgl. ECKHART, Ferenc: Magyar állam- és jogtörténet [Ungarische Staats- und Rechtgeschichte]. Hg. v. Barna MEZEY. Budapest 2000 (Millenniumi magyar történelem), 251-252.

sogar mit der Exkommunikation gedroht wurde,[37] konnten zwar in Folge der immer stärkeren Rekatholisierungspolitik der Habsburger nie geltend gemacht werden; doch solange die Fürsten von Siebenbürgen in der Lage waren, sich für die Religionsfreiheit in Ungarn mit Waffen einzusetzen, konnte die protestantische Religionsausübung wenigstens in Teilen des Landes, wo die habsburgische Administration wenig Einfluss hatte, größtenteils erhalten werden.

Die protestantischen Stände gerieten aber bereits seit 1618 in Folge der Konversion vieler Adelsfamilien[38] in die Minderheit auf dem Landtag, der dann das Vorgehen gegen den Protestantismus endgültig entschied.

Der Höhepunkt der Verfolgung bildete bekanntlich die nach der sog. Magnatenverschwörung erfolgte „protestantische Trauerdekade“[39] mit der berüchtigten Verurteilung von 42 Predigern zur Galeerensklaverei.[40] Die Regelung auf dem Landtag zu Ödenburg aus dem Jahr 1681, die eigentlich auf die Konsolidierung der politischen Lage im Königreich abzielte, bestimmte dann bis zum Erlass des Toleranzpatents Josefs II., also für ein ganzes Jahrhundert, die konfessionelle Lage des Landes.

Der Gesetzesartikel 25 bekräftigte zwar die Beschlüsse des Wiener Friedens, also die freie Religionsausübung der Protestanten, allerdings mit der Ergänzung: „*salvo jure dominorum terrestrium*“ (des Rechts der Landesherren unbeschadet), die wegen der Mehrheit der katholischen Großgrundbesitzer für die Protestanten nichts Gutes bedeutete. In Artikel 26 wurden die Ortschaften in den im Jahr 1681 habsburgischen Gebieten aufgezählt, wo die Protestanten Kirchen, Schulen und Predigerhäuser bauen durften, in elf Komitaten je zwei Orte (die sog. Artikularorte). In den übrigen Gebieten wurde die Zugehörigkeit der Kirchen „*pro actualibus possessoribus*“ (zugunsten der aktuellen Inhaber) bestimmt.[41] Diese aktuellen Inhaber waren aber in diesen Gebieten, eben weil sie den Osmanen näher lagen, wie auch das Komitat Wesprim, überwiegend protestantisch. Somit wurde die protestantische Religionsausübung – wenn wir auf unser näheres Thema blicken – auch in Polány für rechtmäßig erklärt.

In Folge der Befreiungskriege änderte aber der Wiener Hof diese Haltung. Bereits der nächste Landtag in Preßburg (1687 – 88) bekräftigte diese Religionsklausel nur „aus königlicher Gnade“, und die in den folgenden Jahren erlassenen königlichen

---

[37] TUSOR, Péter: A magyar hierarchia és a pápaság a 17. században [Die ungarische Hierarchie und das Papsttum im 17. Jh.]. In: Századok 136 (2002), 527-545, hier 535.

[38] Hier soll die Tätigkeit des Kardinalprimas Péter Pázmány betont werden. Zu seiner Tätigkeit siehe u.a. Pázmány Péter és kora [Peter Pázmány und seine Zeit]. Hg. v. Emil HARGITTAY. Piliscsaba 2001 (Pázmány Irodalmi Műhely, Tanulmányok 2).

[39] Vgl. FABINYI, Tibor: Forschungsprobleme des „Trauerjahrzehntes“ der Evangelischen Kirche Ungarns. In: Religion oder Rebellion? Die Vorträge des internationalen Kirchenhistorischen Kolloquiums Debrecen, 12. 2. 1976. Hg. v. Peter BARTON und László MAKKAI. Budapest 1977, 37-46.

[40] Siehe BARTON, Peter F: „Schickt die protestantischen Prediger auf die Galeeren!“ In: Kirche im Osten. Studien zur osteuropäischen Kirchengeschichte und Kirchenkunde. Hg. v. Robert STUPPERICH. Göttingen 1977, 57-71.

[41] GYENGE, Imre: Der ungarische Landtag zu Ödenburg 1681 und die Artikulargemeinden. In: Im Lichte der Toleranz. Aufsätze zur Toleranzgesetzgebung in den Reichen Josephs II., ihren Voraussetzungen und ihren Folgen. Hg. v. Peter F. BARTON. Wien 1981 (Studien und Texte zur Kirchengeschichte und Geschichte), 33-58. – Ferner MÁLYUSZ, Elemér: Magyarország története a felvilágosodás korában [Geschichte Ungarns im Zeitalter der Aufklärung]. Hg. v. István SOÓS. Budapest 2002 (Millenniumi magyar történet), 280-281.

Dekrete, die die „Erläuterung" dieser Beschlüsse enthielten, hoben das Patronatsrecht der Grundbesitzer auf, besonders in den neu erworbenen, von den Osmanen befreiten Gebieten, wo nur das königliche Patronatsrecht galt. Hier wurde bloß die katholische Religionsausübung geduldet. Den Protestanten wurde die öffentliche Religionsausübung lediglich in den 22 Artikularorten zugesichert, Geistliche durften nur in diesen Orten wirken, das Patronatsrecht des protestantischen Adels wurde nur auf die private Religionsausübung beschränkt. Wie Leopold Kardinal Kollonich, einer der Vorkämpfer der Rekatholisierung in seinem „Einrichtungswerk" formuliert: König und Klerus wollten nicht dulden, dass die protestantischen Adligen ihre „*Häuser und Hütten ein Residenz intituliren, den nächsten Diener und Knecht zu einem Seelsorger declariren*", um so eine öffentliche Religionsausübung einführen zu wollen.[42] Die Prediger der Artikularorte durften in anderen Orten keine Tätigkeit ausüben; sie durften zwar von der Bevölkerung nichtartikulierter Orte aufgesucht werden, in diesem Fall mussten aber die Stolgebühren dem zuständigen katholischen Pfarrer bezahlt werden.[43] Die unter Karl III. (Kaiser Karl VI.) erlassene Resolution (1731) erschwerte die Lage der Protestanten in Bezug auf Ehe und öffentliches Amt noch mehr.[44]

Konfessionelle Konflikte in der Herrschaft Zirc

Nach dieser Zusammenfassung ist es nicht verwunderlich, daß die Aussichten der Protestanten in den Herrschaftsgebieten der Zisterzienser von Zirc im Laufe des 18. Jahrhunderts hoffnungslos wurden. Bereits die ersten Siedlungsversuche der Lilienfelder hatten einen Rekatholisierungscharakter, die von den Administratoren aus Heinrichau angesiedelten Bauern änderten dann weitgehend die konfessionellen Verhältnisse des Gebietes. Auch die Protestanten in Polány gerieten im Laufe der Zeit in Minderheit.

Bei der Rekatholisierung der Dörfer fanden die schlesischen Zisterzienser einen einflussreichen Verbündeten in der Person des Bischofs Martin Padányi Biró.[45] Padányi wurde wegen der häufigen Krankheit seines Vorgängers Adam Acsády 1734 Gene-

[42] Dunamelléki Református Egyházkerület Ráday Gyűjtemény (Reformierter Distrikt entlang der Donau, Ráday Sammlung), K-0 104 Augustissimo ac Potentissimo Romanorum Imperatori et Regni Hungariae Regi Leopoldo Imo Relatio una et Opinio subdelegatione Commissionis, in elaborando novitus post Pulsum e Regno Turcam, introducendo Statu Regni Politico, Iuridico, Ecclesiastico, Militari, et Camerali, considentis per Cardinalem Leopoldum Kollonics porrecta 1689, fol. 41v.

[43] FATA, Márta: Ungarn, das Reich der Stephanskrone, im Zeitalter der Reformation und Konfessionalisierung, Multiethnizität, Land und Konfession 1550-1700. Münster 2000 (Katholisches Leben und Kirchenreform im Zeitalter der Glaubensspaltung 60), 279-280.

[44] MÁLYUSZ: Magyarország, 293.

[45] Nur in der Frage der Rekatholisierung war der Bischof ein Verbündeter der Zisterzienser. Über die Jurisdiktion stritt er mit ihnen und mit den anderen exemten Orden während seiner ganzen Amtszeit. PEHM [Mindszenty], József: Padányi Biró Márton veszprémi püspök élete és kora [Das Leben des Bischofs Martin Padányi Biró und seine Zeit]. Zalaegerszeg 1934 (A Veszprémi Egyházmegye múltjából 2), 164.

ralvikar in der Diözese Wesprim,[46] und 1745, nach dem Tod Acsádys, Diözesanbischof und damit Ewiger Obergespan des Komitats Wesprim. Bereits als Kanoniker kämpfte er gegen die Religionsausübung in Felsőörs (am Balaton) und als Bischof unterstützte er die Bemühungen der Zisterzienser, die Protestanten aus dem Komitat Wesprim zu drängen. In Polány, das spätestens seit 1725 bereits nicht mehr lutherisch, sondern calvinisch war,[47] ist die Anwesenheit reformierter Prediger bis zu den 60er Jahren durchgehend belegt. Da die angesiedelten Deutschsprachigen einen anderen Rechtsstatus hatten als die ungarischen Bauern, und weil sie getrennt von den ursprünglichen Einwohnern lebten, wurde das Dorf als zwei Siedlungen betrachtet: Ungarisch- und Deutsch-Polány.[48] Eine separate Ansiedlung der verschiedenen Ethnien war auch anderswo üblich, den Hintergrund dafür bildeten neben den konfessionellen Verschiedenheiten und dem unterschiedlichen Rechtstatus auch kulturelle Unterschiede.[49]

In Deutsch-Polány wurde keine Zisterzienserpfarrei errichtet, das Dorf war eine Filiale von Városlőd, später vom Nachbarort Kislőd, die unter der Jurisdiktion des Bischofs von Wesprim standen. Auf die Initiative Padányis hin wurde der protestantische Schulmeister 1747 aus Kislőd vertrieben und damit die dortige Religionsausübung eingestellt.[50] Die Calvinisten in Polány konnten hingegen ihr Gotteshaus bis 1757 ungehindert benutzen, bis im Juli ein Gewitter im Gebäude erheblichen Schaden verursachte. Sie beantragten die Renovierung der Kirche und machten damit Prior und Bischof auf sich aufmerksam. Bereits im September jenes Jahres verbot der Königliche Statthaltereirat[51] , die Kirche zu renovieren[52] und Padányi als Obergespan ließ im Januar 1748 eine Untersuchung in Polány durchführen. Das vom Stuhlrichter gehaltene Verhör, indem zehn Zeugen befragt wurden, endete mit dem Ergebnis, daß die Kirche in Ungarisch-Polány „seit Menschengedenken" protestantisch und dort kein katholischer Pfarrer tätig gewesen sei. Außerdem berichtete der Stuhlrichter an das Komitat, daß die Bewohner Ungarisch- und Deutsch-Polány für

[46] PETRÁK, Mihály: Acsády Ádám veszprémi püspöksége (1725-1744) [Das bischöfliche Wirken Adam Acsádys in Wesprim]. Veszprém 1949 (A Veszprémi Egyházmegye múltjából 13), 12.

[47] Die Ursachen und die genaue Zeit dieses späten Konfessionswechsels sind nicht bekannt. Vgl. RAINER: Magyarpolány, 21.

[48] EBD., 22.

[49] Die deutschen Kolonisten von Erdeed (Ardud, heute in Rumänien) baten z.B. 1748 ihren Grundherrn, Graf Alexander Károlyi, sich von den ungarischen Dorfbewohnern zu trennen: „Dan es ist Unmeglich Mer hie zue wohnen Undter denen Ungar: den zweyerley natzionen in einem ohrth zue wohnen ist ein verderbliche sah, Man siet Jah in andteren Derfer all woh die Deitsche allein wohnen in allen sachen ein gewisse ordtnung haben." Zitiert in: FATA, Márta: Einwanderung und Ansiedlung der Deutschen (1686-1790). In: Land an der Donau. Hg. v. Günter SCHÖDL. Berlin 1995 (Deutsche Geschichte im Osten Europas), 89-196, hier 133.

[50] Padányi Biró Márton naplója. Függelékül Birónak Rómába tett két jelentése 1752-ből és 1757-ből [Das Tagebuch von Martin Padányi Biró, im Anhang zwei Berichte des Bischofs nach Rom, aus den Jahren 1752 und 1757]. Hg. v. Károly HORNIG. Veszprém 1903, 258.

[51] Der seit 1723 existierende Ungarische Königliche Statthaltereirat (*consilium regium locumtenentiale Hungaricum*) war für die Durchführung der königlichen Dekrete zuständig und beschäftigte sich außer dem Rechts- und Finanzwesen mit der ganzen Verwaltung des Königreichs.

[52] Veszprém Megyei Levéltár [Komitatsarchiv Wesprim]. (fortan: VEML). XII 2 a. Zirci apátsági levéltár [Archiv der Abtei Zirc], Archivum Vetus, C 435 a. 22. September 1757.

zwei Dörfer gehalten hätten.[53] Der Prior von Zirc, Peter Schneider, bat aber das Komitat, den Gottesdienst, den der Prediger Josef Kisvárday bei Privathäusern hielt, zu verbieten, wies darauf hin, daß im Dorf viel mehr Katholiken als Protestanten wohnten und bewies außerdem, daß Ungarisch- und Deutsch-Polány eigentlich eine einzige Siedlung gewesen sei.[54] Die calvinischen Bewohner beantragten Ende Januar nochmals die Renovierung ihrer Kirche, mit dem sie aber nur eine erneute Untersuchung erreichten, die vor dem Bischof in Anwesenheit des Priors durchgeführt wurde.[55] Der weitere Verlauf des Prozesses ist ab diesem Punkt unklar; am 27. Oktober 1760 wurde aber durch den Statthaltereirat ein Befehl erlassen, der die Renovierung des Gotteshauses verbat, und auf die Rechte des Grundherren bezogen die Errichtung einer katholischen Pfarrei mit Anstellung eines Pfarrers und Schulmeisters verordnete.[56] Mit einem weiteren Befehl vom März des folgenden Jahres verbat er jeglichen protestantischen Gottesdienst in Privathäusern.[57] Die seit Jahrhunderten ungebrochene protestantische Religionsausübung wurde also in Polány in knapp drei Jahren vollkommen ausgelöscht. Der Prediger musste das Dorf verlassen und der Zisterzienserpater Martin Faust begann seine Tätigkeit als Dorfpfarrer. Da der Chor der neuen Kirche erst 1769 und das ganze Gotteshaus 1773 aufgebaut wurde, hielt der Pfarrer bis zu diesem Zeitpunkt im Haus des ehemaligen calvinischen Predigers den katholischen Gottesdienst.[58]

Die konfessionellen Verhältnisse änderten sich in Folge der Geschehnisse in Polány rasch: 1775 wohnten im Dorf 90 Reformierte und 665 Katholiken (14% protestantisch),[59] 1851 noch 48 Reformierte und 1122 Katholiken (4% protestantisch).[60]

Die Zisterzienser hatten in der Verdrängung der Protestanten aber nicht in allen ihren Dörfern einen solchen „Erfolg“. Im Wesprim näher liegenden Dorf Sóly, das im Gegensatz zu Polány von Anfang an zur Diözese Wesprim gehörte, hatten die Calvinisten die Mehrheit. Martin Padányi Biró suchte diesen Ort bereits 1734 noch als Generalvikar auf, notierte die konfessionellen Verhältnisse und den Namen des „akatholischen“ Predigers fleißig auf (Adam Kenesey) und vergaß nicht anzumerken, daß das Dorf kein Artikularort war.[61] Die Visitation aus dem Jahr 1757 fand hier 216 Reformierte, 2 Lutheraner, 12 „Apostaten“ (Konfession nicht bekannt), 5 Juden und 75 Katholiken.[62] Der Prediger wurde vom Administrator P. Schneider bereits 1750 vertrieben, weil er die Bevölkerung angeblich gegen den Grundherrn auf-

---

[53] EBD. C 438 a, b. 10. Januar 1748.
[54] EBD. C 435 b, und Januar 1758. Ebd. 438 c. 1757.
[55] EBD. C 438 d, und 2. Juni 1748. Ebd. C 480 a. 30. Januar 1748.
[56] EBD. C 485 a. Preßburg, den 27. Oktober 1760.
[57] EBD. Ebd. C 493 a. Preßburg, den 31. März 1761.
[58] RAINER: Magyarpolány, 22-23.
[59] VEML XII a. C 829. Conscriptio animarum 1775.
[60] Magyarország geographiai szótára [Geographisches Wörterbuch Ungarns]. Hg. v. Elek FÉNYES. Pest 1851, Bd. 3, 247.
[61] Veszprémi Érseki Levéltár [Erzbischöfliches Archiv Wesprim]. (fortan: VÉL). Conscriptiones proventuum, Fasc. 1. Nr. 7. 1734, pag. 16. Mein Dank gilt Herrn Archivar István Hermann für die freundliche Unterstützung meiner dortigen Forschungsarbeit.
[62] VÉL Archivum episcopatus, A 14 Tom. 8. Conscriptio animarum 1757, pag. 101-105.

hetzen wollte,[63] aus einem Verhör ergibt sich aber, daß die Auseinandersetzung hier deswegen ausbrach, weil die Dorfbewohner Prediger und Schulmeister aus den Einnahmen des Dorfes bezahlt und einige von ihnen für den Bau des Predigerhauses aus dem Wald der Abtei Holz gestohlen hätten. Der Diebstahl habe übrigens ein schlimmes Ende gehabt: Neun Bauern seien während der Aktion erfroren und zwei hätten ebenfalls wegen der Kälte Arme und Beine verloren.[64] Dieser Prozess landete auch bei dem Statthaltereirat, der eine Untersuchung in Bezug auf das calvinische Gotteshaus in Sóly verordnete. Der Ausgang der Untersuchung ist nicht bekannt; die Visitation von 1779 erwähnte keinen reformierten Pfarrer oder Schulmeister, die noch aus dem Mittelalter stammende Kirche[65] wurde aber nicht von den Katholiken benutzt.[66] Seit 1787 – also bereits nach dem Toleranzpatent – versuchte die calvinische Bevölkerung für den Prediger Grundstück und Holz zu erwerben.[67] Dieser Versuch scheiterte auch in den kommenden Jahren; die Abtei Zirc verweigerte die Verleihung des Landsitzes auch nach der Artikulierung der Religionsfreiheit der Protestanten auf dem Landtag 1790 – 91, obwohl das Komitat die Rückgabe ehemaliger Besitze der Protestanten verordnete.[68] 1794 konnte aber die Gemeinde erreichen, daß die Zisterzienser dem Prediger ein Waldstück übergaben;[69] hier konnte also die protestantische Religionsausübung nicht aufgehoben werden. Dies beweist auch, daß die konfessionellen Verhältnisse nicht zugunsten der Katholiken geändert werden konnten: 1851 lebten im Dorf 451 Calvinisten mit 254 Katholiken (56% protestantisch).[70]

Die Ansiedlungsbemühungen der Pauliner im Gebirge Pilis

Wo die wiederkehrenden Ordensgrundbesitzer keine (protestantische) Urbevölkerung vorfanden, war die Rekatholisierung der Landsitze natürlich konfliktlos. Dies zeigt die Paulinerherrschaft Pilismarót nördlich der Donau und das hier liegende Dorf Pilisszentlászló (d.h. St. Ladislaus im Gebirge Pilis).[71]

Die Pauliner – bekanntlich der einzige in Ungarn gegründete geistliche Orden – erlebten ihre Blütezeit wie die Zisterzienser im Spätmittelalter. Sie verfügten bis zur osmanischen Eroberung über mehr als hundert Niederlassungen im Königreich Ungarn.[72] Und obwohl die Pauliner in der Periode der osmanischen Eroberung aus Un-

---

[63] VEML XII. a. C 353. 1750.
[64] Der Diebstahl fand am 8. Februar 1749 statt. Untersuchungsprotokoll vom 20. Mai 1750. EBD. C 356.
[65] FÉNYES: Magyarország Bd. 4, 34.
[66] VÉL Archivum episcopatus A 8, Tom. 12. pag. 7-8.
[67] VEML XII. a. C 1227. Februar 1787.
[68] EBD. C 1395. 8. Mai 1793.
[69] EBD. 1426. 6. März 1794.
[70] FÉNYES: Magyarország Bd. 4, 34.
[71] Ich bedanke mich bei Herrn Bürgermeister Dr. György Illés für seine Hinweise bezüglich der Dorfgeschichte.
[72] Vgl. KISBÁN, Emil: A magyar Pálosrend története [Geschichte des ungarischen Paulinerordens]. Bd. 1. Budapest 1938, 321-325.

garn nicht völlig verschwanden, finden wir 1643 lediglich 41 Paulinermönche in sechs ungarischen Klöstern.[73] Das 18. Jahrhundert ist auch für die Pauliner die Zeit der Wiedergeburt; auch sie konnten ihre mittelalterliche Mitglieder- und Klosterzahl nie wieder erreichen, erlebten aber im Laufe des Jahrhunderts einen viel größeren Aufschwung als die oben behandelten Zisterzienser: In den 80er Jahren verfügten sie über 313 Mitglieder in 24 Niederlassungen.[74]

Trotz ihrer gesellschaftlichen und politischen Bedeutung erreichte im 18. Jahrhundert das Ausmaß der Landgüter der Pauliner das der Zisterzienser nicht, doch hatte der Orden bedeutende Grundstücke in sieben Komitaten des Königreichs zerstreut gelegen.[75] Eines davon bildete die Herrschaft Pilismarót mit den Dörfern: Pilismarót, Pilisszentlászló, Pilisszentlélek und Pilisszentkereszt im Besitz des Paulinerklosters in Pest.[76] Die Herrschaft bzw. das Dorf Pilisszentkereszt (d.h. Heiligenkreuz im Gebirge Pilis) hatte übrigens einen gewissen Bezug zu den Zisterziensern: Im ganzen Jahrhundert verlief ein Prozess zwischen den Paulinern und den Zisterziensern über die Zugehörigkeit des Dorfes, da auch die Zisterzienser behaupteten, ihr ehemaliges, 1184 gegründetes Kloster „Pilis" hätte am Ort dieses Dorfes gestanden. Mit Recht, wie später von Archäologen bewiesen wurde.[77]

Da diese Herrschaft zu Ofen (ung. Buda) und den Gefechten der Türkenkriege näher lag als die vorher behandelte Zisterzienserherrschaft Zirc, waren die zugehörigen Dörfer mit Ausnahme von Pilismarót völlig verlassen worden. Bereits im September 1526, also einige Wochen nach der Schlacht bei Mohács, wurden die Dörfer des Gebirges Pilis von den Osmanen geplündert. Wenn Pilisszentlászló nicht in diesem Jahr entvölkert wurde, geschah es nach der osmanischen Besatzung Ofens (1541), da die türkischen Steuerlisten der 40er und 50er Jahre dieses Dorf nicht mehr erwähnen.[78] Die Grundstücke wurden jedoch von den Bewohnern der Nachbardörfer- und -städte genutzt, die vom osmanischen Grundherrn aber auch von den ins Kloster Felsőelefánt (Horné Lefantovce in der heutigen Slowakei) geflüchteten Paulinern besteuert wurden.[79]

Die Neubesiedlung der verlassenen Gebiete begann hier ebenso erst am Anfang des 18. Jahrhunderts. Im Jahr 1701 lebten fünf Familien im Dorf Pilisszentlászló. Die ersten Ansiedler kamen wahrscheinlich aus der Gegend des Klosters Felsőelefánt, da der dortige Vikar, Paul Majtényi, die Herrschaft für die Pauliner zurückgewann.

[73] TÖRÖK, József/LEGEZA, László/SZACSVAY, Péter: Pálosok [Pauliner]. Budapest 2006[2] (Szerzetesrendek a Kárpát-medencében), 24.

[74] EBD. 25. – Über die ungarischen Pauliner im 18. Jahrhundert siehe KISBÁN, Emil: A magyar Pálostrend története [Geschichte des ungarischen Paulinerordens]. Bd. 2. Budapest 1940.

[75] DÓKA: Birtokok, 99.

[76] MAGYAR, Eszter: A pesti pálos rend pilismaróti uradalmának erdőgazdálkodása [Die Forstwirtschaft der Herrschaft Pilismarót der Pauliner von Pest]. In: Magyar egyháztörténeti évkönyv – Annales Historiae Ecclesiae Hungaricae 1 (1994), 109-123, hier 109.

[77] Vgl. HERVAY: Repertorium, 141-147.

[78] ZÖLD, András: Pilisszentlászló története [Geschichte von Pilisszentlászló]. Manuskript (1980), 69.

[79] MAGYAR, Eszter: A Pálos-rend pilismaróti uradalmának újjászervezése a török hódoltság után [Die Wiedererrichtung der Herrschaft Pilismarót des Paulinerordens nach der türkischen Eroberung]. In: Pálos rendtörténeti tanulmányok [Ordensgeschichtliche Studien über die Pauliner]. Hg. v. Gábor SARBAK. Csorna 1994 (Varia Paulina 1), 104-116, hier 104.

1715 bewohnten sechs Hörigen- und fünf Häuslerfamilien das Dorf. Fünf Jahre später fanden die Conscriptores bereits 14 Hörigen- und 11 Häuslerhaushalte vor und 1728 wurden insgesamt 29 Haushalte besteuert;[80] im Jahr 1744 gehörten 34 Familien zu Pilisszentlászló, 1760 fast die doppelte Zahl, nämlich 64.[81]

Nach 1720 versuchte die Ordensleitung zuerst, in Pilismarót deutsche und slawische Bauern anzusiedeln, wegen ethnischer Konflikte wurden aber die Slawen wahrscheinlich um 1722 nach Pilisszentlászló umgesiedelt. In den weiteren zwei Dörfern finden wir erst nach 1740 neue Ansiedler, die Besiedlung des Herrschaftsgebietes endete im nächsten Jahrzehnt.[82]

Eine schwer zu beantwortende Frage ist die genaue Herkunft der slawischen Bevölkerung. Die Kontrakte, die zwischen dem Grundherrn und den Hörigen geschlossen wurden, verschwiegen i.d.R. den Ursprung der Bauern. Die Nennung der Herkunft wäre für die Hörigen gefährlich gewesen, da deren Umzug grundsätzlich verboten war; dem früheren Grundherrn hätte die Anmerkung der Abstammung Gelegenheit geboten, die Hörigen zurückzufordern. Außerdem sind die Listen über die geflüchteten Hörigen sehr lückenhaft und wegen der großen Bevölkerungsbewegung des Zeitalters sehr unzuverlässig, Taufmatrikeln wurden bis zum Ende des Jahrhunderts besonders unterschiedlich geführt.[83]

Gewiss ist aber, dass im Hintergrund der Umsiedlung die schlechten wirtschaftlichen Verhältnisse der verlassenen Gebiete standen. Im Komitat Pressburg war am Anfang des 18. Jahrhunderts die Bevölkerungsdichte fünfmal so groß als in den von den Osmanen befreiten Gebieten und die Quellen berichten uns über grausames Elend der hier gelegenen Dörfer, die u.a. mit der veralteten Bewirtschaftung der Felder (Zweifeldersystem mit durchschnittlich zweifacher Ernte) zusammenhing. Die Mehrheit der umgesiedelten Bevölkerung bildeten also die geflüchteten slowakischen Hörigen der nördlichen Gebiete;[84] die organisierte Kolonisation spielte hier, im Gegensatz zur Herrschaft der Zisterzienser, eine geringere Bedeutung. Nach Transdanubien wanderten wegen geographischer Gründe die Hörigen aus den Komitaten Neutra, Trentschin und z.T. Sohl,[85] nach Pilisszentkereszt kamen die Bauern aus dem Komitat Komorn.[86]

Trotz der Umzugsbereitschaft der Hörigen bedeutete die Ansiedlung für den Grundbesitzer eine enorm schwierige Aufgabe. Dies zeigt sich daran, dass die umgesiedelten Bauern, wenn sie die wirtschaftlichen Verhältnisse nicht ausreichend fanden, im

[80] ZÖLD: Piliszentlászló, 75-83.
[81] EBD. 91, 108.
[82] MAGYAR: Pesti pálos rend, 111.
[83] FÜGEDI, Erik: Szlovák település a török alól felszabadult területen [Slowakische Siedlung auf dem von den Türken befreiten Gebiet]. In: Agrártörténeti Szemle 8 (1966), 313-332 (mit einem dt. Resümee), hier 314.
[84] EBD. 315f. und 319.
[85] FÜGEDI, Erik: Beiträge zur Siedlungsgeschichte der Slowaken im 18. Jh. auf dem Gebiet des heutigen Ungarn. In: Studia Slavica XI (1965), 289-330, hier 294.
[86] EBD., 316, Tabelle 1 (Herkunftsort und Ansiedlungsort).

Laufe der Zeit weiterzogen. In Pilisszentlászló z.B. verließ zwischen 1715 und 1728 mehr als die Hälfte der Dorfbevölkerung ihre neue Heimatsiedlung.[87] Dies geschah trotz der gewissen Standeserhöhung der Neuansiedler. Eben in Pilisszentlászló erhielten die nach 1710 zugewanderten Hörigen ihre Freizügigkeit.[88] Das im Jahre 1733 für die Hörigen erlassene Urbar machte ihnen weitere Zugeständnisse, in dem u.a. der zu bezahlende Zensus ermäßigt, das Kneipenrecht zugesichert und der Holzverbrauch gestattet wurde.[89] Dieser Vertrag wurde dann in den siebziger Jahren, nach den Initiativen der Erlasse Maria Theresias, mehrmals erneuert.[90]

Die Kirche von Pilisszentlászló wurde in der Türkenzeit, wahrscheinlich gleichzeitig mit dem Kloster, völlig zerstört. 1727 begannen zwar die ersten Bemühungen des Wiederaufbaus,[91] erst zwanzig Jahre später wurde aber lediglich eine Holzkirche aufgebaut. Die Bewohner mußten bis 1753 nach Dunabogdány, dann nach Szentendre gehen, um die Messe zu hören; erst ab jenem Jahr wohnte ein Paulinermönch als Seelsorger im Dorf.[92] Die Steinkirche wurde ebenso wie in Polány in den 70er Jahren (1770 – 1772, wahrscheinlich am Ort des mittelalterlichen Klosters) errichtet;[93] im Hintergrund der Verzögerung der Bauarbeiten standen wohl finanzielle aber keineswegs konfessionelle Schwierigkeiten.

Die Teilnahme der Pauliner an der Rekatholisierung der Stadt Pápa

Dass die Pauliner, wenn sie dazu Gelegenheit fanden, sich ebenfalls an der Arbeit der Rekatholisierung beteiligten, zeigt ihre Tätigkeit in Pápa. Die Stadt, wo – wie behandelt – in den vorausgegangenen Jahrzehnten auch die Zisterzienser von Zirc ihre erste Niederlassung hatten, geriet in die Herrschaft der Grafenlinie der Familie Esterházy. Vor der hier thematisierten Epoche war die Gegend überwiegend protestantisch. In der ersten Welle der Verbreitung der neuen Lehre konnte erst die lutherische, danach die calvinische Richtung Fuß fassen. Die Schule wurde protestantisch und die hier tätigen Franziskaner mussten 1560 die Stadt für eine lange Zeit verlassen. Nach der Ausformung der reformierten Kirchenverwaltung hatte Pápa eine wichtige Stellung: Der hiesige „erste Pastor“ erhielt oft das Amt des Superintendenten des Kreises von Transdanubien. Noch unter der Herrschaft von Ladislaus Csáky wurden die Pauliner 1638 in die Stadt gerufen, die hier sofort die Seelsorge über-

[87] FÜGEDI: Szlovák, 323 und Tabelle 6.
[88] FÜGEDI: Beiträge, 309.
[89] MOL E 153 Acta Paulinorum Fasc. 294, Nr. 9. Sedes Dominalis seu Urbarium cum Pagis nostris Bottyán et Sz. László celebratur. 17. Juni 1733.
[90] EBD. Fasc. 296, Nr. 17 (1772), Nr. 28 (1774) und Nr. 36 (1776).
[91] EBD. Fasc. 294, Nr. 6.
[92] ZÖLD: Pilisszentlászló, 96.
[93] AGGHÁZY, Mária (u.a.): Pest megye műemlékei [Kunstdenkmäler des Komitats Pest]. Bd. 1. Budapest 1958 (Magyarország műemléki topográfiája 5), 658f.

nahmen und 1649 eine Schule gründeten.[94] Die gewaltsame Rekatholisierung führte hier nicht der Orden sondern der Grundherr an: Nach einem gescheiterten Versuch wurde 1660 mit Hilfe des Militärs die Zwangskonversion und die Einstellung der reformierten Religionsausübung bewirkt. Genauso wie anderswo wurden hier die reformierte Pfarrkirche und die Einnahmequellen des Predigers beschlagnahmt. In diesem Jahr konnten auch die Franziskaner zurückkehren.[95]

Kein Wunder, dass auch die katholischen Institutionen an den Gewalttaten leiden mussten: 1704 – während des Rákóczi-Aufstandes – wurde das Haus der Zisterzienser von calvinischen Soldaten geplündert und in der Stadt wurden mehrere katholische Geistliche getötet oder verprügelt. Die Pauliner – im Gegensatz zu den Zisterziensern – mussten aber die Stadt nicht verlassen und auch ihre Schule war während des Aufstandes in Betrieb.[96]

Auch in Pápa bedeuteten die Jahrzehnte nach dem Rákóczi-Aufstand für die Pauliner das Zeitalter des Wachstums: Das bereits seit 1701 als Priorat wirkende Kloster erhielt in der ersten Hälfte des Jahrhunderts weitere Grundstücke und zahlreiche Schenkungen. Nach den Gewalttaten des 17. Jahrhunderts schien aber die Tätigkeit der Pauliner in dieser Epoche bereits friedlich zu sein: Sie bestellten mehrere Pfarreien um die Stadt herum, und ihre Prediger (*predicatores*), die deutsch und ungarisch wirkten, hatten in Pápa ein großes Ansehen. Die 1728 gegründete Rosenkranzgesellschaft überlebte auch die Aufhebung des Ordens.[97]

Fazit

Die oben behandelten Beispiele zeigen uns, dass die geistlichen Orden in Ungarn sowohl im Bereich der Besiedlung des Karpatenbeckens als auch bei der Rekatholisierung des Landes eine bedeutende Wirkung aufwiesen. Falls die Gegend in ihrem Herrschaftsbereich stand, wie im Fall der Zisterzienser das Gebiet um die Abtei Zirc und bei den Paulinern die Dörfer im Gebirge Pilis, nutzten die geistlichen Orden ihre Rechte als Grundherren aus und besiedelten ihre Ortschaften mit entweder ausländischer oder einheimischer, aber nur katholischer Bevölkerung. Falls sie vor Ort eine protestantische Urbevölkerung antrafen, stützten sie sich auf das vom König bekräftigte Patronatsrecht der katholischen Grundherren, das, die festgelegten Artikularorte ausgenommen, praktisch die Rekatholisierung des ganzen Königreichs ermöglichte. Außerdem trugen sie zur friedlichen Rekatholisierung bei. Dies zeigt die Wirkung der Pauliner in Pápa, aber auch die der Zisterzienser, die seit dem Anfang

[94] Zur Geschichte der Schule in Pápa BAKONYVÁRI, Ildefonz: A pápai katolikus gimnázium története a pálosok és a bencések idejében [Geschichte des kath. Gymnasiums von Pápa während der Zeit der Pauliner und Benediktiner]. Pápa 1998 (Reprint), 53-81.

[95] SZAKÁLY, Ferenc: Pápa a török korban [Pápa während der Türkenzeit]. In: Tanulmányok Pápa város történetéből. A kezdetektől 1970-ig [Studien aus der Geschichte der Stadt Pápa. Von den Anfängen bis 1970]. Hg. v. András KUBINYI. Pápa 1994, 125-196, hier 161-169.

[96] BÁNKÚTI, Imre: Pápa története a török uralom végétől a szatmári békéig (1683-1711) [Die Geschichte von Pápa vom Ende der Türkenzeit bis zum Frieden von Sathmar]. In: EBD., 201-223, hier 214.

[97] KISBÁN: Pálosrend II, 24-26.

des 18. Jahrhunderts bereits mehrere Pfarreien bestellten[98] und in den 70er Jahren ebenfalls mit der Lehrtätigkeit begannen;[99] beide erzielten die Verstärkung des Katholizismus im Karpatenbecken. Die Pauliner verloren ihre Existenz nach der Aufhebung des Ordens durch Joseph II. in den habsburgischen Gebieten wie auch im Königreich Ungarn;[100] die Zisterzienser überlebten den Josephinismus mit einigen Verlusten und waren auch im nächsten Jahrhundert tätig.

[98] Siehe BÉKEFI: Emlékkönyv, 383-432.

[99] Siehe BÉKEFI, Remig: Hogyan lettek a czisztercziek tanítórenddé Magyarországon [Wie die Zisterzienser in Ungarn ein lehrender Orden wurden]. Budapest 1902 (A Szent István Társulat tudományos és irodalmi osztályának felolvasó üléseiből 45).

[100] Der Orden erschien nach mehreren gescheiterten Versuchen erst in den 30er Jahren des 20. Jahrhunderts wieder in Ungarn, 1948 wurde er aber – diesmal u. a. mit den Zisterziensern – wiederum aufgehoben. Zu den früheren Versuchen HERMANN, Egyed: Kísérletek a pálosok visszaállítására a XVIII. század fordulóján [Versuche zur Wiedererrichtung der Pauliner um die Wende des 18. Jahrhunderts]. In: Theologia (1) 1935, 63-67.

Abbildungen

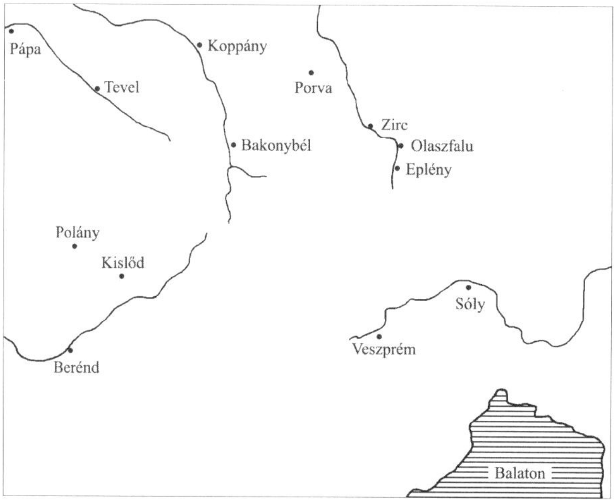

Abb. 1: Die Herrschaft Wesprim der Abtei Zirc
im 18. Jahrhundert

Abb. 2: Die Pfarrkirche von Magyarpolány
(gebaut: 1761 – 1773)

Zoltán Csepregi

Brüderlich verfeindet? Luthertum und Reformiertentum in der neu besiedelten Tolnau

1

Was man von den Anfängen der evangelischen Kirchengemeinden in der sog. „Schwäbischen Türkei" im 18. Jahrhundert und den ersten hier wirkenden lutherischen Pastoren heute weiß, das fußt im wesentlichen auf den unermüdlichen Ermittlungen und dem Datensammeln eines einzigen Forschers, des Pfarrers Johann Schmidt (1889-1958) in Jerking (Györköny H). Er selbst konnte aber vor dem Krieg nur die erste Auswertung der von ihm gefundenen Materialien veröffentlichen,[1] weitere Publikationen anhand Schmidts jetzt im Donauschwäbischen Zentralmuseum in Ulm verwahrter Manuskripte wurden später von Friedrich Spiegel-Schmidt,[2] Gustav Schmidt-Tomka,[3] László Szita[4] und Márta Fata[5] zum Druck befördert.
Der Wert und das Problem der umfangreichen Manuskripte von Schmidt sind demselben Umstand zu verdanken: seine historische Darstellung fußt meistens auf verschollenen Archivalien, was einerseits heißt: man kennt diese Quellen (wie das im zweiten Weltkrieg verbrannte lutherische Senioratsarchiv in Bonnhard, Bonyhád H) nur durch Schmidts Exzerpte, andererseits sind seine Schlüsse nicht immer nachzuprüfen. Kürzlich versuchte Henrik Kéri die bis heute als *opinio communis* geltenden Narrative von Schmidt an einigen wichtigen Punkten zu korrigieren. Seine Korrek-

---

[1] SCHMIDT, Johann: Über die Neubesiedlung der deutsch-evangelischen Gemeinde Varsád. In: Deutsch-ungarische Heimatblätter 4 (1932), 232-241. – DERS.: Hessische Auswanderer nach den Komitaten Tolna, Baranya, Somogy im 18. Jahrhundert. Darmstadt 1934 (Mitteilungen der hessischen familiengeschichtlichen Vereinigung 3,11). – DERS.: Német telepesek bevándorlása Hessenből Tolna-Baranya-Somogyba a XVIII. század első felében [Die Einwanderung deutscher Kolonisten aus Hessen nach Tolna-Baranya-Somogy in der ersten Hälfte des 18. Jahrhunderts]. Győr 1939. – DERS.: Szenicei Bárány György… élete és munkássága [Leben und Werk des György Bárány von Szenice...]. 1682-1757. Paks 1940, 2. Aufl. Sárszentlőrinc 2007.

[2] SPIEGEL-SCHMIDT, Friedrich: Das deutsche Luthertum in der „Schwäbischen Türkei". Auf Grund der Arbeiten von Johann Schmidt. In: Deutsches Luthertum in Ungarn. Hg. v. Heinrich HEIMLER und Friedrich SPIEGEL-SCHMIDT. Düsseldorf 1955, 51-77.

[3] SCHMIDT-TOMKA, Gustav: Beiträge zur Geschichte des evangelischen Seniorats in der Schwäbischen Türkei. München 1976 (Die Deutschen aus Ungarn 10).

[4] SZITA, László: A lutheránus németség bevándorlása és településtörténete Tolna megyében a XVIII. században [Die Einwanderung und Ansiedlung des lutherischen Deutschtums im Komitat Tolna im 18. Jahrhundert]. In: Tanulmányok. Hg. v. Gyula DOBOS. Szekszárd 1996 (Tolna Megyei Levéltári Füzetek 5), 5-163.

[5] FATA, Márta: Von der Ansiedlung zur Auswanderung. Ein Beitrag zur sozialhistorischen Erforschung der Migration der Deutschen in Südostdanubien im 18. und 19. Jahrhundert. In: Die Schwäbische Türkei. Lebensformen der Ethnien in Südwestungarn. Ergebnisse der Tagung des Instituts für donauschwäbische Geschichte und Landeskunde in Tübingen vom 10. und 11. November 1994. Hg. v. Márta FATA. Sigmaringen 1997 (Schriftenreihe des Instituts für Donauschwäbische Geschichte und Landeskunde 5), 15-42.

turen lassen sich folgendermaßen zusammenfassen:
– nicht der Herrscher selbst, nur sein Beauftragter (aber ohne diesbezügliche Ermächtigung) stellte den Einwanderern Kultusfreiheit in Aussicht,
– in den meisten Ansiedlungsverträgen fehlt ein Hinweis auf die freie Religionsausübung,
– die organisatorische Rolle des Grafen Claudius Florimundus Mercy (1666-1733) ist bei Schmidt grob übertrieben, außerdem verwechselt er ihn oft mit seinem Neffen, dem Grafen Anton Ignaz Karl August Mercy d'Argenteau (1691-1767),[6]
– einige mit novellistischen Farben erzählten Geschichten, wie über die Ankunft der Hessen in Kleintormasch (Kistormás H) (1724), oder die über die Auseinandersetzung Mercys mit Bischof Wilhelm Franz Bertram von Nesselrode (amt. 1703-1732) im Jahre 1725 oder die über des Seniors György Bárány (1682-1757) Ausweisung und Rückkehr in den Jahren 1726 und 1729, entnimmt Schmidt gar nicht aus zeitgenössischen Aufzeichnungen, sondern erst im 19. Jahrhundert erstellten Ortsgeschichten,[7]
– auf Quellen derselben Gattung geht die Überzeugung zurück, Mercy selbst sei bestrebt gewesen, auf seinen Besitzungen sprachlich und konfessionell reine Dörfer zu bilden (falls nötig, durch Umsiedeln), um Reibungen und Zank unter der Bevölkerung zu vermeiden.[8]

Kéris Kritik besteht wohl zu Recht. Den „Archiven der Unterdrückung" (dem Komitatsarchiv Tolna, dem Archiv des ungarischen Statthaltereirates) schenkt er aber vielleicht zuviel Glauben und Respekt, viel mehr als den Kirchenbüchern und Korrespondenzen „der Unterdrückten". M.E. liegt es näher an der Wahrheit,
– dass der bischöfliche Obergespan und die Stuhlrichter nur eine lose Kontrolle über die Neusiedlerdörfer auszuüben imstande waren (noch 1737 rechnete man mit einer Rückkehr der Türken),[9]
– dass die Grundherren ihre wirtschaftlichen Interesse gegen die örtlichen oder königlichen Behörden oft erfolgreich zu vertreten wussten,
– dass die Landschaft noch in Bewegung war (falls man in seiner Religion gestört oder behindert wurde, fiel es einem nicht zu schwer, weiterzuziehen, auch vertriebe-

---

[6] SEEWANN, Gerhard: Zur Familiengeschichte der Grafen Mercy und Mercy-Argenteau. In: Südostdeutsches Archiv 19/20 (1976/77), 53-69.

[7] KÉRI, Heinrich: Probleme in der Siedlungsgeschichte des Komitats Tolnau. Suevia Pannonica. Archiv der Deutschen aus Ungarn 14 (1996), 78-94. In: DERS.: Franken und Schwaben in Ungarn: Aufsätze zur Geschichte und Siedlungsgeschichte der Tolnau und der Oberen Baranya. Budapest 2002 (Neue-Zeitung-Bücher 2), 39-55. – KÉRI, Henrik: A Tolna megyei német lutheránusok: megjegyzések egy tanulmányhoz [Über die deutschen Lutheraner in der Tolnau: Eine Richtigstellung]. In: Századok 132 (1998), 916-926. – KÉRI: Franken, 254-268.

[8] WEIDLEIN, János: A tolnamegyei német telepítések [Ansiedlung der Deutschen im Komitat Tolna]. Budapest 1937 (Tolna vármegye múltjából 3), 32. – KÉRI: Franken, 47f.

[9] CSEPREGI, Zoltán: Magyar pietizmus 1700-1756. Tanulmány és forrásgyűjtemény a dunántúli pietizmus történetéhez [Ungarischer Pietismus. Untersuchung und 100 Dokumente zur Geschichte des Pietismus in Transdanubien]. Budapest 2000 (Materialien zur Geschichte der Geistesströmungen des 16-18. Jahrhunderts in Ungarn 36), 212f. (Nr.77).

ne Prediger bekamen sofort einige Dörfer weiter eine neue Anstellung),[10] – und dass die selbstorganisatorische Kraft und das Selbstbewusstsein der Neusiedler noch stärker hervortrat, als bei Schmidt angenommen wurde. Auch die spätere Homogenität der Siedlungen ist langwierigen spontanen Umzügen zu verdanken.[11]

Diese Faktoren ergaben einen – zwar zerbrechlichen – *modus vivendi* im Sinne des Änderungsverbots von Karl III. [VI.] (reg. 1711-1740). Denn der Gesetzesartikel XXXI aus dem Jahre 1715 rief eine vom König und von den Ständen paritätisch beschickte, konfessionell gemischte Religionskommission (*Mixta Religionaria Commissio*), die sog. Kommission von Pest (Budapest H), zur Untersuchung der gegenseitigen Klagen (*gravamina*) der Protestanten und Katholiken ins Leben. Solange diese Kommission tagte, die erst 1721 zusammentrat, sollten am religiösen Status quo keine Änderungen vorgenommen werden.[12] Auf der anderen Seite bedeutete dieses Moratorium praktisch ein Recht auf Duldung für die Gemeinden, die bereits vor der ersten Sitzung der Kommission einen Predigerdienst und Kirchenbesitz nachweisen konnten.[13] In der Formulierung des Predigers in Warschad (Varsád H), Johann Karl Reichard (1700-1753), heisst das folgendermaßen:
„[...] darauf wir unsere Freiheit erlanget, wodurch der hiesige Ort ist in seinem Religions Exercitio confirmiret worden, weil er schon Anno 1719 vor der zu Pest Anno 1721 gehaltenen Commissione Caesarea mit einem Prediger nostrae Confessionis besetzt gewesen, welche aber erst nach dieser Commission sind eingesetzt worden, durften [...] nicht geduldet werden.“[14]
Die vor der ersten Sitzung der Pester Religionskommission formierten evangelische Gemeinschaften konnten also auf Nachsicht hoffen, desto mehr waren also auch die Gutsherren bestrebt, die Ansiedlungen der Protestanten so früh wie möglich zu datieren.

---

[10] Corpus Iuris Hungarici. Magyar Törvénytár. Hg. v. Dezső MÁRKUS. Bd. 4. 1657-1740. Budapest 1900, 644f. (Gesetzartikel CIII/1723). – GALAMBOS, Franz: Glaube und Kirche in der Schwäbischen Türkei des 18. Jahrhunderts: Aufzeichnungen von Michael Winkler in den Pfarrchroniken von Szakadát, Bonyhád und Gödre. München 1987 (Studia hungarica 34) passim. – KÉRI: Franken, 64.

[11] De ortu, propagatione et fatis ecclesiarum evangelicarum in inclyto comitatu Tolnensi et Somogy brevis relatio per reverendum dominum Georgium Bárány, pastorem Szent Lorintziensem producta (1739). In: CSEPREGI: Magyar pietizmus, 226-232 (Nr. 85). – Spätere Fassung: PAYR, Sándor: Egyháztörténeti emlékek. Forrásgyűjtemény a Dunántúli Ág. Hitv. Evang. Egyházkerület történetéhez [Kirchengeschichtliche Denkmäler. Quellensammlung zur Geschichte des Transdanubischen Kirchendistrikts A. B.]. Bd. 1. Sopron 1910, 350-355. – TAFFERNER, Anton: Quellenbuch zur donauschwäbischen Geschichte. Bde. 1-5. München, Stuttgart 1974-1995. Hier Bd. 3, 206-215 (Nr. 530f.).

[12] MÁRKUS: Corpus Iuris, 462-465. – LAMPE, Friedrich Adolf/DEBRECENI EMBER, Pál: Historia Ecclesiae Reformatae in Hungaria. Utrecht 1728, 540-545. – RIBINI, Johannes: Memorabilia Augustanae confessionis in regno Hungariae a Leopoldo M. usque ad Carolum VI. Posonii 1789, 179f und 185f. – LADÁNYI, Sándor: Kétszázötvenéves a Pesti Vallásügyi Vegyesbizottság [Der Pester gemischten Religionskommission 250. Jubiläum]. In: Református Egyház 23 (1971), 200-204. – Die Akten der Kommission sind vorhanden: Országos Széchényi Könyvtár (Széchényi Nationalbibliothek) Budapest, Handschriftenabteilung (im folgenden: OSzK), Fol. Lat. 797 (Originale) und Fol. Lat. 713; 774; 793; 442.

[13] LAMPE/DEBRECENI EMBER: Historia, 547f und 550. – CSEPREGI: Magyar pietizmus, 228 (Nr. 85).

[14] Das Schreiben ist datiert in Warschad, den 6. März 1726. Abgedruckt bei LOTZ, Friedrich: Johann Karl Reichard (1700-1753). Der erste Banater evangelische Pfarrer nach der Türkenzeit. Ein Lebens- und Kulturbild aus der Frühzeit der Südostdeutschen. In: Südostforschungen 22 (1963), 326-346, hier 344f.

Im vorliegenden Beitrag versuche ich diesen durch Schmidts Materialiensammlungen und Kéris Korrekturen geprägten Forschungstand um einige Details zu ergänzen, die aus der Korrespondenz der betroffenen ersten evangelischen Pastoren in der Tolnau/Tolna und der Branau/Baranya stammen.

Im Jahre 1718 waren bereits zwei lutherische Prediger in der neu zu besiedelnden Tolnau tätig: ein Ungar, György Bárány von Szenice,[15] und ein Deutscher aus Kremnitz (Körmöcbánya, Kremnica SK), Jeremias Schwartzwalder (1684-1731).[16] Zwei Hallenser, könnte man sagen, denn Báránys Beziehungen zur Universität Halle sind allgemein bekannt und auch der Name von Schwartzwalder ist in der Matrikel der Academia Hallensis auffindbar.[17] Es ist bemerkenswert, dass beide Prediger sowohl in ungarischen als auch in deutschen Gemeinden dienten. Briefe pastoraler Natur wurden vom hallensischen Professor und Waisenvater August Hermann Francke (1663-1727) sowohl an Bárány als auch an Schwartzwalder geschrieben.[18]
Nach den Schuljahren in Raab (Győr H), Preßburg (Pozsony, Bratislava SK) und Eperies (Prešov SK) hatte Bárány also in Jena und Halle studiert. In Ungarn wurde er 1714 Prediger der Gemeinde zu Nagyvázsony, vertauschte aber diese gute Stelle mit dem Pfarramt der erst noch zu formenden Missionsgemeinden. Einer der erwähnten Pastoralbriefe Franckes hat nämlich positive Anregungen enthalten, indem er auch über die indische Missionsarbeit und die Kriegsgefangenenseelsorge in Sibirien berichtete. Bárány dürfte sich daran ein Beispiel genommen haben, als er seine ruhige Pfarrstelle in Nagyvázsony verließ und zunächst in den Türkenkrieg aufbrach, um die Beichte eines Verwundeten zu hören, sich dann aber von einigen Bauern nach Jink (Gyönk H) rufen ließ und sich endgültig in der von den Türken verwüsteten Gegend niederließ, welche bis in die Gegenwart „Schwäbische Türkei" genannt wird.
Was Bárány, der erste Senior der Südtransdanubischen Lutheraner, hier in 40 Jahren im Zeichen des „praktischen Christentums" trotz des großen Elends und der gegenreformatorischen Maßnahmen aufgebaut hat, sucht seinesgleichen. Bárány organisierte 1720 zunächst sieben Gemeinden in einem Seniorat. 1725 waren es bereits zehn Gemeinden. Auf den Ruinen der zerstörten Dörfer wurden binnen zwei Jahrzehnten 19 deutsche, ungarische und slowakische lutherische Kirchengemeinden gegründet. Die Aufbauarbeit geschah in dem durch den Pietismus propagierten wahren seelsorgeri-

[15] SCHMIDT: Szenicei Bárány; CSEPREGI, Zoltán: György Bárány von Szenicze (1682-1757) und sein Bibelwerk. In: Lutherische Kirche in der Welt 41 (1994), 129-135.
[16] In der weiteren Umgebung gab es noch zwei lutherische Slowaken, nämlich Ján Krmann und Peter Velits. CSEPREGI, Zoltán: Magyar pietizmus 1700-1756. Tanulmány és forrásgyűjtemény a dunántúli pietizmus történetéhez. [Ungarischer Pietismus. Untersuchung und Quellensammlung zur Geschichte des Pietismus in Transdanubien]. Adattár XVI-XVIII. századi szellemi mozgalmaink történetéhez 36. Budapest 2000, 227f. (Nr. 85).
[17] „Schwartzwalder, Jeremias Hungarico-Montano-Cremnicensis 22. 10. 1707. Theol. 16 ggr.". Matrikel der Martin-Luther-Universität Halle Wittenberg. 1690-1730. Hg. v. Fritz JUNTKE. Halle 1960, 412. – Hier publizierte er auch ein deutsches Trauergedicht: Amicorum Lacrymae. Halle: Orbán, 1708. RMK III. 4637.
[18] CSEPREGI: Magyar pietizmus, 129-132 und 143f. (Nr. 32 und 38).

schen Geiste, wie er aus den Schriften und Briefen Báránys und Schwartzwalders zu vernehmen ist.
Das Seniorat Tolnau-Branau-Schomodei/Somogy war, wie bereits angedeutet, sprachlich gemischt. Bárány war Ungar, ihm stand aber ein deutscher Konsenior, Michael Weiß (?-1769), der Prediger der deutschen Gemeinde zu Kleinmangarth (Kismányok H), zur Seite.[19] Nach Báránys Tod übernahm der Konsenior Michael Weiß das Seniorenamt. Auch diese Lösung des Nationalitätenproblems in der Kirchenverwaltung, die zugleich auch das Sprachproblem löste, blieb längere Zeit vorbildlich. Bárány installierte nicht nur Prediger und Lehrer, sondern hat auch, da es weit und breit keinen Superintendenten gab, ordiniert. Die Lehrer ernannte er zu „Lizenziaten" (Lektoren) und gab ihnen das Recht, einzelne kirchliche Funktionen auszuüben.[20] Bárány sorgte auch für geistige Hilfe. Er versorgte nicht nur sein Seniorat, sondern das ganze ungarische Luthertum mit guten Büchern (meistens Übersetzungen) für Kirche und Schule. Katechismen, pädagogische Handreichungen zur Katechese, Gebets- und Gesangsbücher, Neutestamenten durften nicht fehlen.[21]

2

Im Jahre 1722 wurde der Fall von zwei akatholischen Predigern auf der Komitatsversammlung erörtert. Die Amtsleute beschließen, sie zu verhaften und dem bischöflichen Stuhl auszuliefern, und wenn es sich um ein kriminelles handelte, auch eine weltliche Strafe über sie zu verhängen. Der reformierte János Mocsay (?-1737) und der Lutheraner Jeremias Schwartzwalder wurden wegen Blasphemie angezeigt. Beide gerieten bald ins Gefängnis und wurden später des Komitats verwiesen.[22]

Zu Schwartzwalders Person muss soviel Biographisches erwähnt werden, dass er (wie gesagt) aus Kremnitz stammte, in Halle studierte, mit August Hermann Franckes Empfehlungsschreiben nach Schlesien zu Johann Christoph Schwedler (1672-1730), dem frommen Prediger in Niederwiesa,[23] kam, aber die Sehnsucht, seine eigene Landsleute zu bekehren, trieb ihn wieder nach Ungarn in die neu zu besiedelnde Wüste. Schon 1718 hielt er sich in Warschad auf, zu seiner Ordination durch den Superintendenten Daniel Krmann (1663-1740) kam es erst 1720,[24] nach dem Tod

---

[19] Seine Briefe: CSEPREGI: Magyar pietizmus, Nr. 63, 67, 70, 77, 83, 84 und 86. – Sein Album amicorum: OSzK, Oct. Lat. 131.
[20] PAYR: Egyháztörténeti emlékek, 355-358.
[21] CSEPREGI, Zoltán: Pietismus in Ungarn 1700-1758. In: Beiträge zur ostdeutschen Kirchengeschichte 6 (2004), 25-38.
[22] SZITA: Lutheránus németség, 24f und 133f. Zitate aus dem Komitatsprotokoll.
[23] PAASCH, Ernst-Walther: Über den Pietisten Johann Christoph Schwedler. Aus den Kirchenbüchern von Greiffenberg und Nieder Wiesa. In: Jahrbuch für Schlesische Kirchengeschichte 76/77 (1997/98), 227-241. Schwartzwalders Briefe aus Schlesien an Francke: Archiv der Franckeschen Stiftungen Hauptabteilung (AFrSt/H), C 562:1-2.
[24] Evangélikus Országos Levéltár [Evangelisch-Lutherisches Zentralarchiv], Budapest. (fortan: EOL). G III, 44 (43): „Jeremias Schwarzvald n[atus] Cremnicii 1684 patre Mich. matre Sus. Kühlmanniana Varsadinum

des jüngeren Krmanns, Ján, Pastor in Keszi (1669-1720).[25] Schwartzwalder dürfte also einige Jahre hindurch als Lehrer in Warschad gewirkt haben, wovon er schon als Prediger seinem Professor in Halle 1721 so berichtete:

„Ich bin nunmehro in das schwehre wichtige ampt kommen und zwar in einem neuerbauten dorff oder wüsten, welches vorzeiten auch zwar gebaut gewesen, aber durch den türcken und andere völcker verwüstet worden und bis dato wüste gelegen ist. Dergleichen dörffer hieherumb es noch mehr giebt, welche so wohl von päpstischen als evangelischen und reformierten oder calviner bewohnt und gebaut werden, und zwar von leuten unterschiedlicher sprache als deutschen, böhmischen und ungarn, in diesen dreyen sprachen, ungrisch, böhmisch und deutsch, muss ich auch mein ampt verrichten. Allhier in der pusta: Warschad deutsche leute sind aus dem reich herab gezogen, und zwar was evangelisch-lutherische aus dem Heßischen Darmstädtischen, [...] Die gemeinen sind groß, aber arm am gelde, nichts ist hier zu bekommen, von den städten wohnen wir gar weit und ist hier nichts als eine wüsteney. Darumb bitte ich im nahmen meiner armen gemeinden, Varsad, Majusch, Kisch Mányok dergleichen a.m., Sie wollen doch die liebe und barmhertzigkeit erweisen und etliche von besagten büchern, Catech[ismen], N[euen] T[estamenten] oder gesangbüchern schencken, damit wir unverhindert den gottesdienst fortsetzen können. [...] Mein einkommen ist fast nichts und lebe nur so von einem tag zum andern, maßen meine pfarrkinder das gantze jahr von der summa gelebt haben und nun alles weg ist, dass man also nur von dem jetzt bereitten segen der ernte leben und denselben kaum erwarten kan."[26]

Der Fall Mocsay[27] könnte als gewöhnlich betrachtet werden. Regelmäßig erschienen in den evangelischen Pfarrhäusern die römischen Visitatoren, die vor allem zu prüfen hatten, ob die evangelischen Geistlichen die richtigen Kenntnisse über die Taufe besaßen. Daher versuchten sie die Prediger durch die bizarrsten Fragen zum Taufsakrament in Verlegenheit zu bringen, um dann gegen sie vorgehen zu können. Im Visitationsprotokoll des Fünfkirchener (Pécs H) Bischofsvikars lässt sich nachlesen, dass der reformierte Prediger von Nagydorog den katholischen Visitator, den Kanoniker Imre Bohuss, nicht ins Bethaus einlassen wollte, weil er das gesetzlich gewährte Visitationsrecht der geistlichen (römischen) Obrigkeit – mit Berufung auf seinen reformierten Superintendenten János Pathai in Kecskemét – nicht anerkannte. Nach diesem Vorspiel erfolgte ein strenges Examen über das Taufsakrament, wo er – laut Akten – gesagt haben soll, die Absicht des Geistlichen sei dazu nicht unentbehrlich, und wenn sie fehle, schade das nichts dem Getauften. Außerdem soll er

---

ad m[iniste]rium voc. et ord. 1720 circa fest. Michaelis." EBD. AGE, I d 9,34,5,43 mit dieser Ergänzung: „p[astor] Varsadiensis apud Germanos novos incolas".

[25] SCHMIDT-TOMKA: Beiträge, 10-12. – EOL Canonica visitatio Nagyszokoly: „...."...in anno autem immediate subsequenti 1718. soli Lutherani conduxissent praedicantium condam Joannem German, quidam munia per triennium hic exercuisse obiit, in cujus locum successit quidam Jeremias nuncupatus, amoto ipso, successit Andreas Járfás...".

[26] Warschad, den 17. September 1721. CSEPREGI: Magyar pietizmus, 140-143 (Nr. 37).

[27] Zu János Mocsay siehe FÖLDVÁRY, László: Adalékok a Dunamelléki Ev. Ref. Egyházkerület történetéhez [Beiträge zur Geschichte des reformierten Donaudistriktes]. Budapest 1898, Bd. I. 183 und Bd. II. 39, 51 und 78.

gepredigt haben, dass der Name Jesu nicht zu verehren ist, noch dazu, dass nicht alle Menschen erlöset worden sind.[28] Die wohlbegründete Anklage hieß daher Blasphemie.
In demselben Visitationsprotokoll liest man aber, dass derselbe Kanoniker einen Tag früher (1. März 1722) in der Nachbarschaft, nämlich in Jerking, auch den Prediger der Lutheraner, den bereits erwähnten Bárány, besuchte. Er besichtigte das Pfarrhaus bis auf das Schlafgemach und lobte den gebildeten und angesehenen Geistlichen, ohne irgendeinen Einwand hinzufügen.[29] Aus diesem Vergleich stellt sich heraus, dass die einzige Schuld Mocsays darin bestanden haben kann, reformiert zu sein und gegen die bischöfliche Jurisdiktion protestiert zu haben. Nach seiner Ausweisung kehrte der reformierte Pastor zwar heimlich in die Tolnau zurück, wurde aber dann vom eigenen Grundherrn endgültig verjagt.
Diese kanonischen Visitationen waren durch die erwähnten Tätigkeiten der gemischten Pester Religionskommission motiviert. Solange nämlich diese Kommission tagte, sollten am religiösen Status Quo keine Änderungen vorgenommen werden. Der Bischof von Fünfkirchen, Graf Wilhelm Franz Bertram von Nesselrode, versuchte, durch die Ausübung seines auch über die Protestanten geltenden Visitationsrechtes den Beschlüssen der Kommission vorzubeugen und rechtzeitig klare Verhältnisse zu schaffen.[30]
Der Fall Schwartzwalder ist jedoch nicht so klar gewesen. In den Visitationsakten ist zu ihm nichts bemerkt, weil er zur Zeit des Besuches in seiner Gemeinde seit Wo-

[28] Recensio Universi Cleri Dioecesis Quinque-Ecclesiensis, distincte a tempore amotae cum exitu seculi 17-mi tyrannidis turcicae, restitutaeque in his partibus tranquillitatis, adjectis quibusdam aetatem hanc antecedentibus, commentariis historicis illustrata per Josephum BRÜSZTLE. Bde. 1-4. Pécs, 1874-1880, hier Bd. 3, 186: „Die 2. Martii eiusd. an. visitata est parochia conf. helv. in possessione Dorogh, (puta Nagy-Dorogh) ante annos 10. impopulata [...] Visitatio admissa est cum restrictione administratoris, respectu exemtione a jurisdictione eppali ordinarii Quinqueecclesiensis, siquidem palam et publice idem praedicans effutivisset: quod nullatenus eppo Quinqueecclesiensi, sed suo praetenso Patajo eppo subjaceret; unde per consequens contra mandatum suae Mattis excepit. His tamen non consideratis visitata est primo ipsa synagoga recenter in anno 1720. intra spatium 13. hebdomadum erecta, sarta tecta bene scandulis, et picto laqueari affebre tabulato ornata; cujus fundamenta lateritia et lapidea ex antiquae ecclesiae catholicae erutis materialibus genuum tenus jacta sunt. – Hanc administrat a mensibus undecim Joannes Mocsay, annor. 32. novitate hereticorum dogmatum tumens, in Deum et orthodoxos blasphemans; studiosus (ut asserit) intra hoc regnum Enyédiensis, Debreczinensis, Patakensis; extra autem regnum Genevensis, Bernensis, Basiliensis, qui in his partibus studiorum ergo, imputato itinere, duobus annis divagatus est. Examinatus de baptismo respectu intentionis asseruit: nullatenus in ministro esse necessariam, et si desit, nihil nocere baptisato. Hic vir communi fama teste textum S. Pauli »In nomine Jesu« juxta innatam pervicaciae suae arrogantiam pro concione, non sine rudis plebis scandalo, sinistre interpretatus asseruit: hoc SS. Nomen non esse venerandum; ita consimiliter: non omnes a Christo redemtos esse; etc.".
[29] BRÜSZTLE: Recensio 3, 185f: „Anno 1722. 1. Mart. visitata est per Emericum Bohuss canonicum parochia confession. augustanae in possessione Györköny [...] Et primo quidem ipsa domus dni praedicantii, in qua preces solitae ac conciones peraguntur; quae in se continet cubiculum mediocriter honestum, cameram versus occidentem, seu museum etc. [...] Hanc administrat ab anno 1718. (hoc enim anno hic locus impopulari coepit) providus ac circumspectus vir Georgius Bárány, annor. 49. studiosus civitatis Hala in Saxonia. Confessionis augustan. animae sunt 197. Catholici confessionis capaces 35. Calvinistae 13.".
[30] Vgl. BRÜSZTLE: Recensio 1-4. –A váci püspöki egyházlátogatási jegyzőkönyvek protestáns vonatkozású bejegyzései a l8. században [Einträge bezüglich der Protestanten in den Kirchenvisitationsprotokollen des Bistums Waitzen]. Hg. v. Béla HOLL. Budapest 2004.

chen eingekerkert war.[31] Er wurde auch der Blasphemie angeklagt und von der weltlichen Behörde zum Exil verurteilt, während seine Gemeinde mit einer Geldstrafe belegt wurde. Von wem aber und warum Schwartzwalder angezeigt worden ist, verschweigen die Akten. Der Amtsbruder Bárány weiß von seinen zwei Vergehen: er habe erstens das Abendmahl reformierten Christen mit gesäuertem Brot ausgeteilt und zweitens ein mit Wasser aber ohne Anwendung der Taufformel getauftes Kind wiedergetauft (schon wieder das Taufproblem!).[32]

Schwartzwalders Schuld lässt sich anhand eines weiteren an Francke gerichteten Briefes erhellen. Er wurde nicht nur seitens des Domkapitels in Fünfkirchen oder der Komitatsbeamten angegriffen, sondern auch von seinem eigenen Amtskollegen, dem ebenfalls Hallenser Friedrich Samuel Bertram,[33] verketzert:

„Ich bin von etlichen teutschen francken, die aus dem reich in Ungarn gezogen, ad pastoratum beruffen worden. Nach dem ich nun das amt angetreten, habe ichs mit aller treue verwaltet und ihnen Gottes wort geprediget. Weilen sich aber auch etliche reformirte allda eingefunden unter ihnen, als welche mich ansprachen und baten, ich solte ihnen das heilige abendmahl auch reichen, aber NB nach ihrer arten, sagten sie, i.e. sies meineten pane fermentato [mit gesäuertem Brot], da ich denn bedencken trug, hierinnen zu willfahren, doch weil ich in meiner jugend Dieterici Catecheticam[34] gelernet, allwo in einer quaestione de sacra coena stehet responsio: nihil interest sive sit panis NB fermentatus triticeus sive siligineus [es ist gleich, ob der Brot aus Weizen, Roggen oder mit Sauerteig gemacht wird] etc.[35] Also war es mir nur zu thun, umb

[31] BRÜSZTLE: Recensio 4, 471-473.

[32] CSEPREGI: Magyar pietizmus, 228 (Nr. 85): „Fata denique ecclesiae Varsadiensis, utpote: primus pastor fam. Ieremias Schwarzwalder Cremnitziensis, satis religiosus, industrius, satis infelix. Primum, quod reformatos pane domestico ad postulatum eorum communicavit hac imprudentia, quod id publice fecerit una cum evangelicis, quibus hostias altero orbiculo consecravit, non sine offensione infirmorum. Accedit, quod ante ingressum Bertrami omnes Germanicas ecclesias percurrens alicubi offerunt infantem ad baptismum, quem catholicus plebanus iam ante aqua quidem baptismale adsperserit, sed quod librum ritualem non secum haberet, verba usitata adhibere non potuit, ideo mulierculis praecepit, ut mater e puerperio liberata infantem secum accipiat, ac melius baptisabit. Hinc rustici dubitantes infantem recte baptisatum esse, huic forte divertenti afferunt, quod ubi innotescit, capiunt pastorem et Quinque Ecclesiis in aresto detinent, reversalibus acceptis et 50 plagis inflictis dimittunt."

[33] Bertram stammte aus Kalbe/Saale, wurde immatrikuliert in Halle 1712, ordiniert von Krmann für Majosch 1722, wo er seinen guten Ruf in einigen Monaten verlor, 1732-1747 war er Pastor in Geltow. EOL G III 44(48). – Bél Mátyás levelezése [Mathias Béls Briefwechsel]. Hg. v. László SZELESTEI N. Budapest 1993, Nr. 165 und 167. – CSEPREGI: Magyar pietizmus, 228 (Nr. 85): „N.B. Mira fata Maiosiensis ecclesiae cum primo pastore reverendo domino Bertram, qui collectis ad 70 fl. debitis mense Iunio discedit ex ecclesia in summa necessitate propter plurimos morbidos, imo et morientes, sub praetextu, quod velit ad me venire: ille aliam viam elegit. Venit Iaurinum, inde in Saxoniam. Mox post discessum pastoris cursitant alii pro pastore, alii pro pecunia mutuo concessa. Cum lamentationes audiri non possent, nec spes reditus esset, in fine mensis Augusti alius pastor substitit. Reverendus Bertram cum nova coniuge venit mense Novemb., sed redire cogitat".

[34] DIETERICUS, Cunradus: Institutiones catecheticae depromptae e B. Lutheri catechesi, et variis, recenter etiam B. Dn. Christiani Chemnitii notis in usum iuventutis scholasticae illustratae. Lipsiae 1722. (erste Auflage: Gießen 1613).

[35] EBD., 592f.: „De re s. coenae terrena I. Pane. 12. Cujus qualitatis et figurae panis ille erit? Si modo ex aqua et farina pistus est, nihil inter est, sive sit fermentatus, sive triticeus, sive siligineus, sive frumentarius alius, sive itidem rotundus, sive oblongus, sive quadratus, sive alia quacunque formula. / Non enim vel hujus generis panem Christus vetuit, vel illius praecepit. Ideoque omne hoc in Christiana libertate positum".

ihren glauben und meinung von dem hochwürdigen sacrament zu prüfen, ob sie das[selbe] statuiren, was wir [statuiren]. Was ihr esset im sacrament etc.? Da sie dann überall mit ja geantwortet und gesaget: wir glauben das, was ihr glaubet, und da ich sie dann weiter berichtete und catechisirte, auch alle falsche vernunffts schlüsse wiederlegte mit den worten der einsetzung und so weiter, so bald fuhr ich zu und gab ihnen und den unserigen lutheranern zugleich sub duplici pane fermentato et hostio [sowohl mit Brot als auch mit Oblat] das heilige abendmahl. Allein das papsthum, mit welchem unsere lutherische prediger, die meisten zum wenigsten, in Ungarn mit heucheln, und die, die allereifrigsten im christenthum seyn wollen, mich hierinnen verdammten, welches auch der in Mejusch gewesene zungendrescher und scurra, nahmens Bertram, der sich grosse scientiam einbildete, auch that, er war zwar pfarrherr an gedachtem ort, allein er hatte sich ärger aufgeführet, als ein anderer etc. Particularia will ich nicht viel erzehlen. Mit diesem papsthum, sage ich, heucheln anjetzo die meisten pfarrherren, absonderlich 2 in Preßburg. Dieses papsthum lies mich gleich gefangen nehmen als einen neuen ketzer und muste in Fünff-Kirchen 7 wochen im gefängnis liegen und 50 prügeln aushalten und dieses noch, wie das capitel allda vorwandte, aus sonderbahrer grosser gnade. Vitam perdidisti [du hast dein Leben verloren], sagte die pap[stliche] clerisey zu mir, und wolten mich zum verbrennen zum scheiterhauffen verurtheilen, allein da ich die 50 prügeln erlitten, wurde ich darzu ins exilium getrieben und befinde mich anjetzo in Preßburg."[36]

Schwartzwalder wurde ebenfalls aus dem Komitat ausgewiesen, kehrte aber bald zurück nach Majosch (Majos H) und Jink, um dann endgültig vertrieben zu werden. Blasphemie bedeutete in seinem Fall keine Rebellion gegen die Obrigkeit, auch keine rationalistische Sakramentslehre, wie es am Beispiel des reformierten Predigers Mocsay beobachtet werden konnte, sondern nur einen unbedachten Schritt in Richtung der anderen reformatorischen Konfession, das Überschreiten einer überkommenen Grenze. Die Praxis der Interkommunion war nämlich staatlich verboten, daher weder kirchenbehördlich gutgeheißen noch liturgisch geregelt. Sehr selten kam es vor, dass für lutherische Bauern der Dienst eines reformierten Predigers, für Reformierte aber eines lutherischen Geistlichen leichter erreichbar war als der Dienst des eigenen Geistlichen. Für diese Fälle entwickelte sich jedoch eine theologisch nicht legitimierte Praxis: Der lutherische Prediger spendete das Heilige Abendmahl dem reformierten Abendmahlsgast mit gewöhnlichem Brot, der reformierte Prediger dem lutherischen mit der Hostie. Dies waren Lösungen, die weder die Theologen noch die Kirchenleitungen, wohl aber die Bedürfnisse des Gemeindelebens schufen.

Es ist jedoch bemerkenswert, wie reformiertenfreundlich der Warschader Pastor die eindeutig altlutherische Aussage des Dietrichschen Katechismus interpretierte, um eine gelegentliche Altargemeinschaft verwirklichen zu können. Auch Francke hat diesen Fehltritt negativ beurteilt, indem er auf dem Rand des oben zitierten Schreibens bemerkte: „Wenn das negotium unionis allen so übel bekäme, würde es bald cessiren." Schwartzwalder dachte freilich an keine Form der Union, seine Tat barg jedoch

[36] Preßburg, den 14. September 1723. CSEPREGI: Magyar pietizmus, 148-150 (Nr. 42).

die Gefahr, die unionistischen Bestrebungen Christoph Matthäus Pfaffs einzubürgern, zumindest seine Amtsbrüder können einen solchen Verdacht geschöpft haben.
Die Zusammenarbeit der Protestanten in Ungarn war durch die Tätigkeit der erwähnten Pester Kommission bedingt. Trotz der dringenden Not sind die vorsichtigen Annäherungen beiderseitig von Misstrauen begleitet. Christoph Matthäus Pfaff (1686-1760), Professor in Tübingen, der damalige berühmte Vertreter der Idee einer evangelischen Union, korrespondierte in diesen Jahren mit Matthias Bél (1684-1749), der sich (wie auch Francke) die Kooperation nur auf der politischen Ebene vorstellen konnte,[37] Schwartzwalder wagte sich jedoch – obwohl aus einfachen praktischen Gründen – auf das Feld der Liturgik und Dogmatik! Keine Spur davon, dass Schwartzwalder die Pfaffsche Lehre kannte, geschweige favorisierte. In seinem Amt hatte er aber einen Tübinger Studenten als Nachfolger, den späteren Konsenior Michael Weiß, der mindestens eine Eintragung von Pfaff in seinem Album nach Ungarn brachte.[38] Insofern war also die unionistische Frage in Ungarn akut und aktuell, sowie der gegen Schwartzwalder gehegte Verdacht gegründet.
Diese ausführlich angeführten Beispiele verdeutlichen, in welchem Maße die evangelischen Gemeinden des ehemaligen türkischen Eroberungsgebietes der Gewalt und Willkür der örtlichen Behörden – weltlichen oder geistlichen Wesens – preisgegeben waren, falls ihr eigener Grundherr sie nicht zu beschützen wusste. Die Herrschaften der beiden ausgewiesenen Prediger waren Helvetischen Bekenntnisses, was damals Gunst ohne Kunst bedeutete. Sie konnten oder wagten nicht für die Religionsausübung ihrer Untertanen wirkungsvoll aufzutreten. Wenn der Gutsherr aber mächtig genug war, konnte er dem Klerus widerstehen und die ab und zu verjagten akatholischen Geistlichen in seine Güter zurückholen. Gerade auf den Gütern katholischer Herrschaften wie des Fürsten Esterházy, des Grafen Mercy oder des Freiherrn Harruckern entfaltete sich in der ehemaligen Türkei bald ein blühendes evangelisches Kirchenleben.

3

Karl III. bestürmte deutsche Territorialfürsten mit der Bitte, die Werbung von Kolonisten zu gestatten. Den Evangelischen wurde dabei Kultusfreiheit in Aussicht gestellt. Das Gebiet zwischen Donau, Theiß und Mieresch, das sog. Temescher Banat, wurde unter der unmittelbaren Verwaltung der Wiener Regierung seit 1722 neubesiedelt. Karl forderte deutsche Reichsfürsten auf, sie mögen ihre zur Auswanderung entschlossenen Untertanen „ohne Abforderung einiger Mauthzoll, Aufschlag oder derley Anlagen“[39] zu entlassen. Weil die Fürsten die Auswanderungslustigen mit gewisser Sorge vor den Gefahren gewarnt hatten, die ihrer Religionsfreiheit im neu-

[37] SZELESTEI N.: Bél Mátyás levelezése, Nr. 165, 167 und 214.
[38] Országos Széchényi Könyvtár [Széchényi Landesbibliothek]. (fortan: OSzK), Oct. Lat. 131:3.
[39] Karl VI. an den Landgrafen Ernst Ludwig von Hessen-Darmstadt am 20. April 1722. LOTZ: Reichard, 345f.

en Lande drohten, sicherte ein gedrucktes kaiserliches Patent den Lutheranern die freie Ausübung ihrer Religion zu:
„Gleichwie auch in einigen Kayserl. Confin. und Herrschaften die freye Religions=und Gewissens=Freyheit allerdings erlaubt ist, deme zu folg sollen die der Augspurgischen zugethane Hausleuth mit einem Prediger oder Seelsorger aus dem Reich, (welcher sich diesfalls beliebig anzumelden hätte) oder in Ober Hungarn bey dasigem Evangelischen Ministerio mittelst einer vergnüglichen besoldung versehen werden, worauf sich vestiglich zu verlassen ist."[40]
So kamen zu den vorher schon von den neuen Großgrundbesitzern privat angesiedelten Bauern Tausende neuer Kolonisten flussabwärts der Donau, vor allem in den Jahren 1723-1729, aber auch während des ganzen 18. Jahrhunderts hinzu.
Der französische General der Befreiungsarmee, Gouverneur in Temeschwar (Timişoara RO), dann in Esseg (Osijek HR), Graf Claudius Florimundus Mercy, der sich in den Türkenkriegen besonders hervortat, ließ auf die ihm geschenkten Ländereien Siedler aus Bayern, Frankreich, Spanien und Italien kommen. Mercy war katholisch, im Temescher Banat war er nicht nur Kolonisator, sondern auch Reorganisator seiner Kirche. Er fand da fünf Pfarreien vor und erhöhte ihre Zahl bis 1733 auf 39. Nebenbei sei bemerkt, dass er sich auch dadurch verdient machte, dass er in Temeschwar Textilmanufakturen schuf, in den Dörfern aber die Seidenraupenzucht und den Anbau von Reis einführte.[41]

Die fürs Banat bestimmten Ansiedler wurden aber eben von dem Grafen Mercy, bzw. seinem Großneffen und Erben, dem Grafen Anton Ignaz Karl August Mercy d'Argenteau, dezimiert (d'Argenteau vertritt ab 1722 seinen Großonkel in der wirtschaftlichen Administration der Besitzungen und wurde 1725 adoptiert). Nach einem Kaufbrief, ausgestellt am 24. April 1722 in Preßburg, kaufte Mercy an der Donau auf halbem Wege zwischen Wien und dem Banat eine Herrschaft.[42] Beim Ankauf bestand das Mercy-Gut in der Tolnau aus zehn bewohnten Ortschaften und einer Anzahl von unbewohnten Prädien (beim Verkauf 1773 hatte sich die Zahl der bewohnten Dörfer durch die Besiedlung einiger wüster Orte und durch den Kauf zweier weiterer Dörfer auf 23 erhöht). Dann ließ er unter den kaiserlichen Transporten die lutherischen Kolonisten aus dem Hessisch-Darmstädtischen für seine eigene Güter in der Tolnau anwerben, darunter auch geschlossene, disziplinierte Gemeinschaften mit Pastor und Lehrer. Die deutschen Bauern waren es meist zufrieden, zumal das Banat doch in gefährlicher Nähe zur Türkei lag.[43]
Ein Zugeständnis an seine lutherischen Untertanen in Kleinmangarth enthält das erste erhaltene diesbezügliche Schriftstück Mercys (7. Mai 1722). Der Grundherr ver-

[40] EOL AGE, I a 11, 17.
[41] RÖHRIG, Hans Walther: Die Geschichte der deutsch-evangelischen Gemeinden des Banats. Leipzig 1940. – TAFFERNER: Quellenbuch 2, 195f. – BAHLCKE, Joachim: Ungarischer Episkopat und österreichische Monarchie. Von einer Partnerschaft zur Konfrontation (1686-1790). Stuttgart 2005 (Forschungen zur Geschichte und Kultur des östlichen Mitteleuropa 23), 194-196.
[42] TAFFERNER: Quellenbuch 2, 176f.
[43] LOTZ: Reichard, 334. – KÉRI: Franken, 94f.

sprach, „denen drey christlichen Religionen all freyes exercitium zu gestatten“ und bot allen seinen Untertanen den Schutz ihrer Religionsfreiheit an, „so lang in diesem Königreich Hungarn einige dergleichen geduldet sind“.[44] In Abschriften sind uns zwei, annähernd gleichlautende Pfarrverträge erhalten, je einer für das katholische Hőgyész (15. Juli 1724) und das lutherische Kleinmangarth (28. September 1724). Es gibt Hinweise dafür, dass andere Gemeinden ähnliche Verträge erhielten, bzw. sich nach diesen richteten. „...kann bei meinem Salario, welches unsere Herrschaft selbst sowohl deren katholischer Geistliche als uns gemachet hat, wohl stehen“ – berichtete Reichard am 6. März 1726. Wahrscheinlich wurden alle diese von Grafen d'Argenteau veranlasst.[45]

Sehr ähnlich verfuhr der Grundherr Ferenc Kun (1692-1730) in der Grundherrschaft Bonnhard.[46] Die große Anzahl der deutsch-lutherischen Siedlungen in den Dörfern von Mercy und Kun ist dadurch zu erklären, dass beide Grundherren oder ihre Beauftragten erst nach 1720 aktiv wurden. Für die Gutsherren dieser Zeit ist eher eine religiöse Toleranz, mitbestimmt von einer rationalistisch-ökonomischen Denkweise, charakteristisch.

Wie gesagt, wurden die evangelischen Neusiedlerdörfer im Komitat Tolnau vom berühmten Pietisten György Bárány betreut. Bárány deutet in seiner bereits zitierten Senioratsgeschichte an, dass das Nebeneinander von verschiedenen Sprachen und Konfessionen an einigen Orten (wie Kölesd, Jink und Jerking) friedlich und freundlich sein konnte, während anderswo eher Neid und Streit herrschten. Bárány erwähnt ohne weitläufiges Erzählen zwei ursprünglich lutherische Gemeinden, die in den 1730-er Jahren von Reformierten besetzt und unterdrückt (*occupata, oppressa*) wurden: Großsäckel (Nagyszékely H) und Lápafő.[47] Ein ausführlicher Bericht davon ist einem ungarischen Brief des lutherischen Predigers in Lápafő, Ferenc Borbély (Tonsoris: 1702-1750), an den einflussreichen Mihály Ostffy (?-1752) zu entnehmen:

Vergangenen Jahres (1735) sei schon diesem mitgeteilt worden, welcher maßen die winzige lutherische Gemeinde zu Lápafő von Calvinisten bestürmt wird, um den lutherischen Kultus zu erhalten, hätte er sich hinauf nach Abtsdorf (Bátaapáti H), zum Grundherrn, dem Freiherrn László Babocsay begeben müssen. Obwohl er die Lutheraner nicht loswerden wollte, vielmehr sie aufforderte, im alten zu bleiben, hätten aber die Calviner das nicht gewollt, deshalb hätte diesen der Herr, zwar wider Willen, erlaubt, einen Prediger ihres Bekenntnisses am Tage Gregorii einzuführen. Mit diesem Erlaubnis hätten sie sich nicht zufrieden geben, sondern die Lutheraner

[44] LAGLER, Ludwig: Gedenkschrift zur hundertjährigen Gedächtnisfeier des Gotteshauses der evang. Gemeinde Kismányok. Bonyhád 1888, 7f. – KÉRI: Franken, 53-55.

[45] LOTZ: Reichard, 344. – GALAMBOS: Winkler, 368. – KÉRI, Henrik: A Mercy grófok szerződései Tolna megyei jobbágyaikkal. Az úrbérrendezés a hőgyészi uradalomban [Die Verträge der Grafen Mercy mit ihren Tolnauer Untertanen. Die Urbarialregelung in der Grundherrschaft Hőgyész]. In: Tanulmányok. Hg. v. Gyula DOBOS. Szekszárd 1999 (Tolna Megyei Levéltári Füzetek 7), 315-346. – KÉRI: Franken, 56-71.

[46] TAFFERNER: Quellenbuch 3, 136. – KÉRI, Henrik: A hidasi (bonyhádi) uradalom tulajdonosai 1660 és 1740 között. A birtok betelepülése a török kiűzése után [Die Eigentümer der Grundherrschaft Hidasch (Bonnhard) zwischen den Jahren 1660 und 1740. Die Besiedlung der Grundherrschaft nach dem Abzug der Türken]. In: Századok 134 (2000), 323-340. – KÉRI: Franken, 71-93.

[47] CSEPREGI: Magyar pietizmus, 228 (Nr. 85).

desto eifriger verdrängen wollen. Der Gutsherr hätte die viele Klagen und gegenseitigen Anschuldigungen nicht mehr anhören können, sondern an den Komitat weitergeleitet, damit wegen des gefällten Urteils nicht er selbst, sonder der Komitat gescholten würde. So erfuhren über den Streit auch der Komitat und das Domkapitel. Der Dompropst von Fünfkirchen hätte am 24. Mai 1736 auf der Komitatsversammlung dagegen protestiert, nach der Pester Kommission weitere akatholische Gemeindegründungen zu dulden, und sie durch den Stuhlrichter zu verhindern gewünscht. Die lutherische Gemeinde als vor der Kommission entstandene dürfe bleiben,[48] der reformierte Prediger aber als neu angestellter müsse vertrieben werden, was durch den Stuhlrichter auch geschah. Wozu die Calviner hätten gesagt, ohne ihren Prediger entweder die Ortschaft endgültig zu verlassen, oder gerechtigkeitshalber sollten beide Konfessionen ihre Prediger verlieren. Es werde noch der Grundherr herab erwartet, um diesen Streit unter den Protestanten persönlich zu schlichten.[49]
Wie in anderen Fällen,[50] trugen auch in Lápafő die Reformierten einen Sieg davon. Der Prediger Borbély musste schließlich noch in demselben Jahr aus Lápafő weichen und gelangte in die neue Siedlung Meknitsch (Mekényes H).

4

Obwohl die Grundherren die versprochene Kultusfreiheit ernst nahmen, konnten sie die Übergriffe der restaurationseifrigen ungarischen römisch-katholischen Bischöfe nicht immer verhindern. Die Kolonisten konnten sich nur auf das kaiserliche Patent berufen, wenn sie bedrängt wurden, das half ihnen aber manchmal wenig. Der Herrscher war zu weit, um angerufen werden zu können. Die Kleriker nahmen ihrerseits die Verordnung von Leopold I. (reg. 1657-1705) aus dem Jahre 1701 ernst, wonach in den von den Türken wiedereroberten Gebieten allein das römisch-katholische Bekenntnis frei war, und welche den akatholischen Kultus im mit Waffen befreiten Land kategorisch verboten hatte.[51] Die Bischöfe verfügten als Komitatsobergespane über bewaffnete Kräfte, konnten also den Predigern und Lehrern der evangelischen Siedlergemeinden manche trübe Stunde bereiten. In der Tolnau, wo der Bischof von Fünfkirchen das höchste weltliche Amt bekleidete, kam der toleranten Ansiedlungspolitik des einflussreichen Grafen Mercy eine entscheidende Bedeutung zu. In mehreren Ansiedlungsverträgen (z.B. in dem von Kleinmangarth vom 28. Mai 1728) findet sich der Punkt über die Religionsfreiheit: „Den Gottesdienst können sie [die

[48] In den Visitationsakten von 1733 liest sich das anders: „In filiali [ad Szakcs] Lápafő, ubi coloni sunt Slavi, [...] Lutherani oratorium cum ministro habent, quem amovere proxime praeteritis annis clerus nitebatur, cum longe post commissionem Pestiensem subintraverit, sed protectio domini terrestris Lib. Baronis Babócsay non permisit". BRÜSZTLE: Recensio 3, 894.
[49] Magyar Országos Levéltár [Ungarisches Landesarchiv] Budapest. P 533, 4:34:282. Datiert in Lápafő, den 4. Juni 1736.
[50] Im bereits zitierten Brief von Reichard (1726) ist zu lesen: „Die Calviner sind überaus stark in diesem Land, so daß sie auch mit Macht viel tun konnten, und lassen sich dahero wenig nehmen, wie auch ihrer angeborener Hartnäckigkeit bekannt ist". LOTZ: Reichard, 344.
[51] OSzK, Fol. Lat. 2952:1-2. „Copia rescripti Leopoldini." Viennae, 9. Apr. 1701.

Untertanen] vermög ihrer Religion exerciren, bey welcher sie auch allezeit von hoher Herrschaft, soviel möglich seyn kann, wird [!] geschützet werden."[52]
Auf den herrschaftlichen Schutz des katholischen Grafen konnten die evangelischen Kolonisten in der Bedrängnis ihrer Religion rechnen. Als der Bischof von Fünfkirchen gegen ihn klagte, zu viele Protestanten in seine Diözese angeworben zu haben, musste Mercy zum königlichen Verhör, er konnte sich jedoch verteidigen: seine Majestät selbst hätte jene akatholischen Bauern in das Banat angeworben, die jetzt seine Güter besetzt hatten. Nach Kéris Forschungen klang die Verteidigung etwas anders (jedoch mit gleicher Wirkung): der Gutsherr behauptete sein Vorhaben, in seinen Besitzungen den katholischen Glauben zu stärken, die Evangelischen aber waren vor der Übernahme der Herrschaft, also auch vor der Pester Kommission da ansässig.[53]
All das konnte aber den Senior Bárány kurz danach nicht davor bewahren, in Anklage, Verurteilung und Verbannung durch das dem Fünfkirchener Bischof, Wilhelm Franz Bertram von Nesselrode, unterstehende Komitatsgericht (1725) zu geraten.[54] Drei Jahre lebte Bárány in Dörgicse am Plattensee im Exil, erst 1729 durfte er seine Ämter wieder übernehmen.[55]
Auch das Vertrauen in das königliche Änderungsverbot (für die Gemeinden, die bereits vor der ersten Sitzung der Kommission zustande kamen) erwies sich nach dem Erscheinen der ersten *Carolina Resolutio*[56] am 21. März 1731 als eine arge Täuschung. Karl erneuerte nämlich die Gesetzesartikel XXV und XXVI aus dem Jahre 1681, den Artikel XXI vom Jahre 1687, die *Explanatio Leopoldina* von 1691,[57] also alle für die Protestanten nachteiligen Bestimmungen der Ära der Gegenreformation und erlaubte den Evangelischen im Allgemeinen nur den privaten Kult. Der öffentliche Kult wurde nur in den sog. artikularen Orten zugelassen. Die Resolution, die jetzt strengstens durchgeführt wurde, bedeutete die Aufhebung des evangelischen Kultus auch in solchen nicht artikularen Orten, wo dies bisher noch nicht erfolgt war. Im Bericht des schwedischen Gesandtschaftsprediger in Wien, Johann Christian Lerche (1691-1768) liest man: „In den neuen colonien hat man einen feinen prediger, herrn Barany, weil er den gottesdienst so gleich nicht eingestellet, in die eisen geschlagen und fortgeführet."[58]
Selbst die Neusiedler also, denen die Toleranz ausdrücklich versprochen wurde, blieben von der Verfolgung in den befreiten Gebieten nicht verschont. Dort, wo kein weltlicher Patron ihnen zu Hilfe kam, waren sie den rekatholisierenden Bischöfen

---

[52] LAGLER: Gedenkschrift, 10. – KÉRI: Franken, 66 und 68.
[53] KÉRI: Franken, 260, 34f und 45-49.
[54] GEISSLER, Bruno/STÖKL, Günther: In oriente crux. Versuch einer Geschichte der reformatorischen Kirchen im Raum zwischen der Ostsee und dem Schwarzen Meer. Hg. v. Herbert KRIMM. Stuttgart 1963, 317.
[55] CSEPREGI: Magyar pietizmus, 161f und 229 (Nr. 51 und 85).
[56] RIBINI: Memorabilia, 249-253. – KUZMÁNY, Karl: Urkundenbuch zum österreichischen evangelischen Kirchenrecht. Wien 1856, 133-135.
[57] MÁRKUS: Corpus Iuris, 284-287 und 348-351. – [Pál Okolicsányi:] Historia diplomatica de statu religionis evangelicae in Hungaria in tres periodos distincta. Brevissimum compendium Principatus Transylvanici historiae ab anno MDXXVI. usque ad annum MDCCIII. cum variis documentis et diplomatibus. Frankfurt/Main 1710, App. 135f . – RIBINI: Memorabilia, 54-57 und 74f. – KUZMÁNY: Urkundenbuch, 127-129.
[58] Wien, den 9. Juni 1731. CSEPREGI: Magyar pietizmus, 173 (Nr. 57).

wie Nesselrode, Michael Friedrich von Althan in Waitzen (Vác H, 1680-1734), Márton Padányi Biró (1693-1762) in Wesprim (Veszprém H)[59] noch hilfloser ausgesetzt als im alten Königreich, wo die Protestanten sich auf die Hilfe ihrer adeligen Glaubensgenossen stützen konnten.

[59] BAHLCKE: Ungarischer Episkopat, 143-147, 209-213 und 225-242.

Peter Šoltes

„Разлив русской реки". Migrationen und Konfessionen im nordöstlichen Ungarn im 17. und 18. Jahrhundert

Eine der Auswirkungen der bedrückenden sozialen und wirtschaftlichen Verhältnisse im 17. und 18. Jahrhundert war die Instabilität der Bevölkerungsstruktur im nordöstlichen Ungarn. Die Flucht der untertänigen Bauern oder ganzer Familien und der spontane bzw. von den Landesherren organisierte Umzug der Untertanen waren vor allem während der Ständeaufstände charakteristisch und prägnant für die demographische Entwicklung. Die meisten Handels- und Handwerkszentren schrumpften zu kleinen Ortschaften zusammen und eine beträchtliche Anzahl von Dörfern wurde vollkommen entvölkert.[1] Die verheerenden demographischen Folgen während des Kuruzzenaufstandes von Franz II. Rákóczi (1703-1711) wurden in den Jahren 1709 – 1711 von einer zusätzlichen Pestepidemie begleitet. Die übrig gebliebene Bevölkerung, die mehrere Jahrzehnte des wirtschaftlichen Elends und sozialen Niedergangs überwunden hatte, wurde nach der Niederlage der Aufständischen mit neuen Steuern, mit der Einquartierung des Militärs und der Lebensmittelrequirierung belastet. Dies führte zu einer zunehmenden Verschuldung, zur gewaltsamen Steuereintreibung mithilfe des Militärs und zur Vertiefung der wirtschaftlichen Stagnation. Viele Bauern sahen in dieser Situation die einzige Lösung in der Aussiedlung.

Zudem entvölkerte sich infolge der von den Gutsherren organisierten Umsiedlungen eine große Anzahl von Ortschaften. Es handelte sich dabei um Migrationen aus den relativ dicht bevölkerten Dörfern in den nördlichen Teilen der Komitate Zips, Sáros, Zemplin und Ungwar, sowie aus den benachbarten Gebieten von Galizien und der Karpato-Ukraine. Meist waren es Umsiedlungen innerhalb der Güter eines Gutsherrn, zum Vorteil beider Parteien: Die Umsiedler hatten nun genügend Land unter besseren klimatischen und landwirtschaftlichen Bedingungen zur Verfügung, öfter fanden sie sogar leere Landgüter vor. Für die Gutsherren bedeutete zwar jedes einzelne verwaiste Dorf einen ökonomischen Verlust, doch gab es einen großen Unterschied zwischen den Einkünften aus den gebirgigen Landgütern im Norden und denen auf dem Flachland im Süden, wo die Ernteerträge um das Vielfache größer waren.[2]

---

[1] ACSÁDY, Ignác: Magyarország Budavár visszafoglalása korában [Ungarn im Zeitalter der Zurückeroberung Ofens]. Budapest 1886, 25. – SIRÁCKY, Ján: Sťahovanie poddaných z východného Slovenska v 18. a v prvej polovici 19. storočia [Umsiedlung der Untertanen aus der Ostslowakei im 18. Jahrhundert und in der ersten Hälfte des 19. Jahrhunderts]. In: Príspevky k dejinám východného Slovenska [Beiträge zur Geschichte der östlichen Slowakei]. Bratislava 1964, 130-134.

[2] HORVÁTH, Pavol: Poddaný ľud na Slovensku v prvej polovici 18. storočia [Untertanen in der Slowakei in der ersten Hälfte des 18. Jahrhunderts]. Bratislava 1963, 227f.

Das größte Problem beim Wiederaufbau der Komitate nach dem Sathmarer Frieden 1711 war für die meisten Gutsherrschaften der Mangel an Untertanen. Nach den Angaben der Landeskonskriptionen von 1715 und 1720 waren mehr als zwei Drittel der Bauernhöfe im Zempliner Komitat verwaist.[3] In einem ähnlichen Zustand befanden sich die Siedlungen im Ungwarer Komitat.[4] Weniger große Verluste verzeichneten dank ihrer geographischen Lage die Komitate Sáros und die Zips.[5] Den größten Bevölkerungsrückgang gab es in den Städten und den Marktflecken, in den Dörfern des Tieflandes und in der Nähe von Landstrassen. Diese Asymmetrie zwischen dem relativ übervölkerten Norden und dem bevölkerungsarmen Süden hatte im nordöstlichen Ungarn eine große Immigrationswelle zur Folge.

Vor dieser Massenmigration war die Region des nordöstlichen Ungarn horizontal in drei relativ geschlossene Gebiete mit unterschiedlichen ethnischen und konfessionellen Gegebenheiten geteilt. Im Norden bildeten die griechisch-katholischen Ruthenen die absolute Mehrheit der Bevölkerung. Weiter südlich erstreckte sich ein überwiegend mit Slowaken bewohntes Gebiet, das sich konfessionell aufgliederte in römisch-katholische und evangelisch-lutherische Pfarreien sowie aus etwa 20 kalvinistisch-reformierten Pfarreien im Zempliner und im Ungwarer Komitat bestand. Nach einem breiten Streifen gemischt slowakisch-ungarischer Ortschaften änderte sich die ethnische und konfessionelle Zusammensetzung zugunsten der ungarischen und kalvinistisch-reformierten Mehrheit.[6] Die nördliche Grenze des Protestantismus deckte sich in Oberungarn mit der ethnischen slowakisch-ruthenischen Grenze.[7] Die wenigen Belege über die Reformierung von Teilen der ruthenischen Bevölkerung entstammten allesamt dem Zipser Raum.[8] Weiter südlich, nach einem breiten Streifen

[3] BOROVSZKY, Samu: Zemplén vármegye. Magyarország vármegyéi és városai [Zempliner Komitat. Ungarns Komitate und Städte]. Budapest 1905, 43. – ADAM, Ján: Smery útekov poddaných z humenského panstva v 1. polovici 18. storočia [Fluchtbewegungen der Untertanen aus der Herrschaft Homenau in der ersten Hälfte des 18. Jahrhunderts]. In: Obyvateľstvo Karpatskej kotliny [Die Bevölkerung des Karpatenbeckens]. Hg. v. Peter KÓNYA und René MATLOVIČ. Prešov 1997, 22-36.

[4] Im Ungwarer Komitat waren zu dieser Zeit ein Viertel der Ortschaften vollkommen entvölkert, sonst wurden meist zwei bis zehn Bauernhöfe gezählt. Vgl. GABRIEL, František: Pohyb obyvatelstva v bývalé užské župě v první polovině 18. století [Bewegungen der Bevölkerung im ehemaligen Ungwarer Komitat in der ersten Hälfte des 18. Jahrhunderts]. In: Науковый Зборник Товариства Просвита 11 (1936), 1-44, hier 20.

[5] Zur Entvölkerung siehe Sirácky: Sťahovanie poddaných, 51f.

[6] PETROV, Alexej: Národopisná mapa Uher podle úředního lexikonu osad z roku 1773 [Ethnographische Karte Ungarns nach dem amtlichen Lexikon der Orte aus dem Jahre 1773]. Praha 1924, 16f. – ТОМАШИВСКИЙ, Степан: Етнографiчна карта Угорської Руси [Ethnographische Karte von „Ugorska Rus“]. Москва 1910, 44.

[7] Magyar Országos Levéltár [Ungarisches Landesarchiv] Budapest. (fortan MOL). Urbaria et Conscriptiones, Fasc. 31, Nr. 15. – Auch in der Visitation des Munkatscher Bischofs Michal Olšavsky aus der ersten Hälfte des 18. Jahrhunderts gibt es darüber Auskünfte. Vgl. ŠOLTÉS, Peter: Odkedy sú gréckokatolíci na strednom a južnom Zemplíne? [Seit wann gibt es die Griechisch-Katholischen im mittleren und südlichen Zemplin?]. In: Verba Theologica 3 (2004), 12-22, hier 19.

[8] So konvertierten einige orthodoxe Gemeinden der kalvinischen Familie Máriássy zur Konfession ihres Gutsherrn, doch während der Gegenreformation wurden sie griechisch-katholisch. Belege darüber sind in der Visitation des Zipser Propstes aus dem Jahre 1700. „DD. Terrestres sunt Nobiles Máriasy Calvinistae, qui per vim suos subditos multos fecerunt Calvinistas“. HRADSZKY, Josephus: Additamenta ad Initia progressus ac praesens status Capituli Scepusiensis. Szepesváralja 1903/1904, 259. – Mehrere Belege über die Verbreitung des Protestantismus unter den Zipser Griechisch-Katholiken enthält auch die erste griechisch-

der slowakisch-ungarischen Grenzregion, lag das ethnisch ungarische und konfessionell kalvinistisch-reformierte Theißgebiet.[9]

Seit dem Ende des 17. Jahrhunderts erstreckte sich das Terrain der ruthenischen Neusiedlungen immer weiter Richtung Süden. Der Rückgang der autochthonen Bevölkerung machte es ihnen dabei möglich, sich in ursprünglich slowakischen oder ungarischen Ortschaften niederzulassen. Der russische Historiker Alexej Petrov, der sich im 20. Jahrhundert mehr als 30 Jahre mit der Geschichte der Karpato-Ruthenen beschäftigt hatte, benannte mit poetischen Worten diese Immigrationswelle als „Heraustreten des ruthenischen Flusses aus den Ufern" (Разлив русской реки).[10] Er stützte sich dabei in erster Linie auf die Berichte des zeitgenössischen Enzyklopädisten Mathias Bel, vor allem auf sein Monumentalwerk *Notitia Hungariae novae historico geografica.*[11]

Eine feste Siedlungsstruktur ließ sich meist erst nach ein bis zwei Generationen konstatieren, da der *plebs vagabundus*, wie ihn die zeitgenössischen Aufzeichnungen nicht selten benannten, nicht gleich sesshaft wurde.[12] Demnach war auch der häufige Wohnortwechsel ein Merkmal der Ruthenen. Gleichwohl zogen aber auch die benachbarten Slowaken und Ungarn mit.[13]

---

katholische Visitation von Bischof Josef De Camelis. Siehe: ДУЛИШКОВИЧЬ, Иоаннъ: Историческія черты Угро-Русскихь [Historische Züge der Ungarnruthenen]. Унгварь 1877, 20-25. – ГАДЖЕГА, Василій: Канонична визитація в Спишу р. 1701 [Kanonische Visitation in der Zips im Jahre 1701]. In: Подкарпатска Русь 11 (1934), 2-11.

[9] Zur Entwicklung der slowakisch-ungarischen Grenze siehe: VARSIK, Branislav: Národnostná hranica slovensko-maďarská v ostatných dvoch storočiach [Slowakisch-ungarische Volksgrenze in den letzten 200 Jahren]. Bratislava 1940, 77f. – DIENES, Dénes: Szláv ajkú protestánsok Zemplén vármegyében a XVII. században. Adalékok a szláv-magyar nyelvhatár kérdéséhez [Slawischsprachige Protestanten im Zempliner Komitat im 17. Jahrhundert. Beiträge zur Frage der slawisch-ungarischen Sprachgrenze]. In: Zemplén népessége, települései [Bevölkerung und Siedlungen des Zemplin]. Hg. v. Edit TAMÁS. Sárospatak 1999, 104-111.

[10] ПЕТРОВ, Алексей: Материалы до истории Угорской Руси VI [Materialien zur Geschichte der „Ugorska Rus"]. Санкт Петербург 1911, 150. – PETROV, Alexej: Kdy vznikli ruské osady na uherské Dolní Zemi a vůbec za Karpaty? [Wann entstanden die ruthenischen Siedlungen im ungarischen Tiefland und überhaupt hinter den Karpaten?]. In: Český časopis historický 29 (1923), 411-442, hier 436. – Nach der Oktoberrevolution im November 1917 emigrierte Petrov nach Prag, wo er seine Forschungen als Professor der Karlsuniversität fortsetzte.

[11] Über die Stadt Sečovce schreibt Mathias Bel in seinen „Notitia": „[...] ein bevölkerungsstarker aber üblicher Ort der Ruthenen, wo nur wenige von den alten Ungarn anzutreffen sind." Ein ähnliches Dorf war z.B. Ladmovce, wo eine „arme Bevölkerung" lebte. Ein „nicht geringer Teil der Ungarn vermischt sich jetzt mit den Slowaken und den Ruthenen." Zitiert nach BEL, Matej: Zemplínska stolica [Zempliner Komitat]. Hg. v. Martin Slaninka. Bratislava 1999.

[12] Fast in allen Dörfern des Theißgebiets fand Bel in den 1730er Jahren neue Bewohner vor. Einige Beispiele: Veľký Horeš wurde bewohnt „ großenteils aus Einwanderern [...] Ruthenen und Ungarn. Beide sind unbeständig, mal wollen sie hier, mal dort leben." Unweit lag Somotor, ebenfalls von Ungarn bewohnt, „gemischt mit herumziehenden Slowaken". In Zatín lebten laut Bel „herumziehende, unbeständige Ungarn, Slowaken, Ruthenen und Polaken". EBD., kap. I. par. III.

[13] ULIČNÝ, Ferdinand: Notície Mateja Bela o Šarišskej a Zemplínskej stolici [Notizien von Mathias Bel über das Scharoscher und Zempliner Komitat]. In: Nové Obzory 29 (1987), 141-153, hier 149. – Ein Charakteristikum der ruthenischen Bevölkerung – so die zeitgenössische Wahrnehmung – soll demnach ihre „Unfähigkeit" gewesen sein, sich dauerhaft niederzulassen. Dies sei dem Erbe ihrer ursprünglichen, nomadischen Lebensweise als Hirten geschuldet. PETROV, Alexander, Leonidovič: Drevnejšie gramoty po istoriji karpatorusskoj cerkvi i ierarchii 1391 – 1498 [Ältere Urkunden über die Geschichte der Karpato-Ruthenischen Kirche und ihrer Hierarchie]. Praha 1930, 85.

Diese Nord-Süd-Bewegung bewirkte nicht nur die Verschiebung der ethnischen Grenzen zwischen Ruthenen, Slowaken und Ungarn, sondern begünstigte auch die Verbreitung der Katholiken *graeci ritus*. Diese Veränderungen veranschaulicht die Verteilung zwischen konfessionell homogenen, also griechisch-katholischen, und gemischten Gemeinden der Munkatscher Diözese Mitte des 18. Jahrhunderts.[14] Von den 1.129 Ortschaften waren nämlich 40% (453) rein griechisch-katholisch und 60% (676) konfessionell gemischt.[15] Es gibt keine Belege über Migrationen in umgekehrter Richtung bzw. über die Konversionen der griechisch-katholischen Ruthenen in ihren ursprünglichen Gebieten. Bei den konfessionell gemischten Gemeinden handelte es sich also um das Ergebnis der ruthenischen Migration.

Die ersten spärlichen Berichte über die Einwanderer östlichen Ritus in die Neoacquistica-Gebiete stammen aus der ersten Hälfte des 17. Jahrhunderts.[16] Für die 1660er Jahre sind lediglich einzelne griechisch-katholische Siedler bzw. Familien belegt. Dabei handelt es sich vor allem um Nachweise diverser Auseinandersetzungen zwischen protestantischen bzw. römisch-katholischen Altbewohnern und ihren Priestern bzw. den Neuansiedlern.[17] Der Zustrom der griechisch-katholischen Einwanderer stieg Ende des 17. Jahrhunderts erheblich an. Parallel dazu wuchs auch die Anzahl der neugegründeten Pfarreien, zugleich bildeten sich Normen interkonfessioneller Kommunikation heraus. Meist erbauten die neu entstandenen Gemeinden mit der Zustimmung des Gutsherrn aber ohne dessen Patronat eine Holzkirche, aus dem Umfeld ihres Heimatortes luden sie einen Priester zu sich. Neben der existierenden römisch-katholischen und protestantischen Kirche entstand somit eine neue Kirchengemeinde.[18] In vielen leeren oder ziemlich entvölkerten Ortschaften waren die griechisch-katholischen Neusiedler in kurzer Zeit dominierend. Daraufhin stimmten manche Gutsherren zugleich auch als Patronatsherren zu, die leeren und

---

[14] Ukr. Мукачеве, ung. Munkács, sk. Mukačevo.

[15] Es geht um die Angaben aus der Visitation von Michal Manuel Olšavszky aus den Jahren 1750 – 1752. Vgl. ГАДЖЕГА, Василий: Додатки до исторії русинов и руских церквей в Ужанской жупе [Beiträge zur Geschichte der Ruthenen und ruthenischen Kirchen im Ungwarer Komitat]. In: Науковый Зборник Товариства Просвита 2 (1923), 1-63, hier 53. – Zum Anteil der konfessionell gemischten griechisch-katholischen Gemeinden der Munkatscher Diözese siehe auch UDVARI, István: A munkácsi görögkatolikus püspökség lelkészségeinek 1806 évi összeírása [Konskription der griechisch-katholischen Diözese von Munkatsch im Jahre 1806]. Nyíregyháza 1990, 140-154. – BENDÁSZ, István/KOI, István: A Munkácsi Görögkatolikus Egyházmegye lelkészségeinek 1792 évi katalógusa [Katalog der Parochien der Griechisch-Katholischen Diözese von Munkatsch im Jahre 1792]. Nyíregyháza 1994, 147.

[16] 1647 beschwerte sich der orthodoxe Pope aus Trebišov bei den kalvinistischen Visitatoren, dass sein Einkommen seit der Einrichtung der Union von Ungwar/Užhorod 1646 stets zurückginge. Die Gläubigen verteilten sich nämlich seither auf die „Papisten" [pápisták] und „Russen" [oroszok]. DIENES: Szláv ajkú, 108. – DAMJANOVICS, Judit B.: A Munkácsi Egyházmegye papjainak és kántorainak szellemi élete a 16-18. században [Geistiges Leben der Priester und Kantoren der Diözese Munkatsch im 16.-18. Jahrhundert]. In: Levéltári évkönyv 7 (1994), 31-43, hier 33f.

[17] Im Zempliner Dorf Kašov befahlen die kalvinistischen Visitatoren den Ruthenen, den Zehent dem örtlichen kalvinistischen Prediger zu zahlen. Der lutherische Kaplan beklagte, dass in den Filialgemeinden Majerovce und Sedliská sechs ruthenische Familien auf lehren Sessionen lebten und sich weigerten, den Kirchhenzehent zu zahlen mit der Begründung, einer anderen Konfession zugehörig zu sein. Siehe dazu ausführlicher: DIENES: Szláv ajkú, 110.

[18] Beispiele der neugegründeten griechisch-katholischen Pfarreien siehe: ŠOLTÉS: Odkedy sú gréckokatolíci na stredňom a južnom Zemplíne, 16f.

verfallenen Kirchen solchen griechisch-katholischen Gemeinden zu überantworten. Natürlich wurden diese Kirchen dem Bedarf des östlichen Ritus angepasst. Die Visitation des griechisch-katholischen Bischofs Olsavszky von Munkatsch in den Jahren 1750 – 1752 verzeichnete im Zempliner und Scharoscher Komitat 21 – ursprünglich fast ausnahmslos römisch-katholische – Kirchen aus Stein und 274 Holzkirchen.[19] In der Zips gab es zu dieser Zeit 19 Kirchen vom östlichen Ritus, von denen ursprünglich sechs im gotischen Stil erbaute, römisch-katholische Steinkirchen waren.[20]

Bedingungen der Immigration von Griechisch-Katholiken

Die Ausbreitung und die Etablierung des östlichen Ritus in den genannten Gebieten wurde 1646 durch die Union von Ungwar/Užhorod entscheidend vorangetrieben. Obwohl sie anfangs nur von 63 orthodoxen Priestern unterstützt worden war, bestimmte sie bald die konfessionelle Entwicklung im ganzen nordöstlichen Ungarn. Im Unterschied zu den Serben oder teils auch zu Siebenbürgen erwies sich das Unionsmodell als durchaus erfolgreich und definierte tragfähig die Bedingungen für eine gegenseitige Akkulturation. Die Etablierung der griechisch-katholischen Kirche sowie die rasche Errichtung eines ganzen Netzes von Pfarreien ermöglichten zugleich die bis dahin mangelhafte Seelsorge auch unter den traditionellen Konfessionen. Sie war eine der Folgen jener politischen, rechtlichen und sozialen Instabilität, die in dieser Region nach dem Frieden von Sathmar (1711) infolge der Konfiszierung vieler Adelsfamilien und der Ausrottung der protestantischen Elite entstanden war. Der Protestantismus stagnierte, allerdings gab es gravierende Unterschiede zwischen den beiden Konfessionen. Die lutherische verlor nämlich im Laufe des 18. Jahrhunderts viel mehr Kirchengemeinden als die kalvinistische, was in erster Linie mit der großen Anzahl von kalvinistisch-reformierten Kleinadeligen zusammen-

---

[19] HODINKA, Antal: A munkácsi görög-katolikus püspökség története [Geschichte des griechisch-katholischen Bistums von Munkatsch]. Budapest 1910, 783. – Nur im mittleren Zemplin gab es mindestens zehn griechisch-katholische Kirchen, die das gleiche Schicksal ereilte, wie das Gotteshaus im Dorf Pusté Čemerné, in der Nähe von Michalovce. In der Olsavszky-Visitation steht dazu: „Die Steinkirche überging von den Katholiken in die Hände der Lutheraner und stand vor fünfzig Jahren ruiniert da. Ruthenische Pfarrkinder haben sie repariert und benutzen sie auch seither". ГАДЖЕГА, Василий: Додатки до исторії русинов и руских церквей в був. жупе Земплинской [Beiträge zur Geschichte der Ruthenen und der ruthenischen Kirchen im Komitat Zemplin]. In: Науковый Зборник Товариства Просвита 11 (1935), 17-182, hier 71. – Weitere Beispiele siehe ŠOLTÉS: Odkedy sú gréckokatolíci na strednom Zemplíne, 19f.

[20] ŠOLTÉS, Peter: Spiš v dejinách gréckokatolíckej cirkvi v 18. storočí [Die Zips in der Geschichte der griechisch-katholischen Kirche im 18. Jahrhundert]. In: Terra Scepusiensis. Zborník z medzinárodnej vedeckej konferencie, konanej v dňoch 5. – 9. novembra 2002 v Levoči. Hg. v. Martin HOMZA – Michal SLIVKA – Ryszard GŁADKIEWICZ – Michał PUŁASKI, Bratislava 2003, 615-636 hier 617-619. – In sechs anderen Komitaten auf dem Gebiet der Munkatscher Diözese (Abaújvár, Borsod, Szabolcs, Szatmár, Ugocsa und Máramaros) gab es von den 330 Kirchen nur noch 11 aus Stein oder Ziegel, alle anderen waren aus Holz gebaut und mit Schindel oder Stroh gedeckt. Keine einzige davon hatte irgendwelche Pfründe oder Einkommen und war nur „dank der Mühe und Fleiß der Gläubigen intakt". ГАДЖЕГА: Додатки до исторії русинов и руских церквей в був. жупе Земплинской 11 (1935), 168.

hing.[21] In den 13 Komitaten des nordöstlichen Ungarn entwickelte sich der Protestantismus unter besseren rechtlichen Bedingungen als im Westen des Königreiches. Die rechtliche Stellung der Protestanten wurde am 21. März 1731 in der sog. *Resolutio Carolina* definiert. Sie bestätigte nicht nur die Gesetzesartikel 25 und 26 des Ödenburger Landtags von 1681, sondern auch die 21 Artikel der *Explanatio Leopoldina* aus dem Jahre 1691. In den 13 Komitaten, die zwischen 1540–1687 nicht mehr unter der Osmanenherrschaft standen und zu den Schutzbasteien der antihabsburgischen Aufstände avancierten, wurde die Zahl der protestantischen Kirchen nicht auf die zwei sog. Artikularkirchen beschränkt und praktisch die freie Religionsausübung garantiert.[22] Zu diesen Komitaten gehörten auch Zemplin, Scharosch, Ungwar und Abaújvár.[23]

Auch der Wiederaufbau der römisch-katholischen Kirche kam im ersten Drittel des 18. Jahrhunderts nur langsam voran. Selbst in den 30er Jahren konnten weder die Seelsorge noch die wirtschaftliche Absicherung der Pfarreien reorganisiert werden. Die Rekonstruktion der Kirchenorganisation, die Reparatur oder der Aufbau von neuen Gotteshäusern, Pfarr- und Schulgebäuden sowie ihre Besetzung mit Priestern und Lehrern erwiesen sich als schwierig. Die Visitatoren fanden in den Gemeinden der Diözese Erlau (ung. Eger) zwischen 1733 und 1737 mehr als die Hälfte der Kirchen verwahrlost vor, da in den Gebäuden über mehrere Jahrzehnte hinweg keine Gottesdienste mehr gehalten worden waren. Meist waren sie mit liturgischen Gegenständen nicht ausgestattet, in besseren Fällen hatten sie zumindest noch eine Glocke.[24]

---

[21] Von den mehr als 30 lutherischen Pfarreien Ende des 17. Jahrhunderts blieben im Zempliner Komitat 1735 nur noch fünf übrig. Vgl. Acta cassae parochorum. Egyházmegyék 1733–1779. 1 Füzet, Müvészettörténeti adatok [Acta cassae parochorum. Diözesen 1733-1779. Heft 1. Kunsthistorische Daten]. Budapest 1969, 155 und 211. – Von 1763 bis zum Toleranzpatent gab es in Zemplin nur noch eine lutherische Gemeinde. RÁDAY levéltár [Archiv Ráday]. B/1 Archivum agentiale: Collectiones agentialis variae 1718 – 1829, 6 C, f. 526. Dagegen gab es 1773 im gleichen Komitat schon mehr als 60 kalvinistische Pfarreien. Vgl. Lexicon locorum Regni Hungariae populorum Anno 1773 officiose confectum. Publici juris fecit: Delegatio Hungarica pacem tractans. Budapestini E. Typographia V. Hornyánszky 1920, 292-304. – Etliche helvetische Gemeinden bauten nach dem Verlust ihrer Gotteshäuser ein neues. ŠOLTÉS: Náboženská pluralita na Zemplíne v 18. storočí [Religiöse Pluralität in Zemplin im 18. Jahrhundert]. In: Byzantinoslovaca 1 (2006), 256.

[22] BUCSAY, Mihály: Der Protestantismus in Ungarn 1521 – 1978. Ungarns Reformationskirchen in Geschichte und Gegenwart. Teil II. Wien-Köln-Graz 1979, 13.

[23] Im Scharoscher Komitat gab es im Jahre 1722 neunzehn evangelisch-lutherische und fünf kalvinistische Pfarreien, in Zempliner Komitat sogar 53 kalvinistische und fünf evangelische, zugleich mehr als 150 griechisch-katholische und 26 römisch-katholische Pfarreien. SEDLÁK, Peter: Dejiny Košického arcibiskupstva III. Kresťanstvo na území Košického arcibiskupstva od počiatkov do roku 1804 [Geschichte des Kaschauer Erzbistums III. Das Christentum auf dem Gebiet des Kaschauer Erzbistums seit den Anfängen bis in das Jahr 1804]. Prešov 2004, 196.

[24] Die Visitatoren fanden im Zempliner Archidiakonat des Erlauer Bistums noch in 1730er Jahren mehr als Hälfte der Kirchen verwaist, in welchen mehrere Jahrzehnte keine Gottesdienste gehalten wurden, ohne Ausstattung mit liturgischen Gegenständen, in besseren Fällen nur mit Glocken. Am meisten beschädigt waren die Holzkirchen, die zu dieser Zeit auch in römisch-katholischen Kirchen in kleineren oder an der Peripherie liegenden Ortschaften lagen. Brekov: „Est Ecclesia lignea, quod structuram, ruinae proxima". Benkovce: „Est Ecclesia lignea (...) tecto et omnibus necessariis destituta, unum solum campanam habens". Boľ: „Ruinam habet Eclesiam lapideam". Hencovce: „Est Ecclesia lapidea, deserta, nulla habens apparamenta, praeter unicam campanam". Vgl. MOL Acta cassae parochorum. Egyházmegyék szerint besorolt

Die griechisch-katholische Kirche war im Vergleich zu den anderen Konfessionen in mancher Hinsicht im Vorteil: Sie hatte keinen Priestermangel zu beklagen, denn die Strukturen waren anders. In den Priesterfamilien führte der Sohn (oder die Söhne) den Beruf seines Vaters fort, wobei er die dafür relevanten Kenntnisse bereits von seinem Vater erlernt hatte, und nur in wenigen Fällen absolvierte dieser auch eine kurze pastorale und geistliche Ausbildung in einem Kloster.[25] Nur jene wenigen Priester, die ihre Ausbildung an jesuitischen Universitäten oder an den Priesterseminaren in Tyrnau (sk. Trnava, ung. Nagyszombat), Kaschau (sk. Košice, ung. Kassa) oder Erlau absolviert hatten und später im Umfeld des Bischofs oder in größeren Pfarreien ihren Dienst versahen, entsprachen den Anforderungen des Tridentinum. Die Mehrzahl jedoch konnte lediglich lesen und schreiben, davon beides in erster Linie auf Kyrillisch.[26]

Ein weiterer Grund für die schnelle Expansion der griechisch-katholischen Gemeinden waren die im Vergleich niedrigeren Kosten, die die Gründung und die ökonomische Absicherung einer Kirchengemeinde verursachten. Sämtliche Einkünfte einer griechisch-katholischen Pfarrei, das heisst die Pfründe, Zehent und Stolgebühren, betrugen in den 50er Jahren des 18. Jahrhunderts nur selten mehr als 30 rheinische Gulden.[27] Eine Generation später, zur Zeit der ab 1786 eingeleiteten Josephinischen Pfarrregulierung bewegte sich das durchschnittliche Jahreseinkommen eines griechisch-katholischen Pfarrers zwischen 100 und 200 Gulden. Nur in besonders armen und kleinen Pfarreien mussten die Priester mit weniger als 100 Gulden auskommen.[28] Das Jahreseinkommen einer römisch-katholischen Pfarrei dagegen betrug 200 bis 400 rheinische Gulden, in den (Markt-)Städten sogar deutlich mehr.[29]

---

iratok. Egri Egyházmegye 1733-1779, 29, 35, 48 und 146. – Nižný Hrabovec: „Habet Ecclesiam (evangelisch A.B. Bem. PŠ) sub tabulato et tecto commodo, omni interno apparatu caret, praeter campanas tres". Poša: „Est Ecclesia lignea deserta, omnibus apparamentis inno et tecto destituta, duas solum campanas habet". Acta cassae parochorum. Egyházmegyék szerint besorolt iratok Egri Egyházmegye 1733-1779. 2 Füzet, Müvészettörténeti adatok. Laak – Zsuko. Ed. Németh Lajos. Budapest 1976, 155 und 328.

[25] Siehe dazu ausführlicher KONDRATOVIČ, Irenej: The Olsavszky bishops and their activity. In: Slovak Studies 3 (1963), 179-198, hier 185.

[26] Einige Popen waren noch Mitte des 18. Jahrhunderts Analphabeten. Für das Dorf Kalná Ráztoka z.B. notierte der Visitator: „Der Priester führt kein Kirchenbuch, er kann nicht Schreiben." Гаджега, Додатки до исторії русинов и руских церквей в був. жупе Земплинской, 11 (1935), 101 und 119. Siehe dazu ausführlicher: ŠOLTÉS, Peter/ŽEŇUCH, Peter: Sociálne postavenie gréckokatolíckeho duchovenstva a veriacich na východnom Slovensku a v podkarpatskej Rusi v 18.a 19. storočí [Die soziale Stellung des griechisch-katholischen Klerus in der Ostslowakei und in den Transkarpaten im 18. und 19. Jahrhundert]. In: Slavica Slovaca 36 (2001), 133-146, hier 141.

[27] Die statistischen Angaben siehe AACass [Erzbischöfliches Archiv Kaschau], Graeci ritus, nicht signiert, Tabella representans, Districtus Homonensis 1746.; Ebd., Districtus Ujhelyiensis 1746.

[28] MOL Helytartótanácsi levéltár. Számvevőség [Archiv der Statthalterei. Rentenamt]. Allerhöchstresolvierter Pfarregulierungs Vortrag Minkatscher G: K: Diözés. Sign. C 104, A 55.

[29] EBD., Auseinandersetzung zwischen dem Zempliner Komitat und der Erlauer Diözese. Mit Beylagen Sub A. B. C. D. et E dann zwey Tabellen sub No. 1 et 2. Sign. C 104, A 10, Tabelle No. 1 und No. 2, Zempliner Komitat, Erlauer Dioezes. – Von 53 Pfarreien (über eine fehlen die Angaben) lag bei zehn das gesamte Einkommen unter 200 rheinischen Gulden, bei 19 zwischen 200 und 300, bei sechs zwischen 300 und 400 und bei sieben zwischen 400 und 500 Gulden. Die reichsten Pfarreien waren die Winzerstädte Sárospatak (1.698 rh. Gulden), Sátoraljaújhely (1.058 rh. Gulden), Tállya (1281 rh. Gulden), Olaszliszka (872 rh. Gulden), Tarczal (770 rh. Gulden), Nagy Tolcsva (614 rh. Gulden), Mád (500 rh. Gulden) und die Stadt Humenné (599 rh. Gulden). Am besten sieht man den sozialen Unterschied am Beispiel zweier Pfarrer aus

Andererseits musste sich die griechisch-katholische Kirche im Munkatscher Bistum unter für sie ungünstigen sozialen Bedingungen behaupten. Es fehlten fast vollkommen der Adel oder das Bürgertum, deren Förderung für die römisch-katholische Kirche und die beiden protestantischen Konfessionen als selbstverständlich galt. Die wenigen und zudem meist armen griechisch-katholischen Adeligen spielten in der Verwaltung wie auf den Versammlungen des Komitats eine untergeordnete Rolle. Genau das machte diese Kirche von der ökonomischen und politischen Unterstützung des Staats weitgehend abhängig.

Interkonfessionelle Konfliktpotentiale

Die Expansion der griechisch-katholischen Pfarreien engte den seelsorgerischen Wirkungsraum und die ökonomischen Quellen der anderen Konfessionen deutlich ein. In seinem Brief an Kardinal Leopold Kollonich aus dem Jahre 1692 begründete z.B. der apostolische Vikar von Munkatsch, Josef De Camelis, die Konflikte zwischen ihm und dem Erlauer Bischof um das Recht auf den Zehnt.[30] Die interkonfessionellen Beziehungen wurden zudem mit der seelsorgerischen Betreuung der Gläubigen anderer Konfessionen belastet. In den ausschließlich griechisch-katholischen Gemeinden besuchten die Katholiken die kirchenslawischen Gottesdienste und ließen sich von den „Popen" trauen, beerdigen und taufen. Auch die Kirchensteuer zahlten sie der „Konkurrenz".[31] Erheblich seltener ließen die griechisch-katholischen Priester ihre spirituellen Dienste den Protestanten der verwaisten Gemeinden zu-

dem gleichen Dorf. In Sačurov (ung. Szacsur) machten die Einnahmen des griechisch-katholischen Priesters von den 1.095 Gläubigen 87 Gulden aus, während sein römisch-katholischer Kollege von 1.079 Pfarrkindern 263 Gulden erhielt. In Sátoraljaújhely mit Filialien hatte der griechisch-katholische Pfarrer 1.470 Seelen. Sein Jahreseinkommen betrug 259 Gulden. Die römisch-katholische Pfarrei wurde von den Paulinern verwaltet. Die 1.903 Pfarrkinder zahlten hier jährlich 1.058 Gulden in die Pfarrkasse und 55 Gulden in die Kirchenkasse. In Sárospatak hatte der Pope, zusammen mit den Filialdörfern 775 Pfarrkinder und eine jährliche Rente von 241 Gulden. Die Pfarrei wurde erst im Jahre 1728 gegründet und das Patronatsrecht übte die königliche Kammer aus. Der römisch-katholische Pfarrer in dieser Stadt betreute 1.688 Gläubige, er hatte zwei Kapläne und eine jährliche Einnahme von 1.698 Gulden. Angaben über die jährliche Rente der griechisch-katholischen Pfarrer siehe Fußnote 28.

[30] „Ich bin mir dessen sehr wohl bewusst, dass Bischof Fényesi wegen des Zehents sich über mich ärgert [...] obwohl er weiß, dass ich hier der erste, wirklich katholische Bischof bin und keine echte Fundation habe, und dass ich nicht seine Pfarrer, sondern die [protestantischen] Prediger um die Zehenten beraubt habe. Während der langen Jahre, als diese die protestantischen Prediger erhalten hatten, hatte niemand etwas einzuwenden oder fühlte sich beleidigt. Seit ich das tue, passt es ausgerechnet den Katholiken nicht." HODINKA, Antal: A Munkácsi Görög szert. püspökség okmánytára [Urkundensammlung des Munkatscher Bistums griechischen Ritus]. Ungvár 1911, 335.

[31] Die Visitatoren des Erlauer Bistums haben im Jahre 1746 alle griechisch-katholischen Pfarreien auf diesem Gebiet besucht und berichteten in der *„Comportat se cum Parocho Latini ritus quoad jurisdictionalia"* über viele solcherlei Vorfälle. Siehe AACass, Graeci ritus, ohne Signatur, Tabella representans, Districtus Homonensis und Districtus Ujhelyiensis 1746. – Auch in Visitationen der römisch-katholischen Pfarreien aus dem Jahre 1749 findet man viele Belege darüber. AACass, Districtualia, Vol. 3, Fasc 2. Protocollum Canonicae Visitationis 1749, Pars posterior, Districtus Homonensis. – Eine Generation später im Jahre 1772 waren die Visitatoren des Erlauer Bistums mit dieser Praxis konfrontiert. AACass, Districtualia, Vol. 4, fasc. 1, Protocollum Canonicae Visitationis Districtuum Submontani, Ujhelyiensis et Homonnensis I. Comitatui Zempliniensi ingremiatorum Anno Domini 1772.

kommen.[32] Die „Popen" nahmen ausserdem auf die Einhaltung der Reverspflicht nur selten Rücksicht, so dass sie die Trauung konfessionell gemischter Brautpaare vollzogen, falls sie der römisch-katholische Priester abgelehnt hatte, weil der nichtkatholische Teil den Glaubenswechsel nicht unterzeichnen wollte.[33] Besonders heftig kritisierten die Erlauer Bischöfe diese gesetzwidrige Praxis.

Der Terraingewinn der griechisch-katholischen Kirche sorgte von Beginn an für ein spannungsgeladenes Verhältnis zwischen dem Erlauer und dem Munkatscher Bischof. Die polemischen Auseinandersetzungen zielten auf die Frage ab, ob auf dem Gebiet einer Diözese zwei Bischöfe ihre Jurisdiktion ausüben konnten. Die Erlauer Bischöfe waren der Ansicht, dass dies nicht mit dem kanonischen Recht zu vereinbaren sei und hielten den Munkatscher griechisch-katholischen Bischof für ihren *Vicarius graeci ritus unitorum.* Noch Anfang des 18. Jahrhunderts stellten die Existenz des Munkatscher Bistums weder der Kaiserhof noch der Heilige Stuhl in Frage. Kaiser Joseph I. ernannte seinen Favoriten zum Bischof von Munkatsch. Bei der Wahl des nächsten Kandidaten jedoch machte sich Kaiser Karl VI. den Standpunkt des Erlauer Bischofs zu eigen, wonach ein griechisch-katholischer Oberhirt auf dem Gebiet einer römisch-katholischen Diözese lediglich ein Vikar für die Gläubigen des östlichen Ritus sei.[34] Diese Auslegung des kanonischen Rechts bestätigte auch die *Congregatio de propaganda fide* 1718 mit ihrem Dekret.[35]

Der erfolgreiche Terraingewinn der Griechisch-Katholiken gab den Bischöfen von Erlau Anlass, dieser Entwicklung Einhalt zu gebieten. Vor allem sollte der Wirkungsbereich des griechisch-katholischen Klerus beschränkt und die Zahl der neuen Pfarreien reduziert werden. Das sollte nicht nur der „Seelendiebstahl" beenden, sondern in den konfessionell gemischten Familien auch die römisch-katholische Erziehung der Kinder gewährleisten. 1747 unterzeichnete der Erlauer Bischof Franz Barkóczy ein Dekret, das die griechisch-katholischen Priester besonders empfindlich

[32] ГАДЖЕГА, Василій: Додатки до исторії русинов и руских церквей в був. жупе Земплинской [Angaben zur Geschichte der Rusinen und der russischen Kirche im Komitat Semplin]. 11 (1935), 64f. und 82.

[33] Besonders häufig findet man solche Vorfälle im mittleren Zemplin, in den Pfarreien von Budkovce, Dúbravka, Bracovce, Trhovište usw. Siehe AACass, Graeci ritus, Tabella representans, Districtus Homonensis 1746; AACass, Districtualia, Vol. 4, fasc. 1, Protocollum Canonicae Visitationis 1772.

[34] Diese Subordination wurde 1716 auch durch das Dekret von Kaiser Karl VI. anerkannt, in dem er als Patronatsherr dem neuen Munkatscher Bischof nur den Titel *seu honorem Episcopi suprafati Districtus Munkaciensis* und nicht *Dioecesia Munkaciensis* verliehen hatte. PERFECKÝ, Emilián: Boj za náboženskú a národnostnú samostatnosť cirkve v Podkarpatské Rusi [Kampf für die religiöse und nationale Selbstständigkeit der Kirche in Transkarpatien]. In: Prúdy 8 (1924), 147-153, hier 148.

[35] Die *Congragatio de propagaanda fide* argumentierte am 20. Juni 1718 damit, dass, um die „Misshandlungen und Skandale, die im Munkatscher Apostolischen Vikariat des Erlauer Bistums zwischen dem Klerus und dem Volk" zugenommen hatten zu beseitigen 1.) „die Griechisch-Katholiken [...] die Feiertage nach den Geboten der lateinischen Kirche begehen [müssen], 2.) die Priester [...] auf die Bigamie verzichten [müssen] und der Bischof [...] in solchen Fällen nach dem Kanonischen Recht handeln soll. 3.) Neue Priester darf der Munkatscher Apostolischer Vikar nur mit Zustimmung des lateinischen Ordinariats weihen, 4.) nur mit seiner Zustimmung dürfen neue Pfarreien gegründet werden, 5.) griechisch-katholische Priester sollen vom lateinischen Ordinariat ermahnt werden, sich nicht in die lateinischen Ehen einzumischen, und 6.) neue Kirchen dürfen nur mit der Zustimmung des apostolischen Ordinär gebaut und geweiht werden." LUTSKAY, Michael: Historia Carpato-Ruthenorum, Sacra, et Civilis, antiqua et recens usque ad praesens tempus. Tomus 3-ius, 1843. In: Науковий збірник Музею Української культури у Свиднику 16 (1990), 29-256, hier 179-180.

traf. Ein Jahr davor hatte er in seiner Diözese die Visitation der griechisch-katholischen Pfarreien verordnet, um sich ein Bild über die Lage zu verschaffen. Mit seiner Verordnung ließ er die Priester des östlichen Ritus zu regulären Kaplänen der römisch-katholischen Pfarrer degradieren.[36] Für Orte mit zwei katholischen Kirchengemeinden bedeutete dies aber, dass der Kirchenzehnt und die Stolgebühren allein dem römisch-katholischen Pfarrer zugute kamen. In vielen Filialdörfern wurde es den griechisch-katholischen Priestern untersagt, die Sakramente der Trauung oder der Taufe zu spenden; gemäß der örtlichen Tradition bestimmte dies aber über die künftige Zugehörigkeit zur jeweiligen Kirchengemeinde.[37]

Königin Maria Theresia versuchte, die beiden Konfliktparteien miteinander zu versöhnen und verteidigte nicht einmal den griechischen Klerus. 1752 ermahnte sie die Komitatsorgane in den betroffenen Gebieten, die griechisch-katholischen Priester bei der Ausübung ihrer seelsorgerischen Tätigkeit nicht zu hindern.[38] Im September 1756 verlangte sie vom Munkatscher Bischof die vorbehaltlose Anerkennung seiner Unterordnung als *Vicarius graeci ritus unitorum*, im Gegenzug dafür verbat sie dem Bischof von Erlau, sich in die Administration der griechisch-katholischen Gläubigen einzumischen. Über den Bau von neuen Kirchen und die Errichtung von neuen Pfarreien sollte wieder ausschließlich Munkatsch entscheiden.[39]

Die Auseinandersetzung um die Kirchensteuer in den gemischten Gebieten griff der Erlauer Bischof, Karl Eszterházy, wieder auf, als er 1763 mit Hinweis auf die Anordnung seines Vorgängers, Barkóczy, in den Filialkirchen den Zehnt und die Stolgebühren von griechisch-katholischen Gläubigen dem lateinischen Pfarrer zusprach.[40] Die Katholiken des östlichen Ritus wurden damit ausserhalb ihrer Mutterkirchen de jure mit den Nichtkatholiken gleichgestellt.[41] Maria Theresia griff aber erneut ein und bestätigte ihren früheren Standpunkt. In ihrer Verordnung vom August 1768 erklärte sie die griechisch-katholischen Priester mit den römisch-katholischen gleichberechtigt.[42] Ihre Intention war dabei doppelgleisig: Einerseits wollte sie die immanenten Konflikte der katholischen Kirche nicht weiter vertiefen, andererseits aber versuchte sie die Unionsbestrebungen unter den orthodoxen Serben und Rumänen in Serbien und Siebenbürgen zu fördern. Die Vorgänge im Munkatscher Bistum erwiesen ihren politischen Plänen keine Dienste.

---

[36] LUCSKAY, Michael: Historia Carpatho-Ruthenorum in Hungaria, sacra et civilis. In: Наукобий збірник Музею української культури у Свиднику 17 (1991), 27-182, hier 57f.

[37] Vgl. ŠOLTÉS/ŽEŇUCH: Sociálne postavenie gréckokatolíckeho duchovenstva a veriacich na východnom Slovensku, 133-146.

[38] LUCSKAY: Historia Carpatho-Ruthenorum, 84f.

[39] EBD., 84.

[40] ПЕКАР, Атанасій: Нариси історії церкви Закарпаття [Geschichte der Kirche der Karpato-Ukraine]. Том 1. Видання друге, Рим – Львив 1997, 57.

[41] Laut Verordnung der Königlichen Statthalterei aus dem Jahre 1749 waren alle Forderungen der Protestanten nach Aufwertung zur Filialgemeinde gesetzwidrig, und die protestantischen Filialgemeinden der örtlichen römisch-katholischen Pfarrei untergeordnet. Vgl. GRELLMANN, H. M. G.: Rhapsodien über den Gang der protestantischen Kirchenfreyheit in Ungern bis auf Joseph und Leopold II. In: Statistische Aufklärungen über wichtige Theile und Gegenstände der österreichischen Monarchie. Göttingen 1797 (2. Bd.), 1-88, hier 54-56.

[42] ПЕКАР: Нариси історії, 157.

Die Diskriminierungen betrafen die griechisch-katholischen Gläubigen nur in den gemischten, nicht aber in den konfessionell homogenen Gemeinden. Davon zeugen auch die Anmerkungen vom Visitationsprotokoll des Munkatscher Bischofs, Michal Olsavszky, die er explizit für die Königin angefertigt hatte. In den insgesamt 295 homogen griechisch-katholischen Gemeinden der Komitate Zemplin, Zips und Scharosch hatten die Priester keinerlei Benachteiligungen zu beklagen, durchaus aber in den 164 gemischten Dörfern und Städten.[43] Die Frage der Jurisdiktion belastete die interkonfessionelle Kommunikation bis Anfang der 70er Jahre des 18. Jahrhunderts. Eine neue Situation entstand 1771 mit der Errichtung der Diözese Munkatsch.

Entwicklungslinien in der Zips

In einer spezifischen Lage befanden sich die griechisch-katholischen Pfarreien in der Zips. Seit 1662 waren sie mit Zustimmung des Munkatscher Bischofs Peter Partenius Petrovič aus dessen Jurisdiktion ausgegliedert und unter die Aufsicht des Zipser Propstes gestellt worden. Zu dieser Zeit der zugespitzten Konfrontation zwischen Katholizismus und Protestantismus waren dafür folgende zwei Gründe ausschlaggebend: Schwierigkeiten in der Kommunikation des Munkatscher Bischofs mit seinen Pfarrern und eine schwache Kirchenorganisation und die daraus resultierende, mangelhafte Kontrolle der Seelsorge. Die Jurisdiktion des Zipser Propstes zeigte zunächst positive Auswirkungen auf die Griechisch-Katholiken: Entvölkerte protestantische Dörfer konnten von ihnen besiedelt und neue Pfarreien gegründet werden. Der Rest der „autochtonen" Bevölkerung konvertierte nach einiger Zeit zur dominierenden Konfession. Der griechisch-katholische Klerus im Zipser Dekanat stand unter dem disziplinierenden Druck des Propstes, seine theologische Ausbildung wurde auf den Universitäten und Seminaren der Jesuiten vollzogen. Dieser „Vorsprung" gegenüber dem übrigen griechisch-katholischen Klerus in Ungarn wurde auch dadurch bestätigt, dass zwischen 1707 und 1772 von den sechs Munkatscher Bischöfen vier aus der Zips kamen. Ein Viertel der Eliten dieser Diözese wie Chorherren, Vikare oder Archidiakone entstammten im genannten Zeitraum ebenfalls der Zips.[44] Dabei gab es in der Munkatscher Diözese in der zweiten Hälfte des 18. Jahrhunderts etwa 600 griechisch-katholische Pfarreien, im Zipser Dekanat dagegen lediglich 13.[45]
Im Zipser Kapitel betrachtete man die schnelle Verbreitung des östlichen Ritus zunehmend mit Sorge. Die Zahl der griechisch-katholischen Pfarreien hat sich im Lau-

---

[43] ГАДЖЕГА, Василий: Додатки до історії русинов и руских церквей в був. жупе Земплинской [Beiträge zur Geschichte der Ruthenen und der ruthenischen Kirchen im Komitat von Zemplin]. In: Науковый Зборник Товариства Просвита 12 (1937), 37-83, hier 38.
[44] Mehr dazu siehe ŠOLTÉS: Spiš v dejinách gréckokatolíckej cirkvi, 623-630. – Genaue Angaben über die aus der Zips stammenden Eliten siehe LUCSKAY: Historica Carpatho-Ruthenorum, 109-134.
[45] Es ging nur um jene 13 Pfarreien, die zwischen 1662 und 1786 in die Zipser Propstei eingegliedert worden waren. Sechs weitere griechisch-katholische Dörfer waren verpfändet und gehörten bis 1786 kirchenrechtlich zur Diözese Przemysl.

fe der zweiten Hälfte des 17. Jahrhunderts verdoppelt und die Ruthenen drangen folglich immer weiter in andere Gebiete vor. Der demografische Zuwachs wurde durch den Zustrom der griechisch-katholischen Einwanderer aus Galizien gestärkt, was sich im unterschiedlichen Ausmaß das ganze 18. und 19. Jahrhundert hindurch fortsetzen sollte.[46] Der Zipser Propst befürchtete gar, dass der lateinische Ritus großteils durch den griechischen verdrängt werden könnte. Deshalb ergriff er etliche Maßnahmen, um deren Terraingewinn aufzuhalten. Ab 1728 wurde keine neue Pfarrei mehr gegründet, und nur noch einige wenige Dörfer erhielten den Status einer Filialkirche. Wie in der Diözese Erlau wurden also die griechisch-katholischen Gläubigen, die außerhalb von Pfarreien und anerkannten Filialkirchen gelebt haben, kirchenrechtlich den lateinischen Pfarrern unterordnet. Die Kirchensteuer und die Stolgebühren erhielt von diesen der ortsansässige, römisch-katholische Priester. Das hat die wechselseitigen Beziehungen zwischen 1771 und 1786, also der Errichtung der Diözese Munkatsch und der Eingliederung der Zipser griechisch-katholischen Pfarreien, besonders belastet. Auf der einen Seite wurde eine „gezielte Latinisierung" beschworen, auf der anderen Seite war von einer drohenden Wiederkehr der Orthodoxie zu hören. Die königliche Statthalterei, der Kaiserhof sowie der Munkatscher Bischof wurden von den Gläubigen mit Beschwerden überflutet, in denen eine Zurückdrängung des Griechisch-katholischen suggeriert wurde.[47] Die unierten Priester des Zipser Archidiakonats fertigten 1786 eine Liste von mehr als 1.000 Personen an, die in letzten 20 Jahren vom griechischen zum lateinischen Ritus konvertiert seien.[48]

Die Argumente der Gegenseite, die Einschränkungen in der Seelsorge seien notwendig, weil die „orthodoxe Gefahr" von den Griechisch-Katholiken nicht ernst genommen worden sei, waren zu dieser Zeit nicht mehr stichhaltig. Die Erziehung und die Ausbildung des griechisch-katholischen Klerus erfolgten seit mehr als zwei Generationen an den Jesuitenschulen und die „griechische" Seite hielt an der Union aufrichtig fest. Viel mehr hielten etliche römisch-katholische Priester den griechischen Ritus *quasi in minime salvificus esset*.[49] In birituellen Gemeinden weigerten sie sich, den Gottesdienst in der griechisch-katholischen Kirche zu halten, deren liturgischen Gegenstände zu benutzen und sie äußerten sich herablassend über ihre griechisch-katholischen Amtsbrüder. Konvertiten wurden als bis dahin „verirrte Schafe" angesehen. Ähnlich sah es in den protestantischen Ortschaften aus, wo mit

---

[46] HALAGA, Ondrej: Slovanské osídlenie Potisia a východoslovenskí gréckokatolíci [Die slawische Besiedlung des Theißgebiets und die ostslowakischen Griechisch-katholischen]. Košice 1947, 100f.

[47] Nach Angaben des Dekans der Zipser griechisch-katholischen Pfarreien wurden sieben Dörfer mit griechisch-katholischer Mehrheit infolge des „Latinisierungsdrucks" und bis auf wenige Ausnahmen, römisch-katholisch und zwei Pfarreien zu Filialkirchen degradiert. LUCSKAY: Historia Dioecesis Munkatsiensis, Tom. 5., 1995, 155 und 177.

[48] EBD., 143f. Pars pro toto siehe das Dorf Žakarovce: „In possessione Zacharovecz a memoria hominum solum unica domus dabatur Latina, reliqaue omnes Graeci-Ritus Catholicae".

[49] EBD., 150f., 154.

dem Toleranzpatent die Seelsorge der Unierten weiter zurückgedrängt werden sollte.[50]

Dass der östliche Ritus *in minime salvificus* sei, begründeten die lateinischen Priester in erster Linie mit den liturgischen Unterschieden und den verschiedenen Formen der Volksfrömmigkeit: Mit der unterschiedlichen Form der Bekreuzigung, der Verschiebung im Kalender, den Unterschieden im Fasten sowie der Priesterehe. Zusätzlich führte das ungleich höhere Bildungsniveau der katholischen Priester zu mehr gesellschaftlichem Ansehen. Der lateinische Klerus in der Diözese Erlau hatte schon am Ende des 17. Jahrhunderts ausnahmslos das Studium der Theologie an einer Jesuitenuniversität oder an einem Priesterseminar absolviert. Die finanzielle Sicherstellung der Pfarrer hat sich infolge der Konsolidierung der wirtschaftlichen Verhältnisse auch verbessert. Die gesellschaftliche Autorität und verschiedene Variationen der sozialen Figurationen zwischen dem Pfarrer und der Gläubigen haben sich infolge der Disziplinierung und daran anknüpfender sozialer Emanzipation tiefgreifend geändert.[51]

Ganz anders sah es mit dem griechisch-katholischen Klerus aus, der sich in vielerlei Hinsicht keineswegs von seinem sozialen Umfeld unterschied. Dies erfüllte die Erlauer Bischöfe schon Anfang des 18. Jahrhunderts mit Sorge. In seinem Schreiben vom Februar 1718 an den *Vicarius greaci ritus unitorum*, Gabriel Bizanci, warf Bischof Gabriel Erdődy mehreren unierten Priestern Inkompetenz vor. Er beschuldigte den Vikar, vor der Priesterweihe auf Moral und Ausbildung der Kandidaten nicht geachtet, Bigamie toleriert und zwei oder mehr Priester in eine Pfarrei versetzt zu haben.[52] Seit seiner Amtseinsetzung soll der Vikar über 60 Personen mit mangelhafter Ausbildung, ohne die vorgeschriebene Prüfung und ohne Zustimmung des Patronatsherrn geweiht haben. Doch diese Priester kannten sich „weder mit dem christlichen Katechismus, [noch mit der] Form und Materie der Sakramente [aus], und es gibt sogar solche, die sagen, es gäbe so viele Götter als die Personen in der Heiligen Dreifaltigkeit“, so der Bischof.[53] Er griff die griechisch-katholischen Priester besonders wegen deren „Einmischung“ in die bikonfessionellen Ehen an. Besonders in den multikonfessionellen Gebieten kam es nicht selten vor, dass römisch-katholisch-protestantische, aber auch rein protestantische Paare von unierten Priestern getraut wurden, obwohl laut *Resolutio Carolina* dafür nur die römisch-katholischen Priester zuständig waren.[54] Darüber wurde auch der Heilige Stuhl informiert, erneut eine Untersuchung durchgeführt und schließlich schränkte man die Kompetenzen des Mun-

---

[50] Der griechisch-katholische Dekan der Zips beschwerte sich in den 1780er Jahren öfters beim Kaiser und bei der Königlichen Statthalterei, dass die protestantischen Gutsherren und Pfarrer die unierte Seelsorge zunehmend beschränkten. Lucskay: Historia Dioecesis, 171f.

[51] HÖLVÉNYI, György: Katholische Aufklärung und Jansenismus in Ungarn. In: Katholische Aufklärung und Jansenismus. Hg. v. Elisabeth KOVÁCS. München 1979, 93-100, hier 94f.

[52] „Similis etiam casus est ille Hrabócziensis Poppaem, qui primam Uxorem Ruthenam habuit, et jam de facto cum Catholica impie non minus, ac scandalose cohabitat.“ LUTSKAY: Historia Carpato-Ruthenorum, Tomus 3-ius, 1990, 172f.

[53] EBD., 173f.

[54] ŠOLTÉS, Peter: Náboženská pluralita na Zemplíne v 18. storočí [Religiöse Pluralität in Zemplin im 18. Jahrhundert]. In: Byzantinoslovaca 1 (2006), 253-271, hier 258f.

katscher Bischofs deutlich ein. Die griechisch-katholischen Geistlichen wurden zudem auf mehrere Jahrzehnte unter die Aufsicht des Bischofs von Erlau gestellt.
Einer der wichtigsten Faktoren, der dieses religiöse Milieu geprägt hatte, war die Interkonfessionalität.[55] Die Beziehung zwischen den beiden katholischen Kirchen war trotz gegenseitiger „Konkurrenz" bereits nach kurzer Zeit von der Durchlässigkeit konfessioneller Grenzen geprägt. Deutlich wird das an der hohen Zahl von Mischehen, den gegenseitigen Übertritten sowie an der schon erwähnten, gegenseitigen Rezeption der Volksfrömmigkeit und der Spiritualität. Dieser Prozess der Akkulturation intensivierte sich nach der Synode im polnischen Zamość (1720), als die Dekrete des Tridentinums dem östlichen Ritus angepasst wurden. Elemente der barocken Frömmigkeit wie Rosenkranzgebet, Litaneien oder Kreuzwegandacht setzten sich auch im östlichen Ritus durch. Neben der „Barockisierung" der Ikonostasen fand man in griechisch-katholischen Kirchen oft Statuen oder Nebenaltäre vor. Der westlichen Tradition nach passte man zudem auch das liturgische Kleid, die Länge der Bärte und des Haares an.[56] Das Eindringen lateinischer Traditionen vollzog sich im gesamten Munkatscher Bistum, am intensivsten jedoch in den Grenzgebieten, etwa in der Zips. Die mehr als hundert Jahre währende Unterordnung unter den Zipser Propst und später den Zipser Bischof beschleunigte diesen Prozess.[57]
Eine der Ursachen für die zahlreichen Übertritte vom griechischen zum lateinischen Ritus waren nach Meinung der griechisch-katholischen Priester die strengen Fastenregeln der Altgläubigen.[58] Mit der Übernahme der Fastentradition der lateinischen Kirche ging ein wichtiges Zeichen des östlichen Ritus verloren, was allmählich zur Akzeptanz weiterer Charakteristika der lateinischen Kirche und zur Einordnung in die römisch-katholische Kirchengemeinde führte. Die Priester in den am meisten betroffenen Dekanaten forderten vergeblich beim Munkatscher Bischof eine Auflokkerung der Fastenregeln.

---

[55] Interkonfessionalität versteht sich hier als gegenseitiger Austauschprozess zwischen Einzelpersonen oder Gruppen verschiedener konfessioneller Milieus, die für die Rezeption der Konfessionen relevant waren. Mehr dazu siehe KAUFMANN, Thomas: Einleitung. Transkonfessionalität, Interkonfessionalität, binnenkonfessionelle Pluralität – Neue Forschungen zur Konfessionalisierungsthese. In: Interkonfessionalität – Transkonfesionalität – binnenkonfessionelle Pluralität. Neue Forschungen zur Konfessionalisierungsthese. Hg. v. Kaspar VON GREYERZ, Manfred JAKUBOWSKI-THIESSEN, Thomas KAUFMANN und Hartmut LEHMANN. Heidelberg 2001 (Schriften des Vereins für Reformationsgeschichte. Band 201), 9-16, hier 14f.

[56] Siehe dazu Beispiele in LUTSKAY, Michael: Historia Dioecesis Munkatsiensis concinnata per Joannem Pasztelyi Propositum majorem Capituli Munkátsiensis edita vero per Michaelem Lutskay Propositum aulicum Lucensem, tomus 5-tus. In: Науковий збірник державного музею українсько-русинської культури у Свиднику. 20 (1995), 83-185, hier 119.

[57] ŠOLTÉS: Spiš v dejinách gréckokatolíckej cirkvi, 625f. – Die Etablierung der westlichen Spiritualität in der griechisch-katholischen Kirche betonte auch der Zipser Bischof, Joseph Salbeck, in seinem Brief aus dem Jahre 1780 an die *Congregatio de Propaganda Fide*. BOUYDOSH, Ernest: The quadrennial reports of the bishops of Spiš and Banská Bystrica to Rome. In: Slovak Studies 16 (1976), 221-317, hier 251.

[58] „Cujus Sacri Ritus Graeci in Asseclis ruinae, et desolationis principalis, et fundamentalis ratio est, Jejuniorum in Sacra Orientali Ecclesia observari solitorum rigor, quae sacra Jejunia cum Populus Ruthenus in Scepusio degens ob nimiam Plagae suae sterilitatem". In: LUTSKAY: Historia Dioecesis Munkatsiensis, Tom. 5., 1995, 176f.

Perzeptionen der Interkonfessionalität

Die Akkulturation verlief allerdings gegenseitig, auch der westliche Ritus übernahm mehrere Elemente der östlichen Spiritualität und Volksfrömmigkeit, wie etwa die Wallfahrten zu Wunderikonen, das Weihen von Ostergerichten am Ostersamstag oder die doppelte Einhaltung von Feiertagen, nämlich nach dem Julianischen und dem Gregorianischen Kalender, was in mehreren birituellen Gemeinden zum Alltag gehörte. In Ortschaften mit griechisch-katholischer Dominanz übernahm die römisch-katholische Minderheit die Traditionen der östlichen Kirche. Etliche Hirtenbriefe der Zipser und Erlauer Bischöfe aus der zweiten Hälfte des 18. Jahrhunderts ermahnten den Klerus, auf die Übertritte vom lateinischen zum griechischen Ritus zu reagieren und diese Praxis zu unterbinden. So sollten die Gläubigen zumindest bei den wichtigsten Feiertagen die römisch-katholischen Gottesdienste besuchen, die Übernahme der Fastenregeln des griechischen Ritus vermeiden und für den Übertritt in den anderen Ritus die Zustimmung des Bischofs einholen.[59]

In vielen konfessionell gemischten Ortschaften waren die Unterschiede im Kalender die Ursache von schwerwiegenden Konflikten: Während der griechisch-katholische Teil des Dorfes einen Feiertag beging, arbeiteten die Römisch-Katholischen und die Protestanten auf den Feldern. In den gemischten Gemeinden waren die griechisch-katholischen Untertanen dem Druck ihres Patronatsherrn ausgesetzt, der mit dem zweifachen Feiern von Festtagen wirtschaftliche Schäden befürchtete. In griechisch-katholischen Pfarreien mit nur einer Kirche war der Julianische Kirchenkalender maßgebend. In birituellen Gemeinden mit beiden Pfarreien bzw. Gotteshäusern neigte man allerdings dazu, zumindest die wichtigsten Feiertage nach beiden Kalendern zu begehen.[60] Religiöse Vorschriften und bestimmte Begünstigungen der Untertanen standen jedoch im Gegensatz zu den gutsherrlichen Interessen. So entstanden unterschiedliche lokale Normen, die diese Streitpunkte im Hinblick auf die demographische bzw. soziale Schichtung der Gemeinde, auf die Toleranz der Patronatsherren und der Geistlichen sowie auf die Anzahl der Mischehen usw. regulierten. Seit den 1770er Jahren wandte sich dem Problem des Kirchenkalenders auch der absolutistische Staat zu. Kaiser Joseph II. (1780-1790) erließ mehrere Verordnungen, die die Etablierung des Gregorianischen Kalenders in den birituellen Gebieten förderten.[61]

Die große Anzahl von Mischehen im nordöstlichen Ungarn war auch eine der Folgen der leichteren Durchlässigkeit der konfessionellen Grenzen. Die kirchenrechtliche Norm, die die demographische Entwicklung zugunsten der römisch-katholischen Kirche beeinflusste, war die Reverspflicht. Bei Schließung von Mischehen musste der nicht katholische Partner den Revers über die Erziehung der Kinder in

---

[59] BOUYDOSCH: The quadrennial reports, 251.

[60] ZUBKO, Peter: Slávenie sviatkov gréckokatolíkmi na území spoločnom s rímskokatolíkmi podľa relácií z roku 1794 [Feiertage bei den Griechisch-Katholiken auf dem mit Römisch-Katholiken gemischten Gebiet nach der Relation von 1794]. In: Slavica Slovaca 40 (2005), 23-33, hier 31.

[61] Siehe dazu ausführlicher in: ZUBKO: Slávenie sviatkov gréckokatolíkmi (wie Anm. 60), 22-33; LACKO, Michal: The Reduction of the Number of least Days for the Catholics of the Byzantine Rite in Hungary in the XVIII. century. In: Slovak Studies 4 (1964), 197-216, hier 198.

der römisch-katholischen Religion unterzeichnen. Die anfängliche „Nachsichtigkeit“ war Folge der Unfähigkeit seitens der Monarchie, die Verletzung der Reverspflicht zu sanktionieren, und hing mit den interkonfessionellen Beziehungen in diesem Grenzgebiet zusammen. Bis 1768 war laut den Kirchengesetzen die Unterschreibung des Revers vor der Eheschließung „erforderlich“, die Anordnung von Maria Theresia hat den Revers zur unvermeidbaren Bedingung bei allen konfessionsverschiedenen Ehen bestimmt.[62] Die Akzeptanz der Reverspflicht hing in der Praxis von vielen Faktoren ab: von der konfessionellen Verfassung der Gemeinde, von der Konfession des oder der Landesherren oder des Patrons der Kirche, von der gesellschaftlichen Stellung und Autorität der Geistlichen, von der unterschiedlichen sozialen Stellung der Partner usw. In gemischten Ehen haben sich beide Seiten in der Frage der Kindererziehung um einen Konsens bemüht, der den lokalen Usus und die angeführten Faktoren zu berücksichtigen hatte.[63] Es bestand eine im Vergleich zu anderen Gebieten breitgefächerte Skala von Möglichkeiten: Akzeptanz einer, nicht unbedingt römisch-katholischen Konfession, unterschiedliche religiöse Erziehung der Söhne und der Töchter, Nachfolgen des ältesten Sohns (oder wenigsten eines der Söhne) in dem väterlichen Glauben usw. Selten haben die Eltern diese Frage spektakulär zu lösen gesucht. Das Kind wurde lediglich getauft, über seine konfessionelle Zugehörigkeit sollte es zu einem späteren Zeitpunkt selbst entscheiden.

In den konfessionellen Mischehen zeigten vor allem die Griechisch-Katholiken mehr Bereitschaft zu Konzessionen und überließen etwa die Erziehung der Kinder der anderen Seite. Die schwächere Resistenz gegenüber dem Umfeld hing mit der schwächeren sozialen Stellung der Gläubigen und des Klerus sowie der Rolle als „nicht autochthone“ Bevölkerung zusammen.[64] In ursprünglich römisch-katholischen oder kalvinistischen Ortschaften, wo die griechisch-katholischen Neusiedler eine quantitativ dominierende oder zumindest konkurrierende Gruppe gebildet hatten, wurden sie als Kirchengemeinde fast ausnahmslos akzeptiert. Eine wichtige Rolle spielte auch die Abkoppelung von traditionellen sozialen und vor allem familiären Verbindungen. Den wichtigsten Impuls jedoch für die meisten Konversionen gab die Desintegration der Familie, die im entvölkerten und neu besiedelten Gebiet des nordöstlichen Ungarns einen hohen Grad erreichte.[65] Erst nach dem Wiederaufbau der Siedlungsstrukturen konnten sich nämlich die Familienverbindungen festigen. Als „nicht autochthone“ Kirchengemeinde mussten die Siedler verschiedene Beschränkungen auf sich nehmen und den Assimilierungsdruck seitens der Gutsherren und

[62] BUCSAY, Mihály: Das Toleranzpatent in der reformierten Kirche Altungarns. In: Im Lichte der Toleranz. Hg. v. Peter F. BARTON. Wien 1981, 59-104, hier 91.

[63] ŠOLTÉS: Náboženská pluralita na Zemplíne, 258f.

[64] Noch in der zweiten Hälfte des 18. Jahrhunderts waren die Griechisch-Katholiken in der oberen sozialen Schicht einer Dorfgesellschaft – Bauern mit einer ganzen oder einer halben Session – nur selten vertreten. Sie bewirtschafteten am häufigsten eine viertel-, achtel- oder noch kleinere Sessionen, was auch Bischof Michael Olsavszky in seiner Visitation festhielt. ГАДЖЕГА, Василій: Додатки до історії русинов и руских церквей в був. жупе Земплинской 12 (1937), 39f.

[65] VOLKLAND, Frauke: Konfession, Konversion und soziales Drama. Ein Plädoyer für die Ablösung des Paradigmas der „konfessionellen Identität“. In: VON GREYERZ (u.a.): Interkonfessionalität, 91-104.

der Pfarrer anderer Konfessionen abwehren.[66] Oft hatten sie Kirchenzehnt und Stolgebühren dem kalvinistischen Pastor zu entrichten.[67] Die Visitationen des Bischofs von Erlau in den Jahren 1749 und 1772 hielten vor allem in den Gebieten mit einer starken kalvinistischen Kirche viele Beschwerden bezüglich der Verletzung von religiösen Geboten fest. Kalvinistische Prediger sollen demnach ausserhalb ihrer Pfarrei Seelsorge betrieben haben und viele Katholiken beider Riten sowie Lutheraner zur „Apostasie“ veranlasst haben.[68] Im Laufe der nächsten Generationen festigte sich die konfessionelle Identität der Griechisch-Katholiken. Die Umgebung hörte auf, sie als Zuzügler wahrzunehmen, und gleichzeitig mit dem Durchdringen der oberen Gesellschaftsschichten wuchs auch das Selbstverständnis der Einzelnen wie der ganzen Kirchengemeinde an.

Die Anzahl der Mischehen bei den griechisch-katholischen Bewohnern war an der Wende des 18. zum 19. Jahrhundert in gemischten Gebieten beträchtlich. In Dekanaten des mittleren und südlichen Zempli, nämlich in Humenné, Sečovce, Sátoraljaújhely, Bodrogkeresztúr und Tokaj, bewegte sich der Anteil der gemischten griechisch- und römisch-katholischen Ehen zwischen 20% bis 26%. Im Dekanat von Vranov, das einen hohen Anteil an Evangelischen A.B. aufwies, gab es ausser einem häufigen Vorkommen von rituell gemischten Ehen (18%) auch etwa 4% griechisch-katholisch-lutherischer Partnerschaften. In Städten und Marktflecken war der Anteil homogener und rituell gemischter Ehen am höchsten.[69] Im gesamten Zempliner Komitat waren 1806 von allen Ehen, die mindestens ein griechisch-katholischer Partner geschlossen hatte, 86% rein griechisch-katholisch, bei 13% war ein Partner römisch-katholisch, bei 0,7% war er reformiert und bei 0,6% ist er lutherisch gewesen. Für das Dekanat Kaschau (sk. Košice) liegen folgende Zahlen vor: Dort waren im Jahre 1806 nur die Hälfte der Ehen von „rein“ östlichen Ritus, 45% dagegen waren von Katholiken beider Riten gebildet, 3% der Fälle weisen die Partnerschaft mit einem Lutheraner nach und bei 2% ist einer der Partner reformiert gewesen. Im Dekanat von Preschau (sk. Prešov) waren nach Angaben der Kirchenbücher 56% der Ehen von zwei griechisch-katholischen Partnern geschlossen worden, in 41% der Fälle war einer der Lebensgefährten römisch-katholisch und zu 3% war er lutherisch.[70]

[66] Der Munkatscher Bischof Michael Olsavszky wies in seinem Kommentar zur Visitation die Königin darauf hin, dass die griechisch-katholischen Untertanen „wegen Priestermangel ohne die heiligen Sakramente sterben, allmählich die nichtkatholischen [Gottesdienste] besuchen und letztlich zu einer nichtkatholischen Konfession übertreten.” ГАДЖЕГА, Василій: Додатки до исторії русинов и руских церквей в був. жупе Земплинской 12 (1937), 40.

[67] ŠOLTÉS/ ŽEŇUCH: Sociálne postavenie gréckokatolíckeho duchovenstva, 137f.

[68] AACass, Districtualia, Vol. 3, Fasc 2. Protocollum Canonicae Visitationis 1749, Pars Prior, Districtus Submontanus et Ujhelyiensis (nesignované). – AACass, Districtualia, Vol. 3, Fasc 2. Protocollum Canonicae Visitationis 1749, Pars posterior, Districtus Homonensis (nesignované). – AACass. Districtualia, Vol. 4. fasc. 1, Protocollum Canonicae Visitationis 1772.

[69] Einige Beispiele (die erste Angabe bezieht sich dabei auf rein griechisch-katholische Ehen, die zweite auf rituell gemischte Ehen): Humenné 12/30, Michalovce 42/54, Staré 23/29, Budkovce 29/22, Vranov nad Topľou 12/13, Sečovce 105/41. Vgl. UDVARI: A munkácsi görögkatolikus püspökség (wie Anm. 15), 140-154.

[70] УДВАРІ: Причинки до історії підкарпатських Русинів, 153.

Der griechische Ritus hat im 18. Jahrhundert den Übergang aus der konfessionell homogenen Welt des Katholizismus in das Milieu der konfessionellen Pluralität geschafft. Den neuen Bedingungen der gemeinsamen Kirchenorganisation passten sich beide Seiten nach einigen Generationen an. Die Etablierung der dritten, in manchen Ortschaften gar der vierten Konfessionskirche – der griechisch-katholischen – hat dabei die interkonfessionelle Kommunikation tiefgreifend beeinflusst. Während in den Lokalgesellschaften mit der bikonfessionellen Bevölkerungsstruktur die sozialen Normen zur konfessionellen Homogenisierung geführt hatten, war auf dem breiten Gebiet des nordöstlichen Ungarn eine solche Konsequenz schon aufgrund der demographischen Verhältnisse praktisch ausgeschlossen: Die Schließung von konfessionsgemischten Ehen, häufige Nichteinhaltung der Reverspflicht, gemeinsame Benutzung der Glocke, gemeinsame Friedhöfe und andere Formen der interkonfessionellen Kommunikation, die bis zur Vertiefung des Säkularisierungsprozesses im Widerspruch zur kirchenrechtlichen sowie zu staatlichen Normen standen, bestimmten das Zusammenleben. Festzuhalten bleibt, dass sich diese Art des konfessionellen Zusammenlebens auf das Auf- bzw. Vorkommen von konfessionsbedingten Konflikten mildernd ausgewirkt hat.[71]

[71] ŠOLTÉS: Náboženská pluralita na Zemplíne, 259.

Sándor Őze

Städtemigration im Winkel zwischen Theiß, Mieresch und Kreisch nach der Vertreibung der Türken

Ich war etwa zehn Jahre alt, als meine Großmutter – mit dem Familiennamen Csepregi – in den Wintermonaten „szárma" kochte. So nennt man die mit Hackfleisch gefüllten Krautblätter im südlichen Teil der Großen Tiefebene. Das Gericht ist türkischer Herkunft. Üblicherweise bereitete man diese Speise unmittelbar nach dem Sauschlachten und zwar aus der Paprikawurstfüllung zu. Dazu nimmt man den „nagykotla", einen kesselartigen Topf, der in der kalten Kammer (in der Mundart „komra") abgestellt wird. Ja nach Bedarf wird soviel von der halb zubereiteten Speise zur jeweiligen Mahlzeit entnommen wie nötig. Meine Großmutter rührte das Bindemittel aus Paprika und Mehl zusammen und erklärte, dass die Leute aus der nahe gelegenen Stadt Orosháza diese Speise mit Rahm anrühren. Auf meine Frage warum das so sei, erwiderte sie: Weil sie Lutheraner sind wie auch Tante Juli. Bei der Erwähnung ihrer Schwägerin wusste ich, dass die Geschichte ein gutes Ende nehmen würde. Nicht allein weil meine Großmutter katholisch war und somit alle ihre Vorfahren als ersten Vornamen Maria bekommen mussten, sondern auch weil ihre Schwägerin einst ihre Rivalin in einem Erbstreit war. Das Ackerland der Csepregis, „das Feld", befand sich im „Nagykirályság", in den Grenzfluren zwischen Szentes und Orosháza. „Nagykirályság" und „Kiskirályság" waren lediglich durch eine schmale Flur voneinander getrennt, wobei ersterer zu Orosháza, der andere zu Szentes gehörte. Auf beiden Seiten lebten Leute mit dem Familiennamen Csepregi. Die in Orosháza waren evangelisch, die aus Szentes katholisch. Nicht einmal ein Gedanke wurde ihrerseits darauf verschwendet, ob diese Familien einst miteinander verwandt gewesen sein konnten. Zumal die Csepregis in Orosháza einen anderen Dialekt, nämlich den aus Transdanubien, sprachen.

Die ungarische Historiographie nahm das Land zwischen dem Theiß (ung. Tisza), dem Mieresch (ung. Maros) und dem Kreisch (ung. Kőrös) schon im Mittelalter als eine Region wahr. Nach der Vertreibung der Osmanen wurde sie unter den Komitaten Békés, Csanád und Csongrád aufgeteilt. Südlich vom Mieresch erstreckt sich das Banat, nördlich von der Kreisch-Mündung aber der über eine autonome Verwaltung verfügende sog. Kumanen-Bezirk. In dieser Abhandlung thematisiere ich nur die zwei Städte am Theiß, Hódmezővásárhely und Szentes, sowie Szegvár als Herrschaftszentrale und die von diesen östlich liegende Stadt Orosháza. Diese Orte zeigen jeweils unterschiedliche Ansiedlungsmodelle vom Anfang des 18. Jahrhunderts auf und spiegeln vornehmlich die Migrationsbewegungen des ungarischen Ethnikums wider.[1] Die freie königliche Stadt Szeged etwa funktionierte als militärische Verwaltungszentrale und blieb die ganze Türkenherrschaft hindurch eine katholische Stadt. Die Städte Makó, Csongrád, Gyula, Arad, Békéscsaba usw., also Städte im Komitat Békés, Zaránd, Arad etc. wiederum wiesen stets einen großen Anteil von Nichtmagyaren auf und müssten nach anderen Kriterien untersucht werden.

Die Migrationsbewegungen der Nachosmanenzeit sind in dieser Region bis heute nicht erforscht. Lediglich für die Lokalgeschichte bilden sie einen obligatorischen Bestandteil der Vergangenheit, doch sie werden nie regional kontextualisiert. So fehlen auch die methodischen Überlegungen einer gründlicheren Untersuchung dieser Frage. Dabei zeigen schon die ersten Überlegungen nachvollziehbare Regelmäßigkeiten, die Zeit und Raum bedingten: Die in der Osmanenzeit – aus welchen Gründen auch immer – dem Verfall hingegebenen Städte wurden fast immer genau dort wieder besiedelt wie vor der Osmanenherrschaft. In dieser Region z.B. (Békés)Csaba oder Orosháza, die nach einem mehrere Generationen anhaltenden Scheintod wieder zum Leben erweckt wurden. Die größeren Städte der Region wie Szeged, Túr, Vásárhely, Gyula, Wardein (Várad) oder Debrecen behielten weiterhin ihre zentrale Rolle in der ökonomischen Steuerung der Region.

Um schlüssige Kontinuitätslinien ziehen zu können untersuchte ich die Matrikelbücher ausgewählter Gemeinden, sofern dies nicht bereits erfolgt war. Die Namenslisten verglich ich mit den Namen aus den 20er Jahren des 19. Jahrhunderts, um das Verhältnis der Neusiedler und der Abziehenden zu eruieren. Ich sortierte dabei die fremd klingenden Namen sowie jene heraus, die einen Ort oder Region beinhalteten, mit einem Erfolg von 80%. Danach verglich ich sie mit den Namenskonskriptionen der Sandschak Tschanad (Csanád), Gyula und Temeswar (Temesvár), um die Migrationsbewegungen der engeren Region zu rekonstruieren.[2] Im Gegensatz zu meinen ursprünglichen Erwartungen gab es wenige Namen aus Trasndanubien, dafür aber – wider Erwarten – durchaus häufig jedoch Namen aus der Batschka bzw. den Südregionen Ungarn. Auch die Anzahl von Familiennamen, die teils Namen aus mittelalterlichen Siedlungen enthielten, war sehr häufig, bei den Reformierten in Szentes etwa die Hälfte. Auch dies belegt, dass während der Turbulenzen der Türkenkriege die Bevölkerung sich in der Umgebung, meist im Moorland der Theiss, versteckt hatte und nach dem Ende der Gefahr wieder zurückkehrte. Die von Ignácz Acsády und Gyula Szekfű vertretene These des „völlig verwüsteten Landes in der Osmanenherrschaft" kann also nicht bestätigt werden; bereits die Osmanisten verwiesen dar-

[1] Als wichtigste Fachliteratur siehe dazu KÁLDY NAGY, Gyula: A gyulai szandzsák [Der Sandschak Gyula]. Budapest 1980. – DERS.: A csanádi szandzsák [Der Sandschak Tschanad]. Budapest 2002. – KARÁCSONYI, János: Békés vármegye története [Geschichte des Komitats Békés]. Bd. I-III. Gyula 1896. – BOROVSZKY, Samu: Csanád vármegye története 1715-ig [Geschichte des Komitates Tschanad bis 1715]. Budapest 1897. – SZEREMLEI, Samu: Hódmezővásárhely története [Die Geschichte von Hódmezővásárhely]. Bd. III. A leigáztatás kora (1526-1848) [Die Zeit der Unterjochung (1526-1848)]. (Hódmezővásárhely 1907). Reprint Tótkomlós 2001. – Hódmezővásárhely története [Die Geschichte von Hódmezővásárhely]. Hg. v. István NAGY. Hódmezővásárhely 1984. – BLAZOVICH, László: Szeged rövid története [Kurze Geschichte von Szeged]. Szeged 2005.

[2] Leider fehlen die Namenslisten der Sandschak Szeged, Kolotscha (ung. Kalocsa) und Ofen (ung. Buda).

auf, dass vor den Befreiungskriegen (1683-1699) eine Mischbevölkerung von Ungarn und Südslawen sesshaft waren.[3]
Die Familiennamen mit Ortsnamenbezug wiederum zeigen die Handelswege in dieser Region: Dad, der Weg bei Tiszalök von Bátor und Káló über Dobos an der Theiss nach Szentes, Debrecen, Böszörmény, Balmazújváros, Poroszló, und Heves Richtung Gyöngyös bzw. Debrecen, Szoboszló, Nádudvar, Szolnok, auf dem Landweg Richtung Békés und Szeghalom. Die Region war Richtung Szeged nur auf Wasserwegen erreichbar; auch Richtung Becse und Bács wurden die Siedlungen durch die Flüsse miteinander verbunden. An der Donau liegt das kleine Pest, woher der Träger des Namens „Pesti" stammte (und nicht aus der späteren Hauptstadt) oder das benachbarte Bécs (Wien), woher der Immigrant nach Szentes zog nicht aus Österreich.
Das Land, wo die hier behandelten Städte angrenzen, ist eine seit dem Neolithikum bewohnte Tiefebene. Nach den Verwüstungen der Tatareneinfälle (1241) erstreckte sich das Gebiet der kumanischen Siedlungen bis zum Mieresch. Erst die Osmanenherrschaft brachte hier gravierende Veränderungen mit sich. Die Dominanz der Viehzucht wurde hier nie in Frage gestellt, seit dem 16. Jahrhundert erfolgte der Export Richtung Mitteleuropa. Vor den Flussregulierungen im 19. Jahrhundert wurde die Flora wie die Fauna der Puszta von einem dichten System von Gewässern bestimmt. Auf diesen Wasserwegen wurde noch Anfang des 19. Jahrhunderts das Getreide Richtung Südosten transportiert, wie im Mittelalter in die umgekehrte Richtung Stein aus Siebenbürgen geliefert worden war.
Die großen Städte, also Vásárhely, Szeged und Makó bewahrten bis heute ihren autochtonen Dialekt.[4] Die während der Osmanenherrschaft dezimierte Bevölkerung in den Städten wurde nach dem Frieden von Karlowitz (1699) mithilfe von Binnenwanderungen ausgeglichen. Dabei spielten konfessionelle Aspekte eine signifikante Rolle. Nicht wenige Familien von hier lebten in den vergangenen 300 Jahren in einem Umkreis von 20 km um die von mir behandelten Städte herum. Die jeweilige Bevölkerung bildete dabei eine geschlossene, nicht selten introvertierte Gemeinschaft, und bis Ende des 19. Jahrhunderts wurden sie miteinander 4. oder 5. Grades verwandt. Dabei waren konfessionelle aber auch ethnische Mischehen strengstens untersagt. Auch im Alltag machte man einen großen Bogen um die Siedlung einer anderen Konfession.

[3] So urteilte Acsády: „Hinsichtlich der demographischen Entwicklung war sie [die Türkenherrschaft] ein Progrom. Überall wo der Türke hinkam, wurde das Gebiet langsam entvölkert und zur Wüste". ACSÁDY, Ignácz: Magyarország belállapota 1680 [Die inneren Zustände Ungarns 1680]. In: Századok 19 (1885), 549-562, hier 560. – Zu den Rahmenbedingungen siehe besonders für unsere Region DÁVID, Géza: Pasák és bégek uralma alatt [Unter der Herrschaft der Paschas und Begs]. Budapest 2005, 13-52 und 97-184.
[4] So wird bis heute anstatt „e" im Wort meist „ö" gesagt, etc.

Reichtum und Integrationskraft: Hódmezővásárhely

Die drei Städte lagen ungefähr 30 km voneinander entfernt. Von ihnen zählte Hódmezővásárhely mit 60.000 Personen die meisten Bewohner. Diese Zahl stagnierte allerdings ab 1870. Im Gegensatz zu den anderen hier behandelten Städten gab es eine Kontinuität hinsichtlich der Bevölkerung vor der Türkenherrschaft. Die Einwohnerzahl von Orosháza und Szentes machte jeweils die Hälfte der von Hódmezővásárhely aus. Die Burg von Gyula war die letzte bedeutende Festung der Osmanen, die sich sogar bis 1699, also zum Frieden von Karlowitz, halten konnte. Die Bevölkerung der Gegend wurde durch die lange Belagerung der Festung völlig erschöpft. Die Familiennamen der Stadtbewohner waren nicht nur mit den Namen in den türkischen Deftern, sondern auch mit den Namen aus dem Mittelalter identisch. Nach der Türkenherrschaft erhielt die Stadt der spätere Kuruzzengeneral Graf Sándor Károlyi.[5] 1722 wurden in Vásárhely 457 Namen konskribiert, davon 266 alte und 191 neue, aber auch die letzteren stammten aus der unmittelbaren Gegend, also aus einem Radius von etwa 30 km.[6] 1739 fiel etwa die Hälfte der 4.918 Einwohner der Pestepidemie zum Opfer. Doch schon 1747 führten die Matrikelbücher wieder über 325 kalvinistisch-reformierte und mehr als 42 katholische Namen auf. Schätzungen gehen von einer Durchschnittsbevölkerung von 8.000 Menschen aus. Die katholische Bevölkerung machte in der Stadt um die 8-10% aus. 1751 kann eine Einwohnerzahl von 8.524 belegt werden. Im selben Jahr gab es einen größeren Zuzug: 36 Familien aus der in der Nähe von Szeged gelegene Stadt Algyő trafen auf ihren kleinen Ruderbooten mit lautem Psalmensang ein.[7] Doch auch die strategische Planung des Konnubiums führte zum Bevölkerungswachstum: Man wählte seinen Partner aus einer anderen Stadt, doch der gleichen Konfession zugehörig. In der zweiten Hälfte des 18. Jahrhunderts nahm allerdings die Einwanderung deutlich ab und wurde allmählich quantitativ irrelevant. So gab es 1763 291 Neusiedler, zwischen 1764 und 1795 insgesamt 319. Zwischen 1796 und 1825 ließen sich nur noch 194 Personen in der Stadt nieder.[8] Die Kalvinisten behielten dabei stets die Mehrheit, wenn auch der Abstand zu den Katholiken stets abnahm.[9] Im Vergleich zur Immigration war die Auswanderung deutlich kleiner: Immerhin gründeten in den 1770er Jahren Vásárhelyer Kleinhäusler, die sich mit Tabakanbau beschäftigten und auf Steuerbegünstigungen hofften, die Gemeinde Debellias-Torontálvásárhely im

---

[5] Zum Kontext siehe ÉBLE, Gábor: A Harruckern és a Károlyi család [Die Familien Harruckern und Károlyi]. Budapest 1895.

[6] NAGY: Hódmezővásárhely története, 365.

[7] Auch hierbei spielte Konfession die ausschlaggebende Rolle: Das katholische Szeged, das seine katholische Dominanz auch während der Osmanenherrschaft dank den hier lebenden Franziskanern bewahrt hatte, war für die Algyőer ein Konfliktpotential. EBD.

[8] Zu dieser Zeit war Hódmezővásárhely mit ihren 26.000 Bewohnern nach Pest, Debrecen, Pressburg (Pozsony), Szabadka (Subotica), Kecskemét, Szeged und Ofen (Buda) die größte Stadt des Königreiches, 1870 sogar die fünftgrößte Stadt. Die Bewohnerzahl stagniert seither bis heute. Vgl. NAGY: Hódmezővásárhely története, 366.

[9] So gab es 1825 19.111 Kalvinisten, 6.261 Katholiken, 762 Orthodoxe und 32 Juden. 1839 21.313 Kalvinisten, 6.570 Katholiken, 1.038 Orthodoxe und 50 Juden. EBD., 455-456.

Banat. Die verwandtschaftlichen Beziehungen wie auch der alte Dialekt wurden dabei von den Migranten weitergepflegt.[10]
Vásárhely entrichtete an ihren Grundherrn eine Pauschalsumme an Steuern. Dabei führten die Károlyis wegen des Weidelandes, aus dem der Großteil der Einkünfte der Stadtbevölkerung stammte, langjährige Prozesse. Auf Empfehlung des Statthaltereirats wurden schließlich 1777 Katholiken aus Oberungarn angesiedelt, um die Stadt zu teilen. Im katholischen Zentrum am Stadtrand, neben dem Getreidehafen am Theiß wurde eine Statue des Heiligen Johannes von Nepomuk errichtet, die über Nacht von den Kalvinisten verstümmelt wurde. Der Kampf der Konfessionen um die symbolischen Plätze ging weiter: Als die vor 1699 mit einer Mauer umringte, auch militärischen Zwecken dienende Altkirche zu eng wurde, ließ die protestantische Gemeinde die zweitgrößte reformierte Kirche der Großen Tiefebene neben dem katholischen Zentrum erbauen.[11] Der Platz hieß zwar weiterhin Johannesplatz, doch in der Erinnerungskultur wurde er nach Johann Calvin benannt. Die zwecks Teilung der Stadt angesiedelte katholische Bevölkerung wurde in ihren Gewohnheiten, im Verhalten und in ihrer Mundart assimiliert – aber nicht in der Konfession.
Der Wohlstand von Hódmezővásárhely wurzelte im System der freien Puszta, worin die Stadt als modellhaft in ganz Ungarn galt: Nicht das Ackerland sondern das Weideland war der Schlüssel zum Erfolg, da die Bevölkerung traditionell vom Viehzucht lebte. Wer ein Haus in der Stadt hatte, also „Hausbesitzer“ war, wie es im Volksmund hieß, hatte auch das Recht auf Viehzucht auf der unendlichen Weite der Puszta. Wer einen Brunnen in der Puszta gegraben hatte, erhielt auch das Gebiet um den Brunnen von der Stadt zur Nutzung.[12] Zunächst wurden einfache Unterkünfte, Hirtenhütten, später auch größere Bauernhöfe gebaut, wohin die jüngeren Familienmitglieder mit den Hirten und den „Betyáren“ hinauszogen.[13] Die ständige Bevölkerung der Pusztahöfe machte bis zum Ende des 18. Jahrhunderts nicht einmal 10% der Stadt aus.[14]
Ihren Schutz organisierte diese Gesellschaft selbst. Die von den Pusztaburschen der Türkenzeit gebildete Organisation, das so genannte „Bauernkomitat“ mit seinen von der Bevölkerung gewählten „Offizieren“ half der staatlichen wie der Exekutive des Komitates.[15] Das bedeutete natürlich, dass die im 18. Jahrhundert angestrebte Demilitarisierung der Gesellschaft in dieser Region unmöglich war. Diese Form einer bewaffneten Gesellschaft blieb hier als Erbe der Türkenzeit intakt. Der in der Puszta

---

[10] Bis heute pflegt z.B. die Familie Szenti den Kontakt nach Serbien mit ihren im 18. Jahrhundert abgewanderten Verwandten. Freundliche Mitteilung von Tibor Szenti.
[11] NAGY: Hódmezővásárhely története, 612.
[12] Vgl. Dazu ausführlich SZENTI, Tibor: A tanya. Hagyományos és átalakuló paraszti élet a hódmezővásárhely-kopáncsi tanyavilágban [Die Tanya. Traditionelles und sich änderndes Bauernleben in der Tanyawelt von Hódmezővásárhely-Kopáncs]. Budapest 1979.
[13] Als eine Art Vagabunden oder Ruhestörer durften die Betyáren die Stadt nie betreten. Man musste bei der Stadt melden, wollte man einen Betyár in sein Haus einlassen. Viele von ihnen nahmen es tatsächlich mit den Gesetzen nicht so genau, Schmuggel, Raub oder Diebstahl war ihnen nicht fremd. Im 19. Jahrhundert galt der Name bereits als synonym für Viehdieb und Räuber.
[14] NAGY: Hódmezővásárhely története, 456-67.
[15] SZEREMLEI: Hódmezővásárhely, 268-297. – Zu den Bauernkomitaten siehe SZAKÁLY, Ferenc: Parasztvármegyék a XVII. és XVIII. században [Die Bauernkomitate im 17. und 18. Jahrhundert]. Budapest 1969.

lebende Teil der Großfamilie wurde mit den Knechten und Dienstmägden, Freunden und Hirten ergänzt. Diese bildeten im Weideland der vier Städte den Kreis der Nachbarn und der Miteigentümer. Der Leiter einer solchen Siedlung war seit der Türkenzeit bzw. seit der Errichtung der kumanischen Puszta im Mittelalter in der Lage, eine Truppe aus mehreren hunderten bewaffneten Reitern zu mobilisieren.[16]
Die Pusztahöfe waren wie eine Burganlage: In der Mitte stand die „Tscharda", die in der Osmanenzeit eine kleine Kundschafter-Garnison bedeutete, im 18. Jahrhundert allerdings war sie Handelszentrum, Gaststätte mit Unterkunft und Verpflegung für die Herde. Sie konnte verteidigt werden und war oft von einer Ziegelmauer oder einer Planke umgeben. Die Tscharda war also eine Art Karawanserei, der Geist der Türkenzeit lebte hier fort: Sie bedeutete Schutz für Menschen und Tiere auf dem Weg zum Markt, war aber auch geheimer Treffpunkt der Hehler und Schmuggler. Vásárhely verbot der Bevölkerung dieser Bauernhöfe, außerhalb der Stadtgrenze in der Puszta Geschäfte mit Türken, Griechen, Armeniern, also mit Händlern aus dem Balkan, zu betreiben. In der Stadt selbst wurde 1807 eine orthodoxe Kirche für diese vor allem bulgarisch-mazedonische Gemeinschaft gebaut, die etwa 600 Personen zählte und bis 1848 von den Juden verdrängt wurde.

Anpassung ohne Glaubenswechsel: Orosháza

1743 ließen sich evangelisch-lutherische Familien aus Zomba, Komitat Tolna in Süd-Transdanubien, in der riesigen Puszta von Vásárhely nieder.[17] Diese ungarischen Protestanten waren den Umzug gewohnt, denn auch in Zomba fanden sie 20 Jahre zuvor ihre provisorische Niederlassung. Folgende Ortsnamen der einstigen Nádasdy-Güter, die das erste ethnisch ungarische evangelische Gebiet Ungarns gebildet hatten, wurden unter den Familiennamen von Orosháza eingetragen, wie Sitkei, Pápai, Szili, Körmendi usw.[18] Sie sprachen einen transdanubischen Dialekt und brachten auch ihre Esskultur mit. Ein Teil zog später weiter und gründete die evangelische Siedlung in Nyíregyháza. Die wichtigste Sekundärsiedlung von Orosháza jedoch war Fazekasvarsánd zwischen Gyula und Arad.[19]
Die Bevölkerung von Orosháza passte sich sehr schnell an die Gegebenheiten in ihrer neuen Heimat an. Sie hatte auch keine Alternative, sie wurde dazu richtig gedrängt: Es gab nämlich in der Weite weder Stein noch eine größere Wasserfläche

[16] EBD.
[17] VERESS, József: Orosháza történeti és statisztikai adatok alapján [Orosháza anhand von historischen und statistischen Daten]. Hg. v. Ferenc SZABÓ. Békéscsaba 1987. – KOSZORÚS, Oszkár: Orosháza betelepítése [Die Besiedlung von Orosháza]. In: Harruckern emlékülés Orosháza 2001. április 23. [Harruckern Gedenksitzung Orosháza, 23. April. 2001.] Orosháza 2001, hier 32-36.
[18] Vgl. HAJDÚ, Mihály: Orosháza XVIII. századi személynévrendszere [Namensverzeichnis von Orosháza im 18. Jahrhundert]. In: Tanulmányok Orosházáról és környékéről. Orosháza (Békés megyei múzeumok közleményei 7), 43-112. – JÁROLI, József: Orosháza népesedéstörténetének néhány kérdése a XVIII. században [Einige Fragen der Bevölkerungsgeschichte von Orosháza im 18. Jh.]. In: EBD., 23-42.
[19] Siehe dazu ausführlich CSEPREGI, György: Adatok Fazekasvarsánd történetéhez [Angaben zur Geschichte von Fazekasvarsánd]. Arad 1892.

und nur einen einzigen Baum, an dem sich die Neusiedler auch tatsächlich niederließen. In der Erinnerungskultur bildete dieser Baum das Zentrum ihres „Sakralraumes", der identitätsstiftend wirkte.[20] Die Neuankömmlinge lebten zunächst in Zelten, später in Häusern mit gestampften Wänden. Auch die erste Kirche wurde so erbaut. Die Migranten mussten etliche Heimsuchungen über sich ergehen lassen: Nachts wurden sie von den bewaffneten Hirten aus Vásárhely belästigt, indem deren Rinderherden und Gestüt durch ihre Siedlung getrieben und dabei die ganze Gemeinde verwüstet wurde.[21] Für die Neusiedler stellte sich die Frage, ob sie nach Transdanubien zurückkehren und die Puszta den Hirten von Vásárhely zurücklassen, damit sie ihre etablierte Lebensweise fortführen, oder sich mit allen Konsequenzen den gegebenen Verhältnissen anpassen. Die Mehrheit schlug den zweiten Weg ein. Sie eigneten sich die Kunst der Viehzucht an, auch ihre Kleidung wurde den Anforderungen des Klimas und der Arbeitsweise angepasst. Selbst 100 Jahre später gab es nach den Überlieferungen keine Spur von Gärten.[22] Was sie allerdings kompromisslos behielten, was ihre evangelisch-lutherische Konfession.

Die geduldete Koexistenz der Konfessionen: Szentes

Wie in Vásárhely konnte auch die Bevölkerung von Szentes eine Kontinuität seit dem Mittelalter aufweisen. Die Alteingesessenen kehrten nach der Türkenzeit Anfang 1701 in die Stadt zurück, die stürmischen Zeiten des Großen Türkenkrieges (1683-1699) überlebten sie auf den geschützten Inseln der Flüsse Theiß und Kurca. Die Überfahrt bei Böld war nämlich neben Szeged, Szolnok und Tokaj die wichtigste Überfahrt am Theiß, wo sogar in der zweiten Hälfte des 17. Jahrhunderts eine kleine Brücke errichtet wurde. Deshalb wurde hier eine deutsche, katholische Fähren- und Zollkolonie gegründet, die sich später magyarisieren ließ.[23] Die eigentliche Immigration setzte allerdings im 18. Jahrhundert ein.

Die Bevölkerung von Szentes bestand aus reformierten und katholischen Ansiedlern. Die Matrikelbücher der Katholiken beginnen mit 1750, die der Reformierten 10 Jahre früher. Die Ansiedlung erfolgte also etwa zeitgleich mit Orosháza, zumal auch diese Stadt in den Besitz der Familie Harruckern überging.[24] Später ging sie mit der

---

[20] Zur Theorie des „Sakralraumes" siehe ASSMANN, Jan: Kulturális emlékezet. Írás, emlékezés és politikai identitás a korai magaskultúrákban [Das kulturelle Gedächtnis. Schrift, Erinnerung und politische Identität in frühen Hochkulturen]. Budapest 2004, 79-83. – Er stützt sich dabei auf Forschungen von Eliade. Vgl. ELIADE, Mircea: Das Heilige und das Profane. Vom Wesen des Religiösen. Hamburg 1957. – VERESS: Orosháza, 18.

[21] IMPLOM, József: Olvasókönyv Békés megye történetéhez II. (1694-1848) [Lesebuch zur Geschichte des Komiattes Bekesch. Bd.II. (1694-1848)] Békéscsaba 1971, 46. – Veress: Orosháza, 7.

[22] EBD., 30. – Siehe dazu ausführlicher NAGY, Gyula: Hagyományos földművelés a Vásárhelyi-pusztán [Traditionelle Landwirtschaft in der Puszta von Vásárhely]. Budapest 1963, (Néprajzi közlemények Bd. 7/2).

[23] SIMA, Ferenc: Szentes város története [Geschichte der Stadt Szentes]. Budapest 1914.

[24] Der Hofkriegslieferant Johann Georg Harruckern erhielt 1720 die Herrschaft Gyula. Für seine Dienste in den Befreiungskriegen wurde er in den Stand der Reichsritterschaft erhoben. Vgl. dazu IMPLOM: Olvasókö-

Hand von Josefa Harruckern in den Besitz der Familie Károlyi über. Der Statthaltereirat versuchte sowohl die reformierte als auch die im Komitat allmählich einsikkernde orthodoxe Bevölkerung zu katholisieren. 1723 wurden deshalb katholische Paloczen angesiedelt, dennoch gab es 1745 lediglich 23 katholische Familien.[25] Etwa ein Drittel dieser Familien machten laut Matrikelbücher die verschiedenen Zweige der Familie Őze aus, die sich vor allem in dem unteren Stadtteil niedergelassen hatten.[26] Die Herkunftsregion der Neusiedler wie auch jener Region, aus der diese später ihre Ehepartner holten, lassen sich bei beiden Konfessionen genau bestimmen. Bei den Kalvinisten waren dies das Gebiet jenseits der Theiss, nämlich die Städte der Komitate Szolnok, Bihar, Sathmar (Szatmár) und Zaránd, bei den Katholiken die Diözese Waitzen (Vác), vor allem die Siedlungen entlang der Galga. Während bei den Katholiken etwa 25% der Namen fremd klingt und auf slowakische oder deutsche Herkunft schließen lässt, gibt es solche unter den Kalvinisten praktisch überhaupt nicht. Ebenso gibt es bei den Kalvinisten keine nennenswerten Migrationen.

Nach der Ankunft der Paloczen bestand die Stadt aus zwei Teilen: Die kalvinistisch-reformierte „Oberpartei“ separierte sich von der katholischen „Unterpartei“. Zwischen den beiden Teilen gab es nur selten Berührungspunkte oder „Seitenwechsel“. Die Kalvinisten fürchteten nämlich um den Verlust ihrer Vormachtstellung und versuchten die Ansiedlung der Katholiken mit allen Mitteln zu unterbinden. Sogar das Haus eines Neusiedlers wurde über Nacht ruiniert, um ein Exempel zu statuieren. Eine neutrale Koexistenz der Konfessionen charakterisierte die Stadt. Doch die Einwanderung der Katholiken ließ nicht nach, und auch der Stadtrat hatte, nicht zuletzt auf Druck des Gutsherrn, auch katholische Mitglieder. Die Katholiken hielten ihre Prozessionen jedoch stets innerhalb der Kirchenmauer ab. Einmal im Jahr begaben sie sich auf das Ackerland zur Danksagung, dabei durften sie den Stadtteil der Protestanten nicht betreten, um Handgreiflichkeiten aus dem Weg zu gehen.

Szegvár

Die Stadt war das Zentrum der Herrschaft Károlyi. Graf Alexander Károlyi ließ 1726 aus den Ruinen des ehemaligen Renaissance-Schlosses ein neues Palais bauen. Zu dessen Versorgung ließ er einen Garten anlegen, der in dieser Gegend als einzig-

nyv, 38-39. – Mein Dank gilt auch Herrn Géza Nagy, der sich der Erforschung der Geschichte von Szentes gewidmet hat und mir wertvolle Informationen lieferte.

[25] Matrikelbücher der römisch-katholischen Pfarrei 1750-1760, Szentes. – Matrikelbücher der kalvinistisch-reformierten Gemeinde Szentes, 1740-1750.

[26] Der Name war schon im 16. Jahrhundert zwischen Oberungarn und dem Szeklerland verbreitet. Diese Familie stammte wahrscheinlich aus Jazygien oder aus dem katholischen Szeged. Vgl. KÁZMÉR, Miklós: Régi magyar családnevek szótára. XVI-XVII. század [Wörterbuch alter ungarischer Familiennamen. 16.-17. Jahrhundert]. Budapest 1993, 807.

artig galt.[27] Die Bevölkerung auf der Puszta des ehemaligen Dorfes bestand anfangs aus sechs Familien, dann ließen sich 19 Walachen nieder, die aber entweder wieder fortzogen oder sich katholisierten, da sie einige Jahre später in den Konskriptionen nicht mehr vorkommen. Der Gutsherr duldete in Szegvár ausschließlich die katholische Konfession. Die wichtigste Beschäftigung war die Pferdezucht.
Die Károlyis stellten im 18. und19. Jahrhundert ein Husarenregiment, dessen Pferde hier gezüchtet wurden. Zunächst versuchten sie Vásárhely für diese Aufgabe zu gewinnen, worauf die vornehmlich aus freien Menschen bestehende Stadt gar nicht einging. Vielmehr zahlte sie die vereinbarte Taxe als Pauschalsumme.[28] Allein das herrschaftliche Gestüt zählte zu dieser Zeit 1.000 vornehmlich türkische Pferde auf der Puszta von Szegvár.[29]
Die Namen zeigen, wie bunt zusammengewürfelt die Immigranten waren. Wichtigstes Integrationskriterium war die Konfession, sie bestimmte letztlich alles. In Mindszent, in der Nachbarschaft von Szegvár, durften sich Anfang des Jahrhunderts ebenfalls nur Katholiken aus Siebenbürgen niederlassen. Die Fertilität war auch hier sehr hoch, nämlich acht Neugeborene auf 1000 Personen. Die Einwohnerzahl betrug im Jahre 1778 insgesamt 1.723, 1784 schon 1.973 und 1919 3.136 Menschen. 99,8% der Personen waren durchweg katholisch.[30]

Zusammenfassung

Im Winkel zwischen Theiß, Mieresch und Kreisch gab es also vier, voneinander abweichende Immigrationsvarianten: Die erste zeigt Hódmezővásárhely, deren Urbewohner die Gräuel der Türkenkriege überlebt hatten. Die Bevölkerung vermehrte sich schnell und erhielt hauptsächlich reformierte Einwanderer aus der näheren Umgebung. Die auf Viehzucht spezialisierte Stadt konnte durch die Bewahrung der riesigen Pusztagebiete ihre Bevölkerungszahl deutlich erhöhen, gelangte schnell zu Wohlstand und behauptete ihre Selbstständigkeit gegenüber ihrem Gutsherrn. Die aus der Türkenzeit überlieferte Selbstverwaltung der Stadt lebte in vielen Hinsichten fort wie auch die halbmilitärischen Organisationen. Hódmezővásárhely ist vielleicht

---

[27] HERCZEG, Mihály: Szegvár története a török kiűzésétől 1848-ig [Geschichte von Szegvár von der Vetreibung der Türken bis 1848]. In: Szegvár. Tanulmányok a település történetéből. Hg. v. Gyula FARKAS. Szeged 2000, 89-145, hier 125-128. – SZABÓ József: A szegvári nyelvjárás elemzése. In: EBD., 511-532.
[28] Mitte des 18. Jahrhunderts machte sie 1.000 Nutzvieh (Rinder und Pferde) aus. Die Stadt mit einer Bevölkerungszahl von 7-8.000 Personen muss demnach eine Rinderherde von mehreren 10.000 Nutzvieh gehabt haben, wenn sie diese Steuern zahlen konnte. Tausende von selbst gezüchteten Pferden wurden auf den umliegenden Weiden gehalten.
[29] HERCZEG: Szegvár, 93. – Während der Türkenkriege von 1735–38 wurde sogar das königliche Gestüt von Mezőhegyes auf die benachbarte Puszta von Vásárhely gerettet, das für die Zucht zugunsten der Armee eingesetzt wurde. Dies entging nicht der Aufmerksamkeit der Károlyis, und ihre Untertanen in Szegvár wandten sich im großen Stil der Pferdezucht zu. Etwa 100 Jahre sicherte sie der Bevölkerung ein attraktives Einkommen. Um 1800 folgte auch Vásárhely diesem Beispiel. TÁRKÁNY Szűcs, Imre: Gazdaélet a vásárhelyi határban [Wirtsleben auf der Puszta von Vásárhely]. Hódmezővásárhely 2003, 47.
[30] Vgl. KATUS, László: A szegvári római katolikus plébánia története [Geschichte der römisch-katholischen Pfarrei von Szegvár]. In: FARKAS: Szegvár, 333-398, hier 335.

das typischste Beispiel dafür, wie im 18. Jahrhundert die Verbindung zwischen einer Marktstadt und dem System der Pusztahöfe auf der Großen Tiefebene funktionierte. Im Mittelpunkt deren Funktionstüchtigkeit stand die Arbeitsgemeinschaft der Großfamilie. Dieses System blieb bis zum letzten Drittel des 19. Jahrhunderts intakt; es baute auf eine umfangreiche Immigration und wies zugleich eine sehr hohe Fertilität auf. Die Konfession, die Selbstregierung und die autonomen Verwaltungsstrukturen bedingten sich gegenseitig. Die Stadtbevölkerung gehörte der kalvinistisch-reformierten Konfession an, die ohnehin in Ungarn bis zu 95% ethnische Ungarn erfasste, dementsprechend versuchte man auch die Migrationen in diesem Sinne zu kanalisieren.[31]

Eine andere Variante zeigt Szentes, eine Stadt mit bikonfessioneller Zusammensetzung. Die Bevölkerung kehrte nach den Osmanenkriegen zurück, aber die umfangreiche Einwanderung aus mehreren Richtungen setzte endgültig die Festigung der Multikonfessionalität durch, versinnbildlicht im kalvinistischen und katholischen Stadtteil. Da die Immigranten jedoch hauptsächlich aus der näheren Umgebung kamen, blieb die Bevölkerung – abgesehen von den armenischen Händlern – ethnisch und sprachlich überwiegend ungarisch. Die konfessionelle Komponente behielt jedoch ihre auf Trennung und Separierung ausgerichtete Funktion bis zur dualistischen Ära der 1870-er Jahre. Während des 18. Jahrhunderts konnten insgesamt etwa 20 Übertritte registriert werden, trotz der Bemühung des Statthaltereirates und des Komitats, die Katholisierung voranzutreiben. Die zwei Stadtteile sprachen unterschiedliche Dialekte und hatten einen unterschiedlichen Festkalender.

Eine andere Entwicklung belegt Szegvár, das Zentrum der Herrschaft Károlyi. Hier gab es eine ethnisch und konfessionell äußerst differenzierte Einwanderung, die Herkunftsorte und –regionen der Immigranten lassen sich nicht eng begrenzen. Grund dafür war die herrschaftliche Siedlungspolitik: Die Bedürfnisse dieses Zentrums waren auf Untertanen, Handwerker, Administrationsbeamten, Gärtner und Pferdezüchter ausgerichtet, und auch die Immigration wurde dementsprechend gesteuert. Neben den aus den osmanischen Deftern (Steuerregister) des 16. Jahrhunderts bekannten Namen der Ureinwohner lassen sich in den Konskriptionen des 18. Jahrhunderts Namen aus Siebenbürgen, dem Partium, walachischer Hirten wie bulgarischer und serbischer Händler, deutscher Handwerker und slawischer Bauern finden. Eine Nivellierung konfessioneller Vielfältigkeit erfolgte durch die forcierte Katholisierung der Herrschaft, die als Bedingung ihrer Migrationspolitik gegenüber den Einwanderern strikt durchgesetzt wurde.

Schließlich zeigt Orosháza wieder andere Entwicklungslinien. Den Kern der Gemeinschaft bildeten evangelisch-lutherische Ungarn aus Transdanubien, die auf der gewässerlosen, wüsten Puszta angesiedelt wurden. Ihre Einwanderung zog den Paradigmenwechsel in ihrer Lebensführung nach sich, da sie eine weitgehend fremde

[31] Nachdem die Reserven der Puszta erschöpft worden waren, wurden die Höfe aufgeteilt und die Bevölkerung stellte sich auf Ackerbau um. Um zu überleben und die etablierte Lebensführung aufrechtzuerhalten setzte sich eine drastische Geburtenregelung durch, deren Ergebnis eine stagnierende und zunehmend alternde Bevölkerung war. Endogamie und Abschottung gegenüber der Außenwelt waren eine absehbare Folgeerscheinung. Seither werden hier die meisten Selbstmörder und Dichter in ganz Ungarn registriert.

Lebensform vorfanden. Die Verteidigung ihrer Konfession stand aber nie zur Debatte. Wie in Szentes zeigten die katholischen Gutsherren, die Harruckern wie die Károlyis, gegenüber diesen Bedürfnissen Verständnis, da die Besiedlung dieser öden Gemeinden für sie oberste Priorität hatte. So konnten diese transdanubischen Immigranten spätere Einwanderer, vor allem evangelische Slowaken oder Ungarn anderer Konfessionen, schnell und mit Erfolg assimilieren. Zugleich passte sich die ganze Stadt den Bedingungen der Puszta an.

Abbildung

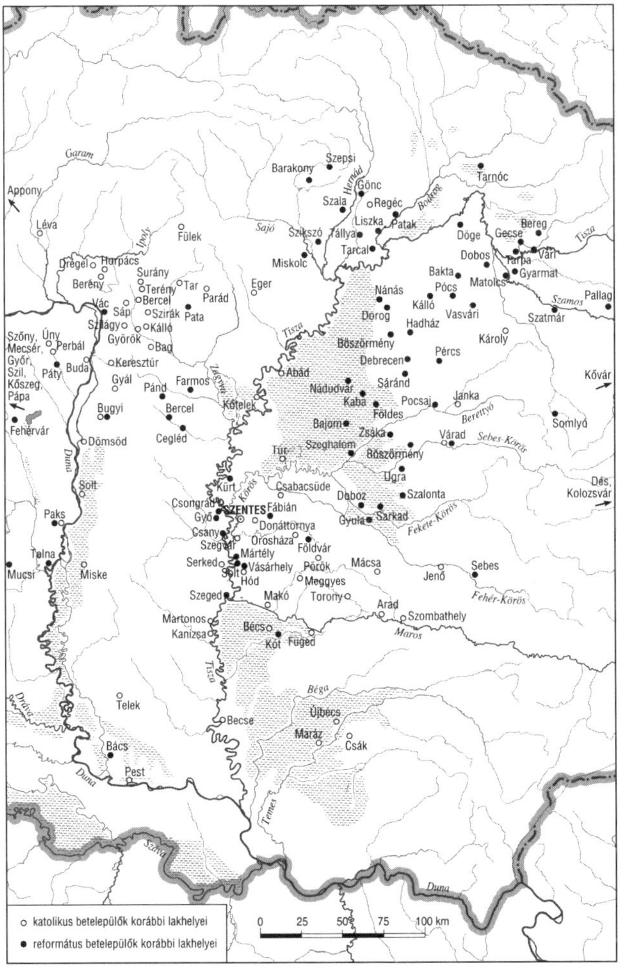

Abb. 1: Herkunftskarte der Neusiedler

helle Kreise: frühere Wohnorte der katholischen Zusiedler

dunkle Kreise: frühere Wohnorte der kalvinistisch-reformierten Zusiedler

Mathias Beer

Konfessionsmigration als identitätsstiftender Faktor. Transmigranten in Siebenbürgen

Ausgangslage: Der Sitzordnungsstreit 1911-1920

Man schreibt das Jahr 1911. Ort der Handlung ist Neppendorf (ung. Kistorony, rum. Turnişor).[1] Die evangelische Gemeinde mit ihrer größtenteils deutschsprachigen Bevölkerung liegt unmittelbar vor den Toren Hermannstadts (rum. Sibiu, ung. Nagyszeben). Im Unterschied zu vielen anderen Gemeinden Siebenbürgens (rum. Transilvania, ung. Erdély) zeichnet sie sich unter anderem dadurch aus, dass in Neppendorf Menschen unterschiedlicher Herkunft zusammen leben, die zu unterschiedlichen Zeitpunkten in den Ort gekommen sind: Siebenbürger Sachsen, die dort seit der Gründung des Ortes im 12. Jahrhundert siedeln,[2] und die Nachkommen österreichischer Zwangsmigranten des 18. Jahrhunderts. Für sie, die aus mehreren Regionen Innerösterreichs Stammenden und in mehreren Etappen nach Siebenbürgen Verbrachten, in der zeitgenössischen Terminologie Transmigranten, hat sich im Ansiedlungsgebiet im Laufe der Zeit der Gruppenbegriff Landler[3] als Selbst- und Fremdbezeichnung herausgebildet. Die Bezeichnung ist Ausdruck der im Ansiedlungsgebiet entwickelten Gruppenidentität. Aufgrund des überdurchschnittlichen Bevölkerungswachstums Neppendorfs im 19. Jahrhundert – auch eine Folge der Ansiedlung der Transmigranten – war es notwenig geworden, die Kirche des Ortes zu erweitern. Mit dem Abschluss der Arbeiten vereinbarte die Kirchengemeinde einvernehmlich eine neue Sitzordnung in der Kirche. Sie war dem Grundsatz verpflichtet, Alter geht vor. Wider Erwarten entfaltete die Entscheidung eine für die Gemeinde ungeahnte

[1] Zu Neppendorf liegt keine Ortmonographie vor. Diese Forschungslücke wird auch durch die keine wissenschaftliche Ansprüche stellende Publikation Neppendorf. Monographie des Ortes. Bearb. v. Renate BAUINGER-LIEBHART. 3 Bde., Linz 2005, 2006 und Eigenverlag 2008 nicht ersetzt, zumal es sich lediglich um den (leider stark fehlerbehafteten) Abdruck von Typoskripten und Quellen aus dem Nachlass des früheren Ortspfarrers Hellmut Klima handelt. – Nach wie vor nützlich ist KLIMA, Hellmut: Neppendorf. Geschichte eines deutschen Dorfes in Siebenbürgen. In: Deutsche Forschungen im Südosten 2 (1943), 118-146. – Zur Person von Klima vgl. STIFT, Inge : Dr. Hellmut Klima (1915-1990), ein siebenbürgischer Pfarrer und Historiker. In: Die Siebenbürgischen Landler. Eine Spurensicherung. Hg. v. Martin BOTTESCH, Franz GRIESHOFER und Winfried SCHABUS. Köln-Weimar-Wien 2002, 793-812.

[2] Zur Geschichte der Siebenbürger Sachsen vgl. ROTH, Harald : Kleine Geschichte der Siebenbürger Sachsen. Köln u.a. 1996. – SCHENK, Annemie: Deutsche in Siebenbürgen. Ihre Geschichte und Kultur. München 1992. – GÜNDISCH, Konrad/BEER, Mathias: Siebenbürgen und die Siebenbürger Sachsen. München 1998, Nachdruck 2005.

[3] BEER, Mathias: Österreichische Protestanten (‚Landler') in Siebenbürgen seit dem 18. Jahrhundert. In: Enzyklopädie Migration in Europa. Vom 17. Jahrhundert bis zur Gegenwart. Hg. v. Klaus J. BADE u.a. Paderborn u.a. 2007, 818-820. – SEDLER, Irmgard: Landler. In: Die Siebenbürger Sachsen. Lexikon. Hg. von Walter MYSS. Thauer bei Innsbruck 1993, 302f.

Sprengkraft. Ein lang anhaltender Streit, der nur vordergründig die Sitzordnung in der Kirche betraf, nahm seinen Anfang.
In einem anonymen Brief an den Pfarrer warnte in jenem Jahr 1911 ein Ortsbewohner: „es würde ihm [dem Pfarrer] schlecht gehn, wenn er dazu rate, die jungen sächsischen Frauen hinabrücken zu lassen.“[4] Der Beschwerdeführer und mit ihm eine beträchtliche, zunächst schweigende Gruppe des Dorfes, wollten sich offensichtlich nicht damit abfinden, dass künftig die jungen sächsischen Frauen hinter den älteren Landler-Frauen sitzen sollten. Der Drohbrief war das Fanal, welches die Zweiteilung der Gemeinde in Alteingesessene und später Dazugekommene offenbarte, in der Sprache von Norbert Elias in „Etablierte und Außenseiter“[5]. Die zahlreichen Versuche, eine für beide Seiten, Sachsen und Landler, akzeptable und damit tragbare Lösung für die Sitzordnung zu finden, scheiterten in der Folgezeit nicht nur, sie bildeten vielmehr den Ausgangspunkt für fast ein Jahrzehnt erbittert geführte Auseinandersetzungen in der Gemeinde. Der Boykott des Gottesdienstbesuches gehörte ebenso dazu wie der Verschleiß von drei Pfarrern. Weder dem eingeschalteten Konsistorium noch dem Landesbischof gelang es, die Wogen zu glätten. Auch der Hinweis auf den ausgebrochenen Ersten Weltkrieg, der alle Parteienunterschiede verschwinden lasse müsse, oder auf den mittlerweile beschädigten Ruf Neppendorfs halfen nicht. Erst 1920 kam quasi als „Volksentscheid“ der weltlichen Gemeinde eine Lösung zustande. Sie war nicht das Ergebnis der Einsicht der beiden sich bekämpfenden Parteien, sondern ist wohl eher als Ergebnis der mittlerweile eingetretenen Erschöpfungserscheinungen zu deuten. Die gefundene Lösung war ein recht komplizierter Formelkompromiss. Er trug der Zugehörigkeit zu der einen als auch anderen Gruppe, dem Alter und dem Geschlecht Rechnung und sah eine getrennte Sitzordnung vor.
Die in Stichworten skizzierte Episode mutet kleinlich und provinziell an, aber nur auf den ersten Blick. Denn der Sitzordnungsstreit war mehr als eine Dorfposse. Einer Revolution gleich stellte er das zur Selbstverständlichkeit geronnene Althergebrachte, die in der Sitzordnung sichtbare Privilegierung der Alteingesessenen gegenüber den später Gekommenen, grundsätzlich in Frage. In der Auseinandersetzung standen sich nicht Gruppen unterschiedlicher, sondern gleicher Konfession gegenüber, die sich aber durch ihre Herkunft, die Art ihrer Migration und die Dauer ihres Aufenthalts in der Gemeinde unterschieden. Damit erhält der Streit um die „richtige“ Sitzordnung einen über den lokalen Rahmen hinausreichenden Stellenwert. Er betrifft nämlich die Rolle frühneuzeitlicher Konfessionsmigration[6], um den

[4] Archiv der Kirchengemeinde Neppendorf, Presbyterialakten 82/12. Zu der damit einsetzenden Auseinandersetzung vgl. BEER Mathias: „Willkürliches Benehmen gegen den ererbten Sitten und Bräuchen“. Zur Aufnahme und Eingliederung der Transmigranten in Siebenbürgen. In: Migration nach Ost- und Südosteuropa vom 18. bis zum Beginn des 19. Jahrhunderts. Ursachen, Formen, Verlauf, Ergebnis. Hg. v. DEMS. und Dittmar DAHLMANN. Stuttgart 1999, 317-335.
[5] ELIAS, Norbert/SCOTSON, John L.: The Established and the Outsiders. A Sociological Enquiery into Community Problems. London 1965. – Auf Deutsch: Etablierte und Außenseiter. Übersetzt von Michael SCHRÖTER. Frankfurt am Main 1990.
[6] SCHILLING, Heinz: Die niederländischen Exulanten des 16. Jahrhunderts. Ein Beitrag zur Typologie der frühneuzeitlichen Konfessionsmigration. In: Geschichte in Wissenschaft und Unterricht 43 (1992), 67-78. –

treffenden, von Heinz Schilling geprägten Begriff zu benutzen, bei der Herausbildung von Gruppenidentitäten. Um die Faktoren zu untersuchen, die dabei eine Rolle gespielt haben, bietet sich der Mikrokosmos einer Gemeinde geradezu an. „Vor Ort", wie in einem Brennglas fokussiert, lassen sich beide Perspektiven, jene von oben und von unten,[7] also jene des Staates und jene des in der Familie und Gemeinde verorteten Individuums, in die Analyse ebenso einbeziehen wie die Rolle des Herkunfts- und des Zielgebietes für die Migranten bei Bewahrung oder Herausbildung einer neuen Identität.

Immer mit Bezug zum roten Faden des Bandes, „Religion als Integrationsfaktor" fragt der vorliegende Beitrag: Welches waren mögliche Ursachen für den grundsätzlichen Streit in der Gemeinde Neppendorf? Warum brach nach über eineinhalb Jahrhunderten friedlichen Zusammenlebens eine solch erbittert geführte und lang anhaltende Auseinandersetzung in der Gemeinde aus? Welche Rolle spielte dabei Religion, in diesem Fall die gleiche Konfession der beiden Gruppen? Wieso erwies sich die gleiche Konfession in diesem Fall nicht als ausreichende Integrationsklammer? Grundsätzlich gefragt, welche Bedeutung kommt dem Faktor Konfession im Rahmen frühneuzeitlicher Migrationsprozesse zu? Wie wirkt er sich auf den der Migration folgenden Eingliederungsprozess und das Selbstverständnis der Migranten aus?

Bei der Suche nach Antworten auf einige dieser Fragen gehe ich am Fallbeispiel Neppendorfs von der These aus, dass die Transmigrationen, also die Zwangsmigration der im 18. Jahrhundert nach Siebenbürgen verbrachten Zuwanderer, und die Umstände, unter denen diese Migration stattgefunden hat, wesentlich den Integrationsprozess und die Herausbildung einer eigenen Gruppenidentität der Landler mitbestimmt haben. In einer spezifischen Form von Konfessionsmigration und deren Folgen scheint mir der Schlüssel für die plausible Deutung des Sitzordnungsstreits in der siebenbürgischen Gemeinde zu liegen. Anders formuliert, die Grundlagen für die Entstehung einer eigenen Landler-Identität und damit auch für die Konflikte in der Gemeinde zu Beginn des 20. Jahrhunderts wurden 200 Jahre früher, im Zeitalter der Konfessionalisierung,[8] gelegt. Erst die konfessionell bedingte Zwangsmigration sowie ihre Charakteristika und die auch davon wesentlich beeinflusste Aufnahme

---

DERS.: Die frühneuzeitliche Konfessionsmigration. In: Migration in der Geschichte seit dem späten Mittelalter. Hg. v. Klaus J. BADE. Osnabrück 2002, (IMIS Beiträge 20), 67-89.

[7] SCHILLING, Heinz: Disziplinierung oder „Selbstregulierung der Untertanen"? Ein Plädoyer für die Doppelperspektive von Makro- und Mikrohistorie bei der Erforschung der frühneuzeitlichen Kirchenzucht. In: Historische Zeitschrift 264 (1997), 675-691. – REINHARD, Wolfgang: „Konfessionalisierung" auf dem Prüfstand. In: Konfessionalisierung in Ostmitteleuropa. Wirkungen des religiösen Wandels im 16. und 17. Jahrhundert in Staat, Gesellschaft und Kultur. Hg. v. Joachim BAHLCKE und Arno STROHMEYER. Stuttgart 1999, 79-88.

[8] Zum Forschungsstand einschließlich der nach wie vor bestehenden Kontroversen zum Konfessionalisierungsparadigma vgl. jüngst SCHMIDT, Heinrich Richard: Perspektiven der Konfessionalismusforschung. In: Staatsmacht und Seelenheil. Gegenreformation und Geheimprotestantismus in der Habsburgermonarchie. Hg. v. Rudolf LEEB, Susanne Claudine PILS und Thomas WINKELBAUER. Wien-München 2007, 28-37. – Zum Zusammenhang von Konfessionalisierung und Transmigration vgl. PREUßE, Christian: „... das Unkraut des Irrglaubens auszureuten ..." Kryptoprotestantismus in den habsburgischen Erblanden und Transmigration nach Siebenbürgen. In: Zeitschrift für siebenbürgische Landeskunde 29/2 (2006), 161-179.

der Transmigranten in Siebenbürgen führten vermutlich dazu, dass sich eine Gruppenidentität der Transmigranten in Abgrenzung zu der eingesessenen siebenbürgisch-sächsischen Bevölkerung herausbildete,[9] die auch in der Bezeichnung „Landler" zum Ausdruck kommt. Insofern bietet die mikrogeschichtliche Analyse die Chance, kurz- und langfristige Folgen von Konfessionsmigrationen des 18. Jahrhunderts aufzuzeigen.

Zur Untermauerung der These wird in einem ersten Schritt auf der Grundlage der neueren einschlägigen Literatur ein geraffter Überblick über die Transmigrationen als einer spezifischen Form von Zwangsmigration geliefert. In Stichworten werden Ursachen, Umfang und Ergebnis dieser Variante von Konfessionsmigrationen vorgestellt. Zweitens werden die Merkmale dieser Migration beleuchtet, in deren Verlauf der Staat als Auslöser der Zwangsmigration ein negativ konnotiertes Bild der Transmigranten erzeugte. Wie sich diese Fremdzuschreibung auf die Aufnahme und Eingliederung der Transmigranten in Siebenbürgen ausgewirkte, darauf soll abschließend eingegangen werden.

Transmigrationen als spezifische Form von Konfessionsmigration

Während des 18. Jahrhunderts wurden in mehreren Schüben rund 4.000 österreichische Kryptoprotestanten[10] aus Kernländern der Habsburgermonarchie nach Siebenbürgen deportiert, vorwiegend in die nördlich von Hermannstadt gelegenen Hauptansiedlungsorte Neppendorf, Großau (rum. Cristian, ung. Keresztényszíget) und Großpold (rum. Apoldu de Sus, ung. Nagyapold).[11] Der entsprechende zeitgenössische Begriff „transmigrieren"[12] weist auf einen Sonderfall von religiös motivierter Zwangsmigration[13] hin. Er gehört in „ein lang andauerndes „konfessionelles Zeital-

[9] Damit setze ich einen anderen Schwerpunkt als Martin BOTTESCH: Identität und Ethnizität der Landler. Zum Selbstverständnis der Landler. In: Die Siebenbürgischen Landler. Eine Spurensicherung. Hg. v. DEMS., Franz GRIESHOFER und Winfried SCHABUS. Köln-Weimar-Wien 2002, 155-177.

[10] HENZE, Barbara: Kryptoprotestantismus. In: Lexikon für Theologie und Kirche Bd. 6. 1997, Sp. 497f. – LEEB, Rudolf: Die Zeit des „Geheimprotestantismus". In: Carinthia 191 (2000), 249-264.

[11] Zum Forschungsstand BEER, Mathias: Die Landler. Versuch eines geschichtlichen Überblicks. In: BOTTESCH (u.a.): Die Siebenbürgischen Landler, 23-80. – Im Unterschied zu dem mittlerweile recht gut erforschten Kontext der Deportationen und der Durchführung der Transmigrationen ist eine Darstellung des Aufnahme- und Eingliederungsprozesses der Transmigranten in Siebenbürgen einschließlich der Herausbildung eigener Landlerkulturen in den drei Hauptansiedlungsorten nach wie vor ein Desiderat der Forschung.

[12] Zum Begriff selbst, seinem Wandel und anderen zeitgenössischen Bezeichnungen für die Transmigranten BEER: Landler, 33-36. – Vgl. auch BUCHINGER, Erich: Die „Landler" in Siebenbürgen. Vorgeschichte, Durchführung und Ergebnis einer Zwangsumsiedlung im 18. Jahrhundert. München 1980, 20f.

[13] Vgl. dazu HELMEDACH, Andreas : Bevölkerungspolitik im Zeichen der Aufklärung. Zwangsumsiedlung und Zwangsassimilierung im Habsburgerreich des 18. Jahrhunderts – eine noch ungelöste Forschungsaufgabe. In: Comparativ. Leipziger Beiträge zur Universalgeschichte und vergleichenden Gesellschaftsforschung 6/1 (1996), 41-62. – Ausweisung – Abschiebung – Vertreibung in Europa. 16.-20. Jahrhundert. Hg. v. Sylvia HAHN, Andrea KOMLOSY und Ilse REITER. Innsbruck-Wien-Bozen 2006. – Vgl. auch KITTEL, Manfred: Vorläufer „ethnischer Säuberungen"? Flucht und Vertreibung in der Neuzeit. In: Geschichtswissenschaft und Zeiterkenntnis. Von der Aufklärung bis zur Gegenwart. Festschrift zum 65. Geburtstag von Horst Möller. Hg. von Klaus HILDEBRAND, Udo WENGST und Andreas WIRSCHING. München 2008, 455-472.

ter“, das bis weit ins 18. Jahrhundert, in manchen Ländern auch darüber hinaus reicht.[14] Transmigrationen verbanden Deportation und Kolonisation innerhalb der Grenzen der Monarchie in sich. Das vom katholischen Wiener Hof unter Kaiser Karl VI. eingeführte und unter Kaiserin Maria Theresia ausgebaute Transmigrationssystem verband die Säuberung der österreichischen Kernländer von Protestanten durch Zwangsumsiedlung mit der Gewährung von Glaubensfreiheit und der wirtschaftlichen Überlegungen folgenden Ansiedlung vor allem in Siebenbürgen. Als Ausdruck katholischer Konfessionalisierung war es das Ziel der von einer intensiven Missionierung begleiteten Transmigrationen, den Protestantismus in den Herkunftsgebieten der Zwangsmigranten auszurotten.[15] Die sich über ein halbes Jahrhundert erstrekkenden Deportationen waren mit einem hohen Maß an Gewalt verbunden. Sie sind sowohl bezogen auf das angestrebte Ziel der konfessionellen Säuberung als auch auf die mit der Deportation verbundenen kolonisatorischen Absichten als Misserfolg zu bewerten.[16] Für die davon Betroffenen waren die Transmigrationen insgesamt betrachtet eine Katastrophe. Darüber dürfen auch die sich in den drei siebenbürgischen Ortschaften herausgebildeten Landlerkulturen nicht hinwegtäuschen.[17]

Die Transmigrationen – zunächst eine begrenzte Zahl von „Rädelsführern“ und deren Familien – setzten im Frühsommer des Jahres 1734 im Salzkammergut ein.[18] Kurzfristig und ohne über das Ziel informiert zu werden, wurden die ersten Transmigranten in Linz eingeschifft. Unter militärischer Bewachung erreichten sie auf der Donau über Klosterneuburg und Ofen den Hafen Titel an der Theiß. Von dort verbrachte man sie nach Temeswar (rum. Timişoara, ung. Temesvár), dann auf dem Landweg über Deva und Mühlbach (rum. Petreşti, ung. Péterfalva) nach Heltau (rum. Cisnădie, ung. Nagydisznód) und schließlich nach Neppendorf. Weil sich die vom Wiener Hof erhoffte abschreckende Wirkung nicht einstellte, wurden die Deportationen in der Folgezeit ausgeweitet. In der ersten, von 1734 bis 1737 dauernden Phase waren davon über 800 Personen betroffen. Die Transmigranten stammten vorwiegend aus dem Salzkammergut (Pfarreien Goisern, Hallstatt, Ischl, Gosau) und

[14] REINHARD: Konfessionalisierung, 85. – Vgl. dazu auch GRÄF, Holger Th.: Gegenreformation und katholische Konfessionalisierung. Epoche(nbegriff) oder Fundamentalprozess der frühen Neuzeit? In: LEEB (u.a.): Staatsmacht, 13-27.

[15] MECENSEFFY, Grete: Geschichte des Protestantismus in Österreich. Graz-Köln 1956. – BARTON, Peter F.: Evangelisch in Österreich. Ein Überblick über die Geschichte der Evangelischen in Österreich. Wien u.a. 1987. – TROPPER, Peter G.: Staatliche Kirchenpolitik, Geheimprotestantismus und katholische Mission in Kärnten (1752-1780). Klagenfurt 1989.

[16] SCHÜNEMANN, Konrad: Österreichs Bevölkerungspolitik unter Maria Theresia. Bd. 1. Berlin o.J. [1935], 104: „So ist die alpenländische Transmigration als Ganzes genommen ein Fehlschlag gewesen. Der österreichische Protestantismus wurde dadurch nicht ausgerottet, sondern eher angefacht. Eine Bevölkerungsverdichtung in Siebenbürgen wurde nur in ganz geringem Ausmaß erreicht.“

[17] Zu der notwendigen Differenzierung des Sammelbegriffs ‚Landler' vgl. BEER: Landler, 65f. – SEDLER, Irmgard: Die Landler in Siebenbürgen. Gruppenidentität im Spiegel der Kleidung von der Mitte des 18. bis zum Ende des 20. Jahrhunderts. Marburg 2004, 89-95.

[18] Neben dem Überblick bei BEER: Landler, 37-72 siehe auch die grundlegenden Publikationen, die den Gesamtvorgang der Transmigrationen betreffen: NOWOTNY, Ernst: Die Transmigration ober- und innerösterreichischer Protestanten nach Siebenbürgen. Jena 1931. – BUCHINGER: „Landler“. – BOTTESCH (u.a.): Die Siebenbürgischen Landler. – SEDLER: Landler.

aus Kärnten, hier insbesondere aus der Herrschaft Paternion.[19] Im Unterschied zu den Deportierten aus dem Salzkammergut wurden bei den Kärntnern die Familien getrennt und die Kinder zurückgehalten.[20] Stellvertretend für die vielen belegten Fälle sei lediglich die Erklärung des deportierten Ehepaares Neubacher vom 9. September 1734 angeführt, in der es sich darüber beschwert, dass der Sohn nicht mit den Eltern mitreisen durfte: „Er hat sich auch mit seinen Kleidern und andern Zeug auf die Reise fertig gemacht, so haben aber die Herren durch die Soldaten ihn mit Gewalt zurück behalten lassen, obwohl er öffentlich bey seinen Eltern Bekennet hat, dass er bey den Catholischen nicht bleiben m[ag].[21]

Darüber hinaus wiesen die Ansiedlungsorte der Kärntner in Siebenbürgen eine breite Streuung auf. Hinzu kam eine hohe Mortalitätsrate. In einem Schreiben des Hermannstädter Magistrats vom 27. August 1733 an den Wiener Deputierten Johann Kinder von Friedenburg, in dem um Hilfe für die Transmigranten angesucht wird, heißt es, „insonderlich aber die elende Cärnther sehr stark mit denen allhier grassierenden Fiebern befallen werden, und grösstenteils wegen Sehnsucht nach ihren hinterbliebenenen Kindern und Mangel an Nahrung dahinsterben."[22]

Die zweite Phase der Deportationen setzte in der Regierungszeit von Kaiserin Maria Theresia ein. Sie betraf über 3.000 Personen und wies betont repressive Züge auf. Die Deportierten stammten aus dem Land ob der Enns sowie in geringerer Zahl aus der Steiermark und Kärnten. Bis auf eine überschaubare Zahl von Steiermärkern, die in den ungarischen Gemeinden Iklad und Keresztúr[23] angesiedelt wurden, war das Ziel aller Transporte Siebenbürgen. Hauptansiedlungsorte waren hier die Gemeinden Großau und Großpold, letztere mit einem verhältnismäßig hohen Anteil an Kärntnern. Die dritte und letzte Phase der Transmigrationen fand in den Jahren 1773 bis 1776 statt. Rund 200 Protestanten deportierte man aus Stadl in der Steiermark.[24]

Kurze Zeit nachdem der letzte Transport nach Siebenbürgen abgegangen war, verfügte Kaiser Joseph II. mit einem Handschreiben an den Präsidenten der böhmisch-

---

[19] Vgl. dazu insbesondere die mikrogeschichtliche Studie von STEINER, Stephan: Reisen ohne Wiederkehr. Die Deportation von Protestanten aus Kärnten 1734-1736. Wien-München 2007. – DERS.: Der Augenblick der Gefahr und die lange Dauer der Geschichte. Die Geburt der Deportation. In: Südostforschungen 63/64 (2004/2005), 170-187. – DERS.: Auf und Davon. Die vergessene Massenflucht aus der Herrschaft Paternion (Kärnten) und ihre Spätfolgen. In: LEEB (u.a.): Staatsmacht, 202-212. – Steiner greift sicher zu hoch, wenn er die karolinischen Transmigrationen als *die* Geburtsstunde der modernen Deportationen deutet.

[20] Zu den Kindeswegnahmen vgl. KÜPPERS-BRAUN, Ute: „Kinder-Abpracticirung". Kinder zwischen den Konfessionen im 18. Jahrhundert. In: Zeitschrift für Geschichtswissenschaft 49 (2001), 208-225. – DIES.: „Und die kleinen Kinder von den Brüsten und Schössen ihrer Eltern gerissen werden." Transmigrantenkinder zwischen Indoktrination und Propaganda. In: LEEB (u.a.): Staatsmacht, 213-229.

[21] Staatsarchiv Hermannstadt. Faszikularakten P II 44, Bl. 6v-7r. Hier zitiert nach POPA, Liliana: Urkunden im Hermannstädter Staatsarchiv zur Transmigration österreichischer Protestanten nach Siebenbürgen 1733-1737. In: BOTTESCH (u.a.): Die Siebenbürgischen Landler, 81-98, hier 87.

[22] Staatsarchiv Hermannstadt. Magistratsakten 38/1735. Hier zitiert nach POPA: Urkunden, 89f.

[23] BRANDTNER, Paul: Beitrag zur Geschichte der Transmigration inner- und oberösterreichischer Protestanten nach Ungarn. Iklad und Keresztúr. In: Deutsche Forschungen in Ungarn 4/1-2 (1939), 71-85. – DEDIC Paul: Die Verpflanzung steirischer Familien nach Ungarn in den Jahren 1752-1765. In: Das Joanneum 2 (1940), 139-150.

[24] Dazu zuletzt KNALL, Dieter: Aus der Heimat gedrängt. Letzte Zwangsumsiedlungen steirischer Protestanten nach Siebenbürgen unter Maria Theresia. Graz 2002.

österreichischen Kanzlei das Ende der Transmigrationen. Von nun an war es in den Erbländern der Monarchie ausdrücklich verboten, „die als Kezer sich angebende oder betrettende Unterthanen oder Inwohner hierwegen ausser Landes verschiket, oder in ein anderes Land wider Willen übersiedelt, sondern vielmehr an ihrer Bekehrung, nach meinen schon bestehenden Anordnungen mit allem Eifer gearbeitet, und derley irrende durch vernünftige und geflissene Verwendung der geistlichkeit von ihrem Irrthum wiederum abgebracht, somit deren Übersiedlung nacher Siebenbürgen oder Hungarn künftig nur in den alleinigen Fall vor die hand genommen werden solle, in sofern Sie selbst auf diesem Verlangen der Transmigration in ein Erbland, wo den Acatholicis das Religionsexercitium gestattet ist, unabweislich bestünden."[25]

Die sich auf die drei tolerierten christlichen Religionen beschränkende „allgemeine Religionsfreiheit" in den österreichischen Erbländern brachte das Toleranzpatent von 1781. Trotz Widerständen von geistlicher Seite schloss es, wie das Hofdekret vom 14. Dezember 1781 zeigt, auch die Transmigranten mit ein.[26] Dennoch blieb die Rückkehr in die Herkunftsgebiete, was viele angestrebt und nicht wenige versucht hatten,[27] auf eine überschaubare Zahl von Fällen beschränkt. Den Gesuchen transmigrierter Eltern, ihnen aufgrund des Toleranzpatents jetzt die bei der Deportation zurückbehaltenen Kinder nach Siebenbürgen nachzuschicken, wurde nicht stattgegeben. Noch zu Beginn des Jahres 1802 heißt es in einem Schreiben des Pfarrers der steiermärkischen Gemeinde Stadl, „seitdem ich hier [bin], versuchten ein und andere von den Stadlerischen Transmigranten in Siebenbürgen, ihre hier zurückgelassene, katholisch erzogene Kinder zu überreden, sich zu ihnen hinab zu verfügen. Allein sie fanden bishero kein Gehör; ich werde auch niemals meine Einstimmung dazu geben."[28]

Dass vom Wiener Hof gerade Siebenbürgen als Zielgebiet der Deportationen bestimmt worden war, hatte mehrere Gründe. Für Siebenbürgen als Ansiedlungsgebiet sprachen die konfessionellen Verhältnisse in diesem Teil der Monarchie. Auf Grund des Leopoldinischen Diploms war die Glaubensfreiheit für die katholischen, lutheranischen und calvinistischen Untertanen in Siebenbürgen gleichermaßen garantiert.[29] Mit der Zugehörigkeit Siebenbürgens zur Monarchie war zudem sicherge-

[25] Österreichisches Staatsarchiv, Allgemeines Verwaltungsarchiv, Wien, Bestandsgruppe Unterricht, Alter Kultus IV A 3, Schreiben vom 7.11.1774. Hier zitiert nach KNALL: Aus der Heimat gedrängt, 258 Anm. 1370. – Vgl. auch NOWOTNY: Transmigration, 109.

[26] NOWOTNY: Transmigration, 91f. – KNALL: Aus der Heimat gedrängt, 267f. – Vgl. das für Oberösterreich erlassene Toleranzpatent in: Der Josephinismus. Ausgewählte Quellen zur Geschichte der theresianisch-josephinischen Reform. Hg. von Harm KLUETING. Darmstadt 1995, 252-255, Nr. 102.

[27] Vgl. dazu die vielen Beispiele bei STEINER: Reisen ohne Wiederkehr, bes. 309-334. – Eine Liste der rückkehrwilligen Transmigranten von 1764 umfasst mehr als 800 Personen. Vgl. dazu CAPESIUS, Bernhard: Die Landler in Siebenbürgen. Bukarest 1962, 26.

[28] Zitiert nach KNALL: Aus der Heimat gedrängt, 270.

[29] ZACH Krista: Politische Motive und Ursachen der Konfessionalisierung in Siebenbürgen. In: Konfessionelle Pluralität, Stände und Nation. Ausgewählte Abhandlungen zur südosteuropäischen Religions- und Gesellschaftsgeschichte. Hg. v. Joachim BAHLCKE und Konrad GÜNDISCH. Münster 2004, 71-82. – ROTH Harald: Von der Nation zum Volk zur Nation. Ethnische Identitäten im Siebenbürgen des 18. und 19. Jahrhunderts. In: Ethnische und soziale Konflikte im neuzeitlichen Osteuropa. Festschrift für Heinz-Dietrich Löwe zum 60. Geburtstag. Hg. v. Ralph TUCHTENHAGEN und Christoph GASSENSCHMIDT. Hamburg 2004, 233-245. – PEPPIN, Volker: Siebenbürgen. Ein kirchenhistorischer Sonderfall von allgemeiner Bedeutung.

stellt, dass die Transmigranten eigene Untertanen sowie Steuerzahler blieben und nicht, wie im Fall der Salzburger Emigration,[30] Preußen oder anderen protestantischen Landesherren als willkommene Kolonisten dienten. „Durch Entblösung Unserer Erb-Landen von Einwohnern die ihrige zu bevölkern“[31], konnte mit der Wahl Siebenbürgens als Deportationsgebiet vermieden werden. Zu den genannten Faktoren kam ein weiterer hinzu. Von der Ansiedlung der Transmigranten in Siebenbürgen versprach sich der Wiener Hof auch einen Beitrag, um das durch Kriege und Aufstände geschwächte Fürstentum wirtschaftlich zu stärken. Zumindest von der Planung her wurden daher den Deportierten „Vorteile“ eingeräumt, die ihre Startbedingungen im Ansiedlungsgebiet verbessern sollten. In einem Referat der Hofkanzlei vom Juli 1734 heißt es, dass den „zur Abreiß destinierten Unterthanen in einem anderen Erbland und zwar in den fruchtbaren und wohl situierten gesunden aber nicht sehr populierten Fürstenthumb Siebenbürgen das freie exercitium religionis würklich verstattet, denen selben anbey mit Entlassung der sonst schuldigen Nachsteuer auch deren sicheren Überbringung in besagtes Fürstenthum nicht weniger für die bedürftige der nöthige Unterhalt auf der reyß und Unkosten des aerarii und bey ihrer Ankunft in Siebenbürgen allen die Gelegenheit zu ihren ehrlichen Fort- und Unterkommen und zwar bey der allda stabilierten deutschen sächsischen Nation, mithin bey ihren jetzigen Glaubensgenossen verschaffet wird.“[32]
Schließlich lag nach Auffassung der Hofkanzlei ein weiterer Grund für die Wahl Siebenbürgens als Deportationsgebiet vor, nämlich, dass beide Gruppen, Siebenbürger Sachsen und Transmigranten, „teutscher Nation und ihres Glaubens Genossen seiyndt.“[33] In der gleichen Volks- und Glaubenszugehörigkeit von ansässiger Bevölkerung und Transmigranten wurde offensichtlich auch eine günstige Voraussetzung gesehen, die die rasche Assimilation der Transmigranten befördern sollte.
Doch trotz dieser von Seiten des Staates als günstig eingeschätzten Bedingungen wurden die Transmigranten dort, wo sie in größerer Zahl angesiedelt wurden, nicht assimiliert. Ihre Eingliederung erfolgte, wenn überhaupt, wie das gewählte Neppendorfer Beispiel zeigt, nur auf lange Sicht und unter den Bedingungen tief greifender

In: Konfessionsbildung und Konfessionskultur in Siebenbürgen in der frühen Neuzeit. Hg. v. DEMS. und Ulrich A. WIEN. Stuttgart 2005, 7-13.

[30] FLOREY, Gerhard: Geschichte der Salzburger Protestanten und ihrer Emigration 1731/32. Wien-Köln-Graz ²1986. – MARSCH Angelika: Die Salzburger Emigration in Bildern. Weissenhorn ²1979. – WALKER, Mack: The Salzburg Transaction. Expulsion and Redemption in Eighteenth-Century Germany. Ithaca-London 1992. – Auf Deutsch: Der Salzburger Handel. Vertreibung und Errettung der Salzburger Protestanten im 18. Jahrhundert. Aus dem Engl. übers. von Sabine KRUMWIEDE. Göttingen-Zürich 1997. – EMRICH Gabriele: Die Emigration der Salzburger Protestanten 171-1732. Reichsrechtliche und konfessionspolitische Aspekte. Hamburg 2002. – LEEB, Rudolf: Die große Salzburger Emigration von 1731/32 und ihre Vorgeschichte. In: Glaubensflüchtlinge. Ursachen und Auswirkungen konfessioneller Migration im frühneuzeitlichen Ostmitteleuropa. Hg. v. Joachim BAHLCKE. Münster 2008, 235-263.

[31] VON ZWIEDINECK-SÜDENHORST, Hans: Geschichte der religiösen Bewegungen in Inner-Österreich im 18. Jahrhundert. In: Archiv für österreichische Geschichte 53 (1875), 460-539, hier 500. – Hier wird aus einem Schreiben Maria Theresias an die protestantischen Reichsstände vom 23.04.1755 zitiert. Darin weißt die Kaiserin entschieden alle Anschuldigungen zurück, sie verstoße mit den Transmigrationen gegen das ius emigrandi.

[32] NOWOTNY: Transmigration, 23.

[33] BUCHINGER: „Landler“, 380.

Spannungen. War also die gleiche Konfession kein die Integration unterstützender und beschleunigender Faktor? In diesem Fall offensichtlich nicht. Weshalb? Mögliche Erklärungen liefern die Charakteristika, die die Transmigrationen als eine spezifische Art von konfessionell bedingter Zwangsmigration ausweisen. Ihr Hauptanliegen war nämlich ein repressives, die Säuberung katholischer Territorien von Protestanten und deren Bestrafung durch Deportation, dagegen war die für den Staat als „gewinnbringend" erachtete Ansiedlung zwar eine willkommene, aber nur eine zweitrangige Folge katholischer Konfessionalisierung.

Charakteristika der Transmigrationen

Die Transmigrationen gehören in ihren Ursachen, ihrer staatlichen Begründung und Durchführung in das konfessionelle Zeitalter. Es zeichnet sich durch massive herrschaftliche und staatliche Eingriffe in allen Bereichen der Gesellschaft zu Lasten der Untertanen aus. Der Willkür des „konfessionellen Zwangsstaates"[34] insbesondere in Glaubensangelegenheiten wurden mit dem Augsburger Religionsfrieden und seit dem Ende des Dreißigjährigen Krieges mit den Bestimmungen der Westfälischen Friedens Grenzen gesetzt. Dennoch gab es auch noch zu Beginn des 18. Jahrhunderts bezogen auf die österreichischen Erblande unterschiedliche Auffassungen darüber, inwiefern der Kaiser als Landesherr durch die Religionsverträge gebunden war. Die beiden wichtigsten und zugleich gegensätzlichsten Meinungen sollen kurz anhand eines Memorandums aus geistlicher Feder und einer Stellungnahme der Hofkanzlei an der Wende von 1733 zu 1734 vorgestellt werden.[35]

Gestützt auf juristische Argumente und untermauert mit politischen Überlegungen stellten die im wesentlichen geistlichen Vertreter der einen Auffassung eine Bindung an die Bestimmungen des ius reformandi[36] und ius emigrandi[37] in Frage. Die oberösterreichischen Protestanten seien ein „aufrührerische[s] Volck" und könnten deshalb keineswegs als Emigranten gelten. Weil sie „allen schuldigen Respect" gegenüber der geistlichen und weltlichen Obrigkeit verloren hätten, seien sie als „Delinquenten" anzusehen. Dieser Status schließe sie von der Gewährung des ius emigrandi aus, wodurch sich die protestantischen Untertanen das Auswanderungsrecht selbst verwirkt hätten. Anstatt sie ziehen zu lassen, sei daher ihre Verschic-

---

[34] REINHARD, Wolfgang: Was ist katholische Konfessionalisierung? In: Die katholische Konfessionalisierung. Hg. v. DEMS. und Heinz SCHILLING. Gütersloh 1995, 419-452, hier 433. – HERZIG, Arno: Der Zwang zum wahren Glauben. Rekatholisierung vom 16. bis zum 18. Jahrhundert. Göttingen 2000.

[35] Bei den folgenden Ausführungen folge ich KÜPPERS-BRAUN: „Und die kleinen Kinder", 215-217. – Hier auch die entsprechenden Nachweise. Für weitere Beispiele, die die beiden gegensätzlichen Interpretationen über die Geltung der Religionsverträge unterstreichen vgl. NOWOTNY: Transmigration, 19-24.

[36] SCHNEIDER, Bernd Christian: Ius reformandi. Die Entwicklung eines Staatskirchenrechts von seinen Anfängen bis zum Ende des Alten reiches. Tübingen 2001.

[37] MAY, Georg: Die Entstehung der hauptsächlichen Bestimmungen über das ius emigrandi (Art. V §§30-43) auf dem Westfälischen Friedenkongress. In: Zeitschrift der Savigny-Stiftung für Rechtsgeschichte 74 (1988), 436-494. – DERS.: Das ius emigrandi nach dem Westfälischen Friedensinstrument. In: Ecclesia militans. Festschrift Remigius Bäumer zum 70. Geburtstag. Hg. von Walter BRANDMÜLLER, Herbert IMMENKÖTTER und Erwin ISERLOH. Bd. 2. Paderborn u.a. 1988, 607-636.

kung innerhalb der Staatsgrenzen vorzuziehen, am besten unter Zurückhaltung der unmündigen Kinder, wodurch deren katholisches Seelenheil gesichert werden sollte. Die aufgrund des Delinquentenstatus zugewiesene „wohlverdiente straff" der Transmigration, „wan sie in Siebenbürgen abgeführet werden", wurde ausdrücklich als obrigkeitlicher Gnadenakt interpretiert.

Im Unterschied zu dieser Auffassung bejahte die Wiener Hofkanzlei in ihrer Stellungnahme ausdrücklich eine Bindung auch der österreichischen Erbländer an die bestehenden Verträge, also auch an das ius emigrandi. Aus der geltenden Rechtslage könne nicht abgeleitet werden, „wie dan in diesen Österr. Ländern, wo keine Leibeigenschafft, ist, wieder einen, so von der Catholischen zu der Lutherischen religion hinumbtritt, in dem selber nicht alß ein Kezer angesehen und ohne anderen verbrechen nicht gestrafft werden kann, anderst procediret werden könne, alß dass selber mit dem seinigen aus dem Land gebracht werde."[38]

Ausdrücklich wurde auch ein Zurückhalten der unmündigen Kinder verneint, da selbst „relegierten Juden ihre unmündige Kinder nicht vorenthalten zu werden pflegen." Vielmehr setzte die Hofkanzlei auf die Überzeugungsarbeit der katholischen Geistlichen, um die „verführten – oder auch unverständigen ohnschuldigen Seelen" zu retten.

So unterschiedlich und gegensätzlich die beiden Interpretationen der Bestimmungen des Westfälischen Friedens auf den ersten Blick erscheinen, stimmen sie dennoch in wichtigen Punkten überein: Erstens in der Verantwortung der Obrigkeit für das Seelenheil der Untertanen und zweitens in dem aus dieser Verantwortung abgeleiteten Gebot des Handelns. Dabei reichte das Spektrum von der seit der Mitte des 18. Jahrhunderts deutlich intensivierten Verfolgung und Missionierung[39] insbesondere durch die Errichtung von Konversionshäusern und Missionsstationen, bis hin zum gewaltsamen Entfernen der Untertanen und deren Verbringen in ein von der Obrigkeit bestimmtes Gebiet. Um die Wirkung beider Maßnahmen zu verstärken, wurden sie gleichzeitig angewandt. Dabei ist eine deutliche Zunahme der Gewaltanwendung bei den Transmigrationen einschließlich der Kinderwegnahme als auch der Missionierung in der Zeit Maria Theresias unverkennbar. Zwei eng miteinander verflochtene Faktoren trugen wesentlich zur Durchführung von Transmigrationen und der Intensivierung der Missionierung bei. Im Bereich der Außenpolitik war es der so genannte „Salzburger Handel"[40], also die Emigration der Protestanten aus dem Erzbistum

---

[38] KÜPPERS-BRAUN: „Und die kleinen Kinder", 217.

[39] Vgl. dazu insbesondere SCHEUTZ, Martin: Die „fünfte Kolonne". Geheimprotestantismus im 18. Jahrhundert in der Habsburgermonarchie und deren Inhaftierung in Konversionshäusern (1752-1776). In: Mitteilungen des Instituts für österreichische Geschichtswissenschaft 114 (2006), 329-380. – TROPPER, Peter G.: Staatliche Kirchenpolitik, Geheimprotestantismus und katholische Mission in Kärnten. Klagenfurt 1989. – PÖRTNER, Regina: Die Kunst des Lügens. Ketzerverfolgung und geheimprotestantische Überlebensstrategien im theresianischen Österreich. In: Kommunikation und Medien in der frühen Neuzeit. Hg. v. Johannes BURKHARDT und Christine WERKSTETTER. München 2005, 385-408.

[40] WALKER: Salzburger Handel. Vgl. dazu auch die in Anm. 30 angeführte Literatur. Zu der nicht zu überschätzenden Bedeutung der Salzburger Ereignisse für den Umgang des Kaisers mit den Portestanten in den eigenen Territorien und der Genese des Transmigrationssystems vgl. zuletzt STEINER: Reisen ohne Wiederkehr, 104f.

Salzburg 1731/32 und das Erstarken Preußens[41]. Hinzu kam im Bereich der Innenpolitik die mit den Reformen des 18. Jahrhunderts erfolgte Durchherrschung der Monarchie, die vom katholischen Glauben als Staatsräson geprägt war. Die bürokratisch untermauerte Festigung des Staates ging mit dem Ziel der Glaubenseinheit einher: „Die Machtentfaltung des werdenden modernen Staates verlangt konfessionelle Intoleranz als Voraussetzung."[42]

Die Antwort des Wiener Hofes auf diese Herausforderung war das System der Transmigrationen, das unter Karl VI. als „Notmaßnahme" eingeführt und dann in der Zeit Maria Theresias systematisch ausgebaut wurde. Es erlaubte, die eingegangenen Verpflichtungen des Westfälischen Friedens einzuhalten und gleichzeitig diese zu umgehen oder zumindest zum eigenen Vorteil auszuhebeln. Aus Gründen der Staatsräson führte an einer Bestrafung der „verstockten Irrgläubigen" durch Deportation kein Weg vorbei. Ökonomische und außenpolitische Gründe geboten es, sie innerhalb der eigenen Staatsgrenzen zu behalten. Mit dem System der Transmigrationen, das sich durch eigens aufgebaute Verfolgungs-, Missions- und Ansiedlungsapparate auszeichnete, gelang es beide Gesichtspunkte zu vereinen. Den protestantischen Untertanen wurde die von ihnen vehement geforderte Religionsfreiheit gewährt, allerdings unter der Auflage, dass der Ort für die freie Ausübung des Glaubensbekenntnisses vom Kaiser vorgegeben wurde, um so mit der Ansiedlung wirtschaftliche Vorteile aus der Deportation zu ziehen. Die Transmigrationen stellten somit einen Versuch dar, den Komplex der Glaubens- und Auswanderungsfreiheit außenpolitischen Implikationen zu entziehen und zugleich die protestantischen Untertanen den politischen, wirtschaftlichen und religiösen Zielen des Staates zu unterwerfen. Aus Sicht des Staates verbanden die Transmigrationen damit die konfessionell motivierte Bestrafung der Untertanen mit der herrschaftlichen „Gnade", in einem anderen Teil der Monarchie den eigenen Glauben frei ausüben zu können. Die Transmigrationen erweisen sich, wie es bereits Wandruszka formulierte, als eine „Kompromisslösung zwischen dem bevölkerungspolitisch-wirtschaftlichen Erwägungen und dem Verlangen der Dynastie nach Bewahrung der erbländischen Glaubenseinheit."[43]

Um einerseits den Bestimmungen der Instrumenta Pacis Osnaburgensis zu entsprechen und sich andererseits die Entscheidungsfreiheit bezüglich der eigenen Untertanen zu behalten, wählte der Kaiser eine Vorgehensweise, die in der schon erwähnten Stellungsnahme der Hofkanzlei vorgeschlagen worden war. Die protestantischen Untertanen wurden außerhalb der anerkannten Religionen gestellt, als Ketzer eingestuft, und damit ihrer verbrieften Rechte entledigt. In der Sprache eines Missionars:

[41] Zum Einfluss Preußens auf die Religionspolitik der Habsburgermonarchie vgl. PÖRTNER, Regina: Propaganda, Conspiracy, Persecution. Prussian Influences on Habsburg Religious Policies from Leopold I. to Joseph II. In: Jahrbuch der Österreichischen Gesellschaft zur Erforschung des 18. Jahrhunderts 18/19 (2004), 457-476.

[42] REINHARD: Konfessionalisierung, 268f.

[43] WANDRUSZKA, Adam: Geheimprotestantismus, Josephinismus und Volksliturgie in Österreich. In: Zeitschrift für Kirchengeschichte 78 (1967), 94-101.

„Vermeine sodan höchst nottwendig zu sein, dass ein so raudiges schaaff und villeicht ein verdekhter reissender wolff von der herde abgesondert werde, damit er nicht mehr andere von der pekherung […] abhalte oder etwan auch andere guette verfüehre.“[44]

Damit wurden die als Ketzer eingestuften Protestanten den rechtlichen Bestimmungen entzogen, die die freie Auswanderung garantierten und zugleich der eigenen Willkür des Staates unterworfen. In einem Schreiben des Wiener Hofes an das Corpus Evangelicorum heißt es ausdrücklich, „dass ein katholischer Landesherr befugt und sein Anbiethen mit alleruntertänigstem Dank zu erkennen sey, wann das exercitium religionis mit dem iure religionis combinieret werden kann, sein recht der Unterthänigkeit zu behaupten, folglich in seinen eigenen Provinzen, die aus nur katholischen Orten Wegbegebenden wiederum zu stabilisieren und beizubehalten, ist nicht zu leugnen, sondern vielmehr vor die größte Gnade zu schätzen, es wäre dann. Dass man malam fidem summi principis, quod tamen absit zu präsuponieren sich bereden lassen wollte.“[45]

Als die beiden letzten Transmigrantenschübe mit rund 200 Personen vorbereitet wurden, war man sich einerseits sicher, dass damit viele der „Irrgläubingen“ aus der Pfarre Stadl entfernt werden. Andererseits wurde befürchtet, es bleibe eine „größere Anzahl der Gleißler zurückh, welche zwar dermahlen sich anstellen, als ob sie eine Unterweisung annehmen wollten, oder sich gänzlich katholisch erklären, immittest aber schon jetzt nicht undeitlich vermerken lassen, dass eine blosse Verstellung verborgen seye.“[46]

Der Missions-Superior empfahl daher, bereits jetzt einen dritten Transmigrantentransport nach Siebenbürgen in Betracht zu ziehen, „wenn anderst die hiesige Pfarr wenigstens größten theils soll gereiniget werden.“ Mit den Transmigrationen wurden, wie es in einem Referat der Hofkanzlei heißt, die Herkunftsgebiete von „Verstockten und Unverbesserlichen vorhero gesäubert“, in dem man Deportationen einleitete. Erklärtes Ziel war die „ausrottung des verderblichen giffts des in hiriges vatterlandt laider eingeschlichenen Luteranisimi.“[47]

Zu der Abstempelung als Ketzer, als „Sectarier“, als räudige Schafe und als getarnte reißende Wölfe , also einer unbedingt zu entfernenden Gefahrenquelle für den vom Herrscher bestimmten „rechten“ Glauben der Allgemeinheit, kam eine weitere Kriminalisierung hinzu. Die Protestanten wurden als „Aufwiegler“, als „lands-Friedensbrüchige“ und als „Verräter“ eingestuft, die gegen die herrschaftliche Ordnung revoltierten.

„Keinem Unterthan kann erlaubt seyn wider des Landes-fürsten Religion zu schmähen, oeffentliche Aergernusse zu geben, der Aufwicklung sich theihafft zu machen, Ruhe störerische Zusammenkunfftten zu halten und sofort an“,[48] heißt es in einem Reskript Maria Theresias vom 17. September 1753. Ungeachtet der von ihnen im-

[44] STEINER: Reisen ohne Wiederkehr, 269.
[45] NOWOTNY: Transmigration, 24.
[46] KNALL: Aus der Heimat gedrängt, 144-147, Zitat 147. – Hier auch die weiteren Belege.
[47] STEINER: Reisen ohne Wiederkehr, 139.
[48] ZWIEDINECK-SÜDENHORST: Geschichte, 498f.

mer wieder bekundeten Kaisertreue wurden die Transmigranten damit zusätzlich als politische Straftäter gebrandmarkt. Zielte die Einstufung als Ketzer auf die konfessionell motivierte Säuberung, so sollten die Transmigranten zusätzlich als unzuverlässige Staatsbürger außerhalb des Rechts gestellt werden.[49] Mit dem bewusst herbeigeführten Zustand der Rechtlosigkeit wurden die anderskonfessionellen Untertanen der Willkür des Herrschers, in diesem Fall der Deportation ausgeliefert. Die Transmigrationen konnten dadurch mit dem der Herrschaft zustehenden Recht der Sicherung der Ordnung gegenüber den im „Corpus Evangelicorum"[50] zusammengeschlossenen protestantischen Reichsständen begründet und durchgeführt werden.

Mit einer solchen Vorgehensweise erfolgte unter dem Banner der Konfessionalisierung eine doppelte Kriminalisierung der protestantischen Untertanen. Das damit verbundene negative Erscheinungsbild der Transmigranten wurde durch die daraus abgeleiteten Maßnahmen verstärkt. Sie durften nicht auswandern, konnten also weder über den Zeitpunkt noch über das Ziel der Migration entscheiden. Sie wurden deportiert, wie Verbrecher unter militärischer Gewalt an einen ihnen zugewiesenen Ort verbracht. In einer offenen Ordre des kaiserlichen Kriegsrats an die nach Siebenbürgen abkommandierten Truppen von 1734 wurde der Befehl erteilt,

„dass sie besagte transmigranten von hiraus nacher widerholtes Fürstenthumb Sibenbürgen abwechselungsweis von Station zu Station escortiren, alle Entweichung deren selben sambt und sonders abhinderen, ansonsten keine Ausschweifungen gestatten, in dem Fürstenthumb selbst aber nach Ordre des commandirenden G[ene]ralens [...] abgeben."[51]

Ihren Bestimmungsort Siebenbürgen durften die Transmigranten nicht verlassen, wofür entsprechende Überwachungsmaßnahmen sorgten. Die Richter in den siebenbürgisch-sächsischen Dörfern hatten „auf diese Leuthe stets genaue Acht zu geben", dass „keiner von ihnen künftig abschleichen möge". Abreisende Transmigranten waren unbedingt den Behörden zu melden, „um zu wiedereinholung derer Entwichenen die gehörige Veranstaltung zu machen."[52] In die gleiche Richtung zielte die strenge Briefzensur.[53]

Zur Überwachung kam die Pauperisierung der Transmigranten hinzu. Sie wurde entweder billigend in Kauf genommen, durch mangelnde Aufsicht geduldet oder aber auch bewusst betrieben. Die hinterlassenen Vermögen wurden den Deportierten äußerst schleppend, unter vielerlei Abzügen und manchmal gar nicht ausgehändigt, was ihre Startbedingungen im Ansiedlungsgebiete deutlich verschlechterte. Die Klagen von Transmigranten, endlich das eigene Restvermögen ausbezahlt zu bekom-

---

[49] EBD., 107-111.
[50] HAUG-MORITZ, Gabriele: Corpus Evangelicorum und deutscher Dualismus. In: Alternativen zur Reichsverfassung in der Frühen Neuzeit? Hg. v. Volker PRESS. München 1995, 189-207.
[51] Staatsarchiv Hermannstadt, Faszikularakten P 145, 16.08.1755. Hier zitiert nach SEDLER: Landler, 248f.
[52] Staatsarchiv Hermannstadt, Magistratsakten 48/1736, Bl. 7f. Hier zitiert nach POPA: Urkunden, 94f.
[53] Beispiel bei SEDLER: Landler. – STEINER: Reisen ohne Wiederkehr.

men, und die Bitten sächsischer Behörden, die Deportierten in die Lage zu versetzen, wirtschaftlich auf eigenen Beinen zu stehen, füllen Bände.[54]
Mit diesen rechtlich abgesicherten Kriminalisierungsmaßnahmen erzeugte der konfessionelle Zwangsstaat ein in jeder Hinsicht negatives Bild der Transmigranten: Religiös nicht festgelegt, Ketzer eben; als Untertanen unzuverlässig und aufmüpfig, Unruhestifter eben; ohne wirtschaftliche Potenz, Menschen also, die dem Ansiedlungsgebiet zur Last fallen. Dieses den Protestanten angeheftete, in jeder Hinsicht negative Gesamtbild ging den Transmigranten voraus. Im Ansiedlungsgebiet lastete es geradezu wie ein Kainsmal auf ihnen und wirkte sich auf die „reservierte" Aufnahme, den zögerlich verlaufenden Eingliederungsprozess und letztendlich auch auf die Herausbildung einer eigenen Landler-Identität aus.

Folgen für die Integration

Als sich im Vorfeld der karolinischen Transmigrationen Siebenbürgen als Zielgebiet der Deportation abzeichnete, äußerten sich die siebenbürgisch-sächsischen Behörden zu den Ansiedlungsplänen. In einem Brief vom 29. Juli 1733 erläuterte der Bürgermeister von Hermannstadt gegenüber dem Deputierten der Sächsischen Nation in Wien den siebenbürgisch-sächsischen Standpunkt. Zunächst bejahte er grundsätzlich die Notwendigkeit der Zuwanderung von „Emigranten" in die siebenbürgisch-sächsischen Territorien:
„Was nun übrigens die bewusste Emigranten- und projective allenfalls hieher in die Nation zu stabilisierende Familien anbetrifft, so liegt ja klar am Tage, wie diese sächsische Nation allbereit sich in einem solchen Verfall befinde, und von ihren alten sächsischen Insassen dergestalt abgekommen sey, dass dieselbe auch nur zum Theil zu bevölkern und mit deutschen Colonien zu recrutieren wohl über 10 m[ille] Familien mögten erfordert werden."[55]
Trotz des zweifellos bestehenden Bedarfs an Zuwanderern sei man aber nach „viel und wolhbedächtig[em] Überlegen" zum Schluss gekommen, das Vorhaben abzulehnen:
„[S]o können unmöglich dazu rathen oder aber uns resolvieren an diesem etwa über kurtz oder lang eventualiter noch geschehen könnenden Emigrations Werck unserseiths sollicitando theil zu nehmen."
Für den ebenso eindeutigen wie klaren Beschluss des Magistrats führte der Bürgermeister zwei, im von mir erörterten Zusammenhang bemerkenswerte Argumente an. Erstens:
„Diese invito suo Domino et cum scandalosa offensione suorum concivium emigrierende Leute ein großmächtiges Odium auf sich laden werden, welches ihnen auch

[54] Vgl. dazu die Beispiele bei BUCHINGER: „Landler", 344-362. – SEDLER: Landler und KNALL: Aus der Heimat gedrängt sowie STEINER: Reisen ohne Wiederkehr.
[55] Staatsarchiv Hermannstadt, Magistratsakten 56/1733, Bl. 2r-3r. Hier zitiert nach NOWOTNY: Transmigranten, 95. – SEDLER: Landler, 224f. Aus diesem Dokument stammen auch die folgenden Zitate.

mit dahin, wohin sie sich recipieren, mitfolgen, consequenter auch die recipienten dessen mittheilhafftig werden müssen".
Demnach wurde befürchtet, dass der den Transmigranten anhaftende Makel, religiös nicht festgelegt und zudem als aufrührerische Untertanen zu gelten, auch auf die Bevölkerung des Zielgebiets ausstrahlen würde. Die Gefahr, dass der „Schandfleck" auf die Siebenbürger Sachsen übergriff, wollte man unbedingt vermeiden und zog es daher trotz des Bedarfs an Siedlern vor, sich gegen die Aufnahme der Transmigranten auszusprechen. Hinzu kam ein zweites wichtiges Argument, mit dem der Hermannstädter Magistrat seine ablehnende Haltung begründete:
„Diese Leuthe wohl nicht anders als bettler, die weder zu ihrem Unterhalt noch auch zu ihrem fernern Stabiliment etwas mit sich bringen zu considerieren sind, folglichen wir nationaliter durchaus nicht im Stande wären, die erforderliche Hülffe ihnen zu leisten".
Offensichtlich auf Grund der unzutreffenden Informationen aus Wien über die wirtschaftlichen Verhältnisse der Deportierten befürchtete der Hermannstädter Magistrat finanzielle Nachteile für die aufnehmende Gesellschaft. Die als Bettler eingestuften fielen aus Sicht des Bürgermeisters dem Gemeinwesen der Siebenbürger Sachsen doppelt zur Last. Die Mittellosen waren bei der Ankunft zu versorgen und zudem konnte von ihnen auf lange Sicht weder ein Beitrag zu ihrer Integration noch zur wirtschaftlichen Stärkung der Siebenbürger Sachsen erwartet werden.
Zu der ablehnenden Haltung der Siebenbürger Sachsen trug offensichtlich die Kriminalisierung der Potestanten in ihren Herkunftsgebieten bei. Sowohl die Einschätzung religiös zumindest Ungefestigte als auch die Abstempelung als unzuverlässige und zudem arme Untertanen finden sich in der Stellungnahme wieder. Dieses den Transmigranten vorausgehende Bild veranlasste den Hermannstädter Magistrat, dem Deputierten in Wien in der Angelegenheit äußerste Zurückhaltung nahe zu legen. Friedenberg wurde empfohlen sich „in diesem Emigrations Negotio passive [zu] verhalten und weder hir noch dort gar nicht poussieren, noch sollicitieren mögen." Sollte aber der Kaiser dennoch darauf bestehen, Transmigranten zur Kolonisation nach Siebenbürgen und, damit verbunden, zur „Säuberung" Siebenbürgens von den Walachen zu schicken, sollte zunächst ein Versuch mit ein bis zwei Tausend Familien durchgeführt werden, um auf dieser Grundlage die weitere Vorgehensweise abzustimmen.
Dass es sich bei den angeführten Gründen nicht lediglich um vorgeschobene, sondern ernst gemeinte, von der staatlich betriebenen Kriminalisierung der Deportierten hervorgerufene Argumente handelte, zeigte sich, als die ersten Transmigrantentransporte in Siebenbürgen eintrafen. Weil die Unterbringung in den für sie bestimmten Ansiedlungsorten zunächst nicht gewährleistet war, wurden die ersten Transmigranten vorübergehend in Heltau untergebracht. Offensichtlich weil man an dem wahren lutherischen Glauben der Neuankömmlinge zweifelte, unterzog man die Transmigranten des ersten Transports aus dem Salzkammergut einer Glaubensprüfung, die sie mit Bravour bestanden. Diese Praxis fand auch in späteren Jahren An-

wendung.[56] Konnten auf diese Weise vorhandene Vorurteile gegenüber den Transmigranten abgebaut werden, so bestätigten sich gleichzeitig ein Teil der vom Hermannstädter Magistrat geäußerten Befürchtungen. Aufgrund der schlechten Voraussetzungen, unter denen die Umsiedlung der Kärntner in karolinischer Zeit stattgefunden hatte, fielen „die elende Cärnthner", von denen wenige überlebten, den Gemeinden zur Last. Sie würden gleichsam als Bettler angesehen, heißt es in einem Bericht. Der Magistrat, der wie das Beispiel Neppendorfs zeigt, um die Transmigranten bemüht war, ersuchte Wien um Hilfe, damit „sie also auß dem Elende in einen nährhaften Stand gesetzt werden mögen, damit sie dermalainst [...] noch gute getreue Unterthannen und Contribuenten mögen abgeben können".[57]

Eine ablehnende Haltung der siebenbürgisch-sächsischen Stände-Nation ist auch gegenüber den Zuwanderern der maria-theresianischen Transmigrationen zu beobachten. Im Vorfeld der ersten Umsiedlungen wurde die Regierung des Fürstentums um eine Stellungnahme zu der geplanten Ansiedlung der Transmigranten aus Oberösterreich, der Steiermark und aus Kärnten gebeten.[58] Hatte man es vor knapp 20 Jahren noch für erforderlich gehalten, eine große Zahl von Kolonisten, allerdings keine Transmigranten, anzusiedeln, so wurde jetzt argumentiert, in Siebenbürgen sei der für die Ansiedlung notwendige Boden nicht vorhanden, es herrsche Landmangel. Allodialbesitz auf Komitatsboden komme dafür nicht in Frage, weil er die Ansiedler zu Arbeitsdienst gegenüber den Grundherren und zur Abgabe des Zehnten verpflichte. Zudem bringe die Ansiedlung dem Land keine wirtschaftlichen Vorteile. Im Gegenteil: Wenn überhaupt, könne man die Transmigranten nur anstelle der ansässigen Walachen ansiedeln. Dies würde aber angesichts der den Transmigranten gewährten Freijahre einen erheblichen Steuerausfall nach sich ziehen. Neben den wirtschaftlichen Argumenten führte man auch die besonderen klimatischen Verhältnisse und die unterschiedliche Lebensweise an. Abschließend wurde auch angesichts der schlechten Erfahrung, die man mit den aufgenommenen Durlachern[59] gemacht hatte, die Ansiedlung der Transmigranten im Banat vorgeschlagen.

Doch auch dieses Mal gelang es den siebenbürgisch-sächsischen Vertretern nicht, die Ansiedlung der Transmigranten abzuwehren. Größeres Gewicht als solche, die siebenbürgischen Verhältnisse betreffenden Gründe hatten für die Kaiserin die Säuberung der Erblande von Ketzern. Die Transmigranten seien nach Siebenbürgen zu

---

[56] Dass die Befürchtung, nicht Lutheraner sondern „Sectierer" aufzunehmen, nicht unbegründet war, zeigen die Kärtner Hutterischen Brüder, die während der Transmigrationen in der Zeit Maria Theresias nach Siebenbürgen kamen. Vgl. dazu BUCHINGER, Erich: Die Geschichte der Kärtner Hutterischen Brüder in Siebenbürgen und in der Walachei (1755-1770), in Russland und Amerika. In: Carinthia 172 (1982), 145-303. – ROTH, Harald: Von den Hutterer zu den Landlern in Siebenbürgen. In: Glaubensflüchtlinge im frühneuzeitlichen Europa. Hg. v. Joachim BAHLCKE. Münster 2008, 335-343.

[57] GROSS Julius: Kärtner Emigranten im Burzenlkand. In: Korrespondenzblatt des Vereins für siebenbürgische Landeskunde 34 (1911), 105-107. – Weiterführend hierbei STEINER: Reisen ohne Wiederkehr.

[58] Sowohl im Schreiben des Guberniums an die Kaiserin als auch in jenem der katholischen Fraktion des Guberniums sowie einer Denkschrift des katholischen Bischofs Baron von Sala wird eindeutig gegen die Ansiedlung der Transmigranten in Siebenbürgen argumentiert. Vgl. dazu NOWOTNY: Transmigranten, 48-50, dessen Ausführungen gefolgt wird.

[59] GÜNDISCH, Gustav: Zur Einwanderung der Baden-Durlacher in Mühlbach. In: Zeitschrift für siebenbürgische Landeskunde 72 (1978), 59-70.

schicken, „weil selbes zur Abschneidung der Korrespondenz am weitesten entlegen, an der Population Mangel leidet und von diesem transmigrierenden arbeitsamen Volk mehr Kultur und Treu als von den mit der sächsischen Nation untermischten Walachen zu erwarten stehet".[60]

Über die widerwillige Aufnahme hinaus blieben die bei der sächsischen Nation vorhandenen Vorbehalte gegen die Transmigranten erhalten. Die Verhandlungen des eigens für die Beschleunigung der Ansiedlung und Eingliederung eingerichteten Transmigranten-Inspektorats[61] mit den sächsischen Magistraten lassen erkennen, dass diese sich, wo immer sie konnten, gegen die Ansiedlungsmaßnahmen sträubten. Trotz der durchaus vorhandenen positiven Ausnahmen weigerten sich die lokalen Behörden Häuser und Boden zur Verfügung zu stellen oder die Transmigranten in die Zünfte aufzunehmen.[62] Transmigranten beschwerten sich, weil sie bei der Zuteilung von Land nicht auch Besitzurkunden erhalten hatten, mit der Folge, dass ihnen fruchtbar gemachtes Ödland von der sächsischen Bevölkerung wieder abgenommen wurde. Der Transmigranten-Inspektor konnte bei der sächsischen Bevölkerung „kein sonderliches Verlangen" erkennen, „die Zahl ihrer Contribuenten mit diesen Transmigranten zu vermehren." Überhaupt wäre es gut, so sein Bericht,

„wenn so viel als möglich aller Unterschied zwischen Sachsen und Transmigranten aufgehoben und selbe in die Dorfschaften aufgenommen würden, um selbe zu überzeugen, dass man sie als wirkliche freie Sachsen behandle".[63]

Zwar war die rechtliche Gleichstellung bereits 1758 in die Wege geleitet worden, doch eine tatsächliche Gleichheit war damit noch nicht gegeben. Ein Beamter, der mit den Verhältnissen bestens vertraut war, sprach 1773 von einem „National-Hass" zwischen alteingesessener sächsischer Bevölkerung und den zugezogenen Transmigranten.[64] Das gegenseitige Misstrauen wurde nur sehr langsam, im Laufe von Jahrhunderten abgebaut.

Neben den vorhandenen, nicht zu unterschätzenden kulturellen Unterschieden – Sprache[65], Tracht[66], Lebensweise[67] – führte die religiös motivierte und von der Staaträson diktierte Kriminalisierung der Transmigranten dazu, dass sich die Zugehörigkeit zur „teuschen nation" und die Zugehörigkeit zur gleichen Konfession nicht als ausreichend starke Klammern erwiesen, um die Transmigranten einzuschmelzen, zu assimilieren. Die gleiche Stammes- und Glaubenszugehörigkeit führte zugespitzt formuliert nicht zur Erleichterung und Beschleunigung der Integration, sondern eher zu ihrer Verzögerung und der Herausbildung einer eigenen kulturellen Identität der Transmigranten. Wesentlich haben dazu die Art der Zwangsmigration und das mit

[60] NOWOTNY: Transmigranten, 47.
[61] BUCHINGER: „Landler", 354f.
[62] Eine ganze Reihe von Beispielen bei SEDLER: Landler. Vgl. auch BEER, „Willkürliches Benehmen".
[63] NOWOTNY: Transmigranten, 65f und 74.
[64] BUCHINGER: „Landler", 414. – Nowotny: Transmigranten, 94.
[65] Der Forschungsstand ist zusammengefasst bei Wilfried SCHABUS: Die siebenbürgischen Landlerdialekte. In: BOTTESCH (u.a.): Die Siebenbürgischen Landler, 179-276.
[66] Vgl. dazu vor allem SEDLER: Landler.
[67] Vgl. zu den einzelnen Bereiche die einschlägigen Beiträge in BOTTESCH (u.a.): Die Siebenbürgischen Landler.

ihr erzeugte Bild der Transmigranten beigetragen. Die vorhandenen Gemeinsamkeiten wurden offensichtlich vom konfessionell begründeten Bild der „Irrgläubigen", „Ketzer", „Aufwiegler" und „Besitzlosen" überlagert, welches durch die vom Wiener Hof betriebene Kriminalisierung im Zuge der katholischen Konfessionalisierung zuzurechnenden Transmigrationen entstanden war. Die Charakteristika dieser Konfessionsmigration gepaart mit der ablehnenden Haltung der aufnehmenden Gesellschaft trugen im Ansiedlungsgebiet entscheidend zur Verstärkung der kulturellen Differenz und damit zur Herausbildung einer eigenen Landler-Identität bei.

Karl-Peter Krauss

Frauen in Not. Das Ehegericht in der Batschka im Prozess der Konsolidierung und Disziplinierung

Einführend werden drei Fallbeispiele aus dem Ehegericht Kalocsa vorgestellt. Diese Beispiele illustrieren und bereiten die folgende Einordnung und Analyse im Rahmen der Thematik vor.

„...samt meiner Tochter die Ehre beraubt, und dieses in meiner Abwesenheit". Der Fall Anna Maria Müller vor dem Ehegericht

Anna Maria Müller kam am 15. Januar 1798 in Tschonopel (serb. Čonoplja, ung. Csonoplya) in der Südbatschka als achtes von 14 Kindern von Peter und Anna Maria Müller zur Welt. Knapp 23 Jahre später wurde sie aktenkundig im Ehegericht von Kalocsa. Ihr Vater hatte sich im Dezember 1820 an das bischöfliche Konsistorium gewandt. Ziel seines Schreibens war, zu erreichen, dass Johann Preisich, von dem seine Tochter seinen Angaben nach schwanger war, diese auch heiraten solle, weil „obesagter Johan Preisich aber nicht nach Relligions P[f]lichte verhalten, sondern hat einen Betträger [Betrug] gemacht, er hatt mir Alten Ehrlichen Mann samt meiner Tochter die Ehre beraubt, und dieses in meiner Abwesenheit."[1] Er forderte daher wegen der fortgeschrittenen Schwangerschaft seiner Tochter, „die Schande von meiner Tochter zu verdeken". Darunter verstand der Vater eine Eheschließung. Doch, so Peter Müller, habe ihm der Pfarrer Georg Paul[2] leider keine „Satisfaction" erteilt. So sei er „Bemüßiget [...] um Hülfe zu Flehen".

Ein Verfahren begann, das über ein Jahr dauerte. Johann Preisich weigerte sich, Anna Maria zu heiraten. Der empörte Vater wandte sich wieder an das Konsistorium. Er beschwerte sich, dass der Bursche dem Befehl des Pfarrers, seine Tochter zu heiraten, nicht Folge geleistet habe. Er schloss den Brief mit dem Satz: „Wän solche Unzucht gar so unbestraft bleiben solte so werden die Jünglinge so ausgelaßen das wir unsere Kinder immer an der Kette zu halden genöthiget werden [...]".

[1] Dieses Zitat sowie die folgenden Zitate sind den nach Ortschaften geordneten Akten des Ehegerichts der Erzdiözese Kalocsa entnommen: Kalocsai Főegyházmegyei Levéltár [Erzbischöfliches Archiv Kalocsa]. (fortan KFL), I. 2. Kalocsai Érseki Főszentszék (Erzbischöflicher Heiliger Stuhl Kalocsa), a. Feudális kori iratok (Schriften aus dem feudalen Zeitalter), Csonoplya, Johann Preisich – Anna Maria Müller 1820 – 1821.

[2] Georg Paul, Pfarrer von 1811-1833. A Kalocsa-Bácsi Főegyházmegye történeti sematizmus 1777-1923. Schematismus historicus cleri Archidiocesis Colocensis et Bacsiensis 1777-1923. Hg. v. Andor LAKATOS. Kalocsa 2002, 172.

Doch die Sache nahm für den Vater eine wenig erfreuliche Wendung. Schon der Pfarrer hatte ihn beschwichtigt, „daß viele große Hegschaften[3] in solche Fähle gerathen und machen kein solchen großen Lärm ich sol zu Hauß gehn". Das war eine erstaunliche Aussage des Pfarrers und sie schien ein deutlicher Hinweis darauf zu sein, dass der Vorfall zumindest kein singuläres Ereignis war, sondern dass der Pfarrer in seinem Dorf öfters mit vorehelichen Schwängerungen konfrontiert wurde. Was war geschehen? Der zur Heirat verdonnerte Johann Preisich hatte keineswegs klein beigegeben. Um einer Heirat zu entgehen, hatte er weitere Männer dazu gebracht, in sog. „Zeugnissen" schriftliche Aussagen über Anna Maria Müller zu machen. Diese Zeugnisse waren von erheblicher Brisanz und bargen die Gefahr, die Glaubwürdigkeit der jungen Frau zu untergraben. Leicht vorstellbar ist, welche Wirkung die Aussage etwa des Lorenz Kirsch auf den Pfarrer und das erzbischöfliche Ehegericht machte: „Zeugniß. Unterzeichneter bekennet daß ihme mit Nahmen Mariann Müllerin zu sich berufen um mit ihr Hurerey zu treiben, und zwar, so oft er will, welches ich mit meinem eichenen Nahmen, und einem Eid Schwur bezeigen kan, und auch wirklich bei ihr gelegen und Geschlafen habe. Bekenne ich Lorenz Kirsch".

Jetzt befand sich der Vater in der Defensive. Im Februar 1821 schrieb er ein drittes Mal an das Konsistorium. Er bat, „dieses Kind[4] in eine Versorgung dem ehelichen[5] zu übergeben". Der bedrängte Vater räumte ein, dass seine Tochter schon früher von einem „Ehman Namens Mathias Weiss[6] welcher Weib und Kinder, aber weder Relligion noch Ehre besitzet" auf dem Heimweg von Kernia[7] [...] ergriefen" und wie die Tochter sagte „mir die Kleider vom Leibe gerießen, und weil ich zu Schwach ware hatt er mich übermächtigt, und mit Gewalt meine Ehre genohmen." Um seiner Überzeugung, von wem das Kind ist, Nachdruck zu verleihen, endet das Schreiben mit dem Hinweis: „Dieses kan das ganze Dorf Bestättigen, das wer das Kind ansiehet saget dieses Kind siehet dem Johan Preiss gleich und er kan es nicht laug[n]en."

Inzwischen hatte der Pfarrer die Zeugenaussagen mit einem Bericht nach Kalocsa versandt. Aus diesen Aussagen geht hervor, dass Anna Maria Müller schon mehrere Männer zur Unzucht verleitet habe. Um den Fall endlich aufzuklären, lud das Konsistorium Johann Preisich wohl für den September 1821[8] zur Einvernahme vor. Doch dem 20jährigen Johann Preisich war der Boden offensichtlich zu heiß geworden. Jedenfalls legte er ein ärztliches Attest vor, in dem der Chirurgus Georgius Szerentség bestätigte, „Daß der Patient [...] in [...] Fieber ist, [...] kann sich nicht amosvi-

---

[3] Sprachlich besteht wohl ein Bezug zu schwäbisch „Hag(e)n", „Hägel", was Stier bedeutet bzw. zu Hagestolz, ein unverheirateter Mann, Junggeselle. Hier geht es wohl um eine abwertende Ausdrucksweise für voreheliche Beziehungen, bei denen eine Schwangerschaft die Folge ist.

[4] Gemeint ist das inzwischen geborene Kind seiner Tochter Anna Maria.

[5] Damit plädierte er nach wie vor dafür, dass das Kind in ehelichen Verhältnissen aufwuchs und beharrte auf der Heirat.

[6] Auch Mathias Weiss hatte ein – allerdings wenig glaubhaftes – „Zeugnis" verfasst, in dem er sich auf den inzwischen verstorbenen Johann Schock berief.

[7] Kernei, serb. Krnjaja, ung. Kerény, Nachbarort von Tschonopel.

[8] Dieses Schreiben ist nicht überliefert, aber die Datierung des Attests deutet darauf hin, dass er in dieser Zeit zu erscheinen hatte.

ren."[9] Welches Urteil das Ehegericht schließlich fällte, lässt sich den lückenhaften Akten nicht entnehmen. Doch die Heiratsmatrikeln des Dorfes geben den entscheidenden Hinweis.[10] Alles spricht dafür, dass Preisich gegenüber Anna Maria Müller ein Eheversprechen abgegeben hatte. So heiratete er diese im Januar 1822. Und damit leistete er der kirchlichen Anweisung, Anna Maria zu heiraten, schließlich Folge. Sie gebar ihm im Januar 1823 ein weiteres Kind. Doch diese Ehe währte nicht lange. Die junge Frau starb noch im September 1823 im Alter von 25 Jahren. In weniger als zwei Monaten heiratete der Witwer die 21jährige Katharina Kemmer, die ihm noch 14 Kinder gebar, wovon aber nur drei Kinder das heiratsfähige Alter erreichten.

Dieses Beispiel gibt einen Einblick in einige charakteristische Handlungs- und Verfahrensabläufe sowie Wirkungsmechanismen von Ehegerichtsverfahren auf die Dorfgesellschaft. Gleichzeitig beleuchtet der Fall die Erwartungsmuster der verschiedenen Akteure.

„...wandle auf Rosen, vergiß mein nicht": Skandal im Dorf. Untreue und Liebesbeziehung der Josepha Schmidt aus Hajós

Der Rittmeister der im Jahre 1812 in Hajós in der Batschka stationierten Reiterabteilung reagierte schnell. Am 20. Oktober hatte er ein Schreiben des Konsistoriums aus Kalocsa erhalten. Diesem war zu entnehmen, dass ein Wachtmeister seiner in Hajós liegenden Esquadron namens „Joseph Stiasny mit der Josepha Sukovics Gattin des Hajoscher Insaßen Franz Schmiedt einen unerlaubten Umgang gepflogen hat, wie dieß die von ihm an die besagte Frau abgeschickten mehrere Liebsbriefchen hinlänglich beweisen, so findet sich das hierortige Erzbischöfliche Consistorium bemüßiget, wegen der Herstellung des ehelichen Friedens zwischen obgenannten Eheleuten, die in der heutigen Consistorial Session ausgesöhnt sind worden, Herrn Rittmeister, und Escadrons Commandanten um die Übersetzung bemeldten Wachtmeisters auf eine Station dienstfreundlichst zu ersuchen". Der Rittmeister antwortete einen Tag später[11]. In diesem Brief versicherte er, „daß der Umgang des dieseitigen Wachtmeisters mit der Gattin des hießigen Innsaßen Franz Schmid bestmöglichst beseitiget werden wird, und kann sich gedachte Frau, ohne etwas zu befürchten; zu ihrem Mann begeben [...] und mann wird Aufsicht tragen, um ferners Unannehmlichkeiten zu verhüten". Allerdings konnte er die gewünschte Versetzung des Mannes nicht zusagen.

Den Fall ins Rollen gebracht hatte der Ehemann der untreu gewordenen Josepha Schmidt, geb. Sukovitz. Er hatte sich mit diesem (undatierten) Schreiben Hilfe su-

[9] Von lat. amovere, fortbewegen.

[10] FEITH, Johann/KAINRAD, Johann/KEMMER, Johann: Ortssippenbuch Tschonopel 1762 – 1945. Hg. von der Heimatortgemeinschaft Tschonopel in der Batschka. Rödermark Ober-Roden 2003 (Deutsche Ortssippenbücher, Reihe B, Band 100). 4. Auflage, Sonderausgabe auf CD.

[11] KFL, I. 2. a., Hajós, Franz Schmidt – Josepha Sukovitz 1812; Schreiben mit Datum vom 21. Oktober 1812.

chend an das Konsistorium gewandt: „Ein Hochleiblisches[12] Consisterium. Bittsteller anersucht dieweilen das Shükschall[13] mir betrofen hat, und ich als ein Unglüglicher Mann von meinem Weib geworden bin, und so viel Beschwerte habe, mich und meine Kinder in das gröste Unglük zu Stürsen, und sie von mir entwichen ist, mit einem Millitars Mann mich zu hintersetzen, so bitte ein Hoch= löbl: Consistorium mir eine Gaüdige[14] behülflichkeit zu erleisten bereit sein wollen.
Indeme ich meine Wirthschaft mit [größ]ten[15] Schweiß erhalten habe, und sie mit Schlederting[16] zu Grund gericht hat, ist erstlich das sie mir von andern Leuden Geld heraus=flatiert hat; und mit den Millitars Mann angewendet, nicht genung an diesen sontern auch Hemeder[17] wie auch Kleidungs= stüke mit sich genohmen, sogar das Heilige Hochwürdige Sakrament des Ehestandes vor eitel haltet; So Bitte ich ein Fußfälliger Diener mir armen und Betrangter Mann Gnädig zu leisten. Bittsteller Franz Schmid Fleischaker Meister." Dem Schreiben kann entnommen werden, dass Josepha Schmidt schließlich ihren Mann verlassen, Kleider mitgenommen und Geld ausgeliehen hatte.

Die an das Konsistorium versandten Liebesbriefe[18] liegen bis heute als Beweisstükke vor. Sie sind, wenn auch schwer beschädigt, erhalten geblieben. Vieles spricht dafür, dass die von dem Soldaten an die Frau des Metzgers Schmidt versandten, teilweise ohne Namen und Datum versehenen Briefe von Franz Schmidt gefunden wurden und als corpus delicti an das Ehegericht weiter geleitet wurden.[19]

Die Briefe zeugen von einer wohl mindestens von Dezember 1811 bis Oktober 1812 bestehenden Beziehung zwischen dem Reitersoldaten und der Frau des Metzgers. Sie war immer wieder unterbrochen von Einsätzen des Soldaten außerhalb von Hajós. Diese Briefe sind mit zärtlichen Anreden überschrieben wie „Allerliebste Peggi!", „Ewig mein Einziges Vergnügen Theuerste Peggi!", Viel geliebeste meines Herzens", „Unvergeßliche Geliebte!", „Zärtlichst Geliebete einzige Freundin" oder „Liebe Seele meines zweiten Ich!" Der Fall kulminierte darin, dass Josepha ihren Mann verließ. Die Briefe zeugen zugleich von einer intensiven sowie vielleicht auch angesichts der notwendigen zwingenden Geheimhaltung auch von Krisen und von Eifersucht geprägten Liebesbeziehung. So beteuerte Joseph Stiasny am 4. Juni 1812 „Ich war noch nie wie ein Schmetterling, der von einer Blume zu [anderen][20] schwebt, und bin noch nicht entschloßen, als ein solches unbedeutendes Thier angesehen zu werden, Es ist wahr und ich muß mir selbst gestehen daß meine Zurückgezogenheit in den Augen meiner Geliebten Argwohn erregen muß." Auch beschwört

[12] Hochlöbliches.
[13] Schicksal.
[14] Gütige.
[15] Dokument ist beschädigt.
[16] Schlendrian.
[17] Hemden.
[18] Es handelt sich insgesamt um 11 Briefe.
[19] Ein großer Teil der 23 Seiten umfassenden Akten wurde beschädigt. Farbe und Konsistenz des Papiers deuten auf Brandspuren. Gleichwohl kann fast der gesamte Text entziffert werden, weil die Beschädigungen vor allem außerhalb des beschriebenen Bereichs liegen.
[20] Dieses Wort fehlt. Offensichtlich handelt es sich um einen Flüchtigkeitsfehler.

er im gleichen Brief: „Ubrigens versichere ich Ihnen bey meiner heißen Liebe die in mir zu einer großen Leidenschaft gegen Sie entflammt ist, daß in Betreff ihrer geliebten Person Niemand einen Einfluß auf mich hat, und nie wird haben können." Noch nach Ostern gab es eine Krise in der Beziehung, die in dem Satz gipfelt: „Gott, wo sind die Osterfeyertäge, die ich mir so vergnügt vorstellte".[21] Schon am 1. Januar 1812 hatte er unter einem Pseudonym einen wehmütigen, von Liebeskummer geprägten Brief an Josepha geschrieben: „[...] aber von hier muß ich scheuten[22] und Dich muß ich meiden und ich meute[23] auch die ganße Welt aber lieber wer es mir wen Du es mit meins Meser mein Hertz durch stegen dest, auch was ach was sol ich den sagen oder was soll ich denken liebe Seele, wen Du nur einen Brief schreibest und mit Lebe woll und ich verbleib Dein bis in den Todt aufrachtiger: Joseph Hanff[24] [...]". Im Lauf der Monate wurde der Briefschreiber zunehmend unvorsichtiger. Schließlich unterzeichnete er die Briefe mit dem vollen Namen und dem Datum. Ein abruptes Ende schien geradezu vorprogrammiert.

Der Fall war sowohl für das Konsistorium als auch für den vorgesetzten Rittmeister des Soldaten bestechend klar und damit einfach zu lösen. Darauf deuten auch die Akten hin: Außer den Liebesbriefen enthält das Faszikel nur das Gesuch des Metzgers Franz Schmidt, das Schreiben des Konsistoriums an den Rittmeister sowie dessen Antwort. Hier lag eine derart eindeutige Normverletzung vor, dass ohne zu zögern gehandelt wurde. Mit der Aussage des Metzgers Franz Schmidt, dass seine Frau „sogar das Heilige Hochwürdige Sakrament des Ehestandes vor eitel haltet", hatte er ein zentrales Argument vorgebracht, dem sich keine Seite entziehen konnte und wollte. Die Akten geben keinen Hinweis darauf, ob die Beziehung nach dem Aussöhnungsgespräch der Ehepartner am 20. Oktober 1812 tatsächlich endgültig zu Ende war. Vieles spricht dafür, da Joseph Stiasny auch der strengen Militärgerichtsbarkeit unterlag. Auch wenn keine weiteren Eintragungen in den Kirchenbüchern von Hajós über Josepha und Franz Schmidt vorliegen, so lässt der Eintrag vom 16. Oktober 1813 im Taufregister keinen Zweifel, dass die Beiden wieder zusammen waren. An diesem Tag war Taufe von Theresia Schmidt. Als Eltern des Kindes sind Franz Schmidt und Josepha Sukovitz angegeben. Das Fehlen weiterer Einträge der Familie mag darauf hindeuten, dass sie sich woanders nieder gelassen hatte. Nur so konnte sich das Paar der gesellschaftlichen und sozialen Stigmatisierung entziehen.

Anna Nándory, geb. Hoffmann: „wie ein irrendes Schaf in der Welt"

Die Akten des Ehegerichts zeugen in der Regel von Beziehungen aus dem gleichen Stand. In fast allen Fällen stammten die Partner aus relativ homogenen gesellschaftlichen Verhältnissen. Eher selten prallten Lebenswelten mit erheblich differierenden

[21] Undatierter Brief.
[22] scheiden.
[23] meide.
[24] Dieser Name wurde als Pseudonym verwendet.

Wertmaßstäben und Normen aufeinander. Insofern bildet das tragische Schicksal der Anna Hoffmann eine Ausnahme.[25] Sie wurde nicht nur Opfer eines gebildeten adligen Beamten, sondern auch der Unerfahrenheit ihrer einfachen Eltern, die sich von einer scheinbar guten Partie blenden ließen. Ihr Vater war Fleischhacker und hatte sich in Gajdobra (ung. Szépliget), Neusatz (serb. Novi Sad, ung. Ujvidék) und Bulkes (serb. Buljkes, heute Bački Maglić, ung. Bulkesz) aufgehalten.

Am 3. November 1798 wandte sich Anna Nándory, geb. Hoffmann, an den Erzbischof von Kalocsa, Ladislaus Graf von Kollonitsch.[26] Sie bat um Scheidung oder darum, ihren Mann zu zwingen, dass er sie „gehörig versorge". Vor zwölf Jahren war sie verheiratet worden, doch wie sie zu Protokoll gab: „Unsere Ehe dauerte drey Wochen".

Anna Hofmann wurde mit 16 Jahren verheiratet. Sie schrieb, dass ihre Eltern arm, aber einen „ehrlichen und christlichen Lebenswandel" hatten, aber sie es als ihre Pflicht betrachteten, sie „in der möglichsten Einfalt, ohne allen Kenntnißen, selbst – ohne der itzigen Zeit so nöthigen Weltkenntniß erzogen". Jedenfalls wurde sie an einen „äußerlich" „artigen", „gut gewachsenen" jungen Mann verheiratet, der ihr bei der Heirat die stattliche Summe von 700 Talern verschrieb und „1000 Verheißungen" machte. Dies obwohl sie für ihn „nicht das mindeste" fühlte, denn sie hatte „keinen Willen, oder durfte wenigstens keinen haben", was dann „schröckliche Folgen eines ungerechten Zwanges!" nach sich zog.

Die Ehegeschichte von Anna Hoffmann ist schnell erzählt. Ihr 22jähriger, weltgewandter und gebildeter Mann, der beim Grafen Hadik[27] als Verwalter in Diensten stand und lateinisch, ungarisch, deutsch, „ratzisch" (serbisch) und slowakisch sprach, hatte sie hinsichtlich seiner Herkunft getäuscht und sich als „Emerich Nándory ein gebohrner Edelmann von Güns" ausgegeben. Drei Wochen nach der Eheschließung sei dann Militär des Esterhazyschen Regiments nach Gloschan[28], ihrem Wohnort, gekommen. Und da habe sie vom Bataillons Chirurgen einen Hinweis bekommen, der sie vor ihrem Mann warnte. Dieser „sey unfähig, er soll sich eher reinigen, er würde es schriftlich geben, daß mein Mann mit Krankheit behaftet ist", woraufhin sie ein Gesundheitsattestat erhielt. Ist das ein Hinweis auf eine Geschlechtskrankheit ihres Mannes, da sie das Thema nicht offen anspricht? Für diese Hypothese spricht auch sehr deutlich ein hinsichtlich der Schrift wohl später angebrachter Vermerk auf dem Titelblatt der Akten: „morb. vener". Gemeint ist „morbus venereus". Unter dieser Bezeichnung wurden die Geschlechtskrankheiten Syphilis und Gonorrhoe zusammengefasst, bis der französische Arzt Philippe Ricord 1867 nachweisen konnte, dass es sich bei Gonorrhoe um eine eigenständige Krankheit

[25] KFL, I. 2., a., Imre Nándory – Anna Hoffmann, 1795-1799.

[26] Die Akte besteht nur aus zwei Dokumenten. Zum einen aus dem Brief von Anna an den Erzbischof, zum anderen aus dem Protokoll der Befragung von Anna. Gleichwohl bieten die Dokumente einen tiefen Einblick in das Leben einer jungen Frau, die völlig desillusioniert wurde.

[27] Andreas Reichsgraf von Hadik-Futok (1710-1790), Feldmarschall. Berühmt wurde Hadik durch die handstreichartige Besetzung Berlins im Oktober 1757 im Siebenjährigen Krieg und durch die Kontribution einer riesigen Geldsumme. Hadik hatte 1769 von Maria Theresia die Herrschaft Futak (serb. Futog) westlich von Neusatz erhalten und war 1771 in den Adelsstand erhoben worden.

[28] Serb. Hložany, ung. Dunagálos westlich von Neusatz.

handelte. Daraufhin stellte ihr Vater ihren Mann zur Rede, weil er „sich unterstanden ein ehrliches Mädel unglücklich“ gemacht zu haben. Doch dieser war darüber aufgebracht und ging zum Stuhlrichter.[29] Jener meinte zu ihrem Vater nur „Nimm der Herr nur seine Tochter zu Hauß“, versprach aber, das Attestat nach Kalocsa zu schicken – was nie geschah.[30] Unter einem Vorwand wurde sie nach drei Wochen Ehe von ihrem Mann verlassen, den sie nie wieder sah. Zuvor hatte er seine Sachen gepackt und sogar ihre Kleider mitgenommen. Alle Nachforschungen blieben jahrelang ohne Ergebnis. In Güns, wohin sie schrieb, wusste niemand etwas von einem Nándory. Neun Monate danach war ihr Vater gestorben. Dann sei ihre Mutter vor zwei Jahren auch gestorben: „...auch diese einzige Stütze verlohr ich [...], und bin nun von aller Welt verlassen“. Um ihren Lebensunterhalt zu fristen, ging sie in den Dienst und arbeitete bei verschiedenen Dienstherren und in mehreren Orten, unter anderem in Neusatz, Belgrad, zuletzt in Fünfkirchen (ung. Pécs), teilweise unterstützt „von verschiedenen Herrn“. Erst letztes Jahr, als sie nach Fünfkirchen gekommen sei, habe sie erfahren, dass ihr Mann mehrere Jahre dort „beim Kreis-Amte“ unter dem offensichtlich korrekten Namen Nándory gearbeitet habe. Nun solle er sich in Pest befinden, wo er bei der Königlichen Tafel[31] tätig sei. Auf die Frage des Konsistoriums „Quare hactenus non inquisiverit in suum Maritum?“[32] antwortete sie: „1tens Weil ich zu der Heyrath gezwungen worden. 2tens Weil er mit der Krankheit behaftet war. 3tns Weil ich arm war, und unerfahren.“

Das Schicksal der Anna Hoffmann zeigt den tiefen gesellschaftlichen Graben zwischen dem armen, unerfahrenen Mädchen aus der einfachen und unbeholfenen Familie des Fleischhackers Johann Hoffmann und dem hoch gebildeten, viele Sprachen sprechenden ungarischen Adligen, der in ihr offensichtlich ein austauschbares, aber leicht zu bekommendes Spielzeug sah. Scheinbar mühelos wurden die Eltern Opfer einer womöglich von Anfang eingefädelten Heiratsintrige, noch mehr erstaunt ihre gutgläubige Autoritätshörigkeit gegenüber dem Stuhlrichter, der versicherte, er werde das Gesundheitsattest nach Kalocsa dem Konsistorium zusenden. Womöglich hatten sie dieses Beweisstück aus der Hand gegeben. Im Zusammenhang der Fragestellung erhellt der Fall das von der dörflich-untertänigen Werteordnung geprägte Weltbild der Familie des Fleischhackers mit klaren Normenvorstellungen, das offensichtlich außerstande schien, drohendes Gefahrenpotential durch Angehörige eines anderen Standes auch nur annähernd realistisch einzuschätzen.

[29] Die Stuhlrichter (judices nobilium, főszolgabiró) hatten einen Bezirk des Komitats unter sich. Die Stuhlrichter waren mit dem Obergespan Richter des Komitatsgerichtes (forum comitatus). Vgl. CSÁKY, Moritz: Von der Aufklärung zum Liberalismus. Studien zum Frühliberalismus in Ungarn. Wien 1981 (Veröffentlichungen der Kommission für die Geschichte Österreichs 10), 51.

[30] Das ist mithin ein Beispiel für die Adelsnetzwerke innerhalb der Komitatsverwaltung, das den Untertanen insbesondere bei Anliegen, die sich gegen Angehörige des Adelsstandes richteten, wenig Chancen einräumte.

[31] Die Königliche Tafel (Tabula regia, királyi tábla) war neben der Septemviraltafel die zweithöchste Instanz des ungarischen Gerichtswesens. Darüber stand nur die Königliche Kurie (Curia regia, királyi kuria).

[32] Übersetzung: Warum forschte sie bisher nicht nach dem Verbleib des Ehemanns?

Die Quellen zur Ehegerichtsbarkeit im Erzdiözesanarchiv Kalocsa

Der hier untersuchte Raum der Batschka gehörte bis nach dem Ersten Weltkrieg vollständig zur Diözese Kalocsa. In Folge der neuen Grenzziehung nach dem Ersten Weltkrieg wurde für die Südbatschka 1923 die Apostolische Administration von Bács gegründet. Die Akten zur Ehegerichtsbarkeit auch der heute serbischen Südbatschka befinden sich im Erzdiözesanarchiv in Kalocsa. Diese Akten sind erst seit Kurzem offiziell zugänglich. Im Zweiten Weltkrieg waren sie aufgrund einer schnellen Evakuierungsmaßnahme in feuchte Kellerräume umgelagert worden, wo sie massiven Beschädigungen ausgesetzt waren. Nach der Trocknung wurden offensichtlich große Mengen kassiert. Heute sind die noch stattlichen Restbestände wieder vorbildlich nach dem Provenienzprinzip gemäß der ursprünglichen Ordnung nach einzelnen Ortschaften gegliedert und verzeichnet.[33] Die Akten setzen zaghaft in der Mitte des 18. Jahrhundert ein. In Städten wie Neusatz oder Baja in einzelnen Fällen schon in den dreißiger Jahren des 18. Jahrhunderts. Mit früheren Akten ist schon aus dem Grund nicht zu rechnen, weil erst 1733 der erste Erzbischof wieder seinen festen Sitz in Kalocsa hatte. Es war Gábor Patasich (1699 – 1745, Erzbischof von 1733 – 1745). Doch entsprechende Akten aus Dörfern der Batschka beginnen, sofern vorhanden, in der Regel erst um 1800. Der zeitliche Schwerpunkt liegt dabei auf der Zeit um die Mitte des 19. Jahrhunderts. Diese mangelnde Aktenlage ist kein Spiegel für das Fehlen von Auseinandersetzungen in den Ehen oder Trennungen, sondern wohl eher Ausdruck einer mangelnden kirchlich-administrativen Konsolidierung des Raumes. Zudem kamen die deutschen Ansiedler mit wenigen Ausnahmen erst in der zweiten Hälfte des 18. Jahrhunderts in diesen Raum. Und mit diesen zumeist katholischen Siedlern wurde erst in vielen Dörfern das geistliche Versorgungsnetz an Pfarrern und Kirchen notwendig. Damit stand zunächst die Aufbauleistung im Vordergrund.

Im ländlichen Raum dominieren Akten von Siedlungen, bei denen der Anteil der bäuerlichen Bevölkerung geringer war. Dazu gehörten Handels- und Verwaltungsorte wie etwa Apatin oder Palanka. Klagen auf Scheidung unter Angehörigen der bäuerlichen Schicht in dem im kanonischen Recht verankerten Rahmen erfolgten überwiegend wegen Misshandlungen (*saevitia*). Doch auch diese kommen überaus selten vor. Häufiger hingegen sind Klagen wegen Eheversprechens (*sponsalia*) und unehelicher Schwängerung (*impraegnatio*).

Trotz des Mangels an Quellen darf nicht die Schlussfolgerung gezogen werden, dass es keine Ehekonflikte gegeben hätte. Denn auch schon die josephinischen Ansiedlungsprotokolle aus diesem Raum geben immer wieder Hinweise auf Ehezerwürfnisse. So beklagte sich 1785 ein „Kolonist von Karavukova“[34], dass „[...] Ihm seine

[33] Für diese Informationen sei dem Direktor des Archivs, Herrn Dr. Andor Lakatos, gedankt, der sie bereits zu einem Zeitpunkt gab, als die Akten wegen der Ordnungs- und Verzeichnisarbeiten noch nicht zugänglich waren. Die gründliche Verzeichnung führten Viktória Banga und Gabriella Csongrádi durch.

[34] Serb. Karavukovo, ung. Bácsordás.

Eheweib mit 400 fl Geld und Geldwerth durchgegangen seie [...].[35] Daraufhin startete die Kameraladministration einen Fahndungsaufruf: „Die Beschreibung dieser entlaufenen Weibs-Person kommt denen 5 diesseitigen Kaal Verwaltern zu dem Ende mitzutheilen: daß Sie solche in denen unterhabenden Orthschaften aufsuchen, und in Arrest schaffen sollen; diese Beschreibung ist zugleich auch der dirigirenden Landes-Stelle mit der Bitt einzuhändigen, daß Hochselbe dessen Currentirung in Land ehestens zu veranlassen habe".

Vom Verfasser wurden im Rahmen eines Projekts zur historischen Demographie Ehegerichtsakten deutsch besiedelter Dörfer in der Batschka bis zur Mitte des 19. Jahrhunderts untersucht. Räumlicher Schwerpunkt ist die Südbatschka in der heutigen Vojvodina. Auswahlkriterium war diese zeitliche und räumliche Vorgabe sowie das Vorhandensein von Ego-Dokumenten in der sehr weit gefassten Definition von Winfried Schulze.[36] Er versteht darunter auch Schriftgut der Gerichte wie Klagen, Bittschriften sowie Verhörprotokolle. Unter Berücksichtigung der bei der Recherche Anfang August 2006 noch nicht vollständig geordneten Akten wurden schließlich trotz einer insgesamt großen Aktenmenge für den Gesamtraum ein Dutzend Fälle als geeignet für eine nähere Untersuchung erachtet. Dabei sollen hier wenige Einzelfälle im Mittelpunkt der Abhandlung stehen.

Alle Aktenfaszikel haben fragmentarischen Charakter. In Einzelfällen bestehen sie nur aus der Anklageschrift eines Betroffenen. In manchen Fällen liegen bis über zwanzig Seiten vor.[37] Keine Akte ist vollständig in dem Sinne, dass von der Anklageerhebung bis zur Urteilsverkündung alle Dokumente vorhanden sind. Doch ihr eigentlicher Wert ergibt sich, wenn Anklageschriften, Meinungsäußerungen von Familienangehörigen, Zeugenaussagen und Stellungnahmen der Pfarrer überliefert sind. Von Interesse ist auch, wer sich äußert. Nicht selten sind es die Eltern, insbesondere der Vater, von unverheirateten Prozessbeteiligten. Dabei sind die selbst verfassten Äußerungen der beteiligten Personen von besonderem Wert. Sie leuchten nicht selten auch dunkle Ecken des ansonsten verborgenen Familienlebens aus, berichten über Normen und Werte, vor allem über Normverletzungen und geben damit unfreiwillig Hinweise auf Normen. Das macht sie zu einer Quelle für die Alltags- und Sozialgeschichte.

Dabei sind die Klagen und Stellungnahmen natürlich auch eine Folge verfahrenstechnischer und prozesstaktischer Überlegungen und zollen einem gewissen Erwar-

---

[35] Magyar Országos Levéltár [Ungarisches Landesarchiv]. (fortan: MOL). E 125, Magyar kincstári levéltárak (Ungarische Kammer), Mikrofilm, 22244, Nr. 56, ohne Fol.

[36] SCHULZE, Winfried: Ego-Dokumente: Annäherung an den Menschen in der Geschichte? Vorüberlegungen für die Tagung „Ego-Dokumente". In: Ego-Dokumente. Annäherung an den Menschen in der Geschichte. Hg. v. DEMS. Berlin 1996, 11-30. – Zu definitorischen Überlegungen von Schulze sei besonders auf die Seiten 13 bis 15 verwiesen. Diese Definition blieb nicht ohne Widerspruch, zumal sie über die klassischen Selbstzeugnisse wie etwa Briefe oder Autobiographien u. a. hinausgeht. Auch bei dieser Untersuchung wurde auf Dokumente zurückgegriffen, die auf unfreiwilligen und als Folge von Zwängen indizierten Selbstaussagen basieren. Gleichwohl gestattet der Äußerungsspielraum der Verfasser einen Einblick in gesellschaftliche Wertvorstellungen und Denkmuster, was die Akten aus Mangel an anderen Quellen so wertvoll macht.

[37] Das unterscheidet diese Akten aus dem bäuerlichen Umfeld von Akten über Scheidungsfälle aus dem Adel oder reichen Bürgern. Bei letzteren umfasst ein Vorgang nicht selten hundert und mehr Seiten.

tungshorizont Tribut. Auch ist mit der Wiedergabe selektiver Tatbestände zu rechnen. Ebenso muss man sich davor hüten, „nachträglich [...] die Richterrolle“[38] zu übernehmen. Ohne Zweifel wurden oft Argumente vorgebracht, die im Rahmen des kanonischen Rechtes Aussicht auf Erfolg hatten. Neben den oft sehr farbigen Schilderungen der Betroffenen und der Zeugen handelt es sich bei den in der lateinischen Kanzleisprache verfassten Mitteilungen der Pfarrer oft um zusammenfassende, entauthentizierte Texte. Sie geben Auskunft über die Verfahrensabläufe und sind Ausdruck des Bemühens, Fakten zu erschließen. Unter Berücksichtigung dieser limitierenden Faktoren sind die Ehegerichtsakten bunte Gemäldeausschnitte aus der Eheanbahnung und der Mikrogeschichte des aus den Fugen geratenen ehelichen Zusammenlebens.

Forschungsstand und Rechtslage

Wer sich mit Ehegerichtsakten im deutschen Sprachgebiet befasst, dem fällt sofort die Dichotomie der Forschungslage auf. Einerseits liegen recht zahlreiche Forschungsergebnisse aus evangelischen bzw. reformierten Regionen vor. Hier ragt der umfassende Forschungsertrag von Susanne Burghartz über die Ehegerichtsbarkeit in Basel heraus.[39] Andererseits gibt es kaum entsprechende Forschungen über katholische Ehegerichte. Eine Ausnahme stellen die bestechenden Untersuchungen Peter Beckers und Rainer Becks dar.[40] Es lohnt sich in diesem Zusammenhang, Untersuchungen außerhalb des deutschen Sprachraums heran zu ziehen. So geben die „Lettres de cachet“ in Frankreich, eigentlich königliche Verordnungen, wenn sie in Familienangelegenheiten erlassen wurden, ebenfalls einen Einblick in das Innenleben der Familien sowie in Konfliktsituationen in Ehen und Familien. Ähnlich wie beim Ehegericht, wurden diese staatlichen Erlasse in der Regel auf Antrag des Ehepartners oder von Familienangehörigen als Disziplinierungsinstrument eingesetzt. Allerdings lief der Beschuldigte dann Gefahr, festgesetzt zu werden – auf Kosten der

[38] BURGHARTZ, Susanna: Ehen vor Gericht. Die Basler Ehegerichtsprotokolle im 16. Jahrhundert. In: Eine Stadt der Frauen. Studien und Quellen zur Geschichte der Baslerinnen im späten Mittelalter und zu Beginn der Neuzeit (13.-17. Jahrhundert). Hg. v. Heide WUNDER. Basel-Frankfurt am Main 1995, 167-187, hier 173.

[39] BURGHARTZ, Susanna: Jungfräulichkeit oder Reinheit? Zur Änderung von Argumentationsmustern vor dem Basler Ehegericht im 16. und 17. Jahrhundert. In: Dynamik der Tradition. (= Studien zur historischen Kulturforschung 4). Hg. v. Richard VAN DÜLMEN. Frankfurt am Main 1992, 13-40. – Eine umfassende Darstellung bietet: BURGHARTZ, Susanna: Zeiten der Reinheit – Orte der Unzucht. Ehe und Sexualität in Basel während der Frühen Neuzeit. Paderborn u. a. 1999. – Erst kürzlich erschien: LUTZ, Alexandra: Ehepaare vor Gericht: Konflikte und Lebenswelten in der Frühen Neuzeit. Frankfurt am Main 2006.

[40] BECKER, Peter: Leben und Lieben in einem kalten Land. Sexualität im Spannungsfeld von Ökonomie und Demographie. Das Beispiel St. Lambrecht 1600–1800. Frankfurt-New York 1990 (Studien zur Historischen Sozialwissenschaft 15). – BECK, Rainer: Frauen in Krise. Eheleben und Ehescheidung in der ländlichen Gesellschaft Bayerns während des Ancien régime. In: VAN DÜLMEN: Dynamik, 137-212. – Eine ansprechende Diplomarbeit über die Ehegerichtsakten des Konsistoriums von Brixen erstellte TERZER ANEGG, Ute: „bey unserer beysam wohnung kein daurhafter ehefrieden anzuhoffen...“ Die katholische Ehescheidungsvariante der Trennung von Tisch und Bett im Spiegel von Ehegerichtsakten des Konsistoriums von Brixen 1750 – 1800. Diplomarbeit. Innsbruck 2003.

Angehörigen. Die vorhandenen Bittschriften und Untersuchungen machen diese Quellengattung für die Forschung interessant.[41] Für Ungarn sind dem Autor entsprechende Untersuchungen nicht bekannt. Das erstaunt angesichts entsprechender Aktenbestände. Die mangelnde Forschungslage verwundert aber auch im Hinblick auf die Bedeutung der Ehe als konstitutives gesellschaftliches Element, deren Rolle gerade bei sich konsolidierenden gesellschaftlichen und kirchlichen Strukturen nicht unterschätzt werden sollte.

Seit der Gegenreformation verstärkte sich der Zugriff der katholischen Kirche in allen Ehefragen. Es galt, deutliche Akzente gegenüber der protestantischen Haltung zu setzen, die eine Ehe bis zu einem gewissen Umfang, wie Luther es ausdrückte, als „weltlich Ding" ansah. Im „ius canonicum" war die Ehe ein Sakrament.[42] Das führte zum Anspruch der katholischen Kirche, allein über Form und Inhalt dieser göttlichen Institution zu entscheiden. Ein wichtiger Meilenstein war das Konzil von Trient (1563). Neue Normen intensivierten die Überwachung der Heiraten und Ehen. Die streng konfessionelle Ehe etablierte sich, die unauflösbar war oder weniger euphemistisch ausgedrückt, aus der es kein Entrinnen gab. Diese Unauflösbarkeit setzte sofort mit dem Beginn der „copula carnalis" ein. Die Akten gewähren einen Einblick in die von „Überlebensimperativen" aus wirtschaftlichen und sozialen Zwängen geprägten ehelichen Gemeinschaften der einfachen Leute, bei denen Gefühle, Betroffenheit, Liebe hinter dem harten Pragmatismus alltäglichen Überlebens kaum offenbar werden.[43]

Und dennoch gab es Möglichkeiten, aus einer unhaltbar gewordenen Ehe zu entfliehen. Dazu gehörte die „Separatio a thoro et mensa", eine „Trennung" oder „Scheidung" von Tisch und Bett auf Zeit oder auch die lebenslange Trennung, die „separatio perpetua". Dabei wurde der Ehebruch in Ungarn nach dem Kirchenrecht nur dann als trennendes Hindernis betrachtet, wenn entweder die Ehe jemandem versprochen, oder einem Partner sogar nach dem Leben getrachtet wird.[44] „Ex capite saevitiei"[45] werden die Ehepartner nicht „ad tempus indefinitum", sondern nur auf ein Jahr getrennt. Bei einer „separatio" war das „vinculum matrimonii", das Band der Ehe nicht aufgehoben, denn eine Wiederverheiratung war nicht möglich. Anders stellte es sich dar, wenn eine Ehe rückwirkend für „null und nichtig" erklärt wurde. Das war etwa der Fall, wenn „die eheliche Beiwohnung" nicht erfolgte.[46]

[41] FARGE, Arlette/FOUCAULT, Michel: Familiäre Konflikte. Die „Lettres de cachet". Aus den Archiven der Bastille im 18. Jahrhundert. Aus dem Französischen von Chris E. PASCHOLD und Albert GIER. Frankfurt am Main 1989.

[42] Allgemein zur Ehe nach dem kanonischen Recht FAHRNER, Ignaz: Geschichte des Unauflöslichkeitsprinzips und der vollkommenen Scheidung der Ehe im kanonischen Recht. Freiburg im Breisgau 1903 (Geschichte der Ehescheidung im kanonischen Recht, Teil 1).

[43] BECK: Frauen in Krise, 138.

[44] GUSTERMANN, Anton Wilhelm: Öesterreichisches Kirchenrecht in den teutschen, ungerischen, und galizischen Erbstaaten. Wien 1807, 59.

[45] Gemeint ist: Aus Gründen der Grausamkeit, bei Misshandlung des Ehepartners. Das war einer der zentralen Gründe für Frauen, sich an das Ehegericht zu wenden.

[46] GUSTERMANN: Kirchenrecht, 72 und 73.

Hinsichtlich der rechtlichen Situation in Ehefragen bildete die Regierungszeit Josephs II. auch für Ungarn eine Zäsur. Die neue utilitaristische Kirchenpolitik Josephs II., das aufgeklärte Staatskirchentum, brachte die Kirche unter weitgehende staatliche Kontrolle.[47] 1786 hatte Joseph II. gegen starken kirchlichen Widerstand durch ein Reskript die Angelegenheiten der Ehe auch in Ungarn in die Kompetenz des Staates verwiesen.[48] Schon drei Jahre zuvor ließ Joseph II. Eheversprechen für unwirksam erklären mit der Begründung: „Da die Verlobnisse weder für den Staat, noch für den Privaten nützlich, sondern vielmehr für beide in Rücksicht auf die gezwungenen Ehen schädlich sind". Falls doch noch eines verfasst werden würde, hätte dieses „[...]nicht die mindeste rechtliche Wirkung".[49] Diese Verordnung machte die ungarische Statthalterei am 19. September 1783 den Komitaten kund.[50]

Der josephinische Eingriff in die bisherige kirchliche Gerichtsbarkeit wirkte sich auf die Anzahl der kirchlichen Eheprozesse aus. Während für das Jahr 1785 15 Verfahren in Kalocsa überliefert sind und anhängig waren, waren es 1787 vier und 1788 noch zwei Verfahren. Nach Josephs Tod stiegen die Prozesse sprunghaft an. Denn sein Nachfolger Leopold II. überließ die Ehestreitigkeiten wieder den Konsistorien. Er ließ das josephinische Reskript durch eine Verordnung vom 20. April 1790 wenigstens in Teilen aufheben.[51] Auch die Eheversprechen wurden in Ungarn wieder erlaubt und hatten rechtliche Wirkungen.[52] Dieser Tatbestand unterschied sich von der Rechtslage in Österreich. So konnte nach einem vorher erfolgten Eheversprechen auch die Schwängerung einer Frau durch einen anderen Mann das verbindliche Eheversprechen nicht lösen. Das erklärt, warum es zahlreiche Prozesse zur Thematik „sponsalia" im Archiv in Kalocsa gibt. Auch für die folgenden Jahrzehnte war es ein Kontinuum in Ungarn, dass die weltliche Gerichtsbarkeit die kirchliche Zuständigkeit in Ehegerichtsfragen akzeptierte. Die staatliche Zuständigkeit setzte dann, aufbauend auf dem kirchlichen Urteil, in zivil- und strafrechtlichen Fragen ihrer Zuständigkeit ein. Das war in diesem Raum auch der Fall während des Bestehens der „Wojwodschaft Serbien und Temescher Banat" (1849 – 1860).[53]

---

[47] ADRIÁNYI, Gabriel: Beiträge zur Kirchengeschichte Ungarns. München 1986 (Studia Hungarica 30), 18f. – CSÁKY, Moritz: Von der Aufklärung zum Liberalismus. Studien zum Frühliberalismus in Ungarn. Wien 1981 (Veröffentlichungen der Kommission für die Geschichte Österreichs 10).

[48] Dies betraf sowohl die Eheangelegenheiten der Katholiken des lateinischen und griechischen Ritus, wie der nicht unierten Griechen. GUSTERMANN: Kirchenrecht, 125.

[49] Zitiert nach EBD., Kirchenrecht, 25.

[50] Zitiert nach EBD., Kirchenrecht, 29. „[...] quod S. M. S. visum fuerit contractus sponsalisticos, quemadmodum in omnibus ditionibus caesareo – regiis germaniciis, ita etiam in regno Hungariae, et partibus annexis penitus aboliendos, et abrogandos decernere. Benignam hancce resolutionem [...].

[51] EBD., Kirchenrecht, 94.

[52] EBD., Kirchenrecht, 29.

[53] Auch bei Zivilklagen wegen Ehestreitigkeiten um Geld und Besitz wurde auf die kirchliche Gerichtsbarkeit Rücksicht genommen. So heißt es in einer gegenüber dem Bezirksgericht Sombor eingereichten Klageschrift des Forstingenieurs Maximilian Stanovits vom 18. Oktober 1856 wegen einer Körperverletzung und wegen Geldstreitigkeiten: „Hingegen meine Tochter hat bereits unter den 8. September d.[es] J.[ahres] ihre Scheidungs Klage dem hochwürdigsten Karloviczer Archidiecesan Consistorio schriftlich unterbreitet, wozu der consistorial Spruch abzuwarten komme." Istorijski Arhiv Sombor [Historisches Archiv Sombor]. (fortan: IAS). 34, Kraljevski Sreski Sud (Königliches Bezirksgericht) Sombor, kutija 5, ohne Fol.

Die Akteure bei den Ehegerichtsverfahren

Die Akten des Ehegerichts von Kalocsa stellen die Spitze eines Eisberges dar. Erste Anlaufstelle und Schlüsselfigur vor Ort war der Pfarrer. Erst wenn sich hier keine Lösung des Konflikts ergab, wurde entweder von den Beteiligten oder meist vom Pfarrer, das Konsistorium, eingeschaltet.[54] In Kalocsa wurden in zweiter und dritter Instanz auch Fälle aus anderen Diözesen entschieden und das Urteil gesprochen. Der Pfarrer war nicht unbedingt an der Einschaltung des Offizilats interessiert, denn er war gezwungen, dem Konsistorium alle notwendigen Dokumente und Beweisstücke vorzulegen – was mit einigem Aufwand verbunden sein konnte.[55] Es war oft auch im Sinne des Konsistoriums, dass der Pfarrer einen Fall selbst löste. Falls dies nicht möglich war, drohte eine Vorladung der Beteiligten nach Kalocsa. Die nicht seltenen Krankmeldungen, um solchen Vorladungen nicht Folge leisten zu müssen, sprechen eine deutliche Sprache.[56]

Neben den unmittelbar Prozessbeteiligten, die sich zu Klagen äußern mussten, um den Fall bewerten zu können, wurden in fast allen Fällen Zeugen vernommen. Diese Zeugen wurden von Klägern oder Beklagten zur Unterstützung des eigenen Standpunktes requiriert. Sie legten in einem schriftlichen „Zeugnis" ihre Sicht der Dinge dar oder wurden vom Pfarrer bzw. dem Konsistorium vernommen. Die Zeugenaussagen waren oft genug sehr detailliert und drangen nicht selten in intime Bereiche häuslichen und alltäglichen Daseins vor. So schildert Andreas Wilpert von Apatin in seiner Zeugenaussage vom 1. August 1829, dass die Katharina Rahm „mehrmahle nächtlicherweile ohne Erlaubniß über das Hof-Thor hinausgestiegen, und das Wohnhauß offengelaßen [...] und sogestallt ihrer Ausschweifung nachgegangen seye". In einem „Zeugnis" wenige Tage zuvor berichtet er, „daß er einmal [...] das Dienstmädl ruffen mußte, fand aber daß dieselbe in einem Zimmer mit dem benannten Herrn Oberjäger eingesperrt war, nach mehrmaligen ruffen Er aber doch herauskam, wo das Mädl dann im Zimmer das bett zurecht machte."[57] Viele Zeugenaussagen bieten unbeabsichtigt einen Einblick in gesellschaftliche Normen und die mit ihr verbundenen Erwartungshaltungen. Joseph Schmidt aus Waschkut (ung. Vaskut) schrieb in seinem „Jurament Zeigniß" über seine ehemalige Dienstmagd 1823, dass „Sie ohne mein Wißen und erlaubniß alle Nächte in allen Wirtshäusern Herum Flangirt" sei. Er habe zu ihr gesagt, dass er das „Herum laufen [nicht] leude" [...], den mein Haus darf mir Nächtlicher Zeit nicht unaufgespert nicht aufstehen" worauf sie

[54] Der geschilderte Fall von Anna Hoffmann, die mit dem Adligen Emmerich Nándory verheiratet war, stellt einen Ausnahmefall dar.

[55] So heißt es im Fall Prokhert – Rahm, dass der Pfarrer Beweise in der gewohnten Art zu leisten haben wird: „Testimoniales solito modo superinde praestiturae"

[56] So heißt es im chirurgischen Gutachten über den Oberjäger Wenzel Prokhert, der die Dienstmagd Katharina Rahm geschwängert haben soll: „Aertzliches Zeigniß. Nachdeme Herr Venzeslaus Prokerth seit 7t[en] July an einem bößartigen Gallfieber mit Rheumatischen Kopfschmerzen leidet, als Folge dessen gegenwärtig im Reconvalescentem Stand mit einem Schwindel behaftet ist; folglich eine Reise weder zu Wagen, noch zu Fuß zu seinem größten Nachtheil sein wird. Daß deme also nach Gewissenhafter erwägung, bezeige mit Eigener Unterschrift. Sig. Apathin am 31t. July [1]829."

[57] KFL, I. 2., a., Apatin, Wenzel Prokert – Katharina Rahm1829.

„den Vortheil gefunden und ihre Thüre zum Fenster hinaus gemacht nur daß Sie zu ihren Unzucht sachen hat kommen können.“[58]
Auch im eingangs geschilderten Fall spielen Zeugnisse hinsichtlich der Bewertung des Falles eine nicht unerhebliche Rolle. Ausgerechnet der wenig glaubwürdige Vergewaltiger von Anna Maria Müller scheute sich nicht als Zeuge aufzutreten und behauptete, dass der inzwischen verstorbene Johann Schock „[...] im Hofe den Beischlaf zweimal in einer Nacht mit ihr vollzogen habe, indem ich selbst zusah, und benanter Johann Schock, es mier auch selbst bekennet habe [...]“.[59]
Welche kollektive Bloßstellung ein Ehegerichtsverfahren zur Folge haben konnte, zeigt am offensichtlichsten der Fall von Anna Maria Müller und Johann Preisich. Hier ist die Beteiligung von vielen Personen schwarz auf weiß bezeugt. Schließlich waren in die causa Müller – Preisich die Familie des geschwängerten Mädchens, die Familie des Johann Preisich, der Pfarrer, der Schulmeister, der Dorfnotar, mehrere Zeugen, die Familien dessen, der das Mädchen vergewaltigt hatte, und das Konsistorium eingebunden. Für die anderen Beispiele ist die Einbindung der Dorfobrigkeit und vieler Zeugen mangels entsprechender Beweisstücke nicht so offensichtlich, doch sie liegt im dörflichen Umfeld nahe.
Das bedeutete im Dorf eine öffentliche Zurschaustellung. Dass dem so war, geht aus der Aussage des Vaters hervor, der ja betonte, dass „Dieses kan das ganze Dorf Bestättigen, das wer das Kind ansiehet saget dieses Kind siehet dem Johan Preiss gleich und er kan es nicht laug[n]en.“ Offensichtlich war die ganze Mikroebene des Dorfes unmittelbar oder mittelbar in den Fall involviert. Dabei war die Kirche als akzeptierte Entscheidungsinstanz im Sinne der Normenkontrolle gefragt. Doch auch die oben geschilderten weiteren Fälle lassen eine ähnliche Aufmerksamkeit, wenn nicht Stigmatisierung der Betroffenen erahnen, wenn dies aus den Akten auch nicht explizit hervor geht.
Was ehrhaft war und den Ehrkodex verletzte, ergibt sich vor allem aus den Aussagen des, wie er meint, seiner Ehre beraubten Peter Müller, des Pfarrers, aber auch weiterer Personen. Nicht die Schwängerung an sich war die Katastrophe, sondern die Verweigerung der Hochzeit mit Anna Maria Müller durch Johann Preisich. Erst dies löste den sozialen Erdrutsch aus. Das erst machte die Untersuchungen notwendig. Vorher waren die wohl auch vom Pfarrer akzeptierten dörflichen Normen nicht verletzt. Denn sofern ein Eheversprechen vorlag, ging alles seinen Gang. Erst durch das verletzte Versprechen musste die Kirche tätig werden. Insofern war es nur konsequent, dass der Vater der geschwängerten Anna Maria Müller den Johann Preisich aufforderte, die „Schande“ seiner Tochter „zu verdeken“, indem er sie heiraten sollte. Dadurch sei auch seine Ehre wieder hergestellt. Aus heutiger Sicht schockierend ist, dass die Gewaltanwendung des Mathias Weiß gegenüber Anna Maria offensichtlich keinerlei rechtliche Folgen hatte oder Restriktionen der Obrigkeit nach sich zog. Gleichwohl ist es sehr wahrscheinlich, dass auch er einen erheblichen Ehrverlust in

[58] KFL, I. 2., a., Csátalja, Katharina Bauer u. a., 1823.
[59] KFL, I. 2., a., Csonoplya, Johann Preisich – Anna Maria Müller 1820-1821.

Kauf zu nehmen hatte. Darauf deutet die Formulierung von Peter Müller hin, der über ihn sagte, dass er „weder Relligion noch Ehre besitzet". Auch das wenig überzeugende „Zeugnis" des Mathias Weiß war wohl eine Reaktion auf Fragen des Pfarrers und den sozialen Druck.

Im Fall von Anna Maria Müller – Johann Preisich ergibt sich ein Spannungsfeld zwischen Tradition und der fallbezogenen Praxis, weil sich die Konfliktparteien nicht an den dörflichen Sittenkodex hielten. Durch die zunächst erfolgte Verweigerung der Heirat durch den Schwängerer waren die soziale Ausgrenzung der Frau und deren Familie sanktioniert. Der Frau wurde der Erwachsenenstatus als Ehefrau und ihre soziale Rolle vorenthalten. Gleichwohl gab es für Johann Preisich noch Argumentationsspielraum, in dem er seine Rolle der Beziehung zu Anna Maria zu relativieren suchte, indem er andere angebliche Partner ins Spiel brachte. Da ist der Fall des Ehebruchs der Josepha Schmidt aus Hajós hinsichtlich des Handlungsspielraums eindeutig, da „Unzucht" nicht geduldet werden konnte.

Der Anlass für ein Verfahren: „Nun aber das er so ein schlegter mensch ist"

Die zwölf untersuchten Fälle und die bislang vorgestellten drei Beispiele stellen einen Ausschnitt aus einem weiten Spektrum für die Aufnahme eines Ehegerichtsverfahrens dar. Dabei handelt es sich durchweg um die üblichen Anlässe für ein Verfahren. Es geht um zwei Verfahren zum Thema Eheversprechen (sponsalia), um drei Fälle von vorehelicher Schwängerung (impraegnatio), um eine Nichtigkeitserklärung einer Ehe (matrimonialis[60]). Die Mehrzahl der Fälle waren Verfahren wegen einer Scheidung innerhalb des zugestandenen Rahmens (divortialis, divortium).

Da Eheversprechen in Ungarn rechtlich bindend waren, wurde bei einem Bruch des Versprechens dagegen vorgegangen. Um ein solches aufzulösen, verwendete Nikolaus Johann aus Apatin das Argument, er sei getäuscht worden. Er versuchte, die Hochzeit mit Elisabeth Schwarz abzuwenden, indem er anführte: „Man hat mir gesagt, sie sey mit einem sehr großen Reichthume ausgerüstet, und als ich mich aber näher erkundigte, so habe ich erfahren daß sie nichts hat, und daß sie nicht einmal ein ehelich erzeugtes Kind sey, welches auch bewiesen ist. So habe ich eingesehen, daß daraus keine glückliche Ehe entstehen könne; so bin ich mit meinem Versprechen wieder zurückgegangen."[61]

Insbesondere die Verfahren um eine uneheliche Schwängerung können tiefer gehende Einblicke in Verhaltensweisen und Argumentationsmuster geben, weil hier oft, wie im Fall der Anna Maria Müller, Zeugenaussagen heran gezogen werden. Auch im Beispiel von Elisabeth Müller, erfolgt der Rückgriff auf verletzte Normen, indem der gesellschaftliche Status der jungen Frau wegen ihrer unehelichen Geburt in Frage gestellt wird.

[60] Eigentlich: solutio vinculi matrimonialis, die Lösung des Bandes der Ehe.
[61] KFL, I. 2., a., Apatin, Elisabeth Schwartz u. a., 1828.

Bei den Anträgen auf eine Trennung von Tisch und Bett ging bis auf einen Fall die Initiative von der Frau aus. Ursache für deren Eingaben waren fast immer schwere Misshandlungen durch den Ehemann (lat. saevitia, Grausamkeit). Erst in der Öffentlichmachung des Konflikts und in der Anzeige beim Konsistorium sah die Frau die Chance auf eine Lösung. Das war zugleich ein Appell an die dörfliche soziale Kontrolle und an die Autorität der Kirche. Oft gingen jahrelange schwerste Konflikte voraus.

So klagte Elisabeth Blum aus Batschalmas (ung. Bácsalmás) über ihren zweiten Mann: „das er mich schon Vielmal so in die ängsten getrieben mich gesuchet um mein Leben zu bringen mit dem meßer auf mich gangen ist, und dießes schon viel mal geschehen, ist das ich meines lebens keine stund sicher bin, und das Kint ihme nicht vor die augen komen därf, das Kint diese 3 Jahr sich Bey anderen gutte Leuden seine Verflägung und Nahrung hat suchen müßen, dan wan es zu uns komen ist Hat er das Meßer genomen und mich sambt dem Kind gesuchet ums Leben zu bringen, also ist es eine unmöchlig keit mit ihme zu leben, dan er zu mir gesacht hat wan ich ein Kind von ihm erzeigen sol däte er es in muter Leib ums Leben bringen“.[62]

Dabei waren oft schon mehrere Vermittlungsversuche des Pfarrers gescheitert wie bei Elisabeth Philipp, geborene Hoffmann aus Weprowatz (serb. Veprovac, ung. Veprőd), die berichtete, dass der Ehemann versprochen habe, „daß er mich niemahl mehr mit Schlägen behandlen wolle; ich glaubte seinen Verheißungen, und ging gutherzig in Rüksicht auf meine 4. noch unerzogene Kinder wieder zu ihm zurük. Dieses sein Versprechen hielte er aber gar nicht lange, sondern er blieb vielmehr immer bey seiner alten Gewohnheit, und hat mich bereits vor 6. Wochen so jämerlich mishandelt, daß ich bis auf diese Stunde noch nicht genesen kann, werde auch die Täge meines Lebens meine Vorige Gesundheit nicht wieder erlangen, sondern bis in mein Grabe fühlen, daß ich einem Tyrannen untergeben ware, wie solches des in Original beigebogene Chyrurgische Zeugnuß sattsam beweißet.“

Oft verlängerten die Aussöhnungsgespräche der Pfarrer und ihre Anweisungen an die Frauen, dass sie zu ihren Männern zurückkommen sollen, deren Leidenszeit. Dabei reichten die Autorität und der Zugriff der Pfarrer auch über Dorfgrenzen hinweg. Das zeigt das Beispiel der Anna Maria Lebkücher aus Tscheb (serb. Čib, heute Čelarevo, ung. Dunacséb), die vor ihrem Mann nach Gajdobra geflüchtet war. Sie sprach sogar davon, dass sie vom Pfarrer zu ihrem Mann „getrieben“ worden war. In ihrem Schreiben an das Konsistorium vom 13. Mai 1823 führte sie aus, dass sie mit ihrem „Mann Dietrich Lebkieger zwanzig Jahre in Frieden, aber ohne Erzeugung eines Kindes“ lebte. Und sie hoffte „[...] Da nun Gott unsern Wunsch erfüllte, und uns mit einem Knaben segnete [...] daß wir noch besser als vorher leben würden.“[63] Doch diese Hoffnung erfüllte sich nicht. Denn ihr Mann war mit der Nachbarin „in eine sehr große Bekanntschaft gerathen“. Dann berichtete sie, dass ihr Mann dadurch „seine Neigung gegen mich immer mehr und mehr verlohr. Mit diesem war es aber noch nicht genug, sondern die Nachbarin fing so gar an, meinen Mann aufzu-

[62] KFL, I. 2., a., Bácsalmas, Mihály Karácsonyi – Elisabeth Blum, 1828.
[63] KFL, I. 2., a., Dunacséb, Theodor Koch – Anna Maria 1818-1825.

hetzen, und ihn endlich auf den Gedanken zu bringen, daß er der Vater zu meinem Kind nicht sey." Schließlich kam es zu massiven Übergriffen des Ehemannes, wovon die Anna Maria Lebkieger schrieb: „so kam es endlich so weit, daß mein Mann anfing, mich mit Drohungen, mit Verfolgungen, zuletzt mit unmenschlichen Schlägen zu tracktieren; wobei nicht nur die Nachbarin, sondern sogar unser eigener Lehrbub wo nur möglich mich verfolgen mußten – dieses alles dauerte nun beständig so fort, bis ich im Haus keine Ruhe mehr hatte, und endlich die Flucht nehmen mußte; dann war meines Mannes und der liebe[n] Nachbarin Wunsch erfüllt – und ihr Ziel war erreicht." Schließlich ging sie mit ihrem Kind nach Palanka und suchte dort Zuflucht, bis ihr der dortige Pfarrer befahl nach Tscheb zurück zu kehren. Sie suchte dann Zuflucht bei ihrem Pfarrer in Tscheb, welcher sie „mit guter Hoffnung" wieder zu ihrem Mann brachte und einen Versöhnungsvertrag aufsetzte. Doch das trug zu einer Entspannung nicht bei. Vielmehr eskalierte die Situation offensichtlich weiter. Mit folgender Argumentation brachte Anna Maria Lebkücher ihr Anliegen auf Trennung von Tisch und Bett schließlich vor, ohne dabei diesen Wunsch explizit auszudrücken: „Es dauerte aber nicht lang, so wurde unser Vertrag aufs neue von der Nachbarin, welche doch selbst ihren Mann hat, wieder gestöhrt, indem sie meinen Mann auf vorige Art wieder aufwiegelte – auch hat er von selbiger Zeit an nichts von denen Speisen gegessen, welche ich gekocht habe; dennoch war ich mit dem was er that und sagte zufrieden, bis er einmal Thür und Fenster versperte, mich abermals wegen meinem Kind mit Schlägen und Stößen so peinigte, daß ich um mein Leben zu retten die Flucht wieder nehmen mußte; welches der damalige Richter Hornung mit noch 2 Mann bezeugen kann. Als ich nun das zweite und dritte mal wieder zu meinem Mann getrieben wurde, ist er gleichfalls auf nämliche Art wieder mit mir verfahren; und so lebe ich Unglückliche mit meinem Kind nun schon 5 Jahre. Weil nun mein Mann Dietrich Lebkieger ausdrücklich sagt, daß er ohne Lebensgefahr durchaus mit mir nicht mehr leben kann, und auch nicht will; sondern mir lieber einen jährlichen Lebensgehalt geben wollte: So ist mein allerunterthänigst gehorsamstes Bitten, meine traurige Klag allergütigst beim Hochwürdigsten Löbl: Consistorio fürtragen zu mögen, um mich armes ohnehin verfolgtes Weib doch nicht gewaltthätig mit Lebensgefahr zu meinem Mann kommen zu lassen; sondern einen gnädigen Spruch der uns beiden Ruhe bringt, gütigst ertheilen zu wollen. Wofür ewig höchst dankbar seyn wird, Einer Hochwürdigts Gnädigsten Geistlichen Obrigkeit. [...] unterthänigste hoffnungsvolle Dienerin Anna Maria Lebkiegerin dermalen in Gajdobra."

Dabei war die Stellung von Anna Maria Lebkücher erheblich beeinträchtigt durch ein schon 1818 ausgestelltes, mit Siegeln versehenes Attestat, in dem der Richter, sechs Geschworene, drei weitere Zeugen und „mehrere Nachbarn als Orths Vorstand" des Nachbarortes Neštin jenseits der Donau ein wenig schmeichelhaftes Urteil über sie fällten: „Endesgefertigte Richter, und Geschwohrene, samt anderen unterfertigten Nestin Insaßen, bezeigen, und beurkunden hiemit jedermann Gewissenhaft, daß Tidrich Lébkicher jemahlig hiesiger Haus: säßiger Contribuent und Mühler Meister seit seiner 13jährigen Aufenthaltung sich so friedsam, und in allem gebührend verhalten habe, daß mann wirklich ein sattsames Vergnügen schöpfen konnte. Hingegen aber dessen Ehe Gemahlin durch ihre Ausschweifende Lebens Art, und unerlaubte Gegenstände nicht nur ihrem Mann gekräncket, sondern um so viel mehr die Ruhe ihres in Zufriedenheit, und größten Vergnügen gemeßenen Ehestandes stöhrte, und größte Unruhe stiftete. Urkund dessen zur Steuer der Wahrheit gegenwärtiges Zeignuß von uns geben, und im Falle einer Zudrinklichkeit auch immer mit einem körperlichen Eide zu bestättigen bereit sind."

Auch dieser Fall macht deutlich, in welchem Maße neben der kirchlichen Autorität die dörfliche Obrigkeit, Richter und Geschworene und weitere Zeugen und damit wohl indirekt das ganze Dorf den Fall an die Öffentlichkeit zerrten, und die Betroffenen öffentlich zur Schau gestellt wurden, was zur Sozialdisziplinierung beitrug. Besonders demütigend für die Frau war, dass sogar der Lehrjunge an den Übergriffen beteiligt war. All dies war geeignet, das „Geschwätz" im Dorf anzuheizen.[64]

Rückblende: Gesellschaftliche und kirchliche Strukturen beim Aufbau

Welche Argumentationsmuster der Vater von Anna Maria Müller bemüht, um Johann Preisich zur Hochzeit mit seiner Tochter zu zwingen, erinnert an eine Verinnerlichung obrigkeitlichen Argumentierens seitens der Untertanen: „Wän solche Unzucht gar so unbestraft bleiben solte so werden die Jünglinge so ausgelaßen das wir unsere Kinder immer an der Kette zu halden genöthiget werden". Ein Blick in verschiedene Quellen kurz nach der Ansiedlung von deutschen Untertanen wenige Jahrzehnte vor diesem Fall zeigt eine gewisse Kongruenz dieser Aussage zu den damaligen Versuchen von Seiten der kirchlichen, grundherrlichen und staatlich-administrativen Seite, die Untertanen zu disziplinieren. Eine Sozialdisziplinierung neu gegründeter deutscher Dörfer mit ungefestigten Strukturen und noch nicht etablierten sozialen dörflichen Kontrollmechanismen bedurfte einiger, auch gerade kirchlicher Anstrengungen. Dabei spielte das äußere Erscheinungsbild der Kirchen sicher eine Rolle. Lecke, halb verfallene, schlecht ausgerüstete Kirchen, demotivierte, miserabel besoldete Pfarrer gehörten zum Bild neuer Ansiedlungen. Oft gleichen sich die Berichte in verschiedenen Regionen erstaunlich.[65] Pfarrer Michael Winkler bezeichnete die Bewohner von Szakadát in Südtransdanubien nach seiner Ankunft 1759 als „Halbbarbaren". Er beklagte, dass im Gotteshaus jede Ehrfurcht fehlte, dass die „Mädchen und Burschen [...] die ganze Nacht hindurch im Freien bleiben", um das Vieh zu hüten und dass dieses unsittliche Treiben von den Eltern mit dem Satz unterstützt wurde „auch wir haben es in unserer Jugend nicht anders gemacht."[66] Be-

---

[64] Allgemein dazu HOLENSTEIN, Pia/SCHINDLER, Norbert: Geschwätzgeschichte(n). Ein kulturhistorisches Plädoyer für die Rehabilitierung der unkontrollierten Rede. In: VAN DÜLMEN: Dynamik, 41-108 und 271-281.

[65] Dieses Bild vermitteln die Visitationes canonicae.

[66] GALAMBOS, Franz: Glaube und Kirche in der Schwäbischen Türkei des 18. Jahrhunderts. Aufzeichnungen von Michael Winkler in den Pfarrchroniken von Szakadát, Bonyhád und Gödre. München 1987 (Studia Hungarica 34), 49.

sonders Wirthausbesuche und Tanzunterhaltungen prangerte er an, ebenso beklagte er sich über wenig fügsame Richter und Geschworene.[67] Er entsetzte sich, dass die Kirchenbesucher im „betrunkenen Zustand, wenn der Priester den Kelch erhob, auch ihre Becher in die Höhe gehoben". Ebenso berichtete er über zahlreiche abergläubische Sitten.[68]

Bei all diesen Berichten glaubt man sich in die Reformationszeit versetzt. Denn vor dem kultischen Ernst von Reformatoren und Gegenreformatoren ging es während der Gottesdienste oft wenig erhebend zu. Zahlreiche Verordnungen zeigen dies. So klagte der Rat in Konstanz 1537, dass man „durch das gschray der hunden [bei der] an hörung des worts gottes vast verhindert würt".[69] Denn in dieser Zeit hatte das ehrfürchtige Schweigen, das im ausgehenden 17. Jahrhundert einkehrte, noch nicht Einzug gehalten.[70]

Eine hervorragende Quelle sind die Visitationes canonicae. Sie ermöglichen aufgrund ihrer periodischen Anfertigung und des Fragerasters Vergleiche. In der ersten Kanonischen Visitation von Batschsentiwan 1767 heißt es über die Bewohner: „Wir haben erfahren, dass ihre Lebensführung [...] zu keiner Zeit empfehlenswert [ist]. In der Kirche würden die Ehebrecher erst gar nicht erscheinen und an den Sonntagen würden sich die Leute verhalten wie an den Werktagen. Sonntags seien die Wirtshäuser während der heiligen Messe für jedermann offen." Auch die Richter und Geschworenen würden gegen Exzesse nicht einschreiten.[71] Auch in Bukin (ung. Dunabökény) wird die „Widersetzlichkeit der Untertanen" beklagt. In der Gemeinde gäbe es sogar „einige Übeltäter der Blasphemie, die weder von den offiziellen Stellen noch vom Richter verhindert werden". Stark seien nächtliche Trinkgelage „sowohl bei Männern als auch bei Frauen, dann Diebstähle" was nicht einmal bestraft würde. Besonders aufschlussreich ist die Bemerkung, dass es in der Gemeinde „auch Streit zwischen den Eheleuten" gäbe „und wenn der Priester bestrafen will, wird er vom Richter nicht unterstützt oder er lässt nichts mit Bestimmtheit" unternehmen. Hier zeigen sich dramatische Unterschiede zur Stellung der Pfarrer um 1800. Selbst die Verspottung kirchlicher Symbole wird beklagt.[72] Nach dem Bericht einer undatierten Visitation von Apatin hatte das Verhalten der Jugend bedrohliche Ausmaße angenommen, die nicht nur nach dem Gottesdienst, „in Scharen" in „alle zehn Wirtshäuser" [strömte], „um hier die Nacht hindurch unter großem Gedränge und Saufereien, dem Tanz zu frönen [...], sondern auch häufig schwere Schelmenstreiche verübt. So kam es endlich dazu, daß über 300 Burschen mit der gleichen Zahl leicht-

[67] EBD., 162 und 164.

[68] EBD., 49.

[69] Die Statutensammlung des Stadtschreibers Jörg Vögeli. Hg. v. Otto FEGER. Konstanz 1951 (Konstanzer Stadtrechtsquellen 4), 181. – Hier zitiert nach HOLENSTEIN/SCHINDLER: Geschwätzgeschichte(n), 87.

[70] BOSSY, John: The Counter-Reformation and the People of Catholic Europe: In: Past and Present 47 (1970), 60.

[71] Zitiert nach der Übersetzung in: Batschsentiwan. Kirchenchronik St. Johannes der Täufer 1788 – 1988. Kirchengeschichte einer ehemaligen donauschwäbischen katholischen Großgemeinde im Batscherland (Batschka). Hg. von der HEIMATORTSGEMEINSCHAFT. Gaggenau-Freiolsheim 1989, 48-50.

[72] KFL, Visitationes Canonicae, Dunabökény, 1756, § 17 de difficultatibus et gravaminibus parochorum; Quantos ad difficultates et gravamina, ac querelas.

fertiger Mädchen sich allen tierischen und fleischlichen Lüsten bis zum Überdruß hingaben. Dies wurde möglich, weil dem Tanze auch Ortsfremde sich zugesellten, die von ihnen sowohl im Glauben als auch in den Sitten stark verschieden sind. So wurden ganze Nächte hindurch Saufereien, Tanz, Lärm, Streit und Blutvergießen, Gotteslästerungen, Fluchen, Hurereien und Deflorationen sogar auf offener Straße durchgeführt. Ja, man war so sehr darauf versessen, Ehebrüche zu begehen, daß vor ihrer Schamlosigkeit nicht nur die Mädchen, sondern selbst fremde Ehefrauen nicht mehr sicher sein konnten. Man bedrängte diese Frauen indem man die Haustore aufbrach oder die Fenster einschlug. Ging aber der Ehemann, um sie zur Vernunft zu bringen, hinaus, schlug man diesen mit kräftigen Hieben zu Boden und verlangte von ihm, ihnen die Frau zu überlassen".[73]

Ebenfalls in Apatin wurde in der Visitation von 1766 ein Untertan namens Josef Oberauer besonders gerügt: „Er ist darin [im Konkubinat und im Ehebruch] so verstockt und unverbesserlich, daß er, nachdem ihn der Herr Dechant wiederholt ermahnt hatte, dieser ihn bei der Herrschaft verklagen mußte. Dennoch hat er sich wieder nicht gescheut, für sich seine eigene Ehefrau ein Kebsweib und Beischläferin suchen zu lassen".[74]

Doch handelt es sich hier nicht um immer wieder bemühte Topoi, die in der „Küche" des Verhältnisses zwischen Kirche und ihren „geistlichen Untertanen" zusammen gebraut werden und die so oder in ähnlicher Form auch in deutschen Territorien anzutreffen sind? Kommt hier nicht ein Rasterdenken zum Ausdruck, das mehr den beurteilenden Geistlichen als die zu beurteilende Gemeinde charakterisiert und entlarvt? Barg die sich konsolidierende Stellung des Pfarrers als Vertreter der Kirche vor Ort, der eine gewisse Monopolstellung in der geistlichen Betreuung beanspruchte und sie durchzusetzen versuchte, nicht a priori erhebliches Konfliktpotential? So berichten bayerische Pfarrer des 17. und 18. Jahrhundert immer wieder von ähnlichen Vorkommnissen: „Die Bauernmenscher[75] gehen zu den Buben und Knechten ins Bad hinein und baden miteinander, was vor Sachen vorbey gehen ist nit zu sagen und wissen und gedulden die Bauern und Hausväter".[76] Diese und zahlreiche Beispiele lassen deutliche Parallelen zu den Verlautbarungen aus der Anfangszeit in den deutschen Ansiedlungsgebieten in Ungarn erkennen.

Sicher wurden diese Stellungnahmen in Ungarn, hier in der Batschka, auch durch die Tatsache angeheizt, dass die Neusiedler für viele einheimische Pfarrer Fremde waren, deren Sitten sie wenig verstanden, die aus verschiedenen Regionen mit unterschiedlichen Traditionen kamen. Und die nicht zuletzt nicht mehr der Sozialkontrol-

---

[73] Kanonische Visitation, undatiert (nach 1771?). Hier zitiert nach der Übersetzung in Kanonische Visitationen der Apatiner Pfarrei im 18. und 19. Jahrhundert. Hg. v. Anton SELGRAD (Donauschwäbisches Archiv 17), 49.

[74] EBD., 36.

[75] Mägde.

[76] Dieser Bericht eines Benefiziaten aus Prittriching (Gericht Landsberg) ist entnommen BECK, Rainer: Der Pfarrer und das Dorf. Konformismus und Eigensinn im katholischen Bayern des 17./18. Jahrhunderts. In: Armut, Liebe, Ehre. Hg. v. Richard VAN DÜLMEN. Frankfurt am Main 1988 (Studien zur historischen Kulturforschung), 107-143, hier 133. – Beck zitiert aus zahlreichen diesbezüglichen Berichten.

le unterlagen wie zu Hause, weil die herkömmlichen sozialen Kontrollinstanzen zu Hause zurück geblieben waren.
Gleichwohl kann davon ausgegangen werden, dass die Berichte der Anfangszeit den Beginn eines Prozesses markieren, der zwar nicht linear ohne Kontinuitätsbrüche verläuft, aber schließlich doch in eine wachsende Konsolidierung mündete. Denn wenige Jahrzehnte später kann man durchweg deutlich entspanntere Beurteilungen lesen. So steht bspw. über Batschszentiwan (serb. Prigrevica Sveti Ivan, ung. Bácsszentiván) 1813 nicht ohne ein fast überhebliches Selbstbewusstsein: „Der Pfarrer hat im Augenblick in der Ausübung seiner seelsorgerischen Pflichten keine Schwierigkeiten mit seinen Pfarrkindern. Sollten solche entstehen, werde man sie bequem überwinden.“[77]

Wirkungsmechanismen von Konsolidierung und Disziplinierung

Das Ehegericht steht hier beispielhaft für den Komplex Wertevermittlung und Normenkontrolle sowie die Funktion der Kirche als Deutungs- und Vermittlungsinstanz. Hier zeigt sich auch der Übergang von der sakralen zur gesellschaftlichen Funktion der Kirche. Die Kirche trug zur Sozialdisziplinierung bei, wobei es um die Lenkung der Bevölkerung geht mit der Absicht, gesellschaftliche und politische Zielvorgaben durchzusetzen. Die Kirche wurde zum Funktionsträger durch ihre Selbstwahrnehmung, durch ihren Anspruch, über das Sakrament der Ehe zu wachen, aber auch durch den staatlichen und grundherrlichen Auftrag. Dazu gehörten im Untersuchungsraum der Aufbau und die administrative Vervollkommnung kirchlicher Strukturen. Vertreter vor Ort und Inhaber des Monopols der geistlichen Betreuung war der Pfarrer, der mit der Verkündung der Ehen und mit der Segnung zur wenig umstrittenen Autorität wurde. Teil der kirchlichen Strategie musste ebenso die Etablierung eines von der Bevölkerung verinnerlichten religiösen und sozialen Wertekanons sein. Auf dieser Ebene musste die Akzeptanz der Kirche gewährleistet sein, was eine Voraussetzung für eine gegenseitige Sozialkontrolle in der Bevölkerung war. Deren Wirkungsmechanismen werden anhand des Ehegerichts besonders deutlich. Trotz des Bemühens von Beteiligten, so diskret wie möglich die Anliegen vorzubringen, gelingt dies fast nie. Beklagte und Kläger wurden öffentlich bloßgestellt, was mit Sicherheit Teil einer Strategie von Prozessparteien war. Das Ehegericht ist zur Untersuchung von Tatbeständen verpflichtet, der Pfarrer ist immer eingebunden, Richter und Geschworene sind involviert, Zeugen werden gehört, Nachbarn befragt, Dienstherrn, Hebammen, Lehrbuben konsultiert, Personen des Vertrauens heran gezogen. Insbesondere im ländlichen Raum der Batschka erhöhten diese Tatbestände die Hemmschwelle, sich an das erzbischöfliche Ehegericht zu wenden und sich wenigstens nach außen hin konform zu verhalten. Das wiederum stärkte die Autorität des Pfarrers. Denn es drohte Gesichtsverlust, das gesellschaftliche Abseits. Kaum etwas deutet darauf hin, dass die kirchlichen Instanzen hier in Frage gestellt wurden,

[77] Batschsentiwan, 101.

wie dies noch wenige Jahrzehnte zuvor der Fall war. Selbst in den wenigen Fällen, in denen der Pfarrer keine „Satisfaction“ leistete, wurde seine grundsätzliche Autorität kaum in Zweifel gezogen. Insofern ist das Ehegericht ein Baustein innerhalb des Prozesses von Disziplinierung und Konsolidierung im zu Ende gehenden Ancien régime Ungarns. Die Autorität der Kirche wurde als selbstverständliche Deutungs- und Vermittlungsinstanz herangezogen, wenn die inzwischen akzeptierten „Spielregeln“ nicht eingehalten wurden. Die Institution „Ehegericht“ setzt an einem für den Aufbau stabiler und sich konsolidierender Strukturen besonders wichtigen konstitutiven Strukturelement an: Der Ehe und der Familie, innerhalb der Normen und Werte vermittelt und verinnerlicht werden.

Quellenanhang

Anna Maria Müller – Johann Preisich, Tschonopel

1820 – 1821, impraegnatio.[78]

1. 15.12.1820
   Tschonopel

Der Vater der geschwängerten Anna Maria Müller, Peter Müller aus Tschonopel wendet sich an das erzbischöfliche Konsistorium Kalocsa. Er bittet, dass der mutmaßliche Schwängerer seine und seiner Tochter Ehre wieder herstellt, indem er seine Tochter heiratet.

An Ein Hoche Löbl: Bischöfliche Ministerium <u>Kallutsa Gehorsamste Bitte</u>.

Endes unterzeichneter nehme mir die Ehrfurchts volle Freyheit Hohen Löbl: Ministerium meine Traurige Lage ganz Unterthänigst vorzustellen und Kniefallend zu Bitten.
Da ein Junger Bursche Nahmens Johan Preisich ofters mein Hauß besucht? fragte ich einstens um die Ursache. Dies er mir auch ohne zu läugnen gleich vorgab, ich komme zu ihrer Tochter, und Wünsche die selbe zur Ehe zu erhalten, welches also in Ehren auch nicht zu währen wäre.
Nun aber hat sich obesagter Johan Preisich aber nicht nach Relligions P[f]lichte verhalten, sondern hat einen Weltbürger gemacht, er hatt mir Alten Ehrlichen Mann samt meiner Tochter die Ehre beraubt, und dieses in meiner Abwesenheit.
Da nun meine Tochter Hohes Leibes ist, und ich selben auf vordere die Schande von meiner Tochter zu verdeken so Äusert selber sich mit verschiedenen Lugen, bis ich selben zum Herrn Pfarer Georg Paul Cittirte alwo ich keine Satisfaction erhalten habe, so bin ich Bemüßiget mich an eine Hoch Löbl: Bischöfliches Ministerium zu

[78] Quellennachweis für diese und die folgenden Quellen KFL I. 2., a.

wenden, und um Hülfe zu Flehen, und zu Bitten worü ich Einen Hoch Löbl: Ministerium ein stetter Unter than und Knecht.
Verbleibe Petter Müller
Sig:[natum] Tsonoplya d:[den] 15ten xmbr [Dezember] 1820.

2. 09.02.1821
Tschonopel

Von insgesamt fünf werden hier zwei „Zeugnisse" veröffentlicht. Diese Berichte waren geeignet, die Glaubwürdigkeit von Anna Maria Müller in Frage zu stellen. Ihre Intention war, zu verhindern, dass Johann Preisich Anna Maria heiraten musste.

Zeugniß

[...] 4tens Ich Endes gestellter bekenne daß mich benante Mariana Müllerin zum Beischlaf selbst begehret habe, welches ich auch um ihr nicht zu wiedersprechen, den Beischlaf auch volzogen habe, welches ich mit meinem Handzeichen und meinem Eidschwur bestättigen kan.
Bekenne ich Peter Csiacsek.

5tens ich Endes gestellter bekenne und bezeige, daß ich mit eigenen Augen gesehen, und selbst gegenwärtig war, wie der benante, und nach der Hand verstorbene Johann Schock bei der oft besagten Mariana Müllerin im Hofe den Beischlaf zweimal in einer Nacht mit ihr vollzogen habe, indem ich selbst zusah, und benanter Johann Schock, es mier auch selbst bekennet habe, da ich ihme abgewartet habe hatte, und er mit mir nach Hauß ginge, das er benante zweimal in einer Nacht beschlafen habe, welches ich auch mit 10 Eidschwüren, wen es erforderlich, oder erfordert würde, und mit eigener Unterschrift bestättigen kan. [...]
Bekenne ich Matheis Weis als Zeigen.

3. 18.11.1821
Tschonopel

Bestätigungsschreiben des Notars von Tschonopel, dass er Beweisschriften des Kantors und Schulmeisters Johann Rittlinger in der Sache der Klagen des Peter Müller mit Siegel ausfertigte.

Infrascriptus praesentium per vigorem fidem facio, quod Joannes Ritlinger Cantor et Ludimagister Germanicus Csonoplensis anno isthoc currente 1821, Certa scripta Consignatoria, quo quaerulatorie Contra Petri Miller Senioris Csonoplensis inhabitoris puellam impregnatam exhibuerit, item quod Scriptum ad petitum ejusdem tran-

sumpserint eidemque iterum resignaverint praesentes, usuali Sigillo munitas extrado Litteras Testimoniales. – Sig[natum] Csonopla Die 18o[79] *9bris*[80] *1821.*

[L. S.][81] *Antonius Homanyi Csonoplensis Notarius.*[82]

Josepha Sukovics – Franz Schmidt, Hajós

1812, divortialis.

4. Undatiert
   Hajós

Dieser Liebesbrief des Soldaten Joseph Stiasny an die Josepha Schmidt wurde wohl schon zu einem späteren Zeitpunkt der Beziehung im Laufe des Jahres 1812 verfasst und ist schon mit dem Namen des Verfassers unterzeichnet.

Unvergleiches Herz

Deinen Wunsch zu erfüllen sollst Du das Vergnügen haben in meine Dich eben so liebende Arme geschloßen zu werden, nach den Abend Rapport komme ich, mich bei Dir einige Zeit Aufheiterung zu gewähren: indeßen dankt Dir für das überschickte und küßt Dich Dein Stiasny Joseph.

5. 31.08.1812
   Ortsnamen unleserlich[83]

Aus einem Einsatz außerhalb von Hajós schrieb Joseph Stiasny diesen Brief an Josepha Schmidt.

Theuerste Geliebte!

Ich kann bey dieser Gelegenheit unmöglich unterlaßen, Dich mit diesen Zeilen zu belasten, und wenn Du auch darüber ungehalten seyn solltest; welches, wenn Du mich noch liebst nicht möglich ist. Ich will nicht viel Schwärmen was nützt es mich

---

[79] Duodevicesimo.
[80] Novembris.
[81] Locus Sigilli.
[82] Für die kompetente Unterstützung bei der Transkription und Übersetzung der lateinischen Texte dankt der Verfasser Frau Andrea Hauff, Tübingen. Übersetzung: Ich als Unterzeichner bezeuge kraft der Anwesenden, dass Johannes Rittlinger, deutscher Kantor und Lehrer von Tschonopel, in diesem laufenden Jahr 1821, in Bezug auf die Klage gegen das schwangere Mädchen, Tochter des Tschonoplenser Einwohners Peter Müller der Ältere, gewisse Schriften ausführte, ebenso dass die Anwesenden die Eingabeschrift übernahmen und demselben wiederum bestätigten. Die mit dem gewöhnlichen Siegel versehenen Beweisschriften fertige ich aus. Unterzeichnet in Tschonopel am 18. November 1821. Anton Homanyi, Notar von Tschonopel.
[83] Randbeschädigung des Dokuments.

da es doch nicht andres seyn kann, sondern daß ich Dich unaussprechlich ja mehr, als mich selbst liebe ist gewiß, die Abwesenheit von Dir ist mir eine unerträgliche Last die ich erst in 3 Wochen von mir abschitteln werde, wenn ich mich nach allen ausgestandenen Plagen und Beschwerden in deine Arme, an Deinen liebenden Küßen wieder erholen werde, dann Theure werde ich dir wieder mündlich sagen ich liebe Dich! noch mehr als vorher, und werde die Bestättigung deiner Liebe und Treue gegen mich von deinen liebe vollen Lippen brünstig hinweg küßen.
Die Zeit wird bald vergehen, ich zähle jede Minute, und nur die Hofnung, dich wider zu umarmen, und von dir geliebt zu werden, wie vorhin, macht mir meine jetzige Lage erträglich.

6. Undatiert (Oktober 1812)
Hajós

Der Fleischhackermeister Franz Schmidt wendet sich an das Konsistorium, berichtet über den Ehebruch seiner Frau mit einem Angehörigen des Militärs und bittet um Einleitung der nötigen Schritte.

Ein Hochleiblisches[84] *Consisterium*

Bittsteller anersucht dieweilen das Shükschall mir betrofen hat, und ich als ein Unglüglicher Mann von meinem Weib geworden bin, und so viel Beschwerte habe, mich und meine Kinder in das gröste Unglük zu Stürsen, und sie von mir entwichen ist, mit einem Millitars Mann mich zu hintersetzen, so bitte ein Hoch= löbl: Consistorium mir eine Gaüdige[85] *behülflichkeit zu erleisten bereit sein wollen.*
Indeme ich meine Wirthschaft mit [größ?]ten Schweiß erhalten habe, und sie mit Schlederting[86] *zu Grund gericht hat, ist erstlich das sie mir von andern Leuden Geld heraus= flatiert hat; und mit den Millitars Mann angewendet, nicht genung an diesen sontern auch Hemeder wie auch Kleidungs= stüke mit sich genohmen, sogar das Heilige Hochwürdige Sakrament des Ehestandes vor eitel haltet; [...]*
So Bitte ich ein Fußfälliger Diener mir armen und Betrangter Mann Gnädig zu leisten.

Bittsteller Franz Schmid Fleischaker Meister.

Anna Hoffmann – Imre Nándory, Futak

1795 – 1799, matrimonialis.

---

[84] Hochlöbliches.
[85] Gütige.
[86] Schlendrian.

7. Undatiert (1798)
Kalocsa

Protokoll der Befragung von Anna Hoffmann durch das erzbischöfliche Konsistorium

Responsa Anna Nándory ad propositas sibi coram Venerabili Consistorio Interrogationes deprompta.[87]

Nomen et Cognomen?[88]

Ich heiße Anna Hofmann

Ubi nata, ubi educata? Quod nomen et cognomen Parentum? Qua conditio eorum? Ubi habitaverint? An vivant, aut mortui sint, et quando?[89]

Ich bin geboren in Peterwardein, und wuchs dorten bis ins neunte Jahr heran: Dann sind meine Eltern auf Gaydobra gezogen, und ließen sich dort nieder. ich bin schon 27. Jahre alt. Mein Vater Johann Hofmann war ein Fleischhacker, meine Mutter hieß Anna Pirschin, sie brachten in Gaydobra 5. Jahre zu, von wo sie auf Neusatz gezogen sind, und sich in Neusatz 3. Jahre aufhielten, dann sind sie auf Bulkeß, wo mein Vater nach drey Jahren gestorben ist. Meine Mutter hat noch im vorigen Jahr um Martini gelebt in Neusatz.

Quod nomen Mariti, qua Conditio ejus, aetas item forma, statura, et unde oriundus? Ubi et per quem copulati?[90]

Mein Mann hat sich lassen verkünden unter diesem Namen: Emerich Nándory ein gebohrner Edelmann von Güns gebürtig[91]*, der Herr Futaker Pfarrer hat uns verkündet. Mein Mann war beim Grafen Hadik in Diensten als Comissair, er hat 6. oder 7. Dörfet unter sich gehabt. er sagte sich damals 22. Jahre alt, wir sind in Gaydobra kopulirt durch Grist. Herrn Wielandt. Mein Mann hatte ein längliches Gesicht, lange Nase, blaue Augen, blondes Haar, kurzes Gsicht [?], mittelmäßige Statur, wir lebten miteinander in Gloschan, er sprach mehrere Sprachen, Lateinische, Ungrische, Deutsche, Ratzische, Slowakische.*

---

[87] Übersetzung: Die von Anna Nándory geäußerten Antworten auf die ihr vor dem ehrwürdigen Konsistorium vorgelegten Fragen.
[88] Übersetzung: Namen und Vornamen?
[89] Übersetzung: Wo wurde sie geboren, wo wurde sie erzogen? Welchen Namen und Vornamen haben die Eltern? Welchen Beruf haben sie? Wo wohnten sie? Leben sie, oder sind sie gestorben und wann?
[90] Übersetzung: Was ist der Namen des Ehemanns? Welchen Beruf hat er, wie alt ist er, wie sieht er aus, was für eine Statur hat er und woher kommt er? Wo und durch wen wurden sie verheiratet?
[91] Unterstreichung wie im Original.

Quandim convixerint, et quare fatentem deseruerit Maritus?[92]

Unsere Ehe dauerte drey Wochen. In der dritten Woche ist Militär auf Gloschan gekommen vom Esterhazyschen Regement. Ein Bataillons Chrirurgus warnete mich, ich soll trachten zu meinen Eltern zu kommen, und dann zu seiner Excellenz auf Kalotscha zu schreiben; denn mein Mann sey unfähig, er soll sich eher reinigen, er würde es schriftlich geben, daß mein Mann mit Krankheit behaftet ist. Der Chirurgus gab mir die Schrift, und so nahmen mich meine Eltern zu Haus. Mein Mann kam mir nach, und fragte um die Ursache meiner Abreise. Mein Vater gab ihm einen harten Verweiß, daß er sich unterstanden ein ehrliches Mädel unglücklich zu machen. Auf das wurde mein Mann aufgebracht, und gieng auf [unles. Abkürzung] zum Stuhlrichter Stepanovits. Wir erschienen vor ihm auch. Aber der Stuhlrichter sagte zu meinem Vater: Nimm der Herr nur seine Tochter zu Hauß, ich werde das Attestatum nach Kalotscha schicken, wenn die Antwort kömmt, so werde ich ihm`s berichten. Mein Mann gab hernach vor, er hätte von Pest von seinem Bruder einem Ober-Lieutenant Briefe erhalten, worin er auf Pest berufen worden, um sein Erbtheil in Empfang zu nehmen, er sagte, er würde in 14 Tägen wiedrum zurück kommen. Dann führet er mich zu meinen Eltern auf Bulkeß, gieng auf Gloschan zurück, packte seine Sachen, mit sammt meinen Kleidern ein, und ist die nehmliche Nacht entwichen. Ich blieb bey meinen Eltern. Im neunten Monath ist mein Vater in Bulkeß gestorben.
Nachdem Tode meines Vaters gieng ich mit meiner Mutter auf Neusatz zurück: Dann begab ich mich in Dienste. Ich diente 1tens in Peterwardein bey einer Hauptmannin 1. Jahr, und 5. Monath. 2tens bey einer kranken Frau 8. Monath. 3tens Bey einem Stabs- [unles. Wort] 1. Jahr und 6. Monath. 4tens. Bleib ich in Semlin bey einer Burgers frau 2. Jahre. 5tens Im Belegrad mit meiner Mutter anderthalb Jahr. 6tens Gieng ich mit meiner Mutter auf Neusatz zurück, und bleib dorten 5. Jahre. 7tens Ein Jahr ist, seit dem ich von meiner Mutter weg bin. Unterdeßen lebte ich in Fünfkirchen, 3. Monath beym Herrn Fangi aus Gnaden, und bekam Unterstützung von verschiedenen Herrn, dann wohnte ich beim Herrn von Reiß 6. Monath.

Quare hactenus non inquisiverit in suum Maritum?[93]

1tens Weil ich zu der Heyrath gezwungen worden. 2tens Weil er mit der Krankheit behaftet war. 3tens Weil ich arm war, und unerfahren.

[92] Übersetzung: Wie lange lebten sie zusammen und warum verließ der Ehemann die Aussagende?
[93] Übersetzung: Warum forschte sie bisher nicht nach dem Verbleib des Ehemanns?

Abbildungen

Abb. 1

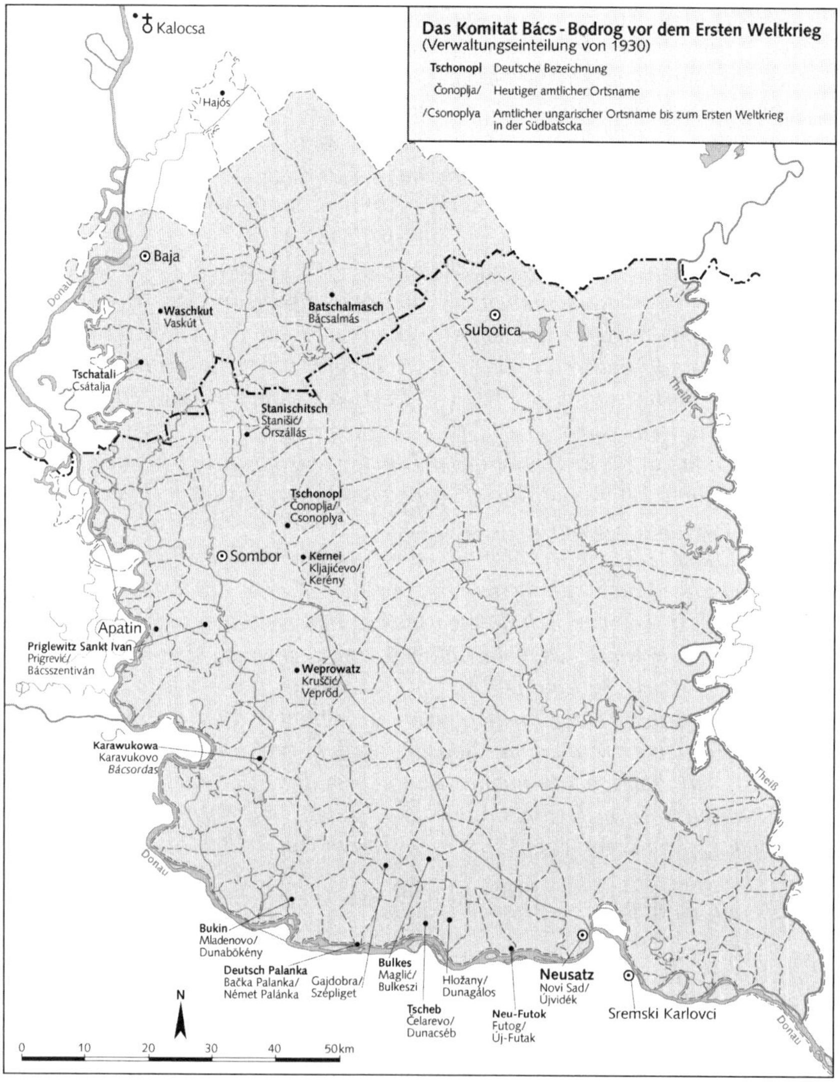

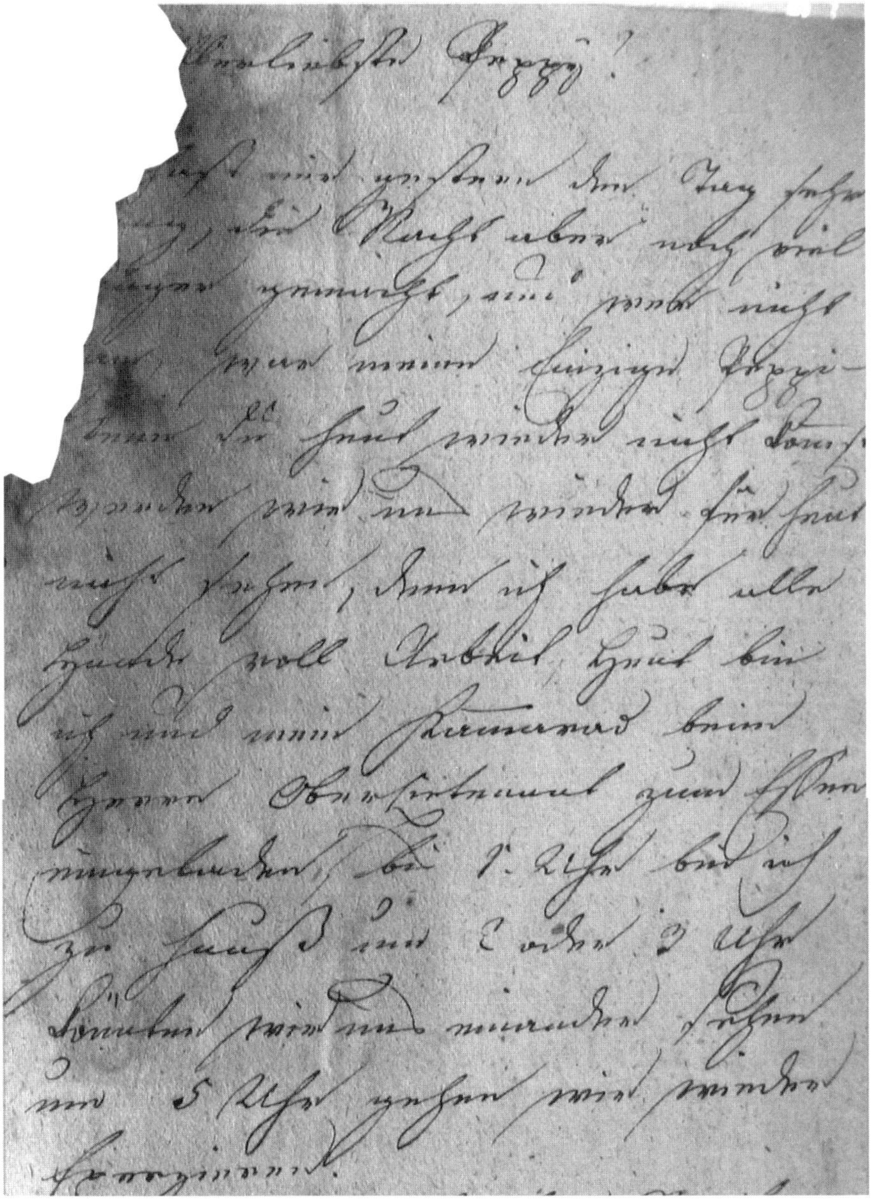

Abb. 2: Ausschnitt aus einem der Liebesbriefe des Soldaten Joseph Stiasny an seine Geliebte Josepha Schmidt, Frau des Fleischhackers Franz Schmidt aus Hajós. Die Überschrift des teilweise zerstörten Dokuments lautet: „Allerliebste Peggy!“

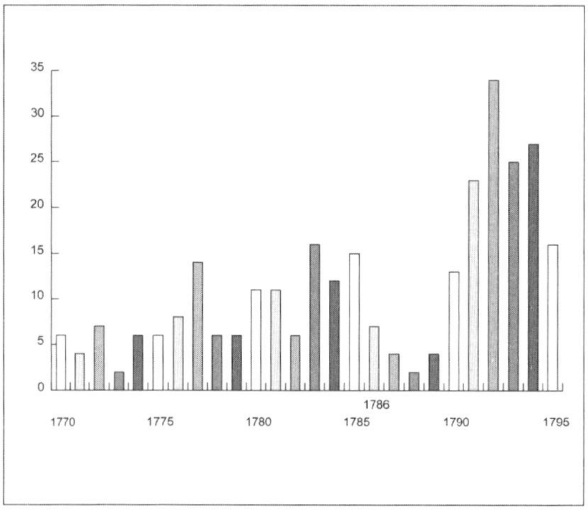

Abb. 3: Die Anzahl der kirchlichen Eheprozesse im Erzbistum Kalocsa 1770 – 1795

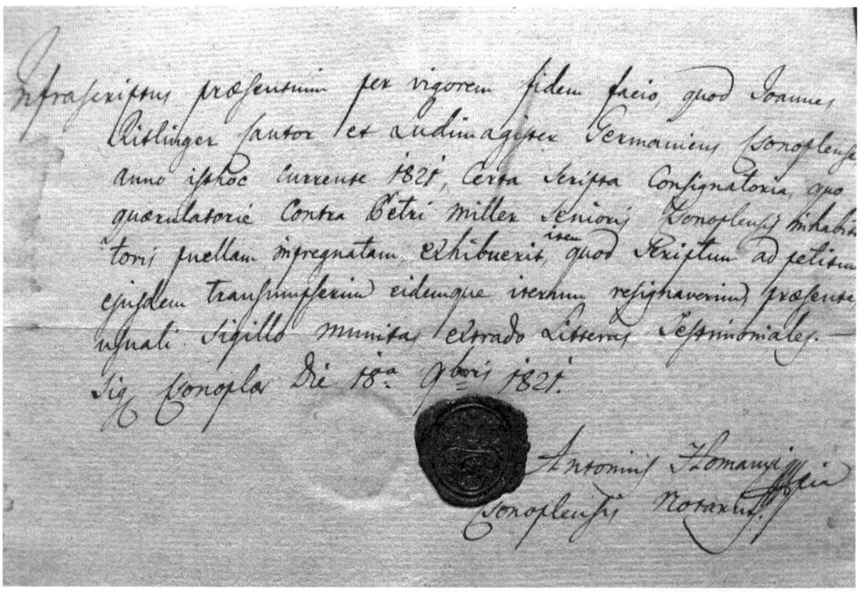

Infrascriptus praesentium per vigorem fidem facio, quod Joannes Ritlinger Cantor et Ludimagister Germanicus Csonopliensis anno isthoc currente 1821, certa scripta consignatoria, quo querulatorie contra Petri Miller senioris Csonopliensis inhabitatori puellam impregnatam exhibuerit, quod scriptum ad petitum ejusdem transumpserim eidemque iterum resignaverim, praesentes usuali sigillo munitas extrado Litteras Testimoniales.
Sig. Csonoplae Die 18a 9bris 1821.
Antonius Szomanyi
Csonopliensis Notarius

Abb. 4: Bestätigungsschreiben des Notars von Tschonopel

György Kurucz

Religion und ethnische Vielfalt: Das Evangelische Seniorat im Banat 1836

Der erste Krieg, den Karl III. (als deutsch-römischer Kaiser Karl VI.) gegen die Türken führte und der mit dem Friedensschluss von Poscharevatz 1718 abgeschlossen wurde, befreite endgültig die Gebiete zwischen den Flüssen Marosch und Donau, d.h. zwischen dem linken Flussufer der Theiß und dem Komitat Hunyad in Siebenbürgen, von der Türkenherrschaft. Dennoch wurde erst mit dem königlichen Erlass von 1778 die Zugehörigkeit jener Teile des Landes zum ungarischen Königreich anerkannt, welche die Gebiete der einstigen Komitate Torontal, Temesch und Kraschowarer umfassten und zeitgenössisch als Banat bezeichnet wurden. Um die spärlich besiedelten Gebiete, die Jahrzehnte lang der Habsburgischen Militär- und Kammerverwaltung unterstellt waren, mit Nachschub zu versorgen – selbstverständlich mit dem Bestreben vor Augen, aus dem Banat ebenfalls wirtschaftliche Erträge zu erzielen – wurde vom Wiener Hof in mehreren Wellen die Ansiedlung einer hauptsächlich deutschsprachigen Bevölkerung unternommen.[1]

[1] Über die Geschichte dieses Gebietes sind mit der Zeit ganze Bibliotheken füllende Bände erschienen. Als erstes sei das Werk GRISELINI, Franz: Versuch einer politischen und natürlichen Geschichte des Temeswarer Banats in Briefen an Standespersonen und Gelehrte. Wien 1780. – Ab Mitte des 19. Jahrhunderts erschienen immer mehr zusammenfassende bzw. ortshistorische Werke, die in Folge der begrenzten Zugänglichkeit der einschlägigen Quellen sowie von den Fachkenntnissen der einzelnen Autoren abhängig recht unterschiedliches Niveau aufweisen. Unter diesen seien nur die wichtigsten genannt wie BÖHM, Leonhard: Geschichte des Temeser Banats. Leipzig 1861. – BÖHM, Lénárd: Délmagyarország vagy az úgynevezett Bánság külön története [Die Sondergeschichte Südungarns, oder des sogenannten Banats]. Bd. 1-2. Pest 1868. – HETZEL, Samuel: Kurzgefasste Lokalgeschichte des Marktfleckens Liebling im Temeser Comitate. Liebling 1870. – SCHWICKER, Johann Heinrich: Geschichte des Temeser Banats. Pest 1872. – SZENTKLÁRAY, Jenő: Száz év Dél-Magyarország újabb történetéből [Hundert Jahre aus der neueren Geschichte Südungarns]. Temesvár 1879. – BARÓTI Lajos: A legrégibb német település története. Ismeretlen kútfők alapján [Die Geschichte der ältesten deutschen Siedlung. Aufgrund unbekannter Quellen]. Temesvár 1892. – BARÓTI, Lajos: Adattár Dél-Magyarország XVIII. századi történetéhez [Quellensammlung zur Geschichte Südungarns im 18. Jahrhundert]. Bd. 1-2. Temesvár 1900-1904. – KAINDL, Friedrich: Geschichte der Deutschen in den Karpatenländern. Gotha 1907. – SZENTKLÁRAY, Jenő: Mercy kormányzata a Temesi Bánságban [Die Regierung von Mercy im Temeser Banat]. Budapest 1909. – SCHIF, Peter: Heimatgeschichte. Geschichte des Banats. Temesvár 1920. – Möller, Karl: Wie die schwäbischen Gemeinden entstanden sind. Temesvar 1923. – KRAUSHAAR, Karl: Kurzgefasste Geschichte des Banats und der deutschen Ansiedlung. Wien 1923. – HESS, Nikolaus: Heimatbuch der drei Schwestergemeinden Sveti-Hubert, Charlevil und Soltur im Banat (1700-1927). Veliki Betschkerek 1927. – BUSSHOFF, Lotte: Wandlungen im Landschafts- und Siedlungsbild der Banater Heide. München 1938. – Von den neueren Werken TAFFERNER, Anton: Quellenbuch zur Donauschwäbischen Geschichte. Bd. 1-4. München-Stuttgart 1974-1982. – FELDTÄNZER, Oskar: Joseph II. und die donauschwäbische Ansiedlung. München 1990. – Mit einer umfassenden Bibliographie versehen sind die folgenden Werke CALINCOF, Eleonora: Streiflichter zum Siedlungsbild des Banats im 18. Jahrhundert. In: Das achtzehnte Jahrhundert und Österreich. Jahrbuch der Österreichischen Gesellschaft zur Erforschung des achtzehnten Jahrhunderts 10 (1995), 125-140. – Über

Unter den Siedlern waren nur wenige Protestanten. Innerhalb des Königreichs Ungarn wurden sie an ihrer Religionsausübung oft mit Gewalt, auch mit Einsatz des Militärs, gehindert. Als im Frühling 1724 deutsche Familien evangelischen Glaubens ein Gesuch um eine Niederlassungsgenehmigung an den militärischen Gouverneur dieses Gebietes, General Graf Claudius Florimund Mercy, richteten, wandte sich Mercy hinsichtlich der Frage der Religionsausübung dieser Familien an den Hofkriegsrat. Obwohl der Rat eine abweisende Haltung zeigte, kann es als eine Tatsache angesehen werden, dass im Banat bereits zu der Zeit evangelische Gemeinden angesiedelt waren, die allerdings zahlenmäßig nur schwer greifbar sind. Diese Tatsache belegen die Daten, die in den Ausgaben mit der Nummer 28 und 32 des Wienerischen Diarium aus dem Jahr 1728 zu lesen sind und die über die erfolgreiche Bekehrungstätigkeit der Kapuziner unter den Deutschen evangelischer Religion berichten.[2] Für die folgenden Jahre stehen uns keine zugänglichen Quellen über das Leben und den Alltag der evangelischen Gemeinden im Banat zur Verfügung.[3] In den letzten Jahrzehnten des 18. Jahrhunderts bildeten sich wiederum kleinere oder größere evangelische Gemeinden, deren Mitglieder ethnisch eher gemischt, aber vorherrschend deutschsprachig waren. Die Herausbildung dieser Gemeinden ist ohne Frage eng mit der letzten großen Ansiedlungswelle des Jahres 1782 bzw. der toleranten Religionspolitik, also mit dem Namen Kaiser Joseph II. verbunden.[4]

In den Jahren zwischen 1782 und 1791 übten die acht lebensfähigen Mutterkirchen ihre Tätigkeit im Rahmen des Seniorats Pest-Bekesch aus, welches einem der vier evangelischen Seniorate im Königreich Ungarn, dem Bergischen Kirchendistrikt angehörte. Die Synode von 1791 entschied über eine neue territoriale Aufteilung und das Seniorat Bekesch-Banat wurde eingerichtet, das somit nicht länger dem Se-

---

die Siedlungsstrategie der Habsburger in den verschiedenen Epochen sowie über die ethnische Zugehörigkeit der Siedler siehe WELLMANN, Imre: Magyarország népességének fejlődése a 18. században [Die Entwicklung der Bevölkerung Ungarns im 18. Jahrhundert]. In: Magyarország története [Die Geschichte Ungarns 1686-1790]. Bd. 1. Hg. v. GYŐZŐ Ember und GUSZTÁV Heckenast. Budapest 1989, 46-59.

[2] Die Ausübung des evangelischen Glaubensbekenntnises unterstand einem Verbot, der vom Amtmann zu Weisskirchen (ung. Fehértemplom, heute Bela Crkva, Serbien) über die Bewohner von Langenfeld verhängt wurde; die Missachtung dieses Verbotes drohte ihnen sogar die Todesstrafe an, „die verdiente Ketzerstrafe." BARÓTI, A legrégibb német település története, 29-30, 59 und 65.

[3] Der evangelische Pastor György Szeniczei Bárány (1682-1757) konnte erst in das Banat zurückkehren, als Mercy 1729 wieder zum Gouverneur des Gebietes ernannt wurde. BUCSAY, Mihály: Magyar református papok a bácskai német telepesek között [Die ungarischen reformierten Pastoren unter den deutschen Ansiedlern]. In: A Ráday Gyűjtemény Évkönyve 4-5 (1984-1985) 51-58, hier 52.

[4] Die deutsche Geschichtswissenschaft bezweifelt nunmehr seit einem Jahrhundert die Authentizität des Textes, welcher vom einstigen Siedler Johan Eimann 1822 als das Ansiedlungspatent von Joseph II veröffentlicht wurde. Die Memoiren von Eimann im Reprint siehe: EIMANN, Johann: Der deutsche Kolonist oder die deutsche Ansiedlung unter Kaiser Joseph dem Zweyten in dem Jahren 1783 bis 1787, absonderlich im Königreich Ungarn in dem Bácser Comitat... Pesth 1822. Hg. v. Friedrich LOTZ. München 1965. – Eine Zusammenfassung der Diskussion siehe FELDTÄNZER: Joseph II., 6. – Zur Siedlungsstruktur der hier behandelten Gebiete, den Daten bezüglich des zu leistenden Frondienstes der Bauern nach der Einführung des Urbariums von 1780, der Gesellschaftsstruktur der feudalen Bevölkerung, sowie der Aufgliederung der bebauten Gebiete siehe KOVÁCH, Géza: A Bánság településhálózatáról és mezőgazdaságáról az 1780-as úrbérrendezés és az 1828-as általános összeírás alapján [Über das Siedlungsnetz und die Landwirtschaft des Banats aufgrund der Urbarregulierung 1780 und der Landesvermessung 1828]. In: Korunk 2 (1994), 94-100.

niorat Pest-Bekesch unterstand. Seit Beginn des 19. Jahrhunderts waren die Gemeinden im Banat zweifellos bestrebt, wegen der bedeutenden Entfernung zu den größeren Gemeinden in Bekesch sowie aufgrund ihrer Verstärkung ein unabhängiges Seniorat zu errichten.[5] Diesbezüglich wandten sie sich im Jahre 1824 zum ersten Mal mit einem Gesuch an die Vorsteher des Kirchendistrikts, blieben aber bis 1834 erfolglos. Ihren Austritt betreffend reichten sie in jenem Jahr wiederholt ein Gesuch ein und zwei Jahre später veröffentlichte der Superintendent János Szeberényi in seiner Abschrift vom 21. Januar 1836 die Entscheidung, dass die Banater Kirchen aus ihrem derzeitigen Seniorat austreten und einem unabhängigen Seniorat unterstellt würden.[6]

Es stehen uns kaum zeitgenössische Quellen über die Tätigkeit des unabhängigen evangelischen Seniorats im Banat, über die Pastoration der Gemeinde, ihre finanzielle Lage und ethnische Zusammensetzung zur Verfügung, wie uns auch keine Daten zur Untersuchung des kulturellen Lebens in den Gemeinden überliefert worden sind.[7] Im Zweiten Weltkrieg wurden die Archivbestände der Evangelischen Kirche in Ungarn sowie die Dokumentensammlungen der hier behandelten Gemeinde schwer beschädigt.[8] Aus diesem Grund gilt das im Budapester Evangelischen Landesarchiv (Evangélikus Országos Levéltár – EOL) aufbewahrte Banater Protokoll der kanonischen Visitation [9] als eine einzigartige Quelle, die im Jahre 1836, also im gleichen Jahr, in dem das Banater Seniorat errichtet wurde, von einem Komitee unter der Leitung des Superintendenten János Szeberényi verfasst wurde.[10] Hinsichtlich des oben erwähnten Dokumentenverlustes tragen die im Protokoll enthaltenen und nach einem einheitlichen System erfassten Daten grundlegend zum besseren Verständnis der zeitgenössischen Charakteristika der Bereiche Kirchen-, Gesellschaft- und Bildungsgeschichte bei, gerade weil die zeitgenössischen Schematismen

---

[5] Grunddaten für den Zeitraum um 1810 mit Bezug auf die Aufteilung der Kirchenbezirke und Diözesen, die Vorsteher, die Pastoren und die Größe der Gemeinden können folgendem Werk entnommen werden: Schematismus Ecclesiarum et Scholarum Evangelicorum Augustanae Confessioni in Inclyto Regno Hungariae Addictorum. Pro Anno 1820. editus a Joanne Csaplovics. Viennae 1820.

[6] POSZVÉK, Sándor: A magyarországi ág. hitv. evang. keresztyén egyház névtára az 1903. évben [Almanach der ung. aug. evang. Kirche aus dem Jahre 1903]. Sopron 1903, 27.

[7] Zur Geschichte des Seniorats siehe: KERNUCH, Károly: A bánáti ágostai-evangélikus hitvallású esperesség monográfiája [Die Monographie des augustinisch-evangelischen Seniorats des Banats]. Temesvár 1886. – RÖHRIG, Hans Walter: Die Geschichte der deutsch-evangelischen Gemeinden des Banats. Leipzig 1940.

[8] Beachtenswert erscheint, dass die uns aus den ersten Jahrzehnten des 19. Jahrhunderts überlieferte Matrikel der evangelischen Gemeinde der Ortschaft Homokos (dt. Mramorak), welche dem Banater Evangelischen Seniorat untergeordnet war, sich im Donauschwäbischen Museum in Ulm befindet.

[9] Evangélikus Országos Levéltár [Evangelisches Landesarchiv] Budapest. (fortan: EOL). L. IX. Protocolla visitationis Canonicae Ecclesiarum Eglicarum in Senioratu Banatico, institutae anno 1836-to mense Junio

[10] Der Slowake János Szeberényi oder Jan Szeberinyi (1780-1856) wurde 1834 vom Banater Kirchendistrikt zum Superintendenten ernannt. Fünf Jahre später erhielt er den Doktortitel der Theologie an der Universität in Jena. Er beteiligte sich an der Bewegung, die mit Hilfe des Herrschers die Rechte der slowakischen Sprache zu sichern versuchte. 1848 nahm er aber zu den, auch vom Herrscher anerkannten Gesetzen Stellung, die den konstitutionellen bürgerlichen Wandel in Ungarn zu erzielen wünschten, und er wandte sich von der panslawischen militanten Bewegung ab, welche von den Habsburgern unterstützt wurde. Zu seinem Leben und Wirken siehe KERTÉSZ, Botond: Evangélium és szabadság. Az evangélikus egyház Magyarországon 1848-49-ben [Evangelium und Freiheit. Die evangelische Kirche in Ungarn 1848-49]. Budapest 2002.

und Kirchenquellensammlungen in Druckformat bedeutend weniger Informationswert besitzen.[11] Im Weiteren unternehmen wir den Versuch, dieses besondere Quellenmaterial mit Blick auf den uns hier zur Verfügung gestellten Rahmen zu untersuchen.[12]

****

Das oben erwähnte, zum Besuch bestellte Komitee fand sich im Zeitraum zwischen 13. Mai und 16. Juni 1836 insgesamt in zwölf Kirchengemeinden ein, laut den auf Lateinisch verfassten 68 Folien des Protokolls in Folgenden: Tótaradác (Torontaler Komitat), Nagybecskerek (Torontaler Komitat), Antalfalva (slow. Kovačica, Deutsch-Banater Regiment), Ferenchalom (Franzfeld, Deutsch-Banater Regiment), Homokos (Mramorák, Deutsch-Banater Regiment), Nagylajosfalva (Ludwigsdorf, Deutsch-Banater Regiment) Istvánfalva (slow. Hajdusica, Torontaler Komitat), Temesbökény (Komitat Temesch), Kisszemlak (Komitat Temesch), Kedvenc (Liebling, Komitat Temesch), Temesukovár (Komitat Temesch), Temesvár (Komitat Temesch).

Abgesehen vom Superintendenten Szeberenyi setzte sich das Komitee jeweils unterschiedlich aus kirchlichen und weltlichen Vorstehern zusammen. Das Komitee zählte in den meisten Fällen sechs Mitglieder, manchenorts sogar neun. Als Vertreter der Kirche waren selbstverständlich Mátyás Ambrózy, der Pastor der Ortschaft Nagybecskerek, der Senior sowie Dániel Abaffy als Visitator aus der Ortschaft Tótaradác anwesend, wobei Letzterer sich als Notar des Komitees betätigte.[13] Es kam auch vor, dass Pastoren aus dem benachbarten Batscher Seniorat an der *canonica visitatio* teilnahmen. So war z.B. János Körösy, der evangelische Pastor der Ortschaft Jarek, in Tótaradác anwesend; Peter Kramár, der Pastor von Nagylajosfalva, nahm sowohl in Antalfalva als auch in Ferenchalom an den Visitationen des Komitees teil. Beachtenswert ist, dass Abaffy der Pastor der ersten vom Komitee aufgesuchten Gemeinde war und das Protokoll von Tótaradác in seiner Handschrift zu lesen ist. Hierbei wurden aber die Zeilen über die Beschreibung der Person und die Tätigkeit des Pastors vom Superintendenten Szeberényi sowohl verfasst als auch eigenhändig zu Papier gebracht. Er beschrieb Abaffy als guten Redner, der die ihm anvertrauten Mittel treu verwaltete, doch oft von seinen Emotionen ergriffen würde.[14] Hier soll noch ver-

[11] Zwei Jahre nach der hier erwähnten canonica visitatio wurde die nächste evangelische kirchliche Quellensammlung veröffentlicht in Schematismus Generalis Ecclesiarum & Scholarum Evang. Aug. Conf. In Hungaria … a Joanne Kollár. Pestini 1838.

[12] Hier möchte ich meinen Dank an Miklós Czenthe, Direktor des Evangelischen Landesarchivs, aussprechen, der meine Aufmerksamkeit auf das erwähnte Protokoll lenkte.

[13] Laut der 1838 veröffentlichten Quellensammlung war Ambrózy zwei Jahre später bereits der Pastor von Andrásfalva, wobei die Stelle des Pastors in Nagybecskerek nicht neu besetzt wurde, also „vacat" blieb (Vgl. Schematismus Generalis Ecclesiarum, 164-165). Ambrózy begann seine geistliche Tätigkeit in Neusatz, wegen seiner Jagdleidenschaft geriet er bereits dort in Gerede. Er war in der Gegend nur als der „Nimrod von Neusatz" bekannt. Belohorszky, Gabriel: Die Königliche Freistadt Neusatz nebst einer Kurzgefassten Geschichte der hiesigen evangel. Kirchengemeinde und ihres Kirchenbaues. Neusatz 1886, 30.

[14] „Vir solide doctus, orator bonus et pius, in munere fidelis, sed visus est mihi facile affectu abripi" EOL L. IX. Protocolla f. 5.

merkt werden, dass teilweise ein Geistlicher, der einer anderen Konfession angehörte, bei den Sitzungen des Komitees anwesend war. Nach dem am 13. Juni in Temesvukovár aufgenommenen Protokoll war Nicolai Popovici, der Pfarrer der örtlichen rumänischen Gemeinde, ebenfalls Mitglied des in Vukovár zusammengerufenen Komitees.[15]

Die weltlichen Personen, die an der Visitation teilnahmen, waren innerhalb der zeitgenössischen Gesellschaft Beamte oder renommierte Persönlichkeiten, die in Folge ihres Wohlstands oder ihrer Besitztümer hohes Prestige genossen. Sie waren Stuhlrichter des Komitats, Tafelrichter oder gar Grenzschutzoffiziere, Advokaten, Lehrer, Notare, Beamte der Hofkammer oder der Statthalterei, reiche Händler. Während der am 4. Juni 1836 gehaltenen Visitation in Antalfalva war k.u.k. Kapitän Szaniszló Novákovics, am 13. Juni in Temesvukovár József Kolozsváry, der örtliche Notar, am 16. Juni in Temesvár Ezékiel Meskó, der Stuhlrichter des Komitats Temesch, bei der Sitzung des Komitees anwesend.[16] Die stets wechselnde Zusammensetzung der Visitationskomitees, abgesehen von den festen Mitgliedern, kann mit den Aufgaben und Verpflichtungen der weltlichen und geistlichen Personen erklärt werden. Aber auch der straffe Terminplan, der alle ein bis drei Tage Sitzungen an einem neuem Ort vorsah, sowie die örtlichen Verhältnisse mit Hinblick auf das Patronat und das Verwaltungswesen tragen zum besseren Verständnis dieses Umstands bei.

Laut den Protokollen sammelten die Komitees Daten über die einzelnen Gemeinden einheitlich in einer bestimmten Reihenfolge zu bestimmten, vorher festgesetzten Themenkreisen. Die in Punkte gefassten, thematischen Einheiten können wie folgt zusammengefasst werden; hierbei sollen die lateinischen Benennungen der im Protokoll enthaltenen Fragenblöcke beibehalten werden:

I. *Ecclesia / Gemeinde*

1. Herkunft – kurze Geschichte der Gemeinde
2. Ereignisse, z.B. Totenfälle wegen Cholera
3. Anzahl der Gemeindeglieder
4. Kirche – kurze Beschreibung, Einzelheiten, Größe usw.
5. Kleinodien-Turm
6. Finanzen der Gemeinde – Einkommen, wie wird es behandelt, Stiftung, usw.
7. Matrikeln, Dokumente und Bücher
8. Friedhof
9. Filialen

II. *Regimen Ecclesiae / Inspector, Curator, Presbyterium*

III. *Status Ecclesiae /Gottesdienste*

IV. *Verbi Dei Minister / Beschreibung der Aktivität des Pastors*

---

[15] EOL L. IX. Protocolla f. 56.

[16] EOL L. IX. Protocolla ff. 15, 56 und 62.

A. Pastoration
1. Seine Predigten
2. Katechese
3. Gottesdienst
4. Sakramente
5. Betreuung von Sterbenden
6. Impfung – ob Mithilfe des Pastors
7. Besuche in den Schulen
8. Familienbetreuung, Beratung
9. Beerdigungen
10. Matrikeln, Rechnungen

B. Charakter des Pastors

C. Seine Bibliothek

D. Pastorenwohnung

E. Verdienst des Pastors

V. *Schola / Schule*

A. Lehrer

1. Vorbildung
2. Was er unterrichtet über Bibel und Religion, was er anders unterrichtet,

B. Anzahl der Schüler

C. Schulgebäude

D. Gehalt des Rektors

E. Stiftung für die Schule

F. Inspektor

VI. *Obstetrices / Hebammen/*

VII. *Vespillones / Totengräber*

VIII. *Instituta pauperum / Armenfürsorge*

IX. *Annuae devotiones / Andachten*

X. *Gravamina / Klagen*

XI. *Abusus / Missbrauch*

Die wichtigsten Punkte der Protokolle, vor allem die identischen bzw. abweichenden Angaben, verweisen auf weit mehr als die mit der Ausübung der Religion verbundenen Daten. Auffallend ist vor allem, dass die Abstammung der Gemeindemitglieder betreffend – obwohl die Bevölkerung überwiegend infolge der Ansiedlung in das Banat gekommen war – nur in zwei Fällen Verweise gefunden werden können. Die Verfasser der Protokolle beziehen sich lediglich in einem einzigen Fall, nämlich in Verbindung mit der Gemeinde Kedvenc (Liebling), auf das Ansiedlungspatent von Joseph II. – die Bevölkerung der Gemeinde und die Sprache des Gottesdienstes war hier ausschließlich Deutsch. Die Gründung der Gemeinde wird auf 1786/1787 datiert, als nämlich „den Patenten des glücklich in Erinnerung gebliebenen Josephs II." folgend aus verschiedenen Teilen Deutschlands die Menschen in diese Gegend ausgewandert waren.[17] In Verbindung mit Tótaradác verweisen die Mitglieder des Visitationskomitees darauf, dass der Grossteil der slowakischen Mitglieder der Gemeinde aus dem Komitat Nograd stammte.[18] Die in den Protokollen vermerkten Gründungsdaten sind aus dem Grund von Interesse, weil der von Jan Kollár 1838 herausgegebenen und oben bereits erwähnten evangelischen Kirchensammlung nicht immer das nachweisbare Gründungsjahr der Gemeinde entnommen werden kann.[19]

Tafel 1

Ortsname	Jahr	Filialen	Seelen	Sprachen
Tótaradác	1786	Elemér	1738	slow., dt., ung.
(		Törökbecse		
Becskerek	1790	Écska	594	slow., dt., ung.
		Lukácsfalva		
Antalfalva	1802	-	2160	slow.
Ferenchalom	1793	-	1819	dt., ung., slow.
Homokos	1820	Weisskirchen	406	dt.
Nagylajosfalva	1806	-	2525	slow.
Istvánfalva	1829	Sándorfalva	536	slow.
(				
Temesbökény	1814	-	714	slow.
Szemlak	1806	Füzes	366	slow., dt., ung.
		Königsgnad		
		Szkula		
Kedvenc	1786	-	2320	dt.

[17] „Hoc repetenda est ab anno 1786 et 1787. quibus anni beatae memoriae Josephi IIdi patentalibus vocati advenerunt incolae … ex diversis partibus Germaniae." EOL L. IX. f. 51.

[18] EOL IX. f. 1.

[19] Schematismus Generalis Ecclesiarum, 164-167. Das Attribut „tót" [slowakisch] führt keine negative Konnotation mit sich, da es im zeitgenössischen Sprachgebrauch auf die Bevölkerung mit slawischem Ursprung verweist. Siehe Tótkomlós.

Temesvukovár	1832	-	778	slow., ung., dt.
Temesvár	1795	Elemér Törökbecse	486	dt., ung., slow.

Verglichen mit den oben erwähnten zwei Gemeinden wurde die evangelische Kirchengemeinde in Temeschvukowar als Letzte gegründet. Dies kann aufgrund der in den Protokollen festgehaltenen Daten festgestellt werden. Es scheint ebenfalls eindeutig zu sein, dass die Anzahl der den Muttergemeinden untergeordneten Filialen nicht von der Anzahl der Gläubigen beeinflusst wurde. Betrachten wir die benutzten Sprachen in den Gemeinden, so sehen wir: In vieren dominierte das Slowakische und in zweien wurde ausschließlich Deutsch gesprochen. Ungarisch kam in vier Gemeinden vor, trat dort aber neben dem deutschen und slowakischen Sprachgebrauch auf. Annähernde Daten zur ethnischen Zusammensetzung der vorwiegend von slowakischen bzw. deutschen Gläubigen dominierten, aber dennoch in Hinsicht auf die ethnische Zugehörigkeit gemischten Gemeinden können heute nicht mehr rekonstruiert werden.

Tafel 2

Ortsname	Pastor	Studien	Sprache
Tótaradác	Dániel Abaffy	Neusohl Debrecen Pressburg Jena	ung., dt., slow., frz.
Becskerek	Mátyás Ambrózy	Neusohl Eperjes Schemnitz	ung., dt., slow., frz.
Antalfalva	Martin Hamaliar (starb Sept. 1835)		
Ferenchalom	Bányász Sámuel	Neusohl Losonc Pressburg Jena	ung., dt., slow., lat.
Homokos	Philip Poltz	Mezőberény Oedenburg	ung., dt., slow., lat.
Nagylajosfalva	Petr Kramár	Perőcsény Schemnitz Pressburg Oedenburg	slow., dt., ung.
Istvánfalva	Stephan Jesztrebinyi	Eperjes	slow., dt., ung., und orientalische Spr.
Temesbökény	Josef Wodár	Mezőberény Neusohl	ung., dt., slow., lat., kroat., rumän.

Szemlak	Josef Wodár (ex missus)		
Kedvenc	Johann Hermann	Bistritz Pressburg	dt.,lat., rumän., etw. ung.
Temesvukovár	Jan Szalmovszky	Eperjes Rosenau Preßburg	slow., dt., ung.
Temesvár	Wilhelm Karner	Oedenburg Wien	dt., ung., lat., ital., slow., frz.

Die oben angeführte Tabelle bietet einen Einblick in die ethnische Zugehörigkeit, die Schulbildung und die Sprachkenntnisse der in den Gemeinden tätigen Pastoren. Letzteres ist von Bedeutung, weil hieraus ersichtlich wird, wie sehr die Mitglieder der Komitees über weitreichende Kenntnisse verfügen mussten, d.h. es wurde von vornherein als erstrebenswert erachtet, dass die Pastoren die Muttersprache ihrer Gemeindemitglieder beherrschten. Die Tabelle berichtet über eine einzige Ausnahme: Johann Hermann, seiner Herkunft nach ein Sachse aus Transsylvanien, war Pastor in der ausschließlich deutschsprachigen Ortschaft von Liebling. Er besaß recht spärliche Kenntnisse der ungarischen Sprache, wobei ihm dieser Mangel an Sprachkenntnis bei der Verrichtung seiner Tätigkeit sicherlich kein Hindernis war.
Allgemein kann festgestellt werden, dass jeder Pastor Deutsch, Slowakisch, Ungarisch, bzw. je nach ethnischer Zusammensetzung der jeweiligen Ortschaften in der Region, eventuell Rumänisch oder Kroatisch sprach.
Von besonderem Interesse sind die Einträge hinsichtlich der sonstigen Sprachkenntnisse, vor allem im Vergleich mit dem Sprachenumfeld der Heimatgebiete der Pastoren. Die in der Tabelle festgehaltenen Daten vermitteln uns Informationen über die Hintergründe der Elementarausbildung der Pastoren, ihre Ausbildung in der Mittelstufe sowie ihre Hochschulstudien. Der Senior Abaffy, gleich Ambrózy, besuchte das evangelische Lyzeum in Neusohl bzw. in Pressburg und beherrschte wie dieser die französische Sprache. Auffallend ist, dass Sámuel Bányász, der Pastor der Ortschaft Franzfeld, der eine ähnliche Ausbildung genoss, dennoch nicht Französisch sprach. Offensichtlich scheint dagegen, warum der in Ödenburg geborene Wilhelm Karner über umfassende Kenntnisse in zahlreichen Sprachen verfügte. Nachdem er das Ödenburger evangelische Lyzeum besucht hatte, studierte er in Wien Theologie und belegte sogar im „institutum polytechnicum" technische Fächer. Im Weiteren verdient der aus dem Komitat Abaujwar stammende Stephan Jesztrebinyi unsere Aufmerksamkeit, der neben der Beherrschung der „heimischen Sprachen" auch über Kenntnisse nicht näher definierter, östlicher Sprachen verfügte.[20]
Der Grossteil der Pastoren erlangte seine Ausbildung in der Mittelstufe und seine theologische Ausbildung vor allem in den in der näheren Umgebung des Heimatgebietes befindlichen evangelischen Lehranstalten. Eine Ausnahme bildet Dániel

[20] „Coluit etiam linguas orientales." EOL L. IX. f. 38v.

Abaffy, der das Reformierte Kollegium von Debrecen besuchte. Besonders auffallend ist, dass lediglich zwei Pastoren, Abaffy und Bányász, an ausländischen Universitäten studierten, und zwar in Jena. Der Umstand, dass Karner infolge seiner Studien in Wien in den Besitz vielseitiger Kenntnisse gelangte, ist beachtenswert, da er zu der Zeit ebenfalls als Ingenieur, als Landvermesser eine Anstellung hätte finden können. Neben den Verweisen auf die Ausbildung kann es ebenfalls als vielsagend gewertet werden, dass die mit der Konskription der Protokolle beauftragten Komitees, mit einer Ausnahme, es nicht für nötig hielten, Angaben über die Nationalität der Pastoren niederzuschreiben, obgleich die Namen vieles über die nationale Zugehörigkeit verraten – die Anmerkung „slowakischer Geburt“ ist lediglich bei Ambrózy zu lesen.[21] Bedauerlich ist, dass in den Quellen und daher in der Tabelle keine nennenswerten Daten über die Bibliotheken der Pastoren zu verzeichnen sind. Die Konskriptoren der Protokolle verweisen eher nur allgemein auf theologische Studien und Katechismen, die im Besitz der Pastoren waren.

Nennenswert ist wiederum, dass die Pastoren betreffenden, kurzen Texteinträge zur Charakterisierung ihrer Person, ihres theologischen Wissensstandes, der Bewertung ihrer oratorischen Fähigkeiten, ihrer Verlässlichkeit in Hinsicht auf die ihnen anvertrauten Güter, ihre Fähigkeiten bei der seelischen Betreuung stets vom Superintendent Szeberényi mit eigener Hand in die Protokolle der *canonica visitatio* vermerkt wurden. Diese Bewertungen sind jedes Mal wohl ausgeglichen, wobei neben den lobenswerten Zügen und Charakteristiken ebenfalls die Mängel aufgelistet werden. Bereits das Protokoll der ersten Station der Visitation zeigt, wie konsequent diese Vorgehensweise eingehalten wurde, wobei der Pastor der zuerst aufgesuchten Gemeinde der Senior Abaffy selbst war. Obwohl das Protokoll von Tótaradác seine Handschrift trägt, wurden die Zeilen über seine Person und Tätigkeit von Superintendent Szeberényi formuliert und eigenhändig verfasst, mit der Bemerkung, dass Abaffy ein pflichtbewusster, guter Redner sei, treuhändig die ihm anvertrauten Güter verwalte.[22] Nach der Meinung von Szeberényi ließ allerdings der Wissensstand des Pastors von Istvánfalva, Jesztrebinyi, einiges zu wünschen übrig.[23] Zur Beschreibung der Person des Pastors von Temesvár, des in Ödenburg geborenen Wilhelm Karner, wandte man die Attribute weise und enthusiastisch an, vermerkte aber , dass er kaum Slowakisch spreche.[24] Hier sollte darauf hingewiesen werden, dass es ebenfalls eindeutig zur Beurteilung der Tätigkeit und Leistungen der Pastoren gehörte, welche Moral in der Gemeinde vorherrschte, ob einzelne Personen im Gefängnis der Gemeinde inhaftiert waren bzw. ob die Pastoren im Kreise ihrer Gemeinde aufklärende , volkserzieherische Kenntnisse vermittelten. Letzteres verdient unsere Beachtung, weil diese Aufgaben laut heutigen Vorstellungen streng genommen nicht zum Kompetenzbereich der Kirchen zählen. In Verbindung mit dem Pastor von Tótaradác wurde z.B. detailliert beschrieben, wie er, mit den Behörden kooperie-

---

[21] „V[erbi] D[ei] M[inister] modernus est Matthias Ambrosz … 1796 genuit Slavum…" EOL L. IX. f. 11v.
[22] " EOL L. IX. f. 5.
[23] „… in officio fidelis. Catecheta miserabilis, orator qualis sine solida eruditione theologica esse potest." EOL L. IX. f. 38v.
[24] „… prudens, zelosus, modestus … dolendum quod linguae Slavicae ignarus…" EOL L. IX. f. 64v.

rend, in seinen von der Kanzel gehaltenen Reden die Aufmerksamkeit der Gläubigen auf die Vorzüge der Pockenimpfung lenkte.[25] Die Einträge zur Gemeinde von Liebling geben wieder, dass die Impfung bereits in weiten Kreisen der Gläubigen verbreitet war und der Pastor es aus diesem Grund nicht länger für nötig erachtete, im Rahmen des Gottesdienstes auf ihre Bedeutung hinzuweisen.[26]

Betrachten wir die Herkunft und die Ausbildung der Lehrer, so erhalten wir ein umfassenderes Bild, vor allem aufgrund der Namen der Lehrer, welche auf einen Grossteil deutscher Herkunft hinweisen.[27] Die Daten zu den Sprachkenntnissen der Lehrer lassen vermuten, dass diesbezüglich an sie die gleichen Anforderungen gestellt wurden wie im kirchlichen Dienst. Als Beweis hierfür sei Jakob Lauf angeführt, der in Kakaslomnic im Zipser Komitat geboren wurde und bei seinen Studien von dem anerkannten, an der Wende zum 19. Jahrhundert tätigen Fachautor, dem kleinadligen Gergely Berzeviczy Unterstützung erfuhr. Lauf besuchte nach seinen im evangelischen Lyzeum zu Käsmark verbrachten Jahren auch das reformierte Kollegium in Sárospatak.[28] Auf eine ähnlich bewusste Vorbereitung zum Amtsantritt in den ungarischen Gebieten lässt die Schulwahl des Rektors von Temesvár, Karel Lukl, schließen. Lukl stammte nämlich aus Mähren, besuchte aber seit seinem zehnten Lebensjahr die Schule in Losonc, später in Nagykőrös und setzte dann seine Ausbildung im Reformierten Kollegium von Debrecen fort.[29]

Anhand der Sprache der beigelegten biblischen Texte und Gottesdienstthematiken, die den Anhang der *canonica visitatio* bilden, kann indirekt rekonstruiert werden, zu welcher ethnischen Gruppe der Grossteil der Gemeinde gehörte, in der die Pastoren und Lehrer ihre Dienste verrichteten bzw. welche die dominante Sprache in den einzelnen Gottesdiensten war. Die administrative, die Sammlung von Daten anzielende Tätigkeit des Vistationskomitees wurde nämlich jedes Mal mit einem entsprechenden Gottesdienst, mit der feierlichen Verkündigung der Worte Gottes begonnen. Von den zwölf Gemeinden wurde die Predigt in Tótaradác, Antalfalva, Nagylajosfalva, Istvánfalva, Temesbökény und Temesvukovár auf Slowakisch, in Ferenchalom, Homokos, Szemlak, Kedvenc (Liebling) und Temesvár auf Deutsch sowie in Nagyberecsk auf Ungarisch gehalten.[30]

Neben der Beschreibung der Tätigkeit der Pastoren und der Lehrer hielten die Verfasser es für wichtig, in den Protokollen ebenfalls Verweise auf die mit dem Leben der Gemeinde eng verbundenen, also im Alltag der Gemeinde präsenten, daran teil-

---

[25] EOL L. IX. ff.4v-5.

[26] EOL L. IX. f. 52. „Vaccinatio est in usu nec commendatione de cathedra indiget."

[27] Die Lehrer der Kirchengemeinden waren namentlich die Folgenden: Tótaradác – Sándor Bakó, Antalfalva – Johannes Lauf, Nagybecskerek – Imre Raksányi, Temesbökény – Pál Darulya, Franzfeld – Lucas und Tobias Fetter, Istvánfalva – vakant, Nagylajosfalva – András Wodár, Liebling – Josef Hermann und David Greisinger, Mramorák – Lucas Fetter, Szemlak – vakant, Temesvár – Karel Lukl, Temesvukova – Jakob Imrich.

[28] EOL L. IX. f. 16.

[29] EOL L. IX. f. 65v.

[30] EOL L. IX. ff.66v-67v. Die Grundlage des Textes des in Nagyberecsk gehaltenen Gottesdienstes war: 2. Korinther 4. 5-6. „Nekünk keresztény lelki tanítóknak Krisztust prédikálni kötelességünk."[Wir christlichen Geistlichen sind verpflichtet, Jesus Christi zu predigen].

nehmenden Personen festzuhalten. Beachtenswert ist hierbei die Erfassung der in den einzelnen Gemeinden tätigen Hebammen. In Tótaradác gab es z.B. zwei Hebammen, deren Bezahlung für den Beistand bei der Geburt eines Kindes jeweils 8 Groschen und ein Brot betrug.[31] Die Hebamme der deutschen Gemeinde Franzfeld, erhielt als Gegenleistung für ihre Dienste einen Forint, aber in ihrem Fall wurde zusätzlich noch vermerkt, dass sie ihre Ausbildung an der Universität in Pest erhalten hatte.[32] In Homokos betrug die Bezahlung der örtlichen, evangelischen Hebamme 48 Kruzigen sowie jährlich 5 Klafter Holz.[33] In der ausschließlich deutschen Gemeinde Liebling gab es keine festgesetzte Bezahlung für den Hebammendienst.[34] Allgemein gilt es als bemerkenswert, dass in den zwölf Gemeinden, mit der Ausnahme der Ortschaft Istvánfalva, jeweils eine oder mehrere Hebammen tätig waren. In Temesvár hatte die evangelische Gemeinde keine eigene Hebamme, weil hier gleich den anderen königlichen Freistädten ausreichende und vertrauenswürdige Hebammen tätig waren.[35]

Obwohl mit Blick auf die gesellschaftliche Stellung die Totengräber den Hebammen bei Weitem unterlegen waren, wurde es dennoch für wichtig erachtet, das Vorhandensein oder gerade den Mangel an Totengräbern in den Protokollen festzuhalten. Im Laufe der Visitation wurde in den meisten Fällen festgestellt, dass in den Gemeinden – ähnlich wie es in anderen Teilen Ungarns der Brauch war – das Grab von den Freunden und Nachbarn des Verstorbenen ausgehoben wurde.[36]

*****

Die Protokolle erlauben ebenfalls einen Einblick in die finanziellen Bestände der einzelnen Gemeinden. Sie mussten jeweils eigenständig dafür Sorge tragen, dass der Pastor und der Lehrer die ihnen jeweils zugesprochene Bezahlung erhielten, sie mussten für die Instandhaltung der Schule aufkommen sowie die nötigen finanziellen Mittel für die Aufrechterhaltung eines zeitgenössischen Pflegeheims bereitstellen, in dem für die Armen und Hilflosen gesorgt wurde. Eine weitere finanzielle Belastung stellte in dieser Zeit die Errichtung von Kirchen dar, die an Stelle der früheren Gebetshäuser gebaut wurden, oder gar die Erweiterung bzw. der Umbau der Pfarrhäuser. Es ist offensichtlich, dass diese letzteren Ausgaben die größten Posten bei den Kostenaufzählungen ausmachten. Die in der folgenden Tabelle erfassten Daten bieten einen Überblick zu den Kirchengebäuden und Kleinodienbesitztümern der Muttergemeinden sowie zu ihren vorhandenen finanziellen Möglichkeiten, die als eine unmittelbare Voraussetzung für jeweilige Kirchenbauvorhaben galten.

---

31 EOL L. IX. f. 6.
32 EOL L. IX. f. 22v.
33 EOL L. IX. f. 30.
34 EOL L. IX. f. 52.v. „Obstetrices sunt duae … salarium fixum nullum habent."
35 EOL L. IX. f. 65.
36 In der ausschliesslich deutschsprachigen Gemeinde von Liebling war dies ebenso Brauch. EOL L. IX. f. 52v.

Tafel 3

Gemeinde	Kirche	Finanzen	Kleinodien
Tótaradác	neue Kirche 16 mal 7 Klafter Turm: 20 Klafter	Einkommen: 343Fl 35Kr Ausgaben: 337 Fl 7Kr	vergoldeter Silber- kelch mit Schüssel, 4 Kandelaber, Kanne
Nagybecskerek	Betsaal neue Kirche mitTurm im Bau	Einkommen: 4.909Fl 42Kr bleibt 2.458Fl 26Kr	Versilberter Kelch mit Schüssel
Antalfalva	Kirche gebaut 1828 22 mal 9,5 Klafter	keine Angaben	Vergoldeter Kelch und Schüssel aus Silber, 6 Kandelaber
Ferenchalom	17 mal 10 Klafter und 6 Klafter hoch Turm: 10 Klafter	Einkommen: 334 fl keine Schulden	Kelch und Schüssel aus Kupfer, 4 Kan- delaber
Homokos	Betsaal 8 mal 5Klafter	Einkommen: 514fl keine Schulden	Kelch und Schüssel, Kreuz, 4 Kandelaber
Nagylajosfalva	neue Kirche im Bau 22 mal 10 Klafter 7 Klafter hoch	Einkommen: 10.000 fl Ausgaben: 8.000 fl keine Passiva	Vergoldeter Kelch, Kanne aus Blei
Istvánfalva	Betsaal/Schule 5 mal 3 Klafter	Einkommen: 67fl Ausgaben: 48Fl 10Kr	Kelch aus Blei, Deckel
Temesbökény	Betsaal 9 mal 5 Klafter Orgel, Taufbecken, Altar	Einkommen: 190fl 12Kr Ausgaben: 181fl 32Kr	Kelch und Schüssel aus Kupfer
Szemlak	Betsaal 6,5 mal 3,5 Klafter	Einkommen: 442fl Ausgaben: 609fl	Kelch und Schüssel, Kanne aus Blei, 4 Kandelaber aus Kupfer
Kedvenc	Kirche 20 mal 8 Klafter, seit 1823 mit Orgel, Turm seit 1833	Einkommen: 8.090fl 55Kr Ausgaben: 7.086fl 44Kr	2 versilberte Kelche aus Kupfer mit Schüsseln

Temesvukovár	keine Kirche, nur die Schule	Einkommen: 72fl 40Kr Ausgaben: 37fl 8Kr	Kelch, Schüssel, Kanne aus Blei
Temesvár	Betsaal 7 mal 5 Klafter	Einkommen: 587fl 8Kr Ausgaben: 587fl 19Kr	Kelch, Schüssel aus Silber

Anhand der in der Tabelle erfassten Daten können wir feststellen, dass Nagylajosfalva und Liebling, die zwei zahlenmäßig größten Gemeinden, über die besten Wirtschaftsdaten verfügten. In Nagylajosfalva wurde der Bau einer neuen Kirche bereits zugesagt, außerdem lassen die Aktiva der Einnahmen verglichen mit der Summe der Ausgaben auf eine für die Verwirklichung der Bauvorhaben beständige finanzielle Lage schließen. Hier soll ebenfalls vermerkt werden, dass das Visitationskomitee es für wichtig erachtete zu betonen, dass die Gemeinde, der eine Einnahme von 10.000 Forint zur Verfügung stand, keine Schulden hatte.[37] In Liebling wurde eine bedeutende Einnahme in Höhe von 8.000 Forint pro Jahr verbucht. In der Gemeinde von Nagyberecsk, deren Mitglieder überwiegend ungarischsprachig waren, wurde eine Summe für den Bau einer Kirche zurückgelegt.

Im Vergleich mit den Gemeinden, deren Finanzen bis auf den letzten Kreuzer in konkreten Summen erfasst werden, enthalten die ähnlichen Spalten des Visitationsprotokolls der Ortschaft Antalfalva keine Informationen. Vermerkt wird lediglich, dass die die Gemeinde belastenden Passiva nicht bedeutend seien,[38] wobei man auf die durch den Kirchenbau der Vorjahre entstandenen Schulden hinweist. Offensichtlich reichten die begrenzten finanziellen Möglichkeiten der kleineren Gemeinden lediglich für die Aufrechterhaltung von Gebetshäusern aus. Ähnliches sehen wir in Verbindung mit den Kleinodien, d.h., die der Gemeinde zur Verfügung stehenden Mittel bestimmten, ob die Kleinodien der jeweiligen Gemeinde aus Edelmetall, Kupfer oder vielleicht aus Zinn angefertigt wurden.

In enger Verbindung mit der Untersuchung der finanziellen Lage der Gemeinden steht die Erfassung der Einkommen der Pastoren und Lehrer. Die detaillierte Beschreibung der vertraglich festgesetzten Bezahlung wurde den Visitationsprotokollen jeweils hinten angehängt. Hierbei soll festgehalten werden, dass es in der protestantischen Kirche allgemein geltende Praxis war, die Bereitstellung der Unterkunft in die jährliche Bezahlung einzuberechnen; die einzelnen weiteren Aufzählungen wurden in den Einkommensbriefen, die Auszahlungen in Geld und in Naturalien überall genauestens vermerkt. Im Allgemeinen wurde den Pastoren und Lehrern ein Einkommen bereitgestellt, das ihnen jährlich 150-500 Forint an Bargeld, im Weite-

---

[37] EOL L.IX. f. 31v.

[38] „Debitis ecclesiae non est onerata" EOL L.IX. f. 15v.

ren Getreide, Holz, Gartenbenutzung, Warentransport sicherte; hinzu kamen Summen, die bei Taufen, Begräbnissen, Hochzeiten zuvor festgesetzt wurden.
Auffallend ist aber, dass die Einkommen nicht unbedingt im Verhältnis mit der Mitgliederzahl der einzelnen Gemeinden und der allgemeinen finanziellen Lage der Gemeinde standen. Im Verhältnis zu der Anzahl der Gemeindemitglieder in Nagyberecsk verfügte der örtliche Pastor über ein außerordentlich hohes Einkommen in bar, welches 500 Forint betrug. Hinzu kamen 14 Pressburger Maß an Getreide, 8 Pressburger Maß an Gerste, 8 Pressburger Maß an Mais sowie 40 Klafter Holz. Für ein Begräbnis mit Gesang und Predigt erhielt er 1 Forint 48 Kruzigen, für eine Taufe 24 Kruzigen.[39] In der gleichen Ortschaft verfügte der Lehrer, Imre Raksányi, über ein jährliches Einkommen von 100 Forint an Bargeld und 24 Pressburger Maß an Weizen. Für ein Begräbnis mit Ansprache wurden dem Pastor 48 Kruzigen gezahlt, für eine Hochzeit erhielt er 24 Kruzigen. Im Gegensatz zu den vorigen Beispielen zahlte die zahlenmäßig viermal überlegene, zu den größten Gemeinden zählende und ausschließlich aus deutschsprachigen Gläubigen bestehende Gemeinde Liebling dem Pastor lediglich 280 Forint pro Jahr aus.[40] Hinzu kam allerdings die Bebauung seines Feldes, was aufgrund der Urbariumsregelung mindestens 24 Morgen Ackerland, 6 Morgen Wiese und 3 Morgen Weide bedeutete.[41] In Franzfeld, einer zahlenmäßig großen Gemeinde, der vorwiegend deutschsprachige Gläubige angehörten, wurde die Höhe der Bezahlung von der Anzahl der zur Gemeinde gehörenden Familienoberhäupter abhängig gemacht. Hier wurde pro Familienoberhaupt eine Summe von 2 Forint 20 Kruzigen an Bargeld festgesetzt, was mit 940 männlichen Kirchenmitgliedern gerechnet um die 150-200 Haushalte ausmachte – somit lag die Bezahlung schätzungsweise zwischen 400 und 500 Forint. Ähnlich der Gemeinde von Liebling waren auch in Franzfeld die Gemeindemitglieder bereit, das Land des Pastors zu bebauen.[42] Im Einkommensbrief der Gemeinde Temesvár, einer weit kleineren Gemeinde, wurden dem Pastor jährlich 300 Forint in bar zugesprochen, im Weiteren erhielt er ungleich den anderen Gemeinden – vielleicht um ihn für die fehlenden Abgaben in Naturalien zu entschädigen – das an den ersten Tagen der Weihnachts-, Oster- und Pfingstfeiern eingeflossene Geld aus der Sammelbüchse.[43]

*****

Zusammenfassend kann festgestellt werden, dass in keinem der Visitationsprotokolle von Seiten der Mitglieder der Komitees vermerkt wurde, dass irgend ein Umstand die angemessene Religionsausübung, die finanzielle Lage der Gemeinde, das karitative Gemeinschaftsleben, mitunter das Zusammenleben der Gläubigen verschiedener ethnischer Zugehörigkeit negativ beeinflusst hätte. Die bereits erstellten bzw. noch

---

[39] EOL L. IX. ff. 14-14v.
[40] EOL L. IX. f. 53.
[41] Kovách: A Bánság, 94.
[42] EOL L. IX. ff. 19, 24.
[43] EOL L. IX. f. 66.

geplanten Kirchenbauten belegen, dass die Gemeinden fähig waren, sich zur Verwirklichung von gemeinsamen, ernsthafte Anstrengungen fordernden Zielsetzungen zusammenzuschließen. Die finanziellen und personellen Bedingungen für die elementare Schulausbildung wurden gewährleistet, welche den zeitgenössischen Anforderungen und Möglichkeiten entsprach, und es wurde ebenfalls für die Armen der Gemeinde Sorge getragen.

Die meisten der unter die Zuständigkeit des Seniorats fallenden Pastoren – von den zwei oben genannten Ausnahmen abgesehen – hatten bei ihrer Tätigkeit keine sprachlichen Barrieren zu überbrücken, die die entsprechende Ausübung ihrer Tätigkeit im Kreise ihrer multiethnischen Gläubigen behindert hätte.

KULTURLANDSCHAFTEN UND ERINNERUNGSKULTUR

Klaus J. Loderer

Kreuzweg und Kalvarienberg im Königreich Ungarn im 18. Jahrhundert

Die Darstellung von Christus am Kreuz gehört zu den zentralen Themen der christlichen Ikonographie. Häufig vorkommend ist auch die Darstellung des gesamten Leidensweges Christi, was als Kreuzweg bezeichnet wird. Diese zumeist in 14 Einzelbilder aufgeteilte Darstellung gehört zum festen ikonographischen Programm katholischer Kirchen und findet sich üblicherweise im Kirchenschiff, wo sie einen eigenen Andachtsweg bildet. Eine Sonderform bilden die von Kirchenbauten unabhängigen Kreuzwege, sog. Kalvarienberge, auf die nachfolgend näher eingegangen werden soll.[1]
Den biblischen Hintergrund der Kalvarienberge liefern die letzten Stunden im Leben Christi von der Verurteilung bis zur Grablegung. Dafür wurde als Bildprogramm eine gewissermaßen normierte Aufteilung in 14 Szenen plus die Kreuzigung herausgebildet. Die Gläubigen sollen den Weg der Kreuztragung von Station zu Station meditierend und betend nachvollziehen. Die Hauptnutzung der Kalvarienberge liegt in den Andachten während der Osterzeit und steht in einem engen Zusammenhang mit Karfreitag, weitere wichtige Tage sind die Kreuzauffindung (3. Mai) und die Kreuzerhöhung (14. September). Kalvarienberge finden sich im gesamten Verbreitungsbereich des römisch-katholischen Glaubens. Die nachfolgende Betrachtung soll sich auf den Bereich des ehemaligen Königreichs Ungarns und den Zeitraum vom 17. bis zum 19. Jahrhundert beschränken.
Kalvarienberge beziehen sich auf lokale Situationen in Jerusalem wie etwa das Haus des Pilatus, die *Via Dolorosa*, den Golgatha oder das Grab Christi. Nachbauten des Heiligen Grabes, die ihrerseits den Rang von Wallfahrtsstätten einnahmen, finden sich in Europa bereits im Mittelalter.[2] Zu den frühen Darstellungen der Kreuztragung in einzelnen Szenen gehören die Reliefs auf dem Weg zum Johannesfriedhof in Nürnberg von Adam Krafft (1490). Frühe Formen des Kreuzwegs besaßen sieben Stationen.[3] Der thematische Schwerpunkt lag hierbei in den sog. Fußfällen, die ei-

[1] Der Begriff kommt vom lateinischen Wort *calvaria* (Schädel), womit eine Übereinstimmung mit dem biblischen *Golgatha* für „Schädelstätte" besteht. Kunsthistorisch sind die räumlich angelegten Kalvarienberge der Neuzeit zu unterscheiden von den spätmittelalterlichen Gemäldedarstellungen, für die der Begriff „volkreicher Kalvarienberg" üblich ist.
[2] RÜDIGER, Michael: Nachbauten des Heiligen Grabes in Jerusalem in der Zeit von Gegenreformation und Barock, ein Beitrag zur Kultgeschichte architektonischer Devotionalkopien. Regensburg 2003.
[3] Nach Kramer wurde die Anzahl der sieben römischen Stationskirchen auf den Passionsweg übertragen. KRAMER, Ernst: Kreuzweg und Kalvarienberg. Straßburg 1957 (Studien zur deutschen Kunstgeschichte 313), 17.

gentliche Kreuzigung gehörte damals noch nicht dazu.[4] Diese Form war im 16. Jahrhundert fast ausschließlich in Deutschland verbreitet.[5] Später wurde das Programm um weitere Stationen erweitert. 1731 legte Papst Clemens XII. auf Betreiben des Franziskaners Leonhard von Porto Maurizio die Kreuzwegandacht als kirchliches Gebet fest.[6] Damals wurde die Zahl der Stationen auf 14 festgelegt.[7] Diese Form breitete sich vom deutschen Sprachraum ausgehend schließlich weltweit aus.[8] Intensiv um die Verbreitung dieser Form des Kalvarienbergs bemüht war der Franziskanerorden. Dem bereits erwähnten Franziskaner Leonhard wird die Anlage von 572 Kalvarienbergen nachgesagt.[9] Der Orden besaß tatsächlich einen direkten thematischen Bezug, oblag die Grabeskirche in Jerusalem doch in seiner Obhut. Seit der osmanischen Eroberung war diese bedeutendste Wallfahrtsstätte der Christenheit jedoch für Pilger nicht mehr erreichbar. Zur Pflege des Kreuzwegs in Europa legten Franziskaner bewusst Nachbauten dieses Wegs an. Dabei ist zu beachten, dass keine Kenntnisse über die tatsächlichen architektonischen Gegebenheiten oder die Wegführung vorhanden waren. Kalvarienberge sind also freie Nachschöpfungen der biblischen Situationen, im Gegensatz etwa zu Nachbauten des Grab Christi, der Heiligen Treppe in Rom oder des Hauses Mariä in Loreto. Wichtiger als der Wallfahrtsaspekt war in der Regel die meditative Andacht. Die Entfernungen zwischen den biblischen Stätten waren nicht bekannt, auch wenn die Kreuzwegliteratur zum Teil Maßangaben enthält. Entsprechend verzichtet man bei der päpstlichen Festlegung der Kreuzwegandacht auf Maßvorgaben.
Kalvarienberge des 18. Jahrhunderts stehen in der Regel im Zusammenhang mit Franziskanerniederlassungen bzw. mit diesen verbundenen oder von ihnen betreuten Bruderschaften. Bereits 1668 wurde den Franziskanermönchen und -nonnen und den Mitgliedern der von ihnen betreuten Bruderschaften das päpstliche Privileg verliehen, dass sie bei Begehung eines Kreuzwegs in einer Ordenskirche dieselben Ablässe gewinnen konnten, wie beim Besuch der heiligen Stätten in Jerusalem. 1723 wurde dieses Privileg auf alle Gläubigen ausgeweitet, die den Kreuzweg bei den Franziskanern besuchten.[10] Die Möglichkeit, einen Ablass zu gewinnen, erklärt die Verbreitung der Kalvarienberge. Zur starken Verbreitung der Kalvarienberge trugen im 18. Jahrhundert auch die zahlreichen Kreuzwegbüchlein bei.[11] Sonderformen

---

[4] 1. Christus trägt das Kreuz, 2. Christus fällt zum ersten Mal zu Boden, 3. Begegnung mit der Mutter, 4. Christus fällt zum zweiten Mal, 5. Veronika reicht das Schweißtuch, 6. Christus fällt zum dritten Mal, 7. Grablegung. – Nach: SACHS, Hannelore [u.a.]: Christliche Ikonographie in Stichworten, 5. Aufl. München [u.a.] 1994, 228.
[5] KRAMER: Kreuzweg und Kalvarienberg, 19.
[6] EBD., 25.
[7] 1. Christus wird verurteilt, 2. Christus nimmt das Kreuz, 3. Christus fällt zum ersten Mal, 4. Begegnung mit der Mutter, 5. Simon Cyrenäus hilft beim Tragen des Kreuzes, 6. Veronika reicht das Schweißtuch, 7. Christus fällt das zweite Mal, 8. Christus spricht zu den weinenden Töchtern Jerusalems, 9. Christus fällt das dritte Mal, 10. Christus wird der Kleider beraubt, 11. Christus wird an das Kreuz genagelt, 12. Christus stirbt am Kreuz, 13. Kreuzabnahme, 14.Grablegung. – Kleines Baum-Gärtchen 1867, 118-145.
[8] KRAMER: Kreuzweg und Kalvarienberg, 20.
[9] EBD., 25.
[10] EBD.,89.
[11] EBD., 24.

sind Stationswege, die mit der Geburt Christi beginnen, das Leben des hl. Franziskus von Assisi darstellen oder sich auf den Rosenkranz beziehen.

Literatur und Forschungsstand

Gemessen an der Vielzahl der vorhandenen Kalvarienberge ist die Zahl der Literaturnachweise im wissenschaftlichen Bereich eher gering. Das mag daran liegen, dass viele Objekte von der Kunstgeschichte als zu banal und von der Volkskunde als zu katholisch angesehen werden. Ernst Kramer bot 1957 einen ersten Gesamtüberblick.[12] Weiterhin vermitteln Paul und Richilde Werner einen geschichtlichen Überblick sowie eine regionale Übersicht zu Oberbayern.[13] Als erstes Korpuswerk ist der *Atlante dei sacri monti, calvari e complessi devozionali europei* zu betrachten.[14] Ansonsten ist die Zahl wissenschaftlicher Veröffentlichungen gering.[15] Für Österreich entstanden allerdings an der Universität Wien in den letzten Jahren mehrere wissenschaftliche Arbeiten.[16]

Für den Bereich des ehemaligen Königreichs Ungarn bildet István Szilágyis 1980 erschienenes Buch *Kálváriák*, das sich allerdings nur auf den heutigen Staat Ungarn bezieht, als überhaupt einzige zusammenfassende Betrachtung immer noch das Standardwerk.[17] Überblicke geben Lexikonartikel in ungarischen Kunst- und Volkskundelexika.[18] Selten sind Einzelstudien wie jene über den Schemnitzer Kalvarienberg[19] oder jene von Hajnalka Márkusne Vörös über Pápa.[20] Der Pester Kalvarien-

---

[12] EBD. – Kramer führt im Katalog ca. 200 Kalvarienberge auf, darunter aus unserem Untersuchungsbereich Budapest, Eisenstadt und Gödöllő.

[13] WERNER, Paul/WERNER, Richilde: Vom Marterl bis zum Gipfelkreuz. Flurdenkmale in Oberbayern. Berchtesgaden 1991, 329-376.

[14] Atlante dei sacri monte, calvarie e complessi devozionali europei. Hg. v. Amilcare BARBERO. 2001.

[15] Vgl. FABIAN, Gunther: Spätmittelalterliche Friedhofscrucifixi und Kalvarienberge im Rheinland und in Westfalen. Bonn Univ. Diss. 1983. – HEUER, Ludger: Ländliche Friedhöhe in Unterfranken. Dettelbach 1995 (Kasseler Studien zur Sepulkralkultur 6). – LANDGRAF, Gabriele: Die Sacri Monti im Piemont und in der Lombardei. Zwischen Wirklichkeitsillusion und Einbeziehung der Primärrealität. Frankfurt am Main 2000. (Europäische Hochschulschriften 28/362).

[16] Darunter SPERR, Josef: Kalvarienberge in Oberösterreich. Wien Univ. Dipl.-Arb. 1993. – UHL, Erika: Hernals „Feste Burg" und Kalvarienberg. Wien Univ. Dipl.-Arb. 1993. – VSEDNI, Karl: Der Pilgerweg nach Hernals mit der Nachbildung des Heiligen Grabes in Jerusalem und dessen Bezüglichkeiten. Wien Univ. Dipl.-Arb. 1999/2000. – VSEDNI, Karl: Die architektonische Umsetzung des Kalvarienberggedankens zu Beginn des 18. Jahrhunderts im ostösterreichischen Raum unter besonderer Berücksichtigung der Kalvarienberganlagen von Lanzendorf und Eisenstadt mit Verweisen auf Hernals und Heiligenkreuz. Wien Univ. Diss. 2002.

[17] SZILÁGYI, István: Kálváriák, Budapest 1980. – Für die heutige Slowakei ist Martin Cico zu nennen. Vgl. CICO, Martin: Kalvárie a Krízové cesty na Slovensku [Kalvarienberge und Kreuzwege in der Slowakei]. Bratislava 2002.

[18] Magyar művelődéstörténeti lexikon. Középkor és kora újkor [Ungarisches kulturgeschichtliches Lexikon]. Bd. 5, Budapest 2006, 54-61. – Magyar néprajzi lexikon [Ungarisches volkskundliches Lexikon]. Bd. 3. Budapest 1980, 5-6.

[19] SZILÁGYI, István: A selmecbányai kálvária és ábrázolásai [Der Schemnitzer Kalvarienberg und seine Darstellungen]. Budapest 2006.

[20] MÁRKUS VÖRÖS, Hajnalka: A pálosok szerepe a pápai kálvária építésében, a hitélet megújításában [Die Rolle der Pauliner im Bau des Kalvarienberges in Pápa und in der Erneuerung des Glaubens]. Manuskript.

berg geriet durch eine ungeklärte Zuschreibung in den 1920er Jahren in den Blick der Kunstgeschichte und neuerdings durch seine Renovierung.[21] Der Kalvarienberg in Eisenstadt wurde seit seiner Entstehung regelmäßig von geschichtlichen Darstellungen begleitet.[22] Zu nennen wäre noch der Bildband *Kreuze, Heilige, Kalvarienberge, Friedhöfe* von László Tám.[23] Wichtige Nachweise finden sich in den Kunstinventaren Ungarns. Außerdem ist noch auf die lokalgeschichtliche Literatur und die Heimatbücher der vertriebenen Ungarndeutschen zu verweisen. Eine der wenigen Einzelstudien zu einem dörflichen Kalvarienberg ist jene von Maria Herein-Körös über Wudigeß (ung. Budakeszi).[24] Tüskés und Knapp dagegen gehen auf Kalvarienberge nicht ein.[25]

Kalvarienberge in Ungarn

Die erstaunliche Anzahl von Kalvarienbergen in den Nachfolgestaaten des ehemaligen Königreichs Ungarn zeigt eindrücklich die dem *Atlante di Sacri Monti* beiliegende Karte, die für Ungarn immerhin 376 Kalvarienberge aufzählt, für die Slowakei 97, für Kroatien 33, für Serbien 83 und für Rumänien 42. Diese Zahlen sprechen, auch wenn sie nichts über die Entstehungszeit aussagen, für eine starke Verbreitung der Kalvarienberge in diesem Kulturraum.

Das früheste Vorkommen eines Kalvarienbergs in Ungarn ist nicht belegt. Es gibt den Hinweis, dass sich der Bischof von Weißbrunn (ung. Veszprém) in der ersten Hälfte des 17. Jahrhunderts Kopien von Passionsbildern, die in der Wiener Akademikerkirche aufgestellt gewesen seien, besorgt habe.[26] Eine Verwendung ist aber nicht nachgewiesen. Für den osmanisch besetzten Teil des Königreichs Ungarn kann wohl davon ausgegangen werden, dass dort keine Kalvarienberge errichtet wurden. Nach der Rückeroberung und einer gewissen Zeit der wirtschaftlichen Konsolidierung entstanden dort die ersten Kalvarienberge nach 1700. Im nicht osmanisch besetzten Teil dagegen gab es sie bereits früher. Für den Kalvarienberg bei Schemnitz (sk. Banská Štiavnica) wurde der Grundstein angeblich bereits im Jahre 1571 ge-

[21] Az epreskerti kálvária. Egy kétszázötven éves barokk müemlék újjászületésének története [Der Kalvarienberg im Epreskert, Die Geschichte der Wiedergeburt eines 250jährigen barocken Kunstdenkmals]. Budapest 2006.

[22] Zu den Publikationen des 18. Jahrhunderts siehe unten. Geschichte des Calvarienberges und Wallfahrtsortes Maria-Eisenstadt. Győr 1912. – SCHMIDT, Leopold: Die Bedeutung der Wallfahrt Maria Einsiedeln auf dem Kalvarienberg bei Eisenstadt in den ersten Jahren ihres Bestandes. Wien 1948 (Burgenländische Forschungen 2). – RITTSTEUER, Josef: Kalvarienberg und Haydnkirche in Eisenstadt. Eisenstadt 1995. – SOFFNER, Monika: Kalvarienberg Eisenstadt, Haydnkirche. Passau 2002 (Peda-Kunstführer 191).

[23] TÁM, László: Keresztek, szentek, kálváriák, temetök, a magyarországi németek szakrális emlékei [Kreuze, Heilige, Kalvarienberge, Friedhöfe, sakrale Denkmäler der Ungarndeutschen]. Pécs 1999.

[24] HEREIN-KÖRÖS, Maria: Sakrale Denkmäler in Wudigeß/Budakeszi, der Kalvarienberg. In: Suevia Pannonica 34 (2006), 70-89.

[25] TÜSKÉS, Gábor/KNAPP, Éva: Volksfrömmigkeit in Ungarn. Beiträge zur vergleichenden Literatur- und Kulturgeschichte. Dettelbach 1996 (Quellen und Forschungen zur europäischen Ethnologie 18).

[26] VSEDNI, Karl: Der Pilgerweg nach Hernals. Ein Beitrag zu dessen Rekonstruktion. In: Steine sprechen. Zeitschrift der österreichischen Gesellschaft für Denkmal- und Ortsbildpflege 119/4 (2000), 3.

legt.[27] In Wandorf (ung. Sopronbánfalva) ist für 1662 ein früher Kalvarienberg mit fünf Stationen nachgewiesen. Mehrere Anlagen entstanden in den 1690er Jahren, darunter Páli 1696.
Die meisten Kreuzwege Ungarns sind Anlagen mit 14 freistehenden Stationen mit Bildnissen in Form kleiner Gemälde oder Reliefs. Die Stationen sind entweder beidseits des Wegs oder einseitig angeordnet. Den Abschluss bildet die Kreuzigungsgruppe. Hierbei handelt es sich um die in Europa häufigste Art der Anlage überhaupt. Diese Form ist nicht auf das 18. Jahrhundert beschränkt, sondern ist als recht einheitliche Struktur allenfalls mit dem Wechsel der stilistischen Details vom 17. bis zum 21. Jahrhundert zu finden. Die im 18. Jahrhundert häufigste Form der Stationskapellchen ist die eines gemauerten und verputzten Pfeilers mit einer Bogennische für das Stationsbild, der von einem Satteldach bedeckt ist.
Oft wurde der Kalvarienberg mit einer Kapelle bzw. mit einem Grab Christi kombiniert. Die Anlage erfolgte gelegentlich in Friedhöfen, häufig jedoch als völlig selbständige Anlage außerhalb der Gemeinde. Tatsächlich scheint man in Ungarn darauf geachtet zu haben, die Anlage auf einer Anhöhe zu errichten, vielleicht um den Gläubigen einen Bezug zur biblischen Situation auf dem Golgatha zu vermitteln. Nicht selten scheint man auch nicht landwirtschaftlich nutzbare Flächen bebaut zu haben. Dies deutet der überaus steile Hang in Nadasch (ung. Mecseknádasd) an. Auch für Ofen (ung. Buda) mag es nicht erstaunen, dass der Kalvarienberg auf dem die Stadt überragenden Blocksberg (St. Gerhardsberg, ung. Gellért-hegy) errichtet wurde. Die Topographie Ungarns weist tatsächlich eine große Zahl kahler und steiniger Hügel auf, die nicht selten geradezu idealtypisch mit einem Kalvarienberg besetzt wurden. Markante Beispiele hierfür sind Bodajk, Wudersch (ung. Budaörs) und Totis (ung. Tata).

Pilgerweg

Eine Besonderheit stellen Kalvarienberge dar, deren Kreuzweg von der Gemeinde entlang einer Straße oder eines Wegs zu einer weit außerhalb gelegenen Kreuzigungsgruppe führt. Hintergrund ist der Versuch, die vermeintliche Länge des Leidenswegs Christi erlebbar zu machen. Ob zum hoch über der Stadt thronenden Kalvarienberg in Güns (ung. Kőszeg), der ab 1686 angelegt wurde, bereits ab der Anfangszeit ein Kreuzweg führte, ist fraglich. Nachgewiesen sind die Stationen erst seit 1763.[28] Die heutige Form wurde erst 1890 vom Architekten Ludwig Schöne geplant.[29] Der Kreuzweg zieht sich über mehrere Windungen zur erhöht und außerhalb der Stadt gelegenen Kalvarienbergkapelle. Wenig später, genauer 1692, entstand ein Kalvarienberg oberhalb des Ofener Stadtbezirks Landstraße (heute ein Teil des II. Budapester Bezirks), der von der Alten Hauptgasse (heute ung. Margit körút) ent-

[27] Die österreichisch-ungarische Monarchie in Wort und Bild. Ungarn. Bd.5. Abt. 2. Wien 1900, 84.
[28] SZILÁGYI: Kálváriák, 139.
[29] EBD., 139. – BARISKA, István: Kőszeg Güns. Szombathely 1997, 117.

lang der späteren Franzensgasse (ung. Zárda utca, heute ung. Rómer Flóris utca) den Hügel hinaufführte.[30] Die Kreuzigungsgruppe und die Marienkapelle befanden sich an der heutigen Veronika utca.[31] Noch weitläufiger dürften die Stationen am Kalvarienberg von Raitzenstadt (ung. Tabán) den Blocksberg hinaufgeführt haben, der ebenfalls nicht mehr erhalten ist.[32] Entlang der Straße zum Steinbruch sollen die Stationen des Pester Kalvarienbergs gestanden haben, auf den später noch genauer eingegangen werden soll.[33]

Weiterhin zu nennen wären noch die Kalvarienberge in Raab (ung. Győr) um 1720 und Pápa um 1740. Nicht genau datiert ist der Kalvarienberg in Badeseck (ung. Bátaszék), dessen Stationen ursprünglich auch entlang der Landstraße standen, heute aber zusammengefasst nahe der Kreuzigungsgruppe stehen, wodurch der ursprüngliche Gedanke des Andachtswegs nicht mehr nachvollziehbar ist.[34] Das Visitationsprotokoll von 1828 gibt für die Entfernung von Ort und Kalvarienbergkapelle etwa 1000 Schritte an.[35] Auch in Baja wurden die Stationen Anfang des 19. Jahrhunderts in eine neue Anordnung gebracht. Ursprünglich folgten sie der Rochusgasse.[36] Doch gehen wir etwas genauer auf Raab und Pápa ein, die gewisse Ähnlichkeiten aufweisen. Bei beiden stehen die Kapellen mit großen Nischen entlang der Straße. Beide besitzen fast lebensgroße figürliche Darstellungen. Den Abschluss der Anlagen bildet eine künstlich aufgeschüttete, erhöhte Terrasse mit der Kreuzigungsgruppe, auf die im nächsten Kapitel noch eingegangen werden soll. Die Anzahl der Stationen ist in Raab mit sieben gering, was auf eine eigentlich altertümliche Form des Kalvarienbergs verweist. In Pápa stehen sechs Stationen entlang der Straße, die letzten sind in den abschließenden Bau eingebunden.

Mehrere Elemente der Kalvarienberge in Raab und Pápa könnten auf den Wiener Kalvarienberg in Hernals verweisen, wie etwa das Motiv des Pilgerwegs und die großen Stationskapellen mit ihren fast lebensgroßen Figuren. Erstmals scheint in Wien 1639 ein Kreuzweg von der Gemeinde zum weit außerhalb gelegenen Kalvarienberg geführt worden zu sein. Der Weg begann bei St. Stephan und führte bis nach Hernals. Unterwegs standen sieben Stationskapellen.[37] Für den Pilgerweg nach

---

30 Die Stationen der Anlage sind auf Fotos aus dem späten 19. Jahrhundert noch zu sehen. Vgl. SIKLÓSSY, László: Hogyan épült Budapest (1870-1930) [Wie wurde ausgebaut Budapest (1870-1930)]. Budapest 1931, 564.

31 Die Kapelle wurde 1690 errichtet, 1692 drei Holzkreuze, 1757-58 wurde die Kapelle erweitert und 1951 abgerissen. – Budapest Műemlékei 2 [Denkmalschätze Ungarns 2]. Budapest 1962 (Magyarország műemléki topográfiája 6), 310-311.

32 Dort wurde 1715 eine Kreuzigungsgruppe errichtet. 1795 stiftete ein Raitzenstädter Bürger eine Kapelle und die Stationen. 1950 wurde der Kalvarienberg entfernt. – GRESZL, Franz: Ofen-Buda. Entwicklungsgeschichte der königlichen Residenzstadt Ungarns im 18. Jahrhundert. Eine kirchen-, pastoral-, kultur- und kunstgeschichtliche Untersuchung im Lichte der Graner (Esztergomer) erzbischöflichen Visitationsprotokolle im Zeitraum zwischen 1686 und 1822. München 1984, 70. – Budapest műemlékei 2, 528.

33 SZILÁGYI: Kálváriák, 137.

34 Nach dem Visitationsprotokoll von 1754 sind außerhalb des Orts auf einem Hügel drei Kreuze und drei Statuen aufgestellt. HERMANN, Ägid: Kapellen, Kreuze und Statuen. In: Heimatbuch der Großgemeinde Bátaszék/Badeseck im Komitat Tolnau (Ungarn). Bd. 2. Hg. v. Johannes GÖBELT. Bátaszék 1991, 133.

35 HERMANN: Kapellen, 133.

36 Im Stadtplan von 1803 ist noch ihre ursprüngliche Anordnung eingezeichnet.

37 Heute ist nur noch die zweite Station erhalten, die in die Alserkirche integriert ist.

Hernals wurde kolportiert, dass seine Länge genau dem Passionsweg Christi entsprechen würde.[38] Obgleich das Maß nicht unbedingt stimmte, kann man vermuten, dass auch in Raab und Pápa die weite Reihung der Stationen den Gläubigen das Gefühl der Entfernung der echten *Via Dolorosa* geben sollte. Übrigens weist auch der eigentliche Kalvarienberg in Hernals Bezüge zu Raab und Pápa auf.

Terrasse mit Kreuzigungsgruppe

Betrachten wir deshalb die Kreuzwege in Raab und Pápa abschließenden Kreuzigungsgruppen genauer. Künstlich aufgeschüttete Anlagen bilden deren Unterbau. In Raab wurde in Ermangelung eines Bergs ein künstlicher Hügel aufgeschüttet, dessen Spitze nochmals durch einen Aufbau mit Terrasse erhöht ist, zu der eine breite, einläufige Treppe hinauf führt. Auf der Terrasse erhebt sich die Kreuzigungsgruppe, die ohne die heute vorhandene umliegende Bebauung früher weithin sichtbar war. In Pápa ist die Treppenanlage komplizierter. Entlang der mehrläufigen Stufen sind noch einige Stationen angeordnet. Außerdem ist dort die Kreuzigungsgruppe von einer überdachten Bogennische in der Art einer Kirchenapsis umfangen. In Pápa ist an der Rückseite der Terrasse in einem Grottenraum ein Heiliges Grab angelegt, während in Raab das Heilige Grab ein freistehendes Gebäude an der Rückseite des Kalvarienbergs bildet, das sich deutlich an das tradierte Bild des Christusgrabs in Jerusalem anlehnt. Es steht quer zur Hauptachse der Anlage, wohl um die Westausrichtung des Originalbaus zu übernehmen.[39] Das erste errichtete Gebäude der Raaber Anlage war 1714 wohl die ungewöhnlich große Dismaskapelle, die eine prominente Stelle einnimmt und durch ihren Dreikonchenchor eine bemerkenswerte Form besitzt.[40] Als Architekt der Anlage wird der Karmeliter Martin Wittwer angenommen.[41]

Auch der barocke Vorgängerbau der heutigen Kalvarienbergkirche in Hernals wies durch seine an ein Bollwerk erinnernde hohe Terrasse zumindest von der Rückseite Ähnlichkeit mit Raab und Pápa auf und könnte Vorbildwirkung besessen haben. Das Aussehen des von 1709 bis 1714 entstandenen Kalvarienbergs ist in einem Stich von Salomon Kleiner erhalten geblieben.[42] Man kann darauf erkennen, dass der Kalvarienberg seinerseits aus 14 Stationen bestand, die von der Kreuzigungsgruppe überragt wurden und mit einer Kirche und einem Heiligen Grab kombiniert waren. Durch die Reihenfolge der Entstehung kann man annehmen, dass der Wiener Kalvarienberg (1709-14) jenen in Raab (1718-22) und dieser den in Pápa (1740) beeinflusste. Die von einer Apsis geschützte Kreuzigungsgruppe auf einer erhöhten Ter-

[38] VSEDNI: Der Pilgerweg nach Hernals, 3.

[39] Zum Heiligen Grab vgl. Rüdiger: Nachbauten des Heiligen Grabes, 220-222.

[40] Dismaskapellen finden sich gelegentlich bei Kalvarienbergen. Der hl. Dismas war der reuige Schächer zur Rechten Jesu bei der Kreuzigung. Seine Verehrung wurde im Mittelalter vor allem vom Franziskanerorden gepflegt. – Biographisch-bibliographisches Kirchenlexikon 16, 394.

[41] SZILÁGYI: Kálváriák, 138.

[42] KLEINER, Salomon: Wahrhaffte und genaue Abbilung aller Kirchen und Clöster (...). Augsburg 1724.

rasse, wie etwa in Pápa, findet man in ähnlicher Form in der nahen Gemeinde Klein Mariazell (ung. Celldömölk) (1755). Dort beginnen die Treppenaufgänge hinter zwei wohl später angefügten Türmen, wodurch heute der Gesamteindruck einer unvollständigen Kirche entsteht.

Dass die Kreuzigungsgruppe durch eine kleine Ummauerung optisch zusammengefasst und durch eine leichte Erhöhung hervorgehoben wurde, lässt sich bei vielen Kalvarienbergen beobachten. Waren die bisherigen Beispiele der erhöhten Terrasse für die Kreuzigungsszene in ihrer Ausformung recht grob, so lassen sich in Ungarn auch ausgesprochen raffinierte Anlagen finden. Zu den bemerkenswertesten Beispielen gehört der Kalvarienberg von Pest, der sich ursprünglich weit außerhalb der besiedelten Stadt in der Nähe der ab 1732 angelegten Siedlung Lerchenfeld befand. Die auf den Abbildungen des 19. Jahrhunderts gezeigten Stationen sind durch ihr neogotisches Äußeres markant für diesen Zeitraum. Ursprünglich sollen die Stationen entlang der Straße zum Steinbruch, der späteren Stationsgasse (ung. Baross utca) gestanden haben.[43] Ob sie allerdings im 18. Jahrhundert schon bestanden, ist fraglich, erst ein Visitationsprotokoll von 1822 erwähnt vier Statuen an den Häuserwänden und drei andere entlang der Straße.[44] Die Terrasse für die Kreuzigungsgruppe wurde 1744-49 errichtet. Als Baumeister wird seit Reh-Révhelyi Andreas Mayerhoffer[45] angenommen. Vorher wurde die Anlage oft auf früher datiert und wechselweise Johann Bernhard Fischer von Erlach oder Johann Lucas von Hildebrandt zugeschrieben.[46] Die Terrasse versetzte man 1893 in den Garten der Kunstakademie, in den sog. Maulbeergarten (ung. Epreskert), wo sie sich noch heute befindet und unter dessen Name sie heute als „Epreskerti kálvária“ bekannt ist. Am ursprünglichen Standort in der Josefstadt (ung. Józsefváros, VIII. Budapester Bezirk) erinnert nur noch bzw. wieder der Name des Platzes an den religiösen Ursprung: Kálvária tér.[47] Der Grundriss der barocken Anlage basiert auf einem Kreis. Im Zentrum des Erdgeschosses befindet sich ein runder Raum, der ursprünglich als Kapelle diente.[48] Umgeben ist er von einem Arkadengang. Diesen Umgang, von dem aus unter dem zweiten Podest zwei Türen in die Kapelle geführt haben sollen, interpretiert Ritoók wegen der neun gleich hohen Arkadenöffnungen als Aufstellungsort von neun Sta-

---

[43] SZILÁGYI: Kálváriák, 137.

[44] RITOÓK, Pál: Az epreskerti kálvária a források tükrében. [Der Kalvarienberg im Maulbeergarten im Spiegel der Quellen]. In: Művészettörténeti Értesítő 52 (2003), 7.

[45] Andreas Mayerhoffer, ist 1690 in Salzburg geboren und 1771 in Pest gestorben. Zu seinen Hauptwerken gehört das Treppenhaus im Schloss Gödöllő 1744-1750, die Paulinerkirche (Universitätskirche) in Pest, die Kathedrale von Kalocsa 1735-1754 sowie das Komitatshaus Gran (Esztergom). Budapest Lexikon Bd. 2, 126. – Deutsche in Budapest. Hg. v. Wendelin HAMBUCH. Budapest 1999, 683. – RÉH (Révhelyi), Elemér: Adatok a régi pesti kálvária történetéhoz. [Angaben zur Geschichte des alten Pester Kalvarienbergs]. In: Archaeológiai Értesítő 63 (1929), 202-222.

[46] GRIMSCHITZ, Bruno: Az epreskerti kálvária. [Der Kalvarienberg im Maulbeergarten]. In: Archaeológiai Értesítő 62 (1928), 188-197. – Eine Zusammenfassung der Diskussion der Baumeisterfrage bietet RITOÓK: Epreskerti kálvária, 19.

[47] 1952-1991 hieß der Platz Kulich Gyula tér. Vgl. Budapest Lexikon. Bd. 1. Budapest 1993, 635.

[48] Nicht dieser diente als Karzer Christi, wie Kramer annimmt, sondern ein anschließender kleiner Raum, der von einem kleinen Fenster an der Stelle der heutigen Tür beleuchtet wurde, betont Ritoók. Vgl. KRAMER: Kreuzweg und Kalvarienberg, 103. – RITOÓK: Epreskerti kálvária, 9.

tionsbildern.[49] Eine mehrläufige Treppe führt zur erhöhten Terrasse. Ihre interessante Wegführung entsteht durch den vorgegebenen Richtungswechsel: zwei Treppenläufe vereinigen sich auf halber Höhe in einem Podest, von dem aus weitere Treppenläufe über dem Umgang bis zur vollen Höhe führen. Von besonderer Qualität ist der plastische Schmuck von Pfeilern und Geländer. Die Treppenanlage erinnert mit ihrem symmetrischen Aufbau und den zahlreichen Zwischenpodesten an Freitreppen barocker Schlösser. Das Bauwerk steht in der ungarischen Architektur des 18. Jahrhunderts durch seine Kreisform einzigartig dar. Runde Bauwerke entstanden im Königreich sonst erst in der Epoche des Klassizismus. Dabei ist die Grundrissstruktur geradezu idealtypisch angelegt. Die insgesamt 16 Öffnungen bzw. Pfeiler unterteilen den Kreis so, dass über Quer- und Längsachsen und sogar über den Diagonalen jeweils eine Öffnung liegt. Mayerhoffer schuf dadurch eine ausgeklügelte Symmetrie. Für ein mögliches Vorbild der Grundrissstruktur sei in einem vielleicht gewagten Vergleich an Bramantes Tempietto bei San Pietro in Montorio in Rom verwiesen, der diese Teilung des Säulenumgangs ebenfalls aufweist. Ähnlichkeiten der beiden Grundrisse treten besonders dann auf, wenn man ältere Darstellungen des „Tempelchens“ betrachtet, bei denen üblicherweise noch die in die Krypta führenden Treppen eingezeichnet sind. Eine Kenntnis römischer Renaissance-Architektur ist bei Mayerhoffer allerdings nicht direkt nachweisbar. Interessanterweise gibt das Patrozinium noch einen Bezugspunkt zum Kalvarienberg, wurde doch der Tempietto über der Stelle errichtet, an der Petrus gekreuzigt worden sein soll.

Eine ähnliche Anlage mit wesentlich einfacheren Formen findet sich in Promontor (ung. Budafok, heute XXII. Budapester Bezirk), die nicht genau datiert ist.[50] Wieder erhebt sich die Kreuzigungsgruppe auf einer kreisrunden Plattform. Zwei Treppenläufe führen gegenläufig zu ihr hinauf und treffen sich in der Mitte. Unter diesem Podest befindet sich ein Heiliges Grab. Diese heute von Gebäuden umgebene Anlage erhob sich ursprünglich frei auf einem Hügel über der Gemeinde. Der Weg mit den Stationen zieht sich unregelmäßig den Hang hinauf.

Ein Werk Johann Mayerhoffers ist der 1771 von Anton Grassalkovich gestiftete Kalvarienberg in Gödöllő, der 1775 geweiht wurde.[51] Eine quadratische Terrasse mit in spätbarocker Manier abgerundeten Ecken wird von zwei Treppen erschlossen, die sich in ihrem Schwung um die Rundungen der Terrasse schmiegen. Schon Kramer weist auf die Ähnlichkeit mit der Pester Anlage hin.[52] Hervorzuheben ist die aufwendig gegliederte Balustrade. Im hinteren Teil polygonal und vorn halbrund ist die Terrasse in Sankt-Andrä (ung. Szentendre) abgeschlossen. Um den halbrunden Abschluss ist konzentrisch eine symmetrische Freitreppe gelegt, deren Läufe über dem Eingang zum Kapellenraum auf einem Podest zusammentreffen. Komplizierter ist die Anlage in Baderseck. Dort sind an die Terrasse seitlich gegenläufige Treppen

[49] Ebd., 7.
[50] Das Kunstinventar datiert die Anlage nur allgemein auf das 18. Jahrhundert und gibt eine Restaurierung für 1934 an. – Budapest műemlékei 2, 607.
[51] Szilágyi: Kálváriák, 138. – Pest megye műemlékei [Denkmäler des Komitates Pest]. Bd. 1. Budapest 1958 (Magyarország műemléki topográfiája 5), 388-389.
[52] Kramer: Kreuzweg und Kalvarienberg, 110.

angesetzt. Die Terrassenfassade schwingt vorne leicht vor und bildet hinten einen halbrunden Abschluss. Am hinteren Teil ist außerdem ein Turm angefügt, der die gesamte Anlage überragt. Im Erdgeschoss befinden sich mehrere gewölbte Räume. Unter dem Turm ist ein kleiner Raum mit einer „Ecce-Homo" Darstellung. Allerdings ist fraglich, ob die bestehende Anlage überhaupt aus dem 18. Jahrhundert stammt.[53] Die vergleichbare Kalvarienberganlage in Gyöngyös entstammt wohl erst dem späten 19. Jahrhundert.[54]

Kreuzigungsgruppen auf erhöhten Terrassen scheinen also typisch für Ungarn gewesen zu sein. Schon Kramer bemerkte, dass „Kalvarienberggruppen über großen Freitreppen auf hoher Bastion" typisch für Ungarn seien.[55] Vereinzelt finden sich diese auch in Deutschland, so am Kalvarienberg beim Franziskanerkloster in Fulda (1737) und in Altstadt bei Hammelburg in Unterfranken (1733). Wurden sie dort benutzt, um die Kreuzigungsgruppe noch mehr hervorzuheben, bestand in Ungarn an vielen Orten in Ermangelung natürlicher Erhebungen die Notwendigkeit, einen künstlichen Hügel zu errichten, um die Situation eines Berges nachvollziehbar zu machen. Bei den bisher besprochenen Bauten waren Kreuzigungsgruppe und Stationen räumlich getrennt. Es gibt jedoch einige Beispiele, bei denen alle Stationen in ein architektonisches Gesamtkonzept eingefügt sind.

Künstliche Berge

Das heutige Burgenland weist einige bemerkenswerte Kalvarienberge auf, bei denen versucht wurde, den Weg auf einen Berg anhand eines entsprechend geformten Bauwerks nachzuahmen. Von 1685 bis 1695 errichteten die Franziskaner neben ihrem Kloster in Frauenkirchen (ung. Boldogasszony) einen Kalvarienberg in der Form einer räumlich nach oben gezogenen Spirale: Eine Rampe mit den Stationen steigt im Uhrzeigersinn gleichmäßig sanft an und führt zum erhöhten Mittelpunkt mit der Kreuzigungsgruppe. Diese ästhetisch anspruchsvolle und gleichzeitig sehr kompakte Lösung scheint im deutschsprachigen Raum singulär geblieben zu sein. Profane Schneckenberge erfreuten sich besonders um die Mitte des 18. Jahrhunderts in Parkanlagen großer Beliebtheit. Beispiele haben sich bei Schloss Mirabell in Salzburg, Wilhelmsbad bei Hanau und der Eremitage bei Bayreuth erhalten. Wie erwähnt ist im Vergleich dazu die Anlage in Frauenkirchen wesentlich älter.

Die opulenteste Ausformung eines Kalvarienbergs in Form eines künstlichen Berges befindet sich in Eisenstadt (ung. Kismarton). Dort hatte Fürst Paul I. Esterházy am

[53] Unsicher ist die Datierung der Kapelle. Für 1762 ist der Neubau einer von Valentin Thes (Deeß) gestifteten Marienkapelle überliefert. Das Visitationsprotokoll von 1776 vermerkt einen Turm, jenes von 1811, dass das Flachdach der Kapelle durch die herrschaftliche Pächterfamilie Kliegl und die Einwohner als Kalvarienberg ausgebildet worden sei. Das Visitationsprotokoll von 1828 vermerkt noch ein Wächterhaus, das 1980 abgerissen wurde. HERMANN: Kapellen, Kreuze und Statuen, 133.

[54] Die Bauarbeiten an einer Kapelle beginnen 1721. Turm und Einsiedelei sind für 1827-32 datiert. 1861 wird der alte Kalvarienberg abgerissen und neu errichtet. SZILÁGYI: Kálváriák, 138.

[55] KRAMER: Kreuzweg und Kalvarienberg, 70.

22. September 1701 den Grundstein zum Bau gelegt. Als Vorbild kann der kurz zuvor errichtete Kalvarienberg im unweit gelegenen Maria Lanzendorf angenommen werden, zumal beide vom Baumeister, Tischler und Franziskanerlaienbruder Felix Niering geplant wurden.[56] Nach der Niederschlagung des Kuruzzenaufstands 1705 wurden in Eisenstadt die Arbeiten fortgeführt. 1707 weihte der Bischof von Wardein, Emmerich Csáky, den Kalvarienberg. 1711 übertrug der Fürst die Obsorge des Kalvarienbergs und die Betreuung der Pilger den Franziskanern der ungarischen marianischen Ordensprovinz. Der neue Kalvarienberg entwickelte sich schnell zum Zentrum der Wallfahrt in Maria Eisenstadt, wie man damals sagte. Dies belegt etwa folgendes Lied: „Zu dem Wunderthätigen Gnaden-Bild auf dem Berg Calvarij bey Eysenstadt in Granitzen des Königreichs Hungarn bey dem Wohl-Ehrwürtigen P.P. Franciscanern Verwahret und von Tag zu Tag mehr und mehr mit grossen Miraculen Leichtet".[57] 1732 erschien eine „wahrhaffte Beschreibung der vielfältigen, und seltsahmen Wunderthaten, welche 1714 [...] Biss auf gegenwärtigen Augenblick, auf dem Welt-berühmten Hoch-Fürstl. Calvari-Berg gewürcket hat".[58] Unmittelbar neben dem Kalvarienberg befand sich die später abgetragene Apolloniakapelle. Eine Beschreibung der ursprünglichen Struktur des Kalvarienbergs gibt eine 1716 „Allen Liebhabern dieser Andächtigen Wahlfahrt zu einem Geistliche n Trost in Druck gegeben Durch die Residenz deren P.P. Franciscanern der Marianischen Provintz bey dem Berg Calvari nebst Eysenstatt daselbst" herausgegebene Schrift.[59]

Einen starken Eingriff in das Gefüge bildete der Bau der neuen Kirche, für deren Chor mehrere Kapellen an der Westseite abgerissen wurden. Insgesamt soll ein Fünftel der ursprünglichen Bausubstanz abgetragen worden sein. So ist der Kapellenkranz, der den Kalvarienberg ursprünglich umgeben hat, heute nicht mehr nachvollziehbar. Von Osten fallen diese Eingriffe nicht auf. Dort befindet sich bis heute der Hauptzugang. Eine Freitreppe führt zur ovalen Gnadenkapelle. Links daneben beginnt der Weg durch den Kalvarienberg. Der erste Teil führt durch enge Gänge. In grottenähnlichen Räumen sind die ersten Szenen dargestellt. Mit der Geißelung Christi überschneidet sich die Heilig-Grab-Kapelle in der Mittelachse, die vermutlich ursprünglich von außen zugänglich war. In der Querachse befindet sich ein hoher Raum mit „Scala Santa" und „Ecce homo". Von hier aus geht der Weg ins Freie den künstlichen Berg hinauf. Treppen führen hierbei über die einen Berg andeutenden geschwungenen Dächer. Den höchsten Punkt bildet die Kreuzkapelle. Von hier aus führt der Weg hinab und endet an der Gnadenkapelle.

Die Anlage mit 24 Stationen und mehreren Kapellen erscheint auf den ersten Blick völlig verwirrend. Das Zentrum nehmen in der Hauptachse Gnadenkapelle, Heilige

[56] Ernst führt an, dass Fürst Paul den Kalvarienberg in Maria Lanzendorf bei einem Besuch 1687 bewundert habe. Dies scheint kaum möglich, da der Kalvarienberg erst 1699-1701 entstanden ist. Trotzdem kann man annehmen, dass der Fürst den Kalvarienberg bei einem anderen Besuch besichtigt haben wird, da Maria Lanzendorf an der Straße von Eisenstadt nach Wien liegt. – ERNST, August: Am Heiligen Berg Eisenstadt-Oberberg. Eisenstadt 1996, 46.

[57] Zwey schöne neue Geistliche-Lieder. Das Erste: Zu dem Wunderthätigen Gnaden-Bild (...). Wiener Neustadt 1715.

[58] Persianisch-Marianisches Gnaden-Brünnl (...). Wiener Neustadt 1732.

[59] Zwey Tractätlein Von Berg Calvari bey Eysenstatt.

Stiege, Heiliges Grab und Kreuzkapelle ein. Um diese nicht begehbare Symmetrieachse ist der Weg herumgelegt. Er beschreibt zuerst im Uhrzeigersinn einen fast vollständigen großen Kreis entlang der Außenwand. Zur Heiligen Treppe führt der Weg hinab in die Tiefe des Bauwerks (dabei hinauf und hinab), wieder heraus und ab hier hinauf. Knapp vor Erreichen der Mittelachse (also ohne den Kreis vollständig zu schließen) ist eine Kehrtwendung notwendig, nach zwei weiteren Kehrtwendungen, während derer steile Treppen nach oben beschritten werden müssen, ist die Kreuzkapelle auf der Höhe erreicht. Dann führt eine Schneckendrehung in die Tiefe. Die beschriebene Bewegung im Kalvarienberg ist eine wesentlich kompliziertere als die Spirale in Frauenkirchen. Die Wegführung in Eisenstadt scheint vielmehr die räumliche Umsetzung eines Labyrinths im Sinne der mittelalterlichen Andachtswege zu sein. Hier sei nur auf die Labyrinthe in den Fußböden mittelalterlicher Kathedralen verwiesen. Die Wegführung in Eisenstadt ist zwar letztlich einfacher, doch entsprechen die Richtungswechsel den Strukturen des Labyrinths.

Heilige Berge

Ein Kalvarienberg, der tatsächlich einen existierenden Berg umformt, befindet sich bei der Bergbaustadt Schemnitz in der heutigen Slowakei. Das *Kronprinzenwerk* beschreibt ihn wie folgt: „Der Calvarienberg befindet sich auf einer Kuppe östlich der Stadt und ist einer der schönsten im Lande. Seine jetzige Gestalt ist vom Jahre 1744, der Grundstein aber wurde schon 1571 gelegt. Es gehören dazu drei Kapellen: die untere, die mittlere und die auf dem Gipfel. Zur mittleren führt die sogenannte »Heilige Treppe« hinauf, welche die Gläubigen kniend hinanrutschen. Rings um die drei Kapellen ziehen sich, den Abhang hinan, in schöner Ordnung 24 Stationen, zum Theil mit geschnitzten Darstellungen. Bei Wallfahrten wimmelt die Stadt von vielen Tausend Gläubigen, die von fernher kommen und den Calvarienberg ersteigen. Dann wird in der unteren Kapelle slowakisch, in der mittleren ungarisch, in der oberen deutsch gepredigt."[60]

In symmetrischer Anordnung ziehen sich in Schemnitz die Stationen den Berg hinauf, verbunden mit einem symmetrischen Wegenetz. Den höchsten Punkt nimmt die umbaute Kreuzigungskapelle mit zwei Türmen und Einsiedelei auf einer erhöhten Plattform ein. Zu ihr führen auf der einen Seite sieben Stationen hinauf (Leidensweg Christi) und auf der anderen Seite sieben Stationen hinab (Schmerzen unserer Lieben Frau). Im unteren Teil des Bergs führen drei Stationen zum Kalvarienberg hin. Die Mittelachse der Anlage nehmen mehrere Kapellen ein, darunter die Heiligkreuzkapelle und die Heilige Treppe. Eine zeitgenössische Beschreibung führt weiter an: „Kirchen für die Teutsche Nation, ganz in Fresco gemahlen [...] Kirchen für die Schläwäkische Nation, ganz in Fresco gemahlen".[61] Der Weg führt, von der

[60] Die österreichisch-ungarische Monarchie in Wort und Bild. Ungarn. Bd. 5. Abt. 2. Wien 1900, 84.
[61] Wahre Abbildung des zu Schemnitz Neu errichteten heil. Calvary berg (...). Abgebildet in SZILÁGYI: A selmecbányai kálvária, 47.

Slowakischen Kirche und der Kapelle der schmerzhaften Muttergottes ausgehend im Zickzack den Berg hinauf und symmetrisch im Zickzack wieder hinab. Die gedachte Mittelachse kann außer im Bereich der Heiligen Stiege nicht beschritten werden. Die Möglichkeit, sechsmal jährlich einen vollkommenen Ablass zu erhalten, wird zum Erfolg der von 1744 bis 1751 auf Initiative der Jesuiten angelegten Wallfahrtsstätte beigetragen haben. Dass die Mittelachse nicht gänzlich beschritten werden kann, ist eine Gemeinsamkeit mit dem Kalvarienberg *Käppele* in Würzburg. Im Gegensatz zur Liturgie in der Kirche, wo die Mittelachse der Prozessionsachse des Priesters mit dem Ausgangspunkt des Hochaltars eine wichtige Bedeutung besitzt, ist diese liturgische Notwenigkeit beim Kalvarienberg nicht gegeben.

Man kann in Ungarn weitere Beispiele von Kalvarienbergen finden, die als eine Art „Heiliger Berg" angelegt wurden. Wesentlich bescheidener ist der Kalvarienberg in dem kleinen Wallfahrtsort Polan (ung. Magyarpolány). Dort beginnt neben der am oberen Rand der Gemeinde befindlichen Pfarrkirche eine steile Treppe, die in geradem Lauf den Berg hinaufführt. An jedem Treppenabsatz steht eine Stationskapelle. Der Kalvarienberg soll um 1770 von den Brüdern Listner geschaffen worden sein. Bemerkenswert sind die fünf großfigurigen Szenen, die von dem nur wenige Kilometer entfernten Kalvarienberg in Pápa beeinflusst sein könnten.[62] Den oberen Abschluss bilden ein Kreuz und eine Kapelle.

Da sich in ländlichen Gebieten spätbarocke Formen zum Teil bis nach 1800 erhielten, sei hier ein Vorgriff gestattet: um und nach 1800 entstanden in vielen Gemeinden Kalvarienberge mit symmetrisch angeordneten Stationen. Frankenstadt, Nadasch, Mohatsch (ung. Mohács), Bonnhard (ung. Bonyhád), Városlöd, Deutschbohl (ung. Bóly) und Waschkut (ung. Vaskút) sind frühe Beispiele einer Anordnung, die im Laufe des 19. Jahrhunderts in vielen Gemeinden tradiert wurde.[63] Besonders in ungarndeutsch geprägten Gemeinden scheint sich dieser Typus besonderer Beliebtheit erfreut zu haben. An Nadasch, Bonnhard, Városlöd und Deutschbohl, die allesamt eine symmetrische Anordnung der Stationen, Kreuzigungsgruppe und Kapelle aufweisen, wird die Idee der nun in bescheidenem Umfang ausgeführten lokalen Fassung des „Heiligen Bergs" deutlich. Die gestaffelte Anordnung und die Ausrichtung der Stationen zum Tal – und nicht wie üblich zum ansteigenden Weg – steigern noch die räumliche Wirkung.[64] Effektvoll wurden die Kalvarienberge in Baja und Waschkut am Ende einer Straße errichtet. Beide Anlagen sind mit ihrer symmetrischen Anordnung der Stationen auf einer breiten Rampe, die einen künstlichen Hügel hinaufführt, ähnlich. In Waschkut befindet sich der Kalvarienberg am Ende der

[62] Die Stationen sind: 1. Christus am Ölberg, 2. Geiselung, 3. Geiselung, 4. Christus trägt das Kreuz, 5.Christus wird an das Kreuz genagelt.

[63] In zahlreichen Gemeinden finden sich spätere Kalvarienberge mit symmetrischer Anlage, z.B. Bawarz (ung. Babarc), Gödre, Waschkut, Kislöd, Vöröstó, Kemend (ung. Máriakéménd), Boschok (ung. Palotabozsok) etc.

[64] Hier könnte wieder der Kalvarienberg in Hernals als Vorbild in Frage kommen, bei dem die Stationen ebenfalls nicht zur ansteigenden Treppe, sondern zur Eingangsseite gewandt waren. In Schemnitz und Klagenfurt ist dies ebenfalls der Fall.

breiten „Großgasse".[65] Durch ihren symmetrischen Aufbau unterscheiden sich diese Kalvarienberge deutlich von anderen Gebieten, in denen eher die einseitige Anordnung der Stationen üblich war.

Ummauerte Kalvarienberge und ein Gefängnis mit Kreuzigungsgruppe

Eine seltene Gruppe stellen die ummauerten Kalvarienberge dar, bei denen die Stationen in eine Mauer integriert sind, die einen geschlossenen Hof bildet, in dessen Zentrum die Kreuzigungsgruppe oder eine Kirche steht. In Sankt-Andrä erhebt sich inmitten eines ummauerten Ovals, das nur einen Zugang besitzt, eine erhöhte Terrasse, zu der eine geschwungene Treppe führt. Die Stationen sind an der den Hof umgebenden Mauer untergebracht. In Veľké Úľany (ung. Nagyfödémes) ist die Anlage fast kreisförmig umschlossen und läuft hinter der Kapelle spitz zu. In Sárvár bildet das Zentrum des 1784 entstandenen Kalvarienbergs eine mehrstufige Terrasse, auf der sich eine Kapelle erhebt, während die auf der Abschlussmauer aufsitzenden Stationen außen herum einen Kreis bilden. In Zalaegerszeg wurden die Stationen 1756 in die unregelmäßig verlaufende Friedhofsmauer integriert. In Deutschtewel (ung. Nagytevel) ist der Kreuzweg um die Kirche gruppiert. Diese steht auf einer rechteckigen, im hinteren Teil halboval abschließenden Terrasse, die rings ummauert ist. Entlang der seitlichen Umfassungsmauern sind links und rechts je sieben Stationen angebracht.

Eine selbständige Kreuzigungsgruppe sei noch besonders erwähnt. Den Eingang des Komitatsgefängnisses im Hof des Komitatshauses in Erlau (ung. Eger) rahmt, in die Fassade integriert, eine Kreuzigungsgruppe, bestehend aus dem zentralen Kreuz mit Christus über der Tür und den flankierenden Kreuzen. Die steinernen Kreuze und die drei aus grobem Putz angedeuteten Hügel kontrastieren mit dem gelben Feinputz der Fassade. Die Bauzeit wird von 1760 bis 1766 datiert.[66] Strittig ist der Name des Architekten: Franz Matthias Gerl[67] oder Josef Ignaz Gerl[68]. Der Name Gerl verweist auf eine Wiener Baumeisterfamilie dieses Namens.[69] In Wien befand sich auch das Vorbild für die ungewöhnliche Fassade. Die Frontseite des „Amtshauses der Malefizpersonen", wie das Gefängnisgebäude in der Unterschrift zu einem Stich Salomon Kleiners genannt wird, besaß eine den Eingang rahmende Kreuzigungsgruppe. Neben den drei Kreuzen waren dort noch Statuen von Maria Magdalena und Johannes aufgestellt. Das 1722 in der Rauhensteingasse nahe der Himmelpfortgasse errichtete Gebäude wurde bereits zur Regierungszeit Kaiser Josephs II. abgerissen.

[65] In Waschkut weist das Visitationsprotokoll von 1783 einen Kalvarienberg aus. 1831 wurde eine Kapelle gestiftet, 1831 die Stationen. FLACH, Paul: Waschkut. Beiträge zur Geschichte einer überwiegend deutschen Gemeinde in der Batschka/Ungarn. München 1983, 536-537.
[66] Heves Megye [Das Komitat Heves]. Budapest 2005, 49.
[67] EBD., 49.
[68] LENGYEL, László: Der Barock in Eger und im Komitat Heves. Veszprém 1992, 14.
[69] Allgemeines Lexikon der bildenden Künstler. Bd. 13. 1920, 468-469.

Bildprogramm

Es wurde in den Ausführungen deutlich, dass neben dem in Ungarn am häufigsten verbreiteten Typus mit 14 Stationen einzelne mit sieben Stationen existieren. Sieben Stationen besaß etwa der Kalvarienberg an der *Landstraß* in Ofen.[70] Weitere Beispiele sind die Kalvarienberge in Raab und Polan. Kalvarienberge mit sieben Stationen waren nach Kramer besonders im deutschsprachigen Raum vertreten und stellen eine für das 18. Jahrhundert eigentlich bereits altertümliche Form dar.[71] Dies ist für den Kalvarienberg in Raab der Fall. Noch augenfälliger wird dies beim Kalvarienberg in Polan, der erst um 1770 entstanden ist. Betrachtet man das Bildprogramm, wird deutlich, dass der Schwerpunkt der Darstellungen in den Fußfällen Christi liegt, was für Kalvarienberge mit sieben Stationen typisch ist. Bewusst hat man sich in Polan einer älteren Tradition verschrieben und sich über die inzwischen erfolgte Festlegung auf 14 Stationen hinweggesetzt. Ob dies wegen der topographischen Begebenheiten des steilen Bergs erfolgte oder mit dem Bauherrn, dem Zisterzienserkloster Sirtz (ung. Zirc) zusammenhängt, ist noch zu untersuchen.
Die bisherige Untersuchung hatte ihren Schwerpunkt in der Wegführung und der architektonischen Struktur der Kalvarienberge. Kurz soll jedoch noch auf die Bildwerke eingegangen werden. Die meisten ungarischen Kalvarienberge aus dem 18. Jahrhundert besitzen heute neuere Stationsbilder. Ursprünglich waren dies Gemälde oder Holzreliefs, also im Freien schwierig zu konservierende Objekte. In Frauenkirchen wurden die Stationsbilder als großformatige Steinreliefs ausgeführt. Eine Sonderstellung nehmen die Kalvarienberge mit großfigurigen vollplastischen Stationsszenen ein so zu finden in Eisenstadt, Raab, Pápa und Polan. Dort sind die Figuren in Holz ausgeführt. Gemeinsam ist ihnen die für das 18. Jahrhundert typische bewegte und teilweise drastische Darstellungsweise.
Die abschließende Kreuzigungsgruppe ist in der Regel in Stein ausgeführt. Zumeist ist das zentrale (und größere) Kreuz von den Kreuzen der Häscher flankiert. Direkt um das Kreuz Christi gruppieren sich Maria, Maria Magdalena und Johannes. Dabei lässt sich eine gewisse Gemeinsamkeit der Darstellungsweise beobachten. Neben der zeittypischen Bewegtheit der Figuren, scheinen Felsen andeutende Sockel der Kreuze sich großer Beliebtheit erfreut zu haben. Gelegentlich finden sich auch Holzkreuze. Eine Ausnahme bildet etwa Raab. Dort sind die drei Kreuze aus Holz mit naturalistisch bemalten, aber flachen Figuren versehen.

[70] Die Stationen waren: 1. Christus am Ölberg, 2. Vespottung, 3. Geißelung, 4. Dornenkrönung, 5. Zimmern des Kreuzes, 6. Ecce-Homo (Steinfigur), 7. Kreuzigung Christi, (8.) Kreuz Christi mit Maria, Maria Magdalena und Johannes. Greszl: Ofen-Buda, 60-61.
[71] KRAMER: Kreuzweg und Kalvarienberg, 20.

Die Auftraggeber

Auch für Ungarn lässt sich festhalten, dass die Franziskaner die Initiatoren zahlreicher Kalvarienberge waren. Im Zusammenhang mit Franziskanerklöstern errichtete Kalvarienberge sind z.B. in Maria Radna und in Frauenkirchen zu finden. Daneben gab es weitere Stiftungen von privater Hand. Die Familie Esterházy scheint sich dabei für den Bau von Kalvarienbergen besonders eingesetzt zu haben. Herausragendes Beispiel einer solchen Stiftung ist Eisenstadt. Der Zusammenhang mit dem Franziskanerorden, den Fürst Paul I. besonders förderte, wurde bereits deutlich. Hier ist auch noch das Kloster Frauenkirchen zu nennen, ebenfalls eine wichtige Esterházystiftung. Aber auch die gräfliche Linie Esterházy stand in enger Beziehung zur Anlage von Kalvarienbergen, darunter in Totis (ung. Tata) und Pápa. Weitere adlige Geldgeber waren die Grafen Széchenyi (z.B. Wandorf) und die Grafen Almássy (z.B. Szentkút bei Mátraverebély). Auch privaten Stiftungen aus bürgerlichen Kreisen ist die Entstehung zahlreicher Kalvarienberge zu verdanken. Es seien ein paar Beispiele angeführt: In Pest verwandte man die Geldmittel von Maria Anna Schwartz zur Errichtung einer ersten Anlage, die wir oben als *Kalvarienberg in der Josephstadt* kennengelernt haben. Allerdings basiert sie auf dem tragischen Lebensverlauf der Spenderin. Nachdem nämlich die wohlhabende Maria Anna Schwartz ihren Mann im Streit umgebracht hatte, büßte sie ihre Strafe im Paulinerkloster ab und stiftete einen neuen Kalvarienberg. Dieser wurde allerdings erst nach ihrem Tod gebaut.[72] 1715 stiftete ein Ofener Bürger die Kreuzigungsgruppe am Blocksberg, 1795 kamen durch den Raitzenstädter Bürger Michael Fühl die Kapelle und die Stationen hinzu, die nach seinem Tod von seinen Nachkommen erhalten wurden.[73] Auch der Kalvarienberg beim Kloster Kleinzell (ung. Kiscell) oberhalb von Altofen (ung. Óbuda, heute III. Budapester Bezirk) geht auf eine Privatinitiative zurück: Zwischen 1770 und 1780 stiftete der Müllermeister Anton Kühtreiber die Gruppe „Christus auf der Wiese". Sein Sohn Emmerich Kühtreiber schenkte diese 1810 der Kirche Neustift (ung. Budaújlak).[74] In all diesen Beispielen zeigt sich die breite Verankerung der Kalvarienberge im Bewusstsein der Gläubigen.

Der Zusammenhang zwischen religiösen Bruderschaften und der Errichtung von Kalvarienbergen wurde für Ungarn noch nicht eingehend untersucht. Es ist aber bemerkenswert, dass nach Tüskés und Knapp von 1304 nachgewiesenen Bruderschaften die weitaus größte Gruppe von 362 dem hl. Franziskus zuzuordnen ist.[75] Da in Deutschland solche Bruderschaften die Errichtung von Kalvarienbergen initiierten, kann dies sicherlich auch für Ungarn angenommen werden. Nachgewiesen ist in Ofen die Bruderschaft der *Todesangst Christi* (Agonia Christi) als Erbauer der Ka-

[72] RITOÓK: Epreskerti kálvária, 3.
[73] Nach dem Visitationsprotokoll von 1822. Greszl: Ofen-Buda, 70.
[74] 1812-14 wurde dann die Kapelle errichtet und 1822-22 die Stationen. – Budapest műemlékei 2, 330-331.
[75] TÜSKÉS/ KNAPP: Volksfrömmigkeit in Ungarn, 292.

pelle auf dem „Kalvarienbergl“ im Bezirk Landstraße.[76] Diese Bruderschaft wurde von den Jesuiten der Ofener Liebfrauenkirche (ung. Mátyástemplom) gefördert.[77] Auch für Raab ist eine von Josef Gastinger geleitete und von den Jesuiten betreute „Todesangst-Christi-Bruderschaft“ als Erbauer des Kalvarienbergs bekannt.[78] Eine ebenfalls von den Jesuiten geförderte Bruderschaft gleichen Namens ist in Gyöngyös 1721 als Initiatorin des Kalvarienbergs genannt.[79] Ab ca. 1640 entstanden „Todesangst-Christi-Bruderschaften“ in Ungarn. Tüskés und Knapp weisen 44 Bruderschaften nach, die überwiegend von Jesuiten betreut wurden.[80] Eine der wichtigen Aufgaben der „Todesangst-Christi-Bruderschaft“, die sich vor allem aus der erwachsenen Stadtbevölkerung rekrutierte, war die Meditation über die Passion Christi.[81] Insofern kann man annehmen, dass diese Bruderschaft auch an anderen Orten Kalvarienberge errichteten.

In Ungarn hat die Vorliebe für Kalvarienberge also auch andere Orden ergriffen, wie etwa die Jesuiten, die etwa die Kalvarienberge in Raab, Schemnitz und auf dem Ofener Blocksberg initiierten. Aber auch die Pauliner in Pápa und die Zisterzienser in Polan handelten so. Ob die starke Verbreitung der Kalvarienberge in Ungarn mit der Ansiedlung der deutschen Bevölkerung, die parallel erfolgt, zusammenhängt, wurde noch nicht untersucht. Im 18. Jahrhundert angesiedelte Deutsche könnten in ihren Heimatorten bereits die Errichtung einiger Anlagen erlebt haben. Außerdem könnten sie Mitglied einer Bruderschaft gewesen sein.[82] Gerade die für die Errichtung von Kalvarienbergen so wichtige „Todesangst-Christi-Bruderschaft“ scheint in den Städten besonders unter dem deutschsprachigen Bürgertum ihre Mitglieder gehabt zu haben. Insofern könnte das Bedürfnis nach einem Kalvarienberg über das deutschsprachige Bürgertum nach Ungarn gelangt sein. Ist wäre also zusamenfassend noch zu klären, ob es sich bei der Anlage von Kalvarienbergen um eine allgemeine Modeerscheinung handelte oder ob eventuell deutschstämmige Franziskaner oder andere Ordensleute die neue Strömung mitbrachten. Für das 19. Jahrhundert kann man aber auf jeden Fall feststellen, dass Kalvarienberge gerade in ungarndeutsch geprägten Gemeinden besonders häufig vorkamen.

Mehrere Kalvarienberge entstanden im Zusammenhang mit Wallfahrtsstätten. Als Beispiel sei Bodajk genannt. In Klein Mariazell entstand der Kalvarienberg im Zusammenspiel mit der Wallfahrtskirche Klein-Mariazell. Auch in Szentkút bei Mátraverebély wurde 1750 ein Kalvarienberg neben einer Wallfahrtskirche errichtet.

---

[76] Laut Visitationsakte der Pfarrei St. Stephan von 1822. GRESZL: Ofen-Buda, 60. – Einen Bezug zu den Franziskanern erhielt der Kalvarienberg erst 1785, als dieser das Augustinereremitenkloster und damit die Pfarrei St. Stephan übernahm.

[77] GRESZL: Ofen-Buda, 35.

[78] RÜDIGER: Nachbauten, 220f.

[79] SZILÁGYI: Kálváriák, 138.

[80] TÜSKÉS/ KNAPP: Volksfrömmigkeit in Ungarn, 292ff.

[81] EBD., 310.

[82] Die Zeit der Auswanderung fällt in etwa in die größte Blütezeit der Bruderschaften in Deutschland. Diese ist in Bayern nach dem Dreißigjährigen Krieg, in Österreich ab 1660 und in Franken zwischen 1720 und 1740. In Ungarn ist die Blütezeit zwischen 1720 und 1770. 1788 erfolgte die Aufhebung der Bruderschaften unter Joseph II. TÜSKÉS/ KNAPP: Volksfrömmigkeit in Ungarn, 320.

Frauenkirchen und Maria Radna sind weitere Beispiele. In Eisenstadt umgibt der Kalvarienberg selbst die Gnadenkapelle und ist so Teil der Wallfahrtsstätte. Auch in Schemnitz war der Heilige Berg selbst Ziel der Wallfahrt. Man kann sogar sagen, dass heute zu jeder Wallfahrtsstätte in Ungarn ein Kalvarienberg gehört. Ob dies bereits im 18. Jahrhundert der Fall war, wäre noch zu prüfen.
Im Unterschied zu Deutschland flachte die Neuanlage von Kalvarienbergen im 19. Jahrhundert nicht ab. Ganz im Gegenteil wurden besonders in ungbarndeutsch geprägten Gemeinden zahlreiche neue Anlagen errichtet. Dabei erfreuten sich besonders Kalvarienberge mit symmetrisch angeordneten Stationen (ein ansonsten für dörfliche Anlagen eher seltener Typ) großer Beliebtheit.

Abbildungen

Abb. 1: Kalvarienberg in Eisenstadt

Abb. 2: Kalvarienberg in Eisenstadt

Abb. 3: Kalvarienberg in Magyarpolány - Gesamtansicht

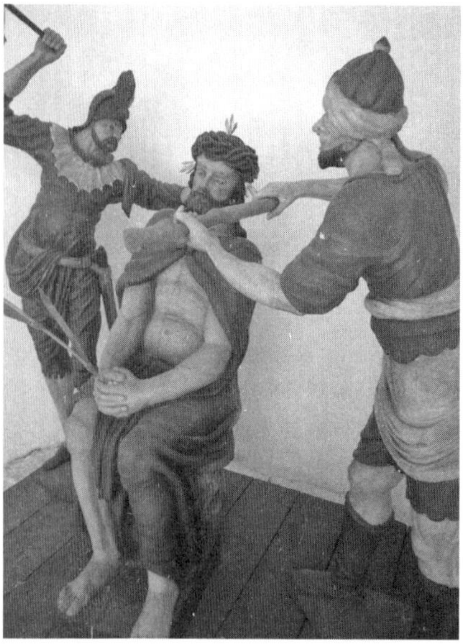

Abb. 4: Skulpturengruppe in Magyarpolány

Abb. 5: Skulpturengruppe in Magyarpolány

Abb. 6: Kapelle und Kreuzigungsgruppe auf dem Kalvarienberg in Güns (Köszeg)

Abb. 7: Kalvarienberg in Frauenkirchen im Burgenland

Swantje Volkmann

Kirchenbau im Banat des 18. Jahrhunderts als Erziehungsstätten des Staates

Die historische Region Banat wurde in besonderer Weise durch die politischen und kulturellen Entscheidungen des 18. Jahrhunderts bestimmt. Innerhalb der Eroberungen des 18. Jahrhunderts, mit dem das Haus Habsburg die größte Gebietsausdehnung seiner Geschichte erreichte, bildete die Region durch die Erhebung zur Kron- und Kammerdomäne, die direkte Unterstellung aller Eigentums- und Rechtsverhältnisse unter den Kaiser, eine Ausnahme in der Vielvölkermonarchie. Grundlegende Voraussetzung für die neuzeitliche Kulturlandschaftsgestaltung des Banats im 18. Jahrhundert war die in den Ideen der Aufklärung und des Absolutismus begründete Überzeugung einer umfassenden Planbarkeit der gesamten materiellen und ideellen Bereiche der Gesellschaft. Die aus diesen Überzeugungen entwickelten Zielvorstellungen betrafen den Willen zur Neuordnung der eroberten Region und die Entwicklung des Gebietes zu einem politischen und militärischen Machtfaktor. In den einzelnen Bereichen wurden spezifische Zielvorstellungen entwickelt, die bezüglich der neuzeitlichen Raumgestaltung und der Bauproduktion eine nahezu ausschließliche Planung und Lenkung realisierte.

Das Tschanader Bistum wurde um 1030 durch König Stefan den Heiligen gegründet. In der ersten Hälfte des 14. Jahrhunderts umfasste es bereits 228 organisierte Pfarreien und 24 Klöster. Mit der osmanischen Eroberung im Jahr 1552 wurde es weitgehend zerstört, und die Diözese existierte fortan nur noch als Titularbistum.[1] Mit der Rückeroberung des Gebietes durch die kaiserlichen Truppen 1716 wurden die Osmanen auch aus dem Kerngebiet der Diözese vertrieben. Als das Banat 1718 der Wiener Hofkammer unterstellt wurde, endete für das Gebiet südlich der Marosch die bis dahin allen ungarischen Diözesen gemeinsame Verwaltung. Zugleich begann eine neue Religionspolitik der Habsburger: Während die Religionspolitik des 17. Jahrhunderts vor allem durch eine indirekte Einflussnahme über die katholische Missionsarbeit gekennzeichnet war, konnten nun – bedingt durch die neue verfassungsrechtliche Stellung des Banats – weitaus zielgerichteter die religionspolitischen

[1] Vgl. NISCHBACH, Josef: Kirchengeschichte. In: Handwörterbuch des Grenz- und Auslandsdeutschtums. Bd. 1. Hg. v. Carl PETERSON. Breslau 1933, 253-261, hier 253f. – DIPLICH, Hans: Die Domkirche in Temeswar. Ein Beitrag zu ihrer Baugeschichte. München 1972, 33-36. – SPONNER, Waltraut: Kirchenpolitik im Banat von 1717-1778. Wien 1941, 3-5. – JUHÁSZ, Coloman: Das Tschanad-Temesvarer Bistum während der Türkenherrschaft 1552-1699. Dülmen 1938, 1-42. – JUHÁSZ, Coloman: Das Tschanad-Temesvarer Bistum im frühen Mittelalter 1030-1307. Münster 1930, 35, 49, 57 und 62f. – ROOS, Martin: Maria-Radna. Ein Wallfahrtsort im Südosten Europas. Bd. 1. Regensburg 1998, 22.

Interessen des Hauses durchgesetzt werden.[2] Der Wiederaufbau des kirchlichen Lebens im Banat vollzog sich ebenso zielbewusst wie die gesamte Neuorganisation und Einrichtung des Landes. Bereits 1734 gab es neunundzwanzig Pfarreien, die, wie fast alle im 18. Jahrhundert eingerichteten Pfarreien, meist infolge der Neubesiedlung des Landes entstanden.[3] Da zunächst der Südteil des Landes besiedelt wurde, entstanden hier auch die ersten Pfarreien, die von Ordenspriestern wie Franziskaner-Observanten, Franziskaner-Konventualen, Jesuiten und von weltlichen Pfarrern betreut wurden.[4] Den Festlegungen des kaiserlichen Diploms aus dem Jahre 1723 entsprechend standen die Pfarrer in strenger Abhängigkeit zu den administrativen Stellen. Sie durften erst nach der „von Hof einhollender genehmhaltung“ in ihr Amt eingesetzt werden.[5] Außerdem hatte allein der Kaiser das Recht, „Pfarrer und anderer geistliche *beneficia successive* in dem Banat“ zu errichten.[6] Darüber hinaus erfolgte die Besoldung des gesamten Klerus – vom Bischof bis zum Landpfarrer – durch das Ärar.[7] Die unmittelbare Abhängigkeit des gesamten Banater Klerus von den administrativen Behörden der Monarchie sicherte eine strenge Kirchendisziplin, die vor allem in theresianischer Zeit als entscheidende Grundlage für die Weiterentwicklung des Landes und angesehen wurde.[8] Die Banater Kirchen sollten als Erziehungsstätten des Staates fungieren.

Die Ziele der habsburgischen Kirchenpolitik im Banat waren erstens, die hier vertretenen Religionsgemeinschaften der Monarchie gegenüber in ein enges Abhängigkeitsverhältnis zu bringen und zweitens das Banat zu einem katholischen Land zu entwickeln.[9] In diesem neu erworbenen Gebiet schien es vorteilhaft die kirchliche Ordnung völlig neu aufzubauen. Somit sollte auch die Abhängigkeit des Klerus effizienter als in den österreichischen Erbländern erreicht werden. Hinzu kam, dass der Kaiser im Banat bis 1778 alleiniger Patronatsherr war und daher keine fürstlichen Zwischengewalten berücksichtigen musste. So waren die katholischen Geistlichen im Banat von Beginn an besoldete Beamte. Das hing einerseits mit der besonderen Struktur des erst neu zu besiedelnden Landes zusammen, in der die Bewohner der neugegründeten Orte und die Kolonisten meist nicht in der Lage waren, ihr kirchliches Leben selbst zu finanzieren, andererseits verhinderte aber der absolutistische

[2] Vgl. MERDZANOV, Ivan: Die Habsburgermonarchie und die katholischen Missionen in den bulgarischen Landen im 18. und 19. Jahrhundert. In: Bulgarian Historical Review 22 (1994), 31-60.
[3] SPONNER: Kirchenpolitik im Banat, 46.
[4] KALLBRUNNER, Josef: Das kaiserliche Banat. Einrichtung und Entwicklung des Banats bis 1739. München 1958, 75. – Teilweise waren die Pfarrer mit den Kolonisten ins Banat gekommen. Vgl. DIPLICH: Die Domkirche, 139. – WOLF, Josef: Die Ordenslandschaft des Banats im 18. Jahrhundert. Quellen. Regensburg 1996.
[5] Hofkammerarchiv Wien (fortan HKA). B. A. r. Nr. 138. Fol. 247-251/7. 7. August 1723.
[6] EBD.
[7] SPONNER: Kirchenpolitik im Banat, 40.
[8] EBD., 49-52. – FREIHOFFER, Heinrich: Geschichte der evangelischen Kirche im Banat. In: Das Banat und die Banater Schwaben. Kirchen. Kirchliche Einrichtungen – Kirchliches Leben. Bd. 1. Hg. v. Landsmannschaft der Banater Schwaben aus Rumänien in Deutschland e.V. München 1981, 23-26, hier 24f.
[9] Die Protestanten, die ins Banat einwanderten, wurden bis 1780 immer wieder nach Siebenbürgen abgeschoben. Die Juden waren ausschließlich in Temeswar geduldet.

Staat so erfolgreich eine Beteiligung der Kirche am wirtschaftlichen Aufbauprozess.[10]

Gegenreformation und Kirchenbau

Die Basis der österreichischen Kirche im Barockzeitalter, die bis heute die Landschaft prägt und künstlerisch dominiert, stammt aus dem hohen und späten Mittelalter. Dies betrifft in erster Linie die kirchliche Territorialstruktur, die Funktion des Landesfürsten als Princeps in *ecclesia* sowie die theologischen Doktrinen und Eigenarten des religiösen Lebens im 17. und 18. Jahrhundert.[11] Für das Banat sind diese Determinanten gleichfalls zutreffend, allerdings mit der entscheidenden Einschränkung, dass hier – wegen des Verlustes der mittelalterlichen Organisation – die Strukturen neu geschaffen werden mussten. Dies gilt sowohl für die kirchliche Organisation als auch für die künstlerische Ausprägung architektonischer Formen im Bereich der sakralen Bautätigkeit. Dass der Aufbau der neuen Strukturen von der Auseinandersetzung mit der calvinistisch-reformierten Religion Ungarns, der lutherischen Reformation Siebenbürgens und dem Islam des Osmanischen Reiches gekennzeichnet war, wurde zu einem der wichtigsten Merkmale der Gestaltung. Unter diesen Bedingungen entstanden Bauwerke, die sehr deutlich einen direkten Bezug zu früherer beziehungsweise gleichzeitiger Bautätigkeit in den österreichischen Erblanden hatten.

Für die entwicklungsgeschichtliche Darstellung der kirchlichen Bautätigkeit im Banat sind vor allem die Bereiche der Enkomiastik oder Panegyrik sowie die verwaltungstechnischen Grundlagen bedeutsam. Die zeitgenössische panegyrische Literatur ist aufschlussreich für die Intention der vom kaiserlichen Hof initiierten Bautätigkeit in der neuen Provinz. Die verwaltungstechnischen Grundlagen vermitteln die Funktionalität des praktischen Baubetriebs sowie die Verantwortlichkeiten der jeweiligen Hofstelle und der ihr untergeordneten Künstler. Vor allem der letztgenannte Bereich hatte einen erheblichen Einfluss auf die Entstehung formaler Strukturen und künstlerischer Formen.

Mit Ausnahme der Reiterstandbilder verzichteten die Habsburger in der Regel auf dauerhafte Denkmäler der eigenen Person. Ihre Denkmäler waren anderer Art. Kunst- und Bauwerke, die in der Regierungszeit Kaiser Karls VI. auf dessen unmittelbare Veranlassung entstanden, sollten die Vorzüge des Herrschers und seine Leistungen in der Öffentlichkeit repräsentieren. Diese Herrschertugenden und deren Ausübung wurden in manifester Weise vor allem an Bauwerken demonstriert.[12] In

[10] LEBER, Reinhard: Politische Kultur und Systemtransformation in Rumänien. Lokalstudie zu der Stadt Temeswar. Frankfurt/Main u.a. 1996, 46f.

[11] KOVÁCS, Elisabeth: Die österreichische Kirche im Zeitalter des Barock. In: Welt des Barock. Bd. 2. Hg. v. Rupert FEUCHTMÜLLER und Elisabeth Kovács. Wien-Basel-Freiburg 1986, 123-140, hier 140.

[12] EHALT, Hubert Ch.: Schloss- und Palastarchitektur im Absolutismus. In: Architektur und Gesellschaft von der Antike bis zur Gegenwart. Hg. v. Hannes STEKL. Salzburg 1980, 161-249, hier 222-229. – MATSCHE, Franz: Die Kunst im Dienst der Staatsidee Kaiser Karls VI. Bd. 1. Berlin 1981, 22 und 62.

diesem Sinn stellte der Jesuit Antonius Höller in seinem Traktat 1733 die realpolitischen und künstlerischen Unternehmungen Karls VI. als Auswirkungen seiner Tugenden dar. Der Traktat gibt damit die Auffassung über die Programmatik der Kunstunternehmungen des Kaiserhofes authentisch wieder. Auch die Betonung der sakralen Bautätigkeit ist wegen der erstrebten Wirkung zielbestimmt. Hintergrund dieser ist die integrierende Wirkung der gemeinsamen Konfession. Die Hierarchie durchziehend besteht ein Integrationszusammenhang zwischen Monarch und Untertan in der Religion, wobei Frömmigkeit und Gottesfurcht sowohl beim Herrscher als auch bei den Untertanen den gesellschaftlich beherrschenden Faktor bilden. Dabei war das Verhältnis der Habsburger zur Kunst einem spezifischen Grundzug der gegenreformatorischen Literatur verpflichtet, in der die zur Frömmigkeit anregende Funktion der Kunst eine beherrschende Rolle spielte, die schließlich auch zur primären Förderung der kirchlichen Bauwerke führte. Diese sollten zwar *ad majorem Dei gloriam* dienen, brachten aber zugleich die wichtigste Herrschertugend, die Frömmigkeit, zur Geltung. Hier wird eine typisch habsburgische Art der Denkmalsetzung deutlich, die in der Verbindung des Ruhmes Gottes mit dem Herrscherlob gipfelte.[13] Dieser Aspekt beeinflusste die Bautätigkeit mit dem Ziel, die Einheit des Glaubens in den Ländern der Monarchie wiederherzustellen bzw. in den neuen Provinzen erneut zu etablieren.[14]

Vor dem Hintergrund der militärischen und politischen Erfolge gegenüber Frankreich und dem Osmanischen Reich erhielt die Durchsetzung der Interessen als katholische Großmacht in den eroberten Provinzen eine neue Qualität. Dementsprechend wurde die sakrale Bautätigkeit besonders gefördert, die zugleich die wichtigste Herrschertugend – die Frömmigkeit -- zur Geltung brachte. Diese besondere Beziehung zwischen Tugendkanon der habsburgischen Dynastie, realpolitischen Ereignissen und Kunstunternehmen des Hauses wird in der zeitgenössischen Literatur besonders betont.[15] So schrieb Küchelbecker 1730: „Ehemal waren die Lutheraner und Reformierten im Reiche die stärcksten, nachdem es aber denen Türcken entrissen wurden, führete man daselbst überall die Römisch=Catholische Religion ein."[16] Neben dem besonderen Stellenwert der neuen Provinzen formulierte auch Höller sehr deutlich den Zusammenhang zwischen sakraler Bautätigkeit, christlicher Religionsfürsorge und öffentlicher Wohlfahrt. Diese Aspekte stehen im Mittelpunkt des ersten Kapitels in Höllers Traktat. Bezeichnenderweise beginnt der Jesuit mit einem Lob auf die Taten des Kaisers für die Religion und besonders seine diesbezügliche Fürsorge für den katholischen Kult in Ungarn, vor allem in den neu eroberten Gebieten. Dabei leuchte die überaus gottesfürchtige Frömmigkeit des Kaisers im Komitat Temeswar

[13] EBD., 65-66.

[14] EBD., 64. – RASSEM, Mohammed H.: Gesellschaft und bildende Kunst. Eine Studie zur Wiederbelebung des Problems. Berlin 1960, 43, 47.

[15] Dabei ist zu berücksichtigen, dass im Gegensatz zu anderen Herrscherhäusern in den „österreichischen" Kunstwerken nicht die Person des Herrschers, sondern seine Tugenden, deren ausgewählter Vertreter der Herrscher ist, verherrlicht wurden. Vgl. MATSCHE, Franz: Kunst Karls VI.

[16] KÜCHELBECKER, Johann Basilius: Allerrneueste Nachricht vom Römisch-Kayserl. Hofe. Nebst einer ausführlichen historischen Beschreibung der Kayserlichen Residentz-Stadt Wien und der umliegenden Oerter. Hannover 1730, 62. – Unter „Reich" verstand Küchelbecker das Königreich Ungarn.

am meisten hervor. Neben einer allgemeinen Beschreibung der kirchlichen Organisation ist an Höllers Traktat vor allem bemerkenswert, dass er detailliert die bereits bis um 1730 errichteten Kirchen im Banat aufführt.[17]
Nach der Bestellung einer Kameraleinrichtungskommission für das Banat erging an diese am 7. Oktober 1717 eine erste Instruktion seitens der Hofkammer. Dabei wurde auch die Notwendigkeit der Bereitstellung von Gotteshäusern zur Ausübung der Seelsorge betont. Die Verfasser schlugen vor, die vorhandenen Moscheen für den römisch-katholischen Ritus zu nutzen. „Die sowohl in der Statt und Vestung als in denen Vorstätten disen beederley Missionarien einraumende Moscheen vor nichts als lahre Mauren anzusehen, und wann sie christliche Kirchen seyn und zum üblichen Gottesdienst dienen sollen, erst darzu zuzurichten und auszurüsten seyn, also dass auf Glokhen, Uhren, Sacristeyen, Predigtstühle, Taufstein, Altäre, Tabernakel und ihre Ausstaffirung mit allem Geräthe, so zur Celebrirung der Sacramente und Verkündigung des Worth Gottes erforderlich ist, gedacht werden muss."[18] (Abb. 1)
Bereits in den ersten Ausführungen zum Aussehen der Banater Kirchen wurde vor allem darauf hingewiesen, dass bei deren Bau und Ausstattung nach dem Willen des Kaisers die größte Sparsamkeit walte, „damit weder auf Pracht noch Überfluß, sondern nur auf die ohnentpährliche und decente Notturft angetragen" werde.[19]
Darüber hinaus sollten die Kommissare einen Vorschlag einreichen, wie die finanzielle Dotierung zur Erhaltung der Kirchengebäude („*fabrica ecclesiae*") einzurichten sei. Laut dieser Instruktion sollten auch den Unierten Gotteshäuser, vorzugsweise ehemalige Moscheen, zur Verfügung gestellt werden. Die notwendigen Mittel dafür sollten aber nicht vom Ärar, sondern von der Bevölkerung erbracht werden, weil diese schon „lange genug" im Land seien und „über Vermögen verfügten". Allerdings wurden Bauholz und Robotleistungen vom Ärar in Aussicht gestellt, allerdings nur „was ohne Auslage paaren Gelts geschehen kann".[20] Eines der zentralen Dokumente für den Kirchenbau war eine Verordnung Kaiser Karls VI. aus dem Jahr 1731, worin er sich verpflichtete, zusätzlich zu seinen Patronatsrechten auch die Lasten, die aus der Dotierung von Pfarreien sowie der Erbauung neuer Kirchen entstanden, zu übernehmen.[21] Diese Verpflichtung hatte weit reichende Folgen für den Kirchenbau in der Region.
Während man noch 1717-1718 von einer strikten Trennung zwischen kameralem und militärischem Bauwesen ausgegangen war, etablierte sich das kamerale Bauwesen schon in den zwanziger Jahren als Bestandteil des Fortifikationsbauwesens. Nach dem Bericht des Gouverneurs Graf Hamilton, der 1734 als kommandierender General und Landespräsident der Banater Administration die Nachfolge des Grafen

[17] Damit ist Höllers Traktat eines der wenigen Dokumente, die sich in einer derart detaillierten Art und Weise mit den baupolitischen und -praktischen Ereignissen im Banat auseinandersetzt. HÖLLER, Antonius: Augusta Carolinae virtutis monumenta seu aedificia a Carolo VI. [...]. Wien 1733, 11-27.
[18] HKA. Wien. B. A. r. Nr. 1. Fol. 158-217. 7. Oktober 1717.
[19] EBD.
[20] EBD.
[21] JUHASZ, Coloman: Nikolaus Stanislavich O. F. M., Bischof von Csanád. In: Franciscanum Historicum 52 (1959), 427-470, hier 438.

Mercy antrat[22], hatte es zwar zu Beginn einen Kameral-Bauschreiber gegeben, „welcher aber vermuthlich der Ursachen halber vor einigen Jahren in Abgang kommen, weiln deßen zu verrechnen gehabter Cameral-Bau Fundus fast iederzeit zu den Fortificationali genommen worden ist".[23] Aus dem Bericht geht auch hervor, dass es zwar eine Kameral-Baukasse gab, die jährlich mit 40.700 Gulden dotiert war, der Fundus aber in keinem Jahr für die Errichtung von Kameral-Gebäuden ausgenutzt und daher das Geld der Fortifikations-Kasse übergeben wurde.[24] Der Kirchenbau bleibt in Hamiltons Bericht unerwähnt. Er verweist lediglich darauf, dass die Administration als auch eine in „Politicis angestelte Landes Obrigkeit auf das Punctum Religionis ein obdachtsames Auge" haben müsse.[25] Darüber hinaus wird lediglich die Einrichtung von Schulen in den schon bestehenden katholischen Orten des Banats angemahnt sowie die Unterstützung der Jesuiten, die die Einrichtung einer Schule in Temeswar planten, in Aussicht gestellt.[26] Auch nach 1740 wurden die Kosten für den Stadtkirchenbau wie für alle öffentlichen Gebäude gänzlich vom Ärar übernommen. Dabei wurde aber für die Stadt- und Ordenskirchen in der Regel ein erheblich umfangreicherer Fond veranschlagt als für die dörflichen Bauaufgaben.[27] Nach 1718 konnte sich in engem Zusammenhang mit der neuzeitlichen Kulturlandschaftsgestaltung im Banat eine neue Hochblüte religiösen und kulturellen Lebens entwickeln.[28]

Fester Bestandteil österreichischer Barockfrömmigkeit war die Verehrung der Eucharistie, die Verehrung des Kreuzes sowie die Marien- und Heiligenverehrung.[29] (Abb. 2) Neben dem Besuch der Messe waren Prozessionen und Wallfahrten das Herzstück dieser neuen Frömmigkeit. Die Sakramentsprozession an Fronleichnam bildete den Höhepunkt eucharistischer Frömmigkeit. Darüber hinaus fand die wachsende Marienverehrung, die zunehmend in den Vordergrund trat, ihren Ausdruck in zahlreichen Marienheiligtümern. Dabei waren nicht nur Denkmäler sondern vor allem die Wallfahrtskirchen und Klöster Ziel von Prozessionen und Wallfahrten.

Dabei ist aber zu beachten, dass Prozessionen und Wallfahrten zwar innerhalb der Barockfrömmigkeit einen neuen Aufschwung erlebten, der Höhepunkt aber zu dem Zeitpunkt, als die Wallfahrt nach Maria-Radna im Komitata Arad begann, bereits überschritten war. Wallfahrten und Prozessionen wurden nämlich von Maria Theresia und Joseph II. deutlich zurückgedrängt. Noch bei Kaiser Karl VI. war das Erbe der *Pietas Mariana* wie die Eucharistie- und Immaculataverehrung ungebrochen erhalten. Während der Regierungszeit Maria Theresias (1740-1780), deren Muttergottes-Verehrung vor allem einen persönlichen Bezug hatte, klang jedoch diese Tradi-

---

[22] PETRI, Anton Peter: Biographisches Lexikon des Banater Deutschtums. Marquartstein 1992, Sp. 635.

[23] HKA. Wien. Hs. 424. Choreographia Bannatus Temesiensis sub auspiciis novi gubernatoris edita. 1734. Fol. 65, 66.

[24] EBD., Fol. 65.

[25] EBD., Fol. 84, 85.

[26] EBD., Fol. 86, 87.

[27] EBD., B. A. Fasz. r. Nr. 19. (Dezember 1740).

[28] Vgl. HANTSCH, Hugo: Der geistige Gehalt der Barockzeit. In: Christliche Kunstblätter 97 (1959), 1-5.

[29] ROMBACH, Heinrich: Die Welt des Barock. Versuch einer Strukturanalyse. In: Welt des Barock. Hg. v. Rupert FEUCHTMÜLLER und Elisabeth KOVÁCS. Wien 1986, 9-23 hier 11.

tion aus, auch wenn etwa die Wallfahrten nach Mariazell beliebt waren. Doch Maria Theresia verehrte in Maria vor allem die Gnadenmutter und Schutzfrau.[30] Dass die Sicht Marias als Herrscherin, Königin und Siegerin, wie sie vor allem seit der Gegenreformation verehrt wurde, dabei verblasste, ist nicht auf die Person Maria Theresias zu reduzieren. Hier besteht ein enger Zusammenhang zu einer neuen Auffassung des Herrschertums. Das Übernatürliche wurde zwar weiter um Hilfe angesucht, es war aber nicht mehr die ausschließliche Basis der Herrschaft. In der vom Sinn für das Praktische geprägten Religiosität der Königin bedeutete dies eine Betonung des Wesentlichen, die entscheidenden Einfluss auf die Reform des Gottesdienstes hatte. Bereits Lodovico Antonio Muratori, dessen Einfluss auf die josephinische Reform des Gottesdienstes von Eleonore Zlabinger nachgewiesen wurde[31], verwies dezidiert darauf, dass die Marienverehrung zwar ihre Existenzberechtigung hatte, diese aber „im Sinne der Kirche“ und ohne „Übertreibungen und Auswüchse“ praktiziert werden sollte. Scharfe Kritik übte Muratori auch an der hohen Zahl von Prozessionen, deren äußeres Gepränge doch „nur der Befriedigung der Schaulust“, keineswegs aber der „wahren Frömmigkeit“ diene.[32]
Aus dieser Gesinnung heraus ergingen schon in den sechziger Jahren des 18. Jahrhunderts die ersten Anweisungen zur Regelung der Prozessionen und schließlich zur Gestalt der Kirchenbauten. Der bereits in der Auffassung Maria Theresias angedeutete und bei Joseph II. endgültig zutage tretende veränderte religiöse Standpunkt äußerte sich darin, dass er sich als absolutistischer Herrscher einzig und allein Gott verantwortlich fühlte. Dabei anerkannte er aber nicht wie seine Vorfahren sein Herrschertum als ein von Gott geschenktes Amt. Seine Religiosität bezeichnete Hollerweger als aufgeklärt in der Art eines „gereinigten“ Glaubens.[33] Begründet wurde die Neuordnung damit, dass die katholische Religion wieder zu ihren Ursprüngen zurückgeführt werden müsse, um dem Vorwurf vor allem von protestantischer Seite zu begegnen, dass wegen der übertriebenen Anwendung des unschicklichen Gepränges die Frömmigkeit nur auf äußerliche Zeichen, nicht aber auf innere Andacht gegründet sei. Mit der Reform wurde in umfassender Weise die Gestalt des Gottesdienstes verändert. Darüber hinaus führte sie auch zu erheblichen Einschränkungen der Wall-

---

[30] Vgl. CORETH, Anna: Pietas Austriaca. Österreichische Frömmigkeit im Barock. München 1982, 45, 62 und 69.
[31] Vgl. ZLABINGER, Eleonore: Lodovico Antonio Muratori und Österreich. Innsbruck 1970.
[32] MURATORI, Lodovico Antonio: Die wahre Andacht des Christen. Wien, Prag, Triest 1760, 230-245. – Die Sinnenfreude und Schaulust des barocken Menschen, die sich auch in den ausgesprochen zahlreichen Wallfahrten und Prozessionen äußerte, erlebte schon durch die beginnenden Reformen Maria Theresias entscheidende Einschränkungen. Auch hier war die persönliche Auffassung der Königin hinsichtlich dieses Bereiches liturgischer Übungen wohl von maßgebender Bedeutung. Auf die Bitte eines Offiziers, der um die Genehmigung einer Romfahrt ersuchte, schrieb sie: „Ich halte nichts auf die Kirchfahrten, Gott ist überall“. Vgl. WALTER, Friedrich: Die religiöse Stellung Maria Theresias. In: Theologisch-praktische Quartalschrift 105 (1937), 34-47, hier 42.
[33] CORETH: Pieta, 87. – Joseph II. sah in der Reform der Kirche die wichtigste Herrscheraufgabe überhaupt, sie ist der eigentliche Inbegriff der als Josephinismus in Österreich definierten Reformbestrebungen, die nahezu alle staatlichen, gesellschaftlichen und kulturellen Bereiche umfasste. Ein zentraler Bestandteil der Kirchenreform war die Neustrukturierung der gottesdienstlichen Ordnung. Diese hatte neben den unmittelbaren Auswirkungen auf die Liturgie auch entscheidenden Einfluss auf Formen der Frömmigkeit sowie auf die architektonische Gestalt der Gotteshäuser.

fahrten und Prozessionen. Es ist beachtlich, dass im Banat dennoch eine Tradition der Wallfahrt entstehen konnte und Wallfahrtskirchen errichtet wurden. Allerdings bleibt zu berücksichtigen, dass es sich bei den beiden hier diskutierten Wallfahrtskirchen auch um eine Kloster- beziehungsweise Pfarrkirche handelte.

Der Banater Behördenapparat und die Bauproduktion

Ziel des Kaiserhofes war der Auf- und Ausbau einer wirtschaftlich leistungsfähigen Region, die innerhalb der Monarchie im Sinne des Merkantilismus Autarkie erreichen sollte. Diese wirtschaftliche Autarkie war eine Grundvoraussetzung für das zweite Charakteristikum der Region, die aufgrund ihrer geopolitischen Lage einen bedeutenden militärischen Stellenwert gegenüber dem Osmanischen Reich aber auch gegenüber Siebenbürgen und dem Königreich Ungarn besaß. Die konfessionelle Bindung der Nachbargebiete des Banats – das kalvinistisch geprägte Ostungarn, das deutlich lutherisch geprägte Fürstentum Siebenbürgen und der Islam des Osmanischen Reiches – führten schließlich auch zu dem Grundsatz, hier prinzipiell nur katholische Untertanen anzusiedeln. Folge dieser Forderung war, dass sich das Banat – bis 1782 – zunächst als vorwiegend katholisch geprägte Region präsentierte. Diese Prägung beeinflusste wiederum die Bauproduktion in hohem Maße. Voraussetzung war eine „kostengünstige“ Ansiedlung von Immigranten. Ein weiterer wichtiger Faktor für die neuzeitliche Kulturlandschaftsgestaltung war, dass das Banat mit seiner Erhebung zur Kron- und Kammerdomäne innerhalb der Länder der Habsburger Monarchie über eine verfassungsrechtliche Sonderstellung verfügte. Die direkte Abhängigkeit von Wien und die daraus resultierende Weisungsgebundenheit der Länderstellen gegenüber den Behörden des Hofes führten im Bereich des Auf- und Ausbaus des Landes zu einer umfassenden Einflussnahme administrativer Funktionsmechanismen.[34] (Abb. 6) Analog zur Einrichtung der staatlichen Verwaltung des Landes erfolgte der Aufbau eines Behördenapparates. Zu den wichtigsten Kriterien dieses Behördenapparates wurden die dekretierte Abhängigkeit von den Wiener Zentralstellen sowie die umfassende Einflussnahme der militärischen Behörden des Landes. Die in den Instruktionen festgelegte Trennung zwischen militärischem und zivilem Bauwesen konnte allerdings in der Praxis nicht durchgesetzt werden. Das Bauamt blieb zunächst dem Generalkommando in Temeswar unterstellt und zivile Bauangelegenheiten unterstanden ebenso der Einflussnahme des Hofkriegsrates wie der Hofkammer.[35]

[34] Österreichisches Staatsarchiv, Hofkammerarchiv Wien. Hoffinanz Ungarn. r. Nr. 499. Fol. 213-214. (30. Dezember 1716). – TAFFERNER, Anton: Quellenbuch zur Donauschwäbischen Geschichte. Stuttgart 1978 (Bd. 3), 131. – Feldzüge des Prinzen Eugen von Savoyen. Hg. v. Kriegsgeschichtliche Abteilung des k. und k. Kriegsarchivs. Bd. XVII. Wien 1891, 70.

[35] Beispiele wie der Kirchenbau des Ordens der Barmherzigen Brüder beweisen, dass dieser administrative Funktionsmechanismus auch die Baugestalt erheblich beeinflusste. Vgl. MRAZ, Henrike: Die Einrichtung der kaiserlichen Verwaltung im Banat von Temeswar. Diss. masch. Wien 1984. – KALLBRUNNER: Das kaiserliche Banat.

Die zentralistische Organisation des Banater Behördenapparates – hier vor allem des Bauamtes der Landesadministration – ermöglichte von Beginn an eine umfassende Einflussnahme auf das gesamte Baugeschehen der Provinz. Das Banater Bauamt wurde so zu einem Garanten für die neuzeitliche Kulturlandschaftsgestaltung nach den Intentionen des Wiener Hofes. (Abb. 3) Während jene Zielvorstellungen, die die bebaute Umwelt betrafen, relativ problemlos in die Praxis umgesetzt werden konnten, erwiesen sich die sozio-kulturellen Determinanten als entscheidende Begrenzungsfaktoren. Der Anspruch auf alle Lebensbereiche planend Einfluss nehmen zu können, ließ sich nicht im gewünschten Umfang verwirklichen.[36]

Stadt- und Ordenskirchen im Banat. Planung und Baupraxis

Der administrative Funktionsmechanismus und die stilkritische Analyse der bauhistorischen Zeugnisse verdeutlichen, dass die Banater kirchliche Architektur von zwei wesentlichen Gegensätzen geprägt wurde: Einerseits erfolgte die bewusste Errichtung einer Vielzahl von Kirchenbauten und kirchlichen Anlagen mit dem Ziel der gegenreformatorischen Erneuerung, andererseits zeigt die formale Anlage der Bauten eine administrativ geforderte Säkularisierung, die die Funktionalität des Baues in den Vordergrund treten ließ. Im Unterschied zu den Landkirchenbauten ist für die Stadt- und Ordenskirchen im Banat innerhalb des Baugeschehens der Provinz eine Primärstellung nachzuweisen, die sich aus der Konzentration der Bautätigkeit auf Festungen und Siedlungen mit städtischem Charakter ergab. Bereits bei den ersten Bauten zeigte sich aber, dass ein akribischer Verwaltungsweg eingehalten werden musste, um den Bau einer Kirche zu realisieren. Dabei blieb bedeutungslos, ob es sich um eine Ordenskirche oder eine städtische Pfarrkirche handelte.
Beispielhaft für diese Vorgehensweise ist die Baugeschichte der Jesuitenkirche in Temeswar. Der im Sommer 1717 ins Banat berufenen *Societas Jesu* wurde von der Administration ein Gebäude zugewiesen, das zu den baulichen Bestandteilen des mittelalterlichen Temeswar gehörte.[37] Bereits 1726 bat der Superior, Antonius Perger, Graf Mercy um Hilfe für den Neubau von Kirche und Residenz. Mercy unterstützte das Vorhaben vor dem Hofkanzleirat und beantragte, den Kloster- und Kirchenbau der Jesuiten „ab aerario" zu ermöglichen. Dazu sollten „bau-Materialien und Requisiten, alß Holtz, Kalck, und ziegl" kostenlos bereitgestellt werden.[38] Die Kirche war in den 1730er Jahren so stark beschädigt, dass der Orden 1739 den Bau

---

[36] Diese Feststellung betraf sowohl den kameral wie den militärisch verwalteten Teil des Landes. Vgl. ROTH, Erik: Die planmäßig angelegten Siedlungen im Deutsch-Banater Militärgrenzbezirk 1765-1821. München 1988 (Buchreihe der Südostdeutschen Historischen Kommission, Bd. 33), 340.

[37] Grundlage der Zuweisung war, dass die Jesuiten innerhalb des Festungsbezirkes die reguläre Seelsorge übernahmen. Vgl. HÖLLER: Augusta Carolinae virtutis, 11-27. – HKA. Wien. B. A. r. Nr.1. Fol. 92, 97, 98.; Temeschburg-Temeswar. Eine südosteuropäische Stadt im Zeitenwandel. Hg. v. Heimatortsgemeinschaft Temeschburg-Temeswar. o.O. 1994, 145.

[38] HKA. Wien. B. A. r. Nr. 137. Fasz. 30. Fol. 141, 150, 151. Schreiben Mercys vom 9. April 1726. Hier wird deutlich, dass der Orden eine Art Gewohnheitsrecht in Anspruch nahm, nach dem das Ärar die Bauten des Ordens schon einmal finanziert hatte.

eines neuen Gotteshauses beantragte. Jesuitenkirche und -kloster befanden sich im südlichen Zentrum der Stadt am Jesuitenplatz. In der Beschreibung des Stadtplanes aus dem Jahr 1752 heißt es dazu: „Neü erbaute aber noch nicht vollendete Residenz deren P.P. Jesuitern, nebst der alten großen zu haltung des Gottes Dienst applicirten Mosche".[39] Im Stadtplan aus dem Jahr 1758 wurde die Jesuitenkirche aber schon mit verändertem Grundriss dargestellt.

Der zum Teil detailliert überlieferte Schriftverkehr des Jesuitenordens hinsichtlich der Errichtung einer Kirche und einer Residenz erlaubt Rückschlüsse zum verwaltungstechnischen Modus, der der Banater Baupraxis zugrunde lag. In der Regel stellte der Pater Superior den Antrag bei der Landesadministration, die diesen dann an die Banco-Hofdeputation weiterleitete. Diese verfasste ein Memorandum für die Eingabe an die Königin, die handschriftlich ihre Bemerkungen hinzufügte. Von Maria Theresia erfolgte der Weg zurück bis zur Banater Landesadministration, die die Angelegenheit dann erneut innerhalb ihrer Baukommission behandelte. Die gesamten Kosten für die Bauarbeiten wurden – wie für die Kirche der Barmherzigen Brüder – gänzlich von der Kameralkasse übernommen.[40]

Der Kirchenbau wurde nach einer Darstellung des Provinzialingenieurs Steinlein erst im Jahr 1755 begonnen, und erst im Verlauf der sechziger Jahre wurde verstärkt an der Kirche gearbeitet. Dies hängt auch mit der Baugeschichte des Domes zusammen, dessen Errichtung vor allem in den fünfziger Jahren des 18. Jahrhunderts hohe Kosten verlangte und den Baufond erheblich belastete.[41] Da für den bisherigen Bau nur 8.000 Gulden verbraucht wurden, waren bei der bewilligten Gesamtsumme von 42.000 Gulden noch 34.000 Gulden übrig, die nach Steinleins Darstellung auch benötigt wurden. Diese Gelder wurden offensichtlich nie vollständig bereitgestellt. Über den Verbleib der für die fünfziger Jahre des 18. Jahrhunderts bewilligten Summen ist nichts bekannt. Aus den Akten wird ersichtlich, dass eine Bewilligung von Geldern noch nicht bedeutete, dass diese dann auch tatsächlich ausgezahlt wurden.[42]

---

[39] PETRI, Anton Peter: Die Festung Temeswar im 18. Jahrhundert. München 1966, 31.

[40] Diese Vorgehensweise zeigt, mit welcher Akribie auch minimale Angelegenheiten in Wien verhandelt oder begutachtet wurden, und dass sämtliche Entscheidungen von den jeweiligen Zentralstellen abhängig waren. Ursprünglich bewilligte die Königin am 17. August 1753 dreitausend Gulden aus der Kameralkasse. Bis 1754 hatten die Jesuiten 8.000 Gulden für den Bau erhalten, siehe: BARÓTI, Lajos: Adattár Délmagyarország 18. századi történetéhez [Datensammlung zur Geschichte Südungarns im 18. Jahrhundert]. Bd. 3. Temesvár 1896, 155.

[41] Darüber hinaus gab es offenbar Schwierigkeiten bei der Errichtung der Kirche durch die Einbeziehung der alten Grundmauern. In Steinleins Darstellung waren „anfangs jeniger architecten ing. nicht von der alten türckischen Maüer, sondern das ganze neüe Haubt=Kirchen gebäu von solchen decliniret, folglich bey damaligen Fon so nicht angelegten Pfeilern ... nicht figur zu nutzen in antrag gebracht worden sint", die alten Mauern wurden also zunächst nicht in den Neubau einbezogen. Dieser Plan entstand wohl erst später, nach dem schließlich die Kirche „mit adaptirung der alten Moscheé Mauer" errichtet wurde. Dafür mussten aber jetzt erhebliche Änderungen vorgenommen werden, die sich vor allem auf das tektonische Stützsystem bezogen. Die Pfeiler sollten nicht wie bisher aus Ziegeln, sondern aus Quadersteinen errichtet, die Kuppel hingegen aus Ziegeln hergestellt werden.

[42] HKA Wien. B. A. Fasz. 30. r. Nr. 137. Fol. 1, 4, 5, 9-20, 45, 100, 106. – Vgl. WOLF : Die Ordenslandschaft des Banats, 4. – Nach einem Protokoll des kaiserlichen Rates vom 16. Dezember 1767 wurde festgestellt, dass den Jesuiten bereits am 9. August 1717 und wiederholt am 20. November 1741 für ihre Missi-

Die veränderten Pläne wurden bereits im Mai 1767 eingereicht. Die Zeichnungen, angefertigt von Franz Anton Platl, Maurermeister in Temeswar, zeigen Grundriss, Längsschnitt und Fassadenaufriss der Kirche.[43] Bis zum Herbst des Jahres 1767 war die Kirche bis auf den Dachstuhl, das Dach, den Turm und die Fassade fertig gestellt. Im gleichen Jahr reichte die Landesadministration auf Verlangen der Wiener Zentralbehörden erneut Pläne für die bereits im Bau befindliche neue Pfarrkirche in Temeswar ein, die einen Kostenüberschlag zur Reparatur der baufälligen Residenz für eine Summe von 19.594 Gulden und 33 Kreuzern enthielten. Der dazugehörige Schriftverkehr endet zunächst ohne ausdrückliche Bewilligung der Summe. Am 29. August 1767 beantragte der Pater Superior Petrus Körner nochmals die Bewilligung der Kosten, jetzt aber direkt bei Maria Theresia, die schließlich ihre Zustimmung gab. Die Fertigstellung der Kirche konnte dennoch zunächst nicht realisiert werden, weil die bewilligte Summe offensichtlich nicht zur Verfügung gestellt wurde. Wiederholte Anträge der Societas Jesu in Temeswar „zur Herstellung ihrer baufälligen Residenz, und daringewinnten Pfarr-Kirchen gebitten und das deshalb allerunterthänigsten Anträgen abgestattet worden", wurden bis zum Februar 1768 abschlägig beschieden.
Die Auseinandersetzung wurde zunächst nochmals durch Maria Theresia beendet, die am 7. Februar 1768 allerdings mit einem unverhohlenen Ultimatum in Wien schrieb: „Dem Pater Provinciali ist per Decretum zu bedeüten, dass ungeachtet Mein aerario ... Ich dennoch ex speciali und pro ultimato zu dem gebäu sechs tausend gulden zu bewilligen geneigt wäre: im Fall aber die Patres Jesuiten sich damit nicht begnügten, so wären meine Willensordnung, die Stadt-Pfarren der Cathedral-Kirchen einzuverleiben, und ihnen P.P. Jesuiten aus dem bisherigen Genuß zu: 2.280 G. zu unterhaltung der nöthigen Professoren für die bisherigen Schulen 1500:G. beyzulassen." Offensichtlich war auch diese Summe noch nicht ausreichend. Denn am 2. Mai 1769 beantragten die Jesuiten nochmals eine Summe von 9.735 Gulden und 10 Kreuzern. Dieser Antrag wurde vom Kameralbauamt an die Landesadministration weitergeleitet, die am 17. Mai 1769 einen Antrag bei der Banco-Hofdeputation stellte. Der Antrag wurde befürwortet, die Kosten sollten von der Kameralkasse getragen werden. Am 6. Juni 1769 erteilte Maria Theresia die Genehmigung in einem Reskript an die Hofdeputation: „Dass denen P.P. Jesuiten zu Temeswar den zu ihrem Kirchen bau nöthige Materialien in den sogenannten ex arial gemaß verabfolgt werden sollen".[44] Während die Pfarrkirche der Jesuiten bis zum Ende des Jahres 1769 fertig gestellt werden konnte, wurde die Residenz infolge der Auflösung der Gesellschaft 1773 nicht mehr vollendet.[45] Die Finanzierung des Kirchenbaues für

---

onstätigkeit in Temeswar und den angrenzen Ländern eine jährliche Summe von 2.280 Gulden bewilligt worden war. In den dazugehörigen Schriftstücken der Societas Jesu wird aber berichtet, dass keine Person oder Institution für dieses Geld mehr zuständig sei und sowohl die Anträge an den Hofkriegsrat als auch an die Hofkammer bisher ergebnislos gewesen seien.

[43] Vgl. PETRI: Biographisches Lexikon, Sp. 1473. – HKA. Wien. B. A. Fasz. 30. r. Nr. 114. Fol. 112-240. – Kartensammlung Rb. Rb 63/1-2.

[44] HKA Wien. B. A. Fasz. 30. r. Nr. 137. Fol. 4, 5, 45, 68-72. r. Nr. 136.; Fol. 59-63, 74, 75.

[45] Pläne zu diesen Gebäuden hatte Franz Anton Platl ebenfalls im Jahr 1767 eingereicht. Eine weitere Kirche der Jesuiten wurde bereits in den zwanziger Jahren des 18. Jahrhunderts in Kraschowa errichtet. Vgl.

die katholische Kirche erfolgte in der Regel – im Unterschied zu den anderen Konfessionen im Banat – gänzlich durch das Ärar.[46] (Abb. 4)
In der karolinischen Ansiedlungsperiode waren für die zivilen und sakralen Bauwerke Provinzialingenieure verantwortlich, die auch an den Fortifikationsaufgaben arbeiteten. An dieser Praxis scheint sich in der Folgezeit wenig geändert zu haben. Im Klosterarchiv des Franziskaner-Klosters zu Maria Radna befindet sich ein Dokument, das beweist, dass noch 1771 in Maria Radna Baumeister bauten, die der Arader Festungsbaugesellschaft angehörten.[47] Die überwiegende Zahl der Bauwerke wurde allerdings von ortsansässigen Maurermeistern errichtet. Von diesen konnte zum Teil nachgewiesen werden, dass sie aus dem Reich oder den Ländern der Habsburger Monarchie eingewandert waren. Die meisten Baumeister wählten Zeit ihres Lebens ihren Aufenthalt im Banat. Nur von wenigen ist bekannt, dass sie in Wien studiert hatten. Sicher ist aber, dass auch im Banat Künstler aus Westeuropa arbeiteten, die für die Ausstattung der Kirchen verantwortlich waren.[48]
Gerhard Egger stellte innerhalb der Wiener Architekturgeschichte für das 18. Jahrhundert einen allgemeinen Zug zum Spannungslosen, Dekorativen und Zeichnerischen fest. Dieser stand in gewisser Weise gegen die Monumentalität des älteren Fischer, begünstigte Hildebrandt und feierte beim jüngeren Fischer Triumphe. Dass Künstler wie Jean-Nicolàs Jadot und besonders Nicolò Pacassi, der als Leiter des Wiener Hofbauamtes das Baugeschehen entscheidend prägte, diesen Stil über die Jahrhundertmitte hinaus fortsetzten, bedeutete eine entscheidende Wende in der Wiener Architekturgeschichte. Sie umfasste vor allem die Abkehr vom monumentalen, phantasievollen Stil des römischen Hochbarock und die Hinwendung zum kühlen klassizistischen Barock Frankreichs. Diese Hinwendung war derart ausschließlich, dass die französische und süddeutsche Spätform des Rokoko in Wien fast gar nicht in Erscheinung trat.[49] Auch die Banater Architektur zeigt jenen zeichnerischen Stil, der die Bauwerke relativ ruhig und spannungslos erscheinen lässt. Daher wurde die Baukunst der zweiten Hälfte des 18. Jahrhunderts von einer Stilauffassung dominiert, die in der Fortsetzung und Variation barocker Bautraditionen bestand.
Auch in der Banater Architektur wurde dem Stilwandel der Jahrhundertmitte nicht nur Rechnung getragen, sondern er fand hier sehr früh Eingang. Mit dem Tod Kaiser

---

PETRI: Die Festung Temeswar, 68.; HKA. Wien. B. A. Fasz. 30. r. Nr. 3. (Juni 1767). – Kartensammlung, Sign. Rb 38.

[46] HKA. B. A. r. Nr. 1. Fol. 158-217.

[47] Vgl. ROOS: Maria-Radna. – Auch die Baugeschichte des Temeswarer Domes beweist, dass hier die Bauaufsicht von der gleichen Person übernommen wurde, die auch den Temeswarer Festungsbau verantwortete.

[48] So malte Johann Nepomuk Schöpf aus Regensburg alle Blätter für die Seitenaltäre des Temeswarer Domes. Ferdinand Schiessl hingegen arbeitete als Freskant in Radna und malte außerdem das Hochaltarblatt für die alte Minoritenkirche in Arad. Das Bild für den Hochaltar des Temeswarer Domes wurde von dem Wiener Künstler Michael Angelo Unterberger gemalt. So weit bekannt, war Unterberger nie im Banat. Inwiefern in diesem Bereich ein kontinuierlicher Austausch zwischen den Provinzen und Westeuropa stattfand, ist weiter zu untersuchen.

[49] EGGER, Gerhard: Geschichte der bildenden Kunst in Wien. Geschichte der Architektur in Wien. Von der Renaissance bis zum Klassizismus. In: Geschichte der Stadt Wien. Hg. v. Verein für Geschichte der Stadt Wien. Wien 1973 (Neue Reihe Bd. VII, 3), 56 und 70.

Karls VI. verlor der *Kaiserstil* der beiden Fischer mit seiner römischen und palladianischen Ausprägung endgültig an Bedeutung. Ausgehend von den monumentalen Umbauten der Residenzen in Innsbruck, Prag oder Ofen (Buda) – im Gegensatz zur Wiener Hofburg – entwickelte sich eine vereinheitlichende Architektur, die fast gleichartig in allen Ländern der Monarchie auftrat und sich gleichzeitig von den lokalen Traditionen deutlich abhob. Trotz der Übernahme tradierter spätbarocker Elemente entwickelte sich auf architektonischem Gebiet eine spezifische Formensprache, die als Klammer die unterschiedlichsten Gebiete zusammenfasste.[50] Dieses Spezifikum erfuhr im Banat wegen der nahezu ausschließlich administrativ getragenen Bauunternehmen eine besondere Ausprägung, deren Höhepunkt Typisierungsmodelle waren.

Darüber hinaus bot der gerasterte Grundriss der Stadt einen vierflügligen Grundriss der Gebäude, die um einen rechteckigen Innenhof herum errichtet wurden, geradezu zwingend an. Grundsätzlich wurden auch die kirchlichen Bauten von den siedlungstopographischen Vorgaben bestimmt. In einigen Orten verzichteten die Erbauer daher auch auf die kanonische Ostung der Kirche. Übereinstimmungen gab es außerdem hinsichtlich der Grundrissdispositionen sowie in der Gestaltung der Schauseite. Hier dominiert eindeutig die Einturmfassade, wobei der Fassadenturm, über quadratischem Grundriss errichtet, aus der Mitte der Fassade herauswächst. Zweitürmige Fassaden blieben in der Banater Baukunst des 18. Jahrhunderts eine Ausnahme. Diese treten hier vor allem bei außerordentlich repräsentativen kirchlichen Bauwerken wie der Domkirche in Temeswar und der Wallfahrtskirche Maria-Radna auf. Beide Kirchen zählen hinsichtlich ihrer Baugeschichte und ihrer stilistischen Prägung zu den Höhepunkten kirchlicher Baukunst im Banat bzw. im Komitat Arad.[51] So lässt sich konstatieren, dass trotz der nachgewiesenen Verwendung einer barocken Formensprache das Hauptmerkmal der Banater Baukunst ein dem Klassizismus zuneigender Spätbarock ist.

Landkirchen im Banat und das Phänomen der Typisierungsmodelle

Analog zu den Reformbestrebungen im kirchlichen Bereich erfuhr auch die Gestaltung der Landkirchenbauten ab der Mitte des 18. Jahrhunderts erhöhte Aufmerksamkeit. (Abb. 10, 11) Dies wiederum spielte im Banat eine Schlüsselrolle, da dort von den Habsburgern fast ausschließlich römisch-katholische Gotteshäuser errichtet

[50] Vgl. POLLEROß, Friedrich: Kunstgeschichte oder Architekturgeschichte. Ergänzende Bemerkungen zur Forschungslage der Wiener Barockarchitektur. In: Fischer von Erlach und die Wiener Barocktradition. Hg. v. Friedrich POLLEROß. Wien-Köln-Weimar 1995 (Frühneuzeit-Studien, Bd. 4), 59-116, hier 68. – WAGNER-RIEGER, Renate: Die Kunst zur Zeit Maria Theresias und Josephs II. In: Wiener Jahrbuch für Kunstgeschichte 34 (1981), 7-22, hier 12.

[51] Vgl. BORN, Robert: Die Domkirche in Temeswar (Timişoara). Eine kunstgeschichtliche Interpretation. Berlin 1999 (Manuskript). – BUZILA, Adriana: Bisericile baroca din Banatul [Barocke Kirchen im Banat]. Diss. masch. Cluj-Napoca/Klausenburg 1999. – ROOS: Maria-Radna. – Barocul in Banat. Catalog de Expozitie [Barock im Banat. Ausstellungskatalog]. Hg. v. Rodica VÂRTACIU und Adriana BUZILÁ. Timişoara 1992.

wurden. Dem Anspruch der römisch-katholischen Lehre entsprechend regelt die Liturgie nicht nur gottesdienstliche Formen sondern auch die Gestalt des Raumes. Ausgehend von den Bestimmungen des tridentinischen Konzils, mit denen Papst Pius V. die gesamte katholische Welt auf den römischen Ritus verpflichtet hatte, entwickelte sich vor allem im Landkirchenbau eine Bauweise, die liturgischen Forderungen sehr direkt Rechnung trug, weil sie weniger verschlüsselt und in einer pragmatischen Art und Weise in Architektur umgesetzt wurde.[52] Grundlage dafür war die Neuordnung der Liturgie innerhalb der josephinischen Kirchenreform, die auch zur Einschränkung von Schmuck und Aufwand im Kirchenbau führte. Die Tendenz, nicht nur die Liturgie, sondern auch die äußeren Zeichen der katholischen Religion zu reformieren, wirkte sich zuerst im Bereich des Kirchenbaues aus. Die traditionellen Formen blieben zwar weiter bestehen, allerdings wurden diese einer schlichten und einfachen Gestaltungsweise unterworfen.[53]

Der stilkritische Vergleich mit der Frage nach der Herkunft der architektonischen Formen ergibt, dass im Banat keine eigenständigen stilistischen Lösungen nachgewiesen werden können. Offensichtlich bestand ein enges Abhängigkeitsverhältnis vor allem zur Architektur der Erbländer aber auch zu den oberdeutschen Lösungen. Hier überzeugt vor allem die bemerkenswerte Vielzahl der Einturmfassaden, die im Banat zu den typischen Merkmalen der Kolonistenkirche gehört. Einturmfassaden finden sich gleichzeitig auch bei der Mehrzahl der Stadtkirchen. Diese Feststellung entspricht vollständig jener Entwicklung, die auch in Wien in der zweiten Hälfte des 18. Jahrhunderts zu beobachten ist. Die Entwicklung reicht von der Zweiturm- zur Einturmfassade und führt schließlich zur turmlosen Fassade. Allerdings wurde im Banat diese Fassadenentwicklung bis zur letzten Konsequenz nicht durchgeführt. Auch die in Wien nachweisbare Vereinfachung der Fassade, um den Baukörper sichtbar zu machen, spielte wohl im Banat keine Rolle. Immerhin fanden jedoch die wesentlichen Entwicklungsstufen barocker Architekturgeschichte – wenn auch zeitversetzt – statt.

Die entscheidende Erkenntnis innerhalb der Untersuchung und Darstellung des Banater Landkirchenbaues ist der Nachweis, dass Typisierungsmodelle für den Sakralbau im Banat vorgeprägt und entwickelt wurden. Damit konnte die These von Elisabeth Springer partiell widerlegt werden, dass die Entwicklung von Typisierungsmo-

[52] Lehre und Konsens über das Messopfer. 22. Sitzung des Konzils von Trient, 17. September 1762. Vgl. Kompendium der Glaubensbekenntnisse und kirchlichen Lehrentscheidungen. Hg. v. Peter HÜNERMANN. Freiburg 1991, 561-565.

[53] Dabei wurde unter anderem gefordert, dass nur noch ein Altar errichtet werden sollte. Die Beweggründe für die Reform erhellt ein Vortrag der Hofkanzlei im Jahr 1781, der vom Kaiser genehmigt wurde. „Die katholische Religion gewinnt ungemein vieles, wenn sie nach und nach in ihre ernsthafte, einfache und mit dem vorhabenden Endzwecke eines öffentlichen Gebethes zu Gott übereinstimmende Verfaßung bey dem culto externo wiederum zurückgeführet wird; denn eben derley übertriebene Anwendung des unschicksamen Gepränges ist der Vorwurf in allen protestantischen Büchern, woraus sie den Schluß ziehen, dass unsere Frömmigkeit vielmehr äußerliche Zeichen, als auf innerliche Andacht gegründet seye." Vgl. HOLLERWEGER, Hans: Die Reform des Gottesdienstes zur Zeit des Josephinismus in Österreich. Regensburg 1976, 482.

dellen erst mit der unstrukturierten Tätigkeit des Wiener Hofbauamtes begann.[54] Ursprung und Anlass dieses kunsthistorischen Phänomens in der Architekturgeschichte des Habsburgerreiches waren unter anderem die spezifischen Bedingungsfaktoren im Banat. Hier entstand wegen der Notwendigkeit einer umfassenden Einrichtung beziehungsweise Wiederbelebung kirchlicher Strukturen zuerst und ausschließlich eine modellhafte Bauweise. Von dieser ausgehend konnten entscheidende Impulse für die josephinische Pfarrreform vermittelt werden, so dass in diesem Bereich eindeutig von einer Beeinflussung des Zentrums durch die Peripherie auszugehen ist.[55] (Abb. 5)

Im Spannungsfeld zwischen einfachsten Bauten, die vom Kriterium der Nützlichkeit geprägt waren und Bauten, die Formenvielfalt und Architekturgeschmack verraten, entwickelten die Banater Provinzialingenieure – hier in erster Linie Steinlein, Kostka und Sax – bereits Mitte der 1760er Jahre Pläne für Pfarrkirchen, die in mehreren neugegründeten Orten errichtet werden sollten. Ursache für diese vereinheitlichenden Kriterien waren die kaiserliche Pfarrreform und die daraus entstandene Notwendigkeit der Errichtung einer Vielzahl von Pfarrkirchen sowie die Entwicklungen im kirchlichen Baugeschehen im Banat. Auch die besonderen Determinanten des Banater Kolonisationswesens waren wichtig, das die Vereinheitlichung der Dorfanlagen, der Kolonistenhäuser und der öffentlichen Gebäude durch administrative Planung erfasste. Entsprechend den ästhetischen und funktionalen Forderungen nach geometrischer Klarheit und einfacher Parzellierung entstanden schließlich Dörfer und vor allem Kolonistenhäuser, die nahezu seriell wiederholt wurden, so dass die einzelnen Orte kaum noch unterschiedliche Merkmale aufzuweisen vermochten. Genauso sollten auch die Kirchen einheitlich und vor allem nach funktionellen Prinzipien gebaut werden. Doch dies ließ sich so nicht realisieren.

Grundlage für die Pläne blieb jene Bestimmung, nach der die Planungen der Bauwerke erst vom Wiener Hofbauamt begutachtet und genehmigt werden mussten. Individuelle Lösungen waren weder möglich – denn die Finanzierung des öffentlichen Nutzbaues erfolgte von Beginn an durch das Ärar – noch erwünscht. Spätestens ab dem Zeitpunkt, als auch die Kosten für den Hausbau vom Ärar übernommen wurden und die Bauweise für Orte und für die Häuser vorgeschrieben war, begannen die Verantwortlichen im Banat mit Typisierungsmodellen zu arbeiten. (Abb. 6) Während für die formale Ausgestaltung der josephinischen Musterkirche keine konkreten Vorschriften überliefert sind, gibt es eine Fülle von Material zur Ausgestaltung der Kirchen in den Neoacquisitica.[56] Der Antrag der Landesadministration an Maria Theresia den künftigen Kirchenbau in den Kolonistendörfern betreffend wurde dahingehend beantwortet, dass „die Kirchen daselbst nicht zwar allzu kostbar, doch mit dem anständigen Decoro hergestellet werden sollen.“ Eine gewisse Handlungsfreiheit des Baumeisters wurde nur insofern gestattet, dass „in besprochenen fällen

[54] Vgl. SPRINGER, Elisabeth: Die Josephinische Musterkirche. In: Das achtzehnte Jahrhundert und Österreich. Jahrbuch der österreichischen Gesellschaft zur Erforschung des achtzehnten Jahrhunderts. 11 (1996), 67-99.
[55] Vgl. POLLEROß: Kunstgeschichte, 79-83.
[56] Vgl. SPRINGER: Die Josephinische Musterkirche, 73.

einige modification" vorgenommen werden könne. Ausgehend von den Richtlinien Kempelens wurde zu Beginn der 1770er Jahre dazu übergegangen, sogenannte Idealpläne für den Bau von Kolonistenkirchen in den Neoacquisitica zu erstellen. In seiner Impopulations-Hauptinstruktion hatte Kempelen auch definiert, wie die Kirchen in den Kolonistendörfern auszusehen hatten. „Solche müssen zwar solide, aber nicht zu prächtig, und mit unnützen Zierath überhäufet werden".[57] Die Diskrepanzen zwischen Plan und Ausführung betrafen in der Regel nur Details. Allgemein ist festzustellen, dass es sich meist um eine einfachere und dann wohl auch kostengünstige Ausführung handelte, was für Wien durchaus wichtig war. Im Gegensatz zu den von Joseph II. unmittelbar beeinflussten Hofburgprojekten, die von einem Klassizismus strenger Observanz geprägt waren, bildeten die Landkirchen bereits in der Regierungszeit Maria Theresias innerhalb der Monarchie eine eigene Stilgruppe. Sie wurden in großer Zahl in relativ kurzer Zeit errichtet und erhielten als Erziehungsstätten des Staates zunehmend den Charakter von Nutzbauten.

Die einzelnen Bautypen im Banat unterschieden sich zwar in individuellen Details, stimmten aber in der Grundstruktur überein. Die Kolonistenkirche wurde mit übersichtlichem Saalraum geplant, gebaut und von Ort zu Ort stereotyp wiederholt. Die Bedeutung dieses Typus liegt vor allem darin, dass die Form auch in den Pfarrkirchen der zweiten Hälfte des 18. Jahrhunderts innerhalb der Erblande Verwendung fand. Bereits am 2. Dezember 1740 schrieb Maria Theresia über deren Funktionalität: „(...) wodurch die Ehre des Allerhöchsten beförderet, der Unterthan in Gottes-Forcht und guten Wandel eingeleithet und darinnen erhalten, wie nicht minder auch die Jugend in denen sittlichen Lehren unterweisen, folglichen successu temporis ein Gott dem Allerhöchsten wohl gefälliges Landvolck erzielet werden möchte".[58]

Im Banater Landkirchenbau können trotz der vereinheitlichenden Tendenzen mehrere Stilgruppen festgestellt werden. Eine erste Gruppe betrifft die sogenannten Bethäuser, die zunächst im Verlauf der neuzeitlichen Kolonisation des Banats in großer Zahl vor allem in den ländlichen Siedlungen errichtet wurden. Beherrschendes Merkmal waren einfachste Konstruktionen, die sehr eng an den Kolonistenhäusern orientiert waren und durch die Verwendung des landesüblichen Baumaterials wie Lehm und zum überwiegenden Teil ungebrannten Ziegeln lediglich durch ihre Funktionalität den Sakralbauten zuzuordnen sind. Es wurde bei Beginn der Ansiedlung verfügt, „... dass die Kirchen in den Colonisten-dorfschaften nur aus gestampfter Erde hergestellet und höchstens 150 Gulden ausgelegt werden sollen ...". Steinkirchen sollten erst dann errichtet werden, wenn die Bevölkerung eigene Mittel dazu beisteuern konnte.[59] Ursprünglich wurde sogar gefordert, zunächst in den Kolonistenorten nur Schulen zu errichten und zunächst auf den Kirchenbau zu verzichten. In den Neubauten sollte zunächst auf die Einziehung der Trennwände verzichtet

[57] HKA. Wien. Administrationsratsprotokolle. Banat. Bd. 163. Fol. 105. (Februar 1769). B. A. Fasz. 30. r. Nr. 137. Fol. 120/2. – TAFFERNER: Quellenbuch zur Donauschwäbischen Geschichte I., 257.
[58] HKA. Wien. B. A. r. Nr. 10.
[59] EBD., r. Nr. 137. Fol. 120-150.

werden, damit hier neben dem Schulunterricht auch der Gottesdienst abgehalten werden konnte.

Für die Größe des Kirchenbaues wurde stets die Zahl der Gemeindemitglieder zugrunde gelegt. (Abb. 7) Die Kosten für die Neubauten beliefen sich in der Regel auf 3.500 bis 5.000 Gulden, dabei wurde der Baufond für die Landkirchenbauten mit 10.000 Gulden nach 1774 jährlich nahezu ausgeschöpft. (Abb. 19) Von Bedeutung erscheint auch, dass die von Kempelen angeratene Hinzuziehung der Gemeindemitglieder zum Kirchenbau von der Administration konsequent eingeplant wurde. Das Ärar übernahm in der Regel Kosten in Höhe von 2.700 bis 3.700 Gulden, die Gemeinde musste hingegen Hand- und Zugrobot im Wert von etwa 1.000 Gulden leisten.[60]

Doch selbst unter den Landkirchen, die aus festem Material errichtet wurden, können trotz stereotyper Wiederholungen Stilgruppen konstatiert werden. Neben den Bethäusern entstanden zunächst einfachste Bauten, die vor allem vom Kriterium der Nützlichkeit und durch das Ringen um eine möglichst kostengünstige Ausführung geprägt waren. Diese Bauten weisen in der Regel einen orthogonalen Grundriss mit apsidalem Chor auf. Die Eingangsseite wird mit einem Dachreiterturm versehen, wie die ersten Kirchen beziehungsweise Kapellen in Neubeschenowa und Sanktandreas beweisen. Eine weitere Gruppe umfasst jene Bauwerke, die dem stilistischen Empfinden der Jahrhundertmitte zuneigt, wie die Pfarrkirchen in Saska, Ulmbach, Tschatad und in Großjetscha zeigen. (Abb. 8) Diese Kirchen gehören gleichzeitig zu jenen Bauten, die aufgrund ihrer außergewöhnlichen Grundrissstruktur und ihrer Dekorationselemente nicht vollständig in die Gruppe der Banater Kolonistenkirchen einzuordnen sind. Zu den beherrschenden Merkmalen zählt außerdem, dass der Innenraum nicht wie sonst üblich mit einer Flachdecke, sondern mit einem Tonnen- oder Spiegelgewölbe ausgestattet wurde.

Die umfangreichste Gruppe bilden jene Bauten, die wegen ihrer übereinstimmenden Merkmale als Typisierungsmodelle definiert werden können. (Abb. 9) Trotz nachweisbarer Einzelentwürfe signalisieren Grundrisssituation, formale Auffassung und Dekorationssystem Einheitlichkeit und dies in einer derartigen Fülle, dass von einer seriellen Bauproduktion gesprochen werden darf. Dabei weisen sowohl die Planungen als auch die ausgeführten Pfarrkirchen durchgehend im Grundriss eine Saalkirche mit eingezogenem Chor und eine Westfassade, die als Schauseite gestaltet wurde, auf. Das relativ niedrige Kirchenschiff wird von einem hohen Turm beherrscht, der über quadratischem Grundriss als eingezogener Fassadenturm in der Mitte der Westfassade errichtet wurde. Die Schauwand wurde durch Pilaster gegliedert, eine

[60] Allerdings wurde strikt auf die Leistungsfähigkeit der Kolonisten geachtet. In einem Schreiben der Temeswarer Landesadministration vom 1. April 1769 hieß es: „Auf einen Beitrag der Kolonisten, um mit der Zeit eine Kirche aus guten Materialien ohne Beschwerung des Ärars herstellen zu können, könne man sich um so weniger verlassen, als die meisten Kolonisten bekanntermaßen sehr arme Leute sind, die nicht das geringste Vermögen mit sich bringen. Folglich wird man zufrieden sein können, wenn man den Ersatz der ihnen geleisteten Anticipationen auch erst nach langen Fristen wieder erhalten wird. Auch würde es niemals rätlich sein, sie zur Reichung eines Beitrags zum Kirchenbau anleiten zu lassen, weil sich viele aus einem unvernünftigen Andachtseifer zu Bettlern machen könnten". EBD., r. Nr. 137. Fol. 21-56. r. Nr. 45.

Gliederung der Seitenwände unterblieb in der Regel. Beispiele wie die Planungen beziehungsweise die ausgeführten Bauten in Guttenbrunn, Jahrmarkt, Perjamosch, Sackelhausen, Bogarosch, Deutsch-Sanktpeter, Billed und Bruckenau zeigen die genannten Analogien, die im wesentlichen den Merkmalen klassizierender Barockarchitektur entsprechen.

Neben der Verwendung fast rein klassizistischer Stilelemente, wie sie die Pfarrkirche in Lowrin zeigt (Abb. 10), dominieren in der letzten Gruppe der Banater Landkirchen die nahezu schmucklosen mit vollkommen vereinfachten Formen. Tradiert werden weiterhin der Saalkirchengrundriss mit eingezogenem Chor sowie die Gestaltung der Westwand mit einem Fassadenturm. Allerdings bleibt diese – wie in der Regel auch der Innenraum – fast ungegliedert. Die Wand wird lediglich durch das meist rechteckige Eingangsportal, partiell ein rechteckiges Fenster oder eine einfache Giebelverdachung definiert und in Einzelfällen durch sehr flache Pilaster zeichnerisch profiliert. Exemplarisch genannt seien hier die Pfarrkirchen in Engelsbrunn und Grabatz. (Abb. 11, 12)

Die Ursachen für diese Vereinfachungen, die im Übrigen die gesamte Architekturgeschichte des Banats begleiten, sind außerordentlich vielschichtig. Eine Komponente war die verstärkte Einflussnahme Kaiser Josephs II., auch wenn ihm unterstellt wurde, kein persönliches Verhältnis zur bildenden Kunst zu haben und diese nur „nach Maßgabe des mehreren und minderen Verhältnisses betrachtete, das sie auf das allgemeine Beste des Staates haben könne".[61] Doch allein die Förderung eines Architekten wie Isidor Canevale, der Elemente des radikalen Klassizismus in seinen Bauwerken verwirklichte, ist Indiz für die neue Richtung der josephinischen Architektur. Eine weitere Ursache ist zweifellos die Einflussnahme Kaiser Josephs II. auf diese Provinz, der das Banat noch vor Beginn seiner Regierungszeit mehrfach bereiste.[62] Von den Ergebnissen der Kolonisation zeigte er sich enttäuscht, so dass er eine weitere außerordentlich sparsame Vorgehensweise in dieser Provinz empfahl, die schließlich nach 1780 zum Verkauf zahlreicher Banater Güter an adelige Grundherren führte. Allerdings nicht nur im Banat, wo dies hinreichend nachweisbar ist, sondern auch in den Erblanden der Monarchie erfolgte die Adaptierung spätbarocker Elemente vor allem auch aus fiskalischen Gründen. Der spätbarock-konservativ geprägte Stil folgt demnach nicht nur dem Mangel qualitätsvoller Möglichkeiten, sondern auch finanziellen Erwägungen.

Ein weiteres Phänomen Banater Architekturgeschichte betraf die lange Tradierung stilistischer Möglichkeiten, die weit in das 19. Jahrhundert hineinreichte. Dabei wurden im Banat noch in der ersten Hälfte des 19. Jahrhunderts Kirchen errichtet, deren Planungen entweder schon auf das letzte Drittel des 18. Jahrhunderts zurückgingen oder die mit Kirchen, die in der zweiten Hälfte des 18. Jahrhunderts gebaut wurden, übereinstimmten. Dies ist umso überraschender, weil zeitgleich auch Kirchen gebaut wurden, die an neuesten stilistischen Auffassungen orientiert waren. Insgesamt ist eine retardierende Verwendung barocker Bauformen zu konstatieren.

---

[61] WAGNER-RIEGER, Renate: Wiens Architektur im 19. Jahrhundert. Wien 1970, 25.
[62] Vgl. NEIDENBACH, Sieglinde: Die Reisen Kaiser Josephs II. ins Banat. Diss. masch. Wien 1967.

Das vielfach für die Banater Architektur konstatierte Phänomen einer außerordentlich langen Tradierung spätbarocker und klassizierend-barocker Stilmerkmale ist im Prinzip ein österreichisches. Bedingt durch die historischen Determinanten konnte sich der Spätbarock hier erst spät durchsetzen, doch diese Entwicklung traf auf das Gesamtreich zu. Walter Seitter nannte Österreich ein „Land der Spätstile".[63] Dem kurzzeitigen Durchbruch klassizierender Tendenzen folgte nach dem Tod Josephs II. eine Reaktion im Sinne einer aufwendigeren und prunkvolleren Gestaltung. Diese Entwicklungslinien sind auch für die Banater Architektur des 18. Jahrhunderts nachzuweisen. Übernommen wurden erprobte Modelle, die teilweise aber vor allem in Dekorationselementen jenen kraftvollen Zusammenhang vermissen lassen, den barocke Bauten noch am Beginn des 18. Jahrhundert atmeten.

Der Kirchenbau im Banat ist ein Phänomen innerhalb der Architektur dieser Region. Seine Bedeutung ergibt sich aus der Baugeschichte, aus seiner Funktion innerhalb der Kulturlandschaft und seiner Rolle im Glaubensleben. Vor allem der Landkirchenbau war wegweisend für die Architekturgeschichte der Monarchie. Hier an der Peripherie des Reiches wurden Lösungen gefunden, die die Neubesiedlung des Landes zu einem gewinnbringenden Ergebnis brachten und die bis heute das Banat prägen. Ob die Monarchie ihr Ziel, „ein Gott dem Allerhöchsten wohl gefälliges Landvolck" zu erziehen, erreichte, ist nicht Gegenstand dieser Abhandlung. Sicher ist aber, dass die Habsburger im Banat eine einzigartige Kulturlandschaft schufen.

Abbildungen

[63] Vgl. SEITTER, Walter: Schwierigkeiten mit dem Barock. In: Barockberichte. Informationsblätter des Salzburger Barockmuseums zur bildenden Kunst des 17. und 18. Jahrhunderts 18/19 (1998), 125-127, hier 125.

Abbildungen

Abb. 1: Dognecea/Dognatschka,
Kirche "Maria Geburt", 1735

Abb. 2: Ciclova Montana/Montan-Tschiklowa,
Kirche „Erscheinung Mariens", 1776/77

Abb. 3 Arad, Franziskanerkirche
„Maria, Königin der Engel", 1775 - 1781

Abb. 4: Timişoara/Temeswar,
St.-Georgs-Kathedrale, 1736 - 1774

Abb. 5: Plan einer Kirche im Banat, 1765

Abb. 7: Fântânele/Engelsbrunn, Kirche „Hl. Schutzengel“, 1779/80, Innenansicht

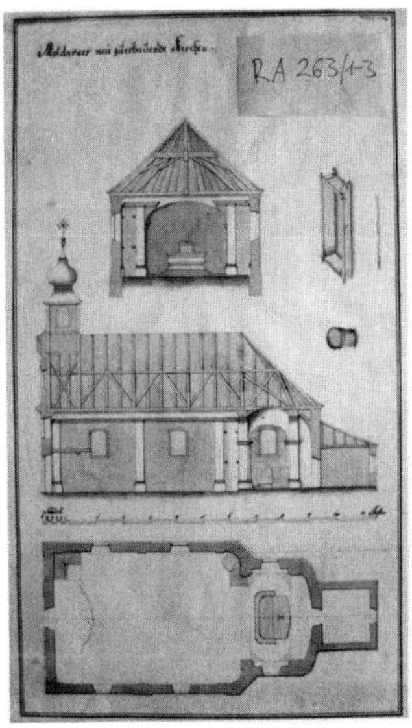

Abb. 8: Lenauheim, Kirche „Hl. Jungfrau Theresia“, 177/78

Abb. 6: Neumoldowa, Kirche „Hl. Johannes der Täufer“, 1777-1778, Querschnitt des Chores, Profil, Grundriß, 1776

Abb. 9: Periam/Periamosch, Kirche „Hl. Johann von Nepomuk", 1772/73

Abb. 10: Lovrin/Lowrin, Kirche „Hl. Peter und Paul", 1785 - 1789

Abb. 11: Grabaţ/Grabatz, Kirche „Maria von der immerwährenden Hilfe", 1780

Abb. 12: Fântânele/Engelsbrunn, Kirche „Hl. Schutzengel", 1779/80, Außenansicht

Tiborc Fazekas

Reflexion und Selbstreflexion: Migration und Erinnerungskultur im Spiegel der Literatur

Anmerkungen zum Thema

Das im Titel meines Vortrags implizierte Thema ist in all seinen Aspekten sehr umfangreich, dem Forscher bietet sich sowohl im historischen als auch im kulturellen Hinblick eine solche Fülle von einschlägigen Vorstudien, publizierten Ergebnissen und überlegenswerter methodologischer Annäherungsmöglichkeiten an, dass diese in dem gegebenen Rahmen natürlich nicht alle wahrgenommen werden können. Meine Darstellungen müssen in diesem Zusammenhang also als „Reflexion über die Reflexionen" aufgefasst werden. Der durch die gegebenen Umstände notwendig gewordenen Einschränkung zur Folge werde ich bei meinen Ausführungen hauptsächlich über die Deutschen in der Batschka-Banat-Gegend sprechen und lasse die übrigen, an sich mindestens ebenso interessanten und wichtigen deutschen Siedlungsgebiete des historischen Ungarn außer Acht. Ich werde die anderen Siedlungsgebiete bei meinen Ausführungen lediglich hin und wieder als Kontrast oder Vergleich zu den Feststellungen heranziehen, die ich bezüglich des thematischen Kerns meines Vortrages gefunden habe.

Die Entstehungsgeschichte

Die in den südlichen Regionen des Königreichs Ungarn eine neue Heimat findenden deutschen Siedler haben zur Zeit ihrer Aussiedlung aus dem Gebiet des Deutschen Reiches, also grob gesagt im 18. Jahrhundert, nicht gewusst, dass sie ins „Ausland" ziehen, denn sie waren der Überzeugung, lediglich aus einem Gebiet des (kaiserlichen) Reiches in ein anderes Gebiet desselben zu ziehen. Die historisch definierte *rechtliche Lage der als neue Heimat geltenden Region* innerhalb des Imperiums war für sie unbekannt. Dass das Königreich Ungarn rein rechtlich betrachtet nicht mit den deutschen Erbländern identisch ist, hat sich für sie erst im Laufe der folgenden Zeit nach und nach und als Begleiterkenntnis der sich wiederholenden Freiheitskämpfe der Ungarn herausgestellt. Die deutschen Siedler des 18. Jahrhunderts mussten im Laufe der Geschichte im Gegensatz zu den von früheren ungarischen Königen nach Ungarn „geladenen" Gästen, den Sachsen in Siebenbürgen und den Zips in Oberungarn, mit verständlichem Unmut zur Kenntnis nehmen, dass das von ihnen besiedelte Land, ihre Heimat, sich sozusagen Stück für Stück zum „Ausland" entwickelte bzw. in den ungarischen Bestrebungen nach Selbständigkeit des Landes als solches definiert wurde. Im Gegensatz zu diesen früher nach Ungarn gelangten Gruppen waren die neuen Siedler weder rechtlich noch materiell mit vergleichbaren Privilegien und Formen des bürgerlichen Lebens ausgestattet. Sie wurden für die Siedlungsaktionen in erster Linie als landwirtschaftliche Fachkräfte an- und vorgesehen, ohne einen vergleichbaren technisch-zivilisatorischen Auftrag, wie ihn die früheren Siedler etwa in der Formierung und Förderung des städtischen Lebens in all seinen Belangen (Recht, Handwerk, Handel, Bildung etc.) gefunden haben. Ihre Situation wurde zunehmend kompliziert, als die Zeit des nationalen Erwachens eingetreten war und der feudalistisch definierte Begriff der Nation durch eine neue Auffassung abgelöst und von jetzt an überwiegend auf die dieselben Sprachen sprechenden menschlichen Gemeinschaften verwendet wurde.[1]

Paradox und in ihren Folgen ganz besonders tragisch war jene Tatsache, dass das, was die deutschen Siedler als ihr ureigenes Recht, nämlich die uneingeschränkte Benutzung ihrer Muttersprache in sämtlichen öffentlichen und kulturellen Funktionen, angenommen und praktiziert haben, zu dieser Zeit, als die Voraussetzungen für eine moderne Nation zunehmend in der Nationalsprache gesehen wurden, mit dem gleichen Anspruch der Ungarn in Konflikt geriet, die ihrerseits die Bevorzugung der deutschen Sprache in den Angelegenheiten des ungarischen Königreichs als eine Verletzung der nationalen Souveränität ansahen und infolge dessen andauernd und vehement ablehnten. Eine unter den gegebenen Umständen und Bewusstseinszuständen unlösbare Reihe von gefährlichen Auseinandersetzungen entstand und verwandelte im Laufe der Zeit das Zusammenleben der verschiedenen Sprachen und Kulturen zum Schauplatz wachsender Spannungen. Soweit die Ungarn im Laufe des 18. und noch mehr des 19. Jahrhunderts ihre politische und kulturelle Souveränität über ihre einst verloren gegangenen südlichen Gebiete wiederherstellen konnten, schränkten sie mit der Durchsetzung ihrer politisch-kulturellen Vorstellungen zum Nationalstaat die Rechte der auf dem Gebiet seit längerem lebenden oder zwischenzeitlich angesiedelten Nicht-Ungarn ein und verletzten sie sogar. Sobald diese nicht ungarischen Landesbewohner die Anerkennung ihrer – vor allem sprachlich definierten – Eigenartigkeiten artikulierten oder später sogar deklarierten, unternahmen sie in den Augen der Ungarn etwas gegen die Souveränität des Landes Ungarn. Die beiden Bestrebungen waren in der gegebenen Konstellation und unter den gegebenen historischen Umständen nicht zu harmonisieren, ja, sie blieben über Jahrhunderte bis in unsere Tage hinein ein festes und zunehmend explosives Element der Konflikte. Auch die universellen Ziele des ungarischen Freiheitskampfes von 1948/49 zur Erkämpfung der Freiheit aller Menschen konnten sehr schnell mit der Hervorhebung der partikulären, sprachlich-kulturellen Identitätsunterschiede zwischen den Menschengruppen erfolgreich entstellt werden. Beim Aufeinandertreffen dieser Konflikte erlebte die politische Elite Ungarns einen nachhaltigen Schock und war nicht mehr imstande die späteren Bestrebungen der Nationalitäten im Spannungsfeld des 19. Jahrhunderts objektiv, ohne einen Verdacht auf Gefahr für die ungarische

[1] Siehe dazu SZEKFÜ, Julius: Der Staat Ungarn. Eine Geschichtsstudie. Stuttgart-Berlin 1918. – Bezüglich der Entwicklung des Nationalitätenbegriffs insbesondere 145-154.

Nation zu beurteilen. Dagegen erlebten z.B. nach 1877 die Deutschen im Lande die in ihren Folgen unumstritten stark repressiven Bestrebungen der ungarischen Politik („Magyarisierung“) zur Schaffung einer ungarischen politischen Nation als Gefährdung ihrer eigenen kulturellen Identität, und etliche Jahrzehnte später erlebten wiederum (auch) die meisten Ungarn die Bestrebungen Deutschlands nach 1933 zur Schaffung einer neuen mitteleuropäischen Ordnung („Germanisierung“) als eine reelle Gefährdung der ungarischen Identität. Die widersprüchlichen Erfahrungen der Einzelnen wurden oft in eine kollektive Phobie dem Anderen gegenüber transformiert, was wiederum nur zur Vertiefung der eigenen Traumata führen konnte.
Das eigentliche Verhältnis der Ungarn zu den Deutschen und umgekehrt können wir unter anderem auch deshalb nicht durch Untersuchungen der interethnischen Beziehungen ermitteln, weil das jeweils konkrete Verhältnis zwischen ihnen immer zugleich eine Resultante der jeweils herrschenden Verhältnisse zwischen den die Deutschen und die Ungarn vertretenden, sehr verschiedenen, und zugleich sich dauernd ändernden Staatsformationen gewesen ist. Insbesondere nach der Zerstörung der Österreich-Ungarischen Monarchie als politisch einheitlichem, kulturell und sprachlich jedoch sehr buntem Raum, also nach 1920, fanden sich alle Akteure unter vollständig neuen Bedingungen wieder. Einerseits hatten die Deutschen, die innerhalb der Monarchie durchaus lebendige und auch geographisch weit reichende Kontakte untereinander besaßen, diese durch die neuen Staatsgrenzen verloren, wodurch jedes deutsches Siedlungsgebiet noch stärker isoliert wurde. Andererseits veränderte sich die Dynamik gravierend: während sich früher die verschiedenen Nationalitäten der Monarchie hatten in ihren Emanzipationsbestrebungen gegen die Staaten bildenden Nationen (meistens gegen die Ungarn und die Österreicher) verbünden können, befanden sich die Deutschen in den neuen Staaten der Region nach 1920 in einer wesentlich schlechteren Position. Ihre einzige Hilfe existierte im Ausland, im stärker werdenden und sich dem Nationalsozialismus zuwendenden Deutschland. Die Folgen dieses fast zwanghaft entstandenen Bündnisses haben die im Laufe der Geschichte organisch entstandenen wirtschaftlichen und gesellschaftlichen Lebensbedingungen aller mitteleuropäischen deutschen Siedlungen entweder völlig zerstört oder nachhaltig beschädigt.

Literatur als Mittler der Traditionen und Vermittler bei Spannung

Wie kann in dieser konfliktträchtigen, kaum veränderbaren Situation die Formulierung der eigenen Vorstellungen literarisch erfolgen, und wie wird diese Artikulation von den ungarischen Literaten in ihren Werken aufgenommen? Dieses Zusammenspiel, die Reflexion der ungarischen Literatur auf die Selbstreflexion der deutschsprachigen Literaten im Laufe des 19. und 20. Jahrhunderts unter den sich ständig ändernden allgemeinen Bedingungen soll den Kern meines Beitrags ausmachen. Denn eine Äußerung, eine Artikulation trifft immer zugleich auf eine Umgebung, ein Publikum, trifft Umstände, die die Artikulation motiviert haben und sie zugleich qualifizieren werden. Die ereignisreichen Zeiten der vergangenen nahezu drei Jahrhunderte haben viel von dem, was geschrieben wurde, relativiert, vieles beinahe unverständlich, unnachvollziehbar für einen heutigen Leser gemacht, und trotzdem sind diese literarischen Werke Zeugen und Begleiter eines einmaligen Prozesses: des Zusammenlebens von sehr unterschiedlichen Menschen.

Die komplexen und verwobenen Motive und Arten der literarischen Reflexion in dieser Zeit werden außer von ästhetischen Gesichtspunkten von weiteren, vielfach dialogisch aufeinander Bezug nehmenden Positionen bestimmt. Ferenc Szász schreibt dazu: „In der ersten Hälfte des 19. Jahrhunderts erschien in der Beziehung der ungarischen und der deutschen Literatur ein neues Element, das man am besten mit dem Wort „Bewusstseinsspaltung“ charakterisieren könnte. Nachdem sich die gesellschaftliche Entwicklung in Mittel- und Osteuropa im Vergleich zu der der westeuropäischen Staaten verspätet hatte, bildete sich das Nationalbewusstsein in diesen Ländern nicht nur aus der eigenen Tradition heraus, sondern es baute auch Bewusstseinselemente in sich ein, die sich aus dem Vergleich mit anderen, bereits selbstbewussten Nationen ergaben. Um das Gefühl des Verspätetseins zu kompensieren, brauchte sie die Bestätigung der eigenständigen Charakterzüge, die auf gewissen Gebieten wertvoller sind als die der benachbarten Nationen. Diese Rivalitätsbestrebung der Ungarn richtete sich in erster Linie gegen die Deutschen, und in dieser Hinsicht machten sie im 19. Jahrhundert keinen Unterschied zwischen Österreich und den anderen deutschen Staaten. Dieses Minderwertigkeitsgefühl, das nach Kompensation strebte, hatte natürlich nicht nur massenpsychologische, sondern auch politisch-wirtschaftliche Gründe, denn bis zum Ende des Zweiten Weltkrieges bestand die tatsächliche Gefahr, dass Ungarn unter den politischen Einfluss des wirtschaftlich stärkeren westlichen Nachbarn gerät und seine staatsrechtliche Unabhängigkeit verliert.“[2]

Die Deutschen Ungarns in der ungarischen und in der deutschsprachigen Literatur

Die deutsch-ungarischen Beziehungen sind in der Kultur und besonders in der Literatur seit Anbeginn immer sehr intensiv und fruchtbar gewesen.[3] Trotz dieser engen und prägenden Kontakte ist eine themenspezifische, kontinuierliche Kommunikation zwischen der deutschen und der ungarischen Literatur bezüglich der deutschen Siedler in Ungarn in der „hohen Literatur” des Landes nicht nachweisbar: die Deutschen werden entweder von ihren eigenen Schriftstellern thematisiert oder spielen in den Werken ungarischer Autoren eine marginale oder die couleur locale der Handlung

[2] SZÁSZ, Ferenc: Die Wirkung der deutschsprachigen Literaturen in Ungarn. In: Hungaria litterata, Europae filia. Hg. v. Gyula KURUCZ und László SZÖRÉNYI. Budapest 1986, 55-70, hier 63.

[3] Siehe etwa JUHÁSZ, Ferenc: Auf deutschen Spuren zum ungarischen Parnass. Einfluss der deutschsprachigen Literatur auf die Entwicklung des ungarischen Schrifttums zu einer Literatur klassischer Höhe von 1772 bis 1848. München 1982 (Studia Hungarica 21). – Studien zur Geschichte der deutsch-ungarischen literarischen Beziehungen. Hg. v. Leopold MAGON u.a. Berlin 1969.

unterstreichende Rolle.[4] Es ist jedoch bekannt, dass im Ungarn des späten 19. Jahrhunderts auf lokaler oder regionaler Ebene vornehmlich in den mit städtischen Einrichtungen (Theater, Redaktionen, Verlage etc.) ausgestatteten Siedlungen die Literaten beider Sprachen lebhafte Kontakte zueinander zu halten pflegten. Langanhaltende, private Briefwechsel, öffentliche, in der örtlichen Presse publizierte Diskussionen der Schreibenden, Reflexionen auf die kulturellen Ereignisse (Veranstaltungen, Vereinsleben, Lesungen, Buchpublikationen etc.) der die jeweils andere Sprache sprechenden Gemeinschaft waren alltägliche Normalität. Die Zeugen dieses bunten und lebhaften Zusammenwirkens, die Dokumente dieser Zeit sind teilweise vernichtet, teilweise waren sie in den vergangenen Jahrzehnten nur schwer für die Forschung zugänglich.[5] Aber nach dem Muster der in unseren Tagen in der Region laufenden Erschließung und Veröffentlichung der verschiedenen kirchlichen Dokumente dieser Zeit wäre auch die Aufarbeitung der erhalten gebliebenen Quellen und Fora der „regionalen literarischen Beziehungen" in einem international koordinierten Forschungsprojekt dringend notwendig.

Außerhalb Ungarns wurden die deutschen Siedler des Landes verständlicherweise vor allem in der deutschsprachigen Literatur geschildert, teilweise durch ihre eigenen, zur größeren Bekanntheit gelangten Schriftsteller, aber auch durch jene nicht aus Ungarn stammenden Literaten, die das Thema „von außen her" betrachteten. Je nach den wechselhaften historischen Gegebenheiten wurden in den deutschen Texten romantische und heroische Elemente oft tendenziell in einer „Ideologie des Deutschtums" als des einzigen Kultur schaffenden Volks in der Region in unterschiedlichem Ausmaß miteinander verknüpft. In der Zeit zwischen den beiden Weltkriegen unterstützten sie damit einerseits direkt die völkischen Gedanken, andererseits unterstützte Nazi-Deutschland ebenso deutlich und wirksam die lokalen Protagonisten, Organisationen und Fora dieser Gedanken. Die tragischen und lang anhaltenden Folgen dieser Praxis können am Beispiel Jakob Bleyers und seines Werks, sowie dessen widersprüchlicher Aufarbeitung exemplarisch illustriert werden. Über ihn schreibt Dezső Keresztury in seinem rückblickenden Text. „Ein Germanist der Bleyer-Schule wollte ich tatsächlich nicht werden, hatte er doch die Weichen der ungarischen Germanistik eindeutig in die Richtung der Bestandsaufnahme der provinziell-dilettantischen deutschsprachigen Literatur in Ungarn gestellt und damit den Abstieg dieser so wichtigen Disziplin angebahnt."[6]

---

[4] Zu dieser Reflexion aus verschiedenen Blickwinkeln siehe z.B. WEBER-KELLERMANN, Ingeborg: Zur Interethnik. Donauschwaben, Siebenbürger Sachsen und ihre Nachbarn. Frankfurt 1978. – RIEDL, Franz Hieronymus: Das Bild des Deutschen in der madjarischen Literatur. Referat bei den 7. Ostdeutschen Kulturtagen in Mainz am 19. November 1960. In: Südostdeutsche Vierteljahresblätter 10 (1961), 72-88. – SCHERER, Anton: Die Literatur der Donauschwaben als Mittlerin zwischen Völkern und Kulturen. In: Lenau-Forum 3 (1971), 111-127.

[5] Siehe dazu: KESSLER, Dieter: Geschichte der deutschen Literaturen Siebenbürgens, des Banates und des Buchenlandes. Von der Revolution bis zum Ende des Ersten Weltkrieges (1848-1918). Köln 1997.

[6] KERESZTURY, Dezsö: Mein Weg zum Deutschen. In: KERESZTURY, Dezsö: Menschen, Werke, Verbindungen. Literatur- und kulturgeschichtliche Studien. Hg. v. Eve-Marie KALLEN. [Pécs][1999], 179-197, hier 180.

In der ungarischen Belletristik bekommen die deutschen Bürger des Landes für lange Zeit keine solch hochwertige Darstellung wie z.B. die in Nordungarn lebenden Slowaken in den Novellen und Romanen von Kálmán Mikszáth. Auch die bürgerliche Entwicklung der nordungarischen Städte und traditionsreichen Bergbausiedlungen werden zu verschiedenen Zeiten von namhaften Autoren (Ferenc Kazinczy bis Sándor Márai) mehrfach reflektiert. Der als „Einsiedler von Stósz (Štós)" apostrophierte Zoltán Fábry ist im 20. Jahrhundert über Jahrzehnte hinweg unter ständig wechselnden, aber zumeist bedrohlichen Bedingungen ein konsequenter Verfechter der „vox humana", der menschlichen Verständigung zwischen Sprachen und Kulturen gewesen, nicht zuletzt in der geistigen Tradition der in Oberungarn ansässigen deutschen Minderheit.

Ähnliches kann über die Sachsen in Siebenbürgen berichtet werden. Im 20. Jahrhundert haben sie in Zsigmond Móricz bzw. in seiner Siebenbürgen-Trilogie einen hochrangigen ungarischen Literaten gefunden, der die historischen Leistungen der Siebenbürger Sachsen auch mit ihren Fehlern großartig schildert, während Károly Kós in seinem kulturgeschichtlichen Werk „Siebenbürgen" (1934) das Zusammenleben der verschiedenen Völker und Kulturen als Ideal beschreibt.[7] Die Selbstreflexion zahlreicher deutschsprachiger Autoren aus Siebenbürgen, die lange und reiche kulturelle Tradition der sächsischen Städte haben im Laufe der Jahrhunderte eine selbständige regionale Literatur auf Deutsch geschaffen, deren Reichtum und Entwicklung zu schildern an dieser Stelle unmöglich ist.

Die zerstreut in Ungarns Mitte angesiedelten Deutschen lebten im Vergleich zu den früher erwähnten älteren Siedlern in Oberungarn und in Siebenbürgen eher in bäuerlicher Umgebung, inselartig, kulturell und auch sprachlich ziemlich isoliert und teilweise für sich belassen. Ihre eigene deutschsprachige „hohe" Literatur, ihre Selbstreflexion ist typischerweise erst im 20. Jahrhundert hervorgetreten.

Einen besonderen Fall bedeuten in dieser Hinsicht die deutschen Siedlungen in der Batschka-Banat-Gegend. Obwohl in bäuerlicher Umgebung lebend, die Landwirtschaft pflegend, aber von rasch sich entwickelnden Städten umringt, erlebte die Bevölkerung dieser Gegend in den kulturellen Angelegenheiten eine sehr schnelle, nahezu sprunghafte bürgerliche Entwicklung. Der Experte dieser Entwicklung, Horst Fassl, behauptet sogar: „Es kommt hier zum ersten Mal überhaupt zur Herausbildung eines selbstbewussten deutschen Schrifttums."[8] Wenn die von deutschen oder ungarischen Autoren verfassten Texte des ausgehenden 19. Jahrhunderts eine(n) Deutsche(n) schildern, dann wird das soziologisch und mental gleichermaßen typische Motiv der Zeit, die Position des Einzelnen und seiner Gemeinschaft zwischen Sprachen und Kulturen, stark betont. Eine spezifische Dynamik in den Auffassungen ist sogar für mehrere Literaten und Gelehrte im Laufe des Lebens gleichermaßen typisch gewesen: zunächst kann eine nahezu kindliche, idealisierende Identifikation

---

[7] KÓS, Károly: Siebenbürgen. Budapest 1989.

[8] FASSL, Horst: Die Donauschwäbische Literatur und ihre Entwicklung vom 18. bis zum 20. Jahrhundert. In: Die Donauschwaben. Deutsche Siedlung in Südosteuropa. Bearb. v. Immo EBERL. Sigmaringen 1989, 289-291, hier 289.

mit der engeren Heimat (meistens mit der Dorfgemeinschaft mit ihren Figuren, Leben und Konflikten) festgestellt werden, die der Persönlichkeit die Grundlagen, die Sicherheit für das Leben gewährt. Dann, meistens durch Bildung und öfter durch den damit verbundenen Ortswechsel, entsteht in den Studenten oder jungen Erwachsenen eine gewisse Entfernung, ja ein Befremden bezüglich des verlassenen Dorfes und schließlich, eher in der reifen Phase des Lebens, kehren viele Autoren zu ihrer ursprünglichen Umgebung thematisch zurück. Doch der Blickwinkel hat sich nun wesentlich geändert, komplexere, kontrast- und polemikträchtige Elemente mischen sich mit harmonisierendem Rückblick und weisem Verständnis. Diese individuelle Entwicklungsdynamik stellte die Schriftsteller allerdings zu einem bestimmten Punkt ihres Lebens vor eine schwere Wahl, die oft über ihre gesamte Laufbahn entschied: die Wahl der Sprache. Je nachdem, ob sie für ihre literarische Arbeit die deutsche oder die ungarische Sprache wählten, fielen ihre Resonanz, ihr Erfolg und ihre Bedeutung unterschiedlich aus. Alle, die sich für die deutsche Schriftsprache entschieden, mussten zunächst eine enorme Kluft zur deutschen Kultur und Literatursprache hin überwinden, diejenigen, die sich fürs Ungarische entschieden, mussten kulturell und sprachlich eine neue eigene Identität entwickeln. Für beide Entscheidungen gibt es viele Beispiele, aber es ist zugleich festzustellen, dass von den deutschsprachigen und auf Deutsch schreibenden Literaten aus Ungarn nur sehr wenigen der Weg in die kanonisierte deutsche Literaturgeschichte gelang (z.B. Nikolaus Lenau), während in der modernen ungarischen Literaturgeschichte mehrere bedeutende, allerdings auf Ungarisch schreibende Schriftsteller mit deutscher Herkunft bekannt sind. Hier kann man z.B. auf Ferenc Herczeg hinweisen, dessen „Ungartum-Auffassung [...] die adlige Ungartum-Auffassung [ist]: den Verkörperer des nationalen Eidos sieht er im Adligen, im Herrn, und den vornehmlichstem Charakterzug des Ungartums im herrischen Trotz, in der Herren[úri]-Empfindsamkeit, in der verzichtenden Geste, mit der er sich zurückzieht, wenn die Welt mit ihrer Berührung die Reinheit seiner Ideale beschmutzt."[9] Einen anderen Weg betrat der Prosaist Géza Gárdonyi: Dessen „väterlicherseits geerbtes deutsches Geblüt offenbart sich in seiner metaphysischen Rastlosigkeit, seiner Gottsuche. Zuerst ist er Atheist, hernach findet er Ruhe [megnyugszik] im Glauben an die Seelenwanderung. Seine Bücher durchwebt er noch und noch mit Reflexionen, die nach den letzten Fragen forschen: in seinen Antworten spürt man zumeist den Autodidakten, das Fehlen der regulären philosophischen und formalen Bildung."[10]

Der aus Werschetz (Versec/Vrsac/Vršac/Vârșeț) stammende anerkannte und populäre Schriftsteller Ferenc Herczeg (1863-1954) reflektierte 1916, inmitten des Ersten Weltkrieges, in einem romantisch-pathetischen Roman (A hét sváb / Die sieben Schwaben) die Zeit des ungarischen Freiheitskampfes von 1848/49 in der Banater Gegend. Im Mittelpunkt der Geschichte stehen die Deutschen, aber hin und wieder werden auch andere Nationalitäten der Region in das Geschehen des Romans einbezogen. Über diesen patriarchalisch und zugleich patriotisch anmutenden Text hat

[9] SZERB, Antal: Ungarische Literaturgeschichte I-II. Youngstown, Ohio 1975. Band II, 339.
[10] EBD. II, 340.

1941 Jenő Pintér, der führende Literaturhistoriker Ungarns, geschrieben: „[Die Helden des Romans „A hét sváb" (1916) – die Deutschen in Südungarn – haben ihr Schicksal zur Zeit des Freiheitskampfes 1848 mit ihrem Blutopfer an das Ungarntum geknüpft. In ihrer Entscheidung manifestiert sich die Dankbarkeit ihrer Rasse dafür, dass sie sich vor hundert Jahren auf ihrem reichen Boden haben niederlassen können. Der durch die Erfahrungen des Lebens alt gewordene schwäbische Bürger drückt seine deutsche Treue wie folgt aus: „Wir sind Deutsche und werden uns so verhalten, wie es die deutsche Ehre verlangt. Die Ehre verlangt: wenn wir in Frieden mit den Ungarn zusammengelebt haben, dann sollen wir auch in der Gefahr zu ihnen halten. Wenn wir sie in der Not verlassen würden, wären wir keine ehrenhaften Deutschen sondern eine zusammengerottete Schurz.']"[11] Aus dem obigen Zitat wird einerseits deutlich, wie einseitig und falsch, aus dem Blickwinkel der Folgezeiten geradezu unhaltbar, ein literaturhistorisches Urteil ausfallen kann, wie nachhaltig negativ es sich auf das Werk eines Schrifttellers auswirken kann. Deshalb muss man hinzufügen, dass die Berühmtheit, die Bedeutung Herczegs in der ungarischen Literatur *nicht* auf dem oben erwähnten Werk ruht, in erster Linie haben seine Gesellschaftskomödien, Novellen und historischen Romane seine Popularität begründet. Darüber hinaus hat Herczeg auch eine beachtliche Rezeption im deutschen Sprachraum erreicht – zwischen 1894 und 1937 sind nahezu 40 Bücher von ihm auf Deutsch erschienen –, aber er konnte im Gegensatz zu anderen, auf Deutsch schreibenden Autoren niemals als „Schriftsteller der Donauschwaben" o.ä. bezeichnet werden.

Diese Kategorie, der Schriftsteller, die Stimme, etc. einer sprachlich-kulturellen Gruppe (meistens eine Minderheit, am häufigsten eine nationale Minderheit) zu sein, ist sowieso eine mehrfach problematische Erscheinung. Die konfliktträchtigen letzten zweihundert Jahre haben trotzdem oft, aber immer für nur eine relativ kurze, aktuelle Konstellation solche Persönlichkeiten hervorgebracht und nicht nur in Bezug auf die deutschen Minderheiten. Auch in der ungarischen literaturhistorischen Tradition findet man die gängige Bezeichnung, dass jemand die „Stimme der Gegend X, der Menschen soundso, oder des echten Y-tums" sei. Diese problematischen Attribute verursachen oft großen Schaden, denn ein Autor kann mit lokalem Kolorit in seinem Werk durchaus auch dann von allgemeiner Bedeutung sein, wenn er/sie in erster Linie eine kleinere Gruppe, die Bewohner der eigenen engeren Heimat anspricht, „nur" für die dort lebenden Leser schreibt und keine Mittler- oder Vertreterrolle der breiteren Öffentlichkeit gegenüber einnehmen möchte.

Etwas komplizierter wird es, wenn der Schriftsteller über die Lage dieser „engeren Heimat" für ein Publikum jenseits dieses Raumes berichten möchte. In diesem Falle ist nämlich sowohl die Möglichkeit eines Weges in die Weltliteratur als auch der künstlerische Verfall in die Rolle eines aktuellen, sehr häufig manipulierten und selbst manipulierenden, vermeintlichen Sprachrohrs gegeben. Für beide Schicksale

---

[11] PINTÉR, Jenő: Magyar irodalomtörténet [Ungarische Literaturgeschichte] (VIII/1). Budapest 1941, 378. (Der zitierte Textabschnitt wurde von mir übersetzt – T.F.)

können wir im Kreis der aus dem Banat stammenden deutschsprachigen Schriftsteller Beispiele finden.

Besonders auffallend ist beim Vergleich des Lebenslaufs solcher Autoren, dass sie, nahezu ausnahmslos das früher erwähnte Muster befolgend, erst durch eine Distanz zur engeren „Heimat" ihre Zugehörigkeit erkennen und sie dann zu formulieren beginnen. Eine der zentralen Figuren der donauschwäbischen Literatur, Adam Müller-Guttenbrunn z.B., hat nach vielen Entbehrungen und Enttäuschungen in den Jugendjahren im Südosten (im Banat: ungarische Grundschule; in Hermannstadt: deutsches Gymnasium) erst in Linz und dann in Wien seine Berufung erkannt: „Durch ihn wurde nach 1900 das Gemeinschaftsbewusstsein aller Donauschwaben bestärkt. Seine Romane („Glocken der Heimat" 1910; „Der große Schwabenzug" 1913; „Meister Jakob und seine Kinder" 1918) erscheinen seinen Landsleuten noch heute als die gültige Darstellung ihrer eigenen Vorstellungen von donauschwäbischem Wesen und donauschwäbischer Geschichte."[12] Den Unterschied, der den jungen Müller-Guttenbrunn vom reiferen unterscheidet, können Texte aus seinen Erinnerungen und Briefen zeigen. Nahezu reformatorischer Eifer und Feuer klingen aus seinen Zeilen und dem Affekt heraus, als er über die Figur Christi in einem Brief nach 1873 schreibt: „Sie glaubten an die Göttlichkeit Christi – glaubten das Unglaublichste, das menschlicher Wahnsinn ausgebrütet. Sie glaubten an die Gegenwart Christi im „Allerheiligsten"! Ich sage Ihnen, Jesus sei ein Mensch, ein großer, herrlicher Mensch gewesen, der nie eine Ahnung hatte von dem heillosen Unfug, den man mit seinem Namen, seiner Lehre einst treiben werde. Er sprach in Bildern wie Poeten sprechen; wie es besonders damals und auch heute noch unter Orientalen gebräuchlich ist. Man nahm diese schönen Bilder wörtlich, und daraus entstand dann das Gegenteil von dem, was Jesus wollte. Der Buchstabe war da, der Geist verflogen. Und dieser kopflose „Buchstabenglaube" hat ungeheures Elend über die Menschheit gebracht, hat Ströme von Blut vergossen, und das alles zu Ehren Christi, des sanftmütigsten, edelsten „Menschensohnes"."[13]

Als er wenige Jahre später, etwa um 1877, aus dem Banat einen Brief verschickt, formuliert er nahezu resigniert die Empfindung seiner literarischen Berufung gegenüber: „Sie erwarten ländliche, idyllische Bilder von mir? Ländliche, ja; idyllische nicht. Zur Idylle fehlt hier alles, selbst der Charakter der Landschaft ist dazu hier ein viel zu ernster, fast melancholischer. Auch wohnt kein Volk von Hirten hier, sondern ein ackerbauendes, das sich im strengsten Sinne des Wortes im Schweiße seines Angesichtes sein Brot erwirbt und von Vergnügungen, welcher Art immer, kaum den Namen kennt. Dazu wird das Volk hier von einem elenden Beamtengesindel ausgesaugt, bestohlen und betrogen, wo es sich hinwendet. Infolgedessen ist ein Zug von Misstrauen und Verbitterung im Charakter dieses Volkes bemerkbar, der mich oft unangenehm, ja peinlich berührt. Ich weiß nicht, war ich früher blind oder war es nicht so arg wie jetzt, aber ich bin sehr ernüchtert, fast möchte ich sagen,

[12] FASSL: Die donauschwäbische Literatur, 290.

[13] MÜLLER-GUTTENBRUNN, Adam: Der Roman meines Lebens (Aus dem Nachlass zusammengestellt von seinem Sohne). Leipzig 1927, hier 79-80.

enttäuscht von meiner Heimat, und ich weiß nicht, ob ich sie je wieder sehen werde."[14]

Der andere große Dichter, der aus dieser Gegend, aus Lenauheim (Csatád) stammt und in Pest herangewachsen zur Symbolfigur der Weltliteratur wurde, war Nikolaus Lenau (1802-1850). Er ist einer der wahrlich Größten, die den Weg vom Partikularen zum Universellen haben beschreiten können und dafür in den Wertungen der Literaturgeschichte einen hohen Preis bezahlt haben. „Germanistische Forschung und Pädagogik haben nämlich, vor allem im deutschen Sprachraum, Lenaus Persönlichkeit und Dichtung während eines Jahrhunderts zerfleischt, verstümmelt, zielbewusst oder wohlgemeint grundlegend umfunktioniert. Aus dem Dichter, der als erster ein breites, sowohl gesellschaftskritisch als auch künstlerisch wirkungsvolles Bild der osteuropäischen Legende und Wirklichkeit seiner Zeit heraufbeschwor, aus dem Dichter, der eine aufrichtige, auch in ihrer Brüchigkeit so kräftig-echte Nachricht von den Bewegungen im großen unruhigen Lebensraum der fragwürdigen Nationen mit den zum Menschentum erwachenden Völkern und mit den ehrfürchtig-stolz bewahrten historischen Bewusstseinsformen der fortschrittlich gesinnten, revolutionsträchtigen Intelligenz des Westens vermittelte, aus diesem Dichter wurde ein „Sänger des Weltschmerzes", der „sinnenden Melancholie", ein psychologisch interessanter Vorläufer modernster Existenzialismen, ein durch seltene, wenn auch etwas herbstlich-welk schimmernde Feinheit der Sprache ausgezeichneter Lyriker. Kurz: an der Stelle eines bedeutenden politischen Dichters trat der Problematiker, der an den Klippen der Wirklichkeit zerschellende Zerrissene; ein Wehklagender Sänger des „mal du siecle".[15] Lenau ist auf jeden Fall ein phänomenales und dementsprechend eher eine Ausnahme darstellendes Beispiel für einen Literaten, der unter Bewahrung der ureigenen und lokalen Erfahrungen mit Hilfe der deutschen Kultur und Sprache über die die Region markierenden Landesgrenzen hinweg in die Universalität Zugang fand.

Die meisten anderen auf Deutsch schreibenden Schriftsteller aus Ungarn haben sich innerhalb anderer Koordinaten bewegt und stellen gerade deshalb eine eher geschlossene, in Zeit und Raum nur begrenzt wirkende und auch in Bezug auf den ästhetischen Wert ihrer Werke besondere Gruppe dar. Ganz grob, jedoch ohne eine mechanisch wirkende Kategorisierung aufstellen zu wollen, kann man unter ihnen grundlegend zwei verschiedene schriftstellerische Verhaltensmuster unterscheiden. Die zahlenmäßig größere Gruppe der Literaten erkannte unter Berücksichtigung der sprachlichen, dialektalen Unterschiede, dass ihr Werk ein klar begrenztes regionales Publikum erreichte, und deshalb stellten jene Schriftsteller sich die Aufgabe, für genau diese Leserschaft zu schreiben. Man könnte sagen, dass sie nicht auf breitere Bekanntheit hin arbeiteten. Das kann auch an ihrer Themenwahl, Sprache, Lebensführung usw. erkannt werden.

---

[14] MÜLLER-GUTTENBRUNN: Aus meinem Leben, 104.

[15] KERESZTURY, Dezsö: Lenau und die ungarische Reformbewegung. In: DERS.: Menschen, Werke, Verbindungen, 139-140.

Die andere, zahlenmäßig deutliche kleinere Gruppe von Schriftstellern erkannte – meistens unter den Einwirkungen der Kaiserstadt Wien –, dass hinter oder über den lokalen deutschen Sprach- und Kulturvarianten eine deutsche Hochsprache und Hochkultur existiert. Diese Erkenntnis animierte sie dazu, eine Verbindung zwischen dem Lokalen und dem Kultur(Nationalen) herzustellen. Dieses Bemühen ist hoch zu schätzen, doch dem späteren Betrachter ist klar, dass die Künstler sich durch diese Entscheidung – meistens ungewollt – auch an eine die gleichen Ziele befolgende Politik anbanden. Und je nachdem, ob diese Politik friedlich und rücksichtsvoll oder eher gewaltsam und ungeduldig agierte, waren die Umstände des literarischen Wirkens sehr unterschiedlich. Im übrigen hat diese politische Komponente immer wieder dafür gesorgt, dass einzelne Schriftsteller in unterschiedlichen Situationen ihren sonst „gewohnten" künstlerischen Wirkungskreis zeitweilig oder endgültig verließen und meistens, nach dem Größeren strebend, versuchten, mit ihren (durch die aktuelle Politik aufgewerteten) Romanen das gesamte deutschsprachige Lesepublikum anzusprechen. Nur unter Berücksichtigung solcher Umstände können z.B. die Romane von Mia Munier-Wroblewska, einer erfolgreichen Schriftstellerin, deren Oeuvre zwischen 1917 und 1940 die deutschen „Schicksale" von Kurland über Lettland bis zur Saar thematisierte und dabei 1933 in einem Roman ganz einfühlsam und innig die Probleme der Banater Schwaben schilderte, objektiv beurteilt werden.[16] Im Fall dieses Werkes ist z.B. eine durchaus glaubwürdige, aus heutigem Blickwinkel nahezu emanzipatorisch anmutende, in innerem Monolog verfasste Schilderung des schweren Lebens einer Frau immer wieder mit Gedanken und Reflexionen durchwoben, die *damals,* als das Buch erschien, einem Leser glaubwürdig erscheinen mochten, heute aber weder motiviert noch glaubwürdig wirken. Die historisch gegebene Zeit und die Entscheidung der Autorin, „Sprachrohr" und Quelle der „Aufklärung" zugleich zu sein, ruinierten nicht nur das künstlerische Vorhaben: sie führten bei sehr vielen anderen Autoren der Zeit und *bei den damaligen Lesern in der deutschen Diaspora zu der falschen Annahme, dass diese und ähnliche Werke die deutsche Hochliteratur repräsentierten!* Auch heute kursieren bei den Deutschen in der Region noch informell ganz merkwürdige deutsche Buchtitel und Autoren aus der Zeit vor dem Zweiten Weltkrieg, die als lesenswert und die Wahrheit beschreibende Werke gelten, die kaum jemand noch kennt, während die kanonisierten Größen der deutschen Hochliteratur bei den gleichen Lesern kaum Aufmerksamkeit finden.

Charakteristik der Selbstreflexion der deutschsprachigen Literatur aus Ungarn

Im Gegensatz zu anderen organisierten oder spontanen Umsiedlungsaktionen des 18. Jahrhunderts außerhalb Ungarns (z.B. in die Bukowina oder in das Moldau-Gebiet) und zugleich zur Stärkung des konfessionellen Gewichts des Katholizismus in der

[16] MUNIER-WROBLEWSKA, Mia: Der Mensch lebt nicht vom Brot allein. Erzählung aus dem Banat. Heilbronn 1933.

Region, bekamen die Gemeinden der Siedler im Banat recht bald ihre eigene Dorfgeistlichen zur Verfügung gestellt. Die Kirche konnte damit unmittelbar das Leben der Einzelnen und auch das der Gemeinden von Anfang an mit beeinflussen, sie wurde im Laufe der Zeit zu einer bedeutenden Säule der Identität und der Gemeinschaft. „Sie lieferte nicht nur das verbindliche Modell zur Welt- und Lebensdeutung, sondern griff auch unmittelbar in den Alltag ein durch ihre Abfolge von Werk- und Feiertagen, durch die Spendung von Sakramenten, durch Vorschriften über Fasten- und Abstinenzzeiten, durch ihre Lehren vom sittlichen und sozialen Verhalten, durch ihr Bildungsangebot usw. Diese Eingriffe oder Anregungen waren nie eng begrenzt, auf die Bedürfnisse eines Dorfes oder einer Landschaft zugeschnitten, sondern immer übergreifend (Hartinger l992a)".[17]

Insbesondere die Fähigkeit, Seelsorge und Betreuung der Menschen in ihrer Muttersprache zu gewähren, war ein wesentlicher Vorteil gegenüber anderen Siedlungsregionen, in denen die Bewohner häufig keine oder, sprachlich betrachtet, „fremde" Pfarrer in den Dörfern hatten. So konnte im Laufe der Zeit ein echtes Gefühl des „Zuhause seins" in größeren Regionen entstehen, das sogar die Trennungen durch die neuen Grenzen des 20. Jahrhunderts zu überleben vermochte. „Die Erinnerung an die Zusammengehörigkeit, an die einstige „Unbegrenztheit", ist heute noch bei den im Banat bzw. in der Südslowakei ansässigen Ungarn, aber auch in den Rumänen, den Deutschen, den Slowaken und den Serben lebendig. In diesem Gebiet wird so z.B. das aus spezifischen mentalen Landkarten kreierte Banat-Bewusstsein offenbar [...], das durch die Anziehungskraft des Wallfahrtortes Maria-Radna zudem eine sakrale Legitimation erhält [...]".[18]

Die Bedeutung der deutschsprachigen Kirche für die Siedler wird mit der Zeit durch vielerlei Veränderungen relativiert, aber dadurch entsteht die Möglichkeit zur Gegenüberstellung der idyllisch reinen „alten" und den verfallenen sündhaften, gottlosen „neuen" Zeiten. Dieser Kontrast ist ein zentrales Element der Werke der (nicht nur auf Deutsch geschriebenen) „regionalen" Literaturen, und natürlich wird auch immer nach den Ursachen dieses vermeintlichen Verfalls gefragt. Die Antwort auf diese Frage fällt sehr von der jeweiligen Zeit abhängig und unterschiedlich aus, als ein gemeinsames „verderbendes" Element stellen sich allerdings bei den meisten Schilderungen die jeweiligen Fremden dar, die in diese geerbte Idylle eindrangen. Da in der gesamten südosteuropäischen Region historische, religiöse, sprachliche, kulturelle und politische Grenzen nicht übereinstimmend, sondern einander kreuzend verlaufen, müsste die Konfrontation mit dem Fremden der alltägliche und natürliche Zustand sein. Die aus diesen Alltagserfahrungen organisch entstandenen weitertradierten Normen, Verhaltensmuster und Rollendefinitionen ermöglichten auf Gemeinde- und Lokalebene für lange Zeit das Zusammenleben der unterschiedlichen Gruppen, die Identität des Einzelnen war nämlich durch eine „höhere" Komponente (vom Herrscher oder vom Lehnherr der Region) bestimmt worden; unter-

[17] HARTINGER, Walter: Die Fiktion von den engen Grenzen der Volkskultur. In: Jahrbuch des Forschungszentrums für Europäische Ethnologie (2000-2001), 109-121, hier 111.
[18] BARNA, Gábor: Reale Grenzen – symbolische Welten. In: EBD., 23-35, hier 31.

halb dieser Ebene waren die Menschen gleich. Seit der Reformation kann man dagegen ein bis in unsere Tage hineinreichendes Abbröckeln der früheren Strukturen feststellen, an Stelle der Homogenität setzt sich eine wachsende Heterogenität durch, die zugleich das Konfliktpotential zwischen den neuen Protagonisten massiv steigert. In der so entstandenen neuen narrativen Konstellation ist jeder, unabhängig von den konkreten eigenen Merkmalen, in erster Linie ein Betroffener, der lediglich die Aktivitäten anderer erleidet und eigentlich ein unschuldiges Opfer ist.

Eine beispielhafte, tendenziöse Darstellung dieses Konfliktes findet man trotz der die Authentizität steigernden, fein und korrekt ausgewählten sprachlichen Merkmale des Textes z.B. bei Munier-Wroblewska: „Nach dem Essen half ich der Magd beim Geschirrwaschen; da erfuhr ich, dass der Stein-Michel schon seit zwei Monaten nicht mehr bei seiner angetrauten Frau lebe, sondern mit einem blutjungen, blutarmen Mädchen zusammen hause, das bereits ein Jahr lang seine Liebste sei. Die Magd tat mir kund, der Stein-Michel sei der schönste Mann im Dorf, er habe vor zehn Jahren die Hafner-Lena nur wegen ihres väterlichen Anwesens genommen, er sei kreuzunglücklich gewesen mit der kränklichen und mürrischen Person, was ihm keiner im Dorf verübele. Auch jetzt stünde mancher insgeheim auf seiner Seite.

Ich frug erstaunt, wie denn solch eine ehebrecherische Handlungsweise vor der öffentlichen Meinung, zumal vor der heiligen Kirche, bestehen könne. Da lachte die Magd spöttisch und meinte, man hänge hier im Dorf nicht so am Priesterrock wie anderweitig. Hochwürden wisse selber, dass er kein allzustrenges Regiment führen dürfe. Zum Lohn für seine Milde drücke man ja auch ein Auge zu oder gar alle beide Augen. Es sei noch keine Beschwerde an den Bischof nach Temesvar gegangen wegen der hübschen Haushälterin, die er mitgebracht, als er vor zwei Jahren sei ins Dorf gekommen, und wegen der Nichte, die ihn in den Ferien immer besuche. Ei, ei, Hochwürden solle fein stille schweigen. Man sei hier aufgeklärter und kümmere sich nicht viel um die Kirche.

Ich war fassungslos. Zum erstenmal vernahm ich solche freigeistigen Worte und empfand sie als sehr frevelhaft.

„Aber wie kann der Stein-Michel denn zur Beichte gehn, wenn er in seinem Tun beharrt und nicht von dem Mädchen lässt?"

„Viele gehn bei uns nicht zur Beichte," lachte das Mädchen, „von den Herrischen tut es keiner. Wozu ist das denn nötig? Der Stein-Michel ist glücklich mit seiner Liebsten und dem kräftigen Jungen, den sie von ihm hat. Was gibt es da zu beichten?"

Ich schauderte. „Aber wenn er stirbt, bekommt er kein christliches Begräbnis,"

„Wär noch nicht das schlimmste. Aber da werden seine Anverwandten schon dafür sorgen, dass er auf dem Sterbebett die Absolution bekommt. Sie werden der Kirche eine Stiftung machen." Sie schnippte mit den Fingern. „Das lässt sich alles einrichten, teuer oder billig."

Es tat sich mir eine neue Welt auf. Ich kannte die schöne, echte Frömmigkeit der Anna-Neni und die gedankenlose Scheinfrömmigkeit meiner Zieheltern. Dass es Menschen gab, die der Kirche und ihren Satzungen spottend gegenüberstanden, ohne sofort mit dem allgemeinen Bann belegt zu werden, das erschütterte meinen

Glauben an die Kirchenmacht aufs tiefste. Zudem konnte ich der Magd in manchem Stück nicht widersprechen. Die üblichen Bauernheiraten ohne Liebe um des Besitzes willen erschienen mir sündhaft, zumal jetzt, da der Philipp die Schmied-Resi nehmen sollte. Warum rügte die Kirche solche Heiraten nicht aufs allerschärfste?
Am Abend dieses Tages dachte ich über vieles nach und begann zu begreifen, welch böse Schäden in unserem schwäbischen Leben steckten, wie wenig unsere Kirche dawider zu wirken vermochte.“[19]

Veränderungen des Inhalts und des Narrativen nach dem Zweiten Weltkrieg

Die Ereignisse des zweiten Weltkriegs und der darauf folgenden repressiven Maßnahmen (Zwangsumsiedlungen, kollektive Schuldzuweisung, Verbot der Benutzung der deutschen Muttersprache) einerseits und die drastischen Veränderungen in der Wirtschaft und in der Gesellschaft (Kollektivierung, Industrialisierung, Migration in die Städte etc.) während der als sozialistisch bezeichneten Jahrzehnte danach haben in der südosteuropäischen Region das Leben radikal verändert und ihre traditionellen Inhalte und Formen weitgehend zerstört. In Folge dieser Veränderungen war zunächst eine literarische Reflexion der unmittelbaren Erfahrungen nicht möglich, denn die Politik und somit die Kulturpolitik gab den (vermeintlichen) Problemen der ganzen Gesellschaft den Vorzug, alles, was sich auf individuelle, regionale oder überhaupt partielle Angelegenheiten des Menschen gerichtet hätte, wäre als retrograd-bürgerlich oder gar als feindlich eingestuft worden. In der bezeichnenderweise in der jeweiligen amtlichen Landessprache publizierten Literatur der fünfziger und frühen sechziger Jahre erscheinen in allen sozialistischen Ländern die deutschen Minderheiten lediglich als bunte „Begleiter" eines größeren, ja weltweiten Klassenkampfes für eine neue Welt. Insofern zeigt diese Literatur eindeutige Ähnlichkeiten mit den zwischen der beiden Weltkriegen in der Sowjetunion von der „Verlagsgenossenschaft ausländischer Arbeiter" publizierten Werken. Die in dieser Literatur geschilderten Figuren und ihre Handlungen sind bemüht, ihre mannigfaltigen Eigenarten völlig zu vernichten, damit sie in der universellen Gemeinschaft von Menschen, also in der Arbeiterklasse, aufgehen können.
Erst im Laufe der sechziger Jahre erschienen in den sozialistischen Ländern Ostmitteleuropas solche deutschsprachigen Publikationen, die sowohl sprachlich als inhaltlich auch das unmittelbar Vergangene reflektierten. Diese Bücher sind jedoch oft im eigenen regionalen Dialekt publiziert worden und können deshalb zunächst eher als Kinderliteratur, als ethnographische, dialektologische oder sprachhistorische Veröffentlichungen, nicht als Belletristik angesehen werden. Dann wurden zunehmend repräsentativ gedachte Anthologien herausgegeben, die von den literarischen Aktivitäten der deutschen Minderheiten in diesen Ländern Zeugnis ablegen sollten.[20] Diese

[19] MUNIER-WROBLEWSKA: Der Mensch, 44-46.
[20] Siehe dazu unter anderen den Dokumentationsband: Ungarndeutsche Literatur der siebziger und achtziger Jahre. Eine Dokumentation. Hg. v. János SZABÓ und Johann SCHUTH. München-Budapest 1991 (Veröffent-

Reflexionen der deutschsprachigen Schriftsteller haben in Ungarn, in Rumänien, in Jugoslawien eine jeweils andere Funktion gehabt, sie galten aber immer als Zeugen der – wie auch immer zu verstehenden – „liberalen" Kulturpolitik des Landes, und nicht selten hatten sie die unmittelbare Aufgabe, die Beziehungen zur Bundesrepublik Deutschland zu „ebnen". Ganz auffällig ist in dieser Phase bei den belletristischen Publikationen die Dominanz der Dichtung, der subjektiven Reflexion der Welt.'[21]

Die achtziger Jahre haben auch weitere, positive Entwicklungen eingeleitet, insbesondere in der hier behandelten Banater Region. Einerseits setzte sich zwar der Exodus der deutschen Siedler fort, andererseits entwickelten sich aber individuelle und institutionelle internationale Beziehungen, die nach dem Wegfall des Eisernen Vorhangs ein Auferstehen der deutschsprachigen Literatur und viel Hoffnung versprachen. Balázs Végh hat dazu geschrieben: „Ob eine neue Literatur aus den Ruinen entstehen wird? Zunächst ist soviel sicher, dass die Zeitschrift *Neue Literatur* an der Adresse Str. Berthelot 41 – 70749 Bucuresti 1 abonniert werden kann."[22] Ein bis dahin nicht bekannter, aus der unmittelbaren kulturellen Umgebung sich befreiender und in die deutschsprachige „Hochliteratur" aufsteigender Typ von Autoren ist auf der Bildfläche erschienen, auch wenn seine bekanntesten Vertreter, Richard Wagner und Herta Müller, sehr verschiedene individuelle Laufbahnen eingeschlagen haben. Gemeinsam ist ihrem literarischen Wirken jedoch, dass sie eine neue Perspektive und damit auch eine neue Sprache in ihren Werken entwickelt haben. Die traditionellen Probleme des dörflichen Lebens, der Familien und Generationen, der Sprachen und Kulturen bekommen neue, nicht mehr bloß lokal geltende Dimensionen; diese Texte reflektieren den Wandel und die Krise der humanen Existenz. Auch sprachlich ist ein kurzes Zitat von Herta Müller imstande, den gewaltigen Unterschied zu den früheren Narrativen eindeutig zu illustrieren, obwohl der von ihr geschilderte Konflikt fast uralt genannt werden kann: „Der Wind hatte einen Ärmel meines Kleides ausgerissen. Er schwebte hauchig und schwarz in der Luft.

Ein Mann lehnte seinen Gehstock an einen dicken Stein. Er legte das Gewehr an und schoß den Ärmel ab. Als er vor meinem Gesicht niedersank, war er voller Blut. Die Leichenversammlung klatschte Beifall.

Mein Arm war nackt. Ich spürte, wie er an der Luft versteinte.

Der Redner gab ein Zeichen. Der Beifall verstummte.

Wir sind stolz auf unsere Gemeinde. Unsere Tüchtigkeit bewahrt uns vor dem Untergang. Wie lassen uns nicht beschimpfen, sagte er. Wir lassen uns nicht verleumden. Im Namen unserer deutschen Gemeinde wirst du zum Tode verurteilt.

---

lichungen des Südostdeutschen Kulturwerks, Reihe B: Wissenschaftliche Arbeiten 60). – Siehe auch die Anthologie: Bekenntnisse eines Birkenbaumes. Ungarndeutsche Anthologie. Dortmund 1990.

[21] Siehe dazu z.B. Balogh, András: Siebenbürgisch-deutsche Dichtung. Budapest 1994 (ELTE-Chrestomathie 6).

[22] Siehe dazu VÉGH, Balázs: Romániai német irodalom vagy német irodalom Romániában? [Rumäniendeutsche Literatur oder deutsche Literatur in Rumänien?] Neue Literatur. Zeitschrift der Querverbindung. In: Regio 4 (1993), 199-201, hier 201. (Der zitierte Textabschnitt wurde von mir übersetzt – T.F.)

Alle richteten ihre Gewehre auf mich. In meinem Kopf war ein betäubender Knall."[23]

Zusammenfassung

Aufgrund der oben dargestellten Merkmale kann man einige Besonderheiten der literarischen Reflexion der deutschsprachigen Schriftsteller in der ungarischen Literatur und ihre eigene literarische Selbstreflexion in ihren soziologischen und kulturellen Zusammenhängen besser verstehen. Dabei fällt auf, dass

- sowohl die deutschsprachigen Autoren Ungarns als auch ihre Werke bis auf wenige und seltene Ausnahmen immer nur eine regionale und temporale Bedeutung erreichen konnten.
- Sie (Autoren und Werke) sind kein fester Bestandteil der nationalen oder weltliterarischen Kanones geworden.
- Ihre Bücher wurden äußerst selten in die Sprache der Mehrheit in ihrem Wirkungsland übersetzt.
- Ihre eigenartige Isoliertheit beeinträchtigt gleichzeitig ihre Beurteilung: für den engeren, betroffenen Umkreis ihres Wirkens vergrößert dieser Umstand ihre Bedeutung, denn sie funktionieren als Artikulation der Stimme einer (meistens) benachteiligten Minderheit.
- Sie wirken sehr oft affirmativ in ihrem unmittelbaren kulturellen und gesellschaftlichen Kontext und zerstören dadurch ihre eigenen Wirkungsmöglichkeiten für eine breitere Öffentlichkeit nicht bloß aus sprachlichen Gründen.
- Kennzeichnend ist wegen der gerade festgestellten Eigenschaften, dass diese Werke meistens keinen konstanten, eigenen literarischen Wert besitzen, sondern fortdauernd „umgewertet" werden.
- Ihre Bewertung, ihre wissenschaftliche Rezeption erfolgt jedoch typischerweise nicht durch bestimmte literarische Instanzen, sondern im Laufe der letzten Jahrhunderte bezeichnenderweise hauptsächlich von ihrem jeweiligen politischen oder gesellschaftlichen Umfeld her.
- Möglicherweise ist diese Situation verantwortlich dafür, dass eine komplexe und objektive Aufarbeitung des ganzen Phänomens bis heute fehlt, lediglich einzelne Zeitabschnitte, Regionen, Autoren, Werke oder Spezialfragen wurden in den Monographien berücksichtigt.

Es bleibt also in allen vorstellbaren Richtungen literaturwissenschaftlicher Forschung auch in Zukunft reichlich zu tun.

---

[23] MÜLLER, Herta: Niederungen. Reinbek 1993, hier 10-11.

FORSCHUNGSBERICHTE

Krista Zach

Konfessionelle Raumkonfigurationen im südöstlichen Europa. Historiographische Anmerkungen zur Frühneuzeit

Einführende Bemerkungen

An den Schnittstellen der im 16. und 17. Jahrhundert mobilen habsburgisch-osmanischen Grenze stellt sich die Forschungs- und Quellenlage als schwierig und komplex dar. Diese Regionen, besonders das türkische Ungarn-Kroatien, bilden den Ort folgender Betrachtungen.

Die hundertsechzigjährige osmanische Herrschaft stellt sich strukturell für den weitaus größten Teil des Reichs der Stephanskrone gegenüber dem Königlichen Ungarn als epochenverschleppt dar – beispielsweise infolge der Kontinuität von spätmittelalterlichen Gesellschaftsformen und verlorener Modernisierungschancen, als Verlust der Gleichzeitigkeit, als Diskontinuität. Das Fehlen stabiler politischer Grenzen, überschaubarer Rechts- und Verwaltungspraxis bzw. die Überlagerung von unterschiedlichen Rechts- und Verwaltungssystemen im Türkischen Ungarn erzeugte weitere Disparitäten, die durch die Neuordnung der Grundbesitzverhältnisse meist willkürlich vertieft wurden. Diskontinuität ergab sich auch aus anderen Entwicklungen, wie die insgesamt starke räumliche und konfessionelle Mobilität in allen Bevölkerungsgruppen Südosteuropas.

Grund und Boden auch des ungarischen Eroberungsgebiets wurden zum persönlichen Besitz des Sultans, der Teile davon als nichterbliche Lehen an osmanische Würdenträger aus Verwaltung und Militär vergab. Die zumindest intentional zentralistisch organisierte Verwaltung ließ an der lokalen Basis, in den fernen Provinzen des Reiches, mannigfach Spielräume für Willkür, Grausamkeiten und Korruption zu. In diesen Regionen fehlte jegliche institutionelle Verdichtung, wie sie sich im 17. Jahrhundert in west- und auch in mitteleuropäischen Staaten – dem Deutschen Reich und den habsburgischen Erbländern – abzeichnete. Die im osmanischen Herrschaftsbereich eingesetzten Instrumente sozialer Disziplinierung wirkten, da meist willkürlich gehandhabt, vor allem desintegrativ. Käuflich waren etwa sowohl die grundlose Arretierung von Gegnern, wie die Befreiung aus der Haft durch andere Helfer; um Gerechtigkeit zu erlangen, waren höherinstanzliche Interventionen erforderlich.

Dazu bieten die – in der Forschung noch zu wenig berücksichtigten – katholischen Visitationsberichte der Apostolischen Administratoren und Bischöfe sowie die Briefe und Taufregister der Missionare aus dem südosteuropäischen Eroberungsgebiet nach Rom eine aussagestarke Quelle. Die zahlreichen strukturellen Gemeinsamkeiten erfordern daher eine gemeinsame historiographische Betrachtung dieses Raumes während der Türkenzeit.

Gleich ob ein verfügbarer historiographischer Befund oder lediglich ein bestimmter Quellenbestand dargestellt werden soll, rekurrieren Forschungen über das südöstliche Europa in der Frühneuzeit immer auch auf konfessionelle Faktoren. Diese Prämisse gilt in besonderem Maße für das Grenzgebiet, das die osmanischen von den Habsburger Territorien in Kroatien und Ungarn im 16. und 17. Jahrhundert voneinander trennte, wie für die bereits seit dem späten 14. Jahrhundert von den Türken beherrschten historischen Regionen des Westbalkan – Albanien und Mazedonien (1391: Einnahme von Skopje), Serbien (1389, 1459), Bosnien und Herzegovina (1463/1470), aber auch für Montenegro (Zeta, 1499), die rumänischen Fürstentümer Moldau und Walachei, sowie für Siebenbürgen (1541), die unter osmanischer Oberhoheit standen, und gleicherweise auch für Polen-Litauen. Der Religionsfaktor ist beispielsweise bei der Untersuchung von sozialgeschichtlichen Einzelkomplexen wie Integration und Desintegration im Gruppenverhalten innerhalb von pluriethnischen und -konfessionellen Räumen, für die Migrations- und Mentalitätsforschung sowie für zahlreiche weitere kulturhistorische Fragestellungen relevant und für die allgemeine politische Geschichtsbetrachtung als Prämisse vorauszusetzen.
Die Bewertung dieses konfessionellen Faktors unterliegt – so banal das hier Vorausgeschickte erscheinen mag – unterschiedlichen extrahistorischen (was meint hier extrahistorisch?)Prämissen.[1] Diese an einem stetig nach Nordwesten verlegten christlich-muslimischen Grenzbereich im südöstlichen Mitteleuropa anzutreffenden Regionen bildeten auch im Spätmittelalter, als lose Glieder in einer Kette kleinerer Spannungsräume, eine konfliktreiche Zone, denn hier verlief der nicht sichtbare „Limes“ zwischen westlichen und östlichen Kulturen, Mentalitäten, Sprach- und Konfessionsgemeinden (sollte man nicht besser Gruppen sagen?). Mit Blick auf das hier zu betrachtende Material können diesen konfessionell unterschiedlich strukturierten Räumen zumindest vier Kennzeichen zugeordnet werden, die bis heute noch – als Ansatz- wie Ausgangspunkt für die Bewertung dieser Kontakt- und Konfrontationszone – erkennbar sind.[2]
In einem breiten Feld von Zusammenhängen ist in der Frühneuzeit erstens von einem konfessionell unterlegten und oft auch gesteuerten Konflikt- und Konkurrenz-

[1] Dafür stellvertretend zwei Arbeiten aus der deutschsprachigen Südosteuropaforschung: In allen Auflagen seiner Geschichte der Balkanländer, Von der Frühzeit bis zur Gegenwart. München [2]1993 ([1]1988, [4]2002), berücksichtigt Edgar HÖSCH als „Grundlagen und Voraussetzungen der Geschichte Südosteuropas“ gleichermaßen „Ethnische Strukturen ..., Kulturzonen ..., Kirchen und Konfessionen“, hier 13, 19, 26. – Anders Karl KASER, der sich erst angesichts der Kriege im ehemaligen Jugoslawien veranlasst sah, der zweiten Auflage seiner Habilitationsschrift Freier Bauer und Soldat. Die Militarisierung der agrarischen Gesellschaft in der kroatisch-slowenischen Militärgrenze (1535-1881). Wien, Köln, Weimar [2]1997 ([1]1986. Zur Kunde Südosteuropas. Bd. 2, 22), ein neues Kapitel zuzufügen: „Nationale Integration auf konfessioneller Grundlage“, 599-617.
[2] Dazu MAGOCSI, Paul Robert: Historical Atlas of East Central Europe. Toronto 1993, Karte Nr. 13 „Ecclesiastic Jurisdcktion, ca. 1450“, 43 (hier: Abb. 1) und Karte Nr. 18, p. 58 „Occupied Hungary“, wie ebd., Karten Nr. 19b, 61; Nr. 20, 63 und Nr. 20b, 65; Karte Nr. 15, „Protestant Reformation, 16th Century“, 49.

verhalten der Bevölkerungsgruppen bzw. der lokalen Machtträger auszugehen; hier lebten längst vor 1390 schon griechisch-orthodoxe und lateinisch-katholische Gruppen mit religiös, politisch wie mentalitätsmäßig unterschiedlich geprägten Ansprüchen, Institutionen und Ordnungsvorstellungen nebeneinander. Ausschlaggebend waren auch in der Frühneuzeit die konfessionellen und nicht die sprachethnischen Differenzierungen. Vom Großen Kirchenschisma gingen nach 1054 in der Region immer wieder Impulse für latente Spannungen aus, verstärkt in Krisenzeiten, wie es die schrittweise osmanische Eroberung gewesen war. Die Reformation[3] fügte dem im 16. und 17. Jahrhundert durch die Bildung und dauerhafte Etablierung einer größeren Zahl von protestantischen Gemeinschaften neue Konfliktpotenziale hinzu. Diese regionale Gemengelage zeigt Abb. 1.

Zweitens wird eine Bewertung auch davon ausgehen, dass es hier um eine vergleichsweise extrem fragmentierte Vielvölkerlandschaft mit jahrhundertelangen Erfahrungen der Außeneinwirkungen handelt – Fremdherrschaft, *Theatrum bellorum* und Ausplünderung –, wodurch die eigenen politischen Institutionen und Strukturen überformt oder zerstört wurden. Es ist drittens von einer Region auszugehen, in der am Beginn der Neuzeit wichtige Prozesse wie die Nationswerdung und anschließende Nationalstaatsbildung nach westeuropäischem Modell retardiert erfolgten. In Rechnung zu stellen ist ferner die Präsenz einer Bevölkerung mit intensiver Neigung zu volkspoetischer Mythenbildung. Für die fehlende oder schwächer ausgebildete staatliche Verdichtung steht in den meisten nationalen Historiographien der Südosteuropäer – in einem engeren Feld von Zusammenhängen – viertens ein Schlüsselwort – die *„lange Türkenherrschaft"*. Diese wurde in Langzeitperspektive regional gleichzeitig zum Epitheton für alles Fremde und Retardierende, für die „Zurückgebliebenheit" gegenüber Europa schlechthin, und die speiste im Westen seit dem 18. Jahrhundert pejorative Vorstellungen vom rückständigen Balkan[4], die im 19. Jahrhundert in doppelter Hinsicht als Blockade wirkten. (Abb. 1)

Raummerkmale wie diese ergeben unterschiedliche Prämissen für das Verständnis von Geschichte, gleich ob sie in langzeitlicher oder kurzer Wahrnehmungsperspektive betrachtet wird. Die wirtschaftliche wie strukturelle „Rückständigkeit" Südosteuropas im späten 19. Jahrhundert – und das ist die letzte Vorbemerkung – wird in den nationalen Historiographien der Balkanvölker weitgehend bis ausschließlich der langen Türkenherrschaft zugeordnet, selbst dort, wo diese, wie in den beiden rumänischen Fürstentümern, „nur" in einer tributpflichtigen Oberhoheit bestanden hatte. Die Türkenzeit wird auch von westlichen Historikern überwiegend mit dem Negativkoeffizienten für Rückständigkeit versehen.[5] Daraus sind nicht nur im von den

[3] Dazu pars pro toto ein neues Werk von LEPPIN, Volker: Siebenbürgen: ein kirchenhistorischer Sonderfall von allgemeiner Bedeutung. In: Konfessionsbildung und Konfessionskultur in Siebenbürgen in der Frühen Neuzeit. Hg. v. DEMS. und Ulrich A. WIEN. Stuttgart 2005, 7-13.

[4] TODOROVA, Maria: Imagining the Balkans. Oxford 1997, Kap. 4: westeuropäische Wahrnehmungsmuster.

[5] TODOROVA: Imagining. – The Origins of Backwardness in Eastern Europe. Economics and Politics from the Middle Ages until the Early Twentieth Century. Ed. by D. CHIROT. Berkeley 1989. – Differenzierter dazu SUNDHAUSSEN, Holm: Die ‚Modernisierung' der Balkanländer in vorsozialistischer Zeit: Ein Missverständnis und seine Folgen. In: Rumänien im Umbruch. Chancen und Probleme der osteuropäischen Integration. Hg. v. Ilina GREGORI und Angelika SCHASER. Bochum 1993, 23-34. – DERS.: Nation und Natio-

Schulbüchern dieser jungen Nationen gespeisten Alltagsdiskurs, sondern auch in der Historiographie zur regionalen Kultur- und Kirchengeschichte – die letztendlich immer schon die Autorschaft dafür innehatte – langlebige Klischees und Wahrnehmungsstereotype über die Türkenzeit und ihre Folgen entstanden. Diese historiographischen Stereotype und Klischees haben bei allen betroffenen Völkern bis heute einen hohen (De-)Motivations- wie Zirkulationswert beibehalten, und sie werden nicht zuletzt auch in die Diskurse zu den einzelnen Nationsbildungsprozessen integriert. Keineswegs soll hier versucht werden, die Türkenzeit schön zu reden oder ihr das Mäntelchen einer Friedens- oder Reformära umzuhängen. Doch lässt die oben erwähnte Betrachtungsweise jede weiter ausgreifende Kontextualisierung vermissen: Die politische und weitgehend auch die wirtschaftliche Abkoppelung vom restlichen Europa, die diese 160 bis 190 Jahre für Ungarn, Kroatien, Dalmatien, und länger noch für den Balkan sowie z.T. auch für die Donaufürstentümer bedeutet hatte, sollte in der modernen Historiographie nicht mehr den Blick auf jene in der Zeit nach 1800 versäumten oder verzögerten Prozesse des strukturellen Wandels verstellen, die vom 19. Jahrhundert bis in die Gegenwart ein gesellschaftliches Erfordernis gewesen wären. Dieser Aspekt wird in den nationalen Forschungstraditionen übergangen oder fast gänzlich ignoriert.[6]

Quellen, Initiativen und Forschungslage

Im Folgenden verengt sich die Perspektive auf katholische Gemeinden im Türkischen Ungarn und seine unmittelbaren Nachbarregionen. Hierbei handelt es sich um die am besten und intensivsten erforschten Aspekte, welche auf die meisten erschlossenen und auch gedruckten *Primärquellen* aufbauen. Dennoch können auch in diesem eingeschränkten Feld zum Einen bedeutende Defizite bezüglich weiterer bibliographischer Erfassung der verstreuten, vielsprachigen Forschungsergebnissen und Primärquellen festgestellt werden, es weiterhin Lücken in der vergleichenden sozial- wie kulturgeschichtlichen Datenerfassung geben[7], und – am gravierendsten vielleicht – es fehlt noch eine größere Raumsynthese[8]. Zum anderen lässt sich dar-

nalstaat auf dem Balkan. In: Der Balkan. Die europäische Krisenregion in Geschichte und Gegenwart. Hg. v. Jürgen ELVERT. Stuttgart 1997, 77-90.

[6] BAHLCKE, Joachim: Ungarischer Episkopat und Österreichische Monarchie. Von einer Partnerschaft zur Konfrontation (1686-1790). Leipzig 2005, 13-40.

[7] MOLNÁR, Antal: Katolikus missziók a hódolt Magyarországon. [Katholische Missionen im Eroberungsgebiet Ungarns]. Bd. 1 (1572-1647). Budapest 2002, 577f.

[8] Die fehlende Synthese allein schon der europäischen Forschung mahnte der Bamberger Osmanist Klaus Kreiser schon 1983 an: „Bekanntlich fehlt jede zusammenfassende Untersuchung der europäischen Historiographie des Osmanischen Reiches." KREISER, Klaus: Clio's Poor Relation. Betrachtungen zur osmanischen Historiographie von Hammer-Purgstall bis Stanford Shaw. In: DERS.: Türkische Studien in Europa. Istanbul 1998 (Analecta Isisiana 31), 33-52, hier 33, Anm. 2. – Vom Stabilitätspakt für Südosteuropa, dem Auswärtigen Amt der Bundesrepublik Deutschland u.a. internationalen Organisationen gesponsert wurden 2005 alternative, integrierte Lehrbücher für die Geschichte Südosteuropas: Teaching Modern Southeast European History. Alternative Educational Materials. Workbook I: The Ottoman Empire. Ed. by Halil BERKTAY and Bogdan MURGESCU. Thessaloniki 2005. – Hier werden zumindest Elemente für eine solche

über hinaus ein starkes Forschungsungleichgewicht erkennen, vergleicht man die nationalen Forschungstraditionen und -ergebnisse zu den Gruppen von Protestanten mit jenen zu den Katholiken: Letztere sind besonders in Ungarn deutlich defizitär.[9] Die meisten zugänglichen Quellen werden nicht in der jeweils entsprechenden Region aufbewahrt, und sie können wohl auch – wegen zahlreichen sprachlichen und Publikationserschwernissen – der Forschung nur nach intensiver Teamarbeit zugänglich gemacht werden. Zu diesen in unterschiedlichen Vollständigkeitsgraden erschlossenen Quellen gehören in einer ersten, streng systematischer Übersicht entbehrenden Reihung drei große Gruppen:

a. Osmanische Quellen, bestehend aus drei Gruppen:

- *Steueraufzeichnungen* (sog. *Defter*), die erst in Teileditionen zu manchen Regionen, z.B. Bosnien, ediert, aber noch wenig systematisch ausgewertet sind;
- *Chronistik* – sie ist lückenhaft überliefert, z.B. zu einzelnen Feldzügen der Sultane in Südosteuropa (vor allem Süleymans des Prächtigen[10]);
- *Bildquellen* (die den Chroniken beigegeben wurden und z.T. sehr präzise Ortsdarstellungen und Karten enthalten z.B. zu Szigetvár, Eszergom, Temesvár[11]) enthalten.

b. Westliche Quellen nichtkonfessioneller Provenienz, bestehend aus drei Gruppen:

- *Akten* unterschiedlicher Herkunft (zur Militärgrenze, zu Flüchtlingen, Steuern u.a.),
- *Flugschriften* und *Traktate* (hauptsächlich über Türkengräuel, Krieg),
- *Reiseberichte,* z.B. die vorbildlich in Bukarest edierte vielbändige Quellensammlung Călători străini despre ţările române[12] (in rumänischer Übersetzung, z.T. im Original).

Synthese aus den nationalen Historiographien zusammengestellt. Sie sind für die Hand des Lehrers bestimmt. Erschienen sind bislang vier thematische Bände (Workbooks). In ihnen werden Licht- und Schattenseiten der Türkenherrschaft in Südosteuropa mittels Zitaten, Grafiken und Bildmaterial von einem internationalen Autorenteam ausgewogen dargestellt.

9 MOLNÁR: Katolikus missziók, 577. – KÜHLMANN, Wilhelm/SCHINDLING, Anton: Deutschland und Ungarn in ihren wechselseitigen Beziehungen während der Renaissance. In: Deutschland und Ungarn in ihren Bildungs- und Wissenschaftsbeziehungen während der Renaissance. Hg. v. DENS. Stuttgart 2004, Einführung, IX-XII, hier X f. – ASCHE, Matthias: Bildungsbeziehungen zwischen Ungarn, Siebenbürgen und den deutschen Universitäten im 16. und frühen 17. Jahrhundert. In: Ebd., 27-52, hier 39 f. – Dazu liegt jetzt das genannte dreibändige Werk in ungarischer Sprache von Antal MOLNÁR vor, dem instruktive Kartenskizzen beiliegen.

10 Daraus sind in ungarischer Übersetzung fünf Bände erschienen: Török történetírók [Osmanische Geschichtsschreiber]. Bd. 1-5. Hg. v. József THÚRY und Imre KARÁCSON. Budapest 1896-1916.

11 Dazu eine Teilveröffentlichung von FEHÉR, Géza: Türkische Miniaturen. Aus den Chroniken der ungarischen Feldzüge. Wiesbaden 1978.

12 Călători străini despre ţările române. Bd. 1-9. Hg. v. Maria HOLBAN (u.a.). Bucureşti 1968-1997 (und n.F.).

c. Westliche Quellen_konfessioneller Provenienz – insbesondere Archivbestände in katholischen Kirchenarchiven.

Eine genauere Aufstellung dieser konfessionellen Quellen, die allein das historische Ungarn betreffen, lässt sich aus dem erwähnten Werk von Antal Molnár erschließen.[13] Eine nur auf Magyarisch kommentierte Quellensammlung zum historischen Ungarn in vier Bänden legte István Gy. Tóth vor.[14]

Die Quellen zu ostmittel- und südosteuropäischen Regionen zum 16. und 17. Jahrhundert liegen im Wesentlichen in Archiven außerhalb der Region, u.a. in den

- *römischen Archiven* des Vatikan sowie in Ordensarchiven (vor allem der Jesuiten[15], Benediktiner und Franziskaner);
- *dalmatinischen Archiven* (vorwiegend im Franziskanerarchiv in Ragusa/Dubrovnik).
- Weitere Bestände in Wien und *Venedig* betreffen die Berichterstattung der damals neuen *Nuntiaturen*; in ungarischen und rumänischen *Ordensarchiven* sind Einzelfunde noch immer möglich.

Die aktuelle Quellen- und Forschungslage fasst Antal Molnár mit Bezug auf seine eigene inzwischen auf drei Bände gediehene Monographie, der ersten umfassenden Synthese aufgrund von katholischen Archivbeständen überhaupt, zusammen:

„Hinsichtlich des Themas fügt sich die Arbeit in die Reihe von Monographien, die als Ergebnis der traditionsreichen ungarischen Forschungsarbeit im Vatikan entstanden ist, bzw. ist sie Teil der Arbeiten zu Kultur- und Kirchengeschichte in der Zeit der Türkenherrschaft, die in den vergangenen Jahrzehnten entstanden sind. Sie füllt unter dem Gesichtspunkt beider, bestimmender Forschungsrichtungen eine Lücke, da der besetzte Landesteil in den Werken zu den Beziehungen zwischen dem Heiligen Stuhl und Ungarn bisher nur in äußerst geringem Maß präsent war, die Forschungen zur Kulturgeschichte in der Zeit der Besetzung hingegen beschäftigten sich bislang mit der Geschichte der protestantischen Konfessionen und ihren kulturellen Leistungen. Die Quellen dieser Arbeit stellen in entscheidendem Maße unveröffentlichte[16] Arbeitsinstrumente dar, die Monographie stützt sich überwiegend auf Quellen aus kirchlichen Archiven und Bibliotheken in Rom (*Archivio Segreto Vaticano, Bibliotheca Apostolica Vaticana, Archivio della Congregatione per la Dottrina della Fede, Archivio storico della Sacra Congregatione per l'Evangelizzazione*

---

[13] Vgl. Anm. 7.

[14] Litterae missionariorum de Hungaria et Transilvania (1572-1717). Bd. 1-4. Hg. v. István György TÓTH. Roma-Budapest 2002-2004.

[15] In den letzten 20 bis 25 Jahren wurden dazu intensive Forschungsanstrengungen unternommen, um die zahlreich vorhandenen Archivalien zu erschließen bzw. zu publizieren. Dazu u.a.: TÜSKÉS, Gábor: Jesuitenliteratur und Frömmigkeitspraxis in Ungarn im 16. und 17. Jahrhundert. In: Jesuitische Frömmigkeitskulturen. Konfessionelle Interaktion in Ostmitteleuropa 1570-1700. Hg. von Anna OHLIDAL und Stefan SAMERSKI. Stuttgart 2006, 17-36, hier 17f.

[16] Die von Tóth edierte Quellensammlung erschien ab 2002, als Molnárs Monographie vermutlich schon abgeschlossen war.

die Popoli o de „Propaganda Fide“, Archivum Romanum Societatis Iesu), bzw. aus dem Historischen Archiv Dubrovnik.“[17]

Kurz zusammengefasst, ergibt sich folgendes Bild zum Forschungsstand: Neben weitaus zahlreicher und intensiver erschlossenen Quellen zur protestantischen Konfessionsgeschichte im historischen Ungarn, zum Teil auch zu Kroatien, den noch nicht vollständig erarbeiteten Quellen zur Militärgrenze und zur Frühzeit der habsburgischen Ansiedlungsprojekte nach der Rückeroberung Ungarns (mit Kroatien) sowie Reiseberichten unterschiedlicher Provenienz stehen die – nur für Teilbereiche ausgewerteten – osmanischen Verwaltungsakten und Chroniken, einzelne ungarische Archivbestände mit regionalem Bezug und die ebenfalls nur in Auszügen publizierten bzw. teilausgewerteten römischen Archivquellen als wichtigstem Bestand.

Was die *Initiativen* betrifft, die im Verlauf des 19. Jahrhunderts, der Ära der Quellenpublikationen, ergriffen wurden, sind vor allem drei zu erwähnen: Erstens die Sammlung von Quellen zur Darstellung der eigenen Geschichte in nationalen Publikationen, die seit dem letzten Drittel des 19. Jahrhunderts in Ungarn, Kroatien und (dem heutigen) Rumänien erschienen sind. Die geographische Reichweite dieser nationalen Sammlungen wird durch den jeweils eigenen politischen Raum beschränkt.[18] Eine zweite Initiative betrifft die für das südöstliche Europa raumübergreifende Publikation katholischer Quellen im 19. Jahrhundert, vor allem durch Eusebius Fermendžin[19], die nach 1918 aber fast gänzlich abbrach. Dass eine solche Raumperspektive für die südosteuropäische Region erforderlich ist, stellte erst hundert Jahre später wieder Antal Molnár klar.[20] Als dritte Initiative sind schließlich Synthesen neuen Datums für Teilräume zu nennen – insbesondere Molnárs schon genannte dreibändige Monographie und eine italienische Synthese, die der jung verstorbene rumänische Historiker Lucian Periş vorlegte.[21]

Hinsichtlich der immer noch unbefriedigenden *Forschungslage* sei hier nur auf einige wenige kontroverse Fragen und defizitäre Bereiche verwiesen:
In den im 19. Jahrhundert erstmals verfassten nationalen Historiographien wird den „türkischen Gräueln“ aus der Eroberungszeit breiter Raum gegeben, diese finden aber auch in späteren Zeiträumen betonte Erwähnung. Dazu gehören „Gewaltereignisse“ – wie Entführung, Verschleppung, Versklavung und Zwangsbekehrung –

[17] MOLNÁR: Katolikus missziók, 577-587, hier 577.
[18] Dazu ZACH, Krista: Katholische Milieus im multikonfessionellen Raum. Siebenbürgen und ihm benachbarte Regionen. In: Formierung des konfessionellen Raumes in Ostmitteleuropa. Hg. v. Evelin WETTER. Stuttgart 2008, 261-279, hier 277-279.
[19] FERMENDŽIN, Eusebius: Acta Bulgariae ecclesiastica ab a. 1565 usque ad a. 1799. Zagrabiae 1887. – DERS.: Acta Bosnae potissimum ecclesiastica cum insertis editorum documentorum regestis ab anno 925 usque ad annum 1752. Zagrabiae 1892.
[20] MOLNÁR: Katolikus missziók, 577.
[21] PERIŞ, Lucian: Presenze cattoliche in Transilvania, Moldavia e Vallachia (1601-1698). Roma 1999. Das Werk wurde von William Bleiziffer ins Rumänische übersetzt: Prezenţe catolice în Transilvania, Moldova şi Ţara Românească (1601-1798). Blaj 2005.

durch Türkenheere oder Banden, wobei es sich meist, wie KASER nachweisen kann, um nicht quantifizierbare Angaben und vor allem Zahlen handelt.[22] So linear durchgehend negativ gestalteten sich die Bevölkerungsverschiebungen und Gebietsverheerungen, von denen in den Nationalhistoriographien oft die Rede ist, offensichtlich nicht, bezieht man auch Zeiträume in die Darstellung mit ein, in denen Frieden herrschte und betrachtet man sie über einen längeren Zeitraum hinweg. Die wirtschaftlichen und kulturgeschichtlich relevanten Hintergründe sind noch nicht ausreichend beleuchtet worden, wie beispielsweise Schwankungen der Tributleistung und deren Zusammenhänge mit der konjunkturellen Lage zu verschiedenen Zeiten[23] oder die Rolle katholischer Handelskompanien ragusaner wie bosnischer Kaufleute, die sich im türkischen Gebiet bewegten, eigene Niederlassung unterhielten, einander befehdeten und sich dabei nicht selten der Hilfe oder Protektion osmanischer Behörden bedienten.[24]

Ein weiteres kontrovers diskutiertes Thema betrifft die Demographie, insbesondere Migrationsvorgänge (unter gängigen historiographischen Stereotypen wie „Verödung", „Entchristlichung" u.a.). Es handelt sich hierbei um mehrere regional unterschiedliche Felder[25] von großer Komplexität, die meistens noch zu wenig dokumentiert sind. Dazu einige Beispiele:

Im 17. Jahrhundert treten neben die organisierte Umsiedlung durch christliche wie türkische Grundherren vorwiegend andere Migrationsformen. Dazu gibt es in den Augenzeugenberichten von Reisenden und den zahlreich überlieferten katholischen Visitationsberichten im Propagandaarchiv zahlreiche, weit gestreute, oft nur kursorisch gehaltene Angaben. Aufschluss geben auch andere Quellen, z.B. über den Rückzug ins Hinterland oder auf Flussinseln und ins Sumpfgebiet in der Nähe der (auch weiter noch bestellten) Felder und genutzten Weideflächen (Puszten).[26] Es wird auch über Gruppen von Flüchtlingen berichtet, die wieder an ihre Ursprungsor-

---

[22] „Es ist nicht möglich, eine annähernd richtige Zahl über das Ausmaß der gewaltsamen Entführungen zu nennen – zu ungenau sind die Angaben, die das vorhandene Quellenmaterial dazu bietet." KASER: Freier Bauer, 45.

[23] FENEŞAN, Cristina: Der *Harac* Siebenbürgens in der ersten Hälfte des 17. Jahrhunderts. In: Revue des Etudes sud-est européennes 34/1-1 (1996), 97-106, hier 97-100.

[24] Dazu eine Übersichtskarte bei MOLNÁR: Katolikus missziók, der erstmals diese konflikthaften katholischen Wirtschaftsinteressen mit konfessioneller Grundierung beschreibt. EBD., Kap. V und 582f.

[25] Zu den Schwierigkeiten bei Erstellung einer modernen Gesamtdemographie zur osmanischen Periode auf dem Balkan TODOROVA, Maria/TODOROV, Nikolai: The Historical Demography of the Ottoman Empire. Problems and Tasks. In: Scholar, Patriot, Mentor. Ed. by Richard B. SPENCE and Linda L. NELSON. New York 1992, 151-172. – Einzelbeiträge dazu finden sich verstreut in mehreren Studien, wie beispielsweise DŽAJA, Srećko M.: Konfessionalität und Nationalität Bosniens und der Herzegowina. Voremanzipatorische Phase 1463-1804. München 1984 (ergänzte kroatische Fassung Mostar [1]1992, [2]1999). – SEEWANN, Gerhard: Südslawische Süd-Nord-Migration als Voraussetzung für die deutsche Ansiedlung nach der Türkenzeit in Ungarn. In: Jahrbücher für Geschichte und Kultur Südosteuropas 1(1999), 139-160. – ZACH, Krista: Migration und Konfession im Türkischen Ungarn und Siebenbürgen des 17. Jahrhunderts. In: Identitate [Kirche, Gesellschaft, Identität]. In Honorem Nicolae Bocşan. Hg. v. Sorin MITU und Rudolf GRÄF (u. a.). Cluj-Napoca 2007, 727-747.

[26] ANDRÁSFALVY, Bertalan: A Duna mente népének ártéri gazdálkodása Tolna és Baranya megyében [Die von der Bevölkerung entlang der Donau in den Komitaten Tolna und Baranya praktizierte Überschwemmungswirtschaft]. Budapest 1975.

te zurückkehrten.[27] Für die längeren Friedenszeiten im 17. Jahrhundert, nach 1606, ist selbst die Erschließung von Ackerland durch Rodung, etwa in Slavonien, belegt[28], auf dem Halbnomaden und irreguläre Soldaten, überwiegend waren es orthodoxe Walachen und Serben, sesshaft gemacht werden sollten.[29] Orthodoxe Christen aus dem Balkan bildeten im 17. Jahrhundert bereits die Bevölkerungsmehrheit im südlichen Ungarn – wie es auch die Visitationsberichte ausweisen.[30] Ähnliches gilt für die kroatisch-slavonische Militärgrenze.[31] Ungarische Forscher zählten insgesamt acht abgrenzbare südslawische Einwanderungs- bzw. Ansiedlungsbewegungen auf osmanischem Gebiet Türkisch-Ungarns, wodurch die Zahl der Orthodoxen um 1700 auf mindestens eine halbe Million (bzw. etwa ein Achtel der Gesamtbevölkerung Ungarns) angewachsen sei.[32] In Syrmien und Slavonien, dem Temescher Banat, Transdanubien sowie bis hinauf nach Tolna und Somogy, in Fünfkirchen, Kanizsa und auch in Buda findet man sie zur Mitte des 17. Jahrhunderts neben katholischen Südslawen, welch Letztere überall hier von den bosnischen Franziskanern und einigen Jesuiten[33] aus der römischen (Belgrad, 1612 – 1632 und Temeswar, 1614 – 1653) bzw. österreichischen Provinz (Fünfkirchen, Gyöngyös, Andocs, Pest) betreut wurden. Das Nachdrängen der „*scismatici*“, die vielerorts bereits die Bevölkerungsmehrheit bildeten, wird in den Visitationsberichten mit (wahrscheinlich) überhöhten Abgaben in Ostslavonien dokumentiert.[34] Nach türkischen Steuerlisten können mitunter Bevölkerungsschätzungen vorgenommen werden, die tendenziell ebenfalls die stetige Zunahme der Orthodoxen in ehemals überwiegend katholischen ungarischen Gebieten andeuten. Diese Zuwanderung wurde wie folgt beschrieben: Sie bildeten die Mehrheit in Syrmien (um 1450), im Temescher Banat (um 1555), in Ostungarn und Slavonien gegen Ende des 16. und im südlichen Teil Transdanubiens zu Beginn des 17. Jahrhunderts.[35] Eine demographische Wende brachten erst die Kuruzzenkriege (1704 – 1711)[36], in deren Verlauf die Südslawen, wie Gerhard Seewann referierte, vorwiegend die orthodoxen Bewohner weitgehend dezimiert worden wären.

---

[27] KASER: Freier Bauer, 46 f.
[28] EBD.
[29] EBD.
[30] Der Visitationsbericht von Bischof Mato Benlić für 1651-1658 hält dieses u.a. für Belgrad (f. 3v-5r), Temeswar und Lippa (f. 24v-25v), Szeged (f. 38r,v), die Batschka mit Sombor (f. 34r) und Fünfkirchen (f. 14v) fest: APF, Scritt. Rif. Congressi. Misc. Bosna, vol. 1. – Bis zu seiner letzten Visitation (1672) setzt sich diese Entwicklung fort: „Nella diocese di Belgrado non v'è alcun cattolico et la maggior parte sino al fiume Savo sono scismstici“, weiß Missionsbischof Benlić zu berichten (SOCG, Vol. 433, f. 281r-284v, hier f. 281r).
[31] VÖLKL, Ekkehard: Militärgrenze und „Statuta Valachorum“. In: Die österreichische Militärgrenze. Hg. v. Gerhard ERNST. Regensburg 1982, 9-24, hier 12-16. – KASER: Freier Bauer, 133-135 und 187.
[32] SEEWANN: Südslawische Süd-Nord-Migration, 144-148. – Sie kamen überwiegend aus dem Westbalkan, aus Bosnien und Serbien.
[33] Dazu MOLNÁR: Katolikus missziók, Kap. V. und 580-583.
[34] 1652 für Sombor: APF, Scritt. Rif. Congressi. Misc. Bosna, vol. 1, f. 8v und für Belgrad (1672) wie Anm. 30.
[35] SEEWANN: Südslawische Süd-Nord-Migration, 144-145.
[36] Seewann referiert dazu neue Forschungsergebnisse in EBD., 150-155.

Andere Quellen über die hohe Bevölkerungsmobilität im gesamten Türkischen Ungarn sind nicht weniger präzise[37], vieles kann aus den Reiseberichten und aus später angefertigten Verwaltungsakten erschlossen werden. Die Wanderneigung ganzer Gruppen machte auch den Habsburgern bei der planmäßigen Dörferanlage nach den Friedensschlüssen von 1699 und 1718, überall vergleichbar große Schwierigkeiten, z.B. aus dem Banat berichteten dazu die Kommandierenden Generäle Claudius Florimund Graf Mercy 1722 und 1734 sein Nachfolger, General Hamilton – betreffend Serben und Rumänen – nach Wien.[38] Der „Reinkorporation" Ungarns stimmte die Wiener Hofkammer für Slavonien 1745 zu, verweigerte sie aber zunächst (bis 1778) für das Temescher Banat.[39] Die österreichischen Quellen aus der Zeit nach der Rückeroberung erlauben Rückschlüsse auf die Zeit davor – etwa, von der Abwesenheit der Magyaren aus dem Grenzgebiet zum Osmanischen Reich in manchen Regionen im Süden, auf ihre gesteuerte Fernhaltung, oder aus der starken Präsenz nomadisierender Südslawen und „Walachen"[40] im Südosten dieser Region auf ihre Bevorzugung durch die Wiener Verwaltungsbehörden u.a. Die Bevölkerungsschätzungen für das gesamte ehemalige Gebiet der Stephanskrone schwanken entsprechend, wobei bei manchen Autoren auch ethnisch und/oder konfessionell gesteuerte Subjektivität eine Rolle spielen können.

Grundlage für eine umfassende, aussagekräftige demographische Untersuchung, die noch fehlt – so lässt sich zusammenfassen – ist ein weit verstreut liegendes, heterogenes Quellenmaterial. Um eine Gesamtsicht auf das große Migrationenpanorama während der Türkenzeit zu erhalten oder auch nur zeitlich und räumlich begrenzte Einzelabschnitte schärfer erfassen zu können, bedarf es weiterer Forschung. Die Raumkonfigurationen sind immer noch nicht – weder in einzelnen Teilräumen noch im Gesamt dieser europäischen Großregion – einsichtig.

---

[37] Der englische Arzt Edward Brown bereiste 1669 Teile Südosteuropas und verfasste danach die umfangreichste, ausführlichste Beschreibung Ungarns aus dieser Zeit. Sachlich berichtet er u.a. aus der Gegend um Mohács von umherziehenden Menschenkarawanen, darunter Umsiedlern, deren Herkunft und genaues Ziel er nicht kennt, als von einem typischen Phänomen: „Hereabouts we met with a Caravan of two or three hundred persons, some going to a place of Devotion, some having Janitscharies with them to guarde them; others intending, by permission, to seate themselves in other parts of Hungary." BROWN, Edmund: A Brief Account of some Travels in Hungaria, Servia ... London 1673. Hg. v. Karl NEHRING. München 1975 (Veröffentlichungen des Finnisch-Ugrischen Seminars an der Universität München. C Miscellanea. Bd. 2. Hg. v. Gerhard GANSCHOW), hier 36.

[38] „Nichts hat die Bevölkerungspolitik im Banat gerade bei den Nationalisten [dort lebende bzw. als Rückwanderer aus dem benachbarten türkischen und siebenbürgischen Gebiet von Mercy erwünschte Südslawen und Rumänen] so sehr erschwert als ihr Mangel an Sesshaftigkeit, ihr Hang zum „Transmigrieren", wie es in der damaligen Zeit heißt. Die Instruktion [...] vom 31. Dezember 1722 gibt einen tiefen Einblick in den vielfach noch nomadisierenden Zustand der Banater Bevölkerung und ist in ihrem Bemühen um die Sesshaftigkeit dieser Menschen, ihr Wohnen in festgebauten Häusern, in ständigen Dorfgemeinschaften mit umgrenzten Gemeindegebieten ein Kulturdokument ersten Ranges. Da wird das Zusammenhausen unserer Familien in elenden Erdhöhlen oder Erdhütten, die die angeblich in türkischer Zeit eingeschlichene Bigamie und Blutschande fördert, strengstens verboten." KALLBRUNNER, Josef: Das kaiserliche Banat. Bd. 1. Einrichtung und Entwicklung des Banats bis 1739. München 1958, 27-29, hier 28.

[39] EBD., 15.

[40] Über die Mehrschichtigkeit dieses Gruppennamens vgl. DŽAJA: Konfessionalität und Nationalität, 43-47 und SEEWANN: Südslawische Süd-Nord-Migration, 145.

Zur Situation der katholischen Kirche im Türkischen Ungarn

Die Grenzziehungen für ekklesiastische Territorien aus der Zeit um 1450 zeigt mit Abb. 1.[41]

a) Katholische Hierarchien:

Im Mittelalter gab es im historischen Ungarn zwei großräumige Erzdiözesen, Esztergom (Gran) und Kalocsa, denen die zwölf Bistümer des Landes untergeordnet waren.[42] Nicht alle Diözesen lagen um 1500 ausschließlich auf ungarischem Staatsgebiet (s. Abb. 2). Die zahlreichen Bistümer entlang der dalmatinischen Küste[43] waren vor der Türkenzeit Aquileia unterstellt. Nur das bosnische Bistum konnte in der Türkenzeit – gestützt auf eine wechselnde Zahl von Klöstern der bosnischen Observanten, die in der Provinz *Bosna Argentina*[44] vereint waren – fortbestehen. Einige Klöster befanden sich am Ort osmanischer Verwaltungssitze.[45] (Abb. 2 und 3)

b) Ostkirchliche Hierarchien

Die während des Mittelalters in Bulgarien (Preslav, dann Veliko Trnovo) und Serbien (Ochrid, dann Ipek/Peć) entstandenen nationalen *Patriarchate* erloschen bereits Ende des 14. Jahrhundert nach der osmanischen Eroberung dieser Territorien wieder. In der Türkenzeit bestand neben den rumänischen nur eine einzige, weiträumige orthodoxe Metropolie zu Ipek/Peć[46] fort. So genannte „Metropoliten" (Vladikas und Äbte) gab es jedoch zahlreich, im 17. Jahrhundert auch im ungarischen Eroberungsgebiet, d.h., im Türkischen Ungarn.

*

Die folgenden Streiflichter beziehen sich nur auf das historische Ungarn und schwerpunktmäßig auf den südslawisch-katholischen Bereich. Was die Zeit der Türkenherrschaft[47] und der Reformation für das katholische Ungarn und Kroatien bedeutet hat, ist aus zahlreichen Publikationen bekannt, hier genügen einige Stichwörter:

- Der Zusammenbruch der im ungarischen Ständestaat stark ausgeprägten Strukturen einer Episkopalkirche, mit durchgehendem Verlust der gesamten katholischen Hierarchie vor Ort um 1550/1556 bedeutete, dass das gesamte dreigeteilte Ungarn dem Heiligen Stuhl seitdem als „Missionsgebiet" galt. Doch war in Rom die Übersicht über die neue Lage seit dann nicht mehr gegeben:

---

[41] Siehe Seite 292.
[42] Hierarchia Cattolica medii et recentioris aevi. Bd. 3. Hg. v. Guilelmus van GULIK und Konrad EUBEL. Monasterii 1923. – Dazu eine Übersicht der Amtsträger zwischen ca. 1500 und ca. 1650 bei MOLNÁR: Katolikus missziók, 462-468.
[43] Dazu die Amtsträger EBD.
[44] MANDIĆ, Dominik: Franjevačka Bosna [Das Franziskanische Bosnien]. Rim 1968, 164-188. – Karten der bosnischen Klöster im 15. und 17. Jahrhundert bei MOLNÁR: Katolikus missziók, Abb. 4 und 5.
[45] MANDIĆ: EBD. – Dazu auch eine weitere Karte bei MOLNÁR: EBD., Das Vilajet Bosnien um 1600.
[46] Dazu Abb. 1 (S. 292) im Vergleich zu Abb. 3 (S. 293) in: MOLNÁR: Katolikus missziók, Karte Az Ipeki Párierkátus a 17. század derekán [Das Patriarchat zu Ipek Mitte des 17. Jahrhunderts].
[47] Dazu nur MOLNÁR: Katolikus missziók.

- Eine eingehende Kenntnis der konfessionellen Verhältnisse fehlte nicht nur für Ungarn, sondern auch für die ehemals katholischen Diözesen auf dem Balkan (Bosnien, Bulgarien), die Zahl der noch verbliebenen Katholiken war unbekannt.[48] Daher wurden ab 1580 mehrere Missionen dorthin entsandt. Die des albanischen Weltpriesters Pietro Massarecchi von 1623 und 1624 brachten schließlich Aufschluss über die Gesamtlage in den südslawischen, weniger den ungarischen, Gemeinden. Seinen Reformvorschlägen folgte Rom auch bis zum nächsten großen Türkenkrieg (1666).
- Als der Umfang der Vernachlässigung und die Dringlichkeit der benötigten Hilfe für die Katholiken in Südosteuropa bekannt wurde, unternahm die 1622 gegründete Kongregation „de Propaganda Fide“ energische Schritte zur Abhilfe. Damit entstand aber auch das Problem der Doppelhierarchiebildung, das bis zum Ende des 17. Jahrhunderts ungelöst blieb: Der Kaiser in Wien (als König von Ungarn) ernannte in Ausübung seines Patronatsrechts (nicht-residierende) Bischöfe für Ungarn und der Vatikan bestellte Administratoren und ab 1647 Missionsbischöfe für die Diözesen auf osmanischem Gebiet (s. Abb. 2). Zwischen Rom und Wien konnte selten eine Einigung darüber erzielt werden.
- Der konkurrierende Missionseifer der bosnischen Bischöfe und der neuen Missionsträger der Propaganda Fide richtete sich vermehrt auf die wenigen ertragreicheren unter den generell sehr armen Pfarreien, die vor allem in Slavonien und Syrmien lagen, statt auf die Gesamtregion. Grenzstreitereien über Zuständigkeiten und Diözesangrenzen begleiten die Korrespondenz mit Rom bis zum Ende der Türkenzeit für Ungarn 1699 bzw. 1718.
- Die Orthodoxe Kirche, die eine viel großmaschigere hierarchische Struktur besaß und von der muslimischen Obrigkeit toleriert wurde (wie die anderer Reaya-Gemeinschaften der Armenier und Juden auch), erstarkten im 16. und 17. Jahrhundert und breitete sich weit nach Norden aus.
- Die Konkurrenz reformierter Prediger in Ungarn, die ebenso wie die Orthodoxen muttersprachlich offizierten, ließ die katholischen Gemeinden, die oft jahrelang keine seelsorgliche Betreuung erhalten hatten, vor allem in Ungarn und Siebenbürgen stark schrumpfen.
- Für sie kam die Hilfe von Draußen spät, oft zu spät: Es mangelte vor allem an ungarisch sprechenden Seelsorgern und an Schulen. Es gab nur wenige katholische Mittelschulen (Jesuitenkollegs in Gyöngyös und Tyrnau sowie zeitweilig Klausenburg) oder diskontinuierliche Unterweisung, z.B. in Karansebesch und Wardein, dafür aber ein immer dichteres Netz protestantischer Einrichtungen.
- Die Missionsbischöfe mit südslawischer Muttersprache verstanden meist kein Ungarisch und visitierten somit den magyarischsprachigen Norden ihrer riesigen Diözese Belgrad nur gelegentlich, wobei sie meist nur die Firmung spendeten und Altäre, Kelche, Kirchen und Friedhöfe weihten).[49]

---

[48] MOLNÁR: Katolikus missziók, 578 und 581.

[49] Beispielhaft sind die Visitationen der Missionsbischöfe von Belgrad, Marin Ibrišimović und Mato Benlić. Dazu ZACH, Krista: Die Visitation des Bischofs von Belgrad Marin Ibrišimović in Türkisch-Ungarn (1649).

In diesem engen institutionellen Rahmen bewegten sich neben dem bosnischen Bischof, der immer ein Franziskaner aus der einheimischen Provinz *Bosna Argentina* war, und seit 1647 den Missionsbischöfen vor allem die Mönchsmissionare – Franziskaner, Jesuiten, später auch Karmeliter und Pauliner – und einige Weltpriester. Letztere hatten ihre Ausbildung in den modernen italienischen *collegi* für die Missionsarbeit der Propaganda Fide – in Rom, Ancona und Loretto – erhalten. An diesen Kollegien studierten seit den dreißiger und vierziger Jahren des 17. Jahrhunderts auch dalmatinische und bosnische Franziskaner, die den römischen Reformen, wie die Missionsbischöfe, zugestimmt, und damit den Konflikt mit dem bosnischen Bischof in Kauf genommen hatten.

Unter den im Türkischen Ungarn, vor allem im Süden tätigen Missionaren gab es zunächst ragusanische Benediktiner (1587 – 1622), dann Jesuiten aus der Römischen (1612 – 1653) wie der Österreichischen und Polnischen Provinz und schließlich, ab etwa 1630, immer mehr Franziskaner aus der einheimischen Provinz *Bosna Argentina*. Letztere schufen zusammen mit den wenigen italienischen Weltpriestern ein Netzwerk, das der Aufrechterhaltung einer minimalen katholischen Seelsorge in Ungarn, Kroatien, Siebenbürgen und der Moldau diente. Einschränkend muss man festhalten, dass sich dieses Netz schützend fast ausschließlich über Katholiken südslawischer Mundarten ausbreitete. Diese waren im 17. Jahrhundert dank Binnenwanderung und Handel nicht nur in Bosnien, Syrmien und Slavonien, der Batschka sowie in der Diözese Csanád (Temeswar, Lippa, Karaschovo, Karansebesch), sondern auch an anderen Orten des osmanischen Ungarns, so in Fünfkirchen, Pest, Gyöngyös u.a. anzutreffen.

Die bosnische Franziskanerprovinz *Bosna Argentina* gehörte zum Zweig der Minoriten strenger Observanz. Sie waren einerseits sehr viel anspruchsloser als die anderen Missionare im Türkischen Ungarn, selbst auch als die im 17. Jahrhundert dort vereinzelt auftretenden ungarischen Franziskaner, die dem Zweig der Konventualen angehörten. Sie lebten, wie ihre südslawischen Gemeinden, in einfachsten Verhältnissen, betreuten diese auf herkömmliche Weise, wie schon im Mittelalter, und sie scheuten jede Einmischung oder Neuerung „von oben" – wie beispielsweise die Tridentinischen Reformen oder den neuen Kalender.
Die bosnischen Observanten bildeten unter den in der gesamten Region viel zu wenig zahlreichen Betreuer der Katholiken die Mehrheit. Sie hatten es geschafft, im heimatlichen Bosnien mit der Duldung der osmanischen Verwaltung etwa zehn bis zwölf ihrer Klöster in Betrieb zu halten. Vor der Türkenzeit hatte es in der Bosnischen Franziskanerprovinz weitaus mehr Klöster gegeben (Abb. 4 und 5).

In: Konfessionelle Pluralität, Stände und Nation. Ausgewählte Abhandlungen zur südosteuropäischen Religions- und Gesellschaftsgeschichte. Hg. v. Joachim BAHLCKE und Konrad GÜNDISCH. Münster 2004, 207-230, hier 216 f. – DIES.: Konfessionsgruppen in Slawonien und Syrmien 1640-1680. Anmerkungen zur Integration von Christen im Osmanischen Reich anhand römischer Archivquellen. In: EBD., 267-285, hier 269-273.

Die Zusammenarbeit mit Rom verstanden sie als Einmischung in „ihre" türkisch-ungarische Diözese, denn sie hatten im türkischen Teilgebiet Ungarns nicht in einem rechtsfreien Raum agiert. Dafür konnten sie ein päpstliches Breve von 1575 zum Missionieren vorweisen. (Abb. 6)
Die im Wege eines Teilkompromisses mit der Bosnischen Ordensprovinz 1647 von der Propagandakongregation eingerichtete Missionsdiözese Belgrad wurde jeweils mit einem moderner denkenden bosnischen Bruder besetzt. Doch die Grenzen des Missionsbistums Belgrad blieben unpräzise. Im betreffenden päpstlichen Breve hieß es dazu lediglich sehr allgemein, das Missionsbistum Belgrad liege *„in Ungaria Inferiore ... inter quatuor flumina Savi, Dravi, Tibisci et Danubii"*.[50] Damit war zwar ein wichtiger Punkt des Missionsstatuts von Francesco Ingoli SJ, dem mächtigen Propagandasekretär (1622 – 1649), erfüllt – nämlich, in den Missionsgebieten unter zentraler römischer Leitung eine Hierarchiebildung ohne Einmischung weltlicher Instanzen (hier: des Kaisers in Wien als König von Ungarn) zu errichten, aber der Streit um die Grenzen bzw. die besten Pfarreien, ging darob unvermindert weiter.

In den häufigen Konflikten zwischen den Franziskanern Bosniens und allen anderen dort tätigen katholischen Missionaren ging es ihnen allen um die gleichen Ziele – den Besitz der wenigen besser gestellten Pfarreien, die Meidung der osmanischen Verwalter und gute Beziehungen zu den südslawischen katholischen Händlern, in deren Schutz man zu den verstreut liegenden Gemeinden umherreisen konnte. Die bosnischen Franziskaner saßen am längeren Arm, weil sie einen alt hergebrachten Stil der Seelsorge praktizierten und eine entsprechende Ekklesiologie vertraten, die Neuerungen aus Rom verwarf. Damit konnten sie sich auch den Türken als Gegner der römischen und kaiserlichen „Spione" bzw. als loyal empfehlen. So fanden sie leichter Unterstützung bei den osmanischen Behörden, die sie häufig durch Verleumdung gegen ihre katholischen Brüder zu instrumentalisieren wussten.

Fazit

Die Quellenerschließung für Ungarn und Siebenbürgen im Spiegel der Korrespondenz mit der Propaganda Fide und anderen katholischen Instanzen kann dank der Publikationen von István György Tóth als abgeschlossen gelten. Die historiographische Dokumentation schreitet in den letzten beiden Jahrzehnten vor allem dank der Monographien von Antal Molnár und einiger Arbeiten von rumänischer und kroatischer Seite zügig voran, kann aber noch nicht als ausreichend betrachtet werden.
Zu Einzelfragen im Zusammenhang des Raumparadigmas, wie beispielsweise zur Siedlungsgeschichte, Migration oder Demographie, bedarf es weiterer Quellenerschließung und Forschung. Das gilt auch für die Geschichte der ostkirchlichen Bevölkerungsgruppen, die bestenfalls national erfasst wurde und eine vergleichbar ebenso schwierige Quellenfrage aufwirft, wie die der anderen Konfessionsgruppen

[50] Ebd.

im südöstlichen Europa in der Türkenzeit bzw. nach dem Erlöschen der bulgarischen und serbischen Metropolien sowie dem Fall von Konstantinopel. Sie alle sind für die Darstellung der konfessionellen Konfigurationen in dieser Region jedoch unentbehrlich. Nicht zu vergessen ist zuletzt die unbekannte Zahl von noch nicht bearbeiteten Materialien in türkischen Archiven.
Die meisten dieser Forschungsaufgaben bedürfen der übernationalen Zusammenarbeit.

Abbildungen

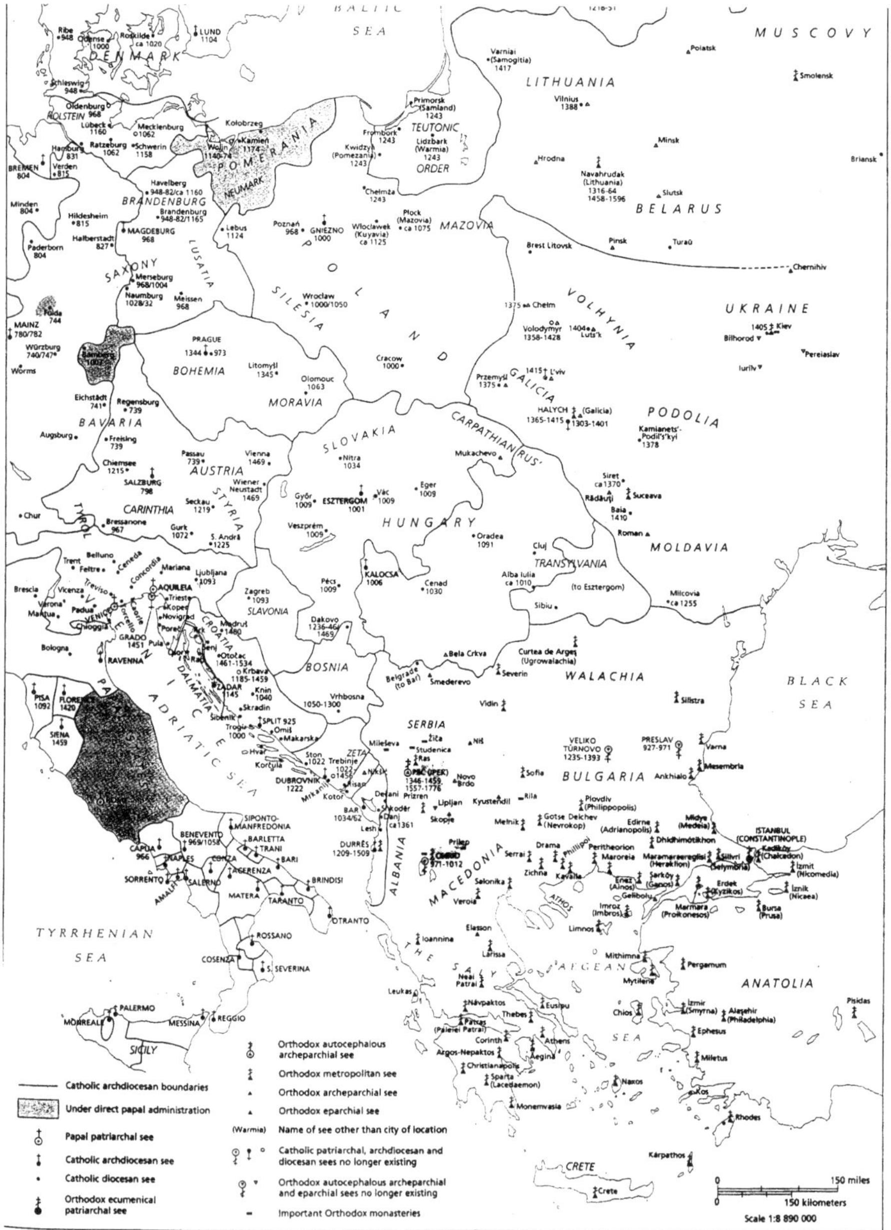

Historical Atlas of East Central Europe

Abb. 1: Geistliche Jurisdiktion um 1450: Die Grenzen der Erzbistümer und Patriarchate. Im 17. Jahrhundert war die Lage bereits eine ganz andere, vgl. Abb. 3.

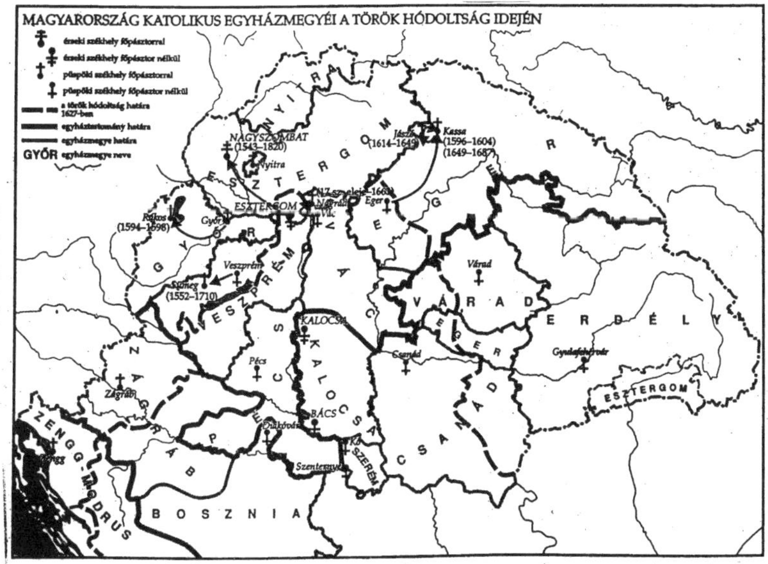

Abb. 2: Die katholischen Diözesen Ungarns um 1550. Die Legende nennt: Erzbistum (besetzt ‡•); Erzbistum (nicht besetzt ‡˙); Bistum (besetzt †•); Bistum (nicht besetzt †˙); Grenzen des Eroberungsgebiets 1627 (— —); Grenzen der Kirchenprovinzen (—); Diözesangrenzen (–); Name der Diözesen (Győr).

Abb. 3: Patriarchat von Ipek im 17. Jahrhundert. Die Legende nennt: Sitz des Patriarchen (‡▪); Bischofssitz (†•); Metropolie (Vranjei)

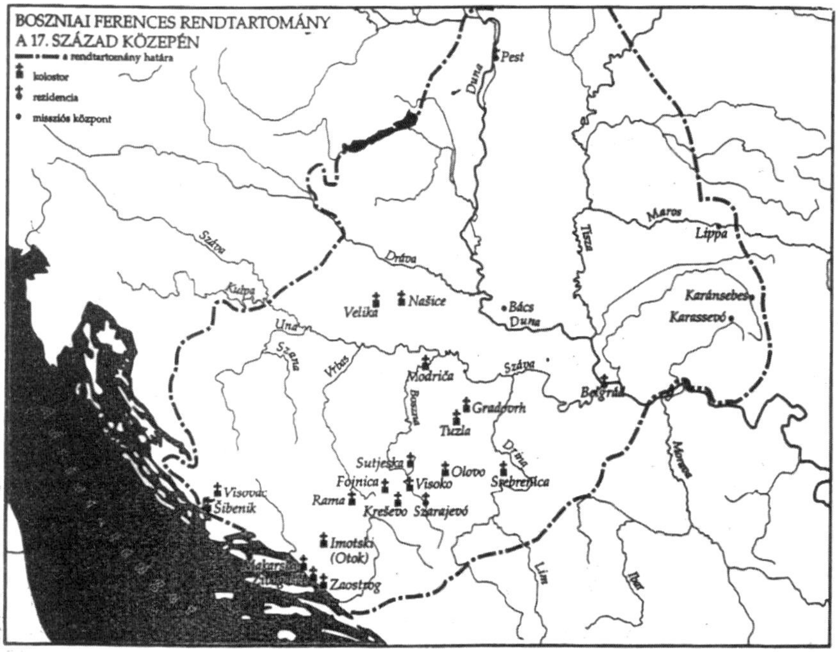

Abb. 4: Bosnische Franziskanerprovinz im 17. Jahrhundert. Die Legende nennt: Kloster (■); Residenz (●); Missionsstation (•).

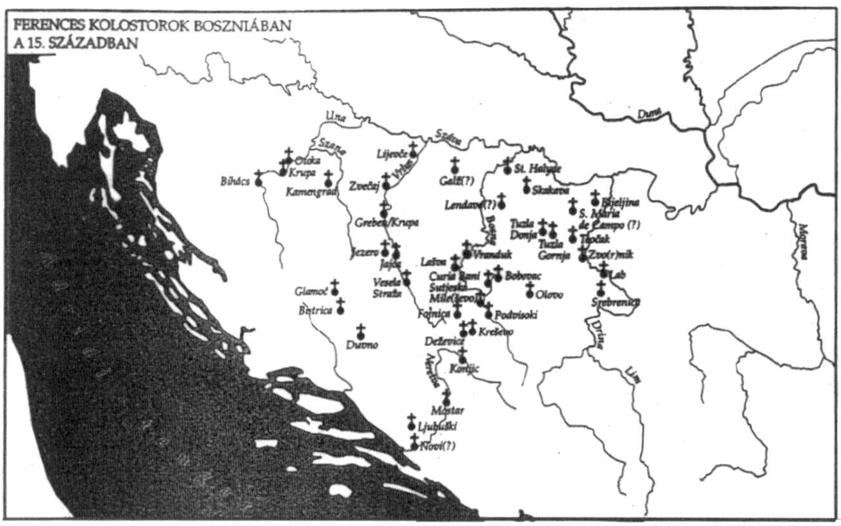

Abb. 5: Bosnische Franziskanerklöster im 15. Jahrhundert

Abschrift eines Apostolischen Breve, ausgestellt unter dem Pontifikat von Innozenz X. für Bischof Marin Ibrišimović – *Rom, ca. *1652
Das Breve nennt die Grenzen des Missionsbistums Belgrad sowie die Titel des Bischofs P. Ibrišimović, der Verwalter der Kirche von Samandria und Apostolischer Vikar der ungarischen (Titular-)Bistümer unter türkischer Herrschaft war. [95]

Innocentius PP. X.

Venerabilis fr[ater] sal[ute]m, et Apost[oli]cam ben[edictionem]. Christi fidelium inter flumina Dravi, [96] Savi, [97] Danubij, [98] et Tibischi, [99] ac in sp[eci]e Bachae [100] usque [ad] Temisvar [101] Regni Hungariae inhabitantium Animar[um] saluti pro Commissi Nobis Pastoralis officij debito paterna Charitate prospicere cupientes, ac de fraternitatis tuae fide, pietate, et Religionis Zelo plurimum in Domino confisi. de Venerabilium fr[atr]um nostror[um] S[anctae] R[omanae] Ecc[lesi]ae Card[ina]lium negotio propagandae fidei praepositor[um] consilio. Te Administratorem Eccl[esi]ae Samandriensis, [102] nec non Vicarium Apost[oli]cum in Ecclesijs Hungariae sub Turcis, Ep[iscop]um residentem non habentibus iuxta t[ame]n Confines supra expressos; Apost[oli]ca authoritate tenore p[raese]ntium ad nostrum, et Sedis Apost[oli]cae beneplacitum facimus, constituimus, et disputamus, Teq[ue] in D[omi]no hortamur, et monemus, ut Curam, et Administrationem Eccl[esi]arum h[uius]mo[d]i illar[um]q[ue] Xpi fidelium sic exercere studeas sollicite, fideliter, et prudenter, ut praeter eternae retributionis praemium nostra[ru]m, et Sedis Apostolicae benedictionem, et gr[ati]am uberius consequi merearis. Mandantes eisd[em] Xpi fidelibus in Virtute Sanctae obedientiae quatenus Te tanquam Patrem, et Pastorem Animar[um] Suar[um] devote suscipientes, et debita honorificentia prosequentes tuis monitis, et mandatis salubribus prompte pareant, et obedienti in contrarium facientibus non obstantibus quibus cumque.

Datum Romae apud Sanctam Mariam Maiorem sub Annulo Piscatoris die 5. Novembris 1647 Pont[ificat]us N[ost]ri anno quatro

Auf der Rückseite:

A tergo Vero. Venerabili fr[atr]i Marino e[piscop]o Belogradens[em]. M. A. Maraldus

[*andere Hand:* Ingoli: [103]] Co[n]cordat cu[m] originalis copia, collationata, in Secretaria Sac[rae] cong[regation]is de prop[aganda] fide existe[n]te. Franciscus Ingolus sec[retari]us.

(f. 109 r)

Abb. 6: Apostolisches Breve von 1652 mit Grenzziehungen der Diözese Belgrad (1647)

Tamás Tóth

Das Wiederaufblühen der katholischen Kirche nach der Osmanenherrschaft unter Gabriel und Adam Patachich, Erzbischöfe von Kalocsa-Batsch (1733-1784)

„Fortuna genitrice satus patruusque neposque;
terminet ut patri grandia coepta nepos."

Grußspruch in Hajosch (ung. Hajós) 1776[1]

Im Festsaal des Erzbischöflichen Palais von Kalocsa sind zwei Grisailles zu sehen. Das erste zeigt die Bauarbeiten an der neuen Barockkathedrale und trägt die Inschrift *Deo*, das zweite zeigt das neue barocke erzbischöfliche Palais mit der Inschrift *Sacerdotio*. Neben diesen beiden Grisailles befinden sich zwei Portraits: Es sind die Abbildungen von Gábor Patachich und seinem Neffen Ádám Patachich, die von 1733 bis 1745 bzw. von 1776 bis 1784 die Erzbischöfe von Kalocsa-Batsch (ung. Kalocsa-Bács, serb. Bač) waren. Die ganze Komposition versucht an die Wiedergeburt der Erzdiözese im 18. Jahrhundert zu erinnern, die nach dem Ende der Osmanenherrschaft erfolgte. Die beiden Patachichs sind die herausragenden Figuren dieser wichtigen Periode von Kalocsa. Auf den Beginn der Amtszeit von Gábor Patachich im Jahre 1733 fällt auch der Beginn von Reformen: So war er der erste Erzbischof seit mehr als 200 Jahren, der seinen festen Sitz wieder in der Diözese hatte. Außerdem begann man unter seiner Regentschaft mit dem Bau der neuen Kathedrale. Ádám Patachich fiel die Aufgabe zu, als letzter Erzbischof diese Ära des *barokken Wiederaufblühens* zu vollenden. Die von ihm erbaute Residenz ist ein Zeichen für die tridentinisch-barocke Erneuerung in einer Zeit, die der Erzdiözese einen starken Impuls und eine neue Struktur gab. Das Ende des 18. Jahrhunderts brachte in dieser Region den Untergang der Barockzeit und so auch den Aufgang einer neuen Epoche mit sich.[2]

Im Folgenden wird der Versuch unternommen, diese für die Kirchen- und Sozialgeschichte wichtige Periode zu thematisieren, in der die Idee einer tridentinisch-barocken Kirche auch in Ungarn verwirklicht werden konnte. Als Beispiel für diese

---

[1] KATONA, Stephanus: Historia metropolitanae Colocensis Ecclesiae. Colocae 1800f. Band II, Kapitel CCV. – Die Sommerresidenz zu Hajosch wurde von Gábor Patachich errichtet. Im Jahre 1776 wurde hier der Festakt der Übergabe von dem Pallium und den Bullen gefeiert.

[2] Der Aufsatz basiert auf der Dissertation „La rinascita della Chiesa d'Ungheria dopo la conquista turca nell'attività di Gábor Patachich e di Ádám Patachich, Arcivescovi di Kalocsa-Bács (1733-1784)." Sie wurde an der Fakultät für Kulturgüter und Kirchengeschichte der Päpstlichen Universität Gregoriana, Rom 2006, erstellt. Betreuer der Arbeit ist P. Luigi Mezzadri, C.M. Die Veröffentlichung in der Reihe „Collectanea Vaticana Hungariae", Budapest-Rom, ist in Vorbereitung.

Studien habe ich die Erzdiözese Kalocsa-Batsch gewählt, die in der osmanischen Zeit großen Schaden genommen hatte und in der beinahe alles vernichtet worden war. Geforscht habe ich in den verschiedenen Bibliotheken und Archiven. Die wichtigsten von mir benutzten Dokumente werden an unterschiedlichen Orten aufbewahrt: in Rom (Archiv des Collegium Germanicum et Hungaricum), in der Vatikanstadt (Vatikanisches Geheimarchiv), in Wien (Österreichisches Staatsarchiv), in Agram (kroat. Zagreb; Kroatisches Staatsarchiv, National- und Universitätsbibliothek, Archiv der Kroatischen Akademie für Wissenschaft und Kultur und die Archive der Erzdiözese und des Kapitels von Agram), in Budapest (Ungarisches Landesarchiv) und in Kalocsa (Archiv der Erzdiözese Kalocsa und Dombibliothek von Kalocsa).

1. Die ungarische Kirche während der Osmanenzeit

Die osmanische Eroberung erfolgte etwa gleichzeitig mit der Reformation und veränderte den Weg Ungarns.[3] Die Niederlage bei Mohatsch (ung. Mohács) im Jahre 1526 war gleichbedeutend mit dem Sturz des mittelalterlichen Königreiches. 1541 wurde schließlich auch die Hauptstadt Buda besetzt. So zerfiel das Königreich in drei Teile: in das so genannte Königreich Ungarn, in das Fürstentum Siebenbürgen und in das türkische Territorium. Es ist wichtig, dass alle Bischofstühle des alten Königreiches durch königliche Nominierungen besetzt blieben, auch wenn die Mehrheit dieser Bischöfe – entweder wegen der Eroberung oder aber der Reformation – nicht in ihr Amt eingeführt werden konnten.[4] Diese alten Bischofstühle blie-

[3] Das Königreich Ungarn und seine christliche Kirche entstanden im 11. Jh. Der Heilige Stefan, erster König von Ungarn (1001-1038), errichtete zehn Bistümer. Gran (Esztergom) erhielt von Beginn an den Rang einer Erzdiözese, aber auch Kalocsa bekam diesen Titel erstaunlich rasch. Es ist bis heute für die Forschung nicht ganz klar, warum die neue ungarische Kirche schon zu Beginn zwei Metropolitanstühle erhielt. Genau so ungewiss ist es, warum die Erzdiözese Kalocsa-Batsch schon ab dem 11. Jh. einen Doppelnamen mit einem doppelten Sitz, mit zwei Kathedralen und zwei Domkapiteln, erhielt.

[4] BEKE, Margit: Esztergomi érsekek a kezdetektől és apostoli adminisztrátorok az újkortól napjainkig [Die Erzbischöfe von Gran vom Anfang und die Apostolische Administratoren von der Neuzeit bis heute]. In: Esztergomi érsekek 1001-2003 [Erzbischöfe von Gran 1001-2003]. Hg. v. Margit BEKE. Budapest 2003. 411-413, hier 412f. – KATONA, István: A kalocsai érseki egyház története. [Übersetzung von: Katona: Historia metropolitanae]. Band II. Hg. v. Imre ROMSICS. Kalocsa 2001-2002, Anmerkungen 57-668. – Az Egri Főegyházmegye névtára 2004. Schematismus archidiocesis Agriensis pro anno Domini MMIV. Hg. v. László FICZEK. Eger 2004 (Az Egri Főegyházmegye ünnepi sematizmusa VII. Schematismus archidiocesis Agriensis VII) 15f. – A Gyulafehérvári Egyházmegye Névtára. Isten Szolgája, Márton Áron püspök születésének századik évében. 1996 [Schematismus der Diözese Weißenburg (Karlstadt, Gyulafehérvár, Alba Iulia) im 100. Geburtsjahr von Diener Gottes, Bischof Áron Márton. 1996]. Gyulafehérvár [1996], 9f. – Váci egyházmegyei almanach [Almanach der Diözese Waitzen (Vác)]. Hg. v. József BÁNK. Vác 1970, 145-180. – A Nagyváradi Egyházmegye történelmi sematizmusa. Schematismus historicus diocesis Magnovaradiensis latinorum. 2003. Hg. v. József FODOR. Nagyvárad 2003, 132. – A Veszprémi Főegyházmegye névtára 2000 [Schematismus der Erzdiözese Wesprim 2000]. Hg. v. Géza GYŰRŰ. Veszprém 2000, 10f. – A Szeged-Csanádi Egyházmegye Névtára 2000 [Schematismus der Diözese Szeged-Csanád]. Hg. v. Endre GYULAY. Szeged 2000. 21f. – Győregyházmegyei almanach. Schematismus diocesis Jaurinensis. Hg. v. Lajos PÁPAI. Győr 2001, 36f. – Schematismus cleri dioecesis Nitriensis pro anno a Christo nato MCMXIII. Nitriae 1912, 10. – A Pécsi Egyházmegye Név- és Címtára 1999 [Schematismus der Diözese Fünfkirchen (Pécs)]. Pécs 1999, 8f. – Schematismus dioecesis Neosoliensis pro anno MCMII. Neosolii 1902, 7. –

ben praktisch als Sitze für Titularbischöfe erhalten. Erlangen konnte man den erzbischöflichen Titel durch eine Würdigung des Einsatzes für die Kirche, das Amt des Titularbischofs erhielt man meist zu Beginn seiner kirchlichen Karriere.

Die Diözesen in Ungarn im 16.-18. Jahrhundert

Diözese	Periode	Dauer (Jahre)	Zahl der Bischöfe
Gran (ung. Esztergom)	1526-1746	220	15
Kalocsa	1527-1732	205	18
Erlau (ung. Eger)	1527-1744	217	23
Neutra (ung. Nyitra, sk. Nitra)	1512-1736	224	20
Raab (ung. Győr)	1535-1732	197	18
Fünfkirchen (ung. Pécs)	1526-1734	208	36
Waitzen (ung. Vác)	1526-1734	208	36
Siebenbürgen	1524-1736	212	21
Wardein (ung. Várad, rum. Oradea)	1535-1732	205	19
Wesprim (ung. Veszprém)	1524-1744	220	27
Tschanad (ung. Csanád)	1526-1739	213	26
Agram (kroat. Zagreb)	1518-1747	229	22
Zengg-Modrus (kroat. Senj-Modruš)	1537-1745	208	20
Sirmium (kroat. Srijem)	1526-1733	207	27
Bosnien	1533-1749	216	18

Unter den Diözesen war die Situation Kalocsas eine spezielle. Schon die Zahl der Erzbischöfe (18) ist im Vergleich zu den anderen Titulardiözesen (Waitzen und Fünfkirchen je 36) erstaunlich gering. Bedenkt man dazu noch, dass sechs Prälaten[5], also ein Drittel, den Sitz nur ein Jahr lang inne hatten, bevor sie der Tod ereilte oder sie zum Erzbischof von Gran ernannt wurden, so ergibt sich ein überraschendes Bild: In Kalocsa waren die obersten kirchlichen Amtsträger überdurchschnittlich lange in Amt und Würde und folglich nicht hohen Alters.

Ein weiterer Unterschied zu den anderen Diözesen bestand darin, dass alle Erzbischöfe von Kalocsa-Batsch zeitgleich auch Bischöfe in einer weiteren Diözese waren. Man kann hierbei jedoch nicht von bloßer Kumulation sprechen, da die admini-

Schematismus venerabilis cleri dioecesis Rosnaviensis pro anno Iesu Christi MCMVI. Rosnaviae 1905, 5. – A Szombathelyi Egyházmegye Névtára 2000. Schematismus dioecesis Sabariensis pro anno Domini MM. Hg. v. Lajos HORVÁTH und Imre RÁBA. Szombathely 2000, 20. – Schematismus almae dioecesis Scepusiensis pro anno a Christo nato MCMXIII. Agriae 1913, 1f. – A Székesfehérvári Egyházmegye névtára [Schematismus der Diözese Stuhlweißenburg (Székesfehérvár)]. Hg. v. Gergely MÓZESSY. Székesfehérvár 2001, 15. – Opći Šematizam Katoličke Crkve u Jugoslaviji. Crkva u Jugoslaviji 1974 [Schematismus der Katholischen Kirche in Jugoslawien. Kirchen in Jugoslawien]. Hg. v. Krunoslav DRAGANOVIĆ et al. Zagreb 1975, 54, 138f und 427f.

[5] Márton Borkovich zum Beispiel war 89 Jahre alt, als er 1686 zum Erzbischof von Kalocsa-Batsch ernannt wurde. Bereits ein Jahr später verstarb er.

strierte Diözese Macht und Einkommen brachte, der erzbischöfliche Titel aber Rang und Ansehen bedeutete. Zu den administrierten Diözesen gehörten die reichen und wenig beschädigten Diözesen Raab und Neutra. Dabei wurden nur die Hälfte der Bischöfe überhaupt von Rom anerkannt.
Die Reformdekrete des Tridentinums konnten die Erzbischöfe von Kalocsa – im Gegensatz zu den administrierten Diözesen – zunächst nicht umsetzen. Erst mit der Vertreibung der Osmanen und der Beendigung der Kuruzenaufstände in der ersten Hälfte des 18. Jahrhunderts begann man unter Erzbischof Imre Kardinal Csáky (1710-1732) mit mancher Reform. Den Höhepunkt fand diese Entwicklung aber, wie erwähnt, in der Ära Patachich, die mit dem Jahre 1733 begann.

2. Bildungswege im Zeichen der Reform

Die Schlüsselfiguren für die Erneuerung der katholischen Verwaltung bzw. der Seelsorge waren Kleriker, die zum großen Teil im *Collegium Germanicum et Hungaricum* (CGH) zu Rom ausgebildet worden waren. Dieses päpstliche Kolleg wurde vom Heiligen Ignatius von Loyola (1491-1556) im Jahre 1552 gegründet, um in der *Urbs Aeterna* gut ausgebildete und katholisch geprägte Priester für die katholische Erneuerung zu formen, die sogleich danach wieder im Heimatland arbeiteten. Darauf wurden die neuen Alumnen sogar vereidigt: der priesterliche Dienst musste nach dem Ende ihrer Studien wieder in der Heimat ausgeübt werden. Rund die Hälfte der ungarischen Diözesanbischöfe des 18. Jahrhunderts hatte in Rom eine solche Ausbildung erhalten.[6]

[6] BEKE: Esztergomi Érsekek, 413. – KATONA: A kalocsai érseki II, 668-1063. Az Egri Főegyházmegye 16; A Gyulafehérvári Főegyházmegye 9f; Váci egyházmegyei 174-188; A Nagyváradi Egyházmegye 132; A Veszprémi Főegyházmegye 10f; A Szeged-Csanádi Egyházmegye 21f; Győregyházmegyei almanach 36f. – Schematismus cleri dioecesis Nitriensis 10. – A Pécsi Egyházmegye 9. – Schematismus dioecesis Neosoliensis 7. – Schematismus venerabilis cleri dioecesis Rosnaviensis 5. – A Szombathelyi Egyházmegye 20. – Schematismus almae dioecesis Scepusiensis 1f. – A Székesfehérvári Egyházmegye 15. – Opći Šematizam 54, 138f und 427f. – VÉGHSEŐ, T.: „Catholice reformare". Ágoston Benkovich O.S.P.P.E. missionario apostolico, vescovo di Várad (1631-1702) Budapest, Roma 2007. (Collectanea Vaticana Hungariae – Series I; Classis II).

Diözesanbischöfe aus dem CGH im 18. Jahrhundert (Alte Diözesen)

Diözese	Periode	Anzahl Bischöfe	Davon aus dem CGH	%
Gran	1695-1799	6	3	50
Kalocsa	1696-1817	8	7	87,5
Erlau	1699-1799	4	4	100
Siebenbürgen	1696-1815	13	5	38,5
Waitzen	1689-1795	10	5	50
Wardein	1681-1802	10	6	60
Wesprim	1687-1802	7	3	43
Csanád	1700-1828	7	4	57
Raab	1696-1802	5	1	20
Neutra	1696-1804	7	4	57
Fünfkirchen	1687-1799	7	2	28,5
Agram	1694-1827	9	4	44,5
Zengg-Modrus	1698-1833	10	1	10
Bosnien	1699-1805	7	1	14,5
Sirmium	1698-1771	8	2	25
Insgesamt		*118*	*52*	*46*

Diözesanbischöfe aus dem CGH im 18. Jahrhundert (Neue Diözesen)

Diözese	Periode	Anzahl Bischöfe	Davon aus dem CGH	%
Neusohl (ung. Besztercebánya , sk. Banská Bystrica)	1776-1813	2	2	100
Rosenau (ung. Rozsnyó, sk. Rožňava)	1776-1799	3	-	0
Steinamenger, (ung. Szombathely)	1777-1804	2	2	100
Zips (ung. Szepes, sk. Spiš)	1776-1806	2	1	50
Stuhlweißenburg (ung. Székesfehérvár)	1777-1811	2	1	50
Insgesamt		*11*	*6*	*60*

In Zahlen verdeutlicht entstammten genau 52 Prälaten (46 %) der älteren ungarischen Diözesen – also solche, die vor 1700 gegründet wurden – bzw. sechs (60 %) der neueren Diözesen – gegründet 1776 und 1777 – der CGH. Für Kalocsa-Batsch waren es sieben von acht.

Gabriel (ung. Gábor) Hermann Anton (ung. Antal) Patachich (1699-1745)[7], Graf von Zajezda[8] und Adam Alexander (ung. Ádám Sándor) Patachich (1716-1784)[9], Baron von Zajezda[10] stammten aus dem kroatischen Adelsgeschlecht der Patačić. Nach dem Doktorat in Philosophie – die Studienorte hießen Tyrnau[11] (ung. Nagyszombat, sk. Trnava) und Wien[12] – studierten sie am *Germanicum-Hungaricum* (von 1718 bis 1722[13] bzw. von 1735 bis 1739[14]), wo ihnen die spezielle kulturelle und religiöse Atmosphäre der Ewigen Stadt, die zu diesem Zeitpunkt das barocke und tridentinische Zentrum war, zu eigen wurde. Beide hatten die Ehre vor dem Heiligen Vater eine predigt zu Allerheiligen abzuhalten (1721[15] bzw. 1738[16]). Gabriel schrieb später in einem Brief: „Ich muss zwar gestehen, dass ich im Kollegium manchen Fehltritt begangen habe, aber zugleich beteuere ich, dass mir das Leben und die Zucht desselben so lieb gewesen ist, dass ich sie auch heute gegen mein Erzbistum eintauschen möchte. Ich sage es in aller Aufrichtigkeit.“[17] Gabriels Neffe Adam interessierte sich früh für Literatur und wurde bald schon Mitglied der Arcadia, eines wichtigen literarischen Kreises in Rom.[18] Nach der Priesterweihe in der Lateranbasilika zu Rom (1722[19] und 1739[20]), kehrten Gabriel und Adam nach Kroatien zurück.

---

[7] Mađarevo, 3. Mai 1699 (Taufe) – Wien, 5. Dezember 1745. Vgl. Vatikanisches Geheimarchiv (Vatikanstadt; Archivio Segreto Vaticano, ASV) Archivum Concistorialis (Arch. Concist.), Processus Concistorialis (Processus Concist.), 117, fol. 748. – KFL I.1.c. Patachich Gábor, Vienna, 5 Dezember 1745.

[8] Bis 1735 war er Baron, danach Erhebung seines Standes in Laxenburg (21. Mai 1735). Királyi Könyvek 1527-1767. Libri Regii 1527-1767. CD-ROM. Hg. v. Zsuzsanna VISSI, Gabriella TROSTOVSZKY et al. Budapest 1998-2002, 37.239. – Eine Kopie im Kalocsai Főegyházmegyei Levéltár [Archiv der Erzdiözese Kalocsa] Kalocsa. (fortan: KFL) I.1.c. Patachich Gábor, Laxenburg, 21. Mai 1735. – Vgl.: Magyar Országos Levéltár [Ungarisches Landesarchiv] Budapest. (fortan: MOL). A 34 Conceptus Referadarum, 1735, N. 36.

[9] Karlstadt (kroat. Karlovac), 18. Februar 1616 (Taufe) – Kalocsa, 19. Juli 1784. ASV Arch. Concist., Processus Concist., 148, fol. 313. – Kalocsai Főszékesegyházi Könyvtár [Bibliothek der Erzdiözese Kalocsa] (fortan: KFK). Manuscript (Ms) 256. Diarium Illustrissimi ac Reverendissimi Domini Domini Francesci Caroli Palma(...), 64f.

[10] Er wurde am 21. Mai 1735 in Laxenburg zum Baron erhoben. Királyi Könyvek 37.240. – Vgl.: MOL A 34 Conceptus Referadarum, 1735, N. 36.

[11] Archiv des Collegium Germanicum et Hungaricum (Rom; ACGU) Historia (Hist.) 2, N. 58. – Marticula et Acta Hungarorum in universitatibus studentium. Vol. 2: Roma, Collegium Germanicum et Hungaricum. I. Matricula (1559-1917). A római Collegium Germanicum et Hungaricum magyarországi tanulóinak anyakönyve és iratai. I. Anyakönyv (1559-1917). Hg. v. András VERESS. Budapest 1917 (Fontes Rerum Hungaricarum. Magyar Történelmi Források II), 128f.

[12] Katona: Historia metropolitanae II, CLXXXIX.

[13] ACGU Hist. 2. N. 58.

[14] ACGU Hist. 2, N. 451.

[15] ACGU Hist. 488, foll. 80f.

[16] ACGU Hist. 2, N. 451.

[17] STEINHUBER, Andreas: Geschichte des Kollegium Germanikum Hungarikum in Rom. Bd. II. Freiburg in Breisgau 1906, 364.

[18] BITSKEY, István: Hungariából Rómába. A római Collegium Germanicum Hungaricum és a magyarországi barokk művelődés [Von Hungaria nach Rom. Das Collegium Germanicum Hungaricum zu Rom und die Barockkultur in Ungarn]. Budapest 1996 (Italianistica Debreceniensis. Olasz Felvilágosodás és Romantica Kutatóközpont Monográfiák 2), 177.

[19] 4. April 1722, von Nunzio Baccari, geweiht von Vizeregenten zu Rom (1721-1738). ASV Arch. Concist., Processus Concist., 117, fol. 749.

[20] 20. Dezember 1739, geweiht von Filippo Carlo Spada, Vizeregenten zu Rom (1738-1742). ASV Arch. Concist., Processus Concist. 148, fol. 314.

Gabriel begleitete ab 1723[21] zunächst das Amt des Pfarrers in Warasdin (kroat. Varaždin), bevor er noch im gleichen Jahr (1723-1733)[22] zum Domherrn von Agram ernannt wurde. Adam war zunächst für zwei Jahre (1739-1741) als Pfarrer in Vrbovec tätig.[23] Danach übersiedelte er ebenfalls nach Agram und nahm seine Tätigkeit als Domherr (1741[24]-1751/1759) auf. Beide übten sich nicht nur in kirchlichen, sondern auch in staatlichen Diensten. So war Adam Militärkommandant an der kroatisch-osmanischen Grenze.[25] Bereits 1729 wurde Gabriel zum Diözesanbischof von Sirmium ernannt[26], seine Weihung erfolgte 1731[27]. Bei Adam dauerte dieser Vorgang etwas länger. Er wurde 1751 Kirchenrat in der Hofkanzlei zu Wien und gleichzeitig gewählter Bischof von Novi.[28] 1759 erhielt Ádám Patachich die Diözese von Wardein[29] (1760[30] zum Bischof geweiht), die er 17 Jahre lang führte. 1776[31] wurde er schließlich von Maria Theresia zum Erzbischof von Kalocsa-Batsch ernannt, ihr Vater Kaiser Karl VI. hatte selbiges 1733[32] mit Gabriel Patachich vollzogen.

---

[21] Kaptolski Arhiv Zagreb [Archiv des Domkapitels Agram] (fortan: KAZ). 10a, 151s. – IVANČAN, Ljudevit: Podatci o zagrebačkim kanonicima od godine 1193-1924 [Das Leben der Domherren von Agram zwischen 1193-1924]. Schreibmaschinenskript im KAZ. Zagreb 1912-1924. III 753. – Es ist möglich, dass Gábor Patachich schon in der zweiten Hälfte des Jahres 1722 in Waraschdin war, doch nachweisbar ist das nicht.

[22] IVANČAN: Podatci o zagrebačkim III, 752. – MAČEK, Pavao: Rod Patačića od Zajezde. Rodoslovna rasprava [Das Geschlecht Patachich von Zajezda. Eine genealogische Studie]. Zagreb 2004, 175. – Marticula et Acta 129. – Vgl. Királyi Könyvek 34.258.

[23] KAZ, 10a, 481.

[24] Das Dekret KFL I.1.c. Patachich Ádám, Agram, 21. April 1741.

[25] Prothocolla Generalium Congregationum Statuum et Ordinum Regnorum Dalmatiae, Croatiae et Slavoniae. Zaklučci Hrvatskog Sabora. Hg. v. Josip BUTURAC et al. Zagrabiae 1960-1980, V 283, 307s, 340.; VI 3.; VI 99.

[26] Királyi könyvek 36.105. – MOL A 35 Conceptus Expeditionum, Juli 1729 N. 5.

[27] Vgl. ASV Arch. Concist., Acta Camerarii, 30, fol. 86. – Er wurde wahrscheinlich von Friedrich Karl von Schönborn, Fürsterzbischof von Bamberg und Fürstbischof von Würzburg (1729-1746) zum Bischof geweiht. „Non fui praesens, dum consecratus fuit, audivi tamen ipsum consecratum fuisse ab Episcopo Herbipolensi tunc temporis in hac Civitate morante." Zeugnis von Nikola Petričević, Domherr von Agram (1730-1756) im Prozess von 1733. ASV Arch. Concist., Processus Concist., 117, fol. 197r.

[28] Das Diplom im KFL VIII.1. b. I. Ádám Patachich, Pozsony, 30. Juli 1751. – Királyi Könyvek 42.166. – Bischof von Novi war ein Bischofstitel, der zwar von den ungarischen Königen verliehen wurde, von Rom aber nicht anerkannt war.

[29] 29. August 1759. Királyi Könyvek 45.92. – MOL A 35 Conceptus Expeditionum, September 1759, N. 30. – Das Präsentationsschreiben (Praesentatio): MOL A 35 Conceptus Expeditionum, September 1759, N. 31. – Das Empfehlungsschreiben (Raccomandatio) im Österreichisches Staatsarchiv Haus-, Hof-, und Staatsarchiv (Wien, ÖStA HHStA) Gesandtschaftsarchiv Rom-Vatikan I. Fasc. 176, Akten des Kardinals Albani – Wien, 29 August 1759, 262f; MOL A 35 Conceptus Expeditionum, September 1759, N. 32.

[30] Wien, 9. März 1760, geweiht vom Freund Christoph Anton Kardinal Migazzi, Erzbischof von Wien (1757-1803) und Bischof von Waitzen (1756-1757, 1762-1803). – KATONA: Historia metropolitanae II CCV.

[31] 8. März 1776. Das Diplom im KFL VIII.1. b. I. Ádám Patachich, Wien, 8. März 1776. – MOL A 57 Libri Regii 50 N. 81. – Vgl. Das Präsentationsschreiben: ASV. Arch. Concist., Processus Concist., 170, 203. – MOL A 57 Libri Regii, 50 N. 82; Das Empfehlungsschreiben: ÖStA HHStA Gesandtschaftsarchiv Rom-Vatikan I., Fasc. 210, Akten des Kardinals Albani, 6. April 1776 – Wien, 8 März 1776. – MOL A 57 Libri Regii 50 N. 83.

[32] 6. Februar 1733. Királyi Könyvek 37.8. – Vgl.: Das Präsentationsschreiben von König Karl III (Kaiser Karl VI) an Clemens XII (1730-1740) MOL A 35 Conceptus Expeditionum, Februar 1733, N. 22. – Das Empählunsschreiben von Karl III (VI) an Kardinal Álvaro de Cienfuegos (1657-1739). – MOL A 35 Conceptus Expeditionum, Februar 1733, N. 23.

3. Neueinrichtung der zentralen Institutionen in der Diözese Kalocsa-Batsch

Gabriel Patachich war im Jahre 1733 nach 207 Jahren der erste Bischof, der die Geschicke der Erzdiözese Kalocsa-Batsch ohne eine parallele Administration in einer anderen Diözese leitete. Außerdem war er der erste seit 1526, der stabil auf dem Territorium seiner Erzdiözese residierte. Er fand sie allerdings in einem sehr kritischen Zustand vor: Neben der geringen und verarmten „Restbevölkerung" – unter ihr waren die Katholiken in der Minderheit – und einem Mangel an Priestern waren auch die Kirchen ruiniert. Drei Gegenmaßnahmen sollten das Erzbistum wieder zu altem Glanz verhelfen: das Priesterseminar, der Neubau einer Kathedrale und die Wiederherstellung des Domkapitels.

Der erste und für Gabriel Patachich gleichzeitig der wichtigste Punkt war die Einrichtung eines Priesterseminars.[33] 1735 verfasste er eine *Regula* für die neue Institution, nach dem Modell in Tyrnau und Rom.[34] In der Zeit seines Neffen Adam Patachich geschah dann die eigentlicheNeugründung des Seminars[35] und manche Korrektur an der *Regula*.[36] Auf Befehl von Joseph II. (1780-1790) musste er das Seminar für einige Jahre schließen.[37] Die Seminaristen stammten aus dem ganzen Gebiet des Königreichs Ungarn, manche kamen auch aus dem Ausland.[38] Nicht alle Kandidaten erwiesen sich dabei als geeignet. Ein Beispiel dafür, wie schwer der Neuanfang an einigen Stellen war, sei hier kurz angeführt: Bei Márton Kállóczy, der wahrscheinlich der erste Priester gewesen war, den Gabriel Patachich in seiner Diözese weihte, stellten sich bereits nach einem Jahr erste Probleme heraus, die zu dessen Versetzung führten.[39] Aber auch am neuen Ort lief es für ihn nicht glatt. Die Pfarrgemeinde erhob Klage gegen den Pfarrer, wie es die Akten des Diözesankonsistoriums bezeugen.[40] Die wichtigsten Beschwerden waren dabei: Erstens stände er der Litanei nur sehr selten vor, da er lieber zur Jagd ginge, zweitens sei die Osterbeichte so skandalös gewesen, dass manche Leute in das nächste Dorf flüchteten. Schließlich wollte er nicht zu einer sterbenden Frau gehen, um ihr die letzte Ölung zu spenden, da sie die Kirchensteuer nicht bezahlt hätte. Aufgrund des gravierenden Priestermangels wurde Kállóczy zunächst nicht suspendiert, sondern nur neuerlich

[33] Er gründete diese Institution noch am Tage seiner Amtseinführung (Fest des Heiligen Karl Borromäus, 4. November 1733). Vgl. KATONA: Historia metropolitanae II XCIX.

[34] KFL I.1.a. Seminarium Archiepiscopalis, Regulae Seminarii, Leges Seminarii, Kalocsa, 5. November 1735.

[35] Das Diplom: KFL VIII.1. b. II. 5. Wien, 8. März 1776; MOL A 57 Libri Regii, 50, N. 86.

[36] Unterschrieben in Kalocsa, 13. August 1777, noch einmal diskutiert am 16. Februar 1781. KFL I.1.a. Seminarium Archiepiscopalis, Regulae Seminarii, Constitutiones Regulae Pro Seminario Cleri Colocensis 1777, 1781.

[37] WINKLER, Pál: A papnevelés története a kalocsai egyházmegyében. Kalocsa 1934 (Árpád Könyvek 47), 23f. – Vgl. KFL I.1.a. Seminarium Archiepiscopale, Acta Seminarii tempore Josephi II.

[38] KFL I.1.a. Seminarium Archiepiscopale, Examen; Ibid., Classificatio; Ibid., Informatio Alumnorum.

[39] KFL I.1.e.A) 1. Protocollum Determinatiorum Venerabilis Consistorii Colocensis 1733-1745, 111f.

[40] Die Sitzung vom 13. Juli 1735. EBD., 65-70.

versetzt.[41] Ein paar Jahre mussten noch vergehen und einige Skandale geschehen, bis er vom priesterlichen Dienst endgültig verabschiedet wurde.[42]
Die Kathedrale ist ein Symbol für Dienst und Würde der Bischöfe. Gabriel Patachich gab daher einen Neubau in Auftrag, der die Prächtigkeit der tridentinischen Kirche zeigen sollte. Der Erzbischof eröffnete die fertig gestellten Abschnitte am 14. August 1738, dem Vorabend des Patroziniums Mariä Himmelfahrt.[43] Wegen abebbender Stiftungen blieb es dann die Aufgabe der Nachfolger, die Bischofskirche zu vollenden. Gabriel Patachich erneuerte neben der Kathedrale auch das Domkapitel. Das Kolleg der Kanoniker assistierte nicht nur bei liturgischen Feiern, sondern es war die bedeutsamste zentrale Führungsorganisation einer Diözese und Beratungsgremium eines Diözesanbischofs. In Ungarn hatte es daneben noch eine spezielle säkulare Aufgabe, kann es doch als Vorgänger des heutigen Notariats (*fidedignitas*) angesehen werden. Patachich war bei dem Versuch einer Erneuerung mit einer Reihe von Schwierigkeiten konfrontiert: Nebst Geldproblemen fand er in der Erzdiözese schlicht zu wenige Würdenträger vor, die er hätte aus dem pastoralen Dienst für die zentrale Leitung bestellen können. Er selbst schrieb 1738 in einem Brief, dass er in der Hoffnung auf Gott die Erneuerung angefangen habe, da „wenn keiner damit anfängt, keiner es beenden wird".[44] So plante er nur ein kleines Domkapitel zunächst mit fünf Personen.[45]
Diese ersten Domherren waren daneben auch als Pfarrer tätig, obwohl ein solches Vorgehen von Rom im Allgemeinen verboten war. Unter seinem Neffen Adam Patachich wurde das Domkapitel erweitert[46], seit dieser Zeit umfasst es bis heute zehn Sitze.

4. Konflikte mit den Franziskanern und den Kalvinisten

Zu Beginn des 18. Jahrhunderts befand sich die Erzdiözese, wie erwähnt, in einer äußerst kritischen Lage. Neben dem institutionellen Wiederaufbau galt es nun auch möglichst schnell die Seelsorge neu zu organisieren. Unverzüglich nahm dies Gabriel Patachich nach seiner Amtseinsetzung in Angriff: So gründete er zehn Pfarrei-

[41] Ebd., 112.
[42] Die Setzungen von 17-20. Juni 1742. Ebd., 183-186.
[43] KFL I.1.e B) 15. Sacrae Ordinationes, Consecrationes, Benedictiones et Caeterae Functiones Ecclesiasticae 1734-1739, 123-129. Kalocsa, 14. und 15. August 1738.
[44] KFL I.1.a. Capitulum, Acta mixta, De jure Patronatus Canonicos Colocensis Ecclesiae nominandi, 2. Von Gábor Patachich an Karl III, Kalocsa, 18. April 1738. – KFL I.1.a. Ecclesia Metropolitana, Acta mixta, Kalocsa, 18. April 1738.
[45] KFL I.1.e B 15. Sacrae Ordinationes, Consecrationes, Benedictiones et Caeterae Functiones Ecclesiasticae 1734-1739, 123-129. Kalocsa, 14. und 15. August 1738.
[46] Wien, 8. März 1776. Das Diplom: KFL VIII.1.B)II) Wien, 8. März 1776. – MOL A 57 Libri Regii, 50, N. 85. Kopie: ASV Arch. Concist., Processus Concist., 170, foll. 204-206. – ÖStA HHStA Gesandtschaftsarchiv Rom-Vatikan I. Fasc. 210, Akten des Kardinals Albani, zwei Kopien zum Schreiben gesandt an den Fürsten Kaunitz (1711-1794), Rom, 20. April 1776 – Wien, 8. März 1776.

en[47], ließ die Stadt Kecel im Donau-Theiß-Gebiet wieder besiedeln (1734)[48], führte Visitationen durch (1734, 1738)[49] und gab der Erzdiözese die bis dahin fehlenden nötigen Vorschriften: das *Rituale Romano-Colocense*[50] (1738) und die *Diözesanstatuten*[51] (1738). Mit manch einem Widerständler musste er sich dabei auseinandersetzen: Nebst Priestermangel und materiellen Nöten bereiteten ihm die Franziskaner, die die Region während der türkischen Zeit betreut hatten, einige Hindernisse.

Folgende Beispiele sollen diese schwierige Situation erläutern. Das erste findet sich im Diözesankonsistorialprotokoll von 1735.[52] Es handelt sich um die Einführung des ersten Pfarrers von Gara. Gabriel Patachich gründete im Dorf, das bislang eine Filialgemeinde der Franziskaner war, eine Pfarrei. Als der Erzbischof feierlich einzog, um den neuen Pfarrer zu bestellen und somit die Franziskaner abzulösen, traf er auf große Widerstände bei den südslawischen Bewohnern und bei diesen Bettelmönchen. Patachich versuchte sie zu überzeugen, musste ihnen aber schließlich mit dem König und den kirchlichen Vorschriften drohen. Als auch das nicht fruchtete, griff er zu einer List: Gabriel lud die Alten des Dorfes zum Essen ein und vollendete mittels Wein das, was weder das gute Wort noch die Bedrohung erreichen konnte. Die Resistenz der Angetrunkenen schwand und sie riefen schon bald mit großer Freude aus: „Es lebe unser Herr Pfarrer!"[53]

Ein weiteres Beispiel kann man den Akten der Pfarrei von Dunapataj entnehmen. Dunapataj war eine kleine Stadt an der Donau, die größtenteils von ungarischen Kalvinisten bewohnt wurde. Hier gründete der Erzbischof im Jahre 1737 eine Pfarrei. Dies störte bald darauf die protestantische Gemeinde: Die Kalvinisten erklärten mündlich und schriftlich, dass sie keinen neuen Pastor benötigen würden, da sie bereits über einen (kalvinistischen) verfügten.[54] Der Erzbischof wollte die Frage der Einführung eines katholischen Pfarrers mit den Bewohnern diskutieren. Die Kalvinisten mochten aber nicht zu Gabriel Patachich gehen, weshalb er sie, dem Recht fol-

---

47 Almasch (ung. Bácsalmás), Besdan (ung. Bezdán, südsl. Bezdan), Dunapataj, Dusnok, Gara, Jánoshalma, Kecel, Nadwar (ung. Nemesnádudvar), Neudorf (ung. Bácsújlak, südsl. Bačko Novo Selo) und Tschatali (ung. Csátalja).

48 DÓKA, Klára: Egyházlátogatási jegyzőkönyvek katalógusa. 1. Kalocsai Főegyházmegye [Katalog der kanonischen Visitationen. 1. Erzdiözese Kalocsa]. Budapest 1994, 50.

49 KFL I.1.a. Visitatio canonica, Prothocollum seu Liber Visitationis Dioecesis Bacsiensis 1734. – Hegedűs, Antal: Patachich Gábor kalocsai érsek élete és restaurációs tevékenysége [Das Leben und die Erneuerungstätigkeit von Gabriel Patachich, Erzbischof von Kalocsa]. Schreibmaschinenskript in der Kathedralbibliothek von Kalocsa, KFK. Budapest 1954, 103-110. – Die von ihm zitierte Primärquelle ist heute leider nicht mehr zu finden.

50 Rituale Romano-Colocense, seu formula agendorum in administratione sacramentorum et caeteris Ecclesiae publicis functionibus rite obeundis observanda. Ac in usum Colocensis, et Com-Provincialium Dioecesium accomodata, et utilibus additamentis aucta. Authoritate, opera, et impensis Reverendissimi P. D. Gabrielis Hermanni Dominici miseratione divina metropolitanae Colocensis, et Bacsiensis canonicae unitarum Ecclesiarum Archi-Episcopi. Budae 1738.

51 KFL I.1.a. Visitatio canonica, Acta generalia, Statuta Dioecesana 1738.

52 KFL I.1.e.A) 1. Protocollum Determinatiorum Venerabilis Consistorii Colocensis 1733-1745, 27-30.

53 EBD., 30.

54 KFL I.1.b. Dunapataj, Acta mixta, Dunapataj, 28. Juni 1737.

gend, mit einer Buße von 100 Gulden belegte.[55] Das war aber nur der Anfang, kurze Zeit später gab es erneut einen Anlass, der 100 Gulden Buße zur Folge hatte: die Kalvinisten ließen die Glocken nicht läuten, als der Oberhirte in die Stadt kam. Die Gemeinde erklärte darauf, dass sie gerne die Glocken hätten läuten lassen, wenn der Erzbischof in die Stadt nicht feierlich sondern still und allein eingezogen wäre.

Aber auch die wenigen Katholiken vor Ort hatten Probleme mit den Protestanten. Mit Verweis auf die Nutzung der ehemaligen katholischen Kirche durch die Protestanten[56] errichteten die Katholiken ein neues Gotteshaus aus Holz.[57] Der Neubau entfesselte infolge einen Jahrzehnte andauernden „Kirchen- und Turmkrieg": Die Protestanten bauten einen Holzturm zu ihrer Kirche. Daraufhin bauten die Katholiken eine neue Kirche aus Ziegelstein, die natürlich einen höheren und schöneren Turm als die protestantische Kirche hatte.[58] Die Kalvinisten beließen es nicht dabei und versuchten, einen neuen Kirchturm zu errichten, diesmal mit Turmruhr.[59] Dieser gefiel den Katholiken wiederum nicht. Der Pressburger Statthaltereirat musste die Frage entscheiden und sprach ein salomonisches Urteil: die Kalvinisten durften einen neuen Turm bauen, aber die Turmuhr sollte die katholische Kirche schmücken.[60]

Die Nachfolger von Gabriel Patachich setzten die angefangene Arbeit fort. Es entstanden weitere neue Pfarreien und Kirchen. In der Zeit von Adam Patachich wurde der erste Diözesanschematismus gedruckt[61] und zehn weitere Pfarreien gegründet.[62]

Allerdings verlor die Erzdiözese nach der Gründung der griechisch-katholischen Diözese von Kreutz Križevci (1777) zwei Pfarreien an den orientalischen Ritus. Während des 18. Jahrhunderts entwickelte sich in der Region eine einzigartige multiethnische und multikulturelle Gesellschaft, deren Spuren auch noch heute – aber leider immer weniger – zu finden sind. Zu Beginn des Wendejahres 1733 hatte die Erzdiözese insgesamt nur zehn Diözesanpriester in 17 Pfarreien[63] und es gab nur einen einzigen Pfarrvikar. Acht Kirchengemeinden wurden von Franziskanern geführt.

[55] Die Grundherrin war damals Katalin Daróczi von Királydarócz. KFL I.1.b. Dunapataj, Acta mixta, Dunapataj, 1. Juli 1738. – Es gibt noch zwei andere Briefe von ihr, wo sie ihre Leibeigenen verteidigt. Ebd., Tétény, 26. Juni 1737 und Tétény, 3. Juli 1738.

[56] EBD., Dunapataj, 30. September 1718.

[57] KATONA: Historia metropolitanae I LVIII., 64.

[58] A Kalocsa-Bácsi Főegyházmegye Történeti Sematizmusa 1777-1923. Schematismus Historicus Cleri Archidioecesis Colocensis et Bacsiensis 1777-1923. Hg. v. Andor LAKATOS. Kalocsa/Coloczae 2002 (A Kalocsai Főegyházmegyei Gyűjtemények kiadványai 3), 181. – Katona: Historia metropolitanae I LVIII 64. – KFL I.1.b. Dunapataj, Visitatio canonica, 1783.

[59] KFL I.1.b. Dunapataj, Acta mixta, Pozsony, 21. Dezember 1772, im Anhang ist das Gesuch. Es gibt noch andere 14 Dokumenten von 1772 bis 1773. – Die Dokumentation ist, im Vergleich zu anderen Affären, umfangreich.

[60] KFL I.1.b. Dunapataj, Acta mixta, Pozsony, 3. Mai 1773.

[61] Calendarium Archi-Dioecesanum Cleri Colocensis, et Bácsiensis Ecclesiarum Canonice Unitarum ad Annum Jesi Christi MDCCLXXVII. Pestini 1777.

[62] Bajsa (kroat. Bajša), Dávod, Felsőszentiván, Kishegyes (Mali Iđoš), Martonos (Martonoš), Nagelsdorf (Bajmok, Bajmok), St. Thomas (Szenttamás, Srbobran), Tataháza, Temerin (Temerin) und Wikitsch (Bácsbokod).

[63] MOL C 38 Acta Cassae Parochorum, Archidioecesis Colocensis, N. 1, 1733, fol. 1-5. – KFL I.1.a. Generalia de Achidioecesi, Pozsony, 21. Oktober 1732 und 13. März 1733. – MOL C 38 Acta Cassae Parochorum, Archidioecesis Colocensis, N. 1, 1733, fol. 10. – Der Monarch war gleichzeitig informiert. EBD., fol. 8f.

Diese Zahlen sind sehr bescheiden, bedenkt man, dass die Diözese vor der türkischen Eroberung nach einigen Schätzungen sogar um die 300 Pfarreien gehabt haben soll.[64] Im Jahre 1784, als Adam Patachich verstarb, gab es schon wieder 72 Pfarreien (3 weitere Pfarreien wurden de jure gegründet), darunter 68, die von Diözesanpriestern geführt wurden.[65]

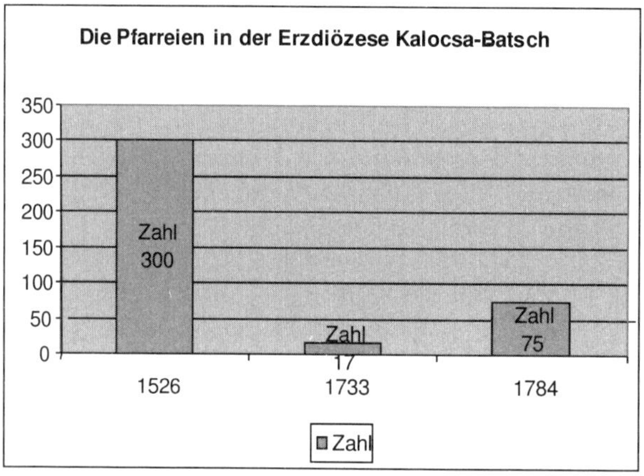

1784 waren allein in den Pfarrgemeinden 82 Diözesanpriester tätig. Es gab Städte, wo sogar 3 Pfarrvikare wirkten. Nach einer Volkszählung von 1733 lebten 14.343 Katholiken (Ungarn, Illyrer – also Südslawen – und Deutsche) in der Erzdiözese, die Mehrheit der Bewohner bestand aus orthodoxen Südslawen.[66]

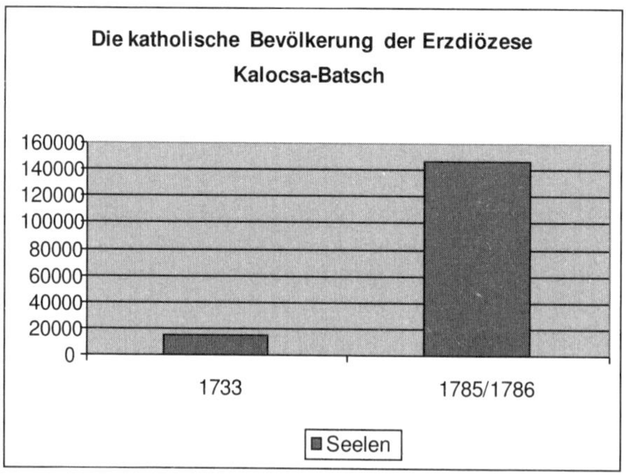

[64] HEGEDŰS: Patachich Gábor, 42f.
[65] Calendarium Archi-Dioecesanum Cleri Colocensis 1784.
[66] MOL C 38 Acta Cassae Parochorum, Archidioecesis Colocensis, N. 1, 1733, fol. 5.

Der staatlichen Pfarrtopographie von 1785/86 zufolge entwickelte sich die Zahl der Katholiken auf 146.794 Seelen[67] und der Katholizismus wurde – auch dank der Immigration und der noch geplanten Ansiedlungen – noch einmal zur größten Religionsgemeinschaft in diesem Raum.

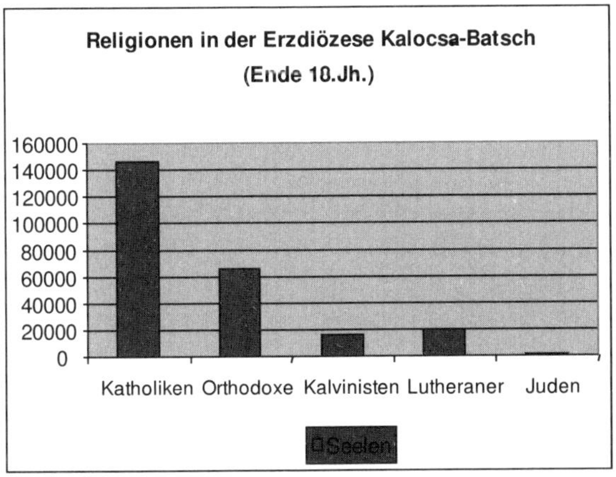

Wie oben zu entnehmen ist, waren die anderen Religionen deutlich geringer vertreten: 66.108 Orthodoxe (1791)[68], 16.135 Kalvinisten (1788)[69] und weniger als 20.000 Lutheraner (11.520 im Komitat Batsch (1803)[70] und 9427 im Komitat Pest-Pilis-Solt (1812).[71] Juden waren in fast allen Gemeinden präsent, allerdings in sehr geringer Anzahl. Insgesamt zählten sie ca. 1300 Gläubige (1216 im Komitat Batsch (1787)[72], 74 im Komitat Pest-Pilis-Solt[73] und 24 im Komitat Csongrád (1785).[74] Es gab durchaus Zusammenhänge zwischen Religion und Ethnie. Wir können im Großen

[67] Daten von 1786. Die Gesamtzahl ergibt sich aus der Gesamtheit der Zahl der einzelnen Pfarreien mitsamt den Filialgemeinden. Das ganze Komitat war unter der Jurisdiktion des Erzbischofs von Kalocsa-Batsch. Magyarország történeti helységnévtára. Bács megye (1773-1808) [Historisches Ortsverzeichnis von Ungarn. Komitat Batsch]. Hg. v. György LELKES. Budapest 2005, 172-177. – Nur die Pfarrei von Horgos (südsl. Horgoš) war unter der Jurisdiktion des Erzbischofs von Kalocsa-Batsch. Magyarország történeti helységnévtára. Csongrád megye (1773-1808) [Historisches Ortsverzeichnis von Ungarn. Komitat Csongrád]. Hg. v. György LELKES. Budapest 2002. 83. – Daten sind von 1785. Die Gesamtzahl ergibt sich aus der Gesamtheit der Zahl der einzelnen Pfarrein der Erzdiözese Kalocsa-Batsch mit den dazugehörigen Filialgemeinden. Einige Filialgemeinden von Frankenstadt (ung. Baja) – mit 1291 Seelen – befanden sich zwar im Komitat Pest-Pilis-Solt, aber sie werden trotzdem zum Komitat Batsch gezählt. Der südliche Teil vom Komitat stand unter der Jurisdiktion des Erzbischofs von Kalocsa-Batsch. Magyarország történeti helységnévtára. Pest-Pilis-Solt megye és a Kiskunság (1773-1808) [Historisches Ortsverzeichnis von Ungarn. Komitat Pest-Pilis-Solt und Kleinkumanien] Hg. v. Aranka SZASZKÓNÉ SIN. Budapest 1998, 197-199.

[68] Die Gesamtzahl ergibt sich aus der Summe der einzelnen Pfarreien. Vgl. Magyarország történeti helységnévtára. Bács megye, 179-181.

[69] EBD., Bács megye, 182f. und Pest-Pilis-Solt megye, 219-223.

[70] EBD., Bács megye, 184f.

[71] EBD., Pest-Pilis-Solt megye, 225-229.

[72] EBD., Bács megye, 186s.

[73] EBD., Pest-Pilis-Solt megye, 213-233.

[74] EBD., Csongrád megye, 91.

und Ganzen feststellen, dass die Ungarn Katholiken oder Kalvinisten waren, ein Teil der Südslawen ist katholisch gewesen, ein anderer Teil orthodox. Die Deutschen und die Slowaken waren entweder katholisch oder evangelisch. Es lebten in der Gegend einige Einsiedler aus den böhmischen Gebieten, die katholisch waren, und noch einige griechisch-katholische Ruthenen und armenisch-katholische Armenier. Teilt man die Pfarreien nach Sprachen auf, so erhält man folgendes Ergebnis:

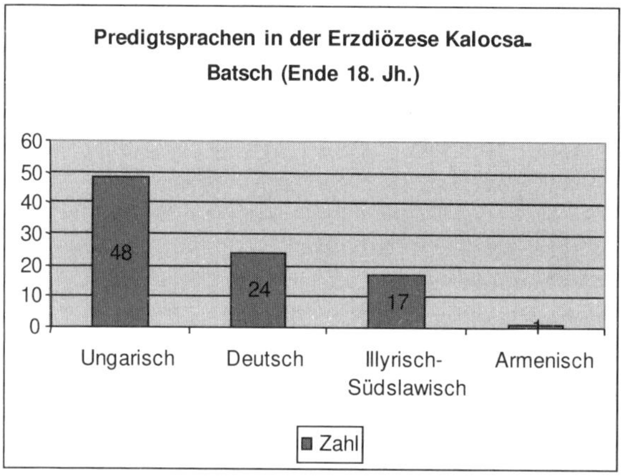

In den Pfarreien, die 1784 bereits existierten oder wenigstens gegründet waren (75), predigte man in 48 von ihnen auf Ungarisch, Deutsch war in 24 Pfarreien vorherrschend, Illyrisch-Südslawisch in 17 Pfarreien und Armenisch in einer Gemeinde.[75] Einige Gemeinden waren zwei- oder mehrsprachig.

5. „Der Vollender" Adam Patachich

Im 18. Jh. wurden die Güter wieder in Besitz genommen, aber die Kirche verlor langsam ihren säkularen Einfluss. Die Bischöfe des Königreichs nahmen an den Reichstagen teil. Gabriel Patachich assistierte bei der Krönung von Maria Theresa.[76] Die Erzbischöfe von Kalocsa-Batsch waren auch Mitglieder am Höchsten Gerichtshof (*Excelsa Tabula Septem-Viralis*)[77] und leiteten das Komitat Batsch als Obergespane bis 1776.[78]

[75] KATONA: Historia metropolitanae I, LXI.

[76] KOLINOVICS, Gabriel: Nova Ungariae Periodus, anno primo gynaeco-cratiae austriacae inchoata, sive Comitiorum Generalium (...). Budae 1790, 220-236.

[77] Am 30. April 1733 wurde befohlen, dass den Erzbischöfen der Lohn eines Assessors zugewiesen werden kann. Österreichisches Staatsarchiv. Finanz- und Hofkammerarchiv. Hofkammerarchiv, Wien (fortan: ÖStA FHKA HKA). Hoffinanz-Protokolle R 1156 199v. – Cfr. KFK Ms 355.

[78] András Hadik (1710-1790), Graf von Futak war der erste nicht kirchliche Obergespan von Batsch. Vgl. der Brief vom Königlichen Kanzler Ferenc Eszterházy an den Bischof Ádám Patachich. KFL I.1.a. Capitulum, Acta mixta, Wien, 2. Februar 1776.

Gabriel Patachich brachte bei Amtsbeginn schlicht zu wenig politische Erfahrung mit, was wohl auf sein noch junges Alter von 34 Jahren zurück zu führen ist. Selbiges kann man über seinen Neffen Adam nicht sagen: dieser übte vor seiner Ernennung mehrere kirchliche und säkulare Würden aus. Dass er als Erzbischof keine politischen Ämter mehr begleitete, muss wohl als ein Spiel des Lebens angesehen werden. Dafür war Adam aber Rektor der Universität von Ofen (ung. Buda).[79] Er nahm an den Reformen der Theologischen Fakultät teil[80] und sammelte eine voluminöse Bibliothek, die zu seiner Zeit eine der größten in Ungarn gewesen war. Im Jahre 1784 umfasste sie 18.992 Bände.[81] Der Erzbischof verfügte über Agenten in ganz Europa, die ihm Bücher kauften, und er pflegte gute Kontakte zu wichtigen Persönlichkeiten, so zum Archivisten und künftigen Kardinal Giuseppe Garampi (1725-1792) und dem Theologen Francesco Antonio Zaccaria (1714-1795).[82] Er schrieb außerdem Bücher, wie das Latein-Rumänische[83] oder das Latein-Illyrisch-Deutsche Wörterbuch[84], aber auch Gedichte in klassischem Latein.[85] Seine Bibliothek und seine Manuskripte fanden ihren endgültigen Aufbewahrungsort im Erzbischöflichen Palais, das er selbst erbauen ließ.[86] Als Adam Patachich 1784 starb, waren alle wichtigen kirchlichen Reformen vollendet. Die Diözese war funktionstüchtig und wuchs beständig.

---

[79] KATONA: Historia metropolitanae II, CCVII.

[80] Die Korrespondenz von Ádám Patachich über den Prozess befindet sich im KFL I.1.a. Seminarium Archiepiscopalis, Regulae educationis, anni 1777-1778.

[81] KÉKESI, János: A kalocsai Főszékesegyházi Könyvtár. 1784-1964 [Die Bibliothek der Erzdiözese von Kalocsa. 1784-1964]. Schreibmaschinenskript in der KFK. Kalocsa 1964, 7. – Die Bibliothek umfasst derzeitig ungefähr 150.000 Bände.

[82] KFK Ms 447.

[83] KFK Ms 706/2 Lexicon compendiarum Latino-Valachicum complectens. Dictiones, ac phrases Latinas cum Valachia earum interpretatione. – KFK Ms 706/1 Institutiones linguae Valachicae sive grammatica compendio exhibita.

[84] KFK Ms 704 Dictionarium Latino-Illyricum-Germanicum.

[85] Über die literarische Tätigkeit von Ádám Patachich siehe: Tóth, Sándor Attila: Rómából a pannon árkádiába [Von Rom in die pannonische Arcadia]. Budapest 2004. – Dieses Werk füllt eine Lücke, wenn auch seine kirchliche Sprache etwas unsicher ist.

[86] JERNYEI KISS, János: A kalocsai érseki székesegyház és rezidencia megújulása a 18. században [Die Erneuerung der erzbischöfliche Kathedrale und Residenz im 18. Jahrhundert]. In: Kalocsa történetéből. Hg. v. László KOSZTA. Kalocsa 2000, 243-282, hier 271-274. – JERNYEI KISS, János: Patachich Ádám és a kalocsai érseki rezidencia [Ádám Patachich und die Erzbischöfliche Residenz]. In: Patachich Ádám érsek emléke. Zajezdai báró Patachich Ádám, kalocsai érsek (1776-1784) halálának 220 évfordulója alkalmából rendezett konferencia és kiállítás emlékkönyve. Kalocsa, 2004. november 17. Hg. v. Adél LAKATOS. Kalocsa 2005. (A Kalocsai Főegyházmegyei Gyűjtemények kiadványai 4), 67-70. – Pál Winkler und andere Wissenschaftler schreiben die Pläne Gáspár Oszwald (1727-1781) zu, allerdings ziehen sie dabei nicht die Änderungen in Betracht, die nach dem Ankommen von Ádám Patachich geschahen. JERNYEI KISS: A kalocsai érseki 270, Anmerkung 73. – Winkler Pál: A kalocsai érseki kastély és főszékesegyházi könyvtár története [die Geschichte vom Erzbischofsschloss und der Kathedralbibliothek von Kalocsa]. Kalocsa 1932, (Árpád könyvek 43), 21f.

Tamás Véghseő

Die Union mit der katholischen Kirche an der Wende vom 17. zum 18. Jahrhundert. Die Unionsbemühungen des Bischofs Augustin Benkovich

Die Union verschiedener Teilkirchen des orientalischen Christentums mit der katholischen Kirche ist im Grunde genommen ein Integrationsprozess, in dem verständlicherweise die dogmatischen und die kanonischen Aspekte die Hauptrolle spielen. Wenn aber diese Unionsprozesse gut definierbare, in spezifischen gesellschaftlichen Situationen lebende und sich in Migrationen befindliche Ethnien betreffen, so sind sie nicht nur Integrationsprozesse im kirchlich-religiösen sondern auch im sozialen Sinn. Im Laufe des 17. Jahrhunderts wurden im historischen Königreich Ungarn mehrere Unionsprozesse eingeleitet, die verschiedene Volksgruppen orthodoxer Konfession betrafen. Während die Unionsversuche unter den Serben nur geringe Erfolge erzielten und nur eine kleine katholische Gemeinde daraus hervorging, wurden aus der Union der Ruthenen ab Mitte des 17. Jahrhunderts und der Union der Rumänen an der Wende zum 18. Jahrhundert zwei lebendige Kirchen geboren, die nicht nur ihre Integration in die katholische Kirche erreichten, sondern auch die soziale und kulturelle Integration der betroffenen Volksgruppen beschleunigten.

Im Folgenden soll ein maßgeblicher Akteur dieser Entwicklung kurz vorgestellt werden. Es handelt sich hierbei um einen Bischof von Wardein (rum. Oradea, ung. Nagyvárad), Ágoston Benkovich[1], der in der zweiten Hälfte des 17. Jahrhunderts und in den ersten Jahren des 18. Jahrhunderts maßgeblich an diesen Integrationsprozessen beteiligt war. Er hatte mehrere Jahrzehnte seines Lebens für die griechisch-katholische Kirche geopfert, die aus der Union von Ungvár/Užhorod hervorging. Später hatte er die Union der Rumänen der Diözese Wardein gefördert. Am 24. April 1646 erklärten 63 orthodoxe Priester unter der Führung ihres späteren Bischofs in der Burgkapelle von Ungwar (ung. Ungvár, ukr.Užhorod) die Einheit mit der katholischen Kirche.[2] Obwohl die Unionsprozesse schon seit Jahren von zwei Basilianermönchen vorbereitet wurden und seit der Rekatholisierung der Familie Homonnai Drugeth Anfang des 17. Jahrhunderts bereits zwei Unionsversuche stattgefunden hatten, waren nur etwa 10% der betroffenen orthodoxen Priester zum feierlichen Akt erschienen. Nachdem Bischof György Jakusich von Erlau (ung. Eger)

[1] Zum Leben und Wirken von Benkovich siehe VÉGHSEŐ, Tamás: Catholice reformare. Ágoston Benkovich O.S.P.P.E. missionario apostolico, vescovo di Várad (1631–1702). Budapest-Roma 2007 (Collectanea Vaticana Hungarae II/2).

[2] Zur Geschichte der Union von Ungwar siehe HODINKA, Antal: A munkácsi görög-katholikus püspökség története [Geschichte der griechisch-katholischen Diözese von Munkatsch]. Budapest 1909. – LACKO, Michael: Unio Uzhorodiensis Ruthenorum Carpaticorum cum Ecclesia Catholica. Roma 1965.

im Namen der katholischen Kirche garantiert hatte, dass der östliche Ritus nach der Union unberührt, der Bischof der Unierten von der Priestersynode gewählt, vom Heiligen Stuhl anerkannt und der unierte Klerus alle Privilegien des katholischen Klerus erhalten werde, legten die Anwesenden das katholische Glaubensbekenntnis ab. Mit diesem Akt wurde die griechisch-katholische Kirche in der Region geboren, die sich heute in den vier Ländern – Nordostungarn, der Ostslowakei, der Südukraine sowie in Nordwest-Rumänien – befindet und über die damals der im Munkatscher Basilianerkloster residierende Bischof die Jurisdiktion ausübte.[3] Die unierte Kirche bestand überwiegend aus den in dieser Region seit dem Ende des 14. Jahrhunderts in immer größer Anzahl angesiedelten Ruthenen, die mit der Zeit auch andere ethnische Gruppen assimiliert hatten. Im Laufe des 17. und 18. Jahrhunderts zogen sie gen Süden und auf Initiative der lokalen Feudalherren besetzten sie in den heutigen ungarischen Komitaten namens Szabolcs-Szatmár-Bereg, Hajdú-Bihar und Borsod-Abaúj-Zemplén eine große Anzahl von Dörfern.

Die Union von Ungwar war gleichwohl eher der Anfang als das Ende der Unionsprozesse. Die Ausbreitung und die Konsolidierung der Union bedurften noch mehrere Jahrzehnte, in denen allerdings auch die drei Unionsbedingungen fast völlig außer Acht gelassen wurden:

1.) Die Unierten mussten nämlich mehrmals Latinisierungsversuche der abendländischen katholischen Missionare abwehren.

2.) Eine Bischofswahl fand nur einmal statt, was im Ungarn der Stephanskrone als unvorstellbar galt.

3.) Die Ausdehnung der kirchlichen Privilegien auf den unierten Klerus scheiterte oft am Widerstand der Feudalherren, welche die unierten Priester als Leibeigene betrachteten.

Erst durch kaiserliche Dekrete ab dem Ende des 17. Jahrhunderts änderte sich sukzessive dieser Zustand für die Unierten. In diesem Zusammenhang muss betont werden, dass im Gegensatz zu den anderen frühneuzeitlichen Unionen die Union von Ungwar nicht auf den Heiligen Stuhl zurückging, sondern auf Initiative einiger ungarischer katholischer Prälaten, Missionare und Feudalherren zustande kam. Das Mitwirken der Feudalherren ist mit ihrer Rekatholisierung zu erklären. Im Gegensatz zur Verbreitung des Protestantismus im 16. und beginnenden 17. Jahrhundert waren sie nach erfolgter katholischer Erneuerung und Gegenreformation aktive Förderer des Katholizismus geworden. Sie zeigten eine Haltung wie die neue Generation ungarischer Bischöfe, unter denen auch die Förderer der Union von Ungwar zu finden waren, wie Jakusich, Lippay oder Kisdy. Während ihrer Ausbildungszeit in Rom, vor allem im *Collegium Germanicum et Hungaricum*, eigneten sie sich den Geist des tridentinischen Katholizismus an.[4] Der tridentinische Katholizismus, gestärkt in

[3] Munkatsch (ukr. Mukatschewe, ung. Munkács).

[4] Zur Bedeutung des *Collegium Germanicum et Hungaricum* in der katholischen Erneuerung Ungarns siehe BITSKEY, István: Hungariából Rómába. A római Collegium Germanicum Hungaricum és a magyarországi barokk művelődés [Das römische Collegium Germanicum Hungaricum und die ungarische Barockkultur]. Budapest 1996. – Auf Italienisch: Il Collegio Germanico-Ungarico di Roma. Contributo alla storia della cultura ungherese in età barocca. Roma 1996. – Zur Ausbildung der Pauliner in Rom siehe VÉGHSEŐ, Ta-

seiner Überzeugung und in seinen Mitteln auch in Ungarn, war in der Lage, nach der Zeit der „Defension gegen den Protestantismus" in die Offensive zu gehen und eine Periode der Expansion in allen Bereichen des Lebens einzuleiten. Schließlich wurden auch die Orthodoxen von den ungarischen Bischöfen für die katholische Kirche gewonnen, womit die protestantische Einflusssphäre weiter zurückgedrängt werden konnte. Wenn auch eine faktische Teilnahme seitens des Heiligen Stuhles fehlte, so wurde diese durch den „tridentinischen Geist" und den *spirito romano* der beteiligten Bischöfe – unter ihnen Benkovich – zum Zeitpunkt der Union und in den folgenden Jahrzehnten ersetzt.

Augustin Benkovich wurde 1632 als Sprössling einer evangelischen Familie geboren. Nach seiner Konversion zum Katholizismus war er Student der Jesuiten in Pressburg. 1652 trat er dem Paulinerorden bei, dessen Ordensgeneral ihn schon ein Jahr später nach Rom ins *Collegium Germanicum et Hungaricum* schickte, wo er Philosophie und Theologie studierte. Der junge Pauliner kehrte 1658 aus Rom zurück und wurde sofort vom Ordensgeneral in das Kloster von Sátoraljaújhely, im heutigen Nordostungarn, geschickt, wo ihn der erfahrene Missionar Prior Alfons Skotniczky in die Missionsarbeit einwies. Die Missionen der Pauliner, die überwiegend in Nordostungarn stattfanden, wurden auf Anordnung der *Congregatio de Propaganda Fide* seit 1642 von Johann Vanoviczi organisiert und sukzessiv erweitert.[5] Bereits nach einigen Jahren wurde Benkovich an die Spitze der Missionsgemeinde von Trebischau (sk. Trebišov, ung Terebes) gestellt. Den eifrigen Missionar hatte Vanoviczi, nach seiner Ernennung zum Missionspräfekt im Jahre 1669, zum Vizepräfekt befördert. Als Vizepräfekt war Benkovich auch Prior des Kloster Máriavölgy, das als das Zentrum des Ordens galt. 1669 wurde er zum Vizegeneral, 1675 zum Ordensgeneral gewählt. 1681 wurde er von Kaiser Leopold I. zum Bischof von Wardein und Probst von Leles (sk. Lelesz) ernannt.

Als Missionar – und später als Bischof – hatte sich Benkovich sehr intensiv mit der Frage einer Union der Katholiken mit den östlichen Christen beschäftigt. Ihm kam zugute, dass er die ruthenische Sprache beherrschte und somit eine erfolgreiche Aktivität unter den östlichen Christen wahrnehmen konnte. Es ist seinem Engagement zu verdanken, dass der 1699 an die Propaganda-Kongregation verfasste Bericht des Missionspräfekten Vanoviczi deutlich mehr Informationen über den Zustand der Union und der griechisch-katholischen Kirche enthielt, als alle anderen vorhergehenden Berichterstattungen.[6] Vanoviczi schilderte darin, dass im restaurierten Kloster von Trebischau Benkovich und seine Mitarbeiter eine Schule eröffnet hatten, die

más: Pálos misszionáriusok római képzése a 17. században: Vanoviczi János és Benkovich Ágoston a Collegium Germanicum et Hungaricumban [Die Ausbildung von Paulinermissionaren in Rom im 17. Jahrhundert: Johann Vanoviczi und Augustin Benkovich im Collegium Germanicum et Hungaricum]. In: Historicus Societatis Jesu. Szilas László Emlékkönyv. Hg. v. István ZOMBORI. Budapest 2007, 188-198.

[5] Zur Vanoviczi's Missionstätigkeit siehe TÓTH, István György: A remeterend vándormisszionáriusa: Vanoviczi János, az első pálos misszionárius levelei, 1642–1677 [Wandermissionär des Eremitenordens: Briefe des erste Paulinermissionärs, Johann Vanoviczi, 1642-1677]. In: Levéltári Közlemények 72 (2001), 187-245. – Zur Geschichte der Missionen der Pauliner siehe VÉGHSEŐ: Catholice reformare, 162-262.

[6] Den Bericht siehe TÓTH, István György: Relationes missionariorum de Hungaria et Transilvania 1627–1707. Roma-Budapest 1994, 141f.

nicht nur den katholischen, sondern auch den protestantischen und orthodoxen Kindern die Möglichkeit zum Studium anbot. Die orthodoxen Kinder wurden dabei von den Missionaren auf „katholische Weise" unterrichtet. Dadurch sollten die Kinder die katholische Liturgie kennen lernen und allmählich für die katholische Kirche gewonnen werden. Über die Kinder konnten die Pauliner auch die Eltern ansprechen, die ihrem Nachwuchs in die Kirche folgten. Diese Methode bewies sich letztlich als sehr effizient: Zwei Jahre später konnte der Missionspräfekt Vanoviczi nach Rom berichten, dass die Anzahl der Griechisch-Katholischen wesentlich gestiegen war. Auf einer Liste aus demselben Jahre finden sich sogar die Namen von zwei orthodoxen Priestern, Szilveszter Skabel und Ignác Szűcs, die zusammen mit ihren Familien auf Anregung der Pauliner die Union mit der katholischen Kirche angenommen hatten.

Auch Benkovich erstattete Berichte an die Kongregation, die Informationen über die Situation des Bistums Munkatsch enthielten.[7] 1673 schrieb er, dass die beiden römisch-katholischen Bischöfe, Ferenc Szegedy aus Erlau und György Bársony aus Wardein, sehr viel zur Verbreitung des katholischen Glaubens beitragen würden. Beide könnten durch den Bischof von Munkatsch Hilfe erfahren, dessen Bischofssitz sei allerdings seit Jahren vakant. Laut Benkovich würden ungefähr 100.000 orthodoxe Christen sowie fünfhundert Priester in dieser Region leben, welche die Union gerne annähmen, wenn sie einen Oberhirten hätten. Am Ende des Berichtes aus dem Jahre 1674[8] kehrt Benkovich – die Bedeutung des Problems betonend – zur Frage der Ernennung eines griechisch-katholischen Bischofs zurück, da in Folge der Nichtbesetzung des Amtes die Disziplin des Klerus nachgelassen habe. Schlimmer noch, gebe es doch viele Priester, deren Ausbildung unzureichend sei: Sie seien kaum in der Lage, die liturgischen Texte zu lesen. Auch um die Priesterausbildung kümmerte sich demnach niemand. Abhilfe konnten laut Benkovich die Kollatoren der Diözese schaffen, namentlich die Familie Rákóczi, der Kaiserhof würde die Ernennung schon approbieren. Es wäre aber notwendig, dass der Heilige Stuhl und der Hof die Auswahl des Bischofs vorantreibe, betonte der Missionar. Unerlässlich sei außerdem, dass der Kandidat der ruthenischen Sprache mächtig sei. Wenn es einen solchen Anwärter in Ungarn, in Wien oder in Rom nicht geben sollte, so könne man den griechisch-katholischen Metropolit von Kiew durch den Nuntius in Polen vom Anliegen in Kenntnis setzen lassen. Benkovich erinnerte im Weiteren daran, dass die Einkünfte der Diözese sehr gering seien, dass aber das Kapitel von Pressburg wichtige Dokumente aufbewahre, die die alten Rechte des Munkatscher Bischofs beweisen würden. Mit diesen Urkunden sollte auch die Reaktivierung dieses Bischofsstuhls begründet werden.

Aus diesen Berichten geht klar hervor, dass Benkovich die Situation und die Probleme der griechisch-katholischen Kirche nicht nur gut kannte, sondern auch etwas zur Lösung beitragen wollte. So berichteten mehrere Geschichtsschreiber seiner Zeit, dass Benkovich sich in diesen Jahren nicht nur als Missionar, sonder auch als

---

[7] Ebd., 185f.
[8] Ebd., 199.

Ritus-Vikar des Bischofs von Erlau betätigte, wie dies der Pauliner Ignác Pongrátz in seinem 1732 veröffentlichten Buch behauptete.[9] Er gilt mit großer Wahrscheinlichkeit auch als Quelle des Ordenshistorikers Nicolaus Benger aus dem Jahre 1743.[10] Der Historiker des Bistums Wardein, Antal Gánóczy, stützte sich auf die Angaben dieser beiden Pauliner.[11] Vince Bunyitay, der Monograph der Bischöfe Wardeins, schrieb zudem, dass Benkovich „vom Erlauer Bischof Szegedy zum Vikar der in den östlichen Regionen der Diözese lebenden katholischen Russen ernannt“ worden war.[12] Diese Aussage wird auch in den Publikationen des 20. Jahrhunderts nicht in Frage gestellt.

In den Quellen findet man hingegen keinen Beweis für die Ernennung von Benkovich zum Vikar durch den Bischof von Erlau. Wenn Benkovich tatsächlich einen solchen Auftrag erhalten hätte, hätte er oder Vanoviczi es der Kongregation mit Sicherheit mitgeteilt. Als er 1681 zum Bischof von Wardein ernannt wurde, berief der Nuntius von Wien, Francesco Buonvisi, zum kanonischen Informativprozess vier Zeugen ein, die Benkovich kannten und sich daran erinnerten, dass er für die griechisch-katholische Kirche sehr viel getan hatte. Keiner von ihnen erwähnte aber, dass Benkovich Vikar des Bischofs von Erlau gewesen sei. Man findet seinen Namen auch nicht unter den Amtsträgern der Diözese Erlau. Die Ursache für das Missverständnis ist wahrscheinlich der Tatsache geschuldet, dass Benkovich zwischen 1669 und 1675 Vizegeneral des Ordens gewesen war und seine Briefe daher als *vicarius generalis* unterzeichnete. Außerdem war seine gute Beziehung zum Bischof Szegedy und sein Einsatz für die orthodoxen Christen offenkundig. Letztlich könnten diese Punkte zur Verbreitung der *opinio generalis* in der Geschichtsschreibung geführt haben.

Obwohl Benkovich kein Ritus-Vikar war, bestätigt sich die seit 1732 stets wiederholte Behauptung, dass er sich mit viel Engagement für die Interessen der griechisch-katholischen Bevölkerung einsetzte. Weitere Einzelheiten hierzu erfährt man aus dem Protokoll des oben genannten Informativprozesses.[13] Der Nuntius Francesco Buonvisi hatte die Jesuiten Mihály Gribóczy und Mátyás Sámbár aus Ödenburg (ung. Sopron) sowie die Pauliner Mátyás Turkovics und György Branich als Zeugen berufen. Auf die Fragen über die vorherigen Tätigkeiten sowie nach der Tauglichkeit des Kandidaten Benkovich für das Amt des Bischofs, gaben Sámbár, Turkovich und Branich seinen Einsatz für die griechisch-katholischen Christen zu Protokoll. Sámbár meinte, dass Benkovich für das Amt des Bischofs unbedingt geeignet sei, da er viele Orthodoxen bekehrt habe. Laut Turkovich konnte man einen besseren Kandidat für das Bischofssitz von Wardein kaum finden, da in jener Diözese viele Ru-

---

[9] PONGRÁTZ, Ignatius: Triumphus Sancti Pauli. Posonii 1732, 312.

[10] BENGER, N[icolaus]: Annalium Eremi-Coenobiticorum ordinis Fratrum Eremitarum S. Pauli primi Eremitae volumen secundum (1663-1727). Posonii 1743, 134.

[11] GÁNÓCZY, A[ntal]: Episcopi varadienses fide diplomatum concinnati opera et studio. Viennae 1776, 350.

[12] A váradi püspökök a száműzetés és az újraalapítás korában (1566-1780) [Die Bischöfe von Wardein in der Zeit der Verbannung und der Neugründung (1566-1780)]. Hg. v. Vince BUNYITAY und Ödön MÁLNÁSI. Debrecen 1935, 145.

[13] Archivio Segreto Vaticano [Geheimarchiv des Vatikans], Fondo Consistoriale – Processus vol 81. fol. 651-664v.

thener leben würden, deren Sprache Benkovich beherrsche und mit denen er gute Beziehungen pflege. Viele von ihnen habe der Kandidat im Sinne der katholischen Kirche bekehrt, was im Land und im Paulinerorden bekannt war. Branich fügte ergänzend hinzu, dass Benkovich unter den griechisch-katholischen Priestern sehr beliebt sei, da er mehrmals für deren Rechte eingetreten war. Auch hätte er verhindert, dass die unierten Priester als Leibeigene der Feudalherren betrachtet worden seien. Auf die Frage also, warum der Kandidat für den Bischofssitz geeignet sei, betonten die Zeugen seine wirksame Tätigkeit für die Union wie für die griechisch-katholische Kirche.

Seit seiner Bischofsernennung lebte Benkovich in der Propstei von Leles, wo er u.a. die Aufgabe hatte, die kirchenpolitischen Maßnahmen des Hofes – vor allem die von Leopold Kollonich – zu verwirklichen. So sollte er 1690 den neuen Bischof von Munkatsch, den Griechen Joannes Josephus De Camillis, in die Eparchie einführen.[14] De Camillis kam aus Rom, wo er Skriptor der Apostolischen Bibliothek und Prokurator der russischen Basilianer gewesen war. Bereits mit 12 Jahren hatte er sein Studium am Collegium Romanum in Rom begonnen. Obwohl er dort in den 50er Jahren Mitstudent von Benkovich gewesen war, kannten sich beide nicht. Nachdem De Camillis den Doktortitel in der Theologie erworben hatte, wurde er von der Propaganda-Kongregation nach Albanien gesandt, wo er fast zehn Jahre als Missionar tätig war. Nach seiner Rückkehr erhielt er in Rom eine Stelle in der Apostolischen Bibliothek, indes war er von den Kardinälen der Kongregation nicht vergessen. Als 1689 Kardinal Kollonich in Rom eintraf und sich bei seinen Kardinalskollegen um einen Kandidat für die Eparchie Munkatsch' erkundigte, wurde seine Aufmerksamkeit auf De Camillis gelenkt. Kollonich bot ihm das Amt an, worauf dieser es annahm, obwohl er über die schwierigen Aufgaben, welche die Stelle mit sich brachte, wohl nicht vollends im Bilde gewesen war. Allerdings war De Camillis bekannt, dass zwei vorherige Kandidaten binnen kurzer Zeit gescheitert waren. Nach seiner Ankunft in Munkatsch korrigierte De Camillis mit der Unterstützung von Benkovich die schwierige Situation der Eparchie mittels der Einberufung von Synoden. Bis zu seinem Tod im Jahre 1706 versuchte er im Dialog für den Aufbau eines tridentinischen Kirchenmodells zu sorgen.

Ab 1687 konnte Benkovich einen Teil seiner Aufmerksamkeit wieder auf die Diözese Wardein richten.[15] In jenem Jahr wurde nämlich ein Teil der Diözese von den Osmanen zurückerobert. Als Obergespan des Komitats Bihar konnte er nun die Wiederherstellung der ungarischen Administration einleiten. Im Jahre 1692 wurden schließlich auch die übrigen Regionen der Diözese sowie sein Bischofssitz durch die kaiserlichen Truppen besetzt. Benkovich musste in der Folgezeit den Wiederaufbau der Diözese von neuem beginnen, da seit 1552 im Komitat Bihar fast 700 Dörfer –

---

[14] Zum Leben und Werk von De Camillis siehe Rómából Hungáriába. A De Camillis János József munkácsi püspök halálának 300. évfordulóján rendezett konferencia tanulmányai [Von Rom nach Hungaria. Studien anlässlich der Konferenz zum 300. Todestag des Bischofs von Munkatsch, Johann Josef De Camillis]. Hg. v. Tamás VÉGHSEŐ. Nyíregyháza 2008. – PEKAR, Athanasius: Tribute to Bishop J. J. De Camillis. In: Analecta Basiliana 18 (1985), 374–418.

[15] VÉGHSEŐ: Catholice reformare, 272-310.

oft spurlos – verschwunden waren.[16] Ein Dilemma stellte das im doppelten Sinne dar: Als Bischof fehlten Benkovich die Gläubigen und als Grundbesitzer hatte er nicht genügend Bauern, um seine Güter zu bewirtschaften. Um beiden Problemen gleichermaßen Herr zu werden, griff er auf das seit 1688 vom kaiserlichen Hof geförderte Programm der organisierten Ansiedlung zurück.[17] Die Widerbevölkerung der Diözese bedeutete für Benkovich auch eine ungewöhnliche pastorale Aufgabe, galt es doch eine anwachsende Volksgruppe zu integrieren, die in immer größerer Anzahl im Komitat Bihar lebte: die Rumänen. Bereits 1773 zählte man im Komitat 130 ungarische und 330 rumänische Dörfer.

Benkovich hatte die Unionsbemühungen der katholischen Kirche den Rumänen gegenüber bereits frühzeitig vorangetrieben. Obwohl er Bischof einer lateinischen Diözese war, gibt es keinen Hinweis darauf, dass er die Integration der Rumänen von einem Latinisierungsprozesses abhängig gemacht hätte. Scheinbar kamen bei ihm Erfahrungswerte zum Tragen, die noch aus seiner Zeit bei der Munkatscher Eparchie stammten, hatte sich doch damals gezeigt, dass die Union der orthodoxen Christen mit der katholischen Kirche nur dann eine Zukunft hatte, wenn der östliche Ritus unberührt blieb und die Gleichberechtigung des Klerus zur Geltung kam. Gleichwohl waren nicht alle römisch-katholischen Bischöfe und Missionare dieser Auffassung. Benkovich scheint da eher eine Ausnahme gewesen zu sein.

Gleich mehrere Quellen dokumentieren die Maßnahmen von Benkovich zugunsten der Unierten. Sein Generalvikar, István Farkas, wurde von ihm beauftragt, über die Rechte des unierten Klerus zu wachen und zu verhindern, dass sie von den lokalen Feudalherren als Leibeigene betrachtet wurden. Der Generalvikar war auch für die materielle Fürsorge des unierten Klerus zuständig. Während Benkovichs Amtszeit wurde weiterhin eingeführt, dass die unierten Priester an der Fronleichnamsprozession teilnahmen und sogar in die Liturgie nach ihrem Ritus miteinbezogen wurden. Mehrmals bat er den kaiserlichen Hof, neue Erlasse zugunsten der Unierten auszugeben, damit ihre Rechte garantiert und dadurch das größte Hindernis der Union beseitigt werde.

Als Benkovich im Oktober 1702 starb, waren die Fundamente für den Wiederaufbau der Diözese und für eine Union mit den Rumänen gelegt. Diese wurden vom sog. Rákóczi-Aufstand (1703-1711) weitgehend zerstört. Doch seine Nachfolger setzten seine Arbeit fort und verwirklichten beide Werke in den folgenden Jahrzehnten. Die Union der Rumänen führte 1777 zur Errichtung der griechisch-katholischen Eparchie von Wardein, die bis zum heutigen Tage Bestand hat.

Wohl oder Wehe des Gelingens einer kirchlichen Union – und damit auch einhergehend die soziale Integration der Unierten – hing entscheidend vom Wohlwollen der lateinischen Seite ab. Karl Esterházy, Bischof der Diözese Erlau, wollte und konnte

[16] Siehe MEZŐSI, Károly: Bihar vármegye a török uralom megszűnése idejében (1692) [Das Komitat Bihar am Ende der Osmanenherrschaft (1692)]. Budapest 1943.

[17] Verwiesen sei auf das sogenannte *Einrichtungswerk des Königsreichs Hungarn* Kardinal Kollonichs aus dem Jahre 1688, das seitens der Habsburger Regierung zwar nie umgesetzt worden ist, gleichwohl aber die Erkenntnis des Königshofes widerspiegelt, in Fragen der Neubesiedelung verödeter Landstriche aktiv zu werden.

beispielsweise die kirchliche, kulturelle und soziale Entwicklung der unierten Kirche innerhalb der Eparchie von Munkatsch verhindern. Die griechisch-katholischen Gläubigen betrachtete er lediglich als zweitrangige Katholiken und – in Tradition des Bildes über die Orthodoxen – weiterhin als zweitrangige Untertanen. Sein Gegenbeispiel ist Augustin Benkovich, der die kirchliche Gemeinde der Unierten, ihren sozialen Stand und ihre ethnische Zugehörigkeit mit Wohlwollen behandelte. Es ist daher kein Zufall, dass die zeitgenössischen Berichte über seinen Tod bemerken: „*in fama sanctitatis*“ verstorben.

Bildnachweise

András Forgó, Ansiedlungspolitik und konfessionelle Konflikte…

Abb. 1: Die Herrschaft Wesprim der Abtei Zirc im 18. Jahrhundert: entworfen nach HERVAY, Ferenc Levente: Repertorium historicum ordinis cisterciensis in Hungaria. Roma 1984 (Bibliotheca Cisterciensis 7), 214.
Abb. 2: Die Pfarrkirche von Magyarpolány (gebaut: 1761 – 1773), Grafik erstellt von András Forgó.

Sándor Őze, Städtemigration im Winkel zwischen Theiß, Mieresch und Kreisch nach der Vertreibung der Türken

Abb. 1: Herkunftskarte der Neusiedler. Sasi, Attila, Kartographisches Institut Budapest.

Karl-Peter Krauss, Frauen in Not. Das Ehegericht in der Batschka im Prozess der Konsolidierung und Disziplinierung

Abb. 1: Das Komitat Bács-Bodrog vor dem Ersten Weltkrieg. Entwurf: Karl-Peter Krauss, Kartographie: Richard Szydlak.
Abb. 2: Ausschnitt aus einem der Liebesbriefe des Soldaten Joseph Stiasny an seine Geliebte Josepha Schmidt, Frau des Fleischhackers Franz Schmidt aus Hajós. Die Überschrift des teilweise zerstörten Dokuments lautet: „Allerliebste Peggy!“. KFL.I.2.a. Hajós, Franz Schmidt – Josepha Sukovitz 1812.
Abb. 3: Die Anzahl der kirchlichen Eheprozesse im Erzbistum Kalocsa 1770 – 1795. Quelle: Viktória Banga; Gabriella Csongrádi, KFL.
Abb. 4: Bestätigungsschreiben des Notars von Tschonopel. KFL.I.2.a. Csonoplya, Johann Preisich – Anna Maria Müller 1820 – 1821.

Klaus J. Loderer, Kreuzweg und Kalvarienberg im Königreich Ungarn…

Abb. 1 und 2: Kalvarienberg in Eisenstadt. Fotos: Klaus J. Loderer.
Abb. 3: Kalvarienberg in Magyarpolány – Gesamtansicht. Foto: Klaus J. Loderer.
Abb. 4 und 5: Skulpturengruppe in Magyarpolány. Fotos: Klaus J. Loderer.
Abb. 6: Kapelle und Kreuzigungsgruppe auf dem Kalvarienberg in Güns (Köszeg) . Foto: Klaus J. Loderer.
Abb. 7: Kalvarienberg in Frauenkirchen im Burgenland. Foto: Klaus J. Loderer.

Swantje Volkmann, Kirchenbau im Banat des 18. Jahrhunderts...

Abb. 1: Dognecea/Dognatschka, Kirche "Maria Geburt", 1735
Abb. 2.: Ciclova Montana/Montan-Tschiklowa, Kirche „Erscheinung Mariens", 1776/77
Abb. 3: Arad, Franziskanerkirche „Maria, Königin der Engel", 1775 - 1781
Abb. 4: Timişoara/Temeswar, St.-Georgs-Kathedrale, 1736 – 1774
Abb. 5: Plan einer Kirche im Banat, 1765
Abb. 6: Neumoldowa, Kirche „Hl. Johannes der Täufer", 1777-1778, Querschnitt des Chores, Profil, Grundriß, 1776
Abb. 7: Fântânele/Engelsbrunn, Kirche „Hl. Schutzengel", 1779/80, Innenansicht
Abb. 8: Lenauheim, Kirche „Hl. Jungfrau Theresia", 177/78
Abb. 9: Periam/Periamosch, Kirche „Hl. Johann von Nepomuk", 1772/73
Abb. 10: Lovrin/Lowrin, Kirche „Hl. Peter und Paul", 1785 – 1789
Abb. 11: Grabaţ/Grabatz, Kirche „Maria von der immerwährenden Hilfe", 1780
Abb. 12: Fântânele/Engelsbrunn, Kirche „Hl. Schutzengel", 1779/80, Außenansicht

sämtliche Fotos: Martin Eichler, Martin Rill

Krista Zach, Konfessionelle Raumkonfigurationen im südöstlichen Europa...

Abb. 1: Geistliche Jurisdiktion um 1450: Die Grenzen der Erzbistümer und Patriarchate. Aus MAGOCSI, Paul Robert: Historical Atlas of East Central Europe. Toronto 1993: „Ecclesiastical jurisdictions ca. 1450", Karte Nr. 13, 43, Text ebd., 42-45.
Abb: 2: Magyarország katolikus egyházmegyéi a török hódoltság idején [Die katholischen Diözesen Ungarns zur Zeit der Osmanenherrschaft]: Aus MOLNÁR, Antal: Katolikus missziók a hódolt Magyarországon. [Katholische Missionen im Eroberungsgebiet Ungarns]. Bd. 1 (1572-1647). Budapest 2002.
Abb. 3: Patriarchat von Ipek im 17. Jahrhundert. Aus MOLNÁR, Antal: Katolikus missziók a hódolt Magyarországon. [Katholische Missionen im Eroberungsgebiet Ungarns]. Bd. 1 (1572-1647). Budapest 2002.
Abb. 4: Bosznai ferences rendttartmány a 17. század közepén [Die bosnische Franziskanerprovinz Mitte des 17. Jahrhunderts]. Aus MOLNÁR, Antal: Katolikus missziók a hódolt Magyarországon. [Katholische Missionen im Eroberungsgebiet Ungarns]. Bd. 1 (1572-1647). Budapest 2002.
Abb. 5: Bosnische Franziskanerklöster im 15. Jahrhundert. Aus MOLNÁR, Antal: Katolikus missziók a hódolt Magyarországon. [Katholische Missionen im Eroberungsgebiet Ungarns]. Bd. 1 (1572-1647). Budapest 2002.
Abb. 6: Apostolisches Breve von 1652 mit Grenzziehungen der Diözese Belgrad (1647). Aus: ZACH, Krista: Die Visitation des Bischofs von Belgrad Marin Ibrišimović in Türkisch-Ungarn (1649). In: DIES.: Konfessionelle Pluralität, Stände und Nation. Ausgewählte Abhandlungen zur südosteuropäischen Religions- und Gesellschaftsgeschichte. Hg. v. Joachim BAHLCKE und Konrad GÜNDISCH. Münster 2004, 216 (Abb. 6).

Namensregister